MUSIC IN THE WESTERN WORLD

A History in Documents

SECOND EDITION

MUSIC IN THE WESTERN WORLD

A History in Documents

PIERO WEISS

Peabody Conservatory of Music
Johns Hopkins University

RICHARD TARUSKIN

University of California at Berkeley

SCHIRMER
CENGAGE Learning™

Australia • Brazil • Japan • Korea • Mexico • Singapore • Spain • United Kingdom • United States

SCHIRMER
CENGAGE Learning

Music in the Western World:
A History in Documents
Piero Weiss and
Richard Taruskin

Publisher: *Clark Baxter*

Assistant Editor: *Emily A. Ryan*

Editorial Assistant: *Nell Pepper*

Technology Project Manager:
Rachel Bairstow

Executive Marketing Manager:
Diane Wenckebach

Marketing Assistant: *Marla Nasser*

Production Manager, Editorial
Production: *Trudy Brown*

Creative Director: *Rob Hugel*

Art Director: *Maria Epes*

Print Buyer: *Nora Massuda*

Permissions Editor: *Roberta Broyer*

Production Service:
Newgen–Austin

Text Designer: *Lisa Henry*

Photo Researcher: *Pamela Carly/
Linda Sykes*

Copy Editor: *Debra Kirkby*

Cover Designer: *Lee Anne Dollison*

Cover Image: *Copyright Biblioteca
Ambrosiana, Milan. MS D. 75.
INF. Auth. No F47/05*

Compositor: *Newgen*

For product information and technology assistance,
contact us at **Cengage Learning Academic
Resource Center, 1-800-423-0563**

For permission to use material from this text or
product, submit all requests online at
www.cengage.com/permissions
Further permissions questions can be emailed to
permissionrequest@cengage.com

Library of Congress Control Number: 2006940688

ISBN-13: 978-0-534-58599-0
ISBN-10: 0-534-58599-X

Schirmer Cengage Learning
20 Davis Drive
Belmont, CA 94002-3098
USA

Cengage Learning products are represented in
Canada by Nelson Education, Ltd.

For your course and learning solutions, visit
academic.cengage.com

Purchase any of our products at your local
college store or at our preferred online store
www.cengagebrain.com

Printed in the United States of America
5 6 7 8 9   26 25 24 23 22

CONTENTS

PART THREE

The Renaissance   67

PART FOUR

The Baroque   143

PART FIVE
The Pre-Classical Period   217

PART SIX
The Classical Period   243

PART SEVEN

The Later Nineteenth Century: Romanticism and Other Preoccupations   285

PART EIGHT

The Twentieth Century   355

PART NINE

The Recent Past, and the Present   489

THE FIRST EDITION of this book was actually compiled during 1975–77 and was already slightly behind the times when it first saw the light of day in 1984. In the two-decades-plus that have elapsed since publication, the history of music has not only lengthened, as was inevitable, but has also taken some interesting new twists that have given rise to new issues and controversies. The primary purpose of the new edition, then, is to take note of current events in what amounts to a new closing section, "The Recent Past and the Present," comprising eleven new reading units. Moreover, three new units have been added to the existing twentieth-century readings to reflect the significantly increased interest in the interrelationships among the cultural, social, and political domains that has taken hold in the humanities since the 1980s; also, several units have been augmented. There have been additions elsewhere in the book as well, and three new units have been interpolated into the existing text so as to do justice to the beginnings of public opera performances, the new conceptualization of folklore at the dawn of romanticism, and Verdi's emergence as the giant of nineteenth-century Italian opera. In consequence, the reading units have been renumbered. To assist instructors who have been using this book and now need to adjust their syllabi, we are appending a small conversion table to this preface. We are grateful to those who have paid us the compliment of adoption in the past and hope that a new generation of teachers and students will continue to find *Music in the Western World* a useful adjunct to their studies.

P. W., R. T.
4 October 2006

First edition	Second edition
1–48	unchanged
49–82	50–83
83–107	85–109
108–147	111–150
148–151	152–155
152–155	158–161
–	162–172

THIS BOOK HAS GROWN out of our many years' experience teaching both the introductory music course designed for nonspecialist students and the music history course
offered over several semesters in connection with the major in music. We missed having
a single book that would impart to our students the countless fascinating insights that
come from reading original historical documents such as letters, memoirs, essays, and
reports of all kinds—in short, the reactions of contemporaries to the music we were
studying in class. There was, of course, Strunk's *Source Readings in Music History,* but
that excellent book was never meant for the level of studies we are speaking of here. As
for the standard, expository textbooks, they did not (indeed could not) devote much
space to original source material.

And so we assembled this collection of documents. We assumed, for our *modus
operandi,* no previous knowledge of music on the part of the student. This automatically ruled out readings dependent on a knowledge of musical notation and guided us
when we came to write the paragraphs that introduce the readings. Another guiding
principle was the assumption that our readers would not necessarily follow us from first
page to last; wishing, on the contrary, to make the material as accessible as possible and
amenable to a variety of approaches, we wrote each introductory paragraph as if our
prospective readers were going to land on it out of the blue, so that, in effect, each
reading may be regarded as self-contained. But we have carried neither principle—
assumption of no previous knowledge, independence of each selection—to extremes,
since that would have involved compulsively defining and identifying every single thing
and person, however insignificant. Instead we have resorted to frequent cross-references;
if occasionally we have allowed certain terms or names to pass without explanation, it is
because we did not feel they were of central concern. A glossary at the end of the book
brings together the more obscure technical terms occurring in the body of the text.

The source of each selection has been fully noted, either at the foot of that selection
or, when more practical, after the group of which it forms a part. Because of the variety
of sources and the diversity of authors, the pieces collected here show, naturally, variety
and diversity of writing and editorial styles. Beyond basic typography, no attempt has
been made to impose any artificial consistency of style on this collection. Many of the
texts have been abridged, and we are sure that, given the purpose of our book, this
requires no apology. Some may question our decision to dispense with the customary
points of omission. But scholars, we reasoned, could always go back to the originals

with the aid of our very precise references; the readers for whom our work is primarily intended would only have found a profusion of little dots a hindrance to their concentration. In all other respects, we have striven for the greatest accuracy; where existing translations proved unsatisfactory we amended them or produced new ones ourselves (identifiable by our initials at the end of the source reference).

We have used the book, in its typescript form, and are pleased with its effect. In the introductory course it has helped to humanize our subject. Students inclined to turn a deaf ear to "classical" music because of its remoteness (because they view it as old, artificial, and an upper-class symbol) have unbended upon reading of the very human circumstances that gave it birth, of the passions it has elicited, the needs it has filled. *Tout comprendre c'est tout pardonner* has worked in our favor: prejudices have crumbled, leaving a path open to new musical impressions. In that sense ours has been a textbook of an unorthodox kind, for it has lent depth to the experience of music in our classroom without addressing its technicalities. The latter we have administered in person; other teachers, no doubt, may prefer to avail themselves of the existing textbooks for that purpose.

In the history courses offered for the major in music, our typescript was only one of several teaching tools. We expect students at this level to spend as much time with scores as with books, and as much time with the standard history texts as with these sources. But exposure to the latter has proved an invaluable and enlivening factor in their experience of the music and thus an essential element in their education. The range of our book, both chronological and topical, closely matches that of most history sequences, so that it makes an effective ancillary text through several semesters of work.

Non-matriculated students, finally—and by this we mean music lovers at large, unconfined by classrooms and teachers—are more than welcome to sample our book. We think they will enjoy it. We have done our best not to give it the grim look of a college text, preferring, on this occasion, a touch of Yeats's Tom O'Roughley, who held that "wisdom is a butterfly/And not a gloomy bird of prey."

MUSIC IN THE WESTERN WORLD

A History in Documents

PART ONE

The Heritage of Antiquity

1

Orpheus and the Magical Powers of Music

Very few specimens of music have survived from Greek and Roman times, not nearly enough to give us an accurate idea of how their music actually sounded. By contrast, we know a great deal concerning classical theory and, even more important, classical aesthetics of music. In these fields, the Greek contribution to later Western attitudes is fundamental. To the Greeks, music possessed *ethos;* that is, the power to influence its hearers' emotions and behavior, indeed their morals. This magical power (recognized, by the way, by all of the world's cultures, in countless legends) is nowhere so dramatically illustrated as in the ancient, celebrated myth of Orpheus, given here in the version of the Roman poet Ovid. The son of a Muse by a Thracian prince, Orpheus acquired such skill at singing and playing the lyre that nothing animate or inanimate could resist his music. An early instance of his powers occurred when, as one of the Argonauts bringing home the Golden Fleece, he saved himself and his fellow mariners from drowning by singing more persuasively than the seductive Sirens. His death was tragic: he was torn to bits by the jealous women of Thrace, who were driven to frenzy by the power of his song and enraged by his lack of attention to them. For all his thoughts remained with his twice-dead wife Eurydice, of whom we read in the selection that follows.

Hymen, clad in his saffron robes, was summoned by Orpheus [to his wedding], and made his way across the vast reaches of the sky to the shores of the Cicones. But Orpheus' invitation to the god to attend his marriage was of no avail, for though he was certainly present, he did not bring good luck. His expression was gloomy, and he did not sing his accustomed refrain. Even the torch he carried sputtered and smoked, bringing tears to the eyes, and no amount of tossing could make it burn. The outcome was even worse than the omens foretold: for while the new bride was wandering in the meadows, with her band of water nymphs, a serpent bit her ankle, and she sank lifeless to the ground. The Thracian poet mourned her loss; when he had wept for her to the full in the upper world, he made so bold as to descend through the gate of Taenarus to the Styx, to try to rouse the sympathy of the shades as well. There he passed among the thin ghosts, the wraiths of the dead, till he reached Persephone and her lord, who hold sway over these dismal regions, the king of the shades. Then, accompanying his words with the music of his lyre, he said:

"Deities of this lower world, to which all we of mortal birth descend, if I have your permission to dispense with rambling insincerities and speak the simple truth, I did not come here to see the dim haunts of Tartarus, nor yet to chain Medusa's monstrous dog, with its three heads and snaky ruff. I came because of my wife, cut off before she reached her prime when she trod on a serpent and it poured its poison into her veins. I wished to be strong enough to endure my grief, and I will not deny that I tried to do so: but Love was too much for me. He is a god well-known in the world above; whether he may be so here, too, I do not know, but I imagine that he is familiar to you also. I beg you, by these awful regions, by this boundless chaos, and by the silence of your vast realms, weave again Eurydice's destiny, brought too swiftly to a close. We mortals and all that is ours are fated to fall to you, and after a little time, sooner or later, we hasten to this one abode. We are all on our way here, this is our final home, and yours the most lasting sway over the human race. My wife, like the rest, when she has completed her proper span of years will, in the fullness of time, come within your power. I ask as a gift from you only the enjoyment of her; but if the fates refuse her a reprieve, I have made up my mind that I do not wish to return either. You may exult in my death as well as hers!"

As he sang these words to the music of his lyre, the bloodless ghosts were in tears. Tantalus made no effort to reach the waters that ever shrank away, Ixion's wheel stood still in wonder, the vultures ceased to gnaw Tityus' liver, the daughters of Danaus rested from their pitchers, and Sisyphus sat idle on his rock. Then for the first time, they say, the cheeks of the Furies were wet with tears, for they were overcome by his singing. The king and queen of the underworld could not bear to refuse his pleas. They called Eurydice. She was among the ghosts who had but newly come, and walked slowly because of her injury. Thracian Orpheus received her, but on condition that he must not look back until he had emerged from the valleys of Avernus or else the gift he had been given would be taken from him.

Up the sloping path, through the mute silence they made their way, up the steep dark track, wrapped in impenetrable gloom, till they had almost reached the surface of the earth. Here, anxious in case his wife's strength be failing and eager to see her, the lover looked behind him, and straightway Eurydice slipped back into the depths. Orpheus stretched out his arms, straining to clasp her and be clasped; but the hapless man touched nothing but yielding air. Eurydice, dying now a second time, uttered no complaint against her husband. What was there to complain of, but that she had been loved? With a last farewell which scarcely reached his ears, she fell back again into the same place from which she had come.

2

Pythagoras and the Numerical Properties of Music

The mystic philosopher Pythagoras (sixth century B.C.) and his disciples are credited with the discovery of the numerical relationships governing the basic intervals of music—the octave, the fifth, the fourth, the second. Numbers formed the basis of the Pythagorean universe, and it is here that the notion of a "harmony of the spheres" was born, an inaudible harmony founded on the basic musical proportions. Hence the early intimate association between astronomy and music, later codified by Plato and his followers as related fields of higher learning. Pythagoras himself remains a shadowy, quasi-legendary figure, about whom many remarkable stories were told. Here is one of the most famous, as related by a neo-Pythagorean of the second century A.D.: it accounts for the invention of the monochord (here called *chordotonos*), the one-stringed instrument upon which the Pythagoreans and all later acoustical scientists, up through the Middle Ages, conducted their experiments. (Incidentally, the numerical proportions mentioned in the story are applicable only with regard to the length of strings—not their tension—and certainly not to the weight of hammers! This is further proof, if any were needed, that the ancient legend is a fabrication.)

Pythagoras being in an intense thought whether he might invent any instrumental help to the ear, solid and infallible, such as the sight hath by a compass and rule, as he passed by a smith's shop by a happy chance he heard the iron hammers striking on the anvil, and rendering sounds most consonant to one another in all combinations except one. He observed in them these three concords: the octave, the fifth and the fourth; but that which was between the fourth and the fifth he found to be a discord in itself, though otherwise useful for the making up of the greater of them, the fifth. Apprehending this came to him from God, as a most happy thing, he hastened into the shop, and by various trials finding the difference of the sounds to be according to the weight of the hammers, and not according to the force of those who struck, nor according to the fashion of the hammers, nor according to the turning of the iron which was in beating out: having taken exactly the weight of the hammers, he went straightway home, and to one beam fastened to the walls, cross from one corner of the room to the other, tying four strings of the same substance, length, and twist, upon each of them he hung a several weight, fastening it at the lower end, and making the length of the strings altogether equal; then striking the strings by two at a time interchangeably, he found out the aforesaid concords, each in its own combination; for that which was stretched by the greatest weight, in respect of that which was stretched by the least weight, he found to sound an octave. The greatest weight was of twelve pounds, the least of six; thence he determined that the octave did consist in double proportion, which the weights themselves did show. Next he found that the greatest to the least but one, which was of eight pounds, sounded a fifth; whence he inferred this to consist in the proportion 3:2, in which proportion the weights were to one another; but unto that which was less than itself in weight, yet greater than the rest, being of nine pounds, he found it to sound a fourth; and discovered that, proportionably to the weights, this concord was 4:3; which string of nine pounds is naturally 3:2 to the least; for nine to six is so, viz., 3:2, as the least but one, which is eight, was to that which had the weight six, in proportion 4:3; and twelve to eight is 3:2; and that which is in the middle, between a fifth and a fourth, whereby a fifth exceeds a fourth, is confirmed to be in 9:8 proportion. The system of both was called *Diapason*, or octave, that is both the fifth and the fourth joined together, as duple proportion is compounded of 3:2 and 4:3, or on the contrary, of 4:3 by 3:2.

Applying both his hand and ear to the weights which he had hung on, and by them confirming the proportion of the relations, he ingeniously transferred the common result of the strings upon the crossbeam to the bridge of an instrument, which he called *Chordotonos;* and for stretching them proportionably to the weights, he invented pegs,

Pythagoras, Inventor of Music. In this illustration from a thirteenth-century manuscript containing the famous treatise *De musica* by John of Cotton, the legend of Pythagoras and the blacksmith is depicted in the upper panel. The inscriptions read, "Per fabricam ferri mirum deus imprimit" (By means of a smithy God has imparted a wonder) and "Is Pythagoras ut diversorum/ per pondera malleorum/perpendebat secum quae sit concordia vocum" (It was this Pythagoras by the turning whereof he distended or relaxed them at pleasure. Making use of this foundation as an infallible rule, he extended the experiment to many kinds of instruments, as well pipes and flutes as those which have strings; and he found that this conclusion made by numbers was consonant without variation in all.

John Hawkins, *A General History of the Science and Practice of Music* (London, 1776; reprint of 2nd ed., New York: Dover Publications, Inc., 1963), I, 9–10 (from Nicomachus, *Enchiridion harmonices,* trans. Thomas Stanley [1701]).

3

Plato's Musical Idealism

Its *ethos* made music a powerful force for good or for evil in the view of Greek thinkers. Plato, the most influential of them, dealt with the subject repeatedly. He looked down on the use of music for mere pleasure.

Second-rate and commonplace people, being too uneducated to entertain themselves as they drink by using their own voices and conversational resources, put up the price of female musicians, paying well for the hire of an extraneous voice—that of the pipe—and find their entertainment in its warblings. But where the drinkers are men of worth and culture, you will find no girls piping or dancing or harping. They are quite capable of enjoying their own company without such frivolous nonsense, using their own voices in sober discussion and each taking his turn to speak or listen—even if the drinking is really heavy.

Protagoras 347c–d.

> Plato's nostalgia for an idealized Golden Age of Greece profoundly colored his thinking on music. When virtue and simplicity of customs ruled, music had seen better days. This ideal, probably strengthened by Plato's admiration for the supposed virtues of the disciplined, self-denying Spartans (as against the vices of the pleasure-seeking Athenians), leads him to set down pronouncements that will find echoes whenever, in time to come, men will seek to control or reform music. For to Plato, and like-minded thinkers (including such non-Westerners as Confucius), musical license is but a step away from social chaos.

Our music was formerly divided into several kinds and patterns. One kind of song, which went by the name of a *hymn,* consisted of prayers to the gods; there was a second and contrasting kind which might well have been called a *lament; paeans* were a third

who, by the weights of the various hammers, worked out the consonances for himself). Down below, the monochord, a more "modern" device for tone measurement (see p. 42), is shown, along with a harp (laterally strung like a lyre), which represents music's power of "ethos" (see the readings on Orpheus and David). A vielle, or medieval fiddle, is also included in the design. This was the most widespread and versatile practical instrument in late medieval music (see Johannes de Grocheo, p. 55). *Munich, Bayerische Staatsbibliothek, CIm.2599, fol. 96ᵛ.*

kind, and there was a fourth, the *dithyramb,* as it was called, dealing, if I am not mistaken, with the birth of Dionysus. Now these and other types were definitely fixed, and it was not permissible to misuse one kind of melody for another. The competence to take cognizance of these rules, to pass verdicts in accord with them, and, in case of need, to penalize their infraction was not left, as it is today, to the catcalls and discordant outcries of the crowd, nor yet to the clapping of applauders; the educated made it their rule to hear the performances through in silence, and for the boys, their attendants, and the rabble at large, there was the discipline of the official's rod to enforce order. Thus the bulk of the populace was content to submit to this strict control in such matters without venturing to pronounce judgment by its clamors.

Afterward, in course of time, an unmusical license set in with the appearance of poets who were men of native genius, but ignorant of what is right and legitimate in the realm of the Muses. Possessed by a frantic and unhallowed lust for pleasure, they contaminated laments with hymns and paeans with dithyrambs, actually imitated the strains of the flute on the harp, and created a universal confusion of forms. Thus their folly led them unintentionally to slander their profession by the assumption that in music there is no such thing as a right and a wrong, the right standard of judgment being the pleasure given to the hearer, be he high or low. By compositions of such a kind and discourse to the same effect, they naturally inspired the multitude with contempt of musical law, and a conceit of their own competence as judges. Thus our once silent audiences have found a voice, in the persuasion that they understand what is good and bad in art; the old "sovereignty of the best" in that sphere has given way to an evil "sovereignty of the audience." If the consequence had been even a democracy, no great harm would have been done, so long as the democracy was confined to art, and composed of free men. But, as things are with us, music has given occasion to a general conceit of universal knowledge and contempt for law, and liberty has followed in their train. Fear was cast out by confidence in supposed knowledge, and the loss of it gave birth to impudence. For to be unconcerned for the judgment of one's betters in the assurance which comes of a reckless excess of liberty is nothing in the world but reprehensible impudence.

So the next stage of the journey toward liberty will be refusal to submit to the magistrates, and on this will follow emancipation from the authority and correction of parents and elders; then, as the goal of the race is approached, comes the effort to escape obedience to the law, and, when that goal is all but reached, contempt for oaths, for the plighted word, and all religion. The spectacle of the Titanic nature of which our old legends speak is re-enacted; man returns to the old condition of a hell of unending misery.

Laws 700a–701c.

It is this horror of disorder that underlies the celebrated passages concerning music in the *Republic.* Here, as elsewhere, Plato's use of the word *music* is more comprehensive than ours. It includes lyric poetry and also, sometimes, the general education of the intellect as against gymnastics, the education of the body. In the ideal city-state, says Plato,

The overseers must be watchful against its insensible corruption. They must throughout be watchful against innovations in music and gymnastics counter to the established order, and to the best of their power guard against them, fearing when anyone says that that song is most regarded among men "which hovers newest on the singer's lips" [*Odyssey* i. 351], lest it be supposed that the poet means not new songs but a new way of song and is commending this. But we must not praise that sort of thing nor conceive it to be the poet's meaning. For a change to a new type of music is something to beware of as a hazard of all our fortunes. For the modes of music are never disturbed without unsettling of the most fundamental political and social conventions.

Republic 424b–c.

> A discussion of the Greek modes, or "harmonies," would be too far-reaching for our purposes. Suffice it to say that the Greeks had very definite opinions as to the *effect* of their various modes, which they called by traditional, originally tribal, names. Here, from Book iii of the *Republic*, is part of the famous dialogue between Socrates (as Plato's mouthpiece) and Glaucon concerning the banishment of most of the modes from the ideal city-state. (That the Dorian survived is no surprise, since the Greeks associated the name Dorian with Sparta, the "brave" city-state Plato so admired.) In later passages, most instruments get banished as well. Note the stress Plato places on "imitation." All art, according to him, is imitation of objects perceptible by the senses. And in Book x of the *Republic* he reminds us that all perceptible objects are themselves imitations of eternal originals, so that art consists of nothing more than an imitation of an imitation.

We said we did not require dirges and lamentations in words.
We do not.
What, then, are the dirgelike modes of music? Tell me, for you are a musician.
The mixed Lydian, he said, and the tense or higher Lydian, and similar modes.
These, then, said I, we must do away with. But again, drunkenness is a thing most unbefitting guardians, and so is softness and sloth.
Yes.
What, then, are the soft and convivial modes?
There are certain Ionian and also Lydian modes that are called lax.
Will you make any use of them for warriors?
None at all, he said, but it would seem that you have left the Dorian and the Phrygian.
I don't know the musical modes, I said, but leave us that mode that would fittingly imitate the utterances and the accents of a brave man who is engaged in warfare or in any enforced business, and who, when he has failed, either meeting wounds or death or having fallen into some other mishap, in all these conditions confronts fortune with steadfast endurance and repels her strokes. And another for such a man engaged in works of peace, not enforced but voluntary, either trying to persuade somebody of something and imploring him—whether it be a god, through prayer, or a man, by teaching and admonition—or contrariwise yielding himself to another who is petitioning him or teaching him or trying to change his opinions, and in consequence faring according to his wish, and not bearing himself arrogantly, but in all this acting modestly and moderately and acquiescing in the outcome. Leave us these two modes—the enforced and the voluntary—that will best imitate the utterances of men failing or succeeding, the temperate, the brave—leave us these.
Well, said he, you are asking me to leave none other than those I just spoke of.

Republic 398d–399c.

The distinction between perceptible "objects" and immutable "forms"—so central to Platonic thinking—lies behind the whole doctrine of ethos. Plato is less interested in the audible than in the inaudible—the harmony of the inner man, which, in turn, is a reflection of the harmony of the universe. These ideas are expounded at length in *Timaeus,* the only Platonic dialogue known to the Middle Ages (thanks to a Latin translation by Cicero) and a powerful influence on all medieval musical thought.

The sight in my opinion is the source of the greatest benefit to us, for had we never seen the stars and the sun and the heaven, none of the words which we have spoken about the universe would ever have been uttered. But now the sight of day and night, and the months and the revolutions of the years have created number and have given us a conception of time, and the power of inquiring about the nature of the universe. And from this source we have derived philosophy, than which no greater good ever was or will be given by the gods to mortal man. This is the greatest boon of sight, and of the lesser benefits why should I speak? Even the ordinary man if he were deprived of them would bewail his loss, but in vain. This much let me say however. God invented and gave us sight to the end that we might behold the courses of intelligence in the heaven, and apply them to the courses of our own intelligence which are akin to them, the unperturbed to the perturbed, and that we, learning them and partaking of the natural truth of reason, might imitate the absolutely unerring courses of God and regulate our own vagaries. The same may be affirmed of speech and hearing. They have been given by the gods to the same end and for a like reason. For this is the principal end of speech, whereto it most contributes. Moreover, so much of music as is adapted to the sound of the voice and to the sense of hearing is granted to us for the sake of harmony. And harmony, which has motions akin to the revolutions of our souls, is not regarded by the intelligent votary of the Muses as given by them with a view to irrational pleasure, which is deemed to be the purpose of it in our day, but as meant to correct any discord which may have arisen in the courses of the soul, and to be our ally in bringing her into harmony and agreement with herself, and rhythm too was given by them for the same reason, on account of the irregular and graceless ways which prevail among mankind generally, and to help us against them.

Timaeus 47a–e.

Edith Hamilton and Huntington Cairns (eds.), *The Collected Dialogues of Plato Including the Letters* (New York: Pantheon Books, 1961), 340, 1294–95, 665–66, 643–44, 1174–75.

4

Aristotle on the Purposes of Music

As in most things, so on the subject of music, Aristotle's ideas are more down to earth than Plato's. For him, music is useful not only in education and in ritual, but also as entertainment and relaxation, so long as its use does not become excessive and distracting. Besides the ethical benefits music can impart, Aristotle recognizes a purely aesthetic pleasure (he calls it "enthusiasm") foreign to Plato's scale of values. However, he cautions against too professional an attitude, which can only compromise the "free man's" status.

Our chief inquiry now is whether or not music is to be put into education and what music can do. Is it an education or an amusement or a pastime? It is reasonable to reply that it is directed towards and participates in all three. Amusement is for the purpose of relaxation and relaxation must necessarily be pleasant, since it is a kind of cure for the ills we suffer in working hard. As to the pastimes of a cultivated life, there must, as is universally agreed, be present an element of pleasure as well as of nobility, for the happiness which belongs to that life consists of both of these. We all agree that music is among the most delightful and pleasant things, whether instrumental or accompanied by singing, so that one might from that fact alone infer that the young should be taught it. For things that are pleasant and harmless belong rightly not only to the end in view but also to relaxation by the way. But since it rarely happens that men attain and keep their goal, and they frequently rest and amuse themselves with no other thought than the pleasure of it, there is surely a useful purpose in the pleasure derived from music, and the young must be educated in and by it. And the teaching of music is particularly apt for the young; for they because of their youth do not willingly tolerate anything that is not made pleasant for them, and music is one of those things that are by nature made to give pleasure. Moreover there is a certain affinity between us and music's harmonies and rhythms; so that many experts say that the soul is a harmony, others that it has harmony.

We must now return to the question raised earlier—must they learn to sing themselves and play instruments with their own hands? Clearly actual participation in performing is going to make a big difference to the quality of the person that will be produced; it is impossible, or at any rate very difficult, to produce good judges of musical performance from among those who have never themselves performed. And all that we have been saying makes it clear that musical education must include actual performing; and it is not difficult to decide what is appropriate and what is not for different ages, or to find an answer to those who assert that learning to perform is vulgar and degrading. Since, as we have seen, actual performance is needed to make a good critic, they should while young do much playing and singing, and then, when they are older, give up performing; they will then, thanks to what they have learned in their youth, be able to enjoy music aright and give good judgments. What is needed is that the pupil shall not struggle to acquire the degree of skill that is needed for professional competitions, or to master those peculiar and sensational pieces of music which have begun to penetrate the competitions and have even affected education. Musical exercises, even if not of this kind, should be pursued only up to the point at which the pupil becomes capable of appreciating good melodies and rhythms, and not just the popular music such as appeals to slaves, children, and even some animals.

We reject then as education a training in material performance which is professional and competitive. He that takes part in such performances does not do so in order to improve his own character, but to give pleasure to listeners, and vulgar pleasure at that. We do not therefore regard it as a proper occupation for a gentleman; it is rather that of a paid employee. Inevitably the consequences are degrading, since the end towards which it is directed—popular amusement—is a low one. The listener is a common person and influences music accordingly; he has an effect on professionals who perform for him; the music which he expects of them, and the motions which they have to make to produce it, affect detrimentally their bodies and their minds.

We say then, in summary, that music ought to be used not as conferring one benefit only but many; for example, for education and cathartic purposes, as an intellectual pastime, as relaxation, and for relief after tension. While then we must make use of all the harmonies, we are not to use them all in the same manner, but for education use those which improve the character, for listening to others performing use both the activating and the emotion-striving or enthusiastic. Any feeling which comes strongly to some, exists in all others to a greater or lesser degree: pity and fear, for example, but also this "enthusiasm." This is a kind of excitement which affects some people very strongly. It may arise out of religious music, and it is noticeable that when they have been listening to melodies that have an orgiastic effect they are, as it were, set on their feet, as if they had undergone a curative and purifying treatment. And those who feel pity or fear or other emotions must be affected in just the same way to the extent that the emotion comes upon each. To them all comes a pleasant feeling of purgation and relief. In the same way cathartic music brings men an elation which is not at all harmful.

Aristotle, *The Politics,* trans. T. A. Sinclair, revised and re-presented by Trevor J. Saunders (Harmondsworth: Penguin Classics, rev. ed. 1981), 307–16. The 1962 translation copyright © the Estate of T. A. Sinclair, 1962. Revised translation copyright © Trevor J. Saunders, 1981. Reprinted by permission of Penguin Books Ltd.

5

The Kinship of Music and Rhetoric

The *Institutio oratoria*, a twelve-volume course in rhetoric by Quintilian (Marcus Fabius Quintilianus, first century A.D.), became a cornerstone of late-classical educational curricula. Defending the inclusion of music in the training of an orator, the Roman author cites its power to move and argues that the orator should learn to imitate its inflections. The "musicalization" of speech he advocates in the service of rhetoric was a powerful precedent for the musical humanists of the late Renaissance, who sought to recapture the ethical powers of music by a return to the alliance of music and rhetoric described here. Quintilian's illustrative anecdotes are of the greatest interest: they turn up again and again in classical writings and were dutifully copied by the humanists. See, for example, the story of the nonmusician's after-dinner embarrassment in the extract from Morley on p. 131, and the updating of the story of Pythagoras and the aulos player by proponents of *musique mesurée à l'antique* (p. 139). It is interesting to observe how Pythagoras, popularly supposed to have been the "inventor" of music, is elevated to quasi-Orphic status in these variations on an ancient theme.

Aristophanes shows in more than one of his plays that boys were trained in music from remote antiquity, while in the *Hypobolimaeus* of Menander an old man, when a father claims his son from him, gives an account of all expenses incurred on behalf of the boy's education and states that he has paid out large sums to musicians and geometricians. From the importance thus given to music also originated the custom of taking a lyre round the company after dinner, and when on such an occasion Themistocles confessed that he could not play, his education was (to quote from Cicero's *Tusculanae disputa-*

tiones) "regarded as imperfect." Even at the banquets of our own forefathers it was the custom to introduce the pipe and lyre, and even the hymn of the Salii has its tune. These practices were instituted by King Numa and clearly prove that not even those whom we regard as rude warriors neglected the study of music, at least in so far as the resources of that age allowed. Finally there was actually a proverb among the Greeks, that the uneducated were far from the company of the Muses and Graces. But let us discuss the advantages which our future orator may reasonably expect to derive from the study of Music.

Aristoxenus [fourth century B.C. philosopher whose *Elements of Harmony* is the most important ancient treatise on Greek music] divides music, in so far as it concerns the voice, into *rhythm* and *melody,* the one consisting in measure, the latter in sound and song. Now I ask you whether it is not absolutely necessary for the orator to be acquainted with all these methods of expression which are concerned firstly with gesture, secondly with the arrangement of words, and thirdly with the inflections of the voice, of which a great variety are required in pleading. Otherwise we must assume that structure and the euphonious combination of sounds are necessary only for poetry, lyric and otherwise, but superfluous in pleading, or that unlike music, oratory has no interest in the variation of arrangement and sound to suit the demands of the case. But eloquence does vary both tone and rhythm, expressing sublime thoughts with elevation, pleasing thoughts with sweetness, and ordinary with gentle utterance, and in every expression of its art is in sympathy with the emotions of which it is the mouthpiece. It is by the raising, lowering, or inflection of the voice that the orator stirs the emotions of his hearers, and the measure, if I may repeat the term, of his voice or phrase differs according as we wish to rouse the indignation or the pity of the judge. For, as we know, different emotions are roused even by the various musical instruments, which are incapable of reproducing speech. Further, the motion of the body must be suitable and becoming, or as the Greeks call it *eurhythmic,* and this can only be secured by the study of music.

To proceed, an orator will assuredly pay special attention to his voice, and what is so specially the concern of music as this? Here I will content myself by citing the example of Gaius Gracchus, the leading orator of his age, who during his speeches had a musician standing behind him with a pitchpipe, or *tonarion* as the Greeks call it, whose duty it was to give him the tones in which his voice was to be pitched. Such was the attention which he paid to this point even in the midst of his most turbulent speeches, when he was terrifying the patrician party and even when he had begun to fear their power. I should like for the benefit of the uninstructed, those "creatures of the heavier Muse," as the saying is, to remove all doubts as to the value of music. They will at any rate admit that the poets should be read by our future orator. But can they be read without some knowledge of music? Or if any of my critics be so blind as to have some doubts about other forms of poetry, can the lyric poets at any rate be read without such knowledge? If there were anything novel in my insistence on the study of music, I should have to treat the matter at greater length. But in view of the fact that the study of music has, from those remote times when Chiron taught Achilles down to our own day, continued to be studied by all except those who have a hatred for any regular course of study, it would be a mistake to seem to cast any doubt upon its value by showing an excessive zeal in its defense. It will, however, I think be sufficiently clear from the examples I have already quoted, what I regard as the value and the sphere of music in the training of an orator.

Give me the knowledge of the principles of music, which have the power to excite or assuage the emotions of mankind. We are told that Pythagoras on one occasion, when some young men were led astray by their passions to commit an outrage on a respectable family, calmed them by ordering the piper to change her strain to a spondaic measure, while [the Stoic philosopher] Chrysippus selects a special tune to be used by nurses to entice their little charges to sleep. Further I may point out that among the fictitious themes employed in declamation is one, doing no little credit to its author's learning, in which it is supposed that a piper is accused of manslaughter because he had played a tune in the Phrygian mode as an accompaniment to a sacrifice, with the result that the person officiating went mad and flung himself over a precipice. If an orator is expected to declaim on such a theme as this, which cannot possibly be handled without some knowledge of music, how can my critics for all their prejudice fail to agree that music is a necessary element in the education of an orator?

Marcus Fabius Quintilianus, *Institutio oratorio,* trans. H. E. Butler (Cambridge, Mass.: Harvard University Press, 1922), 169–77. Reprinted by permission of the publishers and the Loeb Classical Library.

6

Music in Temple and Synagogue: The Judaic Heritage

Psalmody (the singing of psalms) is surely the oldest continuous musical tradition in Western civilization. Three phases may be distinguished in its history: the period of temple worship in Jerusalem, the overlapping period of synagogue worship, and the further overlapping period of Christianity. The nature of psalmody in the temple of Jerusalem may easily be inferred from the texts of a number of the psalms themselves:

Make a joyful noise unto the Lord, all the earth; make a loud noise, and rejoice, and sing praise.
    Sing unto the Lord with the harp; with the harp, and the voice of a psalm.
    With trumpets and sound of cornet, make a joyful noise before the Lord, the King.

Ps. 98:4–6.

Praise ye the Lord. Praise God in his sanctuary: praise him in the firmament of his power.
    Praise him for his mighty acts: praise him according to his excellent greatness.
    Praise him with the sound of the trumpet: praise him with the psaltery and harp.
    Praise him with the timbrel and dance: praise him with stringed instruments and organs.
    Praise him upon the loud cymbals: praise him upon the high sounding cymbals.
    Let every thing that hath breath praise the Lord. Praise ye the Lord.

Ps. 150.

The clangorous noise of instruments (fancifully translated, and it is just as well, since so little is known precisely about Biblical instruments) accompanying the songs of praise reminds the modern reader of no Western form of divine service, but rather of some splendid Eastern ritual, as does the following glimpse of David dancing before the ark of God:

And David and all the house of Israel played before the Lord on all manner of instruments made of fir wood, even on harps, and on psalteries, and on timbrels, and on cornets, and on cymbals. And David danced before the Lord with all his might; and David was girded with a linen garment. So David and all the house of Israel brought up the ark of the Lord with shouting, and with the sound of the trumpet. And as the ark of the Lord came into the city of David, Michal (Saul's daughter) looked through a window, and saw king David leaping and dancing before the Lord; and she despised him in her heart.

And Michal the daughter of Saul came out to meet David and said, "How glorious was the king of Israel today, who uncovered himself today in the eyes of the handmaids of his servants, as one of the vain fellows uncovereth himself!"

And David said unto Michal, "It was before the Lord, which chose me before thy father, and before all his house, to appoint me ruler over the people of the Lord, over Israel: therefore will I play before the Lord."

II Sam. 6:5–21.

David, the singer of psalms and hero of the Old Testament, is also the Biblical Orpheus.

But the Spirit of the Lord departed from Saul, and an evil spirit from the Lord troubled him. And Saul's servants said unto him, "Behold now, an evil spirit from God troubleth thee. Let our lord now command thy servants, which are before thee, to seek out a man, who is a cunning player on a harp: and it shall come to pass, when the evil spirit from God is upon thee, that he shall play with his hand, and thou shalt be well."

And Saul said unto his servants, "Provide me now a man that can play well, and bring him to me."

Then answered one of the servants, and said, "Behold, I have seen a son of Jesse the Bethlehemite, that is cunning in playing, and a mighty valiant man, and a man of war, and prudent in matters, and a comely person, and the Lord is with him."

Wherefore Saul sent messengers unto Jesse, and said, "Send me David thy son, which is with the sheep."

And it came to pass, when the evil spirit from God was upon Saul, that David took a harp, and played with his hand: so Saul was refreshed, and was well, and the evil spirit departed from him.

I Sam. 16:14–19, 23.

King Solomon was seven years building the Temple. Here is the Chronicler's account of the ceremony of dedication, reflecting, no doubt, the wish to trace back to the Temple's origins the musical ceremonial of a much later age.

Thus all the work that Solomon made for the house of the Lord was finished: and Solomon brought in all the things that David his father had dedicated; and the silver, and the gold, and all the instruments put he among the treasures of the house of God. Then Solomon assembled the elders of Israel, and all the heads of the tribes, the chief of the fathers of the children of Israel, unto Jerusalem, to bring up the ark of the covenant of the Lord out of the city of David, which is Zion.

Wherefore all the men of Israel assembled themselves unto the king, in the feast which was in the seventh month. And all the elders of Israel came; and the Levites took up the ark. And they brought up the ark and the tabernacle of the congregation, and all the holy vessels that were in the tabernacle, these did the priests and the Levites bring up. Also king Solomon, and all the congregation of Israel that were assembled unto him before the ark, sacrificed sheep and oxen, which could not be told nor numbered for multitude. And the priests brought in the ark of the covenant of the Lord unto his place, to the oracle of the house, into the most holy place. And there it is unto this day. There was nothing in the ark, save the two tables which Moses put therein at Horeb, when the Lord made a covenant with the children of Israel, when they came out of Egypt.

And it came to pass, when the priests were come out of the holy place (the Levites, which were the singers, being arrayed in white linen, having cymbals and psalteries and harps, stood at the east end of the altar, and with them an hundred and twenty priests sounding with trumpets), and it came to pass, as the trumpeters and singers were as one, to make one sound to be heard in praising and thanking the Lord; and when they lifted up their voice with the trumpets and cymbals and instruments of music, and praised the Lord, saying, For he is good; for his mercy endureth for ever: that then the house was filled with a cloud, even the house of the Lord; so that the priests could not stand to minister by reason of the cloud: for the glory of the Lord had filled the house of God.

Now when Solomon had made an end of praying, the fire came down from heaven, and consumed the burnt offering and the sacrifices; and the glory of the Lord filled the house. And when all the children of Israel saw how the fire came down, and the glory of the Lord upon the house, they bowed themselves with their faces to the ground upon the pavement, and praised the Lord, saying, For he is good; for his mercy endureth for ever. Then the king and all the people offered sacrifices before the Lord. And the priests waited on their offices: the Levites also with instruments of music of the Lord, which David the king had made to praise the Lord, because his mercy endureth for ever, when David praised by their ministry; and the priests sounded trumpets before them, and all Israel stood.

II Chron. 5:1–13; 7:1–6.

In the account given by Nehemiah of the dedication of Jerusalem's new walls in 445 B.C. (they, indeed the whole city, had been burned to the ground by the Babylonians), we meet with the principle of antiphony—the use of split choirs answering back and forth—which, with the responsorial mode of performance (in which one singer and a choir alternate), was to be a mainstay of psalmody in both the Jewish and the Christian service. The practice of antiphonal singing may well have been prompted by the poetic structure of the psalms themselves, with their pairs of hemistichs, or half-lines that state a single thought in different words (for an example see Psalm 150, quoted previously).

And at the dedication of the wall of Jerusalem they sought the Levites out of all their places, to bring them to Jerusalem, to keep the dedication with gladness, both with thanksgivings, and with singing, with cymbals, psalteries, and with harps. And the sons of the singers gathered themselves together, both out of the plain country round about Jerusalem, and from the villages of Netophathi: also from the house of Gilgal, and out of the fields of Geba and Azmaveth: for the singers had builded them villages round about Jerusalem.

And the priests and the Levites purified themselves and purified the people, and the gates, and the wall. Then I brought up the princes of Judah upon the wall, and appointed two great companies of them that gave thanks, whereof one went on the right hand upon the wall, toward the dung gate: and after them went Hoshaiah, and half of the princes of Judah, and certain of the priests' sons with trumpets and with the musical instruments of David the man of God.

And the other company of them that gave thanks went over against them, and I after them, and the half of the people upon the wall, from beyond the tower of the furnaces even unto the broad wall. So stood the two companies that gave thanks in the house of God. And the singers sang loud, with Jezrahiah, their overseer. Also that day they offered great sacrifices, and rejoiced; for God had made them rejoice with great joy: the wives also and the children rejoiced; so that the joy of Jerusalem was heard even afar off.

Neh. 12:27–43.

Antiphonal psalmody is even reflected in the vision by means of which the prophet Isaiah received his call.

In the year that king Uzziah died, I saw also the Lord sitting upon a throne, high and lifted up, and his train filled the temple.

Above it stood the seraphims: each one had six wings; with twain he covered his face, and with twain he covered his feet, and with twain he did fly.

And one cried unto another, and said, Holy, holy, holy is the Lord of hosts; the whole earth is full of his glory.

And the posts of the door moved at the voice of him that cried, and the house was filled with smoke.

Isa. 6:1–4.

The words sung by the Seraphim entered the Jewish liturgy as the *Kedushah* and were later adopted by the Christian church as the Sanctus of the Mass, one more direct musical link between Judaism and Christianity. Like most of the liturgical elements adopted from the older religion, the Sanctus is furnished with an introductory "Christianizing" text (the Preface), rendering it suitable for its new setting:

It is truly meet and just, right and profitable, humbly to beseech thee, O Lord, not to forsake the flock of which thou art the eternal Shepherd; but through thy holy Apostles ever to guard and keep it, so that by those rulers it be governed whom thou didst set over it to be its pastors under thee. And therefore with the Angels and Archangels, with the Thrones and Dominations and with all the array of the heavenly host we sing a hymn to thy glory and unceasingly repeat:

> Holy, Holy, Holy, Lord God of Hosts.
> The Heavens and the earth are full of thy glory.
> Hosanna [Heb.: Save us] in the highest.

Mass and Vespers (Tournai: Desclée & Co., 1957), 13–14.

The early Christian church adopted its rituals not from the pomp and pageantry of the temple (destroyed by the Roman emperor Titus in A.D. 70) but from the far more modest liturgy of the synagogues, which were study houses where Jews met for prayer in small groups. The music of the synagogue did without instruments. After the destruction of the temple and the dispersal of the Jews, an actual ban, still observed by Orthodox congregations, was placed on their use. This ban stemmed from an interpretation of Psalm 137, which dates from the time of the Babylonian exile.

By the rivers of Babylon, there we sat down; yea, we wept, when we remembered Zion.
  We hanged our harps upon the willows in the midst thereof.
  For there they that carried us away captive required of us a song; and they that wasted us required of us mirth, saying, Sing us one of the songs of Zion.
  How shall we sing the Lord's song in a strange land?
  If I forget thee, O Jerusalem, let my right hand forget her cunning.
  If I do not remember thee, let my tongue cleave to the roof of my mouth; if I prefer not Jerusalem above my chief joy.

Ps. 137:1–6.

The Greek-Jewish philosopher Philo of Alexandria, a contemporary of Christ, described the ritual singing of a Jewish sect known as the Therapeutae in his *Treatise on a Contemplative Life.* Their psalm singing seems exceptional in its inclusion of women on an equal footing with men, but except for this detail, what Philo describes is typical of the much modified and scaled-down version of the Jewish liturgy that became the framework for the early Christian vigils. Some scholars maintain, in fact, that the Therapeutae *were* an early Christian sect—at this period Jew and Christian may often have been indistinguishable. And one of the foundations of what has been termed the "sacred bridge" between the two religions was the Book of Psalms—not just the words, but (to an unknown extent) the melodies as well, for modern research has uncovered a close resemblance between certain psalm melodies preserved to this day among Middle Eastern Jews and certain Gregorian chants sung by the Christians of western Europe in the Middle Ages. The singing is antiphonal, and the psalms and hymns are furnished with refrains, which in Christian times became known as *antiphons.*

When, therefore, the presiding worshipper appears to have spoken at sufficient length, some one rising up sings a hymn which has been made in honor of God, either such as he has composed himself, or some ancient one of some old poet, for they have left behind them many poems and songs, and psalms of thanksgiving and hymns, and songs at the time of libation, and at the altar, and in regular order, and in choruses, admirably measured out in various and well diversified strophes. And after him then others also arise in their ranks, in becoming order, while every one else listens in decent silence, except when it is proper for them to take up the refrain of the song, and to join in at the end; for then they all, both men and women, join in the hymn.

  And after the feast they celebrate the sacred festival during the whole night; and this nocturnal festival is celebrated in the following manner: they all stand up together, and two choruses are formed, one of men and the other of women, and for each chorus there is a leader and chief selected, who is the most honorable and most excellent of the band. Then they sing hymns which have been composed in honor of God in many meters and tunes, at one time all singing together, and at another moving their hands and dancing in alternating verses, and uttering in an inspired manner songs of thanksgiving.

Then, when each chorus of the men and each chorus of the women has feasted by itself, like persons in the bacchanalian revels, drinking the pure wine of the love of God, they join together, and the two become one chorus, an imitation of that one which, in old time, was established by the Red Sea, on account of the wondrous works which were displayed there; for by the commandment of God, the sea became to one party the cause of safety, and to the other that of utter destruction. When the Israelites saw and experienced this great miracle, which was an event beyond all description, beyond all imagination, and beyond all hope, both men and women together, under the influence of divine inspiration, becoming all one chorus, sang hymns of thanksgiving to God the Savior, Moses the prophet leading the men, and Miriam the prophetess leading the women.

Now the chorus of male and female worshippers, being formed as far as possible on this model, makes a most delightful concert, and a truly musical symphony, the shrill voices of the women mingling with the deep-toned voices of the men.

The Works of Philo Judaeus, trans. C. D. Yonge, IV (London, 1855), 18–20.

7

Music in the Christian Churches of Jerusalem, c. A.D. 400

A Spanish nun called Egeria visited the holy places toward the end of the fourth century and wrote a vivid account of her pilgrimage for the benefit of the sisters at home. Her description of the ceremonies practiced by the oldest of all Christian congregations throughout the year, an extremely important early document in the history of Christian worship, is full of allusions to the musical portions of the services. We read not only of psalms, but of hymns and antiphons. Scholarly opinion is divided as to whether the last two should be understood in their usual, later, sense or as vague variants of "psalms." For hymns, see p. 25. "Antiphon" here might simply mean a psalm sung antiphonally (see p. 15) or it might already have the later meaning of a text and melody added to such a psalm to be sung between verses as a refrain. In the following excerpt Egeria describes the Sunday Vigil (recognizable as the incipient Matins service) at the Sanctuary of the Resurrection (Church of the Holy Sepulchre) and Sunday Mass at the Church of the Martyrium, or Holy Cross, both built some fifty years earlier by the emperor Constantine. Note that the Mass service is begun at the second church but concluded at the first, to which the catechumens (as-yet unbaptized heathens) are not admitted. This is a clear reflection of the early division of the Mass into two segments: the Mass of the Catechumens contained readings, sermons, and prayers; the Mass of the Faithful, from which the unbaptized were excluded, centered around the sacrament of the Eucharist.

On the seventh, that is, the Lord's day, before cockcrow the whole crowd collects, as many as the place will hold. For, as they are afraid that they may not be there at cockcrow, they come beforehand and sit there. And hymns and antiphons are sung; and after each hymn or antiphon a prayer is offered. For the priests and deacons are always ready there for vigils, on account of the crowd which assembles; and it is their custom not to open the holy places before cockcrow. But when the first cock has crowed, forthwith the bishop descends and enters inside the cave at the sanctuary. All the doors are opened, and the whole crowd streams into the sanctuary. Here innumerable lights are shining; and when the people have entered, one of the priests recites a psalm, and they all respond; then prayer is offered. Again one of the deacons recites a psalm, and again prayer is offered; a third psalm is said by one of the clergy, and prayer is offered for the third time, and the commemoration of all men is made. Then these three psalms having been said, and these three prayers offered, behold censers are brought into the cave of the sanctuary, so that the whole basilica is filled with odors. Then where the bishop stands inside the rails, he takes the Gospel and advances to the door and himself reads of the Lord's resurrection. And when he has begun to read this, there is such a moaning and groaning of all the people, and such weeping, that the most obdurate person would be moved to tears, for that the Lord endured such grievous things for us. Then the Gospel having been read, the bishop comes forth, and is led to the Cross with hymns, and all the people with him. There again one psalm is recited and prayer offered. Again he blesses the faithful, and the dismissal is given. As the bishop comes forth they all approach to kiss his hand; and presently the bishop betakes himself to his own house. From that hour all the monks return to the sanctuary, and psalms and antiphons are sung until daylight; and after each psalm or antiphon, prayer is offered. For every day in turn the priests and deacons keep vigil at the sanctuary with the people. If any of the laity, either men or women, wish it, they stay there till it is light; but if they do not wish to do so, they return to their houses and go to sleep again.

But with the dawn, because it is the Lord's day, they proceed to the Great Church built by Constantine, which is on Golgotha behind the Cross; and all things are done according to the use which is customary everywhere on the Lord's day. But their use here is this, that as many as wish of all the priests who sit shall preach, and after them all the bishop preaches; these sermons are always delivered on the Lord's day, that the people may always be instructed in the Scriptures and in the love of God. And while these sermons are being delivered, there is a long interval before they are dismissed from the Church. They are thus not dismissed before the fourth, or perhaps the fifth, hour [i.e., around 10 A.M.]. But when the dismissal has been given at the Church, in accordance with the use which everywhere prevails, then the monks escort the bishop with hymns from the Great Church to the sanctuary. And when the bishop begins to come with hymns, all the doors of the sanctuary basilica are opened; and all the people enter (that is the faithful; for the catechumens enter not). And when the people have entered, the bishop enters and forthwith proceeds within the rails of the memorial cave. First, thanks are given to God, and prayer is made for all men; next the deacon calls to all to bow their heads where they stand, and the bishop blesses them standing inside the inner rails; and finally he comes out. As the bishop comes out they all approach to kiss his hand. And thus it is that the dismissal is put off nearly to the fifth or sixth hour [i.e., around 11 A.M.]. And in the evening the ordinary daily service is held. This manner of service is then observed every day throughout the year, certain solemn days excepted.

But among all these details this is very plain, that suitable psalms or antiphons are always sung; those at night, those in the morning, and those through the day, whether at the sixth hour or ninth hour or at vespers, being always suitable and intelligible as pertaining to the matter at hand.

John H. Bernard (trans. and ed.), *The Pilgrimage of S. Silvia of Aquitania to the Holy Places* (London, 1896), 47–49.

PART TWO

The Middle Ages

8

The Church Fathers on Psalmody and on the Dangers of Unholy Music

St. Basil the Great (c. 330–c. 379), Bishop of Caesarea in Asia Minor and founder of Christian monasticism, touches on virtually all the beneficial effects attributed to "good" music by the Neo-Platonists in his "Homily on Psalm 1," below, as well as on a peculiarly Christian one: that of joining the worshipers into a unanimous entity.

When, indeed, the Holy Spirit saw that the human race was guided only with difficulty toward virtue, and that, because of our inclination toward pleasure, we were neglectful of an upright life, what did He do? The delight of melody He mingled with the doctrines so that by the pleasantness and softness of the sound heard we might receive without perceiving it the benefit of the words, just as wise physicians who, when giving the fastidious rather bitter drugs to drink, frequently smear the cup with honey. Therefore, He devised for us these harmonious melodies of the psalms, that they who are children in age or even those who are youthful in disposition might to all appearances chant but, in reality, become trained in soul. For, never has any one of the many indifferent persons gone away easily holding in mind either an apostolic or prophetic message, but they do chant the words of the psalms even in the home, and they spread them around in the market place, and, if perchance, someone becomes exceedingly wrathful, when he begins to be soothed by the psalm, he departs with the wrath of his soul immediately lulled to sleep by means of the melody.

A psalm implies serenity of soul; it is the author of peace, which calms bewildering and seething thoughts. For, it softens the wrath of the soul, and what is unbridled it chastens. A psalm forms friendships, unites those separated, conciliates those at enmity. Who, indeed, can still consider him an enemy with whom he has uttered the same prayer to God? So that psalmody, bringing about choral singing, a bond, as it were, toward unity, and joining the people into a harmonious union of one choir, produces also the greatest of blessings, charity. A psalm is a city of refuge from the demons; a means of inducing help from the angels, a weapon in fears by night, a rest from toils by day, a safeguard for infants, an adornment for those at the height of their vigor, a consolation for the elders, a most fitting ornament for women. It peoples the solitudes; it rids the market place of excesses; it is the elementary exposition of beginners, the improvement of those advancing, the solid support of the perfect, the voice of the Church. It brightens the feast days; it creates a sorrow which is in accordance with God. For a psalm calls forth a tear even from a heart of stone. A psalm is the work of angels, a heavenly institution, the spiritual incense.

Oh! the wise invention of the teacher who contrived that while we were singing we should at the same time learn something useful; by this means, too, the teachings are in a certain way impressed more deeply on our minds. Even a forceful lesson does not always endure, but what enters the mind with joy and pleasure somehow becomes more firmly impressed upon it. What, in fact, can you not learn from the psalms? Can you not learn the grandeur of courage? The exactness of justice? The nobility of self-control? The perfection of prudence? A manner of penance? The measure of patience? And whatever other good things you might mention? Therein is perfect theology, a prediction of the coming of Christ in the flesh, a threat of judgment, a hope of resurrection, a fear of punishment, promises of glory, an unveiling of mysteries; all things, as if in some great public treasury, are stored up in the Book of Psalms.

St. Basil, *Exegetic Homilies,* trans. S. Agnes Clare Way, The Fathers of the Church, XLVI (Washington, D.C.: The Catholic University of America Press, 1963), 152–54. Reprinted by permission.

And St. John Chrysostom (c. 345–407), the most famous Greek Father, confirms the importance of psalmody:

In church when vigils are observed David is first, middle, and last. At the singing of the morning canticles David is first, middle, and last. At funerals and burials of the dead again David is first, middle, and last. O wondrous thing! Many who have no knowledge of letters at all nonetheless know all of David and can recite him from beginning to end. And not only in the cities and the churches, in all seasons and for ages past, has David illuminated all our lives, but also in the fields and in the wilderness. In monasteries, in the chorus of the holy angelic host, David is first, middle, and last. And in convents, where virgins gather to imitate Mary, David is first, middle, and last.

Martin Gerbert, *De cantu et musica sacra* ... , I (St. Blasien, 1774), 64. Trans. R. T.

Neo-Platonism also lies at the heart of the Church Fathers' condemnation of all music other than the chaste and unadorned chant. St. Basil even retells the old legend about Pythagoras that we have already met with in Quintilian (p. 12).

Passions sprung of lack of breeding and baseness are naturally engendered by licentious songs. But we should cultivate the other kind, which is better and leads to the better, through his use of which, as they say, David, the poet of the Sacred Songs, freed the king from his madness. And it is related that Pythagoras, too, chancing upon some drunken revellers, commanded the flute player who led the revel to change his harmony and play to them the Doric mode; and that thus the company came back to its senses under the influence of the strain, so that, tearing off their garlands, they went home ashamed. Yet others at the sound of the flute are excited to a Bacchic frenzy. Such is the difference between giving full ear to wholesome and to licentious music. Hence, since this latter is now in vogue, you should participate in it less than in the very basest of things.

St. Basil, *The Letters,* trans. Roy J. Deferrari, IV (London: W. Heinemann, 1934), 419.

As to instruments, the Fathers identify two interrelated evils arising from their use: playing instruments is essentially idle and unproductive, and it can lead to licentious behavior. From the use of flutes it is but a step to "shameful songs," and thence to drunkenness and worse. St. Basil again:

Of the arts necessary to life which furnish a concrete result there is carpentry, which produces the chair; architecture, the house; shipbuilding, the ship; tailoring, the garment; forging, the blade. Of useless arts there is harp playing, dancing, flute playing, of which, when the operation ceases, the result disappears with it. And indeed, according to the word of the apostle, the result of these is destruction.

James McKinnon, "The Church Fathers and Musical Instruments" (Ph.D. diss., Columbia University, 1965), 182. By kind permission of the author.

And St. John Chrysostom:

Marriage is accounted an honorable thing both by us and by those without; and it is honorable. But when marriages are solemnized, such a number of ridiculous circumstances take place as ye shall hear of immediately: because the most part, possessed and beguiled by custom, are not even aware of their absurdity, but need others to teach them. For dancing, and cymbals, and flutes, and shameful words and songs, and drunkenness, and revellings, and all the Devil's great heap of garbage is then introduced.

Philip Schaff, *Nicene and Post-Nicene Fathers,* XII (New York, 1886), 69.

The psalms' many invitations to worship the Lord to the accompaniment of noisy musical instruments needed to be explained away. An easy recourse was to give a symbolic interpretation. Here is one given by Origen of Alexandria (c. 185–c. 254) to Psalm 33:2:

Give thanks to the Lord on the harp; with the ten-stringed psaltery chant his praises. The harp is the active soul; the psaltery is pure mind. The ten strings can be taken as ten nerves, for a nerve is a string. Therefore, the psaltery is taken to be a body having five senses and five faculties.

McKinnon, "Church Fathers," 223.

Or, again, to the same verse, by the "father of ecclesiastical history," Eusebius of Caesarea (c. 260–c. 340):

We sing God's praise with living psaltery, for more pleasant to God than any instrument is the harmony of the whole Christian people. Our harp is the whole body, by whose movement and action the soul sings a fitting hymn to God, and our ten-stringed psaltery is the veneration of the Holy Ghost by the five senses of the body and the five virtues of the spirit.

Gustave Reese, *Music in the Middle Ages* (New York: W. W. Norton & Company, Inc., 1940), 62 (from Eusebius, *Historia ecclesiastica*).

> Most fanciful of all, perhaps, is the following interpretation of Psalm 150 (see p. 12) by Honorius of Autun (died c.1130):

Praise him with timbrel and dance. The timbrel is made from skin that has dried and become firm, which signifies unchangeable flesh, made strong against corruption. Therefore praise God because he has made your flesh, once fragile, to be firm and because it will no longer be subject to corruption.

Praise him with sounding cymbals, Cymbals shine and resound after they have been forged in the fire. This signifies the bodies of the saints who after they have passed through the fire of adversity will glisten as the sun and resound eternally in praise of God.

Indeed, through various instruments are signified different orders of those who praise God in Church. The trumpets are preachers; the psaltery those who perform spiritual deeds, such as monks; the harp those who chastise themselves, like hermits and solitaries. The timbrel is those who have died to their faults, such as martyrs; and the chorus (dance) those living harmoniously in the common life, like the canons regular. By these instruments every spirit, that is everything which has spiritual life, praises God; instruments of that sort will resound during the everlasting nuptials of the Lamb, Alleluia.

McKinnon, "Church Fathers," 239–40.

9

The Testimony of St. Augustine

St. Augustine (354–430), the leading Church Father of Western Christendom, is also one of our major sources of information regarding the uses of music in the liturgy of his day. He himself was immensely susceptible to music, as we learn from several passages in the *Confessions*. Here is the account of his baptism at the hands of his instructor in the faith, St. Ambrose, Bishop of Milan:

We were baptized, and all anxiety over the past melted away from us. The days were all too short, for I was lost in wonder and joy, meditating upon your far-reaching providence for the salvation of the human race. The tears flowed from me when I heard your hymns and canticles, for the sweet singing of your Church moved me deeply. The music surged in my ears, truth seeped into my heart, and my feelings of devotion overflowed, so that the tears streamed down. But they were tears of gladness.

It was not long before this that the Church at Milan had begun to seek comfort and spiritual strength in the practice of singing hymns, in which the faithful fervently united with heart and voice. It was only a year, or not much more, since Justina, the mother of the boy emperor Valentinian, had been persecuting your devoted servant Ambrose in the interest of the heresy into which the Arians had seduced her. In those days your faithful people used to keep watch in the church, ready to die with their bishop, your servant. It was then that the practice of singing hymns and psalms was introduced, in keeping with the usage of the Eastern churches, to revive the flagging spirits of the people during their long and cheerless watch. Ever since then the custom has been retained, and the example of Milan has been followed in many other places, in fact in almost every church throughout the world.

St. Augustine, *Confessions,* trans. R. S. Pine-Coffin (Harmondsworth: Penguin Classics, 1961), 191. Copyright © R. S. Pine-Coffin, 1961. Reprinted by permission of Penguin Books Ltd.

> The hymns mentioned by Augustine were in fact a new musical element in the Western liturgy, and St. Ambrose is remembered as their chief sponsor. They represented a notable departure from other types of chant: the texts were metrical poems, newly composed rather than Biblical, and the music was repeated with each successive stanza (strophic form). Elsewhere, Augustine defines a hymn as a

Song with praise of God: If you praise God and do not sing, you do not utter a hymn. If you sing and do not praise God, you do not utter a hymn. If you praise anything other than God, and if you sing these praises, still you do not utter a hymn. A hymn therefore has these three things: song, and praise, and God.

Martin Gerbert, *De cantu et musica sacra* ... , I (St. Blasien, 1774), 74. Trans. R. T.

> More than any other Father of the Church, Augustine gives evidence of real passion for music. For him it was a powerful carrier of emotional "meaning," at times even better suited than words to express religious ecstasy. The most enthusiastic description of music by any Christian theologian before Luther, in fact, is Augustine's description of the *jubilus,* the lengthy melisma on the last syllable of the word *Alleluia* sung before the Gospel reading at Mass, which sometimes goes on for as many as thirty or forty notes. Far from a merely "decorative" embellishment, the *jubilus* was the most mystically meaningful part of the chant for Augustine.

It is a certain sound of joy without words, the expression of a mind poured forth in joy. A man rejoicing in his own exultation, after certain words which cannot be understood, bursteth forth into sounds of exultation without words, so that it seemeth that he, filled with excessive joy, cannot express in words the subject of that joy.

Gustave Reese, *Music in the Middle Ages* (New York: W. W. Norton & Company, Inc., 1940), 164.

> So much, in fact, was Augustine associated with the enthusiastic and exuberant attitude toward music that characterized the Ambrosian innovations, that a legend sprang up, holding that the greatest of all the Christian hymns of praise, the Te Deum, was created spontaneously by Ambrose and Augustine together in the process of Augustine's baptism. The main source of this legend is an account of the history of the bishopric of Milan by Landulf, who was one of Ambrose's successors as bishop of that city in the eleventh century. His story is a colorful embroidery of Augustine's own account of his baptism, given above. The true author of the Te Deum, by the way, is now generally considered to have been the bishop Nicetas (d. 414), of Remesiana in Dacia (now Romania).

It happened that there was a man named Augustine, a philosopher, later in his life a good Christian and an orthodox bishop, but who had been led astray by the errors of the Manicheans. He came to church one day in the wintertime, not out of interest in the sermon nor to see or hear the mystery of the Lord, but to refute and rebuke the blessed Ambrose, who was preaching and explaining to the people about the Lord's incarnation.

What happened, however, was that Augustine, forgetting both himself and all his philosophy, stood as if transfixed, pale and trembling in the sight of all who were there. Then, when the blessed Ambrose's charge to the people was done, Augustine came to see him in private. Now the Holy Spirit had made known to Ambrose all of Augustine's learning, and revealed to him all his education, and showed him in addition Augustine's excellence in logic, his points of difference with the true faith, and what a faithful and orthodox believer he would become. And so Ambrose received him very gently, and treated him with great kindness.

He rejoiced for Augustine like the father in the Gospel, who, embracing the son he had lost, weeping and placing his ring on his son's finger, kisses him, and then, reproaching his other son for his excessive envy, says to him, "Your brother was dead and now is alive again; he was lost and has been found." So with Augustine. A few days later, by the will of God, at the springs called St. John's, Augustine was finally baptized and confirmed by Ambrose, with God aiding him, in the name of the holy and indivisible Trinity. All the believers of the city stood by and watched, just as formerly many had watched him in his errors and agreed with him. And at these springs the Holy Spirit granted them eloquence and inspiration; and so, with all who were there hearing and seeing and marveling, they sang together the *Te Deum laudamus,* and so brought forth what is now approved of by the whole church, and sung devoutly everywhere. Rejoicing together in God, like men just granted great riches and pearls of great price, they ate together and were very glad; they rejoiced with great joy, and took comfort in God.

Jacques Paul Migne, *Patrologiae cursus completus, Series Latina,* CXLVII (Paris, 1854), cols. 832–33. Trans. for this book by Lawrence Rosenwald.

Finally, we have Augustine's classic analysis of the conflict within his soul engendered by his spontaneous love of music on the one hand and his Christian conscience on the other. Here, in graphically personal terms, is the most articulate statement we have of the characteristic combination of eager acceptance and distrust with which the early Christian church looked upon music.

I used to be much more fascinated by the pleasures of sound than the pleasures of smell. I was enthralled by them, but you broke my bonds and set me free. I admit that I still find some enjoyment in the music of hymns, which are alive with your praises, when I hear them sung by well-trained, melodious voices, but I do not enjoy it so much that I cannot tear myself away. I can leave it when I wish. But if I am not to turn a deaf ear to music, which is the setting for the words which give it life, I must allow it a position of some honor in my heart, and I find it difficult to assign it to its proper place. For sometimes I feel that I treat it with more honor than it deserves. I realize that when they are sung, these sacred words stir my mind to greater religious fervor and kindle in me a more ardent flame of piety than they would if they were not sung; and I also know that there are particular modes in song and in the voice, corresponding to my various emotions and able to stimulate them because of some mysterious relationship between the two. But I ought not to allow my mind to be paralyzed by the gratification of my senses, which often leads it astray. For the senses are not content to take second place. Simply because I allow them their due, as adjuncts to reason, they attempt to take precedence and forge ahead of it, with the result that I sometimes sin in this way but am not aware of it until later.

Sometimes, too, from over-anxiety to avoid this particular trap I make the mistake of being too strict. When this happens, I have no wish but to exclude from my ears, and from the ears of the Church as well, all the melody of those lovely chants to which the Psalms of David are habitually sung; and it seems safer to me to follow the precepts which I remember often having heard ascribed to Athanasius, bishop of Alexandria, who used to oblige the lectors to recite the psalms with such slight modulation of the voice that they seemed to be speaking rather than chanting. But when I remember the tears that I shed on hearing the songs of the Church in the early days, soon after I had recovered my faith, and when I realize that nowadays it is not the singing that moves me but the meaning of the words when they are sung in a clear voice to the most appropriate tune, I again acknowledge the great value of this practice. So I waver between the danger that lies in gratifying the senses and the benefits which, as I know from experience, can accrue from singing. Without committing myself to an irrevocable opinion, I am inclined to approve of the custom of singing in church, in order that by indulging the ears weaker spirits may be inspired with feelings of devotion. Yet when I find the singing itself more moving than the truth which it conveys, I confess that this is a grievous sin, and at those times I would prefer not to hear the singer.

This, then, is my present state. Let those of my readers whose hearts are filled with charity, from which good actions spring, weep with me and weep for me. Those who feel no charity in themselves will not be moved by my words. But I beg you, O Lord my God, to look upon me and listen to me. Have pity on me and heal me, for you see that I have become a problem to myself, and this is the ailment from which I suffer.

St. Augustine, *Confessions,* 238–39.

10

The Transmission of the Classical Legacy

The most coherent summary of classical musical thought, one that was to have a lasting influence on medieval, and even later, attitudes toward music, was that given by the Roman philosopher-statesman Boethius (c. 480–524) in his treatise *De institutione musica.* "Music," here, is to be understood as harmonics, the science of musical sounds, one of the seven liberal arts. More specifically, in this context, it is one of the four arts of measurement that constituted the curriculum of higher education, the others being arithmetic, geometry, and astronomy: the *quadrivium* (a term possibly coined by Boethius himself), as against the *trivium,* or elementary curriculum (grammar, dialectic, rhetoric). Very early in his treatise Boethius separates the various meanings of "music" in a famous three-tiered definition clearly derived from Plato. His use of the word "harmony" shows the author's full awareness of the word's pre-musical root *ar-*, meaning "to fit together."

It seems that one discussing the musical discipline should discuss, to begin with, the kinds of music which we know to be contained in this study. Indeed there are three types of music. The first type is the music of the universe (*musica mundana*), the second type, that of the human being (*musica humana*), and the third type is that which is created by certain instruments (*musica instrumentis constituta*), such as the kithara, or tibia or other instruments which produce melodies.

Now the first type, that is the music of the universe, is best observed in those things which one perceives in heaven itself, or in the structure of the elements, or in the diversity of the seasons. How could it possibly be that such a swift heavenly machine should move silently in its course? And although we ourselves hear no sound—and indeed there are many causes for this phenomenon—it is nevertheless impossible that such a fast motion should produce absolutely no sound, especially since the orbits of the stars are joined by such a harmony that nothing so perfectly structured, so perfectly united, can be imagined. For some stars drift higher, others lower, and they are all moved with such an equal amount of energy that a fixed order of their courses is reckoned through their diverse inequalities. Thus there must be some fixed order of musical modulation in this celestial motion.

Moreover, if a certain harmony does not join together the diversities and contrary qualities of the four elements, how is it possible for them to unite in one body machine? But all this diversity produces a variety of both seasons and fruits, so that the year in the final analysis achieves a coherent unity. Now if you would imagine one of these things that gives such a diversity to everything taken away, then they would all seem to fall apart and preserve none of their "consonance." Moreover, just as lower strings are not tuned too low, lest they descend to a pitch that would be inaudible, and higher strings are not tuned too high, lest they break under the excessive tension, but rather all strings are coherently and harmoniously tuned, so we discern in the universal music that nothing can be excessive; for if it were, it would destroy something else. Everything either bears its own fruit or aids other things in bearing theirs. For what winter confines, spring releases, summer heats and autumn ripens, and so the seasons in turn either bring forth their own fruit, or give aid to the others in bringing forth their own.

Now one comes to understand the music of the human being by examining his own being. For what unites the incorporeal existence of reason with the body except a certain harmony and, as it were, a careful tuning of low and high pitches in such a way that they produce one consonance? What unites the parts of man's soul, which according to Aristotle, is composed of a rational and irrational part? In what way are the elements of man's body related to each other or what holds together the various parts of his body in an established order?

Now the third type of music is that which is said to be found in various instruments. The governing element in this music is either tension, as in strings, or breath, as in the tibia or those instruments which are activated by water, or a certain percussion, as in those instruments consisting of concave brass which one beats and thus produces various pitches.

Calvin Martin Bower, "Boethius's *The Principles of Music:* An Introduction, Translation, and Commentary" (Ph.D. diss., George F. Peabody College, 1967), 44–48. By kind permission of the author.

Echoes of Boethius's musical Platonism can be detected over the next thousand years. Its most elegant embodiment, perhaps, are these famous lines from Shakespeare's *Merchant of Venice,* which poetically summarize not only the three-level definition of music, but also the related concept of ethos:

LORENZO: How sweet the moonlight sleeps upon this bank!
Here will we sit, and let the sounds of music
Creep in our ears: soft stillness and the night
Become the touches of sweet harmony.
Sit, Jessica: look, how the floor of heaven
Is thick inlaid with patines of bright gold:
There's not the smallest orb which thou behold'st
But in his motion like an angel sings,
Still quiring to the young-eyed cherubins;
Such harmony is in immortal souls;
But, whilst this muddy vesture of decay
Doth grossly close it in, we cannot hear it.
—Enter Musicians.—
Come, ho! and wake Diana with a hymn:
With sweetest touches pierce your mistress' ear,
And draw her home with music. [*Music.*

JESSICA: I am never merry when I hear sweet music.

LORENZO: The reason is, your spirits are attentive:
For do but note a wild and wanton herd,
Or race of youthful and unhandled colts,
Fetching mad bounds, bellowing and neighing loud,
Which is the hot condition of their blood;
If they but hear perchance a trumpet sound,
Or any air of music touch their ears,
You shall perceive them make a mutual stand,
Their savage eyes turn'd to a modest gaze
By the sweet power of music: therefore the poet
Did feign that Orpheus drew trees, stones, and floods;
Since nought so stockish, hard, and full of rage,
But music for the time doth change his nature.
The man that hath no music in himself,
Nor is not mov'd with concord of sweet sounds,
Is fit for treasons, stratagems, and spoils;
The motions of his spirit are dull as night,
And his affections dark as Erebus:
Let no such man be trusted. Mark the music.

Merchant of Venice, act V, scene 1, lines 54–88.

To return to Boethius himself, of great interest is his discussion of music as one of the liberal arts. These were "liberal" in that they were considered the only ones worthy of free men, that is, men untainted by the need to work for a living. (Medicine and

A fair measure of the staying power of Boethius's musical cosmology is its representation as the frontispiece of a famous manuscript of polyphonic music of the Notre Dame period, some 800 years later than Boethius's writings. Here we see three panels, in each of which "Musica" points to the different levels of her manifestation. In the top panel she is pointing to a representation of the universe and its four elements: earth, air, fire (stars), and water. The sun and moon represent the periodic movements of the heavens, an aspect of measurable "harmony." In the middle panel Musica points to four men, who represent the four "humors," or temperaments. These were the basic personality types of the human organism, that is, the four types of "human harmony." The architecture, for example, proposed as the eighth and ninth liberal arts by the Roman Varro in the first century B.C., were struck from the curriculum by later writers as being professional disciplines.) In his definition of the true musician, Boethius transmitted to the ages the ancient philosophical bias (see, for example, Aristotle, p. 9) against manual laborers (instrument players) and merely inspired unthinking men (composers) who made tunes.

What a Musician Is

Every art and discipline ought naturally to be considered of a more honorable character than a skill which is exercised with the hand and labor of a craftsman. For it is much better and nobler to know about what someone else is doing than to be doing that for which someone else is the authority. For the mere physical skill serves as a slave, while the reason governs all as sovereign. And unless the hand acts according to the will of reason, the thing done is in vain. Thus how much nobler is the study of music as a rational science than as a laborious skill of manufacturing sounds! It is nobler to the degree that the mind is nobler than the body. For he who is without reason spends his life in servitude. Indeed the reason reigns and leads to right action, for unless reason's commands are obeyed, the action, void of reason, will be senseless.

Thus we can see that rational speculation is not dependent upon an act of labor, whereas manual works are nothing unless they are determined by reason. The great splendor and merit of reason can be perceived in the fact that the so-called men of physical skill are named according to their instrument rather than according to the discipline. But that person is a musician, who, through careful rational contemplation, has gained the knowledge of making music, not through the slavery of labor, but through the sovereignty of reason.

Indeed this fact can be seen in the building of monuments and the waging of wars, since they are given other names; for monuments are inscribed with the names of those with whose authority and reason they were ordained, and military triumphs are also similarly commemorated. But monuments and triumphs are not named or commemorated for the servitude and labor of those who carried these things to completion.

Thus there are three kinds of people who are considered in relation to the musical art. The first type performs on instruments, the second composes songs, and the third type judges the instrumental performances and composed songs.

But the type which buries itself in instruments is separated from the understanding of musical knowledge. Representatives of this type, for example kithara players and organists and other instrumentalists, devote their total effort to exhibiting their skill on instruments. Thus they act as slaves, as has been said; for they use no reason, but are totally lacking in thought.

---

relative proportions of these humors within a person determined his physical and spiritual constitution: the "choleric" temperament is ruled by bile; the "sanguine" by blood; the "phlegmatic" by phlegm; the "melancholic" by black bile. The four humors mirror the four elements; thus, human harmony is a function of the celestial. Finally, in the lowest panel, we find *musica instrumentalis*. Here Musica is reluctant to point; instead, she raises an admonishing finger at the fiddle player, obviously no "musician" in the Boethian sense. *Florence, Biblioteca Medicea Laurenziana, MS Pluteo 29.I. All rights reserved.*

The second type is that of the poets [i.e., *makers* of songs]. But this type composes songs not so much by thought and reason as by a certain natural instinct. Thus this type is also separated from music.

The third type is that which has gained an ability of judging, whereby it can weigh rhythms and melodies and songs as a whole. Of course since this type is devoted totally to reason and thought, it can rightly be considered musical. And that man is a musician who has the faculty of judging the modes and rhythms, as well as the genera of songs and their mixtures, and the songs of the poets, and indeed all things which are to be explained subsequently; and this judgment is based on a thought and reason particularly suited to the art of music.

Bower, "Boethius's *The Principles,*" 101–104.

11

Music as a Liberal Art

The pagan curriculum of the seven liberal arts and, with it, the Latin classics themselves were saved from destruction and oblivion through the efforts of some prominent churchmen (St. Augustine, Cassiodorus, and others) who adapted classical learning to Christian ends. Here, from *Scholia enchiriadis* (a commentary to a musical textbook by an anonymous Frankish clergyman of the ninth or tenth century, famous for its early examples of polyphonic practices—see p. 51), is an example of that adaptation. The subject is the relationship between music and its sister disciplines in the quadrivium.

STUDENT: How, then, is Harmony born of its mother Arithmetic? And are Harmony and Music the same thing?

TEACHER: Harmony is taken to mean the concordant mixture of different sounds. Music is the scheme of that concord. Music, like the other mathematical disciplines, is in all its aspects bound up with the system of numbers. And so it is by way of numbers that it must be understood.

S: What are the mathematical disciplines?

T: Arithmetic, Geometry, Music, and Astronomy.

S: What is Mathematics?

T: Theoretical knowledge.

S: In what way theoretical?

T: In that it considers abstract quantities.

S: What are abstract quantities?

T: Those quantities which exist without matter, without, that is, any touch of the physical, and which one deals with by mind alone. Now quantities include degrees of size and degrees of number, shapes, equalities and equations, proportions, and other things which, to use the words of Boethius, are incorporeal by nature, unchanging substances, things existing by reason alone; and these things are changed by contact with the corporeal, and are, by the touch of the mutable, turned into change and flux. These quantities are treated one way in Arithmetic, another way in Geometry, still another in Astronomy. These four disciplines are not arts of human devising, but are investigations, such as they are, of divine works; and they lead noble minds, by wonderful arguments, to a better understanding of the work of creation. It is inexcusable to come by these means to know God and His eternal divinity, and then not to glorify Him or give thanks.

S: What is Arithmetic?

T: The study of countable quantity in itself.

S: What is Music?

T: It is the study of notes in harmony and in discord according to numbers, which bear a certain relation to what one finds in the sounds themselves.

S: What is Geometry?

T: The study of the magnitude of fixed objects and of shape.

S: And Astronomy?

T: The study of the magnitude of moving objects; it contemplates the courses of the heavenly bodies, and all their figures, and pursues with searching reason the relations of the stars to one another and to the earth.

S: In what way do the three disciplines other than Arithmetic depend on a knowledge of numbers?

T: In that everything in these disciplines arises from the system of numbers, nor can any of it be understood or expressed without numbers. Who, for example, could even hint at what a triangle or rectangle was, or at any matter pertaining to Geometry, without knowing what three was, or four?

S: No one.

T: What in Astronomy can be known without knowing number? How are we to perceive the risings and settings, the relative speeds of the wandering stars? How the phases of the moon, with their manifold variations? How the part of the zodiac occupied by the sun or moon, or any of the planets? Are not all these things to be known according to the fixed and certain laws of numbers? And are they not, therefore, without numbers entirely unknowable?

S: True indeed.

T: What cause brings it about that, in Music, pitches eight steps apart sound alike? That pitches four or five steps apart are harmonious? That pitches fifteen steps apart are like-sounding and pitches eleven or twelve steps apart are harmonious? What are those measurements which join notes to notes so precisely that if a note becomes, in relation to another note, even a little higher or lower, it can no longer be in harmony with it?

S: These measurements, by which the consonances concord, and the remaining pitches are so expertly joined together in order, are indeed wonderful. But go on and discuss what you wanted to discuss.

T: I say, then, that there is a kind of equivalence at the octave, i.e. at the diapason, because the two notes in question stand in a ratio of one to two, e.g. 6:12 or 12:24. The intervals of the octave and the double octave are more perfect than those of the fourth and fifth. It is true, moreover, that the notes corresponding to the ratios in question are like-sounding or consonant because it is precisely these numbers, and these numbers alone, that are measured and counted in all disciplines, not just in Music alone. And it is for that reason that they are assigned to the consonances and to the remaining pitches as well. Or rather, it is the notes that are generated from the aforesaid numbers.

Do you see now that Music cannot be explained except in numerical terms?

S: I do, with all my heart. Arithmetic is unquestionably necessary to a knowledge of Music.

T: Necessary indeed, for Music is entirely formed and fashioned after the image of numbers. And so it is number, by means of these fixed and established proportions of notes, that brings about whatever is pleasing to the ear in singing. Whatever pleasure rhythms yield, whether in song or in rhythmic movements of whatever sort, all is the work of number. Notes pass away quickly; numbers, however, though stained by the corporeal touch of pitches and motions, remain.

Gerbert, *Scriptores ecclesiastici de musica* ... , I (St. Blasien, 1784), 193–96. Trans. for this book by Lawrence Rosenwald.

12

Before Notation

Isidore of Seville (c. 560–636), encyclopedist and historian, defined music as follows:

Music is the practical knowledge of melody, consisting of sound and song; and it is called music by derivation from the Muses. Since sound is a thing of sense it passes along into past time, and it is impressed on the memory. From this it was pretended by the poets that the Muses were the daughters of Jupiter and Memory. For unless sounds are held in the memory by man they perish, because they cannot be written down.

Isidore of Seville, *Etymologiarum sive originum libri xx,* trans. E. Brehaut (New York: Columbia University, 1912), 136.

From this it can be seen that the musical notation of classical antiquity had (except in academic treatises like that of Boethius) been totally lost by the beginning of the Middle Ages, and that all practical music was transmitted by oral tradition. So automatically did medieval thinkers associate music and singing with the processes of memory that St. Augustine employed it in a famous passage from his *Confessions* to illustrate his theory of time. Note that time is conceived of as a kind of moving point, representing the awareness of the present, that constantly encroaches upon the future and turns it into the past. It is not a measurable or divisible quantity; lengths of time are simply collections of successive and discrete "nows." This conception of time is integrally bound up with the "additive" quality of pre-fourteenth-century musical rhythm. The reforms of the Ars Nova in the fourteenth century (see p. 57) depended first of all on the supplanting of this theory of time by the more modern one of time as a systematically divisible entity, a view that arose in connection with the invention of clocks, just as Augustine's theory fits the workings of an hourglass.

The mind performs three functions, those of expectation, attention, and memory. The future, which it expects, passes through the present, to which it attends, into the past, which it remembers. No one would deny that the future does not yet exist or that the past no longer exists. Yet in the mind there is both expectation of the future and remembrance of the past. Again, no one would deny that the present has no duration, since it exists only for the instant of its passage. Yet the mind's attention persists, and through it that which is to be passes towards the state in which it is to be no more. So it is not future time that is long, but a long future is a long expectation of the future; and past time is not long, because it does not exist, but a long past is a long remembrance of the past.

Suppose that I am going to recite a psalm that I know. Before I begin, my faculty of expectation is engaged by the whole of it. But once I have begun, as much of the psalm as I have removed from the province of expectation and relegated to the past now engages my memory, and the scope of the action which I am performing is divided between the two faculties of memory and expectation, the one looking back to what I have already recited, the other looking forward to the part which I have still to recite. But my faculty of attention is present all the while, and through it passes what was the future in the process of becoming the past. As the process continues, the province of memory is extended in proportion as that of expectation is reduced, until the whole of my expectation is absorbed. This happens when I have finished my recitation and it has all passed into the province of memory.

What is true of the whole psalm is also true of all its parts and of each syllable. It is true of any longer action in which I may be engaged and of which the recitation of the psalm may only be a small part. It is true of a man's whole life, of which all his actions are parts. It is true of the whole history of mankind, of which each man's life is a part.

St. Augustine, *Confessions*, trans. R. S. Pine-Coffin (Harmondsworth: Penguin Classics, 1961), 277–78. Copyright © R. S. Pine-Coffin, 1961. Reprinted by permission of Penguin Books Ltd.

The lack of a musical notation became a stumbling block when the Frankish king Charlemagne (742–814) sought alliance with the Pope as part of his strategy to bring about the political unification of Europe under his throne. One of the conditions of that unification was the standardization of the liturgy of the church and its attendant music according to the use of the Roman rite. Local liturgies of northern and central Europe (the so-called Gallican rite) had to be suppressed and supplanted by the imported chant of the Pope's church. In the absence of a way of writing music down, the only means of accomplishing this was by importing cantors from Rome who could teach their chant by rote to the Frankish cantors. The difficulty of the task was compounded by resistance. In order to persuade the northern churches that the Roman chant was in fact better than theirs, it was claimed that Pope Gregory I (reigned 590–604)—who was actually an important reformer of the liturgy but not, as far as we know, a musician— wrote the entire body of "Gregorian" chant directly inspired by the Holy Spirit. As a

The Carolingian propaganda that the Roman liturgy was composed by Pope Gregory the Great under divine inspiration is illustrated in a Frankish Sacramentary (a book prescribing the liturgy for Mass and Office) of *c.* 870. The picture adapts a motif already established in illuminated manuscripts containing Gregory's famous Homilies on Ezekiel. According to this tradition, the Pope, while dictating his commentary, often paused for a long time. This puzzled the scribe, who was separated from Gregory by a screen. So he peeped through and saw the dove of the Holy Ghost hovering at the head of St. Gregory, who resumed his dictation only when the dove removed its beak from his mouth. (It is from such representations of divine inspiration that we get our expression, "A little bird told me.") Such depictions of Gregory in musical connections all date, of course, from a period long after divine rather than a human creation, then, the Roman chant was lent the prestige it needed to triumph eventually over all local opposition. The two accounts given below of the early laborious attempts to reform an orally transmitted chant vividly reflect the situation. One of them gives the Roman side of the story, the other the Frankish. Each side attempts to blame the other for the initial failure. The real culprit, though, was the lack of musical notation.

From John the Deacon, *Life of Gregory the Great* (873–75)

St. Gregory compiled a book of antiphons. He founded a *schola* which to this day performs the chant in the Church of Rome according to his instructions. He also erected two dwellings for it, at St. Peter's and at the Lateran palace, where are venerated the couch from which he gave lessons in chant, the whip with which he threatened the boys, and the authentic antiphonal. Again and again Germans and Gauls were given the opportunity to learn this chant. But they were unable to preserve it uncorrupted, since they mixed elements of their own with the Gregorian melodies, and their barbaric savageness was coupled with vocal crudeness and inability to execute the technicalities.

Charlemagne too was struck, when in Rome, by the discordance between Roman and Gallican singing, while the Franks argued that their chant was corrupted by our chanters with some poor melodies; ours probably showed the authentic antiphonal. On that occasion, so the story goes, Charlemagne asked whether the stream or the source carried the clearer water. When they answered the source, he added wisely, "Then we too, who till now drank the troubled water from the stream, must go back to the clarity of the source." Hence he soon left two of his assiduous clerics with Hadrian. After good instruction they restored for him the early chant at Metz and, by way of Metz, all over Gaul.

But after a long time, when those educated in Rome had died, Charlemagne discovered that the chant of the other churches differed from that of Metz. "We must return again to the source," he said. And at his request—as present-day trustworthy information states—Hadrian sent two chanters, who convinced the king that all had corrupted the Roman chant through carelessness but that at Metz the differences were due to their natural savageness.

From Notker Balbulus, *De gestis Karoli Imperatoris* (Life of Charlemagne)

Deploring the widespread variety in chanted liturgy, Charlemagne got some experienced chanters from the Pope. Like twelve apostles they were sent from Rome to all provinces north of the Alps. Just as all Greeks and Romans were carping spitefully at the glory of the Franks, these clerics planned to vary their teaching so that neither the unity nor the consonance of the chant would spread in a kingdom and province other than their own. Received with honor, they were sent to the most important cities

his death. The actual Gregory could not have dictated music under any circumstances, since in his time there was no way to write it down, as his contemporary Isidore of Seville (see p. 34) advises us quite explicitly. *Paris, Bibliothèque Nationale, MS Lat. 1141, fol. 3. All rights reserved.*

where each of them taught as badly as he could. But in the course of time Charlemagne unmasked the plot, for each year he celebrated the major feasts in a different place. Pope Leo [III, 795–816], informed of this, recalled the chanters and exiled or imprisoned them.

The pontiff then confessed to Charlemagne that, if he would lend him others, they, blinded by the same spite, would not fail to deceive him again. He suggested smuggling two of the King's most intelligent clerics into the papal *schola* "so that those who are with me do not find out that they are yours." This was done successfully. These two chanters returned to Charlemagne; one was kept at court, the other sent to Metz at the request of the bishop. Because of the latter's zeal the chant began to flourish not only there, but throughout Gaul.

Translations of both excerpts slightly adapted and abridged from S.J.P. van Dijk, "Papal Schola *versus* Charlemagne," in *Organicae voces: Festschrift Joseph Smits van Waesberghe* (Amsterdam: Instituut voor Middeleeuwse Muziekwetenschap, 1963), 23–24 (John the Deacon), 27 (Notker).

> Another reason for the success of the Charlemagne-inspired standardization of liturgical music may have been the kind of pedagogical method described below. It will be recalled that one of Gregory's relics mentioned by his biographer was the "whip with which he threatened the boys," so the eleventh-century report given here would seem to describe a time-honored practice.

At Nocturns, and indeed at all the Hours, if the boys commit any fault in the psalmody or other singing, either by sleeping or such like transgression, let there be no sort of delay, but let them be stripped forthwith of frock and cowl, and beaten in their shirt only, with pliant and smooth osier rods provided for that special purpose. If any of them, weighed down with sleep, sing ill at Nocturns, then the master giveth into his hand a reasonably great book, to hold until he be well awake. At Matins the principal master standeth before them with a rod until all are in their seats and their faces well covered. At their uprising likewise, if they rise too slowly, the rod is straightway over them. In short, meseemeth that any King's son could scarce be more carefully brought up in his palace than any boy in a well-ordered monastery.

Costumal of St. Benigne, Dijon (*c.* 1050), in Edward J. Dent, "The Social Aspects of Music," *Oxford History of Music*, I (Oxford: Oxford University Press, 1901), 190–91.

·

13

Embellishing the Liturgy

An interesting sidelight on the practice of music within oral tradition is the invention of the sequence. The monk Notker of St. Gall (called Balbulus, or "the stammerer"), whose biography of Charlemagne is cited above (p. 37), is best remembered as one of the early authors of these lengthy hymns that followed the Alleluia of the Mass. Their origins, as Notker relates, seem to have been humble and eminently practical—simply a way of remembering the *melodiae,* extra melismas that in Frankish times were used to amplify the already-lengthy *jubilus,* the wordless "sound[s] of joy" that so moved St. Augustine (see p. 25). By placing syllables on each of the notes, it was possible to transform the complicated melisma into a simple and easily remembered song. There is irony here, though, for it was the very wordlessness of the *jubilus* that had been, for Augustine, its chief glory. Another irony is the fact that the sequence, which began modestly and "functionally," became one of the lengthiest, most decorative and literary parts of the Mass in the later Middle Ages and remained an integral part of the liturgy until largely eliminated by the Counter Reformation. Had there been an adequate musical notation in Notker's time, perhaps that great flowering of medieval devotional verse might never have been.

To Liutward, who for his great sanctity has been raised in honor to be a high priest, a most worthy successor to that incomparable man, Eusebius, Bishop of Vercelli; abbot of the monastery of the most holy Columbanus, and defender of the cell of his disciple, the most gentle Gallus; and also the arch-chaplain of the most glorious emperor Charlemagne, from Notker, the least of the monks of St. Gall:

When I was still young, and very long *melodiae*—repeatedly entrusted to memory—escaped from my poor little head, I began to reason with myself how I could bind them fast.

In the meantime it happened that a certain priest from Jumièges (recently laid waste by the Normans) came to us, bringing with him his antiphonary, in which some verses had been set to sequences; but they were in a very corrupt state. Upon closer inspection I was as bitterly disappointed in them as I had been delighted at first glance.

Nevertheless, in imitation of them I began to write LAUDES DEO CONCINAT, and further on COLUBER ADAE DECEPTOR. When I took these lines to my teacher Iso, he, commending my industry while taking pity on my lack of experience, praised what was pleasing, and what was not he set about to improve, saying, "The individual motions of the melody should receive separate syllables." Hearing that, I immediately corrected those which fell under *ia;* those under *le* or *lu,* however, I left as too difficult; but later, with practice, I managed it easily. Instructed in this manner, I soon composed my second piece, PSALLAT ECCLESIA MATER ILLIBATA.

When I showed these little verses to my teacher Marcellus, he, filled with joy, had them copied as a group on a roll of parchment; and he gave out different pieces to different boys to be sung. And when he told me that I should collect them in a book and offer them as a gift to some eminent person, I shrank back in shame, thinking I would never be able to do that.

Recently, however, I was asked by my brother Othar to write something in your praise, and I considered myself—with good reason—unequal to the task; but finally I worked up my courage (still with great pain and difficulty) that I might presume to dedicate this worthless little book to your highness. If I were to learn that anything in it had pleased you—as good as you are—to the extent that you might be of assistance to my brother with our lord the Emperor, I would hasten to send you the metrical life of St. Gall which I am working hard to complete (although I had already promised it to my brother Salomon) for you to examine, to keep, and to comment upon.

Richard L. Crocker, *The Early Medieval Sequence* (Berkeley: The University of California Press, 1977), 1–2 (Preface to Notker's *Liber hymnorum*).

The word "trope" is often applied to all medieval explanatory or merely decorative additions to the liturgy, but contemporary definitions are usually more restrictive. "A trope," wrote one thirteenth-century bishop, "is a kind of versicle that is sung on important feasts (for example, Christmas) immediately before the Introit, as if a prelude." The most important of tropes was the so-called *Quem quaeritis* dialogue at the tomb of the risen Christ. It exists as a kind of prelude to the Introit ("Resurrexi") for the Easter Sunday Mass, and, in far more elaborate form, as an appendage to the Matins service, where it became a little play, replete with props and costumes. Thus did the "liturgical drama" of the Middle Ages have its beginnings. We have a remarkably detailed description of the performance of the *Quem quaeritis* play at Winchester Cathedral in England during the latter tenth century from the pen of Ethelwold, the Bishop of Winchester himself.

While the third lesson is being chanted, let four brethren vest themselves; of whom let one, vested in an alb, enter as though to take part in the service, and let him approach the sepulchre without attracting attention and sit there quietly with a palm in his hand. While the third responsory is sung, let the remaining three follow, all of them vested in copes, and carrying in their hands censers filled with incense; and slowly, in the manner of seeking something, let them come before the place of the sepulchre. These things are done in imitation of the angel sitting at the monument, and of the women coming with spices to anoint the body of Jesus. When therefore that one seated shall see the three, as if straying about and seeking something, approach him, let him begin in a dulcet voice of medium pitch to sing:

Whom do you seek in the sepulchre, O followers of Christ?

And when he has sung it to the end, let the three respond in unison:

Jesus of Nazareth, which was crucified, O celestial one.

Whereupon the first:

He is not here; he is risen, just as he foretold. Go, announce that he has risen from the dead.

At the word of this command let those three turn themselves to the choir, saying:

Alleluia! The Lord is risen today; the strong lion, the Christ, the Son of God. Give thanks to God, eia!

This said, let the one seated still, as if recalling them, sing the antiphon:

Come and see the place where the Lord was laid. Alleluia! Alleluia!

And saying this, let him rise, and let him lift the veil and show them the place bare of the cross, but only the cloths laid there in which the cross was wrapped. Seeing which, let them set down the censers which they had carried into the same sepulchre, and let them take up the cloth and spread it out before the eyes of the clergy; and, as if making known that the Lord had risen and was not now therein wrapped, let them sing this antiphon:

The Lord is risen from the sepulchre, who for us hung upon the cross.

And let them place the cloth upon the altar. The antiphon being ended, let the Prior, rejoicing with them at the triumph of our King, in that, having conquered death, He rose again, begin the hymn:

Te Deum laudamus. [We praise thee, O God.]

And this begun, all the bells chime out together.

Ethelwold, *Concordia regularis* (*c.* 975), trans. E. K. Chambers, in W. L. Smoldon, "The Easter Sepulchre Music Drama," *Music & Letters,* XXVII (1946), 5–6.

14

Musical Notation and Its Consequences

The earliest forms of Western notation appeared in the Frankish lands in direct response to the need to transmit the Roman chant to the north (see p. 35). These so-called *neumes* were borrowed from the markings rhetoricians (like Quintilian, p. 10) used to indicate vocal inflections. Placed over lines of text, they gave at best an approximation of pitch, and no indication whatsoever of rhythm. Such notation could serve only as a reminder to a singer who already knew the melody he was to sing. And that singer had to learn the melody in the first place by hearing it and repeating it until he knew it by heart: that is, by the rote method. The idea of being able to sing a melody one had never actually heard was inconceivable. Pitch was eventually fixed by means of the staff, first used in Frankish monasteries in Switzerland. It remained for trainers of choirboys to devise methods to enable a reader to make a direct connection between the sounds of music and the signs that represented them. Among these teachers, Odo of Cluny and Guido of Arezzo were outstanding. Odo made extensive use of the monochord, an "instrument" that was used the way one uses the classroom piano today, to demonstrate the intervals and drill them until the pupil had assimilated them. In his *Enchiridion musices* ("Musical Handbook," c. 935), Odo describes his teaching method and reveals, in his answer to the question "What is music?," a newly practical attitude (compare it with the *Scholia enchiriadis*, p. 32) that suggests the waning of Platonic influence, and with it, the beginning of the end of medieval musical thought.

Here begins the book also called *Dialogus,* written by Dom Odo, and concisely, fittingly, and admirably arranged for the benefit of its users.

My dear brethren: you have asked me most earnestly to set down for you a few rules of music, such rules as children and simple people will understand, and by which they may with God's help quickly acquire skill in singing. You made this request because you had heard that such an accomplishment was possible and had verified those reports carefully. And indeed I have, while I have been with you, succeeded with God's aid in teaching certain children and adolescents that art by those means, in such a way that in a short period of time—sometimes three days, sometimes four, sometimes a week—they learned, by themselves, a great number of antiphons, without having heard them sung by someone else, but having only a proper transcription of them according to the rules. After a little while, they could perform them without hesitation. Just a few days later, moreover, they were able to sing accurately at sight, with no preparation, whatever had been written down in proper musical notation—an accomplishment which the common run of professional singers have not hitherto been able to equal, though many of them have spent fifty years in the study and practice of music and not learned a thing.

At this point, you were even more eager than before. You urged, with vehement prayer and great pressure, that for the honor of God and His holy Mother Mary (in whose convent all this was taking place) rules should be set up, and the whole antiphoner transcribed properly, together with the formulas for the psalm tones.

Trusting in your prayers, and bearing in mind the advice of our common Father, I neither wish nor am able to let this work go. It is true, the theory of this art is a lengthy and difficult study among the scholars of our time; let them cultivate it if they wish, I say, and go the whole length of the course. But those who take this little gift of God on its own terms will be content with the enjoyment of it alone.

And now, so that you may better understand all this, and accept the truth of your own free will, let one of you step up and ask me questions. I will answer them as best I can, and as well as God has made me able.

STUDENT: What is Music?

TEACHER: The knowledge of how to sing accurately, and the direct and easy path toward the acquiring of that skill.

S: How is that learned?

T: Your schoolteacher first shows you all the letters of the alphabet on a slate; just so the musician will reveal to you all the notes used in a melody on the monochord.

S: What sort of thing is the monochord?

T: It is a long, rectangular wooden chest, hollow like a cithara; there is a string placed above it, by sounding which you may easily come to understand all the different notes.

S: How is the string placed?

T: A straight line is drawn lengthwise through the middle of the chest, with a one-inch space left blank at either end. Then a point is marked at either end. Then, in the space left blank, there are placed two bridges, with the string suspended above the line in such a way that the length of the string between the two bridges is equal to the length of the line.

S: But how can just one string produce many pitches?

T: The letters, or notes, which musicians use are placed along the line below the string; and as a movable bridge runs between the line and the string, along the letter, the string becoming longer or shorter, reproduces every song perfectly. When some antiphon or another is sounded out for children by means of these letters, they learn it better and more quickly from the string than they would from a human being. Teach them in this way for a few months, and you can take the string away, and they will sing at sight, unhesitatingly, things they have never heard.

Martin Gerbert, *Scriptores ecclesiastici de musica* … , I (St. Blasien, 1784), 251 ff. Trans. for this book by Lawrence Rosenwald.

Guido of Arezzo's goals were the same as Odo's: to reduce all practical situations to a set of basic principles or rules which could be applied confidently by the pupil. He scorned the monochord as "childish," however, and preferred the use of memorized models of each musical interval, as he describes below in a famous passage from his *Epistola de ignoto cantu* ("Letter on singing unheard songs," c. 1030). This method, too, is still employed by teachers of "ear training."

And so, inspired with divine charity, I have shared this grace that God has given me—unworthy as I am—with you and with as many other people as I could, as diligently and expeditiously as possible. My hope is that posterity will learn with ease those same church chants that I, with all my predecessors, could only learn with difficulty, and will bless us and our colleagues for what we have done. Then, perhaps, there will be, by God's mercy, some remitting of my sins—or at least, from the good will of so many, some prayer on my behalf. Other students, after all, have prayed to God for their teachers, though they have gained from them in ten years of study only an imperfect knowledge of singing. What do you think will be done for us, who can train accomplished singers in a year, or two at most? Perhaps, of course, the habitual wickedness of mankind will be ungrateful for such blessings. But then will not God, who is just, reward us for our labor? Perhaps, again, someone will say that we deserve nothing, on the ground that God is responsible for all, and we can do nothing without Him. Heaven forbid! Even the apostle, knowing that God's grace is at the bottom of everything, writes: "I have fought the good fight, I have finished the course, I have kept the faith; and now there is stored up for me a crown of justice." Secure, then, in our hope of reward, let us pursue this useful work. And since, after all, storms must eventually yield to fair weather, let us set sail cheerfully and with good hope.

In your captivity, however, you cannot, I suppose, easily put your trust in freedom. I will set out what has happened point by point. Pope John [XIX, reigned 1024–33], who governs the Roman church, heard of our schola's reputation. He heard in particular of how, by means of our antiphoners, boys could learn songs they had never heard. He was greatly astonished, and sent three messengers to bring me to him. I went to Rome, therefore, together with Dom Grunwald, the venerable abbot, and Dom Peter, the provost of the canons of the church of Arezzo, a most learned man by the standards of our time. The Pope was most glad to see us, talked much with us, and asked a great many questions. He turned over the pages of our antiphoner as if it were some great prodigy, thinking over in particular the rules prefixed to it. He did not stop, in fact, or move from the place in which he sat, until, fulfilling a vow he made, he had learned to sing one versicle that he had never heard. What he had hardly believed to be true of others he could not but acknowledge in himself. What more is there to say? I had to leave Rome soon—the summer fevers in those wet and swampy places were death to me. We agreed, however, that when the winter returned I would return with it, to explain our work to the Pope, who had already tasted it, and to his clergy.

A few days afterwards, I went to see Dom Guido, the Abbot of Pomposia, our spiritual father, a man beloved of God and men for his virtue and wisdom, and a part of my very soul. He is an intelligent and perceptive man. As soon as he saw our antiphoner, he at once approved it and believed in it. He was ashamed to have been formerly in agreement with our detractors, and begged me to come to Pomposia, saying that for me, a monk, a monastery was preferable to a bishop's church, and this monastery in particular on account of its great intellectual zeal. It is now in fact, by the grace of God and the diligence of Guido, the most eminent, in this respect, in all Italy.

But now, blessed brother, let us turn to the method by which a previously unknown melody is learned. The first and general rule is this: if you sound the letters, or notes, of which each neume is composed on the monochord, and listen to them, you will be able to learn them as if you were hearing them from a teacher. But this rule is for little boys; it is useful for beginners, but harmful for those who go on. I have seen, in fact, a great many very intelligent scholars, men who had sought out as their teachers in this field not only Italians, but even Frenchmen and Germans, who, because they trusted in this rule alone, could never become—not musicians, not even singers—they could never become a match even for our little choirboys. In dealing with an unknown melody, therefore, we ought not to look for the sound from some person or instrument, like blind men who can go nowhere without a guide. Rather we ought to fix fast in our memories the characteristics of every note, every pattern of ascent and descent. Then, indeed, you will have a way of getting at a melody you have not heard sung, and a very reliable way—provided you also have someone to teach the method, and to teach it not only from what has been written down, but also informally, and orally. Indeed, after I began to teach this technique to boys, there were some who could sing new melodies easily in three days, which result could not have been obtained by other means in less than many weeks.

Suppose, then, that you wish to commit some note or neume to memory, in such a way that whenever you wish, in whatever melody (whether one you know or one you don't), it will readily occur to you, and you will be able to reproduce it without hesitation. In that case, you must locate that note or neume in the beginning of some melody you know very well. And for each note to be retained in the memory, you must have a melody of this sort at your beck and call beginning on the note in question. Take this melody, for example, which I use in teaching boys both at the beginning and the end of the course:

UT queant laxis	[O for thy spirit, holy John, to chasten lips sin-polluted, fettered
RE—sonare fibris	tongues to loosen; so by thy children might thy deeds of wonder
MI—ra gestorum	meetly be chanted.
FA—muli tuorum	
SOL—ve reati	—*Hymn for the feast of St. John the Baptist.*]
LA—bii reatum	
Sancte Joannes.	

Do you see how this melody begins, in each of its six phrases, on a different note? Now if someone has studied and learned the beginning of each phrase in such a way that he can sing readily whatever part he wishes, then whenever he sees those same six notes on which the several sections begin, he will be able to sing them properly and exactly. Moreover, hearing some neume without seeing it written, he will think it over, and decide which of the phrases fits best with the end of the neume—fits, that is, so that the last note of the neume and the first note of the phrase in the melody above are the same. Let him be certain, however, that the neume ends on that note on which the phrase above appropriate to it begins.

Now if you begin to sing some melody you do not know beforehand, but do have written out in front of you, you must be careful to end each neume properly, and take care that the end of each neume is well joined to the beginning of that phrase which begins on the same note as that on which the neume ends. If you want to sing new songs as soon as you see them, and to comprehend quickly those that you hear and are to write down quickly, this rule will be of the greatest help to you.

Gerbert, *Scriptores* ... , II, 43 ff. Trans. for this book by Lawrence Rosenwald.

It would be difficult to overestimate the importance of the work of these monks. If there was a single greatest revolution in the history of Western music, this was undoubtedly it. For the conversion of the Western tradition of music into a literate one determined all future development of the art. Innovation was now infinitely facilitated, and so musical style began to change with increasing rapidity. Moreover, the refinement of musical notation and training made the cultivation of polyphony on a grand scale really practicable for the first time, and it is no coincidence that the history of polyphonic music—which above all sets Western music apart from all other traditions—begins at precisely this time. Equally important, the philosophical outlook of Western man on music was fundamentally changed. Music now became for him—we should say for *us*—increasingly what medieval writers called a *res facta,* a "made thing," on which craftsmanship was to be lavished, and whose quality and originality commanded respect. One eventual result of this change was the gradual elevation of the composer, the one who made the *res facta,* over Boethius's speculative "musician" (see p. 31).

Of course, the Guidonian reforms did not take hold instantly; rote method and oral transmission persisted for a long time, witness Chaucer's description of a fourteenth-century English choirboy.

A litel scole of Cristen folk ther stood
Doun at the further ende, in which there were
Children an heep, ycomen of Cristen blood,
That lerned in that scole year by year
Swich maner doctrine as men used there,
This is to seyn, to singen and to rede,
As smale children doon in hir childhede.

Among these children was a widwes sonne,
A litel clergeon, seven yeers of age,
That day by day to scole as was his wone
And eek also, wher-as he saugh th'image
Of Cristes moder, hadde he in usage
As him was taught, to knele adoun and seye
His *Ave Marie* as he goth by the way.

. . . .

The "Guidonian Hand." As a further aid to the "singing of unknown songs," a mnemonic scheme was borrowed from almanac makers (who had invented it to keep track of the calendar), in which the notes of the gamut were assigned to the various joints of the hand. Once the singer had mastered (usually by rote, of course) a table like the one shown here from a musical treatise copied in 1274, the choirmaster had but to point to his hand, and out would come the tune. *Milan, Biblioteca Ambrosiana, MS D. 75. INF.*

This litel child, his litel book lerninge,
As he sat in the scole at his prymer,
He *Alma redemptoris* herde singe,
As children learned hir antiphoner
And, as he droste, he drough him ner and ner,
And herkened ay the wordes and the note,
Til he the first vers coude all by rote.

The Canterbury Tales, "Prioresses Tale," lines 43–56, 64–70.

15

Music in Courtly Life

In the poems of the Provençal troubadours, the German minnesingers, and the other medieval singers of courtly love and the knightly tradition, we may observe a close interrelationship of music with the life of the times that parallels in the secular realm the honored place of music within the church. The knightly life was itself a kind of ritual, courtly love a kind of religion. Like the music of the Church, the poetry and music of the noble troubadour were sober and reflective, and served to elevate and memorialize the permanent values of life, such as were worthy of commemoration in writing. These values included service to lord and lady, the idealization of love, and the fervor of the Crusades. We know a good deal about several of the troubadours, thanks to the way in which their poetry and music were preserved. The songs of knighthood are found in rich manuscripts known as *chansonniers*. These were never used for performance; most performing musicians were still illiterate at this stage. Rather, *chansonniers* were commemorational and honorific in purpose. In them, the songs of the best of the troubadours were arranged by author and were interspersed with introductory and connective prose that related the life of the poet to his songs. It is from these connecting passages that accompany his works in the *chansonniers* that we have assembled the life of the troubadour Raimbaut de Vaqueiras (1180–1207). His span of years was short but nonetheless contained everything that characterized the typical knightly poet's career, all colored by one central and highly unusual fact: Raimbaut was not of noble birth, but managed to advance himself by his art. In him we have the rare phenomenon of one who began as a despised *jongleur,* or professional musician, but was eventually able to call his master his brother in arms and to aspire to the love of the Marquis's sister. His extraordinary gifts of spontaneous invention, which no doubt had a great deal to do with his rise in the world, are amply demonstrated in the concluding anecdote, one of the most famous of all troubadour tales. Notice, too, how every change in the poet's life is reflected, indeed sometimes even brought about, by his art, for a troubadour's art mirrored his life. Like most of the troubadours who served a lady, Raimbaut invents a name to shield her identity, for, as usual in such cases, she was someone else's wife.

Raimbaut was the son of a poor knight from the castle of Vaqueiras in Proensa, called Peirols, who owned no land. And so Raimbaut became a jongleur and served many a year with William of Baux, Prince of Orange [Guillaume IV, 1182–1218]. He knew well the art of song and could make shapely stanzas and praise his master in verse. The Prince of Orange rewarded him with substantial favors and great honors and brought his poetry into high esteem among great personages. But then Raimbaut left his service and went instead to Montferrat in Italy, to his lordship the Marquis Boniface, and remained there a long time. He became so adept at the arts of war that the Marquis made him his knight and brother in arms.

And then did Raimbaut fall in love with Beatrice, the Marquis's sister, who was married to Enrico, lord of Carreto. For her he made his finest songs. And in them he called her Bel-Cavalier, because of an incident which he observed through the crevice of the door to Beatrice's chamber, when she thought herself alone. One day, when the Marquis, returned from the hunt, paid her his usual visit, he left his sword in her apartment. And the lady Beatrice pulled off the long robe she wore, and girding on the sword like a knight, she drew it from the scabbard, tossed it in the air, caught it again with skill and wheeled about to the right and to the left. And Raimbaut, observing this through the crevice in the door as has been said, ever after gave her the name of Bel-Cavalier in his songs.

Then one day, as he had a favorable access to Beatrice, he said to her, "Vouchsafe, my lady, to give me your advice; I stand in great need of counsel. I love a gentle lady, full of grace and merit. I converse with her continually, without daring to let her know my affection; so much do I stand in awe of her virtue. For heaven's and for pity's sake, tell me whether I ought to die for love, from the fear of making it known."

"Every loyal lover," replied Beatrice, "who attaches himself to a lady of merit, whom he fears as well as respects, always explains his sentiments before he suffers himself to die for her sake. I advise you to declare your love, and to request your lady to retain you as her servant and her friend. If she is wise, and courteous, she will neither take it amiss, nor think herself dishonored; for you are so good, that there is no lady in the world, who ought not freely to receive you as her knight."

And Raimbaut, on hearing this advice and the assurance that she gave him, told her that she was indeed the lady whom he so adored. And the lady Beatrice said to him, "Welcome, my new-found lover! Try more and more, by your speech and by your deeds, to make yourself worthy to serve me. I retain you for my knight." And then straightaway did Raimbaut celebrate his felicity in a song.

But then commenced a time of sadness for Raimbaut. The more did Beatrice favor her knight, the more desirous were the envious to ruin him in her esteem. "Who is this Raimbaut de Vaqueiras, then, though the Marquis has made him a knight, that he should presume to love so exalted a lady as yourself? Know, that this does honor neither to you nor to the Marquis." And so much evil gossip was spread about that the lady Beatrice became enraged with Raimbaut. And when Raimbaut besought her for her love and begged her for mercy, she told him that he ought to carry his love to other ladies who were made for him, and that she would never have anything more to say to him. And such became Raimbaut's sorrow as was related above. He ceased to sing of love or to laugh or enjoy any pleasurable thing. But the lovers were reconciled by a song.

At this time there came to the Marquis's court two jongleurs from France, who knew how to play surpassingly well upon their fiddles. And one day they were fiddling an estampie which gave great pleasure to the Marquis and to all the knights and ladies. Only Raimbaut enjoyed it not, which did not escape the notice of the Marquis. He said, "What ails you, Sir Raimbaut, that you do not sing but are so sad in the presence of the sweet sound of the fiddles and also so beautiful a lady as my sister who has taken you for her knight, and who is the most estimable lady in the world?" But Raimbaut answered that he could do nought else. The Marquis knew well the reason and said to his sister, "My lady Beatrice, for love of me and of all the company, I would have you deign to bid Raimbaut, for love of you and for your grace, to cheer up and sing merrily as was his wont." And lady Beatrice showed Raimbaut her mercy and forgiveness, and bade him make her a new song. And straightaway Raimbaut fashioned this song cleverly to the very strains of the fiddlers' estampie:

Kalenda maya	The first of May,
Ni fuelhs de faya	neither leaf of beech
Ni chanz d'auzelh	nor song of bird
Ni flors de glaya	nor gladiolus bloom
Non es que'm playa,	pleases me,
Pros domna guaya,	lady noble and gay,
Tro qu'un ysnelh	until I receive
Messatgier aya	a speedy messenger
De vostre belh	from your fair self
Cors qu'em retraya	who will tell me
Plazer novelh	the new delight
Qu'amors m'atraya	which love brings me,
E jaya	and joy;
E'm traya	and which draws me
Na vos domna veraya.	toward you, true lady.
E chaya	And may he
De playa	die of his wounds,
'L gelos	the jealous one,
Ans que'm n'estraya.	before I take my leave.

Compiled from the *razos* in Camille Chabaneau, *Les Biographies des troubadours en langue provençale* (Paris, 1885), 85–88, collated with versions in S. Dobson, *The Literary History of the Troubadours* (London, 1807) and John Rutherford, *The Troubadours: Their Loves and Their Lyrics* (London, 1873). Text and translation of the song based on Archibald T. Davison and Willi Apel, *Historical Anthology of Music*, I (Cambridge: Harvard University Press, 1946), 16, 241.

Descriptions of scenes of music-making in medieval literature are scanty and usually unreliable. The glimpse of the *carole,* or circle dance, in the *Roman de la rose* (c. 1235), on the other hand, rings true and is for that reason of great value. It confirms the intimate bonds between song and dance in knightly times, and also gives an idea of the dance's instrumental accompaniment. The use of the vielle, or fiddle, is confirmed by Johannes de Grocheo (see p. 55) some seventy years later, and the use of tambourines to accompany dancing is corroborated by many contemporary pictures. A *retrouenge,* the form of the dance described in the text, is a song with refrain, a popular genre (more common ones being the *rondeau* and *virelai*) that was just beginning to find a place in written-down "art music" sources. Its origins were clearly as described here, in impromptu performance by *jongleurs,* who had little to do with the lofty types of music we have referred to above (p. 45) as *res facta.* Thousands of these songs came and went, leaving scarcely a trace in the written records by which we can know the past, save for fleeting "snapshots" like this one.

> Now see the carol go! Each man and maid
> Most daintily steps out with many a turn
> And arabesque upon the tender grass.
> See there the flutists and the ministrel men,
> Performers on the fiddle! Now they sing
> A retrouenge, a tune from old Lorraine;
> For it has better songs than other lands.
> A troop of skillful jongleurs thereabout
> Well played their parts, and girls with tambourines
> Danced jollily, and, finishing each tune,
> Threw high their instruments, and as these fell
> Caught each on finger tip, and never failed.
> Two graceful demoiselles in sheerest clothes,
> Their hair in coifferings alike arrayed,
> Most coyly tempted Mirth to join the dance.
> Unutterably quaint their motions were:
> Insinuatingly each one approached
> The other, till, almost together clasped,
> Each one her partner's darting lips just grazed
> So that it seemed their kisses were exchanged.
> I can't describe for you each lithesome glide
> Their bodies made—but they knew how to dance!
> Forever would I gladly have remained
> So long as I could see these joyful folk
> In caroling and dancing thus excel themselves.

Guillaume de Lorris, *Roman de la rose,* trans. Harry W. Robbins (New York: Dutton, 1962), 16–17 (ll. 753–76).

16

The Emergence of Polyphony

The early history of polyphony is very difficult to trace, and the question of what constitutes its first appearance in the surviving documents has been much debated. The evidence suggests that early polyphony did not consist of "compositions" at all but was a way of amplifying monophonic chants in performance. Ambiguous terminology is also a problem; we cannot say for sure what many crucial words in the texts below actually mean. Our earliest example, from Bishop Aldhelm, could just as easily refer to antiphonal as to polyphonic singing, perhaps more so in view of the author's reference to "men of old" (compare Biblical descriptions of psalmody, p. 14). And

Johannes Scotus Erigena does not explicitly state that the notes he speaks of combining are to be combined simultaneously: he could as well be speaking of melody as harmony. The earliest unquestionable references to simultaneously-sounding consonances are found in the ninth-century writings of Hucbald and Regino given below, and the first treatise to give unambiguous directions for polyphonic singing is the *Musica enchiriadis,* which may date from the early tenth century.

Chanting in voices blending happily together, they sang, "Blessed is he who cometh in the name of the Lord." And we in our humble way, relying on the unquestioned authority of the men of old, observe the same practice with due solemnity: on the holy festival of Palm Sunday we divide into two groups, singing with melodious voices and crying out "Hosanna" with two bodies of singers, in joyful and triumphant melody.

Aldhelm, Bishop of Sherborne (640–709), trans. Anselm Hughes in *The New Oxford History of Music,* II (London: Oxford University Press, 1954), 272.

Just as a melody consists of notes of different character and pitch, which show considerable disagreement when they are heard individually and separately, but provide a certain natural charm when they are combined in one or another of the modes, in accordance with definite and reasoned principles of musical science; so the universe, in accordance with the uniform will of the creator, is welded into one harmonious whole from the different subdivisions of nature, which disagree with each other when they are examined individually.

Johannes Scotus Erigena (*c.* 815–*c.* 877), trans. Hughes, ibid., 273 (from *De divisione naturae*).

Consonance is the judicious and harmonious mixture of two tones, which exists only if two tones, produced from different sources, meet in one joint sound, as happens when a boy's voice and a man's voice sing the same thing, or in that which they commonly call *organum.*

Hucbald (*c.* 840–*c.* 930), in Gustave Reese, *Music in the Middle Ages* (New York: W. W. Norton & Company, Inc., 1940), 253 (from *De harmonica institutione*).

When one hears two strings at once, and one of them sounds a low note and the other a high one, and the two sounds are mixed in one sweet sound, as if the two voices had blended into one, then they are making what one calls a consonance.

Regino of Prüm (d. 915), in Martin Gerbert, *Scriptores ecclesiastici de musica* … , I (St. Blasien, 1784), (from *Epistola de harmonica institutione*). Trans. R. T.

To "improvise" polyphony, of course, no notation is needed, and its practice in oral tradition was presumably widespread, although the evidence is scanty. A valuable testimony is this eyewitness account of the practices of Welsh folk musicians in the late twelfth century:

Among these people I find a commendable diligence on musical instruments, on which they are more skilled than any nation we have seen. For among them, the execution is not slow and solemn as on the English instruments to which we are accustomed, but it is rapid and lively, though the sound is soft and pleasant. It is astonishing that, with such a rapid plucking of the fingers, the musical rhythm is preserved, and with art unimpaired in spite of everything, the melody is finished and remains agreeable, with such smooth rapidity, such unequaled evenness, such mellifluous harmony throughout the varied tunes and the many intricacies of the part music.

When they make music together, they sing their tunes not in unison, as is done elsewhere, but in parts with many simultaneous modes and phrases. Therefore, in a group of singers (which one very often meets with in Wales) you will hear as many melodies as there are people, and a distinct variety of parts; yet, they all accord in one consonant and properly constituted composition. In the northern districts of Britain, beyond the Humber and round about York, the inhabitants use a similar kind of singing in harmony, but in only two different parts, one singing quietly in a low register, and the other soothing and charming the ear above. This specialty of this race is no product of trained musicians, but was acquired through long-standing popular practices.

The Pelican History of Music, Alec Robertson and Denis Stevens, I (Harmondsworth: Penguin Books, 1960), 246–47; and *History of Western Music* ed., Frederick Sternfeld, I (New York: Praeger, 1973), 264 (from Giraldus Cambrensis, *Descriptio Cambriae* [1198]).

> The earliest polyphonic schools were centered around monasteries in France, England, and Spain. The first classic period of Western polyphonic music was reached with the school of Notre Dame in Paris in the twelfth and thirteenth centuries. The Parisian musicians were the first to use a notation that specified rhythm as well as pitch. Their leaders were among the first composers to be honored as "personalities," and who exist as names for us, thanks to a set of lecture notes by an Englishman who either studied or taught at the University of Paris in the second quarter of the thirteenth century. In his brief account, "Anonymus IV" (so called because his is the fourth in a series of anonymous treatises published in 1864) gives us a great deal of information, almost all of which—except the composers' names—is confirmed in the musical sources of the time. Definitions of some of the musical terms Anonymus IV uses will be found in the extracts from Johannes de Grocheo (see p. 53). The word *clausula* is left untranslated, because it has so many meanings. Here it means a section that can be inserted into a preexisting composition, either to amplify it or (as Anonymus IV implies) to replace sections of the earlier composition. The word can also stand for a short independent composition.

Master Leoninus was generally known as the best composer of organum, who made the great book (Magnus Liber) of organa for Mass and Office for the enhancement of the Divine Service. This book was in use until the time of the great Perotinus, who shortened it and substituted a great many better *clausulae,* because he was the best composer of discant and better than Leoninus. Moreover, this same Master Perotinus wrote excellent compositions for four voices, such as *Viderunt* [*omnes,* the Gradual for the third Mass of Christmas Day] and *Sederunt* [*principes,* the Gradual of the Feast of St. Stephen, Martyr], replete with artful musical turns and figures, as well as a considerable number of very famous pieces for three voices, such as the Alleluias *Posui adiutorium, Nativitas,* etc. Besides, he also composed conductus, such as *Dum sigillum summi patris,* and monophonic conductus, e.g. *Beata viscera,* and lots more. The book, or rather books, of Master Perotinus have remained in use in the choir of the Church of Our Blessed Virgin in Paris [i.e., Notre Dame] until the present day.

Sternfeld, *History,* I, 103, 106 (from Anon. IV, *De mensuris et discantu* [*c.* 1272]).

If St. Augustine's candid delineation of his ambivalence to music (see p. 26) reveals a touching sensitivity to the physical beauties of sound, some later representatives of the clergy seem to have been able to rid themselves entirely of such sympathies. The music under discussion below is probably polyphonic; its textures are viewed as a distraction from the real purpose of liturgical music. The strictures of John of Salisbury (d. 1180) constitute an interesting and even more extreme precedent for the more famous protest by Pope John XXII in the early fourteenth century (see p. 60). But then, the singers of his time (and many since) were probably not entirely undeserving of censure.

Music sullies the Divine Service, for in the very sight of God, in the sacred recesses of the sanctuary itself, the singers attempt, with the lewdness of a lascivious singing voice and a singularly foppish manner, to feminize all their spellbound little followers with the girlish way they render the notes and end the phrases. Could you but hear the effete emotings of their before-singing and their after-singing, their singing and their counter-singing, their in-between-singing and their ill-advised singing, you would think it an ensemble of sirens, not of men; and you would be astounded by the singers' facility, with which indeed neither that of the parrot or the nightingale, nor of whatever else there may be that is more remarkable in this kind, can compare. Indeed, such is their glibness in running up and down the scale, such their cutting apart or their con-joining of notes, such their repetition or their elision of single phrases of the text—to such an extent are the high or even the highest notes mixed together with the low or lowest ones—that the ears are almost completely divested of their critical power, and the intellect, which pleasureableness of so much sweetness has caressed insensate, is impotent to judge the merits of the things heard. Indeed, when such practices go too far, they can more easily occasion titillation between the legs than a sense of devotion in the brain.

William Dalglish, "The Origin of the Hocket," *Journal of the American Musicological Society,* XXXI (1978), 7 (from John of Salisbury, *Policratus* [1159]).

17

The Forms and Practices of Music, *c.* 1300

Our most extensive selection from a single medieval source is a series of extracts from the invaluable treatise *De musica* (On Music) by a Parisian musician who lived near the beginning of the fourteenth century. Johannes de Grocheo's treatise is virtually unique among musical writings of the middle ages in that it breaks completely with earlier neo-Platonist traditions. Grocheo deals only with *musica instrumentalis,* and in this he approaches our modern view of what music is. For him a musician is not a philosopher but a craftsman, and he positively blasts the Boethian speculative concept of music (see p. 28) as hypocritical or at the very least outmoded. What is more, he goes on to make his own "division" of the science of music, and this division is ruled by what we might call the "sociological" aspects of the art. In short, Grocheo could not care less how heard melodies relate to the unheard, but he is very much concerned with how they relate to those who hear them. For all these reasons we might in retrospect look upon Johannes de Grocheo as the first "Renaissance man" in the history of musical thought.

Certain people have divided music into three types, as for example Boethius and his followers have done in their treatises. They say that one type is *musica mundana,* another *humana,* and the third *instrumentalis.* Those who make this kind of distinction either invent their opinion, or they wish to obey Pythagoreans or others more than the truth, or they are ignorant of nature and logic. First of all, they say that, as a whole, music is a science concerning measured sound. Nevertheless, celestial bodies in movement do not make a sound. Nor also is sound properly to be found in the human constitution. Who has heard a constitution sounding? Nor is it pertinent for a musician to treat the song of angels, unless he is at the same time a theologian and a prophet; no one can have any experience of such song except by divine inspiration. When they say the planets sing, they seem to be ignorant of what sound is.

For us it is not easy to divide music correctly, since, in a correct division, the dividing factors ought to exhaust the full nature of the whole that is divided. The parts of music are many and diverse according to diverse uses, diverse idioms, or diverse languages in diverse cities or regions. If we, however, will have it divided according to how men in Paris use it, our intention will seem to be sufficiently carried out, since in our day the principles of any liberal art are diligently sought out in Paris and their uses are explored there.

The music which men in Paris use can, so it seems, be broken down into three broad categories. We say that one category is that of simple [i.e., monophonic] music, which they call vulgar [i.e., vernacular] music. Another is that of compound [i.e., polyphonic] music, which they call measured music ["measured," here, does not refer to rhythm but to polyphony, for consonances and dissonances are also measurable]. The third type is called ecclesiastic and is designed for praising the Creator.

Vulgar: Musical forms contained under the first category, which we have named vulgar music, are of two types: either they are performed by the human voice or by artificial instruments. Those which are performed by the human voice are of two types. We call these either a *cantus* or a *cantilena.*

> The context makes it clear that the distinction between *cantus* and *cantilena* is primarily a matter of the presence or absence of a refrain. This, in turn, is an important style and "class" distinction, for music with refrain is essentially popular dance music with or without words (see the extract from the *Roman de la rose,* p. 50), while *cantus* encompasses the more elevated songs of the *trouvères,* the northern French counterparts of the Provençal troubadours. These songs existed in many genres, from epic narratives to songs of courtly love.

A *cantus* is called *chanson de geste* if it relates the deeds of heroes and the achievements of our ancient fathers, such as the life and martyrdom of various saints, the battles and difficulties which men of old underwent for their faith and belief, the life of the Blessed

Stephen, and the history of Charlemagne. This kind of song ought to be provided for old men, working citizens, and for average people when they rest from their accustomed labor, so that, having heard the miseries and calamities of others, they may more easily bear up under their own, and go about their own tasks more gladly.

A *cantus coronatus* is normally composed by kings and nobles and performed before kings and princes of the earth so that it may move their souls to audacity and bravery, to magnanimity and liberality, which lead all things to a good order. This kind of song is about delightful and serious subjects, such as friendship and charity.

A particular kind of *cantilena* is called *round* or *rotundellus* by many, for the reason that it turns back on itself in the manner of a circle and begins and ends in the same way. We, however, call *round* or *rotundellus* only that whose parts do not have a different melody from the melody of their response or refrain. It is the custom in the West, for example in Normandy, for girls and young men to sing a *cantilena* of this type to enhance their festivals and great gatherings.

> The best translation of *rotundellus* would be into French: *rondeau*. This is a dance song with refrain, with the musical structure ABaAabAB (capital letters here standing for the refrain, small letters for repetitions of music to new words). In this scheme the music of the refrain is the same as the music of the verses, just as Grocheo describes it. In the other refrain forms he mentions (the instrumental *ductia* and *stantipes,* both varieties of the dance genre known as *estampie)*, the refrain is musically distinct from the so-called *puncta.* The dance forms are open forms, capable of infinite extension (A-R-B-R-C-R-D-R ... etc.), while the rondeau is "closed" and self-contained.

The method of composing all these types is normally the same. First, words are provided as raw material, afterwards a melody is adapted to the text in an appropriate way. Let us now turn to instrumental forms.

Instruments are divided by some people on the basis of how they generate artificial sound. They say that sound on instruments is made by the breath, as in trumpets, reed instruments, flutes, and organs; or by percussion, as in strings, drums, cymbals, and bells. Among these, stringed instruments occupy the chief place, i.e., the psaltery, harp, lute and fiddle. And here, of all the instruments of the string family, so we feel, the fiddle occupies the main place, for a good performer on the fiddle uses normally every kind of *cantus* and *cantilena* and every musical form. Those, however, that are commonly performed before the wealthy in feasts and games, are, besides the *cantus coronatus* about which we have talked before, the *ductia* and *stantipes.*

A *ductia* is an untexted piece, measured with an appropriate percussive beat. I say *untexted* since, although it can be performed by the human voice and represented in notation, it cannot, however, be written in words, for it is lacking in word and text. But I say with an *appropriate percussive beat* because these beats measure it and the movement of the performer, and excite the soul of man to move ornately according to the art they call dancing. A stantipes is also an untexted piece of a complicated nature; it makes the soul of the performer and also the soul of the listener pay close attention and frequently turns the soul of the wealthy from depraved thinking.

The sections of ductia and stantipes are commonly called *puncta.* A *punctum* is a systematic joining together of two sections alike in their beginning, differing in their end, which are usually called *close* and *open.* To compose *ductia* and *stantipes* is to shape the sound through *puncta* and correct beats. Just as natural material is shaped by natural form, so the sound is shaped by *puncta* and by the artificial form given to it by the craftsman.

Measured music: Certain people, relying on experiment, discovered a kind of song in two voices dependent on both perfect and imperfect consonances. But others, relying on the three perfect consonances, have invented a song in three voices, regulated by a uniform measure, which they have called a *precisely measured song;* it is this type of song that present-day people in Paris use. We divide it into three broad categories according to the custom of people today, that is, *motets, organum* and cut-up song which they call *hocket.*

A *motet* is a song composed of many voices, having many words or a variety of syllables, everywhere sounding in harmony. Each line ought to have a text with the exception of the tenor, which in some has a text and in others not. This kind of song ought not to be propagated among the vulgar, since they do not understand its subtlety nor do they delight in hearing it, but it should be performed for the learned and those who seek after the subtleties of the arts. And it is normally performed at their feasts for their edification, just as the *cantilena* which is called *rotundellus* is performed at the feasts of the vulgar.

Organum is a song composed harmonically of many voices, with only one text. This kind of song is varied in two ways. There is one type which is based on a given [i.e., preexistent] melody, that is, an ecclesiastical one. This is sung in churches or holy places for the praise of God and reverence of His high place. And this kind of song is what is properly called *organum.* The other is based on a melody composed at the same time as the rest [i.e., not preexistent]. This is normally sung at parties and feasts given by the learned and the rich. And, taking its name from this, it is called by the appropriate name *conductus.*

Hocket is a cut-up song, composed in two or more voices. This kind of song is pleasing to the hot-tempered and to young men because of its mobility and speed. Like seeks out like and is delighted by like.

Wishing to compose measured music, one first should arrange or compose the tenor and give to it mode and measure. The principal part ought to be fashioned first, since it is then used to fashion the others. I say *arrange* since in motets and in organum the tenor is taken from an old song and is previously composed, but is laid out by craftsmen in rhythmic patterns. The tenor having been composed or arranged, one ought to compose or arrange the *motetus* above it. Finally the *triplum* [whence our English *treble*] ought to be superimposed on these, to fill out the consonances.

Johannes de Grocheo, *De musica*, trans. Albert Seay (Colorado Springs: The Colorado College Music Press, 1974), 10–11, 15–16, 18–21, 25–27, abridged. Reprinted by permission of The Colorado College Music Press.

The method of composition Grocheo refers to in his discussion of "measured music" is one that is apt to strike us today as somewhat odd. The various lines of a polyphonic texture were not conceived all at once, but were added in layers, "from the ground up," over a preexistent melody usually derived from a favorite Gregorian chant. The little treatise *Tractatus cantus mensurabilis* (Treatise on Measured Song, c. 1400) by the minor theorist Aegidius of Murino is a compact and laconic musical cookbook, in which succinct practical instructions are given for putting together (*componere*) a motet according to this method (called "successive"). About a quarter of this very short manual is given below. Particularly revealing are Aegidius's startling remarks on the relationship between text and music in the medieval motet. It could not be a more casual one: the words are fitted to the music only after the music is completely composed, and then only "as best one can." What a far cry from the intense concern for declamation that was to take hold of musicians during the Renaissance!

First take for your tenor any antiphon or responsory or any other chant from the book of Office chants; and its words should accord with the theme or occasion for which the motet is being made. And then take the tenor and arrange it and put it in rhythm according to what will be revealed below about perfect and imperfect mode: perfect mode is when there are three beats per note of the tenor and imperfect mode is when there are two [see also Jean de Muris, p. 58]. And when the tenor is well laid out, if you wish to make a motet in four parts, your next step is to arrange a contratenor and put it in rhythm over the tenor. And when this is done, take the tenor again, and the contratenor if you are composing in four parts, and arrange a third part, the *triplum,* over them, so that it concords well with the tenor and the contratenor. And if all of the above is to work in the best way possible, then divide the tenor into two segments, or four, or as many as you like; and complete one section over the tenor according to the above rules, and each part should be shaped in this way, from first to last. And this is what is known as setting out a motet.

At this point one can apply all manner of subtlety, that is, one can syncopate the parts, etc. This done, proceed to the *motetus,* that is to say, to the last voice; and arrange its pitches and rhythms to go with the triplum and the tenor, and with the contratenor if the piece is in four parts, and continue thus right to the end.

After the music has been made and fixed, then take the words which are to go into the motet and divide them into four segments; and divide the music into four corresponding segments; and put the first segment of the words over the first segment of the music as best you can, and proceed in this way all the way to the end. Sometimes it will be necessary to stretch many notes over few words in order to make the setting come out right, and sometimes many words must be squeezed into a small amount of time. Just fit it together any way you can.

Charles Edmond Henri Coussemaker, *Scriptorum de medii aevi nova series,* 4 vols. (Paris, 1864–76), III, 124–25. Trans. R. T.

18

The First Musical Avant-Garde

The fourteenth century was a time of trouble all over Europe, marked by strife among nations, between social classes, and in the Church. Even nature herself seemed to conspire against mankind: the Black Death, the most horrible epidemic in history, ravaged the continent and left its inhabitants exhausted and scarred physically, spiritually, and morally. In the face of the heavy blows dealt the Church's authority by the Papal exile and the ensuing schism, a flourishing secularism took hold in the arts. Vernacular literature began to overtake Latin, and the aristocracy began to vie with the Church in art patronage. The works produced under these conditions reflected the values of that rarefied and rather effete social milieu. Enormous technical sophistication was the order of the day, together with a refinement bordering at times on preciosity. Not at all coincidentally, it was precisely at this point that music underwent one of the greatest sudden technical advances in its history. Nowadays we refer to fourteenth-century music generally by the name of a famous treatise by Philippe de Vitry (1291–1361) called *Ars nova—The New Art—which* detailed some of these new musical means. As the name implies, the Ars Nova was a self-consciously "modern" movement, whose technical innovations consisted above all of a new system of musical notation based on a new conception of musical time. Whereas previously the unfolding of music in time was conceived as a perpetual additive process (see St. Augustine, p. 35), the new view of time regarded it—as we do—as an infinitely and systematically divisible continuum. The new notation offered a multitude of ways to divide time, and this gave music an unprecedented rhythmic flexibility and subtlety. An extract from the treatise *Ars novae musicae* (*The Art of the New Music, c.* 1319), by Jean de Muris, the other leading musical theorist of the day, will give the philosophical background. The new theory of time is succinctly stated, and a good summary is given of the significance of the "perfect" number three for medieval thinkers. In this connection it should be emphasized that although the techniques of the Ars Nova represented a breakthrough, they were by no means a revolution. The whole concept of the reform was aimed at the ideal of realizing number in sound, and is therefore very much in the medieval tradition.

Here follows what Master Jean de Muris has to say concerning practical music, also called measured music.

As was shown in the beginning, a note must come into being together with some quantity of motion, because a note belongs by nature to the class of successive things—that is, it exists while it is being produced, but when it has been produced, it does not. Now succession must be accompanied by motion, and time links motions inseparably together; it is necessary, therefore, to measure a note by time. Time is the measure of motion; here, however, time is in particular the measure of a sustained note together with the continuous motion accompanying it. Time [*tempus*] refers also to a single unit of this sort of measurement.

In this last sense, time is sometimes greater, sometimes less [i.e., sometimes triple, sometimes duple]; the greater corresponds to a longer motion, the lesser to a shorter one, other things being equal, and both being measured on the same scale. Our predecessors recognized only that time which had perfection, holding that time to be perfect which could be divided by three, because they believed that all perfection was to be found in threeness. Accordingly, they made *tempus perfectum* [i.e., a three-beat measure] the basic unit of every sort of musical composition, considering that what was imperfect had no place in art.

That all perfection does in fact lie in the ternary number is clear from a hundred comparisons. In God, who is perfection itself, there is singleness in substance, but threeness in persons; He is three in one and one in three. There is, therefore, an extraordinary congruity between one and three. Moreover: in the sun and stars there are the heat, the rays, and the radiance they all give off; in the elements there are agents, things acted upon, and matter; in individuals generation, corruption, and substance; in finite time-spans beginning, middle, and end; in every curable disease onset, crisis, and decline. Three is the first odd number, and the first prime number. It is not two lines but three that can enclose a surface. The triangle is the first regular polygon, the tetrahedron the first regular solid. Every solid body has three dimensions, or it could not support itself.

Since, therefore, the ternary number is to be found everywhere, there is no reason to wonder any further whether it is in fact perfect. The binary number must, by comparison, be called imperfect, even though it may thus fall into ill-repute. But unity, since it is continuous, is divisible not only into three parts, but into many more, ad infinitum.

Martin Gerbert, *Scriptores ecclesiastici de musica* ... , III (St. Blasien, 1784), 292–94. Trans. for this book by Lawrence Rosenwald.

The self-consciously innovative character of the Ars Nova generated the inevitable backlash. The brief passage given below from a mammoth encyclopedic treatise called *Speculum musicae* (*The Mirror of Music*, c. 1330) by one Jacobus of Liège, a protest against the "imperfections" of the new music, is based on a rather clumsily sustained pun: The term *imperfect*, which in the writings of the Ars Nova theorists was merely technical jargon for the newly practicable duple division of the beat, is given all the other connotations of the word. Jacobus's reactionary tirade against the Ars Nova on behalf of the older music (which he conveniently christens "Ars Antiqua"—a term that has also entered the language of music history) set the standard for many future critics who were to bark at the heels of great musical innovators: see, for example, Monteverdi's detractor Artusi (p. 145), who actually—almost as if paraphrasing Jacobus—entitled his polemic "On the Imperfection of Modern Music."

A comparison of the measured music of the Ars Antiqua with that of the Ars Nova with respect to perfection and imperfection:

Now it may seem to some that the Ars Nova is more perfect than the Ars Antiqua on the grounds that it seems to them more subtle and more difficult. It seems subtler to them because it has more ramifications and has a great deal that the Ars Antiqua does not have. So much, at any rate, is clear from all its little notes, its measurements, and its various ways of dividing the beat. That it is more difficult is equally clear from the works of the moderns, from their way of singing and measuring rhythm.

To others, the truth seems to be just the opposite. To them, that art seems the more perfect which follows its fundamental principles more closely and goes against them less often. Now the art of measured music is founded on perfection—so much even the moderns say, and not just the ancients—and the art that uses perfect values more often is, therefore, more perfect. The art that does that is the Ars Antiqua, the art of Master Franco [of Cologne, author of *Ars cantus mensurabilis* (*The Art of Measured Song*, c. 1260), the basic treatise of the Ars Antiqua]. The Ars Nova, as is clear, uses many and varied imperfections in notes, in measurement, and in division. Imperfection insinuates itself practically everywhere. Nor is that enough: the Ars Nova uses imperfection not only in the areas named, but even in counting time.

The Ars Nova, that is, permits imperfect time; the Ars Antiqua never permitted such a thing. The Ars Nova, moreover, applies the imperfection of the basic unit of time to note values of every sort. And more: exponents of the Ars Nova find ways to imperfect the perfect by any number of imperfections. If, however, the Ars Nova were content merely to talk about the imperfections in question, to treat them only theoretically, that would be more acceptable. Unfortunately, that is not the case. They put their theories into practice, and not seldom at that. They use more imperfect values than perfect ones, more imperfect measurements than perfect ones, and that goes for divisions of the beat as well.

If, then, the Ars Nova is said to be more subtle than the Ars Antiqua—and so much may in fact be granted—it cannot be said on that account to be also more perfect. Not every subtlety is an improvement; more subtle is not necessarily more perfect. Subtlety is not among the degrees or kinds of perfection—so much is clear from the fourth book of [Aristotle's] *Metaphysics*. Nor has it even been sufficiently proven that the Ars Nova is in fact subtler than the Ars Antiqua. Granted that the Ars Nova includes certain things that the Ars Antiqua does not, granted that the Ars Nova encompasses a great many more imperfections than does the Ars Antiqua—still, all this is no argument for its being more perfect. Rather it is just this point, namely which of the two arts is the more perfect, that must be looked into most carefully.

It is said, moreover, that the Ars Nova is more difficult than the Ars Antiqua. It is not, however, on that account alone to be judged more perfect. Things are not more perfect because they are more difficult; and art in particular, though it is sometimes said to have essentially to do with what is difficult, has in fact to do essentially with what is good and useful. Art is a virtue that perfects the soul by means of reason. That is why, after all, tradition says that it is easy to teach a good man.

Charles Edmond Henri Coussemaker, *Scriptorum de medii aevi nova series*, 4 vols. (Paris, 1864–76), II, 427–29. Trans. for this book by Lawrence Rosenwald.

The musicians of the "new art" made use of their new technical resources with such relish that "modern music" became a serious problem for the Church. We may read of this in any number of protests along lines familiar from the writings of Augustine and John of Salisbury (see pp. 26 and 53). Most famous of all is the injunction against, among other things, some identifiable Ars Nova practices in Pope John XXII's bull *Docta sanctorum* of 1323.

Certain disciples of the new school, much occupying themselves with the measured dividing of beats, display their rhythm in notes new to us, preferring to devise new methods of their own rather than to continue singing in the old way. Therefore the music of the Divine Office is disturbed with these notes of quick duration. Moreover, they hinder the melody with hockets, they deprave it with discants, and sometimes they pad out the music with upper parts made out of secular songs. The result is that they often seem to be losing sight of the fundamental sources of our melodies in the Antiphoner and Gradual, and forget what it is that they are burying under such superstructures. They may become entirely ignorant of the ecclesiastical modes, which they have already ceased to distinguish, and the limits of which they abuse in the prolixity of their notes. The modest rise and temperate descents of plainsong are entirely obscured. The voices incessantly rock to and fro, intoxicating rather than soothing the ear, while the singers themselves try to convey the emotion of the music by their gestures. The consequence of all this is that devotion, the true aim of all worship, is neglected, and wantonness, which ought to be eschewed, increases. We hasten to forbid these methods, or rather to drive them more effectively out of the house of God than has been done in the past.

Nevertheless, it is not our wish to forbid the occasional use of some consonances [i.e., polyphony], which heighten the beauty of the melody. Such intervals, therefore, may be sung above the ecclesiastical chant, but in such a way that the integrity of the chant remain intact and that nothing in the prescribed music be changed. Used thus, the consonances would, more than any other music is able to do, both soothe the hearer and inspire his devotion, without destroying religious feeling in the minds of the singers.

Henry Raynor, *A Social History of Music* (New York: Schocken Books 1972), 36–37.

> More evidence of the technical preoccupations of fourteenth-century musicians may be found embodied in mock protests against their excesses, which turn up in texts of compositions that often whimsically demonstrate the very practices the text purports to deplore. These include abuse of the smallest divisions of time (*minimae*), hocket, overcomplexity of texture, etc. The "Marchetto" mentioned in the third example below along with Philippe (de Vitry) is Marchetto of Padua, author of theoretical manuals that were the Italian equivalent of Philippe's *Ars nova*.

Certain merchants are now arising amongst the populace. They turn fine gold into lead, and exchange sweet-smelling flowers for foul odors. These men are called, if I am not mistaken, professional singers. When they see some great man in public, they look for their best song, one that they really like. Then they sing it with a great proliferation of little notes, and boast of their singing. They sing not, I think, for the love of God, but for the love of that great man. You are such hypocrites! Have you never looked at the Holy Gospel, where you may read the word of the Lord concerning such matters? So be it then; you have received your price.

Motetus part of the motet "Arae post libamina" (Old Hall MS, c. 1400). Trans. Lawrence Rosenwald.

The science of music sends greetings to her beloved disciples. I desire each one of you to observe the rules and not to offend against rhetoric or grammar by dividing indivisible syllables. Avoid all faults. Farewell in melody.

Rhetoric sends greetings to learned Music, but complains that many singers make faults in her compositions by dividing simple vowels and making hockets; therefore I request that you remedy this.

Motetus and triplum texts of the motet "Musicalis scientia/Sciencie laudabili" (Paris: Bibliothèque Nationale, Coll. de Picardie, MS. 67). Trans. Lawrence Rosenwald.

> A wild bird during the season
> Sings sweet lines in a fine style.
> I do not praise a singer who shouts loudly:
> Loud shouting does not make good singing,
> But with smooth and sweet melody
> Lovely singing is produced, and this requires skill.
> Few people possess it, but all set up as masters
> And compose *ballate,* madrigals, and motets;
> All try to outdo Philippe and Marchetto.
> Thus the country is so full of petty masters
> That there is no room left for pupils.

"Uselletto selvaggio" (poem variously set as madrigal and as caccia by Jacopo da Bologna), trans. Leonard Ellinwood, in *The New Oxford History of Music*, III (London: Oxford University Press, 1960), 75–76.

19

The Life of Francesco Landini

Outstanding composers and theorists of the Ars Nova period enjoyed a personal celebrity unknown to the earlier Middle Ages, except possibly for that of some noble troubadours. Perhaps the first biography of a musician was the account of the life of the blind Florentine organist and composer Francesco Landini (1325–97) which Filippo Villani included in his *Liber de civitatis Florentiae famosis civibus,* a collective biography of the most eminent citizens of fourteenth-century Florence. The author was not a musician, and his life of Landini is filled with irrelevancies, fanciful concoctions, and nonsense. But we include it only slightly abridged as evidence of the new prestige enjoyed by the artist-musician in this age of secular achievement and personal expression.

A good many noted Florentines have excelled in music. Most, however, are now dead. Of those still alive I should mention in particular Bartolo, Ser Lorenzo Masini, and Giovanni da Cascia, as being more outstandingly skillful than the rest.

A creed was to be performed in our principal church, with organ and choir in alternation. Bartholus, however, composed one of such great sweetness and artistry that the usual interruptions by the organ were quite left out, and the piece was performed straight through by human voices in unaccompanied harmony, in the presence of a great crowd of people. It was thus Bartholus who was the first to do away with the former usage of organ alternating with male choir.

Giovanni da Cascia frequented the court of the tyrant Mastino della Scala [of Verona, reigned 1329–51] in search of his fortune. And so he came to take part in a contest for excellence in art with Jacopo of Bologna [leading composer of the generation before Landini and possibly his teacher], a highly skilled musician, the tyrant egging them on with offers of gifts. In that contest, he composed madrigals and many songs, in which his great skill was wonderfully displayed.

None of these, however—nor, for that matter, any composer of fabled antiquity— can measure up to Francesco, who is still alive, and whom I cannot write about truthfully without some fear of seeming to exaggerate.

Francesco was hardly past the middle of his childhood when disaster struck him blind with the smallpox. Music, however, compensated him for his loss with the bright lights of fame and renown. A harsh mischance took away his bodily sight, but his mind's eye was as sharp and acute as an eagle's. All of this, I think, will argue, to those who love the truth, in favor of beating boys who have all their senses and yet are idle in their wretched sloth. Better for them to be abused than to be allowed to fall asleep in miserable ease.

Landini's Tomb, Cappella Ginori, Church of San Lorenzo, Florence. The epitaph says, "Francesco, deprived of sight but with a mind skilled in instrumental music, whom alone Music has set above all others, has left his ashes here, his soul above the stars. Taken from mankind on 2 September 1397."

Francesco was born in Florence. His father, a painter, was named Jacopo, a just man of simple habits and a hater of vice. When Francesco had lived for a while in blindness, and was no longer a child, and could understand how miserable it was to be blind, and wanted some solace for the horrors of his everlasting night, he began, as adolescents will, to make up songs—this by the kindness of Heaven, I think, which was preparing in its mercy a consolation for so great a misfortune. When he was a little older still, and had come to perceive music's charm and sweetness, he began to compose, first for voices, then for strings and organ. He made astonishing progress. And then, to everyone's amazement, he took up a number of musical instruments—remember, he had never seen them—as readily as if he could still see. In particular, he began to play the organ, with such great dexterity—always accurately, however—and with such expressiveness that he far surpassed any organist in living memory. All this, I fear, can hardly be set down without some accusation of its having been made up.

The organ is an instrument made up of a great many pipes, constructed with great ingenuity, put together out of a wide variety of disparate mechanisms. And yet, Francesco would take an ailing organ, and, with all its most fragile pipes exposed and liable to be broken at the least touch, and with all its insides laid bare—so that if one of them were to be moved from its place by the distance of an inch it would be ruined and would make the air introduced by the bellows produce harsh and jangling noises—Francesco would tune it and make it sound sweetly and repair it, correcting whatever had caused the dissonance.

What is more, he played superbly on the fiddle, the lute, all the strings and winds, and every other sort of instrument. And imitating by voice all those instruments that give a pleasant sound in their various ways, and mingling them with the ordinary sounds of human voices, he invented a third species of music, a combination of both of the other two and a source of great charm and delight. In addition, he invented a new sort of instrument, a cross between lute and psaltery, which he called the *serena serenarum,* an instrument that produces an exquisite sound when its strings are struck.

To recount each and every one of the lovely things he did with music I think unnecessary; those who write accounts of this sort are, I fear, too often accustomed to forget the charms of brevity. It is worth mentioning, however, that no one ever played the organ so well. All musicians grant him that. And thus recently, at Venice, he was publicly crowned with laurel by His Majesty the King of Cyprus [this probably happened in 1364]. Just so, once upon a time, poets were crowned by the Emperors of Rome.

Let this be added to his praise, too: he is a master of rhetoric and logic, and has composed poems and novellas.

He has written a great many good things in Italian—a reproach, it seems to me, to the effeminate youth of Florence, the eager pursuers of feminine finery, dissipated in shameful wantonness, whose proud manly spirit has been neglected.

Leonard Ellinwood (ed.), *The Works of Francesco Landini* (Cambridge, Mass.: The Mediaeval Academy of America, 1939), 301–303 (from Filippo Villani, *Liber de civitatis Florentiae famosis civibus*). Trans. for this book by Lawrence Rosenwald.

20

A Letter from Guillaume de Machaut

One of the earliest composers from whom personal letters survive is Guillaume de Machaut (c. 1300–77), the leading poet and musician of fourteenth-century France. The exchange of love letters between the sexagenarian composer and a nineteen-year-old girl named Peronnelle D'Armentières, which was incorporated into Machaut's *Le Livre du Voir-Dit* (*True Tale, c.* 1363), may strike us today as somewhat bizarre. But these letters represent an excellent example of the rather stilted and artificial perpetuation of the traditions and rhetoric of courtly love that characterizes so much of the poetry and song of the Ars Nova period. In this letter, Machaut informs Peronnelle that he is supervising the collection and copying of his own works. Machaut is the first composer known to have done this. It is as good an indication as any of the fourteenth-century artist's new attitude towards his work and its importance.

My sovereign lady, a knight must have no calling or science other than: arms, lady, and conscience. Therefore I swear to you and promise that I shall serve you loyally and diligently to the best of my power with all I do and can do, and all to your honor, as Lancelot and Tristram never served their ladies; and have your likeness as my earthly deity and as the most precious and glorious relic that ever I did see in any place. And henceforth it shall be my heart, my castle, my treasure, and my comfort against all ills in truth. If it please God, I shall see you before Pentecost; for you and your sweet likeness have brought me to such a point that, the Lord be thanked, you have healed me completely. And I should have left before now; but there is a great company of soldiers a few leagues from us; therefore riding is most perilous. I send you my book, *Morpheus,* which they call *La Fontaine amoureuse,* in which I have made a song to your order, and by God it is long since I have made so good a thing to my satisfaction; and the tenors are as sweet as unsalted pap. I beg therefore that you deign to hear it, and learn the thing just as it is, without adding or taking away; and it is to be sung in a goodly long measure [i.e., a broad tempo]; and if anyone play it on the organs, bagpipe, or other instrument, that is its right nature. I am also sending you a *ballade,* which I made before receiving your sweet likeness: for I was a little hurt because of some words which had been said to me; but as soon as I saw your sweet likeness I was healed and free of melancholy. My most sovereign lady, I would have brought you my book to amuse you, wherein are all the things which I have ever made, but it is in more than twenty portions, for I had it made for one of my lords; and so I am having the notes put to it, and that is why it has to be in portions. And when the notes will have been put to it, I shall bring it or send it to you, if it please God. My most sovereign lady, I pray God that he may give you your heart's desire and such honor as I wish you may have; and God give you solace and joy, such as I might wish for myself.

Piero Weiss (ed.), *Letters of Composers Through Six Centuries* (Philadelphia: Chilton Books, 1967), 1–2.

PART THREE

The Renaissance

21

The "Fount and Origin"

We generally date the beginning of the Renaissance style in music from the early fifteenth century and in so doing follow the testimony of many contemporary witnesses. A new sound came to the Continent with the triumphant English army of occupation after the victory at Agincourt in 1415. The Duke of Bedford was made Regent of France, and his secretary was none other than John Dunstable (d. 1453), the foremost English musician of his time, whose music spread like wildfire (it is found in over thirty Continental manuscripts) and had an incalculable influence on local musicians. In the passage below, a chronicler of the court of Burgundy, France's then more-powerful neighbor to the north, bears witness to this impact. The first three names are those of French musicians who led the field immediately before contact with the English sound took place, while Gilles Binchois (d. 1460) and Guillaume Dufay (d. 1474) were the leaders of the first generation of Renaissance composers.

Tapissier, Carmen, Cesaris	Tapissier, Carmen, Cesaris
N'a pas longtemps si bien chanterrent	Not long ago so well did sing
Qu'ilz esbahirent tout Paris	That they astonished all Paris
Et tous ceulx qui les frequenterrent;	And all who came foregathering.
Mais oncques jour ne deschanterrent	But still their discant held no strain
En melodie de tel chois	Filled with such goodly melody—
Ce m'on dit qui les hanterrent	So folk who heard them now maintain—
Que G. Du Fay et Binchois.	As Binchois sings, or Dufay.
Car ilz ont nouvelle pratique	For these a newer way have found,
De faire frisque concordance	In music high and music low,
En haulte et en basse musique,	Of making pleasant concord sound—
En fainte, en pause, et en muance,	In "feigning," rests, mutatio.
Et ont prins de la contenance	The English guise they wear with grace,
Angloise et ensuy Dunstable	They follow Dunstable aright,
Pour quoy merveilleuse plaisance	And thereby have they learnt apace
Rend leur chant joyeux et notable.	To make their music gay and bright.

Gustave Reese, *Music in the Renaissance,* 2nd ed. (New York: W. W. Norton & Company, Inc., 1958), 12–13 (from Martin Le Franc, *Le Champion des dames* [*c.* 1441]).

"Music high and music low," above, refers to loud (dance and outdoor) and soft (court and chamber) music, respectively. The terms listed two lines later have to do with singers' techniques of applying accidentals and of sightsinging. The gist is that the new music is far more consonant and euphonious than the old, a view shared by all the leading writers of the day, including Johannes Tinctoris (1436–1511), whose twelve treatises comprise our richest source of information on the theory and practice of fifteenth-century music. A composer of no small attainments himself, Tinctoris was also a remarkably astute appraiser of the works of others, and the judgments he expressed in his prefaces, of which extracts are given below, hold up very well today.

At present the horizons of music have been so wonderfully extended that it seems a new art, if I may put it so, whose fount and origin is reputed to be among the English, with Dunstable at their head.

Charles Edmond Henri Coussemaker, *Scriptorum de medii aevi nova series,* 4 vols. (Paris, 1864–76), IV, 154 (from Tinctoris, *Proportionale musices* [1476]). Trans. R. T.

In addition, it is a matter of great surprise that there is no composition written over forty years ago which is thought by the learned to be worthy of performance. At this very time, whether owing to the virtue of some heavenly influence or to a zeal for hard work, there flourish, in addition to many singers who perform most beautifully, an infinite number of composers such as Johannes Ockeghem [d. 1497], Johannes Régis [d. 1485], Antoine Busnois [d. 1492], Firmin [or Philippe] Caron, and Guillaume Faugues, who glory in having had as teachers in this divine art the recently departed John Dunstable, Gilles Binchois, and Guillaume Dufay. Almost all the works of those men exhale such sweetness that, in my opinion, they should be considered most worthy, not only of men and heroes, but even of the immortal gods. Certainly I never listen to them or study them without coming away refreshed and wiser. Just as Virgil took Homer as his model in his divine *Aeneid,* so, by Hercules, do I use these as models for my own small productions; I have, in particular, openly imitated their admirable style of composition with regard to the placement of consonances.

Johannes Tinctoris, *Liber de arte contrapuncti* [1477], trans. Albert Seay (Rome: American Institute of Musicology, 1961), 14–15.

22

Music at Church and State Festivities in the Early Renaissance

The dedication of the Florence Cathedral, Santa Maria del Fiore, whose dome by Filippo Brunelleschi (1377–1446) is one of the enduring monuments of Renaissance architecture, was a ceremony important enough for Pope Eugenius IV to officiate in person. Even if we allow for the stupefaction to which our witness confesses, the impression conveyed by the account below, in which music plays a central role, is awesome indeed. The music performed at the Elevation that so moved its auditors was most likely the grand motet "Nuper rosarum flores," one of Dufay's most imposing compositions, which is known to have been written for the occasion.

When these decorations had thus been completely set out, and uncommonly well, lo, the day arrived—the most solemn and most honored of all days instituted by the Roman Church, the day of the angelic Annunciation [25 March 1436, according to Florentine usage the first day of the year], which the Pope a few days earlier, as we said above, had established as an opportune time for the consecration. Along with the fragrant pontifical rose, they bound that most precious altar in wondrous manner with gifts most worthy.

First there was a great line of trumpeters, lutenists, and flutists, each carrying his instrument, trumpet, lute, flute, in his hands, and each dressed in red clothing. Meanwhile, everywhere there was singing with so many and such various voices, such harmonies exalted even to heaven, that truly it was to the listener like angelic and divine melodies; the voices filled the listeners' ears with such a wondrous sweetness that they seemed to become stupefied, almost as men were fabled to become upon hearing the singing of the sirens. I could believe without impiety that even in Heaven, yearly on this most solemn day that marks the beginning of human salvation, the angels sing thus, the more ardently to give themselves up to the celebration of this festive day with sweet singing. And then, when they made their customary pauses in singing, so joyous and sweet was the reverberation that mental stupor, now calmed by the cessation of those sweet symphonies, seemed as if to regather strength from the wonderful sounds.

But at the Elevation of the Most Sacred Host, the whole space of the church was filled with such choruses of harmony and such a concord of divers instruments that it seemed (not without reason) as though the symphonies and songs of the angels and of divine Paradise had been sent forth from the heavens to whisper in our ears an unbelievable celestial sweetness. Wherefore at that moment I was so possessed by ecstasy that I seemed to enjoy the life of the Blessed here on earth; whether it happened so to others present I know not, but concerning myself I car bear witness.

Giannozzo Manetti, in Guillaume Dufay, *Opera omnia,* ed. Heinrich Besseler, II (Rome: American Institute of Musicology, 1966), xxvii.

The court of the dukes of Burgundy was a place where English and Continental musicians met. Although the two greatest fifteenth-century musicians of all—Dufay and Ockeghem—are not believed ever to have been in the court's actual employ, their music was very well known there, to judge from the Burgundian songbooks and choirbooks that survive. An idea of the setting in which these composers worked and in which their music was heard is given by contemporary accounts of the great Banquet of the Oath of the Pheasant, held in Lille on 17 February 1454, at which Philip the Good of Burgundy swore the Knights of the Golden Fleece to a crusade against the Turks, who the year before had captured Constantinople, the seat of Eastern Christendom. The rondeau "Je ne vis oncques le pareille" ("I have never seen the like"), mentioned below, is variously attributed in the sources to Dufay and to Binchois. Since the latter was actually attached to the court at the time of the banquet, perhaps he has the better claim. Another account of the festivities (the *Mémoires* of Olivier de la Marche) tells of the climax: a giant led in an elephant on whose back was a little castle, from which a woman dressed in mourning sang a lament for Constantinople, perhaps one of four composed by Dufay.

In the grand and spacious hall hung with tapestries there were three tables. On one stood a church with a chiming bell and four singers who sang and played the organ when their turn came. On another was pastry in which twenty-eight living persons played on divers instruments, each in turn.

First the church bell sounded, and after the bell had ceased ringing, three little choirboys and a tenor sang a very sweet song. What it was I cannot say, but as for me it seemed a pleasant grace before dining. After those in the church had carried out their task, a shepherd played on a bagpipe in the most novel fashion.

Then, without the slightest pause, a horse came trotting backwards through the entranceway, and on this horse were seated two trumpet players. They played a fanfare on their instruments, as the horse was led up and down through the banquet hall. After this, the organ players in the church began to play most sweetly, and when these had finished, from the pastry there came the sound of a cornett, played in a most unusual way. Then those in the church began again, with a little song which they executed very well and very sweetly. And after this were played, from the pastry, a lute and a sweet pipe, with yet another instrument in harmony, a thing that was good to hear.

After the church musicians and the pastry musicians had played four times each in turn, there entered a stag, wondrously large and fine, and on it was mounted a boy of twelve. And on his entry this boy began to sing the treble part of a song, most loud and clear, and the stag sang the tenor, with no one else visible except the child and the artificial stag. And the song they sang was called "Je ne vis oncques le pareille." After this interlude with the white stag, the singers in the church took up a motet, and afterwards, from the pastry, a lutenist accompanied two good singers. Thus the church and the pastry between them kept things going at all times.

Later, from the pastry, we heard a *chasse* [a song like a round, generally about hunting] that imitated the barking of little dogs and the sounding of trumpets, just as if we were in a forest. And with that *chasse,* the entertainments of the pastry and the church were completed.

Jeanne Marix, *Les Musiciens de la cour de Bourgogne au XVᵉ siècle* (Strasbourg: Heitz & Co., 1937), 38–41 (from Mathieu d'Escouchy, *Chronique*). Trans. R. T.

23

The Triumph of Emperor Maximilian

Political historians may look back on Holy Roman Emperor Maximilian I (1459–1519) as a terribly negligent and wasteful ruler, but he is remembered fondly by historians of the arts: for "Kaiser Max" was one of the most passionate art patrons in all history. His lust for self-aggrandizement and his lifelong obsession with the perpetuation of his memory caused him to commission literally thousands of works from the artists, poets, and architects of his time. More than anyone, Maximilian is responsible for putting the

German-speaking countries at last on the musical map. Not only did he maintain a huge musical establishment at which the best indigenous talent found employment, but he lured one of the best-known Flemish superstars, Heinrich Isaac (see p. 84), to his court from Italy. In 1512 Maximilian planned the ultimate commemoration of himself: a series of woodcuts that would depict the glories of his court in triumphant procession. The text was dictated by the Emperor himself, while the woodcuts, of which 137 were completed, were the work of perhaps the two greatest masters of the medium that ever lived: Hans Burgkmair and Albrecht Dürer. Six woodcuts and captions were devoted to music. The organist Paul Hofhaimer (1459–1537), the senior court musician by title, is given a cart to himself in the procession. Isaac's conspicuous absence is explained by the fact that by 1512 he was no longer in personal residence at the court, although he continued to draw a salary from the lavish Kaiser until his death in 1517. The musical woodcuts in *The Triumph of Maximilian* are a very valuable document about musical life in the early sixteenth century. Among other things, they give modern performers of early music welcome hints as to the appropriate grouping of instruments into "consorts."

What is written in this book was personally dictated by Emperor Maximilian in 1512 to me, Max Treitzsaurwein, His Imperial Majesty's secretary. The following tells how Emperor Maximilian's triumph is to be made, arranged and depicted:

Fifers and Drummers

[Here] shall be depicted Anthony of Dornstätt, the fifer, on horseback, carrying his verse inscription, and he shall be distinguished in his dress from the other fifers; he shall carry his fife case and wear a long sword, and his verse shall read thus:

> I, Anthony of Dornstätt, have played my fife
> For Maximilian, great in strife,
> In many lands on countless journeys,
> In battles fierce and knightly tourneys,
> At grave times or in holiday,
> And so in this Triumph with honor I play.

Music—Lutes and Viols

Then shall be depicted a low little car on small plough wheels; two elks shall draw the car, and a little boy shall be the driver and shall bear the verse inscription.

And on the car shall be five lutenists and viol players. And their leader shall be Artus, master lutenist, and his verse, borne by the boy, shall read how he prepared the lutes and viols in the most artistic way for an entertainment by the Emperor's orders.

> Now lutes and viols harmonize
> In elegant and courtly wise;
> Thus bade by his Imperial might
> Have I produced this fair delight,
> Blending these tuneful instruments
> As well befits such great events.

The lutenists, viol players, and the boy shall all be wearing laurel wreaths.

Music—Shawms, Trombones, Krummhorns
[Reed and brass instruments]

Then depict a low car on small plough wheels, drawn by two buffalo; a boy shall drive them and bear the leader's verse. On the car shall be five shawm players, trombonists and Krummhorn players. And Neyschl, master trombonist, shall direct them, and his verse, borne by the boy, shall read how to the Emperor's joy and by his command he combined such diverse instruments in the merriest way.

> The trombone and the shawm adorn
> The joyous sound of curving horn,
> Each to the others well adjusted.
> Since His Majesty entrusted
> This musical command to me,
> I have performed quite frequently.

All of them and the boy shall wear laurel wreaths.

Music—Regal and Positive [Organs]

Then shall be depicted a similar low little car on plough wheels, drawn by a camel; a little boy shall drive it and bear the leader's verse. On the car shall be a regal and a positive organ and people playing them. Their leader shall be Master Paul Hofhaimer, organist, and his verse shall be as follows, how by order of the Emperor he artistically increased and enlightened music.

> Regal and positive I play with ease.
> The organ, too, with many keys
> I make resound with artful voices
> So that the listener rejoices—
> All with a master's understanding,
> Our noble Emperor thus commanding.

The boy and all of them shall wear laurel wreaths.

Music—"Sweet Melody" [Mixed Consort]

Again depict a similar low, small car with plough wheels, drawn by a dromedary; a boy shall drive it and bear the leader's verse. On the car shall be the "sweet melody," or mixed consort, that is: first, a small drum; a cittern; a large lute; a viol; a fiddle; a small *rauschpfeife*; a harp; a large *rauschpfeife*.

> And now melodious music springs
> From the multifarious hums of strings.
> By Emperor's wish the members are
> The drum, the lute, the sweet guitar,
> And harps and fifes both small and large.
> To lead this consort is my charge.

All of them shall be wearing laurel wreaths.

Music—Choir

Again depict a similar small, low car with plough wheels, drawn by two bison; a boy shall drive them and bear the Kapellmeister's verse. On the car should be the choir, and also cornett players and trombonists arranged in good order. Herr Jorg Slatkany, Bishop of Vienna, shall be Kapellmeister and his verse shall be as follows: how by the Emperor's instructions he arranged the choral singing most delightfully.

> With voices high and low conjoint,
> With harmony and counterpoint,
> By all the laws of music moved,
> My choir constantly improved.
> But not alone through my intent—
> Give thanks to royal encouragement!

Stewdl shall be leader of the trombonists, Augustin of the cornett players, and their verse, borne by a boy in the car, shall read thus: how by the Emperor's instructions they attuned the trombones and cornetts in most joyous manner.

The cornetts and trombones we placed
So that the choral song they graced,
For His Imperial Majesty
Has often in such harmony
Taken great pleasure, and rightly so,
As we have good cause to know.

The Triumph of Maximilian I, trans. and ed. Stanley Appelbaum (New York: Dover, 1964), 1, 4–6. Copyright © 1964 Dover Publications, Inc. Used by permission.

24

Music as a Business

If the development of notation and literacy was the great medieval "revolution" in music, surely the comparable epoch-maker during the Renaissance was the invention of music printing from movable type. Through publication, composers sought and won much broader audiences than before. Their services were no longer the exclusive

An opening from the first book of music to be printed from movable type, Ottaviano Petrucci's *Harmonice musices Odhecaton A.* (The copy shown, now at the New York Public Library, is from the second impression, issued in 1504.) The composition is *Amours, amours, amours,* an instrumental arrangement of an old French song. The composer, Jean Japart, was one of the many Franco-Flemish musicians employed at northern Italian courts in the late fifteenth century.

property of church and court, but could be purchased by anyone with the price of a book. The concept of the "public" was born, and this undoubtedly contributed both to the rise of distinct national schools in the sixteenth century and to the "popularization" of musical style. Moreover, the ease and rapidity with which music could now travel must account in large part for the extraordinary cross-fertilizations and stylistic trans-formations of the period, such as that of the French *chanson,* via the keyboard *canzona francese,* into the Italian *canzona* for instruments. First to solve the problems of printing polyphonic ("figured") music from type was the Italian printer Ottaviano Petrucci. His method was cumbersome and costly, but his results were exquisite and, some would argue, unsurpassed to this day. Petrucci used a triple impression, mean-ing that a sheet would be fed to the presses three times: first for the staves, a second time for the notes and rests, and a third for the texts and decorative capitals. The document given below is the petition by which Petrucci applied to the Venetian government for the equivalent of a patent on his invention. Although the petition was approved immediately, Petrucci did not actually set up shop for three years: the first volume to come from his presses was the famous *Harmonice musices Odhecaton A* of 1501, a collection of Franco-Flemish chansons and instrumental pieces.

Most serene Prince and most illustrious Signory:

There being a most widespread report that your Serenities, through your grants and privileges, invite and inspire all men of mettle to think upon new inventions that add to comfort and to the adornment of public life, Ottaviano dei Petrucci of Fossombrone, an inhabitant of this illustrious City, a very ingenious man, has, at great expense and with most watchful care, executed what many, not only in Italy but also outside of Italy, have long attempted in vain, which is, with the utmost convenience, to print Figured Music. And still more easily, as a result of this, Plainchant: a thing very important to the Christian religion, a great embellishment, and exceedingly necessary: wherefore the above-named petitioner seeks relief at the feet of your Most Illustrious Signory, pleading that the Signory, through its accustomed clemency and benignity, deign to accord him, as first inventor, the special grace that, for twenty years no other be empowered to print Figured Music in the land subject to Your Signory, nor tablatures for organ or lute, nor to import said things, printed outside in any other place whatsoever, nor cause them to be imported or sold in the territories or places belonging to Your Sublime Signory, on pain of confiscation of said works—printed by others, or imported from outside— and a fine of ten ducats for each copy thereof: of which sum half shall be applied to the hospital of St. Anthony, and the other half to the benefit of the new municipal pawnshop, and this he asks as a special grace from Your Illustrious Signory to which he commends himself forever.

1498, the 25th day of May

Gustave Reese, "The First Printed Collection of Part-Music," *The Musical Quarterly*, XX (1934), 40.

Pierre Attaingnant of Paris, the second important music printer–publisher, used a different method: by lining up little bits of type that contained both notes and segments of the staff, an entire page could be set up and printed in one operation—a huge saving. There was a loss in elegance, though, since the staves were now full of annoying gaps. The practicality of the method ensured its success despite its drawbacks, and until copper-plate engraving became popular in the late seventeenth century, Attaingnant's method was the standard one for all printed music. The document below is the royal privilege, or patent, conferred on Attaingnant by the King of France on 18 June 1531.

Francis [I], by the grace of God King of France, to the magistrates of Paris, bailiffs, seneschals, and to all other justices and officers or their lieutenants, greetings. Having received the humble supplication of our well-loved Pierre Attaingnant, printer–book-seller dwelling in the University of Paris, stating that heretofore no person in this our realm had undertaken to cut, found, and fashion notes and characters for the printing of figural music or tablatures for the playing of lutes, flutes, and organs, because of the intricate conception, long consumption of time, and very great expense and labors necessary to that purpose, the said suppliant, by protracted excogitation and mental effort and with very great expense, labor, and genius, has invented and brought to light the method and industry of cutting, founding, and printing the said notes and char-acters both of the said music and of the said tablatures for the playing of lutes, flutes, and organs, of which he has printed, and hopes in the future to print, many books and quires of Masses, motets, hymns, chansons, as well as for the said playing of lutes, flutes, and organs, in large volumes and small, in order to serve the churches, their ministers, and generally all people, and for the very great good, utility, and recreation of the general public. Nevertheless, he fears that after having brought to light his said inven-tion and opened to other printers and booksellers the method and industry of printing the said music and tablatures, these printers and booksellers will similarly wish to attempt printing the said music and tablatures, etc. And by this means the said suppliant would totally lose the merit of his labors and the recovery of expenses and investments which he has made and contracted for the invention and composition of the above said characters, unless he is patented and succored by us, having humbly sought our grace. Thus we, having considered these things, do not wish that the said suppliant's labors, application, expenses, and investments in the said affair go unrewarded. May he succeed in it and experience the benefit. From such causes and others stirring us to this we have willed and ordained: we will and ordain that for the time and term of six years to follow, starting with the date of this present day, others than the said suppliant or those having charge from him, may not print nor put up for sale the said books and quires of music and tablatures for the playing of lutes, flutes, and organs declared above. We charge and command therefore by these present orders that every person look to the said suppliant's enjoying, and fully and tranquilly exercising, the ordinance entreated from our present grace. Making strictures and prohibitions to all booksellers and other persons generally, whatever they may be, to print or put up for sale the said books and quires of music and tablatures for the said time of six years without the express power and consent of the said suppliant. And this on great penalty to be levied by us and loss and confiscation of said books and quires. To the accomplishment of this all those whom it may apply are constrained, that they may enforce it with all due ways and reasonable means. For such is our pleasure, all ordinances, restrictions, charges, or prohibitions to the contrary notwithstanding.

Daniel Heartz, "A New Attaingnant Book," *Journal of the American Musicological Society*, XIV (1961), 22–23. Reprinted by permission of the American Musicological Society.

One of the most interesting documents of the fledgling music business is the monopoly over the printing not only of music but even of all ruled music paper granted by Elizabeth I to Thomas Tallis (1505–85) and William Byrd (1543–1623), the outstanding representatives of two generations of English church composers. Their venture not meeting with the desired success, two years later the partners applied once more to the Queen, this time for a supplementary grant of land to make up their losses. As the note appended by the Queen's secretary attests, she did not refuse them, thus conferring what may be the earliest "government subsidy for the arts."

Elizabeth by the Grace of God, Queen of England France and Ireland

To all printers, booksellers and other officers, ministers and subjects, greeting. Know ye, that we for the especial affection and good will that we have and bear unto the science of Music and for the advancement thereof, by our letters patent dated 22 of January, in the 27th year of our reign [1575] have granted full privilege and license unto our well-beloved servants Thomas Tallis and William Byrd, two of the Gentlemen of our Chapel, and to the assignees of them and survivors of them for 21 years next ensuing, to imprint any and so many as they will of set song or songs in parts, either in English, Latin, French, Italian or other tongues that may serve for music either in Church or chamber, or otherwise to be either played or sung, and that they may rule and cause to be ruled by impression any paper to serve for printing or pricking of any song or songs, or any books or quires of such ruled paper imprinted. Also we straightly by the same forbid all printers, booksellers, subjects and strangers, other than is aforesaid to do any the premises, or to bring or cause to be brought out of any foreign Realms into any of our dominions any song or songs made and printed in any foreign country, to sell or put to sale, upon pain of our high displeasure, and the offender in any of the premises for every time to forfeit to us, our heirs and successors forty shillings, and to the said Thomas Tallis and William Byrd or to their assignees and to the assignees of the survivor of them, all and every the said books, papers, song or songs. We have also by the same willed and commanded our printers, masters and wardens of the Stationers to assist the said Thomas Tallis and William Byrd and their assignees for the due executing of the premises.

To the Queen's most excellent Majesty:

Most humbly beseech your Majesty your poor servants Thomas Tallis and William Byrd, gentlemen of your highness' chapel: That whereas the said Thomas Tallis is now very aged and hath served your Majesty and your Royal ancestors these forty years, and had as yet never any manner of preferment except only one lease which your Majesty's late dear sister Queen Mary gave him, which lease being now the best part of his living is within one year of expiration and the reason thereof by your Majesty granted one unto another: And also for that the said William Byrd being called to your highness' service from the cathedral church of Lincoln where he was well settled is now through his great charge of wife and children come into debt and great necessity, by reason that by his daily attendance in your Majesty's said service he is letted from reaping such commodity by teaching as heretofore he did and still might have done to the great relief of himself and his poor family: And further your Majesty of your princely goodness intending the benefit of us your said poor servants did give unto us about two years past a license for the printing of music. So it is most gracious sovereign that the same hath fallen out to our great loss and hindrance to the value of two hundred marks at the least. It might therefore please your Majesty of your most abundant goodness for the better relievings of our poor estates to grant unto us without Fine a lease in reversion for the term of 21 years of the yearly rent of £30 to the tenant use. So shall we most dutifully pray unto almighty God for the prosperous preservation of your Majesty long to Reign over us.

At Greenwich 27 June 1577

It then pleased her Majesty to signify her pleasure that these petitioners in considera-tion of their good service done to her highness should have (without fine) a lease for 21 years of land in possession on Reversion not exceeding the yearly rent of £30 they abiding such order as should be taken by the Lord Treasurer or Sir Walter Mildmay Knight for the behoof of the tenants in possession.

Edmund H. Fellowes, *William Byrd,* 2nd ed. (London: Oxford University Press, 1948), 7–10.

25

Music in Castiglione's *Courtier*

Baldassarre Castiglione's *Il libro del cortegiano* (The Book of the Courtier, 1528) purports to be a transcription of four evenings' conversation and discourse that supposedly took place in the year 1507 in the castle of the Duke of Urbino. Music comes in for a great deal of praise. Some of this praise is the routine, rhetorical kind, parroted from the classics, that educated persons liked to affect. But Castiglione also offers revealing glimpses of music practiced as a social pastime by ladies and gentle-men of birth and breeding. Revealing, too, are the attitudes that underlie courtly music-making. The old Aristotelian suspicion of "professionalism" is revived in the call for a certain nonchalance (Italian: *sprezzatura*), which the courtier is admonished to adopt in his musical performances. A spontaneous simplicity is admired. There is little appreciation of intricate part-writing, but instead solo singing to the lute is held up as the ideal medium. While a few books of songs with intabulated accompaniments had been published by the time of Castiglione's book (chiefly by Petrucci) in response to this courtly taste, undoubtedly most such performances were spur-of-the-moment affairs, in which part-songs (*frottole*) were turned into solos by singing one line and reducing all the rest to chords. When we read later on of the "monodic revolution" at the end of the sixteenth century, we would do well to bear this important precedent in mind.

The Count began again: "Gentlemen, you must know that I am not satisfied with our Courtier unless he be also a musician, and unless, besides understanding and being able to read music, he can play various instruments. For, if we rightly consider, no rest from toil and no medicine for ailing spirits can be found more decorous or praiseworthy in time of leisure than this; and especially in courts where, besides the release from vexations which music gives to all, many things are done to please the ladies, whose tender and delicate spirits are readily penetrated with harmony and filled with sweetness. Hence, it is no wonder that in both ancient and modern times they have always been particularly fond of musicians, finding music a most welcome food for the spirit."

Then Signor Gasparo said: "I think that music, along with many other vanities, is indeed well suited to women, and perhaps also to others who have the appearance of men, but not to real men; for the latter ought not to render their minds effeminate and afraid of death."

"Say not so," replied the Count, "or I shall launch upon a great sea of praise for music, reminding you how greatly music was always celebrated by the ancients and held to be a sacred thing; and how it was the opinion of very wise philosophers that the world is made up of music, that the heavens in their motion make harmony, and that even the human soul was formed on the same principle, and is therefore awakened and has its virtues brought to life, as it were, through music. Therefore, do not wish to deprive our Courtier of music, which not only makes gentle the soul of man, but often tames wild beasts; and he who does not take pleasure in it can be sure that his spirit lacks harmony among its parts."

As the Count now remained silent for a little, the Magnifico Giuliano [de' Medici] said: "I am not at all of Signor Gasparo's opinion. Indeed I think, for the reasons given by you and for many others, that music is not only an ornament but a necessity to the Courtier. Yet I would have you state how this and the other accomplishments which you assign to him are to be practiced, and at what times and in what manner. For many things which are praiseworthy in themselves often become most unseemly when practiced at the wrong times; and, on the contrary, others which appear to be quite trivial are much prized when done in a proper way."

Then Calmeta said: "Gentlemen, since the hour is late, I think it would be well to put off the rest of this discussion until tomorrow, and let the brief time that remains be spent in some other more modest entertainment."

When everyone agreed, the Duchess desired that madonna Margherita and madonna Costanza Fregosa should dance. Whereupon Barletta, a delightful musician and an excellent dancer, who always kept the court amused, began to play upon his instruments; and the two ladies, joining hands, danced a *bassadanza* with extreme grace, much to the delight of those who watched.

[The next night, Messer Federico, speaking for the Count], went on: "There are certain exercises that can be practiced in public and in private, such as dancing. And in this I think the Courtier should take great care; because, when dancing in the presence of many and in a place full of people, I think he should maintain a certain dignity, though tempered with a fine and airy grace of movement; and even though he may feel himself to be most agile and a master of time and measure, let him not attempt those quick movements of foot and those double steps which we find most becoming in our Barletta, but which would perhaps little befit a gentleman. Yet privately, in a chamber, as we are now, I think he could be allowed to try this, and try *branles* [see p. 110] as well; but not in public, unless he is masquerading, for then it is not unseemly even if he should be recognized by all; for masquerading carries with it a certain freedom and license, which among other things enables one to choose the role in which he feels most able, and to bring diligence and a care for elegance into that principal aim, and to show a certain nonchalance in what does not matter.

"About music I am of the same opinion: hence, I would not have our Courtier behave as many do who have no sooner come into any place (and even into the presence of gentlemen of whom they know nothing) when, without waiting for much urging, they set about doing what they know how to do, and often enough what they do not know how to do; so that it seems they have put in an appearance for that alone, and that that is their principal profession. Therefore, let the Courtier turn to music as to a pastime, and as though forced, and not in the presence of persons of low birth or where there is a crowd. And although he may know and understand what he does, in this also I would have him dissimulate the care and effort that is required in doing anything well; and let him appear to esteem but little this accomplishment of his, yet by performing it excellently well, make others esteem it highly."

Then Signor Gaspar Pallavicino said: "There are many kinds of music, vocal as well as instrumental: therefore I should be pleased to hear which is the best kind of all and on what occasion the Courtier ought to perform it."

Messer Federico answered: "In my opinion, the most beautiful music is in singing well and in reading at sight and in fine style, but even more in singing to the accompaniment of the lute, because nearly all the sweetness is in the solo and we note and follow the fine style and the melody with greater attention in that our ears are not occupied with more than a single voice, and every little fault is the more clearly noticed—which does not happen when a group is singing, because then one sustains the other. But especially it is singing poetry with the lute that seems to me most delightful, as this gives to the words a wonderful charm and effectiveness.

"All keyboard instruments are harmonious because their consonances are most perfect, and they lend themselves to the performance of many things that fill the soul with musical sweetness. And no less delightful is the music of four viols which is most suave and exquisite. The human voice gives ornament and much grace to all these instruments.

"Then, as to the time for engaging in these several kinds of music, I think that must be whenever one finds himself in a familiar and cherished company where there are no pressing concerns; but it is especially appropriate where ladies are present, because their aspect touches the soul of the listeners with sweetness, makes them more receptive to the suavity of the music, and arouses the spirits of the musicians as well.

"As I have said, I favor shunning the crowd, especially the ignoble crowd. But the spice of everything must be discretion, because it would really not be possible to imagine all the cases that do occur; and if the Courtier is a good judge of himself, he will adapt himself to the occasion and will know when the minds of his listeners are disposed to listen and when not; and he will know his own age, for it is indeed unbecoming and most unsightly for a man of any station, who is old, gray, toothless, and wrinkled, to be seen lute in hand, playing and singing in a company of ladies, even though he may do this tolerably well. And that is because the words used in singing are for the most part amorous, and in old men love is a ridiculous thing; although, among other miracles, it sometimes seems that Love delights in kindling cold hearts regardless of years."

26

Josquin des Prez in the Eyes of His Contemporaries

The encyclopedic treatise Dodekachordon (1547) by the Swiss humanist Heinrich Loris, called Glareanus (1488–1563), was one of the outstanding achievements of sixteenth-century music theory. While its major contribution was the justification of the major and minor scales (under the names Ionian and Aeolian) within the system of the "church modes," the book also contains a number of interesting sketches of the composers whose music Glareanus admired most. He gives much space to anecdotes of sometimes dubious veracity and relevance, which, however, have the compensating virtue of vivid characterization—in a word, "human interest." And in this Glareanus reveals the Renaissance inclination to glorify the creator along with his creations. Another sign of the times is Glareanus's occasional impatience with exhibitions of "mere" technical competence at the expense of music's true purpose or content, which the writer sees in terms of music's power to move the "affections." This is a position a medieval thinker would have found incomprehensible, but one that increasingly came to characterize humanist thought. The outstanding personality in Glareanus's account is Josquin des Prez (c. 1450–1521), though even he does not entirely escape humanist censure for excessive cleverness. Josquin's preeminence among early sixteenth-century musicians is confirmed by all contemporary writers and by the surpassingly wide dissemination his music enjoyed and continued to enjoy for a half a century after his death, especially in German-speaking lands.

In the great crowd of talented men, there stands out most particularly in talent, conscientiousness, and industry (unless I am mistaken in my affection) Jodocus a Prato, whom in his native Belgian tongue the ordinary people endearingly call *Josquin*. His talent was so versatile in every way, so equipped by a natural acumen and vigor, that there was nothing in this field which he could not do. But in many instances he lacked a proper measure and a judgment based on knowledge, and thus in some places in his songs he did not fully restrain, as he ought to have, the impetuosity of a lively talent, although this ordinary fault may be condoned because of the otherwise incomparable gifts of the man. Moreover, although his genius is indescribable and we can be amazed at it more than we can treat it worthily, it also seems that not only in genius should he be placed above others, but also in the carefulness of his emendations. For those who knew him say that he published his works after much deliberation and with manifold corrections; neither did he release a song to the public unless he had kept it to himself for some years.

Before becoming generally known, he is said to have done many things. Among many others the following story is told: Louis XII, the French king, had promised him some benefice, but when the promises remained unfulfilled, as is wont to happen in the courts of kings, Josquin became aroused and composed the Psalm "Remember thy word unto thy servant" with such majesty and elegance that, when it was brought to the college of singers and then examined with strict justice, it was admired by everyone. The king, filled with shame, did not dare to defer the promise any longer and discharged the favor which he had promised; but then Josquin, having experienced the liberality of a ruler, immediately began, as an act of gratitude, another Psalm, "Thou has dealt well with thy servant, O Lord." Yet between these two compositions one can see how much more of a stimulus is the uncertain hope of reward than is a securely established benefice. For in my opinion, looked at from the point of view of the affections, the first composition is much more beautiful than the second.

Louis XII is said to have had a very inadequate voice. He had formerly been pleased by some song and asked Josquin if there was anyone who would compose a song in several voices in which he could also sing some part. The singer, wondering at the demand of the king, whom he knew to be entirely ignorant of music, hesitated awhile and finally decided what he would answer. "My king," he said, "I shall compose a song in which your Majesty will also be given a place in the singing." The following day, after the King had had breakfast and was to be refreshed with songs according to royal custom, the singer produced his song composed in four parts. In it I do not approve the skill of his art so much as I praise industry joined with art. For he had composed the song so that two boys would sing the upper part very lightly and delicately in canon, evidently so that the exceedingly thin voice of the King would not be drowned out. He had given the King the next part, consisting of one continuous tone in the alto range, a range suitable to the royal voice. Not content with this device, and so that the King would not waver in pitch, the composer, who was to sing the bass, arranged this part so that at regular intervals he would be supporting the King at the octave. The King laughed merrily at the trick and gladly dismissed the composer with a present and with the desired favor.

And Josquin loved to produce many parts from one [i.e., canon], a practice which many after him emulated. But in compositions of this kind, to say frankly what I believe, there is more display of skill than there is enjoyment which truly refreshes the hearing.

Glareanus, *Dodekachordon*, trans. Clement A. Miller (Rome: American Institute of Musicology, 1965), Chap. 24, abridged. Reprinted by permission of Dr. Armen Carapetyan, Director of the American Institute of Musicology.

Josquin worked for Louis XII of France in the early 1500s; this, apparently, was his last official position. Earlier, like so many other Flemish musicians, he found employment in Italy—first in Milan, then in Rome, and finally at the most musical Renaissance court of all, Ferrara. A fascinating document is the report sent on 2 September 1502 by the singer Gian de Artiganova to Ercole I d'Este, Duke of Ferrara, in which Josquin's merits are weighed against those of Heinrich Isaac (*c.* 1450–1517), his nearest rival in reputation. It is usually taken as a mark of Ercole's artistic discrimination that he hired Josquin despite Gian's recommendation of Isaac; but equally understandable might be the wish to "possess" the musician who by common consent was the best to be had at any price and whose presence might therefore confer the greatest prestige on the court he served.

I hereby inform Your Highness that the singer Isaac has been to Ferrara and has fashioned a very good motet, and finished it in only two days. From this one can reliably conclude that he can compose very quickly and is a fine man besides. One can easily get along with him, and he seemed to me very suitable for Your Highness. Prince Alfonso [Ercole's son, the later Duke] asked him through me whether he would like to enter Your Highness's service. He answered that he would sooner serve you than the other Lords he knows, and that he would not refuse the appointment. He asked to be informed within one month's time whether or not he is hired, and we accepted this term so as to have time to inform Your Highness of these events. We have promised him ten ducats a month, and he is satisfied with that; so would you now be so kind as to send word as to whether you are in agreement with all this or not. He seemed to me far more suitable to serve Your Highness than Josquin, since he is more sociable with his colleagues and composes new things more quickly. It is true that Josquin is the better composer, but he writes only when he pleases, not when he is requested to, and has demanded 200 ducats in salary, while Isaac is content with 120. Your Highness can now choose between them at pleasure.

Helmuth Osthoff, *Josquin des Prez* (Tutzing: H. Schneider, 1962), I, 211–12. Trans. R. T.

Adrian Coclico, the author of the extract given below, may have been merely boasting when he claimed to have taken instruction from Josquin. But the passage has value even if spurious, for it illustrates the new Renaissance attitude that valued the natural, spontaneous gift of the artist over the application of reason and mastery of theoretical doctrine.

My teacher Josquin des Prez never rehearsed or wrote out any musical exercises, yet in a short time made perfect musicians, since he did not hold his students back with lengthy and frivolous instructions, but imparted precepts in a few words, while teaching practical singing. When he had seen his students firmly grounded in singing, able to pronounce neatly, to sing ornately, and to put the words under the notes correctly he taught them the perfect and imperfect consonances and how to improvise counterpoint on plainchant using these. Those whom he noticed to be of high ability and good disposition he taught in a few words the rules of composing in three parts, then in four, five, six, etc., always providing examples for them to imitate. Josquin did not judge everyone capable of the demands of composition. He felt that it should be taught only to those who were driven by an unusual force of their nature to this most beautiful art, since he asserted that many works had been beautifully composed, and only one man out of thousands could compose anything like them, let alone better.

Adrian Petit Coclico, *Compendium musices* [1552], trans. Albert Seay (Colorado Springs: Colorado College Music Press, 1973), 16.

Martin Luther was a great admirer of Josquin's art. The two well-known quotations given below once again emphasize Renaissance humanist ideals of naturalness and spontaneity, governed withal by a sovereign mastery of technique—in a word, the "art that conceals art."

Josquin is a master of the notes, which must express what he desires; on the other hand, other choral composers must do what the notes dictate.

God has His Gospel preached also through the medium of music; this may be seen from the compositions of Josquin, all of whose works are cheerful, gentle, mild and lovely; they flow and move along and are neither forced nor coerced and bound by rigid and stringent rules, but, on the contrary, are like the song of the finch.

W. E. Buszin, "Luther on Music," *The Musical Quarterly,* XXXII (1946), 91.

27

Luther and Music

Few upheavals affected music as directly as did the Lutheran Reformation. For this was a revolution within the church, music's own stronghold in the Renaissance, led by a man whose passion for the art and whose recognition of its powers were exceptional even for a humanist, let alone a theologian. Where the Roman church was traditionally suspicious of it, Luther enthusiastically embraced music as perhaps his most powerful ally in winning souls for God. He gave his musical philosophy its fullest expression in prefaces to the numerous publications that, in the early years of the Reformation, supplied music for use in the Lutheran churches and schools. The most extended and passionate of these is the preface to *Symphoniae jucundae* (1538), a collection of Latin motets issued by the reformer's close friend, the Wittenberg printer Georg Rhaw. A large proportion of the pieces contained in this anthology was the work of pre- and non-Lutheran musicians like Isaac, Mouton, Févin, and, of course, Luther's beloved Josquin (see the preceding selection). That Luther valued their music so highly shows that his love for it was not sectarian, but rather the love of a devotee and amateur practitioner of the art (Luther played the lute and the flute and even composed a few pieces that have survived). When he describes "figural music" towards the end of this essay, Luther has a very specific kind in mind. When he speaks of a simple melody in one voice, with the others "tripping lustily" about it, he is describing the so-called *Tenorlied*, the German part-song of the time, which had provided the model for the earliest Lutheran hymn settings.

Martin Luther to the Devotees of Music: Greetings in Christ! I would certainly like to praise music with all my heart as the excellent gift of God which it is and to commend it to everyone. But I am so overwhelmed by the diversity and magnitude of its virtue and benefits that I can find neither beginning nor end nor method for my discourse. As much as I want to commend it, my praise is bound to be wanting and inadequate. For who can comprehend it all? And even if you wanted to encompass all of it, you would appear to have grasped nothing at all. First then, looking at music itself, you will find that from the beginning of the world it has been instilled and implanted in all creatures, individually and collectively. For nothing is without sound or harmony. Even the air, which of itself is invisible and imperceptible to all our senses, and which, since it lacks both voice and speech, is the least musical of all things, becomes sonorous, audible, and comprehensible when it is set in motion. Wondrous mysteries are here suggested by the Spirit, but this is not the place to dwell upon them. Music is still more wonderful in living things, especially birds, so that David, most musical of all kings and minstrel of God, in deepest wonder and spiritual exultation praised the astounding art and ease of the song of birds when he said in Psalm 104, "By them the birds of the heaven have their habitation; they sing among the branches."

And yet, compared to the human voice, all this hardly deserves the name of music, so abundant and incomprehensible is here the munificence and wisdom of our most gracious Creator. Philosophers have labored to explain the marvelous instrument of the human voice: how can the air projected by a light movement of the tongue and an even lighter movement of the throat produce such an infinite variety and articulation of the voice and of words? And how can the voice, at the direction of the will, sound forth so powerfully and vehemently that it cannot only be heard by everyone over a wide area, but also be understood? Philosophers for all their labor cannot find the explanation; and baffled, they end in perplexity; for none of them has yet been able to define or demonstrate the original components of the human voice, its sibilation and (as it were) its alphabet, e.g., in the case of laughter—to say nothing of weeping. They marvel, but they do not understand. But such speculations on the infinite wisdom of God, shown in this single part of his creation, we shall leave to better men with more time on their hands. We have hardly touched on them.

Here it must suffice to discuss the uses of this great thing called music. But even that transcends the greatest eloquence of the most eloquent, because of the infinite variety of its forms and benefits. We can mention only one point (which experience confirms), namely, that next to the Word of God, music deserves the highest praise. She is a mistress and governess of those human emotions—to pass over the animals—which as masters govern men or more often overwhelm them. No greater commendation than this can be found—at least not by us. For whether you wish to comfort the sad, to terrify the happy, to encourage the despairing, to humble the proud, to calm the passionate, or to appease those full of hate—and who could number all these masters of the human heart, namely, the emotions, inclinations, and affections that impel men to evil or good?—what more effective means than music could you find? The Holy Ghost himself honors her as an instrument for his proper work when in his Holy Scriptures he asserts that through her his gifts were instilled in the prophets, namely, the inclination to all virtues, as can be seen in Elisha. On the other hand, she serves to cast out Satan, the instigator of all sins, as is shown in Saul, the king of Israel [see p. 13].

Thus it was not without reason that the fathers and prophets wanted nothing else to be associated as closely with the Word of God as music. Therefore, we have so many hymns and Psalms where message and music join to move the listener's soul, while in other living beings or when played on instruments music remains a language without words. After all, the gift of language combined with the gift of song was only given to man to let him know that he should praise God with both word and music, namely, by proclaiming the word through music and by providing sweet melodies with words. For even a comparison between different men will show how rich and manifold our glorious Creator proves himself in distributing the gifts of music, how much men differ from each other in voice and manner of speaking so that one amazingly excels the other. No two men can be found with exactly the same voice and manner of speaking, although they often seem to imitate each other, the one as it were being the ape of the other.

But when learning is added to all this, and artistic music, which corrects, develops, and refines the natural music, then at last it is possible to taste with wonder (yet not to comprehend) God's absolute and perfect wisdom in his wondrous work of music. Here it is most remarkable that one single voice continues to sing the tenor, while at the same time many other voices trip lustily around it, exulting and adorning it in exuberant strains and, as it were, leading it forth in a divine dance, so that those who are the least bit moved know nothing more amazing in the world. But any who remain unaffected are clodhoppers indeed and are fit to hear only the words of dung-poets and the music of pigs.

But the subject is much too great for me briefly to describe all its benefits. And you, my young friends, let this noble, wholesome, and cheerful creation of God be commended to you. By it you may escape shameful desires and bad company. At the same time you may by this creation accustom yourselves to recognize and praise the Creator. Take special care to shun perverted minds who prostitute this lovely gift of nature and of art with their erotic rantings; and be quite assured that none but the devil goads them on to defy their very nature which would and should praise God its Maker with this gift, so that these bastards purloin the gift of God and use it to worship the foe of God, the enemy of nature and of this lovely art. Farewell in the Lord.

Martin Luther, Preface to *Symphoniae jucundae* [1538], trans. Ulrich S. Leupold, in *Luther's Works*, LIII (Philadelphia: The Fortress Press, 1965), 321–24. Used by permission of Fortress Press.

> As to the reformer's reforms, they were meant to make church ritual generally, and church music particularly, a participatory, active experience, in keeping with Luther's vision of the church as the community of all believers. Therefore, functions that had traditionally been the province of the monastic or professional choir were now to be shared by the entire congregation. Thus was born the unaccompanied congregational hymn known as the Lutheran chorale, sung in unison and in the vernacular. The passage given below is from a liturgical prescription that Luther wrote in 1523.

I also wish that we had as many songs as possible in the vernacular which the people could sing during Mass, immediately after the Gradual and also after the Sanctus and Agnus Dei. For who doubts that originally all the people sang these which now only the choir sings or responds to while the bishop is consecrating the Host? The bishops may have these congregational hymns sung either after the Latin chants, or use the Latin on one Sunday and the vernacular on the next, until the time comes that the whole Mass is sung in the vernacular. But poets are wanting among us, or not yet known, who could compose evangelical and spiritual songs, as Paul calls them, worthy to be used in the church of God. In the meantime, one may sing after communion, "Let God be blest, be praised, and thanked, Who to us himself hath granted." Another good hymn is "Now Let Us Pray to the Holy Ghost" and also "A Child So Worthy." For few are found that are written in a proper devotional style. I mention this to encourage any German poets to compose evangelical hymns for us.

This is enough for now about the Mass and communion. What is left can be decided by actual practice, as long as the Word of God is diligently and faithfully preached in the church. And if any should ask that all these forms be proved from

Scriptures and the example of the Fathers, they do not disturb us; for as we have said above, liberty must prevail in these matters and Christian consciences not be bound by laws and ordinances. That is why the Scriptures prescribe nothing in these matters, but allow freedom for the Spirit to act according to his own understanding as the respective place, time, and persons may require it. And as for the example of the Fathers, their liturgical orders are partly unknown, partly so much at variance with each other that nothing definite can be established about them, evidently because they themselves used their liberty. And even if they were perfectly definite and clear, they still could not impose on us a law or the obligation to follow them.

Martin Luther, "Order of Mass and Communion for the Church at Wittenberg," trans. Paul Zeller Strodach, ibid., 36–37. Used by permission of Fortress Press.

> A memoir by Johann Walther (1496–1570), Luther's chief musical assistant, shows the reformer himself at work on the task set forth in the foregoing selection. His account was published in 1615 by a Lutheran musician of a later generation, Michael Praetorius (1571–1621), in his three-volume musical encyclopedia *Syntagma musicum.*

Martin Luther, that holy man of God and the prophet and apostle of the German nation, took great pleasure both in plainsong and in polyphonic music. I spent many an hour singing with him and saw how happy and joyful he was then. He could never get enough of music, and he spoke about it magnificently. Forty years ago, when he was arranging the German Mass at Wittenberg, he wrote to the Elector of Saxony and to Count Johansen of beloved memory, asking to have Conrad Rupff [another early Lutheran musician] and me sent to him there. We talked to him at length about church music and the nature of the eight modes. At length he assigned the eighth mode to the Epistle, and the sixth to the Gospel, saying: "Christ is a most amiable Lord, his words are sweet; let us, therefore, use the sixth mode for the Gospel. St. Paul, on the other hand, is a grave and serious apostle; let us use the eighth mode for the Epistle." He himself, moreover, set the notes to the Epistles, the Gospels, and the sacrament of the true body and blood of Christ. He sang them all for me, and asked me for my comments. He kept me at Wittenberg for three weeks, while I set down in proper notation the music for some of the Gospels and Epistles, until the German Mass was sung for the first time in the parish church. I had to stay and hear it, and then take a copy with me to Torgau and, at Luther's request, hand it over to the Elector.

He also had me set the Vesper hymns, which were quite popular at the time, to short, simple melodies for students and children. He wanted poor students, such as beg for their bread from door to door, to have Latin songs, antiphons and responsories, to sing when they had the opportunity. He was not at all pleased at their having nothing to sing but German songs. And let me say here that I do not at all approve of people who want to drive sacred music in Latin entirely out of the church, thinking it not really Evangelical or properly Lutheran. Nor do I think any better of singing nothing but Latin music in church, since in that case the congregation understands nothing. The simple, old Lutheran songs and psalms in German are best for most people; those in Latin, however, are also useful for the benefit of students and scholars.

It is clear, I think, that the Holy Spirit was at work not only with the authors of the Latin chant, but with Luther as well, who wrote most of the German hymns, and set [some of] them to music. Take for example the German Sanctus, *Jesaia dem Propheten das geschah* ["It happened unto Isaiah the Prophet"]. Luther set the notes to the text, with the correct accentuation and prosody throughout—a masterful accomplishment. I was curious, and asked him where he had learned how to do it. He laughed at my simplicity, and said: "The poet Vergil taught me. He was able to fit his meter and diction to the story he was telling. Just so should music fit its notes and melodies to the text."

Michael Praetorius, *Syntagma musicum*, I (Wolfenbüttel, 1615), 451–53. Trans. for this book by Lawrence Rosenwald.

One of the ways in which the Lutheran church met the problem of quickly acquiring a musical repertoire of its own was to take existing songs, often secular ones, and adapt the words to devotional use. This method, known as parody, had its detractors, who held that the inclusion of familiar popular songs in the religious service could only demean it. Luther, on the other hand, saw in their very popularity an asset to the chorales' acceptance and potency. According to what is undoubtedly his most oft-quoted (if probably apocryphal) remark concerning music, Luther could not see why the devil should have all the best tunes. Here is a typical sacred parody, in which a popular song famous in a setting by Heinrich Isaac is converted to Lutheran use.

Insbruck, ich muss dich lassen,	Innsbruck, I now must leave thee,
Ich fahr dahin mein' Strassen	My way takes me far from here,
In fremde Land dahin.	From here to distant lands.
Mein' Freud' ist mir genommen	My joy is taken from me,
Die ich nit weiss bekummen,	I don't know how I'll regain it
Wo ich im Elend bin.	Where I am made to suffer so.

. . . .

O Welt, ich muss dich lassen,	O world, I now must leave thee,
Ich fahr dahin mein' Strassen	My way takes me far from here,
Ins ew'ge Vaterland.	To the eternal Fatherland.
Mein Geist will ich aufgeben,	My soul I'll render up,
Dazu mein Leib und Leben	Likewise my body and life
Setzen in Gottes gnädige Hand.	Will I place in God's gracious hands.

[Trans. R. T.]

And here is a curious reversal of the process: an Italian parody of the Te Deum from about 1530 that uses Luther's method to denounce him savagely. The opening of the original Te Deum text is on the left, the parody on the right, and a translation below.

Te Deum laudamus:	Te Lutherum damnamus:
te Dominum confitemur.	te haereticum confitemur.
Te aeternum Patrem	Te errorum patrem
omnis terra veneratur.	omnis terra detestatur.
Tibi omnes Angeli,	Tibi omnes Angeli,
tibi Caeli et universae Potestates:	tibi justi et universae religiones:
Tibi Cherubim et Seraphim	Tibi clerici et laici
incessabili voce proclamant:	detestabili voce proclamant:
Sanctus, Sanctus, Sanctus	Dirus, dirus, dirus
Dominus Deus Sabaoth.	Blasphemus in Deum Sabaoth!

Pleni sunt caeli et terra 　　majestatis gloriae tuae, Te gloriosus 　　Apostolorum chorus: Te Prophetarum 　　laudabilis numerus: Te Martyrum candidatus 　　laudat exercitus.	Pleni sunt caeli et terra 　　horrendae miseriae tuae. Te adulterinus 　　apostatarum chorus, Te hypocritum 　　damnabilis numerus, Te excommunicatorum male 　　dictus laudat exercitus.

> We curse you, Luther,
> 　　we acknowledge you a heretic.
> The whole world
> 　　detests you, father of error.
> All the angels,
> 　　all just men, all religions,
> Clergy and laity alike,
> 　　all proclaim in a voice of execration:
> "Horrid, horrid, horrid
> 　　blasphemer against the Lord of Hosts!
> Heaven and earth are filled
> 　　with your horrible dirty work!"
> The adulterous choir
> 　　of apostates,
> The damned crew
> 　　of hypocrites,
> The accursed army
> 　　of the anathematized
> Sing your praises.

Bologna, Civico Museo Bibliografico Musicale, MS Q27. Trans. for this book by Lawrence Rosenwald.

28

The Swiss Reformers

Except for Luther, the reformers of the sixteenth century were just as mistrustful of music as was the church against which they rebelled. Zwingli in Zurich and Calvin in Geneva would permit only unison congregational psalm-singing to take place in church, while for home use they sanctioned a few polyphonic psalters whose extremely restrained and simplified, chordal style was as far from the avid Lutheran perpetuation of Franco-Flemish traditions as could be imagined. In his preface to the Geneva Psalter of 1543, Calvin quotes from St. Augustine and from Plato on the need to control and regulate music as strictly as possible. For him, as for the medieval Church Fathers, to perform music in church was to play with spiritual fire.

As to public prayers, there are two kinds: the one consists of words alone; the other includes music. And this is no recent invention. For since the very beginning of the Church it has been this way, as we may learn from history books. Nor does St. Paul himself speak only of prayer by word of mouth, but also of singing. And in truth, we know from experience that song has a great power and strength to move and inflame the hearts of men to invoke and praise God with a heart more vehement and ardent. One must always watch lest the song be light and frivolous; rather, it should have weight and majesty, as St. Augustine says. And thus there is a great difference between the music that is made to entertain people at home and at table, and the Psalms which are sung in church, in the presence of God and His angels. Therefore, if any wish rightly to judge the kind of music presented here, we hope he will find it to be holy and pure, seeing that it is simply made in keeping with the edification of which we have spoken, whatever further use it may be put to. For even in our homes and out of doors let it be a spur to us and a means of praising God and lifting up our hearts to Him, so that we may be consoled by meditating on His virtue, His bounty, His wisdom, and His justice. For this is more necessary than one can ever tell.

Among all the other things that are proper for the recreation of man and for giving him pleasure, music, if not the first, is among the most important; and we must consider it a gift from God expressly made for that purpose. And for this reason we must be all the more careful not to abuse it, for fear of defiling or contaminating it, converting to our damnation what is intended for our profit and salvation. If even for this reason alone, we might well be moved to restrict the use of music to make it serve only what is respectable and never use it for unbridled dissipations or for emasculating ourselves with immoderate pleasure. Nor should it lead us to lasciviousness or shamelessness. But more than this, there is hardly anything in the world that has greater power to bend the morals of men this way or that, as Plato has wisely observed. And in fact we find from experience that it has an insidious and well-nigh incredible power to move us whither it will. And for this reason we must be all the more diligent to control music in such a way that it will serve us for good and in no way harm us. This is why the early doctors of the Church used to complain that the people of their time were addicted to illicit and shameless songs, which they were right to call a mortal, world-corrupting poison of Satan's. Now in treating music I recognize two parts, to wit, the word, that is the subject and text, and the song, or melody. It is true, as St. Paul says, that all evil words will pervert good morals. But when melody goes with them, they will pierce the heart much more strongly and enter within. Just as wine is funneled into a barrel, so are venom and corruption distilled to the very depths of the heart by melody. So what are we to do? We should have songs that are not only upright but holy, that will spur us to pray to God and praise Him, to meditate on His works so as to love Him, to fear Him, to honor Him and glorify Him. For what St. Augustine said is true, that one can sing nothing worthy of God save what one has received from Him. Wherefore though we look far and wide we will find no better songs nor songs more suitable to that purpose than the Psalms of David, which the Holy Spirit made and imparted to him. Thus, singing them we may be sure that our words come from God just as if He were to sing in us for his own exaltation. Wherefore Chrysostom exhorts men, women, and children alike to get used to singing them, so as through this act of meditation to become as one with the choir of angels. Then, too, we must keep in mind what St. Paul says, that devotional songs can only be sung well by the heart. Now the heart implies intelligence, which, says St. Augustine, is the difference between the singing of men and that of birds. For though a linnet, a nightingale, or a parrot sing ever so well, it will be without understanding. Now it is man's gift to be able to sing and to know what it is he is singing. After intelligence, the heart and the emotions must follow, and this can happen only if we have the hymn engraved in our memory so that it will never cease.

And therefore the present book needs little recommendation from me, seeing that in and of itself it possesses its own value and sings its own praise. Only let the world have the good sense henceforth to leave off singing those songs—in part vain and frivolous, in part stupid and dull, in part foul and vile and in consequence evil and destructive—which it has availed itself of up to now, and to use these divine and heavenly canticles with good King David. As for the melody, it has seemed best to moderate it in the way we have done, so as to lend it the gravity and majesty that befits its subject, and as might even be suitable for singing in Church, according to what has been said.

Geneva, June 10, 1543

Jean Calvin, *Œuvres choisies* (Geneva: Chouet & Cie., 1909), 173–76. Trans R. T.

29

The Reformation in England

Surely among the most hostile of all the reformers towards music were the English. During the reign of Edward VI (1547–53), veritable search-and-destroy missions were carried out against books of elaborately polyphonic "popish ditties," which is one reason why the magnificent English music of the Middle Ages and early Renaissance only survives fragmentarily, and why so much of it is better represented in Continental sources than in English ones. A selection of the more stringent cathedral injunctions of Edward's reign will give an idea of the severity of English reformist attitudes.

Lincoln Cathedral, 14 April 1548:

The choir shall henceforth sing or say no anthems of our Lady or other Saints, but only of our Lord, and them not in Latin; but choosing out the best and most sounding to Christian religion they shall turn the same into English, setting thereunto a plain and distinct note for every syllable one: they shall sing them and none other. And after them read the collect for the preservation of the King's Majesty and the magistrates, which is contained and set forth in the English suffrage.

St. George's Chapel, Windsor, 8 February 1550:

Because the great number of ceremonies in the church are now put away by the King's Majesty's authority and act of Parliament, so that fewer choristers be requisite, and the College is now otherwise more charged than it hath been; we enjoin from henceforth there shall be found in this College only ten choristers; and their Informator shall be yearly chosen by the Dean and Chapter.

Whereas heretofore, when descant, prick-song [i.e., polyphony], and organs were too much used and had in price in the church, great search was made for cunning men in that faculty, among whom there were many that had joined with such cunning evil conditions, as pride, contention, railing, drunkenness, contempt of their superiors, or such-like vice, we now intending to have Almighty God praised with gentle and sober quiet minds and with honest hearts, and also the Commonwealth served with convenient ministers, do enjoin that from henceforth when the room of any of the clerks shall be void, the Dean and prebendaries of the church shall make search for quiet and honest men, learned in the Latin tongue, which have competent voices and can sing, apt to study and willing to increase in learning: so that they may be first deacons and afterward admitted priests; having always more regard to their virtue and learning than to excellency in music.

York Minster, 1552:

We will and command that there be none other note sung or used in the said church at any service there to be had, saving square note plain [i.e., unaccompanied hymns], so that every syllable may be plainly and distinctly pronounced, and without any reports or repeatings which may induce any obscureness to the hearers.

We will and command that there be no more playing of the organs, either at the Morning Prayer, the Communion, or the Evening Prayer within this Church of York, but that the said playing do utterly cease and be left the time of Divine Service within the said Church.

Peter le Huray, *Music and the Reformation in England* (Cambridge: Cambridge University Press, 1967), 9, 24–25.

> The English Reformation differed from all the others in one crucial respect: it was led from above. Secular authority was on the side of the reformers, and recusants, those who refused to follow the reform, were persecuted. Many faithful Catholics went underground; William Byrd was among these. Others were exposed and had to flee; among the latter unfortunate group was the greatest English organist of the time, John Bull, who tells his own story in a letter of 1614 written originally in Flemish, to the mayor and aldermen of Antwerp.

Be it humbly known that John Bull, organist, was in the service of the King of England; and how, in the month of October in the year 1613, he was forced to take flight thence hither, since information had been laid against him that he was of the Catholic faith, and that he would not acknowledge His Majesty as Head of the Church. Which is a capital offense there. On account of which Their Highnesses [Albert and Isabel of the Netherlands] took him into their service, granting him a salary of 800 guilders a year, as well as exemption from tax, watch and other civic charges. But when, some time later, they learned that this was very displeasing to the aforesaid King of England, they dismissed him from their service. Wherefore he left some months ago to come hither into this city, as being the most famous in Europe for holding all the arts in higher esteem than elsewhere, and during this time he has given ample evidence to Your Worships and to everyone, in public in the churches, as well as in private houses, of the skill and knowledge of music which the Lord (be it said without boasting) has been pleased to bestow upon him. And since he is resolved to remain in this city, and there to live and die in the Catholic faith; and since he was forced to leave all his goods (with which he was well provided) in England; so he could not fail to offer his humble and willing services to Your Worships and to this city, most humbly craving that you will be pleased to appoint him your organist–pensioner at whatever salary you may think just and reasonable for a person of his quality, granting him in addition exemption from tax, watch and other civic duties. In return for which he will gladly serve Your Worships not only in whatever church services it shall please you to command, but also to play during banquets and feasts at which the city may desire to uphold its renown by means of music, upon the occasions of visits by lords and princes, without involving you in any additional expense.

Thurston Dart, "An unknown letter from Dr. John Bull," *Acta Musicologica*, XXXII (1960), 177.

30

High Renaissance Style

A very significant departure in compositional technique took place around the time of Josquin's maturity. This was the shift from the "successive" procedure of adding voice to voice generally employed by medieval composers of polyphonic music (see Aegidius of Murino's motet recipe, p. 57) to a method in which the composer shaped the texture as a whole, with due regard for each polyphonic strand. Not only does this change in compositional method reveal a new awareness of the "vertical," or harmonic, element on the part of composers, but it also shows a lessened reliance on "authority" such as characterized the attitude of medieval musicians. No longer did a composer necessarily begin with a borrowed melody as foundation for his polyphony. The new ideal was a light and airy texture, in which all the voices participated equally in the presentation of the oft-times freely invented melodic material. The voices were generally brought in one by one, each beginning with the same musical phrase as the preceding voice. Renaissance composers could generate lengthy pieces out of successive "points of imitation," while the technique permitted them to explore all kinds of subtleties in varying the order of entries, the time elapsing between them, and the pitch interval at which imitation took place. Music governed by "simultaneous conception" of parts could serve the Renaissance ideals of naturalness and spontaneity better than any known previously. The new technique was first described by the Florentine theorist Pietro Aron (*c.* 1490–1545) in his compendium Il Toscanello in musica of 1523. Aron's understanding of the older method is clearly imperfect: he imagines composers starting with the top voice and working their way down, while we know the actual practice to have been more nearly the opposite.

[Explanation of Counterpoint]

Through counterpoint a simple song, most beautiful in nature, is artificially varied in many ways and thereby becomes much more beautiful and smooth and of infinite sweetness to the listeners who partake of it. We call counterpoint a procedure containing in itself diverse variations of singable sounds with certain reason in proportions and measure of time. It is called counterpoint from "point against point," that is, note against note, because the notes are placed one against another, and a harmonic concordance of the extreme sounds which correspond together arises.

How the Composer May Give a Beginning to His Song

Many composers used to have the idea that the cantus [soprano] should be fashioned first, then the tenor, and after the tenor the bass. This happened because they lacked the order and understanding of what was required in making the alto part, and thus they made many difficulties in their compositions, because this inconvenience forced them to use unisons, rests, and ascending and descending leaps difficult for the singer, so that their songs had little smoothness or harmony. For when the cantus or soprano was written first and then the tenor, sometimes there would be no room left for the bass after the tenor was written, and after the bass was written, some notes in the alto would not fit. Thus when one considers only part by part, that is, when you attend only to the concord of the tenor when composing that part, and the same for the bass, each part may necessarily suffer the loss of its place in the overall harmony.

The moderns have considered better in this matter, as is manifest in their compositions for four, five, six, or more voices, each of which has its place and moves easily and smoothly. For modern composers consider all the parts together rather than by the method described above. If you prefer to begin by bringing in the cantus, the tenor, or the bass first, this is up to you. But because it might be difficult and troublesome to begin [your point of imitation] now with one part and now with another, until you are somewhat experienced through practice, follow the order and method given above.

Pietro Aron, *Il Toscanello in musica*, trans. Peter Bergquist (Colorado Springs: Colorado College Music Press, 1970), II, 21, 27–28.

> One of the major achievements of High Renaissance music was the regularization of dissonance treatment. Dissonances were carefully controlled within a context dominated by consonance. They were rigorously subordinated to consonance and were "prepared" and "resolved" according to well-defined principles, so as not to disturb the flow of counterpoint. Rules were devised to train composers in handling dissonances in this way, and these rules still survive in academic counterpoint study. What follows is the preliminary discussion that introduces these rules in the great treatise of 1558, the *Istitutioni harmoniche* of Gioseffo Zarlino (1517–90).

As I have said, every composition, counterpoint, or harmony is composed principally of consonances. Nevertheless, for greater beauty and charm dissonances are used, incidentally and secondarily. Although these dissonances are not pleasing in isolation, when they are properly placed according to the precepts given, the ear not only endures them but derives pleasure and delight from them. They are of double utility to the musician. The first has been mentioned: with their aid we may pass from one consonance to another. The second is that a dissonance causes the consonance that follows it to sound more agreeable. The ear then grasps and appreciates the consonance with greater pleasure, just as light is more delightful to the sight after darkness, and the taste of sweets more delicious after something bitter. We daily have the experience that after the ear is offended by a dissonance for a short time, the consonance following it becomes all the more sweet and pleasant. Therefore the musicians of older times held that compositions should include not only perfect and imperfect consonances, but also dissonances; for they realized that their work would achieve more beauty and charm with them than without them. Had they composed solely with consonance, they might have produced agreeable effects, but nonetheless their compositions (being unmixed with dissonance) would have been somehow imperfect; and this from the standpoint of singing as well as of composition, for they would have lacked the great grace that stems from these dissonances.

Though I have said that in composing we use consonances primarily, and dissonances incidentally, it must not be thought that these dissonances can be placed in counterpoints or compositions without rule or order, as is sometimes done, for confusion would result. Care should be taken to use them in an orderly, regular fashion, so that all may turn out well. Two things must be borne in mind above others, and I believe all the beauty and charm of every composition resides in these: the movements of the melodic parts, ascending and descending in similar or contrary motion; and the proper distribution of the consonances in the texture.

Gioseffo Zarlino, *Istitutioni harmoniche,* trans. Guy A. Marco and Claude V. Palisca, in Zarlino, *The Art of Counterpoint* (New Haven: Yale University Press, 1968), 53–54. Copyright © 1968 by Yale University. Reprinted by permission of Yale University Press.

31

Willaert the Reformer

Zarlino's rules (see the preceding selection) were largely derived from the compositional style of his teacher, Adrian Willaert (c. 1490–1562), a transplanted Fleming who stood supreme among musicians in mid-sixteenth-century Italy. He appears to have devoted special attention in his compositions to the regulation of the handling of dissonance and the clarification of text declamation, for which he earned the reputation of a reformer. As cantor of St. Mark's in Venice, Willaert was also an early experimenter with the effects of "split" (antiphonal) choruses later brought to such a peak by his successors the Gabrielis. His accomplishments in reforming the music of his time are celebrated in two passages below, the first by his protégé Zarlino, the second by a German musician of the time, whose testimony shows how far-reaching Willaert's influence was.

God has shown us the favor of causing Adriano Willaert to be born in our day, in truth one of the rarest masters who has ever practiced music and who, a new Pythagoras as it were, after examining thoroughly all music's possibilities and finding a vast number of errors, set to work to eliminate them and to restore it to that honor and dignity which were once its own and which should be its own by right; and he has shown us a reasonable way of composing gracefully any song, providing the most glorious example in his own works.

Alfred Einstein, *The Italian Madrigal* (Princeton: Princeton University Press, 1949), I, 322 (from Preface to Zarlino, *Istitutioni harmoniche*).

Recently, Adrian Willaert seems to have begun, and happily so, a new music, in which he does away altogether with the liberties taken by the older composers in matters of declamation. He so strictly observes well-defined rules that his compositions offer the singer greatest pleasure and no difficulties at all as far as the words are concerned. All modern composers follow him now. As Josquin appears to be the leader of the older school of music, so Adrianus stands out as the summit, the father, leader, and creator of the new style which is now being generally imitated. For he followed not only the precepts of the older composers in many of his published compositions, but he also arrived finally at a more precise understanding of the rules and found a new style which he also taught others such as Orlando [di Lasso] and Cipriano [de Rore] etc. and he himself wrote in this style many compositions partly set to Latin texts [i.e., motets], partly to Italian [i.e., madrigals, of which Willaert was one of the earliest composers].

Gasper Stocker (*c.* 1570, in Edward Lowinsky, "A Treatise on Text Underlay by a German Disciple of Francesco de Salinas," *Festschrift Heinrich Besseler,* ed. Eberhardt Klemm (Leipzig: VEB Deutscher Verlag für Musik, 1961), 245–46.

32

Music at a Medici Wedding

Renaissance court music-making at its most spectacular took place at state weddings, and nowhere more lavishly than in Medici Florence. The celebrations would culminate in the evening with a dramatic spectacle, between the acts of which would be performed a curious kind of diversion known as *intermedio,* where music really came into its own. The Florentine intermedii were allegorical representations that provided a kind of commentary to the main drama. In their mixture of scenic effects, dramatic action, and music they were a notable precursor of opera. Indeed, the famous intermedii of 1589 (for which all the music survives) were the work of many of the same artists who a decade later produced the first genuine specimens of music drama. The description given below is that of an earlier set of intermedii performed at the wedding of Francesco de' Medici and Joanna of Austria in 1565. The music is no longer extant, but so vivid is the account that one can fairly hear the madrigals, solo songs, and dance numbers, with their rich and variegated instrumental accompaniment—the ancestor of the modern orchestra. As for the visual effects, they reveal in their spectacular virtuosity the advanced state the art of stagecraft had reached in Italy by the sixteenth century.

DESCRIPTION

OF THE INTERMEDII

REPRESENTED

WITH THE COMEDY

At the Nuptials of His Most Illustrious and

Excellent Highness the Prince of Florence,

and of Siena.

IN FLORENCE, A.D. 1565

All the Intermedii were taken from the story of Cupid and Psyche, so pleasingly related by Apuleius in his romance "The Golden Ass"; and we proceeded by selecting the parts that seemed to be the most important, and fitting them to the Comedy with all the skill at our command, with the intention of making it appear as if that which is enacted by the Gods in the fable of the Intermedii, is likewise enacted—as it were, under constraint of a higher power—by the mortals in the comedy.

First Intermedio

Accordingly, a brief space after the descent of the curtains which conceal from the eyes of the Spectators the Perspective of the concave Heavens of the opening scene, there is seen to appear a second, most ingeniously contrived Heaven, wherefrom, little by little, a Cloud is perceived approaching, in which there is set with singular ingenuity a gilded

Lavish Spectacle at the Medici Court. From a volume commemorating the wedding of Grand Duke Francesco and Bianca Cappello (*Feste nelle nozze del Serenissimo … Gran Duca …*, Florence, 1579), one of the numerous occasions of state on which all the theatrical arts, including, importantly, vocal and instrumental music, were combined in fanciful recreations of classical myths used in allegorical tribute to the rulers. It is easy to see how the earliest operas grew out of this same tradition.

and gem-encrusted Car, recognized as that of Venus, because it is seen to be drawn by two snow-white swans, and in which, as Mistress and charioteer, is most majestically seated that loveliest of Goddesses, entirely nude, engarlanded with roses and, reins in hand, adorned with the beautiful girdle called Cestus by the ancients.

In her train follow the three Graces and the four Seasons, all distinguishable by their costumes. All of these were seated in charming grouping on the aforementioned cloud, which, descending little by little, seemed to leave behind it in Heaven Jove, Juno, Saturn, Mars, Mercury, and the other Gods, from whose midst was nevertheless heard to issue a Harmony passing sweet, seemingly a thing divine rather than human, while the entire great, dark Hall was filled with the sweetest and most precious odors.

At the same time there was seen at one extremity of the perspective, as though walking on the earth, Cupid approaching with wings and quite nude as he is described by the Poets, in whose company were seen his four principal passions—Hope, Fear, Joy, and Sorrow, all distinguishable by their costumes.

All these having come near the car, which in the meantime had reached the ground, Venus, who had risen to her feet and gracefully turned about, sang a *ballata*, seconded by all the others, in which her envy of Psyche is expressed. In the meantime, Cupid, crossing the Stage with his companions, sang the last stanza of the *ballata*, where he expresses his determination to avenge his mother, all the while letting numerous arrows fly into the crowd of onlookers.

Second Intermedio

The first Act being finished, there is seen issuing, from one of the four passageways left between the scenes for the use of the actors, a tiny Cupid gracefully bearing in one arm the counterfeit presentment of a swan, whereto is most skillfully attached a bass viol of no great size, from which latter, with a willow wand held in the other hand and concealing the Bow fixed beneath it, he, as it were with playful art, drew sweet sounds.

When he had reached his predetermined station, Music was seen approaching, recognizable by the harmonic band which she wore on her head, and by her rich robe all bestrewn with her various instruments, and with divers charts whereon were inscribed all the notes and all the measures of the same, and by the large and handsome bass lyre, on which she played while advancing.

Behind these, four more Cupids were seen to enter all at the same time, playing on four profusely ornamented lutes as they advanced; and after them four others, two with apples in their hands and disporting together, and two who with bows and arrows were shooting at each other with a certain affectionate grace.

All these, now formed into a choir, most sweetly sang and played a madrigal relating how Cupid, taking arms against love, fell victim to himself and to Psyche.

Third Intermedio

While Cupid is bent on another task, namely, the inflaming of human hearts, it appears at the end of the second Act as though the floor of the stage were rising up into seven small Hillocks; whence were seen to issue gradually, at first seven, and then seven more Deceptions. These were readily to be recognized as such, because every one wore as a headdress, each in a different and graceful attitude, a Wolf, forming indeed a pleasing and diverting spectacle for the audience; having, furthermore, their busts all mottled and spotted in the semblance of Leopards, and the rest of the body, and the legs and tails in the guise of serpents. Some held in their hands Nets, others Fishhooks, and others having Paws and Claws, beneath all of which were concealed small Cornetts. And thus they sang a Madrigal of how Cupid sought to deceive his mother Venus, and following that took their most orderly departure by the four passageways of the Stage.

Fourth Intermedio

Offense resulting from the Deceptions, and dissensions with a thousand other ills, instead of the seven hillocks there came to view seven small craters after the third Act. Dark smoke issued forth, followed gradually by Discord, Anger, Cruelty, Rapine, and Vendetta, all of whom could be recognized by their costumes.

And next followed two Anthropophagi, or Laestrygones, whichever one may please to name them, who, blowing two trombones in the form of ordinary trumpets, seemed as though they would excite the spectators to combat. Each of them was placed between two Furies provided with drums having iron drumsticks, and with divers arms, beneath which were hidden divers instruments.

All of them together sang and played a madrigal of arms and war, while executing, in the excitement of combatants, a new and extravagant *Moresca* [Moorish dance] at the end of which, rushing hither and thither across the stage as if in confusion, they fled in simulated terror from the gaze of the spectators.

Fifth Intermedio

Psyche, given over to desperation, is seen approaching, after having been sent by Venus to the Infernal Proserpine, accompanied by malign Jealousy all pallid and doleful, and by Envy, Care, and Scorn, who by their costumes reveal their identity.

Now when these four, while beating her and urging her on, were arrived at the intended spot, the Earth suddenly opened with fire and smoke, wherefrom were marvelously seen to appear four Serpents, the which they seized, however they sought to prevent, and, lashing them right and left with the thorny rods they held in their hands, under which were hidden four little bows, they finally seemed to disappear into the bloody gorge, and immediately there was heard issuing from the interiors a mournful, yet wondrous suave and sweet harmony, for within the Serpents had been set with singular ingenuity four bass Viols, which accompanied Psyche in her madrigal of despair, which she sang with such sweetness that one saw the tears drawn from the eyes of more than one.

Last Intermedio

When the Comedy was finished, there was seen to rise all at once out of the flooring of the stage a small, verdant Mount all adorned with Laurels and divers flowers, which, bearing on its summit the winged Horse Pegasus, was directly perceived to be Mount Helicon, whence little by little was seen descending that charmful band of Cupids, along with Zephyr and Music and Amor and Psyche held by the hand and all joyous and festive, now that she had returned safe from the Inferno, and through the intercession of Jove, moved by the prayers of her Husband, had won pardon and grace from the offended Venus. And with these was Pan, and nine other Satyrs with divers pastoral instruments in their hands, under which various other musical instruments were concealed. These, descending from the aforesaid Mount, led Hymen, the God of Nuptials, along with them, and playing and singing in his praise, and executing a new and most vivacious dance, they formed a graceful close to the festival.

For the satisfaction of curious Musicians, should these lucubrations fall into the hands of any such, we shall add that as the Hall, besides being marvelously beautiful, was of a singular magnitude and altitude, and perhaps the greatest of which we have knowledge today, it was necessary to make the Concerts of Music very full, and therefore the first from which emanated the exceeding sweet harmony of the open Heavens, was formed

> By four double-manual Harpsichords
>
> By four Viols
>
> By two Trombones
>
> By two Tenor Recorders
>
> By one mute Cornett
>
> By one Transverse Flute
>
> And by two Lutes.

The Music for the first two stanzas of the *Ballata* of Venus was in eight parts: only sung on the stage by voices, and accompanied behind the scenes, a feat of singular difficulty, calling for ingenuity,

> By two Harpsichords
>
> By four Bass Viols
>
> By one alto Lute
>
> By one mute Cornett

By one Trombone

And by two Recorders.

Then the last stanza of Cupid was likewise sung by voices throughout in five parts, on the stage, and accompanied behind the scenes

By two Harpsichords

By one large Lute

By one contrabass Viol doubling the bass

By one soprano Viol, also doubling

By one Recorder, also doubling

By four transverse flutes

And by one Trombone.

And this was the first intermedio. The last was in four parts, and most fully quadrupling all the voices, and adding thereto

Two mute Cornetts

Two trombones

One Dulcian

One small Serpent

One bass Lyra da braccio

One regular-sized lyra da braccio

One violin

And two Lutes

playing in the first song, and all singing.

In the second, where all is danced, the lines were sung by only eight voices, and the lyras were played, but in the refrain, refreshing as it were the spirits of the auditors, all were heard joyously playing and singing together with renewed gusto.

Messer Alessandro Striggio wrote the Music for the first, second, and fifth intermedios. That for the third, the fourth, and the last was furnished by Messer Francesco Corteccia, Maestro di Cappella to their most Illustrious Excellencies.

Oscar Sonneck, *Miscellaneous Studies in the History of Music* (New York: Macmillan, 1921), 276–86, abridged (Filippo Giunti, 1593, trans. Theodore Baker).

33

Lasso and Palestrina as Revealed in Their Letters

One of the last of the peripatetic Netherlanders who contributed so much to the development of Renaissance musical style, Roland de Lassus (also known as Orlando di Lasso, 1532–94) was born in Belgium, educated in Italy, and employed most of his life by the Bavarian dukes at Munich. Hired by Albert V in 1556, Lasso became fast friends with his employer's son, who was roughly his age. When the son became Duke William V, the friendship continued, and no greater testimony to the status Lasso enjoyed at the Bavarian court could be imagined than the familiarity with which the musician addressed his patron in a number of surviving letters. Nor could we hope for a better testimony to the cosmopolitan character of Lasso's career and art than the freewheeling mixture of French, German, Italian, and Latin in which the letter given below is playfully cast. The signature (see the fascimile of the letter) is another playful touch: it is a musical rebus, whose solution requires a knowledge of solmization according to the Guidonian hand (see p. 46). In the "soft hexachord," the notes given would be read "la so[1]."

Trehaut, Trepuissant, Jouissant: mons^r mon maistre a Jamais. Ego sum arivatus monacorum con gratia sine privilegio, sanus et gagliardus sicut poltronus. Moi, qui me tiens homme sage, ai mis ici cet image, wie E. F. g. mihi ordinavit; se in altra cosa la posso servire, a lei sta il comandar e a me ubedire. Je prie le Createur quil meine et rameine vre Ex^ce en baviere sain et dispos en tous propos, et quil aporte a madame, un petit filz dedans sa lame, ie le desire sur mon ame. Al gentil prospero mi raccomando, et de salutj Due mille li mando, et anco il mio garson le raccomando. A rivedersi poi ma non so quando. Aies souvenance de moj, e poi del resto fate voj:—

Ma femme, mon petit rudolfe et mon^r mon personage baisons en toutte humile les mains de vre Ex^ce et de madame la princesse: encore qu'elle n'ait mal au fesse. Dieu nous conserve en liesse: De monaco a di .19. du mois d'aoust 1572.

D.V.E.
treshumble serviteur
Orlando di [Lasso]

Most High, Most Mighty, Flighty: lord my master Forevermore: I have arrived at Munich with grace and without privilege, hale, hearty and lazy. I, who think many a deep thought, have hither the picture brought, as Your Princely grace has commanded me; if I can serve you in any other way, you must order and I obey. I pray the Creator may turn and return your Excellency to Bavaria, hale and sound all round, and that he grant my lady's womb a little heir, upon my soul that is my prayer. To your gentle favor I me commend, and of greetings Two thousand I do send, and also my boy to you I commend. Adieu till later, though when I can't portend. Forget me not, I pray, for the rest, have your own way—

My wife, my little Rudolf, and my own person do kiss in all humility the hands of your Excellency and of madam the princess, while her rump feels no distress. God preserve our cheerfulness. From Munich this 19th day in the month of August 1572.

Your Excellency's
most humble servant
Orlando di [Lasso]

Letter of Orlando di Lasso to Willliam V. Munich, Bayerische Staatsbibliothek, CIm 373h.

Facsimile of original in Orlando di Lasso, *Briefe,* ed. Horst Leuchtmann (Wiesbaden: Breitkopf & Härtel, 1977), 40; trans. in Piero Weiss (ed.), *Letters of Composers Through Six Centuries* (Philadelphia: Chilton Books Philadelphia, 1967), 17–18.

Another letter of more than common interest is one in which Giovanni Pierluigi da Palestrina (c. 1525–94), the greatest church musician of the latter sixteenth century, made bold to criticize the efforts of a noble amateur, Duke Guglielmo Gonzaga of Mantua. The circumspect tone of this letter from a musician whose reputation at the time was mainly a local one contrasts markedly with that of Lasso, the international celebrity. It is fitting that Palestrina should have been chosen to judge the Duke's work, for he was a preeminent craftsman, whose contrapuntal style has become the basis for "strict" counterpoint as it is taught to this day. When Palestrina speaks of "scoring" the motet, he refers tacitly to the Renaissance practice of presenting poly-phonic music in separate part-books. In order better to observe the Duke's work, Palestrina had to go to the considerable trouble of copying it out in score himself.

[3 March 1570]

Most excellent lord and very honorable Master

Your virtuoso having favored me with a hearing of Your Excellency's Motet and Madrigal, he ordered me on your behalf to express my opinion freely; I say that just as Your Excellency surpasses nature in all your works, so in Music you exceed those who worthily make it their profession. And the better to contemplate it, I have scored the Motet, and having seen the fair, uncommon artistry, and how the words are given a living spirit, in accordance with the meaning, I have marked some places, for it seems to me that if one could do without them, the Harmony would sound better. Also the use of imitation forces your parts into unisons too often. It likewise seems to me that because of the close imitation the words are hidden from the listener, who cannot enjoy them as in ordinary Music. It is evident that Your Excellency knows all these trifles better than I do, but I have said this in order to obey you, and so shall I obey you whenever you will favor me by commanding your affectionate and most willing servant.

Weiss, *Letters of Composers,* 16–17.

34

The Life of the Church Musician

The major cathedrals of Europe were the leading employers of singers during the Renaissance, and employed them in ever-greater numbers as time went on. In the fifteenth century the average size of a cathedral choir grew from about half a dozen to around fifteen, while by the middle of the sixteenth century a choir of two dozen or more, including men and boys, was by no means exceptional. Foremost both in quantity and in the quality of its singers was the Pope's own choir, that of the Sistine Chapel in Rome. Its members were recruited from all over Europe, and numbered many who later went on to stellar careers as composers. When one considers that Dufay, Josquin, and Palestrina—to name only a few—spent their formative years as singers in the papal choir, the document abstracted below, which details the choris-ters' requirements, rights, and duties, takes on a compelling human interest.

A singer need not be in holy orders but must be a man of honor and of good repute. When a new member is proposed, his character shall first be examined, and then he shall be brought to a musical examination conducted by the choir members themselves. The first requisite is his voice quality; the second, his ability to keep his part in homophony; the third, his sufficiency as a singer of contrapuntal music; the fourth, his ability to sing plainsong; and the fifth his sightreading ability. A secret vote shall be taken after his musical examination, and no singer may be admitted unless two-thirds of the singers, plus one, vote for his admission. After being admitted and having attended to all the financial formalities, he must give himself solely to the daily routine in the pope's chapel and may not sing elsewhere nor carry on other business. His duties as a new singer include moving the heavy choirbooks into place; as soon as a newer singer enters he no longer moves them into place for everyday singing, but he still carries them with his junior novice in the choir during processions. Only when two singers are junior to him can he consider his chores as porter ended. Absolute silence during divine office is required. All business such as requests for leaves of absence must be directed to the most senior member of the choir present. Special requests must be approved in a secret vote by two-thirds plus one. Heavy fines are to be assessed for malingering or other false reports. Every five years an extended leave is granted—five months for Italians; ten for French and Spanish. The feast box from the pope's kitchen is to be awarded in rotation to choristers, who should divide it among their colleagues. Ceremonies for creation of new cardinals, for the exequies of a pope, and for the creation and coronation of a new pope are to follow a prescribed routine. All unusual choir business not covered by clauses in the constitutions shall be entrusted to a committee of three, six, or nine members, composed of Italians, French, and Spanish in equal numbers. The reason for this division by nations is that experience has shown the singers divide always into their own national groups, and speak their own language with each other.

Robert Stevenson, *Spanish Cathedral Music in the Golden Age* (Berkeley: University of California Press, 1961), 27 (*Constitutiones Capellae Pontificiae* [1545]).

Another major center whose cathedral boasted a choir of international standing was Milan, seat of the Ambrosian rite. Josquin sang here, too, for a time, as did such other Renaissance luminaries as Alexander Agricola and Loyset Compère. The chapel master when the rules given below were made (1572) was Vincenzo Ruffo, one of the important musical figures of the Counter Reformation period. Rule 16, which details his compositional duties, also suggests that only Mass and Vespers were graced with polyphonic music. At lesser offices, and most probably on lesser days, Gregorian chant sufficed. Compare the document Ruffo had to sign with the very similar terms of Bach's employment in Leipzig 150 years later (see p. 209).

1. When the chapel master and the singers are obliged to go into the choir to sing they shall first go to the sacristy to dress themselves in cassocks and surplices, and then go up to the choir with decorum; on leaving, when the divine offices are concluded, they shall proceed similarly to the sacristy to disrobe; whoever contravenes this order shall lose that day's wages, if the chapter so desires.

2. Neither the chapel master nor any of the singers shall leave the choir while the divine offices are being celebrated, except for some urgent reason which shall first be approved by the chapel master or his coadjutor.

3. When the Archbishop is participating, neither the chapel master nor the singers shall depart until the divine offices have been completely finished; when the Archbishop does not participate, they may leave after their singing has been concluded, provided the elevation of the body and blood of our Lord has been completed; under penalty of punishment by the chapter.

4. None of the singers may leave Milan or go to sing in any other church of Milan on those days on which they are obligated to be at the Duomo, without permission of the chapel master; he in turn must first notify the cathedral authorities; under penalty to the singer of losing his place in the chapel, if the chapter so desires.

5. The chapel master shall see that the boys remain in their places, and not permit them to go upon the steps of the choir because great disorder results.

6. The chapel master shall not allow anyone to go up into the choir for any reason, except to give someone a trial as a singer; under penalty of punishment at the discretion of the chapter.

7. The chapel master and the singers shall appear in person and not send substitutes at the beginning of the singing, except in case of sickness or some other legitimate cause; due notice shall be given to the authorities by two of the deputies and by the chapel master, and whoever does not appear shall lose his wages for the time he has missed.

8. When the singers are in the choir they shall be proper and modest in action and word, none of them leaving his place; and transgressors shall be punished at the discretion of the authorities.

9. Everyone must obey the chapel master in all things pertaining to his duties; for the first offense the transgressor shall lose a day's wages; for the second, he shall be punished at the discretion of the authorities; for the third, deprived of his place.

10. When the singers are in the chapel they shall utter no blasphemy, under penalty of being punished at the discretion of the authorities; and the chapel master may send any delinquents out of the chapel; the next day he must give notice to the authorities who will determine what steps should be taken.

11. Wherever the Archbishop of the Reverend Chapter of the Duomo shall go to sing Mass, Vespers, offices, or litanies, the singers shall carry their clerical cassocks, surplices, and caps to the place where they will sing; otherwise they shall lose that day's wages.

12. The chapel master shall take care to note all latecomers and all who do not appear at the appointed hours to sing, and each month must present the list to the Treasurer, so that wages can be withheld for the time lost; and in order that the singers may not move the chapel master to take pity on them, there shall be added the testimony of one of the more experienced chapel members, who shall confirm the absence.

13. Wages which have been withheld from those who have been entirely absent from service shall not be returned or given out except by the chapter, in which case they shall not be more than two-thirds of the amount due.

14. The chapel master cannot accept or dismiss any singer without permission of the chapter, except the boys, whom he may release and take on; however, with the knowledge of the authorities.

15. No one shall be admitted to the chapel if he has not first been vouched for by a trustworthy person as to his character and habits: that he lives in a Christian fashion, that he confesses several times a year, that he is not disrespectful, that he is neither a

thief nor a blasphemer, nor stained with any other sin; and if any such individual should be admitted, he shall be immediately turned out of the chapel.

16. The chapel master shall be required every month to compose a Mass and a Magnificat and such hymns as shall be necessary, according to the notice given him by the chorusmaster, and he shall notify the authorities in charge of music as to his compositions.

17. The chapel master shall be required to teach the boys twice a day in the appointed place; and he shall teach the usual number of boys; if he does not do this, he shall be punished at the discretion of the chapter.

18. The chapel master is warned to give notice of the absence of one or more of the three basses, or of the four tenors, or of the four contraltos; in order that they may be replaced by new members to maintain the complement in the numbers stated; this being at our discretion.

Lewis Lockwood, *The Counter-Reformation and the Masses of Vincenzo Ruffo* (Venice: Fondazione Giorgio Cini, 1970), 58–60. Reprinted by the kind permission of the Fondazione Cini and the author.

Writing about singers tends as a rule to fall into an admonitory tone, which suggests that many of the vocal performances to which Renaissance ears were treated fell short of Olympian standards. And this is understandable: for every lutenist hired by a Renaissance prince, ten singers would be employed in the church. Their level of training, skill, and taste was not likely to be uniformly high. Some singers, moreover, attempted to ape the ornamental practices of instrumentalists with less than happy results. Finally, almost everyone who wrote of singing in the sixteenth century cautioned singers not to sing too loudly. As Andreas Ornithoparcus, a German writing in 1517, put it of the Saxon singers with whom he grew up: "Why they should so delight in such clamoring there is no reason, but either because they have a deaf God, or because they think he is gone to the south-side of Heaven, and therefore cannot so easily hear both the Easterlings and the Southerlings" (*Musice active micrologus,* trans. John Dowland, 1609). The most concise and sensible set of guidelines for singers to observe can be found in the passage that follows, from the ever-authoritative Zarlino's *Istitutioni harmoniche* of 1558.

Matters for the singer to observe are these: First of all he must aim diligently to perform what the composer has written. He must not be like those who, wishing to be thought worthier and wiser than their colleagues, indulge in certain rapid improvisations that are so savage and so inappropriate that they not only annoy the hearer but are ridden with thousands of errors, such as many dissonances, consecutive unisons, octaves, fifths, and other similar progressions absolutely intolerable in composition. Then there are singers who substitute higher or lower tones for those intended by the composer, singing for instance a whole tone instead of a semitone, or vice versa, leading to countless errors as well as offense to the ear. Singers should aim to render faithfully what is written to express the composer's intent, intoning the correct steps in the right places. They should seek to adjust to the consonances and to sing in accord with the nature of the words of the composition; happy words will be sung happily and at a lively pace, whereas sad texts call for the opposite. Above all, in order that the words may be understood, they should take care not to fall into the common error of changing the vowel sounds, singing *a* in place of *e, i* in place of *o,* or *u* in place of one of these; they should form each vowel in accord with its true pronunciation. It is truly reprehensible and shameful for certain oafs in choirs and public chapels as well as in private chambers to corrupt the words when they should be rendering them clearly, easily, and accurately. For example, if we hear singers shrieking certain songs—I cannot call it singing—with such crude tones and grotesque gestures that they appear to be apes, are we not compelled to laugh? Or more truthfully who would not become enraged upon hearing such horrible, ugly counterfeits?

A singer should also not force the voice into a raucous, bestial tone. He should strive to moderate his tone and blend it with the other singers' so that no voice is heard above the others. Such pushed singing produces more noise than harmony. For harmony results only when many things are tempered so that no one exceeds the other. The singer should know too that in church and in public chapels he should sing with full voice, moderated of course as I have just said, while in private chambers he should use a subdued and sweet voice and avoid clamor. Singers in such places should use good taste, so as not to leave themselves open to rightful censure. Further, they should refrain from bodily movements and gestures that will incite the audience to laughter as some do who move—and this is true also of certain instrumentalists—as if they were dancing.

But to leave these matters, I shall conclude by saying that if the composer and singer observe those things that pertain to their respective offices, there is no doubt that every composition will be sweet, soft, and harmonious, and the listeners pleased and grateful.

Gioseffo Zarlino, *The Art of Counterpoint,* trans. Guy A. Marco and Claude V. Palisca (New Haven: Yale University Press, 1968), 110–11. Copyright © 1968 by Yale University. Reprinted by permission.

35

The Genres of Music in the High Renaissance

One of the most useful surveys of Renaissance musical genres is Thomas Morley's, in his *Plaine and Easie Introduction* of 1597. He proceeds from vocal to instrumental forms and, within each of these, from the most serious to the lightest genres. A lover of all things Italian, Morley ignores the vernacular genres of French and German music, but except for this omission, and allowing for an occasional clarification of the author's somewhat archaic vocabulary, Morley's descriptions are self-explanatory.

All music for voices [i.e., polyphonic music] is made either for a ditty or without a ditty [i.e., with or without words]. If it be with a ditty it is either grave or light; the grave ditties they have still kept in one kind, so that whatsoever music be made upon it is comprehended under the name of a Motet.

A Motet

A Motet is properly a song made for the church, either upon some hymn or anthem or such like, and that name I take to have been given to that kind of music in opposition to the other which they called *Canto fermo* and we do commonly call Plainsong [i.e., monophonic chant]. This kind of all others which are made on a ditty requireth most art and moveth and causeth most strange effects in the hearer, being aptly framed for the ditty and well expressed by the singer, for it will draw the auditor (and especially the skillful auditor) into a devout and reverent kind of consideration of Him for whose praise it was made. If you compose in this kind you must cause your harmony to carry a majesty, taking discords and bindings [i.e., suspensions] as often as you can, but let it be in long notes, for the nature of it will not bear short notes and quick motions which denotate a kind of wantonness.

Light Music

This much for Motets, under which I comprehend all grave and sober music. The light music hath been of late more deeply dived into so that there is no vanity which in it hath not been followed to the full.

A Madrigal

But the best kind of it is termed Madrigal, a word for the etymology of which I can give no reason [nor can we today]; yet use showeth that it is a kind of music made upon songs and sonnets such as Petrarch and many poets of our time have excelled in. This kind of music were not so much disallowable if the poets who compose the ditties would abstain from some obscenities which all honest ears abhor, and sometimes from blasphemies which no man (at least who hath any hope of salvation) can sing without trembling. As for the music it is, next unto the Motet, the most artificial [i.e., skillfully formed] and, to men of understanding, most delightful. If therefore you will compose in this kind you must possess yourself with an amorous humor (for in no composition shall you prove admirable except you put on and possess yourself wholly with that vein wherein you compose), so that you must in your music be wavering like the wind, sometime wanton, sometime drooping, sometime grave and staid, otherwhile effeminate; you may show the very uttermost of your variety, and the more variety you show the better shall you please.

Canzonets, etc.

The second degree of gravity in this light music is given to *Canzonets*, that is little short songs (wherein little art can be showed, being made in strains [i.e., short repeated sections], the beginning of which is some point lightly touched [i.e., a brief passage of imitation] and every strain repeated except the middle) which is, in composition of music, a counterfeit of the Madrigal. The last degree of gravity (if they have any at all) is given to the *Villanelle* or country songs, which are made only for the ditty's sake for, so they be aptly set to express the nature of the ditty, the composer (though he were never so excellent) will not stick [i.e., hesitate] to write coarsely, for in this kind they think it no fault to make a clownish music to a clownish matter. There is also another kind more light than this which they term *Balletti*, or dances, and are songs which being sung to a ditty may likewise be danced. These, and all other kinds of light music (saving the Madrigal) are by a general name called *ayres*. There be also another kind of Balletts commonly called *fa las*. A slight kind of music it is, and, as I take it, devised to be danced to voices.

Fantasies

The most principal and chiefest kind of music which is made without a ditty is the Fantasy, that is when a musician taketh a point at his pleasure and wresteth and turneth it as he list, making either much or little of it according as shall seem best in his own conceit. In this may more art be shown than in any other music because the composer is tied to nothing, but that he may add, diminish, and alter at his pleasure. Likewise this kind of music is, with them who practice instruments of parts [i.e., instruments which take single parts in *consorts* or ensembles, especially viols], in greatest use, but for voices it is but seldom used.

Pavans

The next in gravity and goodness unto this is called a Pavan, a kind of staid music ordained for grave dancing and most commonly made of three strains, whereof every strain is played or sung twice; a strain they make to contain eight, twelve, or sixteen measures as they list, yet fewer than eight I have not seen in any Pavan. Also in this you must cast your music by four, so that if you keep that rule it is no matter how many fours you put in your strain for it will fall out well enough in the end, the art of dancing being come to that perfection that every reasonable dancer will make measure of no measure.

Galliards

After every Pavan we usually set a Galliard (that is a kind of music made out of the other), causing it to go by a measure consisting of a long and short stroke successively, for as the foot *trochee* consisteth of one syllable of two times and another of one time so is the first of these two strokes double to the latter. This is a lighter and more stirring kind of dancing than the Pavan, consisting of the same number of strains. The Italians make their Galliards (which they call *Saltarelli*) plain, and frame ditties to them which in their masquerades they sing and dance, and many times without any instruments at all, but instead of instruments they have courtesans disguised in men's apparel who sing and dance to their own songs.

Other Dances

The *Alman* is a more heavy dance than this (fitly representing the nature of the people whose name it carries [i.e., the Germans]) so that no extraordinary motions are used in dancing of it. Like unto this is the French *Branle* (which they call "Branle Simple") which goeth somewhat rounder in time than this, otherwise the measure is all one. The "Branle de Poictou" or "Branle Double" is more quick in time but the strain is longer. Like unto this (but more light) be the *Voltes* and *Courantes* which being both of a measure are, notwithstanding, danced after sundry fashions, the Volte rising and leaping, the Courante traversing and running, in which measure also our *Country Dance* is made though it be danced after another form than any of the former. There be also many other kinds of dances, as Hornpipes, Jigs, and infinite more which I cannot nominate unto you, but knowing these the rest cannot but be understood as being one with some of these which I have already told you.

Thomas Morley, *A Plaine and Easie Introduction to Practicall Musicke* (London, 1597), 179–81, abridged. Spelling and punctuation modernized.

Conspicuous by its absence from Morley's genres is the one that usually heads the list— that is, the Mass, which, if sung at all in post-Reformation England, would have been sung only behind closed doors. For a detailed description of High Renaissance Mass composition, we must turn to Padre Pietro Cerone's very late compendium *El melopeo y maestro* of 1613. The kind of Mass Cerone discusses is what nowadays we call "parody," an ingenious compromise between the old-fashioned traditions of Mass composition and the newer, specifically Renaissance, ideal of homogeneous, imitative texture. Since the individual parts of a sixteenth-century composition written in imitation were constantly oscillating between foreground and background, no one of them could provide a suitable cantus firmus for a new composition. Instead, the whole texture was adopted as a model. Its motives were extracted and rewoven into a new fabric, and in the process the composer was given considerable opportunity to show off his skill and resourcefulness by finding all kinds of new contrapuntal possibilities in the borrowed material. In the very last sentence of the extract given below, Cerone refers to the rage for "polychoral" music that seems to have had its origins and its heyday in Venice but rapidly spread wherever the musical forces were big enough to accommodate the style. As Cerone implies, such elephantine compositions demanded a radical simplification of texture in favor of sonority. This was one among many pressures on the "classical" polyphonic style of the Renaissance that eventually resulted in its transformation into what today we describe as early Baroque style.

THE MANNER TO BE OBSERVED IN COMPOSING A MASS

The manner, or style, to be observed in composing a Mass agrees with that of the motet as regards the slow tempo which the parts should maintain, but in other ways it is very different.

—It is necessary and obligatory that the musical theme at the beginnings of the first Kyrie, the Gloria, the Credo, the Sanctus, and the Agnus Dei should be one and the same. The same melody, that is, but not the same treatment or accompaniment. For example, if the treble began the point of imitation in the first Kyrie, let another voice (the tenor, alto, or bass) begin it in the Gloria, another in the Credo, another in the Sanctus, and still another in the Agnus Dei. And should it happen that the treble or some other part begins two or three times, take care that the other parts enter each time at different intervals. Thus all the aforesaid beginnings should maintain variety in the treatment and accompaniment, but not in the invention or subject.

—When the first Kyrie is finished, the Christe may be written upon some subsidiary motive from the same motet or madrigal (whichever it is) from which the principal subject was borrowed. Know also that the composer may here use some motive of his own invention, provided it is appropriate to the tone and not in another style altogether.

—The endings of the last Kyrie, the Gloria, the Credo, the Sanctus, the Osanna (for the Sanctus is always divided, for greater solemnity, into three or four sections), and the third Agnus Dei should all be made alike, following the melody of the motet or madrigal upon which the Mass is composed, preserving the rule which I have said should be preserved in the beginnings, namely, that all these endings be alike as to invention and subject, yet varied in accompaniment and treatment.

—In the course of the Mass, the more use one makes (whether with or without imitation) of motives from the middle or inside of the composition upon which the Mass is written, the better and the more praiseworthy the work will be.

—The Gloria and Credo are composed as continuous movements, without embellishment and with less imitation among the parts, using melodic ideas that are short, clear, familiar, and closely woven, unlike those of the Kyries, the Sanctuses, and the Agnus Dei's, which should be long, elaborate, less familiar, and less closely woven.

—It may be seen that good composers have taken care to make the parts sing all together, using only slow notes and with devout consonances and harmonious intervals, upon the words "Jesu Christe." This is done because of the reverence and decorum due to their meanings. The same is usually observed upon the words "Et incarnatus est" to "Crucifixus" [i.e., the sections of the Credo that relate the life of Christ]. To write points of imitation and lively passages here is a very great error and a sign of great ignorance.

—The composer is free to write the middle sections of all the movements of the Mass for fewer voices than are used in the work as a whole. In other words, if the Mass is for five voices, the aforesaid sections may be written for four or for three; if the Mass is for four voices, they may be written for three or even two. But it should be noted that, being written for fewer voices, these sections should be composed with greater artifice and greater learning and in a loftier, more elegant style. These reduced parts are the flower of the whole work.

—And to conclude their work with greater harmony and greater sonority, composers usually write the last Agnus Dei for more voices, adding one or two parts to the regular parts of the composition, doubling as they find most convenient.

As a rule, the Mass is usually composed upon some motet, madrigal, or chanson, even though by another author; thus it afterwards takes its title from the first words with which the said motet, madrigal, or chanson begins. If the composer does not wish to use the above-mentioned materials, but prefers to write his Mass upon a new invention of his own, he may give it a title of another sort, thus "Missa sine nomine" [Mass without a name], or, if it is short, he may call it "Missa brevis" [Short Mass] or "Missa L'hora è tarda" [Mass for when it's getting late]. He may also name it from the subject of the composition, as was done by some composers who, having contrived Masses dependent upon the notes of the scale, gave them the title "Missa Ut re mi fa sol la"; and Josquin took for a subject or theme the five notes La sol fa re mi. If the Mass is composed upon the formulas of any mode it should take its title from the name of the mode to which the formulas belong, thus "Missa Primi toni," "Missa Secundi toni," etc. If it is written upon a plainsong, that is, if it is formed upon the notes of the Kyries, Glorias, Credos, Sanctuses, Agnus Dei's, or any other chant, but using the various figures of figured [i.e., polyphonic] music, it should be named after the plainsong, namely, "Missa de Beata Virgine" [Mass of the Blessed Virgin], "Missa Apostolorum" [Mass of the Apostles], "Missa Dominicalis" [Mass for Sundays throughout the year], etc.

Masses composed for several choruses should be written with short imitations, plain consonances, and less artifice.

Oliver Strunk (ed.), *Source Readings in Music History* (New York: W. W. Norton & Company, Inc. New York, 1950), 265–68. Reprinted by permission of W. W. Norton & Company, Inc., and Faber and Faber Ltd. Copyright © 1950 by W. W. Norton & Company, Inc. Copyright renewed 1978 by Oliver Strunk.

Genres like the parody Mass tended to blur the boundaries between sacred and secular. Voices were often raised against the intermixture of genres, most often from the clergy (as might be expected). Occasionally, though, a "purist" from among the ranks of lay musicians would express himself on the subject, as in the passage given below, from the treatise *L'antica musica ridotta alla moderna prattica* (*Ancient Music Adapted to Modern Practice*) by the composer and musical scholar Nicola Vicentino (see p. 136). The "secularization" of sacred music is here denounced from a humanistic point of view, it being contrary to the philosophy of Greek music and a trivialization, in Vicentino's eyes, of a noble and heroic art.

Now the composition of Masses and Latin-texted pieces ought to be serious, not frenzied, because Masses and Psalms being ecclesiastical, it is only right that the treatment of these should be different from that of French chansons, madrigals, and the like. Some composers compose Masses on madrigals, on French chansons, and even on battle pieces [e.g., Clément Janequin's *La Bataille de Marignan,* which was the model for many parodies], so that when such compositions are heard in church, they impel everyone to laughter, to the extent that it almost seems as if the temple of God had become a place for the recitation of lascivious and ridiculous things, as if it were a stage where it was permissible to perform every kind of ridiculous and lascivious musical buffoonery. One should not be surprised if music is not held in high esteem nowadays, since it has been applied to such low things as *balli, villanelle,* and other things equally ridiculous, contrary to the thinking of the ancients, who reserved it only for the singing of hymns to the gods and of the great deeds of men.

Henry W. Kaufmann, *The Life and Works of Nicola Vicentino* (Rome: American Institute of Musicology, 1966), 38–39.

36

The Counter Reformation

Tension between composer and clergy had long been a fact of life in Catholic church music (see, for example, pp. 53 and 60). In the sixteenth century a new target for clerical strictures emerged: the technique of imitation, which played havoc with the intelligibility of sacred words. This concern was expressed as early as 1549 by the Roman bishop Cirillo Franco (c. 1500–75) in the letter excerpted below. Although the theme of reforming church music is an old one, the bishop's frame of reference is new. He approaches the problem in the spirit of Renaissance humanism, glorifying the achievements of classical antiquity, much as many secular musicians were also doing at the time. The combined pressures from church and humanist quarters were eventually to undermine the "ars perfecta" of the High Renaissance and transform late sixteenth-century music into something approaching the style of the early Baroque.

I should like, in short, when a Mass is to be sung in church, that its music be framed according to the fundamental subject of the words, in harmonies and rhythms apt to move our affections to religion and piety, and likewise in Psalms, Hymns, and other praises that are offered to God. And the musicians of today should endeavor in their profession to do what the sculptors, painters, and architects of our time have done, who have recovered the art of the ancients, and the writers who have recalled literature from the hell to which it had been banished by corrupt ages, and as the sciences have been explained and given in their purity to our times. Thus should the musicians seek to recover those styles and modes, and the power of the Phrygian, Lydian, Dorian, and Mixolydian songs, with which they would be able to do what they wish. I do not say that they should try to recover the enharmonic, chromatic, and diatonic genera, for these were dismissed by the ancients themselves; but that they should approximate as much as possible the four above-mentioned modes, and that they should lend beauty and individuality to church music. In our times they have put all their industry and effort into the composition of fugues [i.e., points of imitation], so that while one voice says "Sanctus," another says "Sabaoth," still another "Gloria tua," with howling, bellowing, and stammering, so that they more nearly resemble cats in January than flowers in May.

Lewis Lockwood, *The Counter-Reformation and the Masses of Vincenzo Ruffo* (Venice: Fondazione Giorgio Cini, 1970), 128–29. Reprinted by the kind permission of the Fondazione Cini and the author.

At the time of Bishop Franco's letter, no one within the church was doing more about the imperfections of church music than complaining. However, the threat of the Reformation in the North spurred the Roman church to undertake a series of internal reforms, known collectively as the Counter Reformation, which had many profound and far-reaching effects on music. The legislative body that implemented the Catholic church's internal reforms was the Council of Trent, an assemblage of bishops and cardinals that met on and off between 1545 and 1563. Music reform was taken up at a late session, and a canon, or decree, on church music was promulgated on 10 September 1562:

All things should indeed be so ordered that the Masses, whether they be celebrated with or without singing, may reach tranquilly into the ears and hearts of those who hear them, when everything is executed clearly and at the right speed. In the case of those Masses which are celebrated with singing and with organ, let nothing profane be intermingled, but only hymns and divine praises. The whole plan of singing in musical modes should be constituted not to give empty pleasure to the ear, but in such a way that the words may be clearly understood by all, and thus the hearts of the listeners be drawn to the desire of heavenly harmonies, in the contemplation of the joys of the blessed.

Gustave Reese, *Music in the Renaissance*, rev. ed. (New York: W. W. Norton & Company, Inc., 1959), 449.

By the time the decree was published—on 17 September, after another week's debate—these strictures had been whittled down to the bland admonition that Catholic musicians should "banish from church all music that contains, whether in the singing or in the organ playing, things that are lascivious or impure." Nevertheless, we may observe an almost immediate response from composers to the Council's "guidelines" not only in the actual music they wrote, but also in the prefaces to their Mass publications, in which obedience to the Council's decree was expressly acknowledged. Of the three quoted below, most enthusiastic in his submission was Ruffo [see p. 105], who, as *maestro di cappella* at Milan Cathedral, was directly answerable to

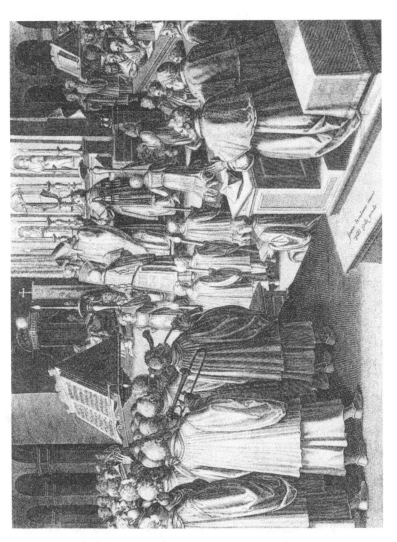

A Sixteenth-Century Mass. This scene, from a famous Flemish book of engravings after drawings by Johannes Stradanus, shows a Mass being celebrated with two choirs (each reading from one huge choir book on a lectern) and wind instruments (the curved horns are cornetts, the slide instruments sackbuts). The moment depicted is the Elevation of the Host, and thus what is probably being performed is a festal motet (see Morley's definition, p. 108). This engraving is one of the very few pictorial documents we have of the kind of extravagant Counter-Reformation musicoreligious festivities described by Thomas Coryat (see p. 117). (From Philipp Galle, *Encomium musices*, Antwerp, *c.* 1595, fol. 17.)

Cardinal Carlo Borromeo (1538–84), Archbishop of Milan and Papal Secretary of State. Borromeo had been one of the guiding forces of the Council of Trent and had taken a leading part in the deliberations concerning music.

Palestrina, *Second Book of Masses* (1567)

I, who have been engaged in this art for many years, not wholly unsuccessfully (if I may rely on the judgment of others more than on my own), have considered it my task, in accordance with the views of most serious and most religious-minded men, to bend all my knowledge, effort, and industry towards that which is the holiest and most divine of all things in the Christian religion—that is, to adorn the holy sacrifice of the Mass in a new manner.

Giovanni Animuccia (c. 1520–71), *First Book of Masses* (1567)

Being led to this by the judgment of these men, I have sought to adorn these divine prayers and praises of God in such a way that the music may disturb the hearing of the text as little as possible, but nevertheless in such a way that it may not be entirely devoid of artifice and may contribute in some degree to the listener's pleasure.

Giovanni Pierluigi da Palestrina, *Pope Marcellus Mass,* ed. Lewis Lockwood (New York: W. W. Norton & Company, Inc., 1975), 22–23.

Vincenzo Ruffo, *Missae quatuor concinate ad ritum Concilii Mediolani* (1570)

When compelled to undertake that task which the Most Illustrious and Most Reverend Cardinal Borromeo had formerly laid upon me: that, in accordance with the decree of the sacred Council of Trent I was to compose some Masses (as they are called) which should avoid everything of a profane and idle manner in worship, and that the powerful and sweet sound of the voices should soothe and caress the ears of the listeners in a pious, religious, and holy way; I was deeply ignorant which way to turn. You [i.e., the Milanese senator to whom the book is dedicated], then, however, who had been of the same sentiments, came forth to me, openly revealed your feelings, and, as it were, showed me the Prototype of this manner of composing music. Accordingly, guided by your help, I composed one Mass in this way: so that the numbers of the syllables and the voices and tones together should be clearly and distinctly understood and perceived by the pious listeners. Thus it was that later, imitating that example, I more readily and easily composed other Masses of the same type. When I had collected a fair number of them, and the Most Illustrious and Most Reverend Cardinal Borromeo ordered that I be allowed to publish them, I wished to dedicate them to you.

Lockwood, *The Counter-Reformation,* 99.

One of the most curious but in its own way most revealing musical developments of the late Renaissance was the revision of Gregorian chant to conform with the guidelines of the Council of Trent. This reform was commissioned in the 1560s by Pope Paul V and completed in 1614 with the publication of the so-called *Editio Medicaea,* which remained the standard version of the chant until the nineteenth century. The chant of the Christian church, which medieval musicians had regarded as the inspired and sacrosanct creation of the Holy Spirit, and which had been an inviolable "authority" in medieval music, was now subjected to a stylistic and aesthetic critique by proud mortals, and amended according to their lights. Nowhere could we hope to find a better illustration of the subjectivity and anthropocentrism of the Renaissance. Below we give one of the prime documents of the chant revision: Pope Gregory XIII's behest to Palestrina and an assistant to continue the work begun under his predecessor.

Beloved sons, greetings and apostolic benediction on you.

It having come to our notice that the books of Office chants, Mass chants, and psalters which contain the music for the plainsong used in all divine services are full of barbarisms, obscurities, inconsistencies, and superfluities as a result of the ineptitude, the negligence, even the malice of composers, scribes, and printers alike, and so that these books may be made to conform with the Breviary and Missal recently published in accordance with the order of the Council of Trent, and so that the superfluities we have mentioned may be pruned away and the barbarisms and obscurities corrected (so that God's name may be the more easily praised with reverence, distinctness, and devotion), and in our desire to help in this matter as far as we may with God's help, we charge you, whose skill in music and in singing, whose faithfulness and diligence, and whose piety towards God have been tested to the utmost, to fulfill this urgent task, trusting confidently that you will fully satisfy our wishes. And thus we give you the responsibility of revising, purging, correcting, and reforming these books of chants, and any others that may be used in the churches according to the rite of the Holy Roman Church. And over all this we give you full jurisdiction and the free exercise thereof by virtue of our apostolic authority. Given at St. Peter's in Rome under the seal of the Fisherman the 25th day of October 1577, the sixth year of our reign, to our dear sons Giovanni Pierluigi da Palestrina and Annibale Zoilo Romano, musicians of our private chapel.

Raphael Molitor, *Die nach-Tridentinische Choral-Reform zu Rom*, I (Leipzig: F. E. C. Leuckart, 1901), 297–98. Trans. R. T.

The high point of color and sonority in late Renaissance church music was reached in Venice under the Gabrielis: Andrea (1510–86) and his nephew Giovanni (1557–1612). The description below by a visiting Englishman of a Vespers service at St. Mark's Basilica reads more like an account of a concert than of a religious observance. This kind of musical feast was one of the ways in which the "Church Militant" of the Counter Reformation sought to attract huge congregations, and to impress worshipers with a show of pomp and glory. When measured against the traditional Renaissance ideals of clarity and refinement, these gargantuan church concerts were indeed "baroque."

Upon Saint Roche's day, I heard the best music that ever I did in all my life both in the morning and the afternoon, so good that I would willingly go a hundred miles on foot at any time to hear the like. This feast consisted principally of music, which was both vocal and instrumental, so good, so delectable, so rare, so admirable, so superexcellent, that it did even ravish and stupefy all those strangers that never heard the like. But how others were affected with it I know not; for mine own part I can say this, that I was for the time even rapt up with Saint Paul into the third heaven. Sometimes there sang sixteen or twenty men together, having their master or moderator to keep them in order; and when they sang, the instrumental musicians played also. Sometimes sixteen played together upon their instruments, ten sackbuts, four cornetts, and two violda-gambas of an extraordinary greatness; sometimes ten, six sackbuts and four cornetts; sometimes two, a cornett and a treble viol. Of these treble viols [most likely violins, in fact] I heard three several there, whereof each was so good, especially one that I observed above the rest, that I never heard the like before. Those that played upon the treble viols, sang and played together, and sometimes two singular fellows played together upon theorboes [large lutes], to which they sang also, who yielded admirable sweet music, but so still that they could scarce be heard but by those that were very near them. These two theorbists concluded that night's music, which continued three whole hours at the least. For they began about five of the clock, and ended not before eight. Also it continued as long in the morning; at every time that every several music played, the organs, whereof there are seven fair pair in that room, standing all in a row together, played with them. Of the singers there were three or four so excellent that I think few or none in Christendom do excel them.

Thomas Coryat, *Coryat's Crudities; hastily gobled up in five moneths travels* (London, 1611), 251–52. Spelling modernized.

37

Palestrina: Fact and Legend

If Vincenzo Ruffo was the church musician most closely identified with the Counter Reformation (see p. 116), in the popular view that distinction has always been accorded Palestrina. A durable legend grew up around Palestrina and the Council of Trent, in which the Council was cast as a kind of tribunal bent on condemning music to abolition (as if it, or any body of men, could accomplish that), while Palestrina was elevated to the station of music's savior through his *Missa Papae Marcelli* (*Mass in Memory of Pope Marcellus II* [d. 1555]), which supposedly showed the cardinals that, yes, polyphonic music could stay out of the text's way. In the quartet of extracts that follows, we may trace the growth of this legend through various stages of embroidery.

Agostino Agazzari (1607):

Music of the older kind is no longer in use, both because of the confusion and babel of the words, arising from the long and intricate imitations, and because it has no grace, for, with all the voices singing, one hears neither period nor sense, these being inter-fered with and covered up by imitations; indeed, at every moment, each voice has different words, a thing displeasing to men of competence and judgment. And on this account music would have come very near to being banished from the Holy Church by a sovereign pontiff, had not Giovanni Palestrina found the remedy, showing that the fault and error lay, not with music, but with the composers, and composing in confirmation of this the Mass entitled *Missa Papae Marcelli*.

Lodovico Cresollio (1629):

Pius IV, a most serious-minded pontiff of the church, had noticed for some time that music and singing in sacred places was very little else than an abundance of delicate diminutions and vain adornments to the words, from which no benefit of piety came forth to the listeners. He then determined to set the question of banishing sacred music from the church before the Council of Trent. When word of this came to the ears of Giovanni Palestrina, he quickly set himself to compose Masses in such a way that not only should the combinations of voices and sounds be grasped by the listeners, but that all the words should be plainly and clearly understood. When the pontiff had heard these works and had seen how useful they could be for the divine service, he changed his mind and determined not to banish sacred music but to maintain it. This was told by Palestrina himself to a certain member of our society [i.e., the Jesuits], from whom I heard it.

Lelio Guidiccioni (1637):

The Tridentine fathers were gathered to consider the resolution to prohibit music in the church by decree. They were motivated, I believe, by the frivolous diminutions and ornaments used in singing, which carried music too far away from the sanctity of the divine service. The day of the session was fixed. On that day they had performed a Mass that was sent thee by Giovanni Pierluigi da Palestrina, who, taking the opposed position, argued in favor of music. The chaste and correct style of the work combined with the sweet harmony and the unanimous eagerness of the singers all aided and sustained the music. And consequently, the fathers changed their opinion and rescinded their decree.

Giuseppe Baini (1828):

Summoning Palestrina before him, Cardinal Borromeo told him face to face to compose a Mass in the desired manner, enjoining on him all possible effort to prevent the possibility that the Pope and the Congregation of Cardinals might be encouraged to ban music from the apostolic chapel and the church. Poor Pierluigi! He was placed in the hardest straits of his career. The fate of church music hung from his pen, and so did his own career, at the height of his fame.

On Saturday, 28 April 1565, by order of Cardinal Vitellozzi, all the singers of the papal chapel were gathered together at his residence. Cardinal Borromeo was already there, together with the other six cardinals of the papal commission. Palestrina was there as well; he handed out the parts to the singers, and they sang three Masses, of which the Pope Marcellus Mass was the last. The most eminent audience enjoyed them very much. But the greatest and most incessant praise was given to the third, which was extraordinarily acclaimed and, by virtue of its entirely novel character, astonished even the performers themselves. Their Eminences heaped their congratulations on the composer, recommending to him to go on writing in that style and to communicate it to his pupils.

Giovanni Pierluigi da Palestrina, *Pope Marcellus Mass*, ed. Lewis Lockwood (New York: W.W. Norton and Company, Inc., 1975), 28–32, 35–36.

It is true that Palestrina's historical role has been exaggerated, partly because his style was adopted by seventeenth- and eighteenth-century pedagogues as the basis for academic counterpoint. But Palestrina was undeniably a musician sincerely dedicated to the spiritual goals of the Counter Reformation and even in his own day regarded as exemplary in his fulfillment of them. A unique document is the dedication to Pope Gregory XIII, Palestrina's patron (see p. 117), of his Fourth Book of Motets (1584), where the composer denounces the effects of secular music, and actually recants his own early madrigals, of which one, "Vestiva i colli" ("Valleys and Hills"), had become one of the century's most popular.

There exists a vast mass of love songs of the poets, written in a fashion entirely foreign to the profession and name of Christian. They are the songs of men ruled by passion, and a great number of musicians, corrupters of youth, make them the concern of their art and their industry; in proportion as they flourish through praise of their skill, so do they offend good and serious-minded men by the depraved taste of their work. I blush and grieve to think that once I was of their number. But, while I cannot change the past, nor undo what is done, I have mended my ways. Therefore I have labored on songs which have been written in praise of Our Lord, Jesus Christ, and His Most Holy Virgin Mother, Mary; and I have now produced a work which treats of the divine love of Christ and His Spouse the Soul, the Canticle of Solomon.

Henry Coates, *Palestrina* (New York: E.P. Dutton, 1949), 4.

38

Madrigals and Madrigalism

The sixteenth-century madrigal was a highly sophisticated part-song that sought to mirror and intensify the imagery and emotional content of a poem, even to the point of obscuring the poem's form. In this the madrigal differed markedly from all other kinds of Renaissance vocal music, and was the highest embodiment of the humanistic teaching that music should "imitate" human passions in all their changeability. This attitude was put succinctly by a minor madrigalist, Marc'Antonio Mazzone da Miglionico, in the Dedication of his First Book of Madrigals (1569):

The notes are the body of music, while the text is the soul and, just as the soul, being nobler than the body, must be followed and imitated by it, so the notes must follow the text and imitate it, and the composer must pay due attention to it, expressing its sense with sad, gay, or austere music, as the text demands, and he must even sometimes disregard the rules.

Alfred Einstein, *The Italian Madrigal,* I (Princeton, N.J.: Princeton University Press, 1949), 223.

Beginning in the 1560s, then, madrigals were a hotbed of musical radicalism and experimentation. Any effect of dissonance or chromaticism (i.e., using tones foreign to a scale or mode), however bizarre, could be justified on the basis of text expression. Because of its aesthetic premises, the late sixteenth-century madrigal has been held up as the earliest embodiment of "Baroque" musical ideals. And indeed, early composers of Baroque music (see Monteverdi, p. 146) tended to look back upon the madrigalists as their predecessors and historical justification. In the passage below, Zarlino—the great teacher of Renaissance style—considers the technical means by which music can "imitate" a text. And recognizing that a text so illustrated must be presented intelligibly, he follows his discussion of "madrigalisms" (illustrative devices, which by the Counter Reformation period were by no means confined to the madrigal) with a plea for good text declamation. Zarlino describes the rather restrained techniques employed by such early madrigalists as his revered teacher Willaert (see p. 96). He little dreamed of the madrigalistic excesses that were to be committed by composers of later generations, and when he learned of them he became a bitter anti-madrigalist. The text (*Istitutioni harmoniche*, IV, Chap. 32) is given in an English paraphrase by Thomas Morley, who included it—without attribution!—in his *Plaine and Easie Introduction* of 1597.

It now followeth to show you how to dispose your music according to the nature of the words which you are therein to express, as whatsoever matter it be which you have in hand such a kind of music must you frame to it. You must therefore, if you have a grave matter, apply a grave kind of music to it, if a merry subject you must make your music also merry, for it will be a great absurdity to use a sad harmony to a merry matter or a merry harmony to a sad, lamentable, or tragical ditty [i.e., text].

You must then when you would express any word signifying hardness, cruelty, bitterness, and other such like make the harmony like unto it, that is somewhat harsh and hard, but yet so that it offendeth not. Likewise when any of your words shall express complaint, dolour, repentance, sighs, tears and such like let your harmony be sad and doleful. So that if you would have your music signify hardness, cruelty, or other such affects you must cause the parts proceed in their motions without the half step, that is, you must cause them proceed by whole steps, sharp thirds, sharp sixths, and such like; you may also use cadences bound with dissonances which, being in long notes, will exasperate the harmony. But when you would express a lamentable passion then must you use motions proceeding by half steps, flat thirds, and flat sixths, which of their nature are sweet, specially being taken in the true tune with discretion and judgment.

But those chords so taken as I have said before are not the sole and only cause of expressing those passions, but also the motions which the parts make in singing do greatly help; which motions are either natural or accidental. The natural motions are those which are naturally made betwixt the notes of the scale without the mixture of any accidental sign or chord, be it either flat or sharp, and these motions be more masculine, causing in the song more virility than those accidental chords which are marked with the sharp and the flat, which be indeed accidental and make the song, as it were, more effeminate and languishing than the other motions which make the song rude and sounding. So that those natural motions may serve to express those effects of cruelty, tyranny, bitterness, and such others, and those accidental motions may fitly express the passions of grief, weeping, sighs, sorrows, sobs, and such like.

Also, if the subject be light you must cause your music to go in motions which carry with them a celerity or quickness of time; if it be lamentable the notes must go in slow and heavy motions; and of all this you shall find examples everywhere in the works of the good musicians.

Moreover, you must have a care that when your matter signifieth "ascending," "high," "heaven," and such like you make your music ascend; and by the contrary where your ditty speaketh of "descending," "lowness," "depth," "hell," and others such you must make your music descend; for as it will be thought a great absurdity to talk of heaven and point downwards to the earth, so will it be counted great incongruity if a musician upon the words "he ascended into heaven" should cause his music to descend, or by the contrary upon the descension should cause his music to ascend.

We must also have a care so to apply the notes to the words as in singing there be no barbarism committed; that is that we cause no syllable which is by nature short be expressed by many notes or one long note, nor no long syllables be expressed with a short note. But in this fault do the practitioners err more grossly than in any other, for you shall find few songs wherein the penult syllables of these words: "Dóminus," "ángelus," "fílius," "miráculum," "glória," and such like are not expressed with a long note, yea, many times with a whole dozen of notes, and though one should speak of forty he should not say much amiss, which is a gross barbarism and yet might be easily amended.

We must also take heed of separating any part of a word from another by a rest. But to show you in a word the use of the rests in the ditty, you may set a short rest above a comma or colon, but a longer rest you may not make till the sentence be perfect, and then at a full point you may set what number of rests you will. Also when you would express sighs you may use a short rest, but a longer one you may not use because it will rather seem a breath taking than a sigh.

Lastly you must not make a close till the full sense of the words be perfect. So that keeping these rules you shall have a perfect agreement and, as it were, an harmonical consent betwixt the matter and the music, and likewise you shall be perfectly understood of the auditor what you sing, which is one of the highest degrees of praise which a musician in dittying can attain unto or wish for.

Thomas Morley, *A Plaine and Easie Introduction to Practicall Musicke* (London, 1597), 177–78, abridged. Spelling and punctuation modernized.

39

Gesualdo, Nobleman Musician

Don Carlo Gesualdo (*c.* 1560–1613), Prince of Venosa, in southern Italy, near Naples, was one of the most extraordinary musical personages of the Renaissance. His name derives equal notoriety from his having murdered his unfaithful first wife, together with her lover, and from his astonishing musical compositions, which carry the use of madrigalisms to unheard-of extremes of dissonance and chromaticism. Because of his high birth and wealth, Gesualdo must be counted a noble amateur, although he published six books of madrigals that went through many printings (as well as three volumes of church music) and although he played many instruments and sang. In 1594 Gesualdo paid an extended visit to the fabulously musical court of Ferrara, in connection with his wedding to his second wife, cousin of Duke Alfonso II. He was escorted there by an emissary of the Duke, who sent on ahead a series of fascinating reports on the princely musician. The passage below, extracted from the most extended and revealing of these reports, contains two especially pertinent remarks. First, it is clear that Gesualdo's "open profession" of music is reported with mild disapproval, it being a violation of the courtly *sprezzatura* of which Castiglione wrote (see p. 80). And when Gesualdo's art is described as "full of attitudes," we may see a reference to the exaggerations and artificialities of late madrigal style, which today, taking our cue from art historians, we call "mannerist."

I met the Prince at the ferry. On leaving the boat he decided to get into a carriage since he wanted to escape the mud so as not to have to change his clothes. He has it in mind to beseech Your Highness most warmly that tomorrow evening you will permit him to see Signora Donna Leonora [Gesualdo's bride]. In this he shows himself extremely Neapolitan. He thinks of arriving at eleven P.M., but I doubt this because he does not stir from his bed until extremely late. With respect to this I shall not send another courier. Suffice it to say that we will come by boat as far as Gaibana, and then we shall go in the direction of the road which Orazio reports to be good for this purpose.

The Prince, although at first view he does not have the presence of the personage he is, becomes little by little more agreeable, and for my part I am sufficiently satisfied with his appearance. I have not been able to see his figure since he wears an overcoat as long as a nightgown; but think that tomorrow he will be more gaily dressed. He talks a great deal and gives no sign, except in his portrait, of being a melancholy man. He discourses on hunting and music and declares himself an authority on both of them. On hunting he did not enlarge very much since he did not find much reaction from me, but about music he spoke at such length that I have not heard so much in a whole year. He makes open profession of it and shows his works in score to everybody in order to induce them to marvel at his art. He has with him two sets of music books in five parts, all his own work, but he says that he only has four people who can sing for which reason he will be forced to take the fifth part himself, although it seems that he is confident that Rinaldo will enter into the singing and do well.

He says that he has abandoned his first style and has set himself to the imitation of Luzzasco [i.e., Luzzasco Luzzaschi (d. 1607), eminent Ferrarese musician], a man whom he greatly admires and praises, although he says that not all of Luzzasco's madrigals are equally well written, as he claims to wish to point out to Luzzasco himself. This evening after supper he sent for a harpsichord so that I could hear Scipione Stella [a musician in Gesualdo's entourage] and so that he could play on it himself along with the guitar, of which he has a very high regard. But in all Argenta we could not find a harpsichord, for which reason, so as not to pass an evening without music, he played the lute for an hour and a half. Here perhaps Your Highness would not be displeased if I were to give my opinion, but I would prefer, with your leave, to suspend my judgment until more refined ears have given theirs. It is obvious that his art is infinite, but it is full of attitudes, and moves in an extraordinary way. However, everything is a matter of taste. This Prince then has himself served in a very grand way and with some little Spanish ceremonies, for example, having the lighted torch brought in before the cup, covering his plate while he drinks, and similar things.

Argenta
18 February 1594

Your most faithful and devoted servant,
Alfonso Fontanelli

Glenn Watkins, *Gesualdo, The Man and His Music* (Chapel Hill, N.C.: The University of North Carolina Press, 1973), 44–46. Copyright © 1973 Glenn Watkins. Reprinted by permission of The University of North Carolina Press and Oxford University Press.

40

The Most Musical Court in Europe

The court of Ferrara in northern Italy maintained an enviable reputation for musical excellence throughout the sixteenth century. A glimpse behind the scenes at the preparations that produced the results that so astounded all who heard them is given by the Italian music theorist Ercole Bottrigari (1531–1612), whose account of the discipline and rehearsal techniques employed by the Ferrarese music masters is the prologue to a detailed discourse on good intonation and principles of effective scoring, for which the Ferrarese *concerti* provided the best model. In the passage that follows, Bottrigari describes this famous Renaissance court orchestra at work.

About the concerts at Ferrara, meaning principally those of the Serenissimo Signor Duca, I will speak. And because I am able to speak of them as a professional, having been several times to hear and see them in public as well as private, at which time I heard them *in camera*, I feel that the conclusion that I will make about them is valid for all the other similar concerts, excellent and rare and worthy to be remembered and prized. Now listen. His Highness has two large, decorated rooms, called the Musicians' Rooms because there the Musician–servitors ordinarily paid by His Highness go whenever they wish; there are many of them—both Italian and Flemish—with good and beautiful voices, and graceful ways of singing, and of the highest excellence in playing as well, some on Cornetts, others on Trombones, Dulcians, Pipes; still others on the Viols, Fiddles, and still others on Lutes, Psalteries, Harps and Harpsichords. The instruments are placed neatly in those rooms. To these rooms, then—which I hope you will not expect me to describe in every particular—the musicians, all or part of them, as they please, may repair and practice both playing and singing. Therefore there are, in addition to musical compositions in manuscript, many, many printed music books, written by all the talented men in the profession, kept in the greatest order in the places provided for them. The instruments are always in order and tuned so that they can be taken and played at any moment; and they are kept thus by capable Maestri who know both how to tune and how to manufacture them most excellently, and who are therefore permanently retained by His Highness, the Serenissimo. Sometimes His Highness the Duke commands Fiorino, his Maestro di cappella and head of all the music (public as well as private, domestic, and *in camera*), to give a *Concerto grande,* for thus it is called. It is almost never commanded by His Highness except on occasions when he entertains Cardinals, Dukes, Princes, or other great personages for whom he may be, as he is almost continually, a most splendid and gracious host. And I may truly affirm that there is no other Prince in Italy who offers such an act of courtesy more willingly, liberally, and magnificently.

Fiorino, as soon as he has received the order from the Duke, confers with Luzzasco [organist and madrigalist: see p. 123] first if the latter had not been present at the command, and then afterwards, with all the other musicians, the aforesaid singers and players; and also he summons every Ferrarese who can sing and play well enough to be judged by Fiorino and Luzzasco good enough to participate in such a concert. With much kindness the Maestro tells them that they must return to the rooms the next day or the day after, according to the length of the foreign Prince's stay. Then they have not one or two, but a number of rehearsals, during which they maintain the highest obedience and attention, and think of nothing except a good ensemble and the greatest possible union without any other consideration; for that reason each performer comes with gracious modesty when he needs to be instructed and corrected by the Maestro di cappella. And the Signor Duca also comes in person, with most kind and serene bearing and brotherly majesty, and when he has heard them often gives them efficacious advice, with his perfect judgment, and admonitions, encouraging them to bear themselves well and do themselves honor. Then, at the time set by His Highness, they meet to give the concert, to the highest delight and infinite pleasure of the foreign Prince who has come to hear them. All the other persons there follow its harmony with great marveling, for it is truly so great that telling about it falls very short of giving its real effect.

Now therefore I will make this true and firm conclusion in its honor, that all of those who try to make similar concerts with so many diverse and various kinds of musical instruments fail to follow the example of close concord and of unanimity attained by these excellent musicians of Ferrara in their Great Concerts. The latter perform no other compositions than one of two written for this purpose only, one by the late Alfonso della Viola, the other by Luzzasco. There will never be any other composition which brings them to a good accord and which, by giving great delight to judicious and intelligent listeners, causes them to deserve praise. The frequent and so to say continuous conversing, singing, and playing together of the singers and instrumentalists work largely to perfect this union and to lessen and minimize the great imperfection of so many kinds of instruments playing at the same time. This is necessary to bring about the sought-after harmony, by which the soul of the listener truly enjoys the hoped-for pleasure and delight.

> Ferrara was also famed for the cultivation of virtuoso solo singing, particularly as practiced by a trio of women singers known throughout Europe as the "ladies of Ferrara." Their new art of decorative accompanied singing was based on the madrigal but advanced vocal technique to levels scarcely dreamt of before. It was the direct antecedent of the "monodic" style of the early seventeenth century, and as such was an important link between the Renaissance and the Baroque. What is noteworthy in the following description of the art of the "ladies of Ferrara" is the strongly implied point that all of the virtuoso devices and artifices that thrilled their listeners were motivated as much by expressive as by purely exhibitionistic aims. Their singing was an object lesson not only in skill but also in taste.

In the Holy Year of 1575, or shortly thereafter, a style of singing appeared which was very different from that preceding. It continued for some years, chiefly in the manner of one voice singing with accompaniment. It inspired composers to write similar works to be sung by several voices in the manner of a single one accompanied by some instruments. But as these acquired greater perfection through more artful composition, so also every composer took care to advance in the style of composition for several voices, particularly Giaches [de] Wert [1535–96] in Mantua and Luzzasco in Ferrara. They were the superintendents of all music for those Dukes, who took the greatest delight in the art, especially in having many noble ladies and gentlemen learn to sing and play superbly, so that they spent entire days in some rooms designed especially for this purpose and beautifully decorated with paintings. The ladies of Mantua and Ferrara were highly competent, and vied with each other not only in regard to the timbre and training of their voices but also in the design of exquisite passages of embellishment delivered at opportune points, but not in excess. Furthermore, they moderated or increased their voices, loud or soft, heavy or light, according to the demands of the piece they were singing; now slow, breaking off with sometimes a gentle sigh, now singing long passages legato or detached, now *gruppi,* now leaps, now with long trills, now with short, and again with sweet running passages sung softly, to which sometimes one heard an echo answer unexpectedly. They accompanied the music and the sentiment with appropriate facial expressions, glances, and gestures, with no awkward movements of the mouth or hand or body that might not express the feeling of the song. They made the words clear in such a way that one could hear even the last syllable of every word, which was never interrupted or suppressed by passages and other embellishment. They used many other particular devices that will be known to persons more experienced than I. And under these favorable circumstances the abovementioned musicians made every effort to win fame and the favor of the Princes their patrons, who were their principal support.

Carol MacClintock (trans.), *Hercole Bottrigari: Il Desiderio* and *Vincenzo Giustiniani: Discorso sopra la musica,* Musicological Studies and Documents, IX (Rome: American Institute of Musicology, 1962), 49–53, 69–70. Reprinted by permission of Dr. Armen Carapetyan, Director of the American Institute of Musicology.

41

Music and Dancing as Social Graces

The group of readings that follows will show how art music was cultivated in the sixteenth century not only in noble courts and churches, but also in bourgeois households as a social pastime, a development made possible by the music printing and publishing business (see p. 75). The scene below is a model singing session as given in a Flemish etiquette book of around 1540. The music books in Master Jacob's cupboard would have come from the presses of Tylman Susato of Antwerp, the leading music publisher of Flanders, who printed most of the works of the two composers named, Nicholas Gombert (c. 1480–1556) and Johannes Lupi (d. 1539), along with those of their contemporaries and the ever-popular Josquin. The main problem the singers have is in getting started. That is because each has his own part book and does not see his companions' music. Also notice that a man sings the highest part. The falsetto voice was widely cultivated at the time, and remained fashionable until the eighteenth century.

MASTER JACOB:	And now, should we not sing us a little song? Willeken, would you go get my books?
WILLEKEN:	What books d'you want, Sir?
MASTER JACOB:	The books in four and three parts.
WILLEKEN:	Where d'you keep 'em, Sir?
MASTER JACOB:	You will find them on the sideboard.

WILLEKEN:	I'll go get 'em, Sir.

(The company drink their wine)

MASTER JACOB:	Now where's that Willeken got to?
WILLEKEN:	I can't find 'em, Sir!
MASTER JACOB:	You go look for them, Antoni, and pick us out something pretty.
ANTONI:	Right, Sir. Would you like to hear a song in four parts?
MASTER JACOB:	It's all the same to me. Sing what you like.
ANTONI:	Dierick, here's the soprano. It's not too high for you? The children can help you out.
ROMBOUT:	Give me the bass part.
ANTONI:	I'll do the tenor.
DIERICK:	Who'll sing alto?
YSAIAS:	I, I'll sing it!
DIERICK:	Who begins? Is it you, Ysaias?
YSAIAS:	No, not I. I've a four-beat rest.
ANTONI:	And I one of six.
YSAIAS:	Well then, you come in after me?
ANTONI:	So it seems. It's up to you then, Rombout!
ROMBOUT:	Yes, I've only a quarter-note rest. But we'd better get the pitch.
DIERICK:	What note do you begin on, Ysaias?
YSAIAS:	I start on E.
DIERICK:	And I on C.
ANTONI:	That makes a sixth. And you, Rombout?
ROMBOUT:	I begin on F.
MASTER JACOB:	Thomas and Felix, you children sing along with Dierick!
FELIX:	Yes, father.
MASTER JACOB:	Have you studied this song?
FELIX:	Yes, father.
MASTER JACOB:	And you, have you learned it?
THOMAS:	No, father, but we'll be able to do it all right.
ROMBOUT:	Steven's not singing with us?
DAME CATELYNE:	No, he's too young yet, but he'll begin soon to learn, and his sister also. Now, Steven and Cecily, you go eat.

(The company sing the song)

MASTER JACOB:	Now, that's what I call a pretty song. Who made it up?
ROMBOUT:	I think it's Gombert.
MASTER JACOB:	Who's he?
ROMBOUT:	He's singing master to the Emperor [Charles V].
MASTER JACOB:	Well, that's really a pretty song. And who made up the other one?
DIERICK:	Johannes Lupi, the singing master at Cambrai.
MASTER JACOB:	That's pretty, too. And now, Ysaias, I drink to your health.

Roger Wangermée, *Flemish Music*, trans. Robert Erich Wolf (New York: F. Praeger, 1968), 134.

Pieds joints

Pieds joints, oblique droit

Pieds joints, oblique gauche

Pieds largis, oblique droit

Pieds largis, oblique gauche

Pieds largis

Pied croisé droit

Pied croisé gauche

Révérence

Illustrations from Arbeau's *Orchésographie*. Showing the various attitudes and courtly gestures described in the text.

The best-known dance treatise of the Renaissance is the *Orchésographie*, the work of a retired astronomer named Jehan Tabourot, who wrote under the pseudonym Thoinot Arbeau, an anagram of his real name. Although first published in 1589, it gives a wealth of information not only on the dances of its time, but even on those of the fifteenth century. Below we give extracts from the introductory dialogue, where a lively impression is conveyed of the place and importance of dancing in Renaissance "society."

CAPRIOL: I come to pay you my respects, Monsieur Arbeau. You do not remember me, for it is six or seven years since I left this town of Langres to go to Paris and thence to Orleans. I am an old pupil of yours, to whom you taught computation.

ARBEAU: Indeed at first glance I failed to recognize you because you have grown up since then, and I feel sure that you have also broadened your mind by manliness and learning. What do you think of the study of law? I pursued it in bygone days myself.

CAPRIOL: I find it a noble art and necessary in the conduct of affairs, but I regret that while in Orleans I neglected to learn fine manners, an art with which many scholars enriched themselves as an adjunct to their studies. For, on my return I have found myself in society, where, to put it briefly, I was tongue-tied and awkward, and regarded as little more than a block of wood.

ARBEAU: You took consolation in the fact that the learned professors excused this shortcoming in recognition of the learning you had acquired.

CAPRIOL: That is so, but I should like to have acquired other skills during the hours between my serious studies, which would have rendered my company welcome to all.

ARBEAU: This will be an easy thing by reading French books in order to sharpen your wit and by learning fencing, dancing, and tennis that you may be an agreeable companion alike to ladies and gentlemen.

CAPRIOL: I much enjoyed fencing and tennis, and this placed me upon friendly terms with young men. But, without knowledge of dancing, I could not please the damsels, upon whom, it seems to me, the entire reputation of an eligible young man depends.

ARBEAU: You are quite right, as naturally the male and female seek one another and nothing does more to stimulate a man to acts of courtesy, honor, and generosity than love. And if you desire to marry you must realize that a mistress is won by the good temper and grace displayed while dancing, because ladies do not like to be present at fencing or tennis, lest a splintered sword or a blow from a tennis ball cause them injury. And there is more to it than this, for dancing is practiced to reveal whether lovers are in good health and sound of limb, after which they are permitted to kiss their mistresses in order that they may touch and savor one another, thus to ascertain if they are shapely or emit an unpleasant odor as of bad meat. Therefore, from this standpoint, quite apart from the many other advantages to be derived from dancing, it becomes an essential to a well-ordered society.

CAPRIOL: You fill me with a longing to learn to dance and I regret that I have not devoted many idle moments to it, for one can take honest pleasure without becoming tainted by vice or evil habits.

ARBEAU: You can quickly regain the time you have wasted, especially as you are a musician and dancing depends on music, one of the seven liberal arts, and its modulations.

CAPRIOL: Then I beg of you to teach me about these things, Monsieur Arbeau, because I know you are a musician, and in your youth won a reputation for good dancing and dexterity in a thousand sprightly steps.

ARBEAU: The noun "dance" comes from the verb "to dance," which in Latin is called *saltare*. To dance is to jump, to hop, to skip, to sway, to stamp, to tiptoe, and to employ the feet, hands, and body in certain rhythmic movements. These consist of leaping, bending the body, straddling, limping, flexing the knees, rising upon the toes, twitching the feet, with variations of these, and further postures. Dancing, or saltation, is both a pleasant and a profitable art which confers and preserves health; proper to youth, agreeable to the old, and suitable to all, provided fitness of time and place are observed and it is not abused. I mention time and place because it would bring contempt upon one who became overzealous like the tavern haunters.

CAPRIOL: Since dancing is an art, it must therefore belong to one of the seven liberal arts.

ARBEAU: As I have already told you, it depends on music and its modulations. Without this rhythmic quality dancing would be dull and confused inasmuch as the movements of the limbs must follow the rhythm of the music, for the foot must not tell of one thing and the music of another. But, most of the authorities hold that dancing is a kind of mute rhetoric by which the orator, without uttering a word, can make himself understood by his movements and persuade the spectators that he is gallant and worthy to be acclaimed, admired, and loved. Are you not of the opinion that this is the dancer's own language, expressed by his feet and in a convincing manner? Does he not plead tacitly with his mistress, who marks the seemliness and grace of his dancing, "Love me, desire me?" And when miming is added, she has the power to stir his emotions, now to anger, now to pity and commiseration, now to hate, now to love.

CAPRIOL: Do not tantalize me by delaying any longer to grant my request to learn how the movements of the dance are performed, in order that I may master them and not be reproached for having the heart of a pig and the head of an ass.

ARBEAU: To please you I will tell you what I know, although it would ill become me, at my present age of sixty-nine, to practice the subject matter.

Thoinot Arbeau, *Orchesography,* trans. Mary Stewart Evans (New York: Dover Publications, Inc., 1967), 11–18. Reprinted by permission of the publisher.

What follows next is an Elizabethan sales puff, a kind of jacket blurb for a music book expressly aimed at the amateur, the *Psalmes, sonets, & songs of sadness and pietie* (1588) by William Byrd , whom we have already seen to have been an astute musical businessman (see p. 78). He certainly hit the mark this time: the book went through two printings and was followed by two sequels, *Songs of sundrie natures* (1589) and

Psalmes, songs and sonnets (1611). The latter two publications, incidentally, enclose between their dates the brief period when England went crazy over the Italian madrigal—home music-making at its most exalted—and produced the torrent of imitations that still constitute the best known, if in some ways the least characteristic, specimens of English music of the period.

Reasons briefly set down by th'auctor, to perswade every one to learne to sing.

First it is a knowledge easily taught, and quickly learned where there is a good Master, and an apt Scoller.

2. The exercise of singing is delightfull to Nature & good to preserve the health of Man.

3. It doth strengthen all the parts of the breast, & doth open the pipes.

4. It is a singular good remedie for a stutting & stammering in the speech.

5. It is the best meanes to procure a perfect pronunciation & to make a good Orator.

6. It is the onely way to know where Nature hath bestowed the benefit of a good voyce: which guift is so rare, as there is not one among a thousand, that hath it: and in many, that excellent guift is lost, because they want Art to expresse Nature.

7. There is not any Musicke of Instruments whatsoever, comparable to that which is made of the voyces of Men, where the voyces are good, and the same well sorted and ordered.

8. The better the voyce is, the meeter it is to honor and serve God therewith: and the voyce of man is chiefly to be imployed to that ende.

Omnis spiritus laudet Dominum.

Since singing is so good a thing
I wish all men would learne to sing.

William Byrd, *Psalmes, sonets & songs* ... (London, 1588), frontispiece.

Byrd might have added the avoidance of social embarrassment to his list, for it is the chief matter treated in the opening dialogue from Thomas Morley's *Plaine and Easie Introduction* of 1597. This passage, reminiscent of the dialogue on the merits of dancing from Arbeau's *Orchesographie* given above, has often been cited as evidence of the universality of musical skill and training in Elizabethan England. Actually, though, here the ever-eclectic Morley has again paraphrased an earlier writer, this time Quintilian (who in turn was citing Cicero—see p. 10).

POLYMATHES:	Stay, brother Philomathes, what haste? Whither go you so fast?
PHILOMATHES:	To seek out an old friend of mine.
POL.:	But before you go I pray you repeat some of the discourses which you had yesternight at Master Sophobulus his banquet, for commonly he is not without both wise and learned guests.
PHIL.:	It is true indeed, and yesternight there were a number of excellent scholars, both gentlemen and others, but all the "propos" which then was discoursed upon was music.

POL.:	I trust you were contented to suffer others to speak of that matter.
PHIL.:	I would that had been the worst, for I was compelled to discover mine own ignorance and confess that I know nothing at all in it.
POL.:	How so?
PHIL.:	Among the rest of the guests, by chance master Aphron came thither also, who, falling to discourse of music, was in an argument so quickly taken up and hotly pursued by Eudoxus and Calergus, two kinsmen of Sophobulus, as in his own art he was overthrown; but he still sticking in his opinion, the two gentlemen requested me to examine his reasons and confute them; but I refusing and pretending ignorance, the whole company condemned me of discourtesy, being fully persuaded that I had been as skillful in that art as they took me to be learned in others. But supper being ended and music books (according to the custom) being brought to the table, the mistress of the house presented me with a part earnestly requesting me to sing; but when, after many excuses, I protested unfeignedly that I could not, every one began to wonder; yea, some whispered to others demanding how I was brought up, so that upon shame of mine ignorance I go now to seek out mine old friend Master Gnorimus, to make myself his scholar. Farewell, for I sit upon thorns till I be gone, therefore I will make haste.

Thomas Morley, *A Plaine and Easie Introduction to Practicall Musicke* (London, 1597), 1–2, abridged. Spelling and punctuation modernized.

Finally, Sonnet CXXVII by Shakespeare, whose delightful scene of flirtation at the keyboard gives us a better glimpse of music in Elizabethan society than many a weighty sociological tome. In Shakespeare's time the virginals—little pentagonal spinets of varying size, often piled one atop another—were fast replacing the lute as the domestic solo instrument par excellence. Its chief repertoire consisted of sets of variations on popular songs meant to please bourgeois tastes and composed by all the foremost musicians of the time, Byrd and Bull being most prolific in this genre.

How oft, when thou, my music, music play'st,
Upon that blessed wood whose motion sounds
With thy sweet fingers, when thou gently sway'st
The wiry concord that mine ear confounds,
Do I envy those jacks that nimble leap
To kiss the tender inward of thy hand,
Whilst my poor lips, which should that harvest reap,
At the wood's boldness by thee blushing stand!
To be so tickl'd, they would change their state
And situation with those dancing chips,
O'er whom thy fingers walk with gentle gait,
Making dead wood more bless'd than living lips.
   Since saucy jacks so happy are in this,
   Give them thy fingers, me thy lips to kiss.

42

Renaissance Instrumentalists

We get our first descriptions of virtuoso instrumentalists in a recently discovered treatise of *c.* 1480 by Tinctoris (see p. 68). Although undoubtedly virtuosos existed from the beginning of time, it was only with the Renaissance that their accomplishments began to be valued as truly artistic ones. Their names began to be celebrated and their spontaneous inspiration admired. In Tinctoris's descriptions of outstanding performances he himself had witnessed on plucked and bowed string instruments, two things stand out. First, instrumentalists were preeminently improvisers, and second, instrumentalists' repertoire consisted in the main of arrangements and embellishments of vocal pieces. Indeed, much of the written-down instrumental music that began to appear, chiefly in Italy, around the turn of the fifteenth century was exactly the kind of piece Tinctoris here describes: florid, freewheeling virtuosic flights over a famous dance tune or over the tenor part of a popular *chanson*.

The lyra commonly called lute, and the various instruments derived from it: The lute is made of wood in the shape of a tortoise-shell, with a hole roughly in the center, and a long neck over which the strings are stretched from just below the hole up to the top of the neck. The player holds the instrument with his left hand, at the same time making the notes by pressure of his fingers, while the strings are struck by the right hand either with the fingers or with a plectrum. The plectrum elicits the notes from the strings.

The [ancient] lyre is described as having seven strings tuned by tones and semitones [i.e., to a scale], analogously to the seven planets, or in honor of the seven Pleiades. But since seven strings differing by tones and semitones do not suffice for every composition, an arrangement of five, sometimes six, principal strings was later adopted, first, I think, by the Germans. According to this, the two middle strings are tuned to a major third and the rest in fourths, thereby making the lute completely perfect. And further, to provide a stronger sound, an additional string may be conjoined to any string and tuned to the octave. The strings are generally of ram's gut, but there is also the German invention by which another set of brass strings, tuned very deeply, is added. By this the sound is rendered not only stronger, but also much sweeter.

Some instruments of the lute family, by reason of the size and number of their strings, are perfectly suitable for rendering all four parts of a composition, or even more if the player has sufficient skill. We use the lute at feasts, dances, and entertainments public and private, and in this many Germans are exceedingly accomplished and renowned. Thus some will take the treble part of any piece you care to give them and improvise marvelously upon it with such taste that the performance cannot be rivaled. Among such, Pietro Bono, lutenist to Ercole, Duke of Ferrara [see p. 84] is in my opinion preeminent. Furthermore, others will do what is much more difficult; namely to play a composition alone, and most skillfully, in not only two parts, but even in three or four: for example, Orbus the German, or Henri who was recently in the service of Charles [the Bold], Duke of Burgundy.

The viol, played with a bow, is also used over the greater part of the world. And it is used not only in the ways we have mentioned, but also in the recitation of epics. Nor must I pass over a recent event, the performance of two blind Flemings, the brothers Charles and Jean, who are no less learned in letters than skilled in music. At Bruges, I heard Charles take the treble and Jean the tenor in many songs, playing the viol so expertly and with such charm that the viol has never pleased me so well. And I am similarly pleased by the rebec, my predilection for which I will not conceal, provided that it is played by a skillful artist, since its strains are very much like those of the viol. Accordingly, the viol and the rebec are my two instruments; I repeat, my chosen instruments, those that induce piety and stir my heart most ardently to the contemplation of heavenly joys. For these reasons I would rather reserve them solely for sacred music and the secret consolations of the soul, than have them sometimes used for profane occasions and public festivities.

Anthony Baines, "Fifteenth-Century Instruments in Tinctoris' *De inventione et usu musicae*," *Galpin Society Journal*, III (1950), 21–25.

> By the middle of the sixteenth century, instrumentalists (particularly lutenists) had a fairly well-developed solo repertoire, consisting, besides song and dance arrangements, of fantasias and ricercars—free-form compositions, sometimes in a strict imitative style, sometimes flashy and full of "inspired" effects like sudden changes of tempo and contrasts of register. It is this latter kind of piece that Francesco da Milano, one of the great instrumentalists of the century, performs in the extract given below, from the travel diary of a visiting Frenchman. This extravagant description of the effect of Francesco's playing on his hearers will hardly be matched until we read of such nineteenth-century virtuosos as Liszt and Paganini.

While staying in Milan I was invited to a sumptuous and magnificent banquet where, among other pleasures of rare things assembled for the happiness of these select people, appeared Francesco da Milano—a man who is considered to have attained the end (if that is possible) of perfection in playing the lute well. The tables being cleared, he chose one, and as if tuning his strings, sat on the end of the table seeking out a fantasia. He had barely disturbed the air with three strummed chords when he interrupted the conversation that had started among the guests. Having constrained them to face him, he continued with such ravishing skill that little by little, making the strings languish under his fingers in his sublime way, he transported all those who were listening into so pleasurable a melancholy that—one leaning his head on his hand supported by his elbow, and another sprawling with his limbs in careless deportment, with gaping mouth and more than half-closed eyes, glued (one would judge) to the strings of the lute, and his chin fallen on his breast, concealing his countenance with the saddest taciturnity ever seen—they remained deprived of all senses save that of hearing, as if the spirit, having abandoned all the seats of the senses, had retired to the ears in order to enjoy the more at its ease so ravishing a harmony; and I believe that we would be there still, had he not himself—I know not how—changing his style of playing with a gentle force, returned the spirit and the senses to the place from which he had stolen them, not without leaving as much astonishment in each of us as if we had been elevated by an ecstatic transport of some divine frenzy.

Jacques Descartes de Ventemille, quoted in Pontus de Tyard, *Solitaire second ou prose de la musique* [1555], trans. Joel Newman, in "Francesco Canova da Milano" (Master's thesis, New York University, 1942), 11.

In Renaissance cathedrals (especially in the Counter Reformation period), instrumentalists often accompanied the choral singing. The document given below suggests how prominent was their role at Seville under the great Spanish church composer Francisco Guerrero (1528–99). This prescription of the "order that must be observed by the instrumentalists in playing" (1586) not only takes instrumental doubling for granted, but grants enormous license to the musicians to embellish their parts soloistically, a license that, to judge from the document itself, they must have frequently abused. It is also clear that the instrumentalists did not merely play along with the chorus, but at times actually replaced the singers, or alternated with them. Documents like this give modern performers of Renaissance music provocative food for thought.

First, Rojas and Lopez shall always play the treble parts; ordinarily on shawms. They must carefully observe some order when they improvise passages both as to places and to times. When the one player adds passages to his part, the other must yield to him and play simply the written notes; for when both together embellish at the same time, they produce absurdities that stop one's ears. Second, the same Rojas and Lopez when they at appropriate moments play on cornetts must again observe the same moderation in embellishing: the one deferring to the other; because, as has been previously said, for both simultaneously to add improvised passages creates insufferable dissonance. As for Juan de Medina, he shall ordinarily play the contralto part, not obscuring the trebles nor disturbing them by exceeding the passages that belong to a contralto. When on the other hand his part becomes the top above the sackbuts, then he is left an open field in which to glory and is free to add all the passages that he desires and knows so well how to execute on his instrument. As for Alvanchez, he shall play tenors and the bassoon. At greater feasts there shall always be a verse played on recorders. At Salves [i.e., at evensong] one of the three verses that are played shall be on shawms, one on cornetts and the other on recorders; because always hearing the same instruments wearies the listener.

Robert Stevenson, *Spanish Cathedral Music in the Golden Age* (Berkeley: University of California Press, 1961), 167.

Musicians were employed not only by noble courts and churches. Municipalities also retained bands of wind players to perform at public and ceremonial occasions. Their duties were not unlike those of musicians employed by the nobility, except that their pay and their discipline—and consequently their level of performance—were no match for those musicians lucky enough to gain a position with a wealthy court. The document reproduced below is a decree by the Town Council of Lucca, Italy, and dates from the year 1577.

Nicolao Dorati is to be the director and head of said musicians, and they must obey him in performing whatever music in whatever manner he may choose. When playing at the city hall, before and after the dinner of the *Signoria*, Messer Bernardino da Padova is to play the first soprano, and Vincenzo di Pasquino Bastini the second soprano; but when playing in the hall or the chambers of the *Signoria*, each one is to play or sing the part assigned to him by said Messer Nicolao, their director. However, outside of the city hall, in church, on the public square, at weddings, feasts, serenades, or other events, where they will number at least six, Messer Giulio is to play the first soprano, Messer Bernardino, his father, the second, and Messer Vincenzo the third, that is, the contralto.

And if by chance, which God forbid, there should arise among them a quarrel, ill-will, or other trouble, Messer Nicolao is to intervene and restore peace, and if anyone should refuse to listen to reason, he is to be reported to the *Signoria* in office at the time, so that steps may be taken accordingly. And since beautiful music and perfect harmony are the result of constant practice, there should be assigned for this purpose a room equipped with tables and benches in which they are to meet for practice twice a week, namely, Wednesdays and Saturdays. From the first of February to the last of September they shall meet in the morning, two hours before dinner, and from the first of October to the last of January, in the afternoon, two hours before supper.

In order to enforce these rules, the *maestro di casa* shall take attendance, and those who are absent shall be fined one *carlino* for each time, except in case of illness or other legitimate excuse.

Carl Anthon, "Some Aspects of the Social Status of Italian Musicians During the Sixteenth Century," *Journal of Renaissance and Baroque Music*, I (1946), 225.

43

Radical Humanism: The End of the Renaissance

When the humanist scholars of the Renaissance sought to investigate the music of antiquity, they were confronted by a frustrating paradox: there was no music to investigate, only, on the one hand, theoretical treatises describing the music's materials, and on the other, accounts of musical performances and music's effects, often miraculous. They noticed that the prodigies of musical *ethos* described by Plato, Quintilian, Boethius, and others (see antiquity readings, especially p. 12) did not seem to happen any more. The more literal-minded among them concluded that the "perfected art" of the High Renaissance, magnificent as it was, had lost something worth far more than its much-vaunted perfection of technique. The problem was how to recapture the powers of ancient music, its intimate bond with men's souls and its miraculous influence on men's character and behavior. One way to attempt this was to revive the theory of Greek music and apply it as far as possible to the music of one's own time. The leading experimenter in this direction was Don Nicola Vicentino (c. 1511–72), who, as early as 1546, attempted to introduce into his madrigals the "chromatic and enharmonic genera" of Greek theory. This meant, to put it as simply as possible, that Vicentino wrote music that made use of a more pervasive chromaticism than any previous, and that even included microtones (i.e., intervals smaller than a semitone). Regarded as a crank by his contemporaries, Vicentino was subjected on occasion to public ridicule, and his ideas, for the most part, died with him. The extracts below, from his *L'antica musica ridotta alla moderna prattica* (1555), an elaborate justification of his attempts to "reconcile ancient music with modern practices," reflect his defiant spirit and the ebullient sense of exploration and discovery that so appealingly mark one whom we may consider perhaps the quintessential "Renaissance man" of music.

Although in these times there can be found some professors of music who disparage the efforts which are made in order to learn, and do not even praise those struggles which were undertaken by so many celebrated philosophers in their desire to understand the ultimate divisions of music, nonetheless, these fellows will not deter me from learning and investigating new things, because knowledge is proper to man; and for this reason, I shall incessantly continue to adapt to modern practice the genera and species [of Greek music]. And if I am unable to make a great gain for that practice, at least I shall give such an impetus to fine minds that they will then come up with their own better solutions. How much one sees in the comparison of music of our time with that which was in use a hundred, fifty, twenty-five, and ten years ago! And similarly with this my effort. How intricate my compositions will seem to our posterity! And the reason will be that it is easy to add to things discovered, but the invention and beginning of all things is very difficult.

The nature of the enharmonic genus allows one to make steps and leaps beyond all reason, and because of this, such a division of pitches is called an irrational proportion. Thus the student ought to learn to compose and sing such steps and leaps in order that he may be a perfect musician and a perfect singer. By this he will show the world that he is a rare artist and that he does with art that which reason has not been able to do.

And here is an ironic footnote by "posterity," in the person of another (and more successful) musical humanist, Vincenzo Galilei (see p. 139).

I doubt if the enharmonic music pleased even Don Nicola himself. I think what happened to him was that which occurs to many other people: and this is that inadvertently, because of their naïveté, they abuse what deserves praise and praise what merits abuse, and afterwards, ashamed to contradict themselves, they remain obstinate; others because of their ambitions boast of being capable of things beyond their powers, and badly as they succeed in their ventures, always wish to sustain them as well done.

Henry W. Kaufmann, *The Life and Works of Nicola Vicentino* (Rome: American Institute of Musicology, 1966), 113, 105–106.

An important center of musical humanism was the Académie de Poésie et de Musique, founded in 1570 by the French poet Jean Antoine de Baïf (1532–89) under the enthusiastic patronage of King Charles IX. Among the musicians associated with Baïf and his academy were Jacques Mauduit (1557–1627), Guillaume Costeley (c. 1531–1606), and one of the greatest French musicians of the day, Claude Le Jeune (c. 1525–1600). Although there was some interest among these composers in "chromatic" experimentation along Vicentino's lines, their main contribution, which they made under Baïf's tutelage, was the *musique mesurée à l'antique,* in which the meters of classical poetry were more or less arbitrarily assigned to French poems and then strictly observed by the composers in their settings. The aims of the academy were set forth years later in the encyclopedic treatise *Harmonie universelle,* by Marin Mersenne (1588–1648), who in his youth was a pupil of Mauduit.

The Academicians did not wish to bring in a new kind of music, unless you call that new when something is restored to wholeness, but wished to recover those effects, which, as we read, were once produced by the Greeks, by joining Gallic verses to our carefully cultivated music. For they hoped to exhilarate the depressed spirit, to reduce the over-elated spirit to modesty, and to stir themselves to other feelings by their own music. And they frequently made trial of these things before the King and the princes, as King Charles testifies in a document signed by his own hand, with the great seal attached, in the year of Our Lord 1570, the tenth of his reign, in which he established himself First Auditor of the Academy, and most willingly approved its rules and constitutions.

When Jean Antoine de Baïf and [his collaborator] Joachim Thibault de Courville labored together to drive barbarism from Gaul, they considered that nothing would be of more potency for forming the manners of youth to everything honorable than if they were to recover the effects of ancient music and compose all their songs on the models of the fixed rules of the Greeks.

Would that that Academy might drive its roots into this our time and put forth flowers and fruits, never ceasing from divine praises and bringing forth musical persons, each of whom should make music with his whole heart. But there is no need for complete despair; it will be possible to start an even better Academy, if the most famous men in every kind of art and science would bring their industry together. Only let envy be absent, on account of which such great labors are wont to come to nought in Gaul.

Florence Yates, *The French Academies of the Sixteenth Century* (London: The Warburg Institute, University of London, 1947), 24–25.

> In the preface to Le Jeune's posthumous *vers mesurés* settings of Baïf's *Le Printemps* (1603), the anonymous editor gave classic expression to the Academy's ideals, and to the musical means for realizing them.

The ancients who have discussed music have divided it in two parts: Harmony and Rhythm. The first consists of the proportional ordering of high and low sounds, the other of short and long durations. Harmony was so little explored by them that they used no other consonances than the octave, fifth, and fourth. From these they would construct a certain chord on the lyre, and sing their poetry to its sound. Rhythm, on the other hand, reached such a peak of perfection with them that with it they achieved marvelous effects. They could move the passions of men's souls at will. Since then, this power of rhythm has been so neglected as to have been lost altogether, while Harmony has been so precisely investigated in the last two hundred years that it has been perfected. It creates effects of beauty and grandeur, but these are not those which antiquity records. This has given many cause for wonder, since the ancients sang only with one voice, while we have the melody of several voices together. Some, perhaps, may have discovered the cause of this situation, but no one has ever been found to attempt a cure before Claude Le Jeune, who is the first to have made bold to retrieve this poor Rhythm from the grave in which it has so long been languishing, and make it Harmony's equal. For Harmony alone with its agreeable consonances is capable of arousing the true admiration of the subtlest minds. But Rhythm can excite them, and moreover, can excite, move, and transport at will by the sweet violence of its orderly movements any soul however coarse and uncouth.

Henri Expert (ed.), *Les Maîtres musiciens de la Renaissance française,* XII (Paris, 1900), unpaginated (fac-simile of original preface). Trans. R. T.

> If the claims of the advocates of *musique mesurée* were valid, then they would have to come up with music that could produce the effects the ancient authors described. And

so we have reports like the one below by the French humanist scholar Artus Thomas, in which a familiar classical musical legend—whose prototype should be well known to readers of this book—is rather transparently brought up to date.

It was with two songs in the Phrygian and Hypophrygian modes that Timotheus gave proof of his power on the person of Alexander, whom, with a Phrygian tune, he caused to rush to his arms when at table, immediately afterwards causing him to return to his former tranquillity with a Hypophrygian tune. I have ofttimes heard it said of Sieur Claudin Le Jeune (who has, without wishing to slight anyone, far surpassed the musicians of ages past in his understanding of these matters) that he had sung an air (which he had composed in parts) at the magnificent fêtes which took place on the occasion of the marriage of the late Duc de Joyeuse in 1581, and that when this air was rehearsed at a private concert it caused a gentleman there to put hand to arms and begin swearing out loud, so that it seemed impossible to prevent him from attacking someone: whereupon Claudin began singing another air in the Hypophrygian mode, which rendered the gentleman as calm as before. This has been confirmed to me since by several who were there. Such is the power and force of melody, rhythm, and harmony over the mind.

Yates, *French Academies*, 59.

What was to prove ultimately the most influential of the neoclassical tendencies of late Renaissance musical thought was that which we associate with the Florentine Camerata. This was a group of noble literati and aesthetes who met at the home of Count Giovanni de' Bardi (1534–1612) to discourse on the arts and sciences generally and on the virtues of ancient music in particular. Among the members of his fraternity was Vincenzo Galilei (1533–91), a lutenist and dilettante composer, who was the father of the great astronomer Galileo. In his *Dialogo della musica antica e della moderna* (*Dialogue on Music Ancient and Modern*) of 1581, Galilei gave the ideas of the Camerata their fullest literary expression. Although he had been a pupil of Zarlino himself and was the author of contrapuntal treatises, Galilei took, in his *Dialogo* (so called because it was cast in the form of a dialogue between Count Bardi and another member of the Camerata, Piero Strozzi), the most extreme and hostile stand against the principles of High Renaissance polyphony. (His book called forth an equally hostile retort from Zarlino, in the *Sopplimenti musicali* of 1588.) The condensation of the central portion of the *Dialogo*, which follows, emphasizes Galilei's three main contentions: (1) that the art of Renaissance polyphony was a worthless diversion from the true meaning and purpose of music as practiced by the ancients; (2) that the madrigal and its "isms" were a perversion of these ideals; and (3) that the recovery of the principles of true music was to be sought in the art of orators and actors, Galilei holding, as Quintilian had ages before, that music was to be viewed above all as a branch of rhetoric. These ideas might have proved as sterile and devoid of issue as Vicentino's or Baïf's had they not stimulated the imagination of some great musicians, beginning with Giulio Caccini and culminating in Claudio Monteverdi. For it was at the Camerata's behest that the first steps were taken in the direction of the "musical speech" known as recitative over a basso continuo, and through the medium of recitative, to the attempted revival of the Greek drama, which actually led instead to the birth of opera around the turn of the century. This, of course, marked one of the great epochs in the history of music, and just as our readings from the Baroque will open with selections dealing with the Camerata-inspired "monody" and dramatic music of the early seventeenth century, so Galilei's tract will make a fitting close to our selection of readings from the Renaissance.

Despite the peak of excellence modern music has achieved, we do not hear or see today the least sign of those effects which ancient music produced, nor again do we read that they were accomplished fifty or a hundred years ago, when music was not so common and accessible to all. Consequently neither its novelty nor its excellence has ever given our modern musicians the power of achieving any of those wondrous effects that ancient music achieved, which were so infinitely desirable and useful. From which we must necessarily conclude that either music or human nature has changed from its original state.

If the use of music was introduced among men for the reason and to that end upon which all the learned agree, that is, none other than that it arose principally to express with the greater efficacy the passions of the soul for celebrating the praises of gods and heroes, and secondarily, to impress these with equal force upon the minds of mortals, for their benefit and welfare, then it will be clear that the rules of modern contrapuntists, which they observe like inviolable laws, as well as those additional rules which they so frequently employ at their discretion and to show off their learning, are altogether contrary to the perfection of the best and truest harmonies and melodies.

Consider each rule of the modern contrapuntists in and of itself, or all of them together if you wish. They aim at nothing but the delight of the ear, if delight it can be truly called. On the ways of expressing the passions of the soul and impressing them with the greatest possible efficacy on the minds of the listeners, modern musicians have no books. Nor do they think—nor have they *ever* thought—about such things since music like theirs was invented, but only how to ruin it all the more, if only given the chance. And that it is the case today that no one gives a thought in the world to expressing the emotions of the words with the proper affect—except in the ridiculous way I will describe later—is proven by the fact that all their rules and techniques cover nothing more than how to move about among the musical intervals, seeing to it that the melody vies with varied harmonies according to their precepts, and without further thought to expression of emotion or the sense of the words.

To this, our practicing contrapuntists will say, or rather hold fast to the idea, that they have indeed expressed the passions of the soul in the manner appropriate, and that they have imitated the words, each time they set to music a sonnet, a madrigal, or other poem in which one finds verses which say, for example, "Bitter heart and fierce, cruel desire," which happens to be the first line of one of Petrarch's sonnets, and they see to it that between the parts that sing it are many sevenths, fourths, seconds, and major sixths, and that by means of these they have made a rough, bitter, grating sound in their listeners' ears. Another time they will say they have imitated the words when among the ideas in the text are some that have the meaning "to flee," or "to fly." These will be declaimed with such speed and so little grace as can hardly be imagined. As for words like "to vanish," "to swoon," "to die," they will make the parts fall silent so abruptly that far from inducing any such effect, they will move their listeners to laughter, or else to indignation, should they feel they are being mocked. Again, having words like "alone," "two," or "together" to set, they will have one voice, then two, and finally all together chime in with unheard-of suavity. Others, setting this particular line from one of Petrarch's sestinas: "And with the lame ox he will go in pursuit of Laura," will have it declaimed with such jerkiness, wavering, and syncopations that it will sound like nothing so much as a case of hiccups. And if mention be made in the words, as it happens now and then, of drum rolls, trumpet calls, or some such instrument, they will seek to represent its sound to the hearer with their song, never mind that in so doing they cause these very words to be pronounced in an unheard-of manner. Finding words denoting contrasts of color, like "dark" versus "light hair," and the like, they will set them to black and white notes respectively, to express their meaning most astutely and cleverly, they say, never mind that they have altogether subordinated the sense of hearing to accidents of form and color which are properly the domain of vision and touch. Another time, they will have a verse like this: "He descended into Hell, into the lap of Pluto," and they will make one of the parts descend so that the singer sounds to the listener more like someone moaning to frighten and terrify little girls than like someone singing something sensible. And where they find the opposite—"He doth aspire to the stars"—they will have it declaimed in such a high register that no one screaming in pain has ever equaled it. Unhappy men, they do not realize that if any of the famous orators of old had ever once declaimed two words in such a fashion they would have moved their hearers to laughter and contempt at once, and would have been ridiculed and despised by them as stupid, abject, and worthless men.

When musicians go henceforth for their amusement to the tragedies and comedies played by the actors and clowns in the theaters, let them for a while leave off their immoderate laughing and instead kindly observe in what manner the actors speak, in what range, high or low, how loudly or softly, how rapidly or slowly they enunciate their words, when one gentleman converses quietly with another. Let them pay a little attention to the differences and contrasts that obtain when a gentleman speaks with one of his servants, or one of these with another. Let them consider how the prince converses with one of his subjects or vassals; again, how he speaks to a petitioner seeking a favor; how one speaks when infuriated or excited; how a married woman speaks, how a girl, a simple child, a witty wanton; how a lover speaks to his beloved seeking to persuade her to grant him his wish; how one speaks when lamenting, when crying out, when afraid, and when exulting with joy. From these diverse observations, if they are carried out attentively and considered with care, one can deduce the way that best suits the expression of whatever meanings or emotion may come to hand.

Vincenzo Galilei, *Dialogo della musica antica e della moderna,* ed. Fabio Fano (Milan: A. Minuziano, 1947), 93–96, 130–31, 153–59, 160–62. Trans. R. T.

The Baroque

44

The Birth of a "New Music"

The singer Giulio Caccini (d. 1618) was one of several claimants to the title of inventor of a new music around the beginning of the seventeenth century. He was, in any case, one of the first musicians to turn the learned theorizing of the Camerata into a living music that could really form the basis of a new style. His songs were not without precedent: the music of the "ladies of Ferrara" (see p. 125) comes to mind, and we know from Castiglione (p. 79) that solo singing to a simple accompaniment had a long tradition in Italian courtly circles. Indeed, Caccini at times seems to paraphrase Castiglione, as when he calls for "a certain noble negligence in the singing." What, then, was new in Caccini's self-consciously titled *Nuove musiche* of 1601? For one thing, the lofty aims: Caccini knowingly made the ideals of the Camerata his own, and strove to achieve the "effects of the ancients" according to Galilei's prescription (p. 139). Caccini's idea of "speaking musically" is the origin of what became known as "recitative," the prime distinguishing feature of early opera (in whose beginnings Caccini also had a hand). And Caccini's references to a certain freedom in the handling of dissonances are related to what Monteverdi was to call the *seconda prattica:* a revolutionary approach that for the first time liberated harmony from linear part-writing. In the preface to *Le nuove musiche,* from which we give an extract below, Caccini mentions two kinds of song: besides the recitative-like "madrigal," he wrote strophic "arias" in various dance meters. Something like this pair of styles was to provide the basic framework for musical drama for centuries to come. But Caccini's ascetic approach to vocal display was to prove short-lived indeed.

In the days when the most excellent Camerata of the Very Illustrious Mr. Giovanni Bardi, Count of Vernio, was thriving in Florence, where not only much of the nobility but also the city's first musicians, intellects, poets, and philosophers met together, I can state, having frequented it myself, that I learned more from their savant speeches than I had in over thirty years' study of counterpoint. For those most knowledgeable gentlemen were always urging me, and with the clearest arguments persuading me, not to prize the sort of music which, by not letting the words be properly understood, spoiled both the sense and the verse, now lengthening, now shortening syllables to suit the counterpoint (that mangler of poetry), but rather to adhere to the manner so much praised by Plato and other philosophers, according to whom music consists of speech, rhythm, and, last, sound—not the contrary. They further urged me to aspire that it might penetrate the minds of others, working those wonders so admired by the ancient writers, which counterpoint, in modern compositions, rendered impossible: and especially so when singers sang alone to a stringed instrument, and the words could not be understood for the profusion of embellishments on both short and long syllables, and in any sort of music whatever, provided by this means the multitude exalted them and cried them up for worthy songsters. Having, I say, observed that such music and musicians afforded no other pleasure than that which the harmony might impart to the sole sense of hearing (the intellect being unaffected so long as the words were incomprehensible), it occurred to me to introduce a sort of music in which one might, so to say, speak musically, making use (as I have said elsewhere) of a certain noble negligence in the singing, passing occasionally through a dissonance, the bass staying firm, and the middle parts reduced to instrumental harmony that expressed some affection, for otherwise they are useless. Wherefore, having made a beginning with songs for one voice alone, since it seemed to me they had more power to delight and move than songs for several voices together, I composed in those days certain madrigals and, in particular, an aria in the very style which was to serve me later for the stories put on stage with singing in Florence [i.e., the first operas]. These madrigals and this aria, having been heard by the Camerata with loving applause and with exhortations to me that I pursue my goal by that path, prompted me to go to Rome so that they might be sampled there too. There I performed the madrigals and aria at Mr. Nero Neri's house in the presence of many gentlemen who frequented it, and all can testify how much they urged me to continue my undertaking, saying that they had never before heard music sung by a single voice to a mere stringed instrument that had as much power to move the soul's affections as did those madrigals, both because of their novel style and because, it being then the fashion to sing many-voiced madrigals with a single voice, it seemed to them that a soprano thus singled out from the other parts was wholly devoid of any affection, the parts having been designed to act upon each other reciprocally. Returning to Florence, and seeing that in those days, too, musicians were accustomed to certain little songs (set for the most part to vile words) which I felt were improper and not relished by connoisseurs, it occurred to me, in order occasionally to lift men's drooping spirits, to compose some little songs by way of airs, to be used with consorts of strings; and having imparted this thought to many gentlemen of the city, I was obligingly favored by them with many rhymes in a variety of meters, all of which I set to different airs from time to time, and they have proved welcome enough to all of Italy, their style having now been found serviceable by anyone wishing to compose for a single voice, particularly here in Florence.

It should be observed that passages [of embellishment] were not invented because they were necessary to the right way of singing, but rather, I think, for a certain titillation they afford the ears of those who do not know what it is to sing with affection; for were this understood, then passages would no doubt be abhorred, since nothing can be more contrary to producing a good effect.

Angelo Solerti (ed.), *Le origini del melodramma: testimonianze dei contemporanei* (Turin: Fratelli Bocca, 1903), 56–60. Trans. P. W.

45

The "Second Practice"

The new freedom of early Baroque composition was received with suspicion by conservative musicians. One such was Giovanni Maria Artusi, who in 1600 published a savage attack on certain madrigals by Monteverdi (unfairly, before the offending works had been published), in which the unnamed composer, the greatest musician of his age, was accused of vaingloriousness and even incompetence because of the licenses he allowed himself in his part writing.

Such composers, in my opinion, have nothing but smoke in their heads if they are so impressed with themselves as to think they can corrupt, abolish, and ruin at will the good old rules handed down from days of old by so many theorists and excellent musicians, who are the very ones from whom these modern musicians have learned awkwardly to put a few notes together. But do you know what generally befalls works like these? As Horace says:

> 'Tis the tall pine that oftenest is tossed by winds:
> Lofty towers fall with heaviest crash;
> Lightnings strike the mountain's peak.

In the end, since they lack a good foundation, they are eaten away by time and fall to the ground, and those who put them up are made a laughingstock.

Of course I recognize that new discoveries are not only a good thing but a necessary one. But first tell me why you want such clashes as they have written? If you would answer, "I wish them to be heard clearly, but not so as to offend the ear," then why not prepare them in the conventional way, as reason dictates? Now, even if you want dissonances to become consonances, they will always remain the opposite of consonant; they are naturally always dissonant and can become consonant, therefore, only if consonances become dissonances. We have reached the point of absurdity, but it is altogether possible that these modern composers will so exert themselves that in time they actually will find a way to turn dissonances into consonances and vice versa. But if one's purposes can be achieved by following the teachings and the good old rules handed down by authority and followed by musicians everywhere, why then go beyond their bounds in search of extravagant novelties? Don't you know that all the arts and sciences have long since been regulated by theorists and that their basic principles and rules have been handed down to us so that, as long as they are kept to, we shall be able to understand one another? Horace says:

> There is a moderate measure in things, there are definite limits
> Which sensible conduct should neither exceed nor fall short of.

Compositions like these, then, are the product of ignorance. For such composers it is enough to set up a great roar of sound, an absurd confusion, an array of defects, and it all comes from the ignorance which keeps them benighted.

L'Artusi, ovvero, Delle imperfezioni della moderna musica (Venice, 1600), fols. 42–43. Trans. R. T. *The Odes of Horace,* trans. A. D. Godley (London, 1898), 37. *The Satires and Epistles of Horace,* trans. Smith Palmer Bovie (Chicago: University of Chicago Press, 1959), 37.

It is Artusi, of course, who has become the laughingstock. Monteverdi's answer, which he issued through his brother Giulio Cesare as a "Declaration" appended to his first book of *Scherzi musicali* (1607), stresses the overriding import of the text and its expression. The phrase "the words [are] the mistress of the harmony" was to become one of the chief slogans of the era, and the term *seconda prattica* (second practice), which Claudio Monteverdi had coined in the preface to his fifth book of madrigals (1605), has been taken over by modern scholars to designate everything that sets early Baroque music apart from that of the Renaissance. (By "harmony" Monteverdi means what we would call polyphony; his *melodia,* which refers to the way the music carries the words, is translated here as "setting.")

My brother says that his works are not composed at random, for, in this kind of music, it is his goal to make the words the mistress of the harmony and not its servant, and it is from this point of view that his work should be judged. But in the event Artusi takes a few details, or, as he calls them "passages" from my brother's madrigals, without any regard for the words, which he ignores as if they had nothing to do with the music. By judging these passages without their words, my brother's opponent implies that all merit and beauty lie in following exactly the rules of the First Practice, in which the harmony is mistress of the words.

"First Practice" refers to that style which is chiefly concerned with the perfection of the harmony; that is, in which harmony is not ruled, but rules, is not the servant but the mistress of the words. Its founders were the first to write down music for more than one voice, later followed and improved upon by Ockeghem, Josquin des Prez, Pierre de la Rue, Jean Mouton, Crequillon, Clemens non Papa, Gombert, and others of those times. It reached its ultimate perfection with Messer Adriano [Willaert] in composition itself, and with the extremely well-thought-out rules of the excellent Zarlino.

"Second Practice"—which was originated by Cipriano de Rore, later followed and improved upon by Ingegneri, Marenzio, Giaches de Wert, Luzzasco, still more by Jacopo Peri, Giulio Caccini, and finally by yet more exalted spirits who understand even better what true art is—is that style which is chiefly concerned with the perfection of the setting; that is, in which harmony does not rule but is ruled, and where the words are mistress of the harmony. This is why my brother calls it "second" rather than "new," and "practice" rather than "theory," for its understanding is to be sought in the process of actual composition. Thus, it is my brother's aim to follow the principles taught by Plato and practiced by the divine Cipriano and those who have followed him in modern times, which are different from the principles taught and laid down by the Reverend Zarlino and practiced by Messer Adriano.

Claudio Monteverdi, *Tutte le opere,* ed. G. Francesco Malipiero, X (Vienna: Universal Edition, 1929), 69–72. Trans. R. T.

Monteverdi's account of how he invented the *tremolo* well illustrates the basic tenets of early Baroque neoclassical musical philosophy: the aim of the composer, no less than of any other artist, is *imitazione della natura,* the imitation of reality. For musicians the way to do this was to copy speech, which was the embodiment of the passions of the soul. And the principles by which this was accomplished were those of the orator—music became once again an art of rhetoric. The spectacular results Monteverdi obtained with his discovery may be heard in his *Combattimento di Tancredi e Clorinda* from the eighth book of madrigals (*Madrigali guerrieri et amorosi,* 1638), from whose preface the following extract is taken:

It has seemed to me that the chief passions or affections of our mind are three in number, namely anger, equanimity, and humility. The best philosophers agree, and the very nature of our voice, with its high, low, and middle ranges, would indicate as much. The art of music clearly points to these three in its terms "agitated," "soft," and "moderate" [*concitato, molle, temperato*]. In the works of past composers I have been able to find examples of the soft and the moderate, but I have never found an example of the agitated style, although Plato describes it as "the harmony which would fittingly imitate the speech and inflections of the brave man going to war" [see p. 7]. In view of this I have exerted myself with no little diligence and effort to recover this style.

Since according to all the best philosophers the fast pyrrhic foot was used for agitated, warlike dances, and the slow spondaic foot for their opposites, I took the whole note and proposed that one whole note correspond to one spondee. Dividing this into sixteen sixteenth-notes, struck one after the other and joined to words expressing anger and scorn, I could perceive in this brief example a resemblance to the emotion I was seeking.

At first, the musicians, especially those whose task it was to play the basso continuo, thought it ridiculous to strike a single string sixteen times in one measure, and so they reduced it all to one stroke per measure, thereby producing the spondee instead of the pyrrhic foot, and destroying all resemblance to agitated speech. Be assured, therefore, that the basso continuo must be played just as written, along with the other parts.

Monteverdi, *Tutte le opere,* VIII (1929), unpaginated. Trans. R. T.

46

The Earliest Operas

The *seconda prattica* (see the preceding selection) was soon put to what was considered the most exalted possible use: the revival of ancient Greek tragedy. These early musical dramas, the first real operas, were the work of Florentines and originally served the same purposes and were performed at the same kinds of functions as the older Florentine *intermedii* (see p. 97). They are described below by Marco da Gagliano (1582–1643), court composer to the Medici, whose *La Dafne* (from whose preface we quote), produced in Mantua for the wedding of the young prince Francesco Gonzaga in January 1608, was a resetting of the libretto of the earliest opera of all.

I think it may not prove useless to remind the reader how and when spectacles of this kind originated; which without any doubt, having been received with so much applause at their birth, will sooner or later attain to much greater perfection, perhaps to the point that one day they may be likened to the celebrated tragedies of the ancient Greeks and

Jacopo Peri in Theatrical Costume. In 1589, a few years before composing *Dafne* (the first opera), Peri participated in the wedding festivities in honor of Ferdinand I de' Medici and Christine of Lorraine. In the fifth *intermedio* to a comedy, he appeared seated at the stern of a ship in the guise of the poet-singer Arion, captured by pirates. After singing a heart-rending lament of his own composition, "he threw himself precipitously, thus fully dressed, into the sea, and the water was seen to splash high into the air at his fall, and it was a while before he was seen emerging, carried by a Dolphin" (from a contemporary account; the costume design is by Bernardo Buontalenti). *Florence, Bibl. Naz. Centrale, MS Pal. C.B.3.53.*

Latins, the more so if great masters of poetry and of music shall put their hands to them, and if princes, without whose aid any art can but ill be brought to perfection, shall be favorably inclined to them.

Having repeatedly discoursed on the manner in which the ancients used to represent their tragedies, how they introduced their choruses, whether they employed song, and of what kind, and similar matters, Signor Ottavio Rinuccini [Florentine poet, 1562–1621] took to composing the play of *Dafne*, and Signor Jacopo Corsi [*c.* 1560–1604] of honored memory, lover of all sciences and of music in particular (so much so that he is rightly called its Father by all musicians), composed some airs to parts of it. And having grown to like these exceedingly, he resolved to see what effect they should make on the stage, and therefore, together with Signor Ottavio, shared his thought with Signor Jacopo Peri [1561–1633], a great expert in counterpoint and a most exquisite singer. The latter, having listened to their purpose and approved of a part of the airs already composed, took to composing the rest. Signor Corsi liked these uncommonly well and, availing himself of a Carnival festivity in the year 1597, he had [*Dafne*] played in the presence of my lord the most excellent Duke Giovanni Medici and of some of the principal gentlemen of our town. The pleasure and the amazement produced in the audience by this novel spectacle cannot be described; suffice it to say that each of the many times it was performed it generated the same admiration and the same delight. This experiment having taught Signor Rinuccini how well singing was suited to the expression of every sort of affection, and that it not only afforded no tediousness (as many might perchance have presumed) but indeed incredible delight, he composed his *Euridice,* dilating somewhat more in the dialogues. Signor Corsi having heard it, and being pleased with the story and the style, he determined to put it on the stage for the wedding of the Most Christian Queen [Maria de' Medici]. Then it was that Signor Jacopo Peri discovered that artful manner of reciting in song which all Italy admires. I shall not go to the trouble of praising it, since everyone praises it to the skies, nor is there any lover of music who does not keep Orfeo's songs before him at all times. I will say, though, that no one who has not heard Signor Jacopo sing them himself can fully comprehend the nobility and force of his airs; for he imparts to them such gracefulness, and so forcefully does he impress on the listener the affection of these words, that we must needs either cry or be cheered as he pleases. It would be superfluous to tell how well the performance of that tale was received, there being the testimony of so many princes and lords who attended those splendid nuptials. I shall only say that among those who commended it, my lord the Most Serene Duke of Mantua was so very pleased with it that, among many admirable festivities ordered by His Highness for the magnificent wedding of the Most Serene Prince his son and the Most Serene Infanta of Savoy, he ordered that a musical tale be enacted. And this was *Arianna,* composed for the occasion by Signor Ottavio Rinuccini, whom my lord the Duke called to Mantua for the purpose. Signor Claudio Monteverdi, a most celebrated musician and chief of His Highness's music, wrote the airs so exquisitely that one may truthfully aver that the virtues of ancient music were reborn, for all the audience was visibly moved to tears.

This was the origin of the musical plays, a spectacle truly fit for princes and delightful beyond any other, being one in which are united all the noblest pleasures, such as the invention and treatment of the tale, sense, style, sweetness of rhyme, musical artistry, consorts of voices and of instruments, exquisite beauty of singing, comeliness in the dancing and gestures; and one should also say that no small part is played therein by painting, through the [scenic] perspective and the costumes; so that, together with the intellect, all the noblest senses are gratified at once by the most delightful arts discovered by human ingenuity.

Angelo Solerti (ed.), *Le origini del melodramma: testimonianze dei contemporanei* (Turin: Fratelli Bocca, 1903), 79–82. Trans. P. W.

L'Orfeo, a "musical tale" by Claudio Monteverdi, to a poem by the court secretary of Mantua, Alessandro Striggio, was first performed during the Carnival season of 1607 in honor of the young prince Francesco Gonzaga. Like its predecessor mentioned by Gagliano, it is based on the legend of Orpheus and Eurydice (see p. 1). And indeed, what could better suit a work that embodied the new recitative style than a story demonstrating the very effects at which that style aimed? Striggio's prologue to the drama hints as much. In its own way it is a kind of manifesto of the *seconda prattica,* sung by "La Musica" herself:

Dal mio Permesso amato a voi ne vegno,	From my beloved Permessus I come to you,
Incliti eroi, sangue gentil de' regi,	Renowned heroes, blood royal of kings,
Di cui narra la Fama eccelsi pregi,	Of whom Fame tells glorious deeds,
Nè giunge al ver, perch'è tropp'alto il segno.	Falling short of truth, so lofty is the theme.
Io la Musica son, ch'ai dolci accenti	I am Music, who with sweet melody
So far tranquillo ogni turbato core,	Know how to calm every troubled heart,
Ed or di nobil ira ed or d'amore	And now with noble anger, now with love
Poss'infiammar le più gelate menti.	Can inflame the most frozen minds.
Io su cetera d'or cantando soglio	I, singing to my golden cittern, am wont
Mortal orecchio lusingar talora,	Sometimes to charm mortal hearing,
E in questa guisa a l'armonia sonora	And in this way cause souls to yearn
De la lira del ciel più l'alme invoglio.	The more for the sonorous harmony of Heaven's lyre.
Quinci a dirvi d'Orfeo desio mi sprona,	A longing spurs me hither to tell you of Orpheus,
D'Orfeo che trasse al suo cantar le fere,	Who attracted the beasts with his song,
E servo fe' l'Inferno a sue preghiere,	And made Hades a slave to his prayers,
Gloria immortal di Pindo e d'Elicona.	Immortal glory of Pindus and of Helicon.
Or mentre i canti alterno or lieti, or mesti,	Now as I vary the songs, now gay, now sad,
Non si mova augellin fra queste piante,	Let no bird stir among this foliage,
Nè s'oda in queste rive onda sonante,	Nor let any wave resound on these banks,
Ed ogni auretta in suo cammin s'arresti.	And let every breeze stop in its path.

47

Basso Continuo and Figured Bass

The popularity of the recitative and the solo song gave rise to a new way of writing music down: only the melodic line and the bass of the accompaniment were notated, the harmonic filler being indicated in a numerical shorthand. This texture was known variously as basso continuo, thorough bass, etc. It remained a standard practice for about a century and a half, roughly the period now designated as the Baroque (sometimes referred to, as a matter of fact, as the "age of the thorough bass"). One of the earliest descriptions of the basso continuo occurs in a treatise by the Italian church musician Agostino Agazzari (1578–1640), entitled *Del sonare sopra il basso con tutti li stromenti ...* (Siena, 1607).

Since the true style of expressing the words has at last been found, namely, by reproducing their sense in the best manner possible, which succeeds best with a single voice (or no more than a few), as in the modern airs by various able men, and as is the constant practice at Rome in concerted music, I say that it is not necessary to make a score or tablature for the organ. A Bass, with its signs for the harmonies, is enough. But if some one were to tell me that, for playing the old works, full of fugues and counterpoints, a Bass is not enough, my answer is that vocal works of this kind are no longer in use.

By the use of this method, the organist is freed from that difficult and tiresome thing, the score, which is indeed a frequent source of mistakes, the eye and mind being so overburdened with following the many parts (especially when on occasion one has to make music on the spur of the moment). And without it, in order to furnish the music for a single year's services, the organist would need a larger library than a Doctor of Laws. Wherefore there is abundant reason for the introduction of such a Bass, after the fashion described above; and, in conclusion, there is no necessity for the player to cause all the parts to be heard as written, as long as he is playing merely to accompany singing.

What was one man's reasonable convenience was another's impoverishment of skill. Adriano Banchieri, a church musician famous for his ribald madrigal comedies, saw the use of the thorough bass as a threat to the organist's musicianship and expressed himself scathingly on the subject in his *Conclusioni nel suono dell'organo* (Bologna, 1609), a book that contains much valuable information on the place of the organ within the church service. Banchieri's strictures were hardly enough to stem the tide, for the figured bass was in fact rooted in the very essence of the new style: the independence of harmony as a full-fledged element of music. And far from stifling improvisation, continuo practice actually liberated the accompanying musician to improvise over the bass line more freely than ever before. From now on, every performance of a Baroque composition contained an element of extemporization.

Because it is easy to play from a Basso Continuo, many organists nowadays are highly successful in concerted playing. But in their great vanity on account of their sureness in playing with others, they give little thought to exerting themselves in improvisation and playing from score, whereas it is in this very domain that many a good man has made himself immortal. So that, in short, we shall soon have two classes of players: on the one hand Organists, that is to say, such as practice good playing from score and improvisation, and, on the other hand, Bassists who, overcome by sheer laziness, are content with simply playing the Bass. I do not mean to say that playing from a Basso Continuo is not useful, and is not easy, but I do say that every Organist ought to seek to play the Basso Continuo in accordance with sound rules.

Frank T. Arnold, *The Art of Accompaniment from a Thorough-Bass* (London: Oxford University Press, 1931), 73–74, 81.

48

From the Letters of Monteverdi

We are indeed fortunate that over fifty letters survive from the greatest musical dramatist of the early Baroque. One of the most interesting is the rebuke Monteverdi sent Striggio (see p. 149) on receiving from him what he considered to be an inadequate libretto. This summation of the aesthetics of early opera was based on a misunderstanding: what Striggio had sent was in fact a set of *intermedii,* traditionally decorative and dramatically inconsequential. Once this had been cleared up, Monteverdi expressed his willingness to set the text to music (though his music, if it was in fact written, has not survived). But as long as he envisioned the work as an opera, Monteverdi insisted on a certain realism, a strong focus on human characters and emotions, and the opportunity to imitate speech tones. Only then could music and drama unite to achieve their first aim: to move the affections.

Venice, 9 December 1616

Most Illustrious Sir and Honorable Master:

I greatly rejoiced at receiving, from Signor Carlo de Torri, your letter and little book containing the maritime fable of Thetis' wedding. You write, Illustrious Sir, that you are sending it to me in order that I may view it diligently and write you my opinion of it afterwards, as it is to be set to music and used at the forthcoming wedding of His Serene Highness [Ferdinando Gonzaga of Mantua, for whose brother *Orfeo* (see p. 149) had been written]. I, Illustrious Sir, having no other desire than to be of some service to His Serene Highness, shall answer first that I am ever ready to attend to anything His Serene Highness will deign to command me and always honored to receive without demur whatever His Highness will command. So that, should His Serene Highness approve this, it would in consequence be both very beautiful and much to my liking. But if you bid me speak, I will obey your orders with all respect and promptness, mindful that what I say is nothing, being a person of little worth in all things and a person who honors all virtue, especially that of the present poet whose name I do not know, and the more so as poetry is not my profession. I would say with all respect, in order to obey you since you so command, I would say, then, first and generally, that a proper imitation of the speech ought in my judgment to rest upon wind instruments rather than delicate stringed instruments, since I should think that the Tritons' and other sea-gods' harmonies belonged to trombones and cornetts, and not to citterns or harpsichords and harps. For this performance, being a maritime one, is in consequence outside the city; and Plato teaches that "the cithara must be in the city, and the aulos in the fields." So that either we use delicate sounds that will be inappropriate, or appropriate sounds that will be indelicate. Besides, I see the speakers are to be winds, Cupids, little Zephyrs and Sirens, and many sopranos will be needed in consequence. To which moreover must be added that the winds are to sing. How, dear Sir, shall I be able to move the affections by their means! Arianna moved the audience because she was a woman, and Orfeo also moved them, being a man and not a wind. Music cannot imitate the undiscoverable speech of winds. The dances, further, which are scattered through this fable are not in a proper dancing meter. And I feel, in my rather deep ignorance, that the whole fable does not move me a whit; and I hardly understand it either, nor do I feel that it will inspire me, by a natural order, to a moving climax. Arianna inspired me to a true lament, and Orfeo to a true prayer, but I know not to what end this will inspire me. And so, Illustrious Sir, what can you expect the music to accomplish in it?

Piero Weiss (ed.), *Letters of Composers Through Six Centuries* (Philadelphia: Chilton Books, 1967), 36–38.

Monteverdi's first major court position was as musician to the dukes of Mantua, who treated him in a high-handed manner and summarily dismissed him in 1612. When, some years later, after his appointment to the Basilica of San Marco in Venice, Monteverdi was wooed by Mantua once more, the now securely established and successful Maestro delivered himself of the astonishing document given below. This letter, addressed again to Striggio, gives a revealing glimpse of an artist whose awareness of his own gifts emboldened him in his dealings with his social superiors. And nowhere do we get a more vivid and detailed picture of the patronage system in action.

Venice, 13 March 1620

I must tell Your Excellency that the singular honor His Highness has done me in making me this exceptionally gracious offer to return to his service has touched me and pleased me so much that I cannot find words to express my gratitude. The years of my youth that I spent in that Most Serene service have implanted in my heart such strong feelings of devotion, goodwill, and reverence towards that Most Serene house that I shall pray to God on its behalf as long as I live, and desire that it may enjoy the greatest prosperity that a devoted servant could hope and wish for. And certainly if I had thoughts only for myself Your Excellency could rest assured that I should feel bound to return, if I could minister to His Highness's commands without taking other matters into consideration.

But there are two factors—one relating to this Most Serene Republic [of Venice], the other to my sons—that cause me to have second thoughts: perhaps you will allow me to say a little more about these two matters, for I know that I can count on Your Excellency's kindness, and that wisdom and brotherly love are among your greatest qualities. I shall therefore ask Your Excellency to bear in mind that this Most Serene Republic, which has never given a salary of more than 200 ducats to any of my predecessors—whether Adriano [Willaert], Cipriano [de Rore], Zarlino, or any other—gives me 400, a favor that I must not lightly set aside without taking it carefully into account; since, Excellent Sir, this Most Serene Signory does not make innovations without careful thought, I must regard this particular act of grace very favorably indeed. Nor, having done this, have they ever had second thoughts: indeed they have honored me further, in that they will accept no singer into the choir without first hearing the opinion of the *maestro di cappella,* nor accept organists or vice-*maestri* without the opinion and report of the *maestro di cappella.* There is no gentleman who does not esteem and honor me, and when I go and perform, whether church music or chamber music, I swear to Your Excellency that the whole city runs to listen. My position is the more agreeable also because the whole choir is under temporary appointment except the *maestro di cappella:* indeed it is up to him to appoint and dismiss the singers and to grant leaves of absence or not; and if he does not go into the choir no one will say anything about it. His position is assured until he dies and is not affected by the death of the procurators or of the prince, provided he gives loyal and devoted service and not the opposite. If he does not go and collect his salary at the right time it is brought to his house. This is his basic income. There are also useful additional earnings outside St. Mark's: I have been asked again and again by the wardens of the confraternities and earn 200 ducats a year, for anyone who wants the *maestro di cappella* to make music for them will pay 30, even 40, or as many as 50 ducats for two Vespers and a Mass and afterwards will also thank him very warmly.

Now, Your Excellency, weigh against this in the balance of your fine judgment what you have offered me in His Highness's name and see whether there are any genuine grounds for my moving or not. In the first place, Your Excellency, kindly consider the damage I would do to my reputation with these excellent gentlemen here and with His Highness the Doge himself if I decided to exchange my present income, assured for life, for that offered by the Mantuan treasury, which ceases with the prince's death or his least displeasure; if I were to give up more than 450 ducats (in Mantuan currency), which is what I receive from the Venetian treasury, in order to accept 300 in Mantua, what would not these gentlemen say about me, and with reason? It is true that on behalf of His Highness you add a further 150 *scudi* from land that would be my freehold. But to this I reply that His Highness cannot give me what is mine: there would not be 150 but rather 50, since His Highness already owes me the 100; so he should not take into account what I have earned in the past by great toil and sweat. There would therefore be 350 ducats altogether; here I earn 450, and 200 more on the side.

So Your Excellency can see that people would undoubtedly speak very ill of me, especially as there are others—though I should not say so—who have hitherto been much more liberally rewarded than I have. How ashamed I should feel beside them to see them rewarded better than me! Compare Venice! Your Excellency should also remember that His Highness made me a better offer, verbally through Signor Capagnolo, when I was staying in the latter's house after Signor Sante's death: this was a salary of 300 *scudi* from land, 200 of which were to be mine up to my death and 100 as a gift as payment of my annual rent. Then when I said I did not wish to have anything to do with the treasury he offered me a pension of 200 more, which came altogether to 600 Mantuan ducats. Now His Highness would like me to settle for so much less, as well as going to the treasurer every day to beg him to give me what is mine! As God sees me, I have never in my life suffered greater humiliation of the spirit than when, almost for the love of God, I had to go and beg the treasurer for what was mine. I would rather go from door to door than submit again to such indignity. (I beg Your Excellency to forgive me if I speak freely and to be so kind, on this occasion, and for the love I bear you as your devoted servant, as to hear me out with your boundless humanity and not in your official capacity.)

When the excellent procurator Signor Landi, together with the other excellent gentlemen, wished to increase my salary by 100 ducats he spoke as follows:

"Excellent colleagues, he who desires an honorable servant must grant him an honorable contract." So if the Duke wished me to come and live honorably it is only right that he should treat me likewise; if not, I beg him not to bother me, since, as Your Excellency well knows, I have acted honorably.

I have said nothing of my sons. Yet Your Excellency, who is also the father of a family, knows very well how zealous a father has to be in desiring that honor for himself and for the household depending upon him which by the laws of nature he feels to be their due.

My conclusion, Excellent Sir, is this. As for Claudio, he is already in every way at His Highness's beck and call. As for the above considerations, he cannot honorably change his situation unless it be for the better and thus feel entirely justified in leaving the service of these excellent gentlemen. His Highness has the opportunity, now that the illustrious Bishop of Mantua has passed to a better life, of satisfying Monteverdi with a pension and a little more land without exposing him to the repugnant practices of an unreliable treasury: in short, a pension of 400 Mantuan *scudi* and 300 from land would be little to His Highness, and to Claudio a truly generous settlement. Perhaps Claudio is asking the impossible? He asks in fact for less than [the singers] Adriana and, possibly, Settimia used to get; he asks for what he is getting now. For it is my duty to leave a little something to my sons. If I were to leave something provided by the Most Serene house of Gonzaga it would be to their eternal honor, for they would have helped a long-serving employee not wholly despised by princes. And if this seems too much to His Highness, let him do me the honor of assigning me a little land so that I may have a little capital, since the 400 ducats I am getting now are in effect a pension. In so doing, His Highness will have paid his servant; and if he will deign to command him, he shall find that I will get up in the middle of the night the more expeditiously to carry out his orders.

Please forgive me, Your Excellency, if I have written at too great a length. It only remains for me to thank Your Excellency with all my heart for the exceptional favor you did me in presenting my madrigals [Book VII] to Her Highness; I am sure that, since they were handed over by no less a person than Your Excellency, they will have been the more gratefully received.

Denis Arnold and Nigel Fortune (eds.), *The Monteverdi Companion* (New York: W. W. Norton & Company, Inc, 1968), 52–56. Reprinted by permission of W. W. Norton & Company, Inc., and Faber and Faber Ltd. Copyright © 1968 by Denis Arnold.

49

Venice, 1637: Opera Opens for Business

If Florence was the birthplace of opera, then Venice became its launching pad. In 1637 one of its theaters engaged a traveling opera company and opened its doors to paying customers, thus charging admission to a musical performance for the first time in modern history and anticipating by some 40 years the establishment of the first public concerts in London (see p. 179). The Venetian public, enlarged even then by throngs of tourists, especially during the Carnival, made the first commercial operas a big success. Within a few years the number of opera houses in Venice grew to four, five, six, and by 1681, when Cristoforo Ivanovich published the following observations, to twelve. Court patronage was replaced in Venice by a new authority, the box office, and opera rapidly adjusted to meet its demands. This Venetian model, dominated by virtuoso singers and lavish scenery and designed to be composed and produced in quantities sufficient to fill each season with new works, spread to the rest of Italy and Europe. By the time Ivanovich wrote his book, however, opera was becoming bad business, and he tells us why.

THE CUSTOM OF RENTING BOXES, AND THE RIGHTS ACQUIRED BY THOSE WHO RENT THEM

The most certain profit accruing to every theater consists in the rental of boxes. These number at least one hundred, not counting the upper tiers, which are divided in several orders. Not all [boxes] have the same price, which is determined by the order and the number indicating their location; therefore one cannot accurately assign a value to each [box] because of the variety of locations, which in turn makes the rents variable. These orders of boxes have easy, well-lit access, and each box has its number. The key bears two marks, the number of the order and that of the box, which averts all confusion and helps one to find the box. When a theater is to be built, it is the custom to establish two sources of revenue from the very beginning. The first consists of a gift of money for each box, and this serves to a large extent to cover the construction costs and has been the principal reason why several theaters have been built with such ease and celerity. The second is the yearly rental; every year in which a theater offers performances, this payment is made to meet the theater's expenses and provide ease and comfort to the renter. It is the right, then, acquired by the owner of that box to hold it as his own property, though without the option of yielding it to others; furthermore to keep it for his own use and lend it at will. Two reasons can make it revert to the owner of the theater: when the rent is not paid during a year of performances, or when [the box] is voluntarily relinquished by its owner; in such cases it can pass on to a new tenant. Otherwise, once acquired, it remains the owner's property for life as well as his heirs' after his death; that is, it passes from father to son, from son to father, from brother to brother, and the obligation contracted in the beginning remains in force without any alterations in the manner in which it was met in the past. This custom is founded on several cases argued in courts of law and is punctually observed. The profit from this practice is considerable, as will be mentioned later, in the discussion on a theater's earnings. There are in addition several boxes at the ground level and in the upper tiers, which, because they are inconvenient and of lesser quality, are not all rented out at the beginning, but instead are rented just for the evening or for the year at the pleasure of the owner, who seeks to realize as much as possible for his own benefit.

THE EXPENSES A THEATER MUST SUSTAIN

A theater, before it earns any profit, must incur many expenses, all of them connected with the performance of the dramas, without which all interest in it would cease completely. The first and most considerable [expense] is that of remunerating the men and women who sing, their pretensions having become excessive, where before they were content to perform for a share of the profit or to receive honest compensation.

One must pay the maestro who sets the drama to music; then come the expenses for the costumes, the scenery, the construction of machines, the contract with the choreographer, the compensation each evening for the stage hands and orchestra players, and for keeping the theater lit. All the above expenses have changed with the times, for when the theaters were just starting, prices were not so high; discretion and honesty were still respected, and the efforts of *virtuosos* were more welcome and appreciated. Today dispositions are so insatiable that loss rather than gain is the rule; and for the most part one spends far more than one gains because of the exorbitant payments to the singers. In earlier days two exquisite voices sufficed, a small number of arias gave pleasure, a few changes of scenery satisfied curiosity; nowadays one unsuitable voice receives more attention than the best voices in Europe. Every scene in the drama is expected to entail a change of scenery, and the invention of the machines must be extravagant. These are the reasons why expenses grow heavier every year; but in reality they do not grow, for payments at the door are diminishing, putting the continuance [of theaters] at risk, unless a better regulation is imposed on current trends.

Piero Weiss (ed.), *Opera: A History in Documents* (New York: Oxford University Press, 2002), 38–39.

50

Schütz Recounts His Career

With the publication of his third book of *Symphoniae sacrae* in 1651, Heinrich Schütz (1585–1672) made this formal request to be relieved of his duties as chapel musician to the Elector of Saxony. His career, as he relates it, reveals much about the musical climate of the early Baroque. Italy was regarded everywhere as the center and seat of musical innovation. Schütz played a leading role in bringing the new styles pioneered by Gabrieli and Monteverdi to northern Europe.

With the present most submissive tribute of my little work, now brought out under Your Highness' exalted name, I am prompted to touch somewhat upon the rather toilsome life I have led from youth until now. I beg with deep devotion that Your Highness will not be wholly undisposed to receive this letter with favor and to examine it at your leisure.

Not long after I had come into this World (in the year 1585, on St. Burckhard's day), indeed already in my thirteenth year, I left my late parents' house in Weissenfels and have always lived abroad from that time forward. First, I served for several years as chorister at the Court Chapel of my Lord the Landgrave Moritz in Cassel, but was kept at School and brought up to learn Latin and other tongues as well as Music.

And as it was never my late parents' wish that I should make music my profession then or later, I betook myself at their prompting to the University of Marburg after I had lost my treble voice, my intention being to pursue, besides music, those other studies in which I had made a beginning, pick a definite profession, and afterwards gain in it an honorable station. But this purpose of mine was soon unsettled (doubtless through the will of God), for my Lord the Landgrave Moritz came to Marburg one day (he may perhaps have observed, while I was employed as chorister at his court, that nature had endowed me with some aptitude for music) and recommended to me the following course of action: since at that time a very famous if elderly musician and composer [Giovanni Gabrieli] was still alive in Italy, I was not to miss the opportunity of hearing him and gaining some knowledge from him. And the aforementioned Princely Highness ordered that a yearly stipend of 200 thalers be presented to me for the journey. Then (being a young man, and eager to see the world besides) I quite willingly accepted the recommendation with submissive gratitude, whereupon I set out for Venice in the year 1609, against my parents' wishes. On my arrival (and after I had stayed with my master for a while), I soon observed the weightiness and difficulty of the study which I was undertaking in composition, and how unfounded and poor a beginning I had made in it till then; and I repented very much, therefore, that I had turned away from those studies which are common at the German universities and in which I had already made some progress. Nevertheless, I resigned myself to be patient and to apply myself to the task that had brought me there. Wherefore I put aside all my previous studies from then on and studied only music with all possible diligence, to see how far I might succeed in it. Then with God's help I made such progress in it, in all modesty, that three [actually two] years after (and one year before I returned from Italy) I had my first small musical work [a book of madrigals] printed there in the Italian tongue, to the particular acclaim of the most distinguished musicians then at Venice, and sent it thence to my Lord the Landgrave Moritz (to whom I also dedicated it in submissive gratitude). Having published my aforesaid first small work, I was exhorted and encouraged not only by my preceptor Gabrieli, but also by the other most distinguished musicians there, to persevere in the study of music, for I should enjoy excellent successes therein. And as I remained one more year after this (although at my parents' expense) in order to learn somewhat more from these studies, it happened that my above-mentioned preceptor died in Venice, whom I accompanied to his place of rest. On his deathbed, he had arranged out of special affection that I should receive one of the rings he left behind as a remembrance of him; this was indeed presented and handed to me after his death by his Father Confessor, an Augustinian monk (from the cloister at which Dr. Luther once sojourned). The grant I had received from my Lord the Landgrave Moritz in Marburg was ended, for whoever wished to learn from that supremely gifted man might not absent himself longer than I had.

Now when I left Italy for the first time in the year 1613 and returned to Germany, I privately resolved to hold back for a few years the good musical foundations I had by then acquired and hide them until I should have schooled them somewhat further, whereupon I could bring honor upon myself through the publication of a meritorious work. Now, too, I did not lack for counsel and inducement from my parents and kinsfolk whose opinion, briefly, was that I should endeavor to use my qualities, slight as they were, and seek advancement by other means, and treat music as a secondary matter. At length I was prevailed upon to heed their repeated, ceaseless admonitions and was on the point of seeking out the books I had previously put aside. But as God the Almighty ordained (who without doubt had set me apart from birth for the profession of music), I was engaged to come here to Dresden and serve at the impending Princely baptism of my Lord and Duke August, the present administrator of the Magdeburg Archbishopric, in the year 1614. And having come here and undergone an examination, I was forthwith most graciously offered the direction of your music in Your Highness' name. Whereupon my parents and kinsfolk, and I too, felt the presence of the unalterable will of God; and so my wandering was at an end. And I was prompted not to reject the honorable condition I had been offered but to accept it with most submissive gratitude and to vow I would take charge of the direction with all the diligence at my disposal. Your Highness will, I hope, recollect in some measure what my slight, yet not careless, functions have been since the year 1615, that is, for over 35 years. And I do indeed praise the charity and mercy God has shown me so far in that, besides my private studies and the publication of various musical works, I have waited most submissively on Your Highness from the beginning of my direction at many and sundry solemnities which have occurred the while, such as imperial, royal, electoral, and princely meetings at home and abroad, but more especially your own beloved children's weddings one and all, no less than their Christian baptisms. Now I most heartily wish that I could continue having charge over Your Highness' court chapel in the manner practiced by me until now; but I cannot by any means trust myself or venture to serve it fittingly any longer, nor uphold at my present age the rather good name I gained in younger years: not only because of the ceaseless studying, traveling, writing, and other constant labors in which I have, in all modesty, been engaged since youth, but also because old age has now come upon me, and my sight and vital strength have waned.

For as my strength declines still further, it may befall me as it did a not badly qualified old cantor living in a noted place. I knew him well, and he wrote to me over a period of time and complained bitterly that his young town councilors were most displeased with the antiquated style of his music, and would, therefore, gladly be rid of him; that therefore they had explicitly told him to his face, at the Town Hall, that a Thirty Years' Tailor and a Thirty Years' Cantor were quite useless in this world [Schütz makes sardonic reference to the Thirty Years' War, which had ended three years previously], for it cannot but be that the young world tends soon to tire of the old customs and fashions, and to change them.

Piero Weiss (ed.), *Letters of Composers Through Six Centuries* (Philadelphia: Chilton Books, 1967), 46–51.

51

The Doctrine of Figures

It remained for the Germans to classify and codify the principles the Italian musicians of the early Baroque had worked out more or less by instinct. Below we give a synthesis of three treatises by Christoph Bernhard (1627–92), a pupil of Heinrich Schütz, who no doubt incorporated into his writings a great deal of his master's teaching. Musical "figures" are equated with figures of speech, to be learned by musicians as the latter were learned by orators. By reducing the devices of the *seconda prattica* to a set of ordered principles, theorists like Bernhard gave them the justification they needed to match the prestige of the First Practice (which Bernhard calls the *stylus gravis*), i.e., Renaissance polyphony. Bernhard is at pains, moreover, to point out that the Second Practice was not a revolt against the first, but an outgrowth of it. His approach of finding the underlying counterpoint behind the modern surface has suggested fruitful analytical methods in our own time (e.g., that of Heinrich Schenker). Bernhard's advice to performers, which might as well have been addressed to actors as to musicians, is reminiscent at times of Zarlino's (see p. 107) and retains its validity to this day.

Composers of the most recent period have begun to set things down that were unknown to men of former times, and which have seemed unacceptable to the unenlightened, but charming to good ears and to professionals. The result is that the art of music has attained such a height in our own day that it may indeed be compared to rhetoric, in view of the multitude of figures, particularly in the newly founded and ever more elaborate style of vocal music. Such figures and works, however, have the old masters as their foundation, and what cannot be justified through them must rightly be weeded out of composition as an abomination.

Since language is the absolute master of music in this style, just as music is the master of language in the *stylus gravis,* this general rule follows: that one should represent speech in the most natural way possible. One should set joyful things joyfully, sorrowful things sorrowfully, swift things swiftly, slow things slowly. In particular, that which is heightened in ordinary speech should be set high, that which passes unemphasized set low. Questions, according to common usage, are ended a step higher than the penultimate syllable. Textual repetition should be employed either not at all, or just in those places where elegance permits. Musical repetition, on the other hand, occurs when two successive utterances are similar in subject matter. Musical repetition a step higher [that is, sequence] occurs in connection with two or more successive questions, when their words correspond in subject matter, and when the last seems to be more forceful than the first.

The figures belonging to this style include the following:

Extension: the rather sizable lengthening of a dissonance.

Ellipsis: the suppression of a normally required consonance.

Tearing off (abruptio): this occurs when, in place of a consonance anticipated as a necessary resolution of a dissonance, the vocal line is either ruptured or broken off altogether.

Performance in this style requires an adequate understanding of the text. Accordingly it is to be deplored that only a few singers concern themselves with a proper and solid grounding in Latin and Italian—two languages which, besides their mother tongue, all singers ought to understand passably, if not indeed to speak well. The anger of learned listeners is all too frequently aroused by singers who apply passagework to a word like "confirmation," or place an ascending run on one like "abyss," thus exposing their ignorance to the light of day.

The words, once understood, suggest what affections, occurring therein, should be elicited. The noblest affections that can be represented in music are Joy, Sorrow, Anger, Contentment, and the like. In Joy, Anger, and similarly strong affections, the voice must be strong, valiant, and hearty. Notes must not be decorated in special ways; rather, they should more frequently be sung as written, for any further application of embellishment would sound somewhat more melancholy than these affections require. On the other hand, for sorrowful, gentle, and like words, it is better to employ a milder, softer voice, to slur and slide between the notes, and to employ frequently the refinements of embellishment. For this type of affection one should also choose a slower tempo, for the other a quicker one. A good singer will derive further rules through his own judgment and from the example of other singers.

Finally, one must know those pitfalls which a good singer and sophisticated musician, familiar with the qualitative and quantitative properties of sound, can avoid: a singer should not raise his voice when the affection is one of humility or love; nor let it fall several tones when anger is to be shown. In the recitative style, one should take care that the voice be raised in moments of anger, and to the contrary dropped in moments of grief. Pain makes it pause; impatience hastens it. Happiness enlivens it. Desire emboldens it. Love renders it alert. Bashfulness holds it back. Hope strengthens it. Despair diminishes it. Fear keeps it down. Danger is fled with screams. If, however, a person faces up to danger, then his voice must reflect his daring and bravery. To conclude, a singer should not sing through his nose. He must not stammer, lest he be incomprehensible. He must not push with his tongue or lisp, else one will hardly understand half of what he says. He also should not clench his teeth, nor open his mouth too wide, nor stretch his tongue out over his lips, nor thrust his lips upward, nor distort his mouth, nor disfigure his cheeks and nose like the long-tailed monkey, nor crumple his eyebrows together, nor wrinkle his forehead, nor roll his head or the eyes therein round and round, nor wink with the same, nor tremble with his lips, etc.

The Treatises of Christoph Bernhard, trans. Walter Hilse, *The Music Forum*, III (New York: Columbia University Press, 1973), 21, 24, 90–91, 110–15. Reprinted by permission.

52

Music and Scientific Empiricism

To the subjective and sense-oriented Renaissance attitude towards music, Baroque thinkers added the emphasis on natural observation and experiment that characterized what scientists like to refer to as the "early modern" period. Sound and its effects were regarded not merely as the embodiment of numerical "truths" in the spirit of medieval rationalism, but as a phenomenon of nature to be investigated both in and of itself and in relation to the hearer (whose responses were also governed by natural law). As René Descartes put it in his *Compendium musicae* of 1618: "The basis of music is sound; its aim is to please and to arouse the affections. The means to this end, i.e., the attributes of sound, are principally two: namely, its differences of duration or time, and its differences of tension from high to low. The quality of tone itself (from what body and by what means it emanates in the most pleasing manner) is in the domain of the physicist." The result of this new objectivity about sound and music was, in the first place, the increasing rejection of Platonic musical ethics, as here, with fine sarcasm, by Milton in his treatise on the freedom of the press (*Areopagitica*, 1644).

If we think to regulate Printing, thereby to rectify manners, we must regulate all recreations and pastimes, all that is delightful to man. No musick must be heard, no song be set or sung, but what is grave and *Dorick*. There must be licensing dancers, that no gesture, motion, or deportment be taught our youth but what by their allowance shall be thought honest; for such *Plato* was provided of. It will ask more than the work of twenty licensers to examine all the lutes, the violins, and the guitars in every house; they must not be suffered to prattle as they do, but must be licensed what they may say. And who shall silence all the airs and madrigals that whisper softness in chambers? The windows also, and the *Balconies* must be thought on; there are shrewd books with dangerous Frontispieces set to sale; who shall prohibit them? Shall twenty licensers? The villages also must have their visitors to inquire what lectures the bagpipe and the rebeck reads, even to the balladry and the gamut of every *municipal* fiddler. To sequester out of the world into Atlantick and Eutopian polities, which never can be drawn into use, will not mend our condition; but to ordain wisely as in this world of evil, in the midst whereof God hath placed us unavoidably.

Sir Arthur Quiller-Couch (ed.), *The Oxford Book of English Prose* (Oxford: Oxford University Press, 1925), 225.

> *Sylva sylvarum* (1626) by Francis Bacon, the father of modern science, contains a fascinating section entitled "Experiments in consort touching music," wherein the properties of sound are thoroughly investigated, at times with an eye towards practical application, at others in a spirit of creative and curious play. What is particularly interesting is that Bacon's "scientific" approach leads him directly to the association of music with rhetoric, to which the practical musicians of the time were led by an altogether different path.

Music, in the practice, hath been well pursued, and in good variety; but in the theory, and especially in the yielding of the causes of the practice, very weakly; being reduced into certain mystical subtilities of no use and not much truth. We shall, therefore, after our manner, join the contemplative and active part together.

[101.] All sounds are either musical sounds, which we call tones; whereunto there may be an harmony; which sounds are ever equal; as singing, the sounds of stringed and wind instruments, the ringing of bells, *etc.* or immusical sounds, which are ever unequal; such as are the voice in speaking, all whisperings, all voices of beasts and birds, except they be singing birds, all percussions of stones, wood, parchment, skins, as in drums, and infinite others.

[111.] The causes of that which is pleasing or ingrate to the hearing, may receive light by that which is pleasing or ingrate to the sight. There be two things pleasing to the sight, leaving pictures and shapes aside, which are but secondary objects; and please or displease but in memory; these two are colors and order. The pleasing of color symbolizeth with the pleasing of any single tone to the ear; but the pleasing of order doth symbolize with harmony. And therefore we see in garden-knots, and the frets of houses, and all equal and well answering figures, as globes, pyramids, cones, cylinders, *etc.* how they please: whereas unequal figures are but deformities. And both these pleasures, that of the eye, and that of the ear, are but the effects of equality, good proportion, or correspondence: so that, out of question, equality and correspondence are the causes of harmony. But to find the proportion of that correspondence, is more abstruse; whereof notwithstanding we shall speak somewhat, when we handle tones in the general enquiry of sounds.

[112.] Tones are not so apt altogether to procure sleep, as some other sounds; as the wind, the purling of water, humming of bees, a sweet voice of one that readeth, *etc.*

The cause whereof is, for that tones, because they are equal and slide not, do more strike and erect the sense than the other. And overmuch attention hindreth sleep.

[113.] There be in music, certain figures or tropes, almost agreeing with the figures of rhetoric, and with the affections of the mind, and other senses. First, the division and quavering, which please so much in music, have an agreement with the glittering of light; as the moonbeams playing upon a wave. Again, the falling from a discord to a concord, which maketh great sweetness in music, hath an agreement with the affections, which are reintegrated to the better, after some dislikes: it agreeth, also with the taste, which is soon glutted with that which is sweet alone. The sliding from the close or cadence, hath an agreement with the figure in rhetoric, which they call *praeter expectatum* [contrary to expectation]; for there is a pleasure even in being deceived. The reports, and fugues, have an agreement with the figures in rhetoric, of repetition and traduction. The triplas, and changing of times, have an agreement with the changes of motions; as when galliard time, and measured time, are in the medley of one dance.

Experiments in Consort Touching the Magnitude and Exility and Damps of Sounds

[151.] I remember in Trinity College in Cambridge, there was an upper chamber, which being thought weak in the roof of it, was supported by a pillar of iron of the bigness of one's arm in the midst of the chamber; which if you had struck, it would make a little flat noise in the room where it was struck, but it would make a great bomb in the chamber beneath.

[159.] Trial was made in a recorder after these several manners. The bottom of it was set against the palm of the hand; stopped with wax round about; set against a damask cushion; thrust into sand; into ashes; into water, half an inch under the water; close to the bottom of a silver bason; and still the tone remained: but the bottom of it was set against a woollen carpet; a lining of plush; a lock of wool, though loosely put in; against snow; and the sound of it was quite deadened, and but breath.

[161.] Let there be a recorder made with two fipples, at each end one; the trunk of it of the length of two recorders, and the holes answerable towards each end; and let two play the same lesson upon it at an unison; and let it be noted whether the sound be confounded, or amplified, or dulled. So likewise let a cross be made of two trunks hollow throughout; and let two speak, or sing, the one longways, the other traverse: and let two hear at the opposite ends; and note whether the sound be confounded, amplified, or dulled. Which two instances will also give light to the mixture of sounds, whereof we shall speak hereafter.

Experiment in Consort Touching Melioration of Sounds

[231.] In frosty weather, music within doors soundeth better. Which may be by reason not of the disposition of the air, but of the wood or string of the instrument, which is made more crisp, and so more porous and hollow: and we see that old lutes sound better than new for the same reason. And so do lute-strings that have been kept long.

[232.] Sound is likewise meliorated by the mingling of open air with pent air; therefore trial may be made of a lute or viol with a double belly; marking another belly with a knot over the strings; yet so, as there be room enough for the strings, and room enough to play below that belly. Trial may be made also of an Irish harp, with a concave on both sides; whereas it useth to have it but on one side. The doubt may be, lest it should make too much resounding; whereby one note would overtake another.

[233.] If you sing in the hole of a drum, it maketh the singing more sweet. And so I conceive it would, if it were a song in parts sung into several drums; and for handsomeness and strangeness sake, it would not be amiss to have a curtain between the place where the drums are and the hearers.

Experiments in Consort Touching the Sympathy or Antipathy of Sounds One with Another

[278.] All concords and discords of music are, no doubt, sympathies and antipathies of sound. And so, likewise, in that music which we call broken music or consort music, some consorts of instruments are sweeter than others, a thing not sufficiently yet observed: as the Irish harp and bass viol agree well: the recorder and stringed music agree well: organs and the voice agree well, *etc.* But the virginals and the lute; or the Welsh harp and Irish harp; or the voice and pipes alone, agree not so well; but for the melioration of music, there is yet much left, in this point of exquisite consorts, to try and inquire.

[279.] There is a common observation, that if a lute or viol be laid upon the back, with a small straw upon one of the strings, and another lute or viol be laid by it; and in the other lute or viol the unison to that string be struck, it will make the string move; which will appear both to the eye and by the straw's falling off. The like will be, if the diapason or eighth [i.e., octave] to that string be struck, either in the same lute or viol, or in others lying by; but in none of these there is any report of sound that can be discerned, but only motion.

[280.] It was devised, that a viol should have a lay of wire-strings below, as close to the belly as a lute; and then the strings of guts mounted upon a bridge as in ordinary viols; to the end that by this means the upper strings struck, should make the lower resound by sympathy, and so make the music the better; which if it be to purpose, then sympathy worketh as well by report of sound as by motion. But this device I conceive to be of no use [N.B.: "partials" were not discovered until *c.* 1700 (see p. 186)], because the upper strings, which are stopped in great variety, cannot maintain a diapason or unison with the lower, which are never stopped. But if it should be of use at all, it must be in instruments which have no stops, as virginals and harps; wherein trial may be made of two rows of strings, distant the one from the other.

Experiments in Consort Touching the Spiritual and Fine Nature of Sounds

[289.] All sounds are suddenly made, and do suddenly perish: but neither that, nor the exquisite differences of them, is matter of so great admiration: for the quaverings and warblings in lutes and pipes are as swift; and the tongue, which is no very fine instrument, doth in speech make no fewer motions than there be letters in all the words which are uttered. But that sounds should not only be so speedily generated, but carried so far every way in such a momentary time, deserveth more admiration. As for example, if a man stand in the middle of a field and speak aloud, he shall be heard a furlong in a round; and that shall be in articulate sounds; and those shall be entire in every little portion of the air; and this shall be done in the space of less than a minute.

[290.] The sudden generation and perishing of the sounds, must be one of these two ways. Either that the air suffereth some force by sound, and then restoreth itself as water doth; which being divided, maketh many circles, till it restore itself to the natural consistence: or otherwise, that the air doth willingly imbibe the sound as grateful, but cannot maintain it; for that the air hath, as it should seem, a secret and hidden appetite of receiving the sound at the first; but then other gross and more materiate qualities of the air straightways suffocate it; like unto flame, which is generated with alacrity, but straight quenched by the enmity of the air or other ambient bodies.

There be these differences, in general, by which sounds are divided: 1. Musical, immusical. 2. Treble, base. 3. Flat, sharp. 4. Soft, loud. 5. Exterior, interior. 6. Clean, harsh or purling. 7. Articulate, inarticulate.

The Works of Francis Bacon, I (London, 1805), paragraphs as indicated.

53

Music in the Churches of Rome, 1639

André Maugars was a French viol player attached to the court of Louis XIII. He was also secretary to Cardinal Richelieu and thereby became involved in many court intrigues. As the result of one of these he found himself banished to Italy for a time. To this circumstance we owe one of the most complete and authoritative descriptions we possess of seventeenth-century music making, Maugars's well-known letter on music in Italy, from which we present some sizable extracts below. Maugars touches on many topics of interest. First we have an admiring description by an outsider of the *seconda prattica*. From there Maugars moves on to a vivid description of polychoral singing at its most impressive, and, most interesting of all, of the early oratorio, in which the recitative style was applied to sacred subjects. A glimpse of Frescobaldi at the organ is followed by Maugars's not overly modest report of his own conquest of musical Rome with a dazzling display of virtuosity on the viol extemporized over a ground bass. This was instrumental music at its most characteristic in the seventeenth century: like jazz musicians, instrumentalists were mainly improvisers who based their flights of fancy on the "standards"—favorite tunes—of the day. What emerges from all of these vignettes with greatest force is that the Roman churches acted as a musical focal point. One went to church in seventeenth-century Rome much as one goes to a concert today, and it was in these public church performances that our modern concert life was first prefigured.

First of all, I find that Italian church music has much more art, learning, and variety than ours; but also more freedom. Speaking for myself, since I cannot find fault with this freedom when it is practiced with discretion and with a skill that carries the senses along unawares, I am, therefore, unable to approve of the stubbornness of our [French] composers, who remain too strictly enclosed in pedantic categories, and who would think themselves guilty of errors against the rules of the art if they were to write two fifths in succession, or if they departed the least bit from their modes. It is surely in these pleasing departures that all the secret of the art lies, music having its figures of speech as well as rhetoric, which tend, all of them, only towards charming and beguiling the hearer without his knowing how. Really, it isn't necessary to be so wrapped up in the rigid observance of these rules that we ruin the proper development of a fugue or the beauty of an air, for these rules were invented only to hold young learners in check and to keep them from throwing off restraints before attaining the age of discretion. That is why a man of good judgment, once he has perfect knowledge of his craft, is not condemned by an irrevocable sentence to remain forever in these narrow prisons. He may skillfully take flight, carried along in some fair pursuit by his fancy, and as the force of the words or the beauty of the vocal lines may prompt. And since the Italians are much more refined than we are in music, they scoff at our adherence to the rules, and thus they compose their motets with more art, more knowledge, more variety, and more charm.

They never sing the same motets twice, although hardly a day goes by without a celebration in some church with its attendant presentation of some good musical composition. The result is that one is certain to hear a new composition every day. That is the most pleasant pastime I have in Rome.

I will give you a description of the very excellent concert I heard in Rome on the eve and feast of St. Dominick, in the church of Santa Maria on the ruins of Minerva [Rome's only Gothic church]. This church is rather long and capacious, and in it there are two great organs built on either side of the main altar, where two choirs had been placed. Along the nave there were eight more choirs, four on each side, placed on scaffolding eight or nine feet high, equidistant from each other and all in view of each other. With each choir there was a portative organ, as is their custom. You mustn't be surprised at this, for there are more than two hundred of them in Rome, whereas in Paris one would hardly be able to find two at the same pitch and tuning. The master composer gave the main beat in the first choir, made up of the most beautiful voices. In each of the others there was a man who did nothing but watch this original beat so as to conform to it with his own; the result was that all the choirs sang to the same beat, without dragging. The counterpoint of the music was elaborate, full of beautiful melodic lines and many pleasing solo passages. At times a soprano of the first choir would have a solo, then one in the third, the fourth, and tenth would answer. At other times two, three, four, and five voices of different choirs would sing together, or the combined sections of all the choirs, each in its turn, would have a solo in rivalry with the other sections. Now two choirs would contend with each other, then two others would answer. Or three to five choirs would sing together, then one to five voices alone. At the Gloria Patri, all ten choirs resumed singing together. I must confess to you that I have never experienced such rapture, especially in the Hymn and in the Prose, where the master ordinarily tries to do his best, and where I did indeed hear perfectly beautiful melodies, cunningly contrived variations, excellent bits of invention, and very charmingly varied rhythms. At the antiphons there were again very good instrumental pieces scored for one to three violins with organ, or for several archlutes playing certain tunes in dance tempo and antiphonally.

But there is another sort of music which is not practiced in France, and which for that reason deserves a special description. This is called the recitative style. The best that I have heard was at the Oratory of San Marcello, where there is a congregation of Brothers of the Holy Cross made up of the greatest nobles of Rome, who, consequently, are able to bring together the best that Italy produces. And indeed, the most excellent musicians take pride in being there, and the most skilled composers vie for the honor of having their compositions heard there and try to offer the best fruits of their labors.

This admirable and delightful music is presented only on Fridays in Lent, from three to six o'clock. The church, smaller than the Sainte-Chapelle in Paris, has a spacious roof-loft at the end with an organ of moderate size, quite mellow in sound and suitable for voices. On the sides of the church, there are two other small galleries, where the best instrumentalists were placed. The singers begin with a psalm motet, and then the players of instruments furnish a very good symphony. Then is sung a story from the Old Testament, in the form of a religious drama, such as that of Susanna, Judith and Holofernes, or David and Goliath. Each soloist represents a character in the story and gives perfect expression to the force of the words. Next one of the most famous preachers delivers the sermon, after which is sung the gospel of the day, such as the story of the good Samaritan, the Canaanite woman, Lazarus, Mary Magdalen, or the passion of Our Lord, with the soloists portraying to perfection the various roles contained in the gospel passage. I cannot praise highly enough this recitative music; one has to have heard it in this setting to be able to appreciate its merit.

Most impressive of all was the great Frescobaldi displaying a thousand kinds of inventions on his harpsichord while the organ stuck to the main tune. It is not without justification that this famous organist of Saint Peter's has won so great a reputation in Europe; for, although his printed works give sufficient evidence of his skill, still, to get a true idea of his deep knowledge, one must hear him improvise toccatas full of admirable refinements and inventions. That is why he deserves to be held up as a model to our organists, to make them wish to come to Rome to hear him.

It was in the talented household of the singer Leonora Baroni that I was first obliged to display in Rome the talent which it has pleased God to give me, in the presence of ten or twelve of the most intelligent people in all Italy. They listened attentively and made a few flattering remarks, not untinged with jealousy. To test me further, they had Signora Leonora keep my viol and ask me to return the following day, which I did; and having been informed by a friend that they said that I did very well with artistically worked-out pieces, I gave them so many preludes and fantasies [i.e., improvisations] on this second occasion that they thought more highly of me than they had on the first. Afterwards, I was visited by curious gentlefolk, my viol being unwilling to leave my room except in deference to the purple, which it has been accustomed to obey for so many years. After winning the esteem of society people, I still had some distance to go before obtaining that of the professionals, who were a bit jaded and much too reluctant to give any praise to foreigners. They admitted, I was told, that I played solos very well, and that they had never heard so many parts played on the viol, but they doubted that I, being French, was able to improvise on a theme. You know, sir, that this is not where I shine the least. These very words having been said to me in the French Church on the eve of Saint Louis when I was attending an excellent concert given there, I resolved the next morning, inspired by the holy name of Louis, by the honor of our nation, and by the presence of twenty-three cardinals who attended the Mass, to go up into a gallery, where, having been received with applause, I was given fifteen or twenty notes on a little organ, after the third Kyrie Eleison, and I improvised on them with so much variety that they were quite happy, and had the cardinals ask me to play again after the Agnus Dei. I thought myself quite fortunate to be able to do so eminent a company such a small favor; they sent me another theme, gayer than the first, which I varied with so much imagination and with so many different rhythms and tempi that they were quite astonished, and came immediately to compliment me, but I withdrew to my room to rest.

This deed won me the highest honor I could have received; for the report of it, having spread throughout Rome, came as far as the ears of His Holiness, who did me the special favor a few days later of sending for me, and said to me, among other things, "We have heard that you have a special talent and we would like to hear you." I will not tell you here how happy His Holiness showed himself to be after having done me the honor of listening to me for more than two hours; some day you will see people worthy of being believed, and they will give you a full account of it.

André Maugars, *Response faite à un curieux sur le sentiment de la musique d'Italie, escrite à Rome le premier Octobre 1639,* trans. Walter H. Bishop, *Journal of the Viola da Gamba Society of America,* VIII (1971), 5–17. Reprinted by permission of Efrim Fruchtman, editor.

54

Music under the Sun King

During the seventeenth century, which the French still call their "grand siècle," music attended the French kings everywhere. They rose in the morning to the sound of the oboes and brasses of the Great Stable (Grande Écurie), they danced to the music of their famous "twenty-four violins" (also known as the Grande Bande), and were regaled at meals by a smaller band of fiddlers, known as the Petits Violons. In the Royal Chapel they heard the crowning musical expressions of their majesty and power: the *grands motets,* often sung by a choir of sixty, accompanied by an orchestra to match. At its height under Louis XIV, the royal musical establishment at Versailles numbered some 120 musicians. The description given by Pierre Rameau, dancing master to Louis XV, of a court ball suggests some of this splendor, and also the rigid formality that governed the proceedings. The dances came in a prescribed order, as in the standardized instrumental dance suite established by the lutenists and harpsichordists of Louis XIV's time.

Of the Ceremonial Observed at the King's Grand Ball

I believed it impossible to give a description more likely to inspire regard for the ceremonies and rules of private balls than first to attempt some brief account of the King's Grand Ball, since it is the most important of all such functions and should serve as a model for private balls in regard to the order of the proceedings, and the respect and politeness to be observed thereat.

In the first place, none is admitted to the royal circle save Princes and Princesses of the Blood Royal, the Dukes and Peers, and Duchesses, and afterwards the other Lords and Ladies of the Court according to their rank. The Ladies are seated in front, while the Lords are placed behind them. Nevertheless, I have ventured to represent the latter standing [see the illustration], to avoid confusion in my figures, and to make them more easily seen.

Everyone being thus placed in order, when His Majesty wishes the ball to begin he rises, and the whole company does likewise.

The King takes up his position at that end of the room where the dancing is to begin, which is near the musicians. In the time of the late King [Louis XIV], the Queen

The King's Grand Ball. The musicians are seated at the rear of the ballroom, near the entrance (that is, closest to the reader), the King at the front. The moment depicted is described in the next-to-last paragraph of the accompanying text, where Rameau details the extremely precise protocol that was observed on such occasions. (Pierre Rameau, *Le Maître à danser*, Paris, 1725, facing p. 1. Engraving by the author.)

danced with him, or in her absence, the first Princess of the Blood, and they placed themselves first. Then the company took up their station behind them, two by two, according to their rank. The Lords stood on the left side, the Ladies on the right. Retaining this order, they made their bows in turn. Afterwards the King and Queen led the *Branle* [a dance in which the couples stand in long sets] with which all Court Balls opened, and all the Lords and Ladies followed Their Majesties, each on their own side. At the conclusion of the strain, the King and Queen went to the end of the line, then the next couple led the *Branle* in their turn, after which they took up their position behind Their Majesties. This continued until all the couples had danced and the King and Queen were at the head again.

Then they danced the *Gavotte* in the same order as the *Branle,* each couple successively retiring to the end of the line. The dance finished, they made the same bows on parting as those with which the Ball opened.

Then came the *danses à deux.* Formerly the *Courante* was danced after the *Branles,* and Louis XIV, of happy memory, danced it better than any member of his Court. But nowadays the *Menuet* is danced after the *Branle.*

Therefore, when the King has danced the first *Menuet,* he goes to his seat and every one sits down, for while His Majesty is dancing all stand. Then the Prince who is to dance next, after His Majesty is seated, makes him a very profound bow, and then goes to the Queen or the first Princess of the Blood, and together they make the same bows as before the dance. Afterwards they dance the *Menuet,* and at the conclusion make the same bows again. Then the Lord makes a very low bow to the Princess on leaving her, because she will not appear again before the King.

But if His Majesty desire another dance to be performed, one of the First Gentlemen of the Bed Chamber announces his wish, which does not prevent the same bows being observed.

Pierre Rameau, *The Dancing Master* [1725], trans. Cyril Beaumont (London: C. W. Beaumont, 1931), 37–39.

55

Rationalistic Distaste for Opera

The French were skeptical of the whole idea of opera during its first century. They possessed a glorious and very intellectualized spoken drama, compared to which the Italian *dramma per musica* seemed a kind of child's babble, in which verisimilitude was impaired, credibility made difficult, and the emphasis placed not on the content of the play but on decorative trappings. Music was admitted to their theaters mainly in an incidental capacity, on a par with the spectacular "machines" on which gods descended or winged chariots took off. And as the great French dramatist Pierre Corneille (1606–84) makes clear in the preface to his *Andromède* (1650), a *pièce à machines,* the machines were far more integral to his conception of that sort of play than the music that accompanied them.

Each act, and the prologue as well, has its own set, and at least one flying machine, with a musical accompaniment which I have only used in order to entertain the ears of the spectators while their eyes are engaged in watching the descent or ascent of a machine, or are focused on something (like the fight between Perseus and the monster) which would prevent their paying attention to what the actors might be saying. But I have been very careful to have nothing sung that is essential to the understanding of the play, since words that are sung are usually understood poorly by the audience, owing to the confusion caused by the multitude of voices which pronounce them at once. It would make for a great obscurity in the body of the work if sung words were to try to impart to the audience anything of importance. But all this does not apply to the machines, which in this play are anything but a dispensable frill; they are the very essence and point of the play, and are so necessary that you could not omit a single one without causing the whole edifice to tumble.

Pierre Corneille, *Œuvres complètes*, I (Paris, 1834), 570. Trans. R. T.

> Opera in French made its real appearance only in the 1670s, with the works of Robert Cambert (c. 1628–77) and Jean-Baptiste Lully (1632–87). In England, outside of a few isolated works, such as Henry Purcell's *Dido and Aeneas* (1689), it was not established until the next century, and then it was an imported Italian opera rather than a native one that found favor. The prejudices that worked against the opera in these countries were nowhere expressed more forcefully than in a famous letter from a Frenchman, the courtier and wit Charles de Marguetel de Saint-Denis, Seigneur de Saint-Évremond (1613–1703), to an Englishman, the Duke of Buckingham. St.-Évremond gives a virtual catalogue of operatic offenses against reason. The points he raises have bedeviled opera throughout its history.

I have long had a desire to tell your Grace my thoughts of operas. The occasion I had of speaking of it, at the Duchesse Mazarin's, has rather increased than satisfied that desire; therefore I will gratify it in the discourse I now send your Grace.

I shall begin with great freedom, and tell your Grace, that I am no great admirer of Comedies in music, such as nowadays are in request. I confess I am not displeased with their magnificence; the Machines have something that is surprising; the Music, in some places, is charming; the whole together seems wonderful: but it must be granted me also, that this Wonderful is very tedious; for where the mind has so little to do, there the Senses must of necessity languish. After the first pleasure that surprise gives us, the eyes are taken up, and at length grow weary of being continually fixed upon the same object. In the beginning of the concerts, we observe the justness of the concords; and amidst all the varieties that unite to make the sweetness of the harmony, nothing escapes us. But 'tis not long before the instruments stun us; and the music is nothing else to our ears but a confused sound that suffers nothing to be distinguished. Now how is it possible to avoid being tired with the *Recitativo*, which has neither the charm of singing, nor the agreeable energy of speech? The soul, fatigued by a long attention, wherein it finds nothing to affect it, seeks some relief within itself; and the mind, which in vain expected to be entertained with the show, either gives way to idle musing, or is dissatisfied that it has nothing to employ it. In a word, the fatigue is so universal, that everyone wishes himself out of the house; and the only comfort that is left to the poor spectators, is the hope that the show will soon be over.

The reason why, commonly, I soon grow weary at Operas, is, that I never yet saw any which appeared not to me despicable, both as to the contrivance of the subject, and the poetry. Now it is in vain to charm the ears, or gratify the eyes, if the mind be not satisfied; for my soul being in better intelligence with my mind than with my senses, struggles against the impressions which it may receive, or at least does not give an agreeable consent to them, without which, even the most delightful objects can never afford me any great pleasure. An extravagance set off with music, dances, machines, and fine scenes, is a pompous piece of folly, but 'tis still a folly. Tho' the embroidery is rich, yet the ground it is wrought upon is such wretched stuff that it offends the sight.

There is another thing in Operas so contrary to nature, that I cannot be reconciled to it; and that is the singing of the whole piece, from beginning to end, as if the persons represented were ridiculously matched, and had agreed to treat in music both the most common, and most important affairs of life. Is it to be imagined that a master calls his servant, or sends him on an errand, singing; that one friend imparts a secret to another, singing; that men deliberate in council, singing; that orders in time of battle are given, singing; and that men are melodiously killed with swords and darts? This is the downright way to lose the life of representation, which without doubt is preferable to that of harmony: for, harmony ought to be no more than a bare attendant, and the great masters of the stage have introduced it as pleasing, not as necessary, after they have performed all that relates to the subject and discourse. Nevertheless, our thoughts run more upon the musician than the hero in the opera: Luigi [Rossi, 1597–1653, chief opera composer in Rome], [Pier Francesco] Cavalli [1602–76, Monteverdi's pupil and successor in Venice], and [Antonio] Cesti [1623–69, leader of Italian opera in Vienna] are still present to our imagination. The mind, not being able to conceive a hero that sings, thinks of the composer that set the song; and I don't question but that in Operas at the Palace-Royal, Lully is a hundred times more thought of than *Theseus* or *Cadmus* [heroes of Lully operas presented in 1675 and 1673, respectively].

I pretend not, however, to banish all manner of singing from the stage: there are some things which ought to be sung, and others that may be sung without trespassing against reason or decency: Vows, Prayers, Praises, Sacrifices, and generally all that relates to the services of the Gods, have been sung in all nations, and in all times; tender and mournful passions express themselves naturally in a sort of querulous tone; the expressions of love in its birth; the irresolution of a soul tossed by different movements, are proper matters for stanzas, as stanzas are for music. Everyone knows that the chorus was introduced upon the Grecian Theatre, and it is not to be denied, but that with equal reason it might be brought upon ours. So far, in my opinion, music may be allowed: all that belongs to conversation, all that relates to intrigues and affairs, all that belongs to council and action, is proper for actors to rehearse, but ridiculous in the mouth of musicians to sing. The Grecians made admirable tragedies where they had some singing; the Italians and the French make bad ones, where they sing all.

Would you know what an Opera is? I'll tell you, that it is an *odd medley of poetry and music, wherein the poet and musician, equally confined one by the other, take a world of pains to compose a wretched performance.* Not but that you may find agreeable words and very fine airs in our Operas; but you will more certainly find, at length, a dislike of the verses, where the genius of the poet is so crampt; and be cloyed with the singing, where the musician is spent by too long a service.

I forgot to speak to your Grace about *Machines,* so easy it is for man to forget that which he would have laid aside. Machines may satisfy the curiosity of ingenious men, who love mathematical inventions, but they'll hardly please persons of good judgment in the theatre: the more they surprise, the more they divert the mind from attending to the discourse; and the more admirable they are, the less tenderness and exquisite sense they leave in us, to be touched and charmed with the music. The ancients made no use of machines, but when there was a necessity of bringing in some God. If men love to be at expenses, let them lay out their money upon fine scenes, the use whereof is more natural and more agreeable than that of machines. Antiquity, which exposed their Gods, even at the gates, and chimney-corners; antiquity, I say, as vain and credulous as it was, exposed them, nevertheless, but very rarely upon the stage. Now the belief of them is gone, the Italians, in their Operas, have brought the pagan Gods again into the world; and have not scrupled to amuse men with these ridiculous vanities, only to make their pieces look great, by the introduction of that dazzling and surprising Wonderful. These stage deities have long enough abused Italy: but the people there being happily undeceived at last, are disgusted with those very Gods they were so fond of before, and have returned to plays, which, in truth, cannot pretend to the same exactness, but are not so fabulous, and which with a little indulgence, may pass well enough with men of sense.

A man runs a risk of having his judgment called in question, if he dares declare his good taste; and I advise others, when they hear any discourse of Operas, to keep their knowledge a secret to themselves. For my own part, who am past the age and time of signalizing myself in the world by a sense of the fashionable, and the merit of new fancies, I am resolved to strike in with good sense, and to follow reason, though in disgrace, with as much zeal, as if it were still in as great vogue as formerly. That which vexes me most at this our fondness for operas, is that they tend directly to ruin the finest thing we have, I mean *Tragedy*, than which nothing is more proper to elevate the soul, or more capable to form the mind.

After this long discourse, let us conclude, that the constitution of our Operas cannot be more faulty than it is. But it is to be acknowledged at the same time, that no man can perform better than *Lully*, upon an ill-conceived subject; and that it is not easy to out-do [Philippe] Quinault [1635–88, Lully's librettist] in what belongs to his part.

John Hayward (ed.), *The Letters of Saint Évremond*, trans. [in 1705] by Pierre Desmaizeaux (London: G. Routledge & Sons, Ltd., 1930), 205–17.

Against the strictures of critics like Saint-Évremond, the famous moralist Jean de La Bruyère (1645–96) expressed a love of spectacle and "machines" that was to become traditional in France, in a passage in defense of *le merveilleux* (what St. Évremond's eighteenth-century translator rendered as "the Wonderful") from his *Caractères* of 1688.

Nothing could be further from the truth than to maintain, as so many do, that machines are nothing but a childish amusement, fit only for marionette shows. Machines augment and embellish the works of the imagination, and aid the spectators in maintaining that sweet illusion which is the whole joy of the theater, and they add a strong dose of the *merveilleux* as well. There is no need for magical flights, chariots, or changes of scenery in plays by Corneille or Racine, but there is in opera. And the purpose of such spectacle is to hold the mind, the eye, and the ear equally enthralled.

Jean de La Bruyère, *Les Caractères* (Paris, 1874), 20–21. Trans. R. T.

56

A New Sound Ideal

The earliest "orchestral" music was that of the seventeenth-century opera theater and of the *vingt-quatre violons du roi*, the twenty-four instruments of the violin family that provided the ballroom music of the French court. The violin, long used by street musicians, was a relative newcomer to high society and the lofty pretensions of the opera. It was warmly greeted by some, like the French encyclopedic theorist Marin Mersenne (see p. 137), who in the third book of his *Harmonie universelle* (1637), which deals with instruments, gave the violin pride of place as the harbinger of a new "sound ideal" in tune with Baroque aesthetics generally.

The violin is one of the simplest instruments that can be imagined, in that it has only four strings and is without frets on its neck. That is why all the just consonances can be performed on it, as with the voice, inasmuch as one stops it where one wishes. This makes it more perfect than the fretted instruments [like the viol and lute], in which one is forced to use some temperament and to decrease or increase the greatest part of the consonances, and to alter all the musical intervals.

To this it can be added that the violin's tones have more effect on the minds of the listeners than those of the lute or of the other stringed instruments, because they are more vigorous and come more into notice, because of the great tension of their strings and their high sounds. And those who have heard the Twenty-four Violins of the King avow that they have never heard anything more ravishing or more powerful. Thus it comes that this instrument is the most proper for playing for dancing as is experienced in the ballet and everywhere else. Now the beauties and graces that are practiced on it are so great in number that it can be preferred to all the other instruments, since the strokes of the bow are so delightful sometimes that one has a great discontent to hear the end, particularly when they are mixed with ornaments of the left hand, which force the listeners to declare the violin to be king of instruments.

For even though many parts are played together on the lute and the spinet, and though consequently these instruments are more harmonious, nevertheless, those who judge the excellence of music and its instruments by the beauty and excellence of airs and *chansons* have rather powerful reasons for maintaining that the violin is the best, from the great effect it has on the passions and affections of the body and soul.

Marin Mersenne, *Harmonie universelle, Book III*, trans. Roger E. Chapman (The Hague: M. Nijhoff, 1957), 235.

But Mersenne tells only one side of the story. As an instrument associated with Italy and things Italian, the violin was met with resistance in many French quarters. Its loudness was taken for stridency, its brilliance for vulgarity. The rivalry between the violin and its Italianate repertoire versus the more traditional French courtly and chamber instruments (particularly the viola da gamba, called *basse de viole* in French) was carried on for over a century before the violin emerged as undisputed victor. A late and particularly bitter opponent of the instrument was the Abbé Hubert Le Blanc who in 1740 wrote a lengthy diatribe entitled *Defense of the viola da gamba against the designs of the violin and the pretensions of the cello*. Le Blanc saw the violin as an agent of the Italian war of musical conquest initiated by the opera, which had given Italian musicians virtual hegemony over Europe by the end of the seventeenth century.

Sultan Violin, an abortion and a pygmy, took it into his head to challenge the universal dominion of the viola da gamba in France. Not content with his portion, Italy, he proposed to invade the nearby States and to do to the viola da gamba what the latter had already done to the lute, theorbo, and guitar (not even excepting King David's harp). In his small body there resided an extraordinary strength, and he could speak of nothing else than of ruining his rivals, of interring his adversaries alive, and of burying their dulcet *pièces* under mountains of his own piercing and piquant compositions.

Sultan Violin's two acolytes were called Monsieur Harpsichord and Sir Violoncello. They joined together to temper the violin's stridency (since without them the sting would be felt too much), like salt or spice which ought, for seasoning, only to be noticed if it is lacking, and should never make its presence too perceptible.

To attack the viola da gamba, to outshout her, to speak louder than she, to jump on her body—Sultan Violin would do it gladly if that were all it took to conquer her, but it was essential to put up a good fight, and above all to make assaults where the viol had long since been established in friendly territory. It would be hard for a parvenu to penetrate among the great who were the viol's protectors. So the violin, who was then neither Sultan nor so proud as he is now, approached the harpsichord and the violoncello and humbly said to them, "Fine sirs, the first of you is already established among the ladies for whom Couperin writes his *piéces* [see p. 200], but the other is relegated to the choir [the early cellos were used mainly in church]. I propose that you join me and that between us, we claim to represent the three instruments which alone are necessary in music, which can surpass all others, and for whose absence nothing can compensate."

They thanked him *affettuoso,* making him the compliment that he was Alexander the Great among instruments. They saluted him as Attila, the scourge of the viola da gamba and exterminator of all half-breed instruments. Thereupon they discussed the methods they would use.

The Violin said, "They are all prepared. With my concertos we will equal the Opera in large audiences, and with solo sonatas and trio sonatas I will annihilate all their asthmatic *pièces.* They'll never get away with saying, 'Ah! I'm not in practice,' not to mention protestations about memory slips. I, the Violin, vow that I will never be caught napping, nor will I make inappropriate excuses for myself."

The Violoncello, who up to now had been regarded as a miserable dunce, a poor hated devil, who had been dying for want of a square meal, now flattered himself that he would receive the viol's caresses. Already he imagined such bliss that he wept tenderly.

The Harpsichord rejoiced at becoming a commercial instrument. The ladies who, in the heyday for *pièces,* only amused themselves on the harpsichord until they got married, would no longer be able to dismiss him after marriage, when sonatas would come to prevail.

The Violin, to be sure, could not compete with the viol in delicacy of moving sound or in chordal playing, so refined in its resonance when heard in the proper place for appreciating its attributes at close range. So to allow themselves to make an impression, the trio moved the setting to an immense hall, where there would be many effects which were as prejudicial to the viol as they would be favorable to the violin.

Hubert Le Blanc, *Défense de la basse de viole contre les entreprises du violon et les prétensions du violoncel,* trans. Barbara Garvey Jackson, *Journal of the Viola da Gamba Society of America,* X (1973), 24–27. Reprinted by permission of Efrim Fruchtman, editor.

57

The Baroque Sonata

The violin's most significant medium was the sonata. The earliest extended genre of "absolute" instrumental music, the sonata had a mixed and complicated ancestry. The canzona and toccata, genres of music traditionally employed as embellishment and filler in the church service, gave way to the *sonata da chiesa,* which originally served the same purposes. The long traditions of dance music for instrumental ensemble in the Renaissance and early Baroque gave rise to the *sonata da camera,* which is really only another term for a dance suite. The two types of sonata did not remain stylistically distinct for long. The Englishman Roger North (1653–1734), writing at the end of the seventeenth century, describes what begins as a typical *sonata da chiesa* (four movements arranged slow-fast-slow-fast, with the fast movements fugal), but in place of the last movement he describes the kind of dances usually found in the *sonata da camera.*

Now in our common Sonatas for Instruments, the entrance is usually with all the fulness of harmony figurated and adorned that the master at that time could contrive, and this is termed *Grave,* most aptly representing seriousness and thought. The movement is as of one so disposed, and if he were to speak, his utterance would be according, and his matter rational and arguing. The upper parts only fulfill the harmony, without any singularity in the movement; but all join in a common tendency to provoke in the hearers a series of thinking according as the air invites, whether Magnifick or Querulous, which the sharp or flat key determines. When there hath been enough of this, which if it be good will not be very soon, variety enters, and the parts fall to action, and move quick; and the entrance of this denouement is with a *fugue.* This hath a cast of business or debate, of which the melodious point is made the subject; and accordingly it is wrought over and under till, like waves upon water, it is spent and vanisheth, leaving the music to proceed smoothly, and as if it were satisfied and contented. After this comes properly in the *Adagio,* which is a laying all affairs aside, and lolling in a sweet repose: which state the music represents by a most tranquil but full harmony, and dying gradually, as one that falls asleep. After this is over Action is resumed, and the various humors of men diverting themselves (and even their facetiousness and wit) are represented, as the master's fancy at the time invites, wherein the instrument or ingredient of the connection with human life is (sometimes the touch or breaking, but chiefly) the measure; as a *Gavott,* which is an old French dance; and so *Minuets, Courants,* and other dancing expressions. There is often the *Andante,* which is an imitation of walking *equis passibus* [with even steps]; there is a *Ricercata,* which is to imitate a looking about as for a thing lost; and divers imitations of men's humors well known to the performers, so need not be described; and for the most part concluding with a *Gigue,* which is like men (half foxed) dancing for joy, and so good night.

John Wilson (ed.), *Roger North on Music* (London: Novello, 1959), 117–18.

But North, like Le Blanc (see p. 174), was not entirely happy with the craze for sonatas. They were a soloist's and professional's repertoire. In the passage below, North describes the music he had loved in his youth: that of the consort of viols, whose "airs" and "fancies" were the cream of English instrumental music from the late Elizabethan period up to the time of the Civil War. This was a gentleman's and an amateur's art, chamber music in the truest sense; that is, a recreational music whose intended audience was the performers themselves.

My Grandfather, Dudley the Lord North, took a fancy to a wood he had about a mile from his house, called Bansteads, situated in a dirty soil, and of ill access. But he cut glades, and made arbors in it. Here he would convoke his musical family, and songs were made and set for celebrating the joys there, which were performed, and provisions carried up for more important regale of the company. The consorts were usually all viols to the organ or harpsichord. The violin came in late, and imperfectly. When the hands were well supplied, then a whole chest went to work, that is six viols, music being formed for it; which would seem a strange sort of music now, being an interwoven hum-drum, compared with the brisk *battuta* [beat] derived from the French and Italian. But even that hum-drum in its kind is well; and I must make a great difference when music is only to fill vacant time, which lies on hand.

And I may justly say, that the late improvements of Music have been the ruin, and almost banishment of it from the nation. Now when Music was kept in an easy temperate air, practicable to moderate and imperfect hands, who for the most part are more earnest upon it than the most adept, it might be retained in the country. But since it is arrived to such a pitch of perfection, that even masters, unless of the prime, cannot entertain us, the plain way becomes contemptible and ridiculous, therefore must needs be laid aside. By this you may judge what profit the public hath from the improvement of Music. I am almost of Plato's opinion, that the state ought to govern the use of it, but not for their reasons, but for the use it may be in diverting noble families in a generous way of country living.

Wilson, *North on Music,* 10–12.

The chamber music of Henry Purcell (1659–95) illustrates the change in taste of which North speaks. One of Purcell's earliest important works was a set of fantasias for a consort of viols in the style of North's "interwoven hum-drum." These were composed, according to notations on the manuscript scores, during the summer months of 1680. A scant three years later, Purcell came forward with his *Sonatas of Three Parts: Two Violins and Bass, to the Organ or Harpsichord.* These were thoroughly and consciously Italianate in style, the first works of the kind to be published in England. Purcell's preface is an interesting document. He takes pains to explain to his readers the Italian tempo markings which he has adopted in keeping with his wholesale espousal of Italianism. These terms, of course, remain with us to this day, a memento of a period in which Italy was the recognized leader in all things musical.

TO THE READER

Ingenuous Reader,

Instead of an elaborate harangue on the beauty and the charms of Musick (which after all the learned Encomions that words can contrive commends itself best by the performances of a skilful hand, and an angelical voice) I shall say but a very few things by way of Preface, concerning the following Book, and its Author: for its Author, he has faithfully endeavour'd a just imitation of the most fam'd Italian Masters; principally, to bring the Seriousness and gravity of that sort of Musick into vogue, and reputation among our Countrymen, whose humor, 'tis time now, should begin to loath the levity, and balladry of our neighbours. The attempt he confesses to be bold, and daring, there being Pens and Artists of more eminent abilities, much better qualify'd for the imployment than his, or himself, which he well hopes these his weak endeavours, will in due time provoke, and enflame to a more accurate undertaking. He is not asham'd to own his unskilfulness in the

Italian Language; but that's the unhappiness of his Education, which cannot justly be accounted his fault, however he thinks he may warrantably affirm, that he is not mistaken in the power of the Italian Notes, or elegancy of their Compositions, which he would recommend to the English Artists. There has been neither care, nor industry wanting, as well in contriving, as revising the whole Work; which had been abroad in the world much sooner, but that he has now thought fit to cause the whole Thorough Bass to be Engraven, which was a thing quite besides his first Resolutions. It remains only that the English Practitioner be enform'd, that he will find a few terms of Art perhaps unusual to him, the chief of which are these following: *Adagio* and *Grave,* which import nothing but a very slow movement: *Presto Largo, Poco Largo,* or *Largo* by itself, a middle movement [i.e., a medium tempo]: *Allegro,* and *Vivace,* a very brisk, swift, or fast movement: *Piano,* soft. The Author has no more to add, but his hearty wishes, that his Book may fall into no other hands but theirs who carry Musical Souls about them; for he is willing to flatter himself into a belief, that with such his labours will seem neither unpleasant, nor unprofitable.

VALE.

Henry Purcell, *Works,* V (London, 1983), Preface (facsimile).

The first French sonatas were the work of François Couperin (1668–1733), called "le Grand" to set him apart from other members of his distinguished musical family. One of the few French musicians not altogether hostile to things Italian, Couperin admired the works of Arcangelo Corelli (1653–1713), and in his own compositions strove to bridge the gap between the French and Italian "tastes" of his day. Although he wrote sonatas as early as 1692, Couperin did not publish them until 1726, in a collection called—fittingly enough—*Les Nations.* In the preface, Couperin revealed the clever ruse by which his sonatas were first introduced. Like most works of their kind, they are scored for two violins and basso continuo, and hence Couperin refers to them as "trios."

It has been some years now since some of these trios have been composed. Several manuscripts containing them have been circulating in use, all of which I consider untrustworthy, owing to the negligent ways of copyists. From time to time I have increased their number, and I believe that true lovers of art will find them to their taste. The first Sonata in this collection was both the first one that I composed, and the first to be composed in France. Its history is rather unusual.

Delighted with the sonatas of Signor Corelli, whose works I shall love as long as I live (even as I shall the French works of Monsieur de Lully), I made bold to compose one myself, which I then had performed in the same concert series where I had heard Corelli's. Knowing the hostility with which the French greet foreign novelties of all kinds, and lacking self-confidence, I did myself a good turn with a little white lie. I pretended that an actual relative of mine in the service of the King of Sardinia had sent me a sonata by a new Italian author: I rearranged the letters of my name in such a way as to form an Italian-sounding name [Rupecino? Pernucio?], which I entered on my sonata. The sonata was devoured enthusiastically, and I will keep silent on the accolades it received. I was encouraged by this, however, and wrote others. And my Italianized name brought me, behind the mask, as it were, great applause. My sonatas, fortunately, have enjoyed sufficient popularity so that my ruse has caused me no embarrassment. I have compared these first sonatas with those I have written since, and I have not seen fit to alter or add anything much. I have merely joined them to grand suites of *piéces*, to which the sonatas serve simply as preludes or as a sort of introduction.

I hope that the impartial public will be pleased with them. For there will always be gainsayers, more to be dreaded than good critics (from whom one often can receive good advice, contrary to their intention). The former are despicable, and I settle herewith with them in advance and with interest! I still have a rather considerable number of these trios; enough to make at some time to come a volume as big as the present one.

François Couperin, Preface to *Les Nations: Sonades et Suites de Symphonies en Trio, en quatre livres séparés pour la comodité des Académies de Musique et des concerts particuliers* (Paris, 1726). Trans. R. T.

58

Modern Concert Life Is Born

Just as it was in every area of political, economic, and social life, the English middle class was far ahead of its Continental counterpart in the active support and consumption of music. A widespread taste for "listener's music" led to the institution of public concerts in London during the reign of Charles II. These began as a kind of collective patronage, whereby, through subscription or the payment of an admission price, the services of musicians could be secured by those who had not the wherewithal to employ them privately. Roger North (see p. 176), an eyewitness to this development, described the earliest concert series anywhere (organized in London in the 1670s by John Banister) in his memoirs, "The Musical Grammarian." The first lasting and significant concert series on the Continent was the Concert Spirituel, organized in Paris in 1725; in the German cities, the trend began about 1740. In Italy, where opera as a form of public entertainment dated back to 1637, concerts continued to be privately organized by learned academies for their members—hence the occasional use of the term "academy" for a concert, both in Italy and elsewhere, as late as the nineteenth century.

But how and by what steps Music shot up into such request, as to crowd out from the stage even comedy itself, and to sit down in her place and become of such mighty value and price as we now know it to be, is worth inquiring after. The first attempt was low: a project of old Banister, who was a good violin, and a theatrical composer. He opened an obscure room in a public house in White friars; filled it with tables and seats, and made a side box with curtains for the music. Sometimes consort, sometimes solos, of the violin, flageolet, bass viol, lute and song *all'Italiana,* and such varieties diverted the company, who paid at coming in. One shilling a piece, call for what you please, pay the reckoning, and *Welcome gentlemen.* Here came most of the shack-performers [i.e., vagabond players] in town, and much company to hear; and divers musical curiosities were presented, as, for instance, Banister himself, upon a flageolet in consort, which was never heard before or since, unless imitated by the high manner upon the violin. But this lasted not long, nor another meeting of like kind near St. Paul's, headed by one Ben Wellington, for voices to an organ, where who would, that was gifted, might perform, and no payment, but the reckoning.

And upon this occasion and further encouragement, a place in York Buildings was built express and equipt for Music, to which was made a great resort and profit to the masters, and so might have continued but for the unfortunate interfering with the plays. I observed well the music here, and although the best masters in their turns, as well solo, as concerted, showed their gifts, yet I cannot say, whatever the music was, that the entertainment was good; because it consisted of broken incoherent parts; now a consort, then a lutenist, then a *violino solo,* then flutes, then a song, and so piece after piece, the time sliding away, while the masters blundered and swore in shifting places, and one might perceive that they performed ill out of spite to one another; whereas an entertainment ought to proceed as a drama, firework, or indeed every public delight, by judicious steps, one setting off another, and the whole in a series connected and concluding in a perfect acme, and then ceasing all at once. All which cannot be done but by an absolute Dictator, who may coerce and punish the republican mob of music masters. So this very good design failed; but ample amends hath been made since.

John Wilson (ed.), *Roger North on Music* (London: Novello, 1959), 302–305.

59

The Mature Baroque: The Doctrine of the Affections

For Baroque musicians, the nature of human emotion (described in terms of "passions" and "affections") was a vital philosophical issue. If emotions could be somehow classified and ordered, their "imitation" in art could be brought under fully rational control. Here the psychological investigations of Descartes laid the essential groundwork. In his *Passions of the Soul* (1645–46), his last published work, the great French philosopher attempted to make the desired classification and tried to go further and explain the workings of the passions in physiological terms. The result was that the passions were rationalized; they became, literally, "objects," as Descartes stresses in paragraph 46, below. They had, in his view, discreteness, perceptible duration, and distinctness. And these attributes made them perfect objects for artistic imitation. Further, Descartes's description of the physiological processes that underlay and determined the passions was extremely suggestive to musicians in search of technical means for analogizing the passions in tones. Below we give Descartes's general introduction to the subject, his classification and definition of the basic affections, and in the case of two (joy and sorrow), his physiological explication of their mechanism.

[1.] On proceeding to treat of the passions, I observe that whatever occurs in the way of novelty or change, is by the philosophers ordinarily termed a passion in respect of the subject to which it happens and an action in respect of what causes it to happen.

Though agent and patient are often very different, the action and the passion are thus always one and the same thing. We are allowing it these two names because of the two diverse subjects to which we can refer it. I note that we are not aware of any subject which acts upon our soul more immediately than does the body with which it is conjoined, and that consequently we ought to recognize that what in the soul is a passion is in the body usually an action.

[28.] Experience shows that those who are the most excited by their passions are not those who know them best, and that their passions are to be counted as belonging to that group of cognitions which the close alliance of mind and body renders confused and obscure. We may also entitle them feelings, as being received into the soul in the same fashion as the objects of the external senses, and otherwise not known by it. But it is best to name them emotions of the soul, not only because this name can be given to all the changes which take place in it, i.e., to all the various thoughts which the soul can know, but especially because, of all the various kinds of thoughts it can have, there are no others which agitate and unsettle it so powerfully as do these passions.

[34.] Let us allow that the soul has its chief seat in a small gland which is in mid-brain and that from there it radiates through all the rest of the body owing to the intervention of the animal spirits, the nerves, and even the blood, which, participating in the impressions of the spirits, can carry them by way of the arteries to all its members.

[35.] If, for example, we see some animal approach us, the light reflected from its body depicts two images of it, one in each of our eyes. The two images, by way of the optic nerves, form two others in the interior surface of the brain which faces its cavities. From these, by way of the spirits which fill these cavities, the images then radiate towards the small gland which the spirits encircle, and do so in such fashion that the movement which constitutes each point of one of the images tends towards the same point of the gland as does the movement constituting that point in the other image which represents the same part of the animal; and in this way the two brain-images form but one image on the gland, which, acting immediately on the soul, causes it to see the shape of the animal.

[36.] Moreover, if this shape is very startling and terrifying, i.e., if it is closely related to things which have previously been hurtful to the body, it excites in the soul the passion of anxious apprehension, and thereupon either of courage, or it may be of fear or terror, according to the varying temperament of the body or the strength of the soul, and according as it has been by defense or by flight that we have hitherto secured ourselves against the harmful things to which the impression stands related. Such past actions so predispose the brain, in certain men, that the spirits reflected from the image thus formed on the gland then proceed to take their course, partly in the nerves which serve in turning the back and in moving the legs for flight, partly in those which enlarge or contract the heart, partly in those which so enlarge or contract the orifices of the heart, or which so agitate the other parts whence the blood is sent to the heart, that this blood, being there rarefied in some unusual manner, conveys to the brain animal spirits suited to the maintenance and fortifying of the passion of fear, suited, that is to say, to the holding open, or to the re-opening, of those pores of the brain which conduct them to those same nerves. And since the pores, by which they pass, mainly operate through the small nerves which serve to contract or enlarge the orifices of the heart, this causes the soul to feel the pain chiefly in the heart.

[37.] This is also true of all the other passions; they are one and all chiefly caused by the spirits which are contained in the cavities of the brain, in so far as these operate by way of the nerves which serve to enlarge or contract the orifices of the heart. From this it can be clearly understood why in my definition I have declared each of them to be caused by some one particular movement of the spirits.

[46.] There is one special reason why the soul is unable to change or suppress its passions in an effortless manner, and this reason is what has led me, in defining them, to say that they are not merely caused, but also upheld and fortified by some particular movement of the animal spirits. They are almost all accompanied by some commotion taking place in the heart, and consequently also in all the blood and animal spirits, so that until this commotion has subsided, the passions remain present to our thought in the same manner as sensible objects are present to us in thought during the time they act on our sense-organs. Just as the soul, in making itself closely attentive to some other thing, can prevent itself from hearing a slight noise or feeling a slight pain, but cannot in the same way escape hearing thunder or feeling fire burning the hand, it is similarly easy to overcome the lesser passions, but not those that are more violent and powerful; we have to await the abating of the commotion in the blood and spirits. The most the will can do while this commotion is in its full strength, is to refuse consent to its effects, and to restrain several of the movements to which it disposes the body. For instance if anger causes the hand to be upraised for striking, the will can usually arrest it from further action; if fear incites the legs to flight, the will can restrain them, and so in all other like cases.

[69.] There are only six simple and primitive passions, i.e., wonder, love, hatred, desire, joy, and sadness. All the others are composed of some of these six, or are species of them. That is why, in order that their multitude may not embarrass my readers, I shall here treat the six primitive passions separately; and afterwards I shall show in what way all the others derive from them their origin.

[70.] *Of Wonder, its definition and cause.* Wonder is a sudden surprise of the soul which causes it to apply itself to consider with attention the objects which seem to it rare and extraordinary. It is thus primarily caused by the impression we have in the brain which represents the object as rare, and as consequently worthy of much consideration; then afterwards by the movement of the spirits, which are disposed by this impression to tend with great force towards the part of the brain where it is, in order to fortify and conserve it there; as they are also disposed by it to pass thence into the muscles which serve to retain the organs of the senses in the same situation in which they are, so that it is still maintained by them, if it is by them that it has been formed.

[71.] And this passion has this particular characteristic, that in it we do not notice that it is accompanied by any change which occurs in the heart and blood like the other passions. The reason of this is that not having good or evil as its object, but only the knowledge of the thing that we wonder at, it has no relation with the heart and blood on which all the good of the body depends, but only with the brain where are the organs of the senses which are the instruments of this knowledge.

[79.] *The definition of Love and Hate.* Love is an emotion of the soul caused by the movement of the spirits which incites it to join itself willingly to objects which appear to it to be agreeable. And hatred is an emotion caused by the spirits which incite the soul to desire to be separated from the objects which present themselves to it as hurtful. I say that these emotions are caused by the spirits in order to distinguish love and hate, which are passions and depend on the body, both from the judgments which also induce the soul by its free will to unite itself with the things which it esteems to be good, and to separate itself from those it holds to be evil, and from the emotions which these judgments excite of themselves in the soul.

[91.] *The definition of Joy.* Joy is an agreeable emotion of the soul in which consists the enjoyment that the soul possesses in the good which the impressions of the brain represent to it as its own. I say that it is in this emotion that the enjoyment of the good consists; for as a matter of fact the soul receives no other fruits from all the good things that it possesses; and while it has no joy in these, it may be said that it does not enjoy them more than if it did not possess them at all. I add also that it is of the good which the impressions of the brain represent to it as its own, in order not to confound this joy, which is a passion, with the joy that is purely intellectual, and which comes into the soul by the action of the soul alone, and which we can call an agreeable emotion excited in it, in which the enjoyment consists which it has in the good which its understanding represents to it as its own. It is true that while the soul is united to the body this intellectual joy can hardly fail to be accompanied by that which is a passion; for as soon as our understanding perceives that we possess some good thing, even though this good may be so different from all that pertains to body that it is not in the least capable of being imagined, imagination does not fail immediately to make some impression in the brain from which proceeds the movement of the spirits that excites the passion of joy.

[104.] *The movement of the blood and spirits in Joy.* In joy it is not so much the nerves of the spleen, the liver or the stomach, or the intestines, which are active, as those which are in the whole of the rest of the body, and particularly that which is round the orifices of the heart, which, opening and enlarging these orifices, supplies the means whereby the blood which the other nerves drive from the veins to the heart may enter there and issue forth in a larger quantity than usual. And because the blood which then enters the heart has already passed and repassed there several times, having come from the arteries to the veins, it dilates very easily and produces spirits whose parts, being very equal and subtle, are proper for the formation and fortification of the impressions of the brain which give to the soul thoughts that are gay and peaceful.

[92.] *The definition of Sadness.* Sadness is a disagreeable languor in which consists the discomfort and unrest which the soul receives from evil, or from the defect which the impressions of the brain set before it as pertaining to it. And there also is an intellectual sadness which is not passion, but which hardly ever fails to be accompanied by it.

[105.] *The movement of the blood and spirits in Sadness.* In sadness, the openings of the heart are much contracted by the small nerve which surrounds them, and the blood of the veins is in nowise agitated, which brings it to pass that very little of it goes towards the heart and yet the passages by which the juice of the food flows from the stomach and the intestines towards the liver remain open, which causes the appetite not to diminish at all, excepting when hatred, which is often united to sadness, closes them.

[86.] *The definition of Desire.* The passion of desire is an agitation of the soul caused by the spirits which dispose it to wish for the future the things which it represents to itself as agreeable. Thus we do not only desire the presence of the absent good, but also the conservation of the present, and further, the absence of evil, both of that which we already have, and of that which we believe we might experience in time to come.

[87.] I know very well that usually in the schools the passion which makes for the search after the good which alone is called desire is opposed to that which makes for the avoidance of evil, which is called aversion. But inasmuch as there is no good whose privation is not an evil, nor any evil considered in a positive sense, whose privation is not a good, and that in investigating riches, for example, we necessarily shun poverty, in fleeing from sickness we make for health, and so on with other things, it seems to me that it is always an identical movement which makes for the search after good, and at the same time for the avoidance of the evil that is contrary to it.

[148.] *The exercise of virtue is a sovereign remedy against the passions.* It is certain that, provided our soul is always possessed of something to content itself with inwardly, none of the troubles that come from elsewhere have any power to harm it, but rather serve to increase its joy, inasmuch as, seeing that it cannot be harmed by them, it is made sensible of its perfection. And in order that our souls may thus have something with which to be content, it has no need but to follow exactly after virtue. For whoever has lived in such a way that his conscience cannot reproach him for ever having failed to perform those things which he has judged to be the best (which is what I here call following after virtue) receives from this a satisfaction which is so powerful in rendering him happy that the most violent efforts of the passions never have sufficient power to disturb the tranquillity of his soul.

[212]. For the rest, the soul may have pleasures of its own, but as to those which are common to it and the body, they depend entirely on the passions, so that the men whom they can most move are capable of partaking most of the enjoyment in this life. It is true that such men may also find most bitterness when they do not know how to employ them well, or fortune is contrary to them. But the principal use of prudence or self-control is that it teaches us to be masters of our passions, and to so control and guide them that the evils which they cause are quite bearable, and that we even derive joy from them all.

Through [46]: Norman Kemp Smith (ed. and trans.), *Descartes' Philosophical Writings* (London: Macmillan, 1952), 285, 292, 295–97, 300–301; by permission of Macmillan, London and Basingstoke. From [69] to the end: Elizabeth S. Haldane and G. R. T. Ross (trans.), *The Philosophical Works of Descartes,* I (Cambridge: Cambridge University Press, 1911), 362, 366, 369–70, 372, 377, 398–99, 427; by permission of Cambridge University Press.

Among the musicians (once again, mainly German) who turned Cartesian psychology into systematic musical theory, Johann Mattheson (1681–1764) was outstanding. A composer and performer of considerable reputation, Mattheson was also an encyclopedic theorist in the tradition of Praetorius and Mersenne. In his *Der volkommene Capellmeister (The Complete Music Master)*, published in 1739, Mattheson openly acknowledged his debt to Descartes and proceeded to apply the Frenchman's teachings to the establishment of precepts for musical composition. This new theory of emotion in music (the *Affektenlehre*, or "The Doctrine of the Affections," as it was often called) was a significant departure from the earlier doctrine of figures. Now the object of imitation was no longer speech, the exterior manifestation of emotion, but the emotion itself, in terms at once more direct and more generalized. Emotions were represented not as transient feelings embodied in a free and flexible recitative, but as monolithic, static, "objective" phenomena to be musically concretized by a whole piece of coherent, often monumental structure. The most direct realization of this theory is found in the *opera seria* of the late Baroque, with its stylized and rigidly classified aria types associated with the various "affections." Many of these were based on recognizable dance rhythms, thus supporting Mattheson's classification of dance types as analogies to the emotional typology he had taken over from Descartes.

The most important and outstanding part of the science of sound is the part that examines the effects of well-disposed sounds on the emotions and the soul. This, as may be readily seen, is material that is as far-reaching as it is useful. To the musical practitioner it is of even more importance than to the theoretician, despite its primary concern with observation. Of much assistance here is the doctrine of the temperaments and emotions, concerning which Descartes is particularly worthy of study, since he has done much in music. This doctrine teaches us to make a distinction between the minds of the listeners and the sounding forces that have an effect on them.

What the passions are, how many there are, how they may be moved, whether they should be eliminated or admitted and cultivated, appear to be questions belonging to the field of the philosopher rather than the musician. The latter must know, however, that the sentiments are the true material of virtue, and that virtue is nought but a well-ordered and wisely moderate sentiment. Those affects, on the other hand, which are our strongest ones, are not the best and should be clipped or held by the reins. This is an aspect of morality which the musician must master in order to represent virtue and evil with his music and to arouse in the listener love for the former and hatred for the latter. For it is the true purpose of music to be, above all else, a moral lesson.

Those who are learned in the natural sciences know how our emotions function physically, as it were. It would be advantageous to the composer to have a little knowledge of this subject. Since, for example, joy is an *expansion* of our vital spirits, it follows sensibly and naturally that this affect is best expressed by large and expanded intervals. Sadness, on the other hand, is a *contraction* of those same subtle parts of our bodies. It is, therefore, easy to see that the narrowest intervals are the most suitable. Love is a *diffusion* of the spirits. Thus, to express this passion in composing, it is best to use intervals of that nature. Hope is an *elevation* of the spirit; despair, on the other hand, a *casting down* of the same. These are subjects that can well be represented by sound, especially when other circumstances (tempo in particular) contribute their share. In such a manner one can form a concrete picture of all the emotions and try to compose accordingly.

Pride, haughtiness, arrogance, etc., all have their respective proper musical color as well. Here the composer relies primarily on boldness and pompousness. He thus has the opportunity to write all sorts of fine-sounding musical figures that demand special seriousness and bombastic movement. They must never be too quick or falling, but always ascending. The opposite of this sentiment lies in humility, patience, etc., treated in music by abject-sounding passages without anything that might be elevating. The latter passions, however, agree with the former in that none of them allow for humor and playfulness.

Music, although its main purpose is to please and to be graceful, must sometimes provide dissonances and harsh-sounding passages. To some extent and with the suitable means, it must provide not only unpleasant and disagreeable things, but even frightening and horrible ones. The spirit occasionally derives some peculiar pleasure even from these.

Mattheson now proceeds to the discussion of dance types as analogies to the affections.

The *minuet*, whether it be made especially for playing, singing, or dancing, has no other affect than *moderate gaiety*.

Next let us look at the *gavotte,* whose affect is truly *jubilant joy.* The *hopping* quality of the *gavotte* is its true property. A melody having a more fluid, smooth, gliding, and connected character than the *gavotte* is the *bourrée.* Such melodies seem contented, obliging, unconcerned, relaxed, careless, comfortable, and yet pleasing. We continue by taking up the *rigaudon,* whose melody is, in my opinion, one of the most pleasing. Its character is one of *flirtatious pleasantry.* Our next examination concerns the *march,* which can be either serious or droll. Its true character is *heroic* and *fearless,* yet it is not wild or running. The composer must form his picture by thinking of a hero, with a firm spirit that is unseated or shaken by nothing. Such a spirit is swayed neither by clever arguments nor by heated passions. The picture the composer should bear in mind is not that of a raging fire but of courageous warmth.

We shall let something fresh and quick follow these serious melodies, namely, the *gigue,* whose special quality is *hot and hurried eagerness,* anger that soon evaporates. The *loures,* or slow and dotted gigues, by contrast, exhibit a *proud* and *pompous* character, which makes them very popular in Spain. The *canarie* must have a very *desirous quality* and quickness, but it should be somewhat simple-minded.

All these remarks are not aimed so much at an understanding of particular dances as at the complete comprehension of the wealth contained in them and the clever use of this wealth. They are useful in many compositions that are seemingly of a more important nature, especially in tasteful vocal music and in the expression of all kinds of passions. The incredible ideas that may flow from these unassuming sources are countless. Bear this remark in mind! There are arias in gigue tempo, just as there are arias based on the other species of melody. This applies to the very effective *loure* type of *gigue* especially. With nothing more than the gigue I can express four important affects: anger or eagerness, pride, simple-minded desire, and flightiness. On the other hand, if I had to set *open-hearted* and *frank* words to music, I should choose no species of melody other than the Polish one, the *polonaise.* In my opinion, this is its quality, character, and affect. A people's character seldom remains hidden in its entertainment and dances, even though it might on other occasions.

Hans Lenneberg, "Johann Mattheson on Affect and Rhetoric," *Journal of Music Theory,* II (1958), 47–84, 193–236, *passim.* Reprinted by permission.

60

The Art of Music Reduced to Rational Principles

A major breakthrough in the investigation of sound was Joseph Sauveur's discovery of the "chord of nature," the phenomenon of vibration we now call the overtone series. His findings were published in 1701, and made the basis of a general theory of music by Jean-Philippe Rameau (1683–1764), whose *Traité de l'harmonie* (1722) was the first musical treatise to embody the new rational empiricism of the Baroque. For the first time the bass was recognized as a harmonic generator in theory, although it had been functioning that way in practice for over a century. Rameau made harmony the center of his musical universe, and was also the first to speak of chord roots and inversions. The contents of Rameau's hugely important work are set out in the preface, which we give here in abridged form.

However much progress music may have made until our time, it appears that the more sensitive the ear has become to the marvelous effects of this art, the less inquisitive the mind has been about its true principles. One might say that reason has lost its rights, while experience has acquired the certainty of authority. But if through the exposition of an evident principle, from which we then draw just and certain conclusions, we can show that our music has attained the last degree of perfection, we shall know where we stand. In short, the light of reason, dispelling the doubts into which experience can plunge us at any moment, will be the most certain guarantee of success that we can expect in this art.

Music is a science which should have definite rules; these rules should be drawn from an evident principle; and this principle cannot really be known to us without the aid of mathematics. Notwithstanding all the experience I may have acquired in music from being associated with it for so long, I must confess that only with the aid of mathematics did my ideas become clear and did light replace a certain obscurity of which I was unaware before. Though I did not know how to distinguish the principle from the rules, the principle soon offered itself to me in a manner convincing in its simplicity. I then recognized that the consequences it revealed constituted so many rules following from this principle. The true sense of these rules, their proper application, their relationships, their sequence (the simplest always introducing the less simple, and so on by degrees), and finally the choice of terms: all this, I say, of which I was ignorant before, developed in my mind with clarity and precision. I could not help thinking that it would be desirable (as someone said to me one day while I was applauding the perfection of our modern music) for the knowledge of musicians of this century to equal the beauties of their compositions. It is not enough to feel the effects of a science or an art. One must also conceive these effects in order to render them intelligible. That is the end to which I have principally applied myself in the body of this work, which I have divided into four books.

The First Book contains a summary of the relationship between sounds, consonances, dissonances, and chords in general. The source of harmony is discovered to be a single sound and its most essential properties are explained. We shall see, for example, how the first division of this single sound generates another sound, which is its octave and seems to be identical to the first sound, and how the latter then uses this octave to form all the chords. We shall see that all these chords contain only the source, its third, its fifth, and its seventh, and that all the diversity inherent in these chords derives from the power of the octave. We shall discover several other properties, perhaps less interesting for practice but nonetheless necessary for achieving proficiency. Everything is demonstrated in the simplest manner.

The Second Book concerns both theory and practice. The source is represented by the part called the *bass* in music, to which the epithet *fundamental* is added. All its properties, together with those of the intervals, chords, and modes depending on it alone, are explained. We also speak of everything which may be used to make music perfect in its construction. To this end we recall, whenever appropriate, the reasoning given in the preceding book, our experience, and the authority of the finest authors in this field, though not sparing them when they have erred. As for the new ideas presented here, we shall try to justify them to the learned by reason, to those who follow only their ear by experience, and to those who show too much submission to the rules of their masters by pointing out the errors found there. Finally we shall try to prepare the reader to receive freely the rules set down here and deduced in order and at length in the following books.

The Third Book contains a specific method for learning composition rapidly. The method has already been tested, but since we are rarely persuaded except by our own experience, I shall remain silent about this. I shall content myself with asking those to whom this method is unfamiliar to see the fruits that can be derived from it before opposing it. Those who wish to learn are not concerned about the method used to instruct them, as long as the method succeeds.

No rules have yet been devised to teach composition in all its present perfection. Every skillful man in this field sincerely confesses that he owes all his knowledge to experience alone. When he wishes to share this knowledge with others, he is often forced to add to his lessons this proverb, so familiar to musicians: *Caetera docebit usus* [Experience will teach the rest]. To this end I shall give a reasoned, precise, and distinct explanation of all harmony through the simple exposition of three intervals, from which are formed two principal chords and the entire progression of the fundamental bass; the latter simultaneously determines the progression of the other parts. Everything else depends on this simple explanation, which as you will see can be understood at the very first reading.

The Fourth Book contains the rules of accompaniment, both for the harpsichord and for the organ. The position of the hand, the arrangement of the fingers, and everything else useful in acquiring practical facility as rapidly as possible is deduced there.

The basic rules for accompanying on the harpsichord can also be used for other similar accompanying instruments.

These last two books have a great deal in common, and will be useful to persons who wish to study either the practice of composition or that of accompaniment. One should also consult Book II, if one wishes to overlook nothing (assuming that I have forgotten nothing). I do not doubt that there are those who could do better than I, however, despite the pains I have taken to let nothing escape me, as my long discourses and repetitions must prove. These defects are due as much to my efforts to make matters clear and intelligible as to the feebleness of my intellect. As for Book I, it will not be of much use in practice. I have placed it at the beginning as proof of everything else contained in this treatise concerning harmony, and one should make whatever use of it one considers appropriate.

Jean-Philippe Rameau, *Treatise on Harmony*, trans. Philip Gossett (New York: Dover Publications, Inc., 1971), xxiii–xxvii. Reprinted by permission.

61

The Earliest Musical Conservatories

The first music schools in the modern sense (as distinct from the ancient choir schools attached to churches and cathedrals) sprang up in Italy, at Venice and Naples, in connection with charitable institutions that cared for orphans and foundlings. By the eighteenth century, Venice was celebrated for its four "hospitals" for girls, Naples for its four "conservatories" (the two words meant the same thing) for boys. The concerts given by the girls at Venice, where musicians as eminent as Vivaldi oversaw the instruction, were particularly admired. Among the many travelers' reports on their prowess is this, by the historian Charles Burney (1726–1814), who visited Italy in 1770.

Sat. Aug. 4

[Venice] is famous for its *conservatorios* or music schools, of which it has four, the *Ospedale della Pietà,* the *Mendicanti,* the *Incurabili,* and the *Ospedaletto a St. Giovanni e Paolo,* at each of which there is a performance every Saturday and Sunday evening, as well as on great festivals. In the evening I went to that of the *Pietà.* The performers, both vocal and instrumental, are all girls; the organ, violins, flutes, violoncellos, and even french-horns, are supplied by these females. It is a kind of Foundling Hospital for natural children, under the protection of several nobles, citizens, and merchants, who, though the revenue is very great, yet, contribute annually to its support. These girls are maintained here till they are married, and all those who have talents for music are taught by the best masters of Italy.

Sun. Aug. 5

In the afternoon I went to the hospital *de' Mendicanti,* for orphan girls, who are taught to sing and play, and on Sundays and festivals they sing divine service in chorus. From hence I went to the *Ospedaletto.* The performers here too are all orphan girls; one of them, *la Ferrarese,* sung very well, and had a very extraordinary compass of voice, as she was able to reach the highest E of our harpsichords, upon which she could dwell a considerable time, in a fair, natural voice.

At the Hospitals and in Churches, where it is not allowed to applaud in the same manner as at the Opera, they cough, hem, and blow their noses, to express admiration.

Frid. Aug. 10

I had this morning a long visit from Signor [Gaetano] Latilla [1711–88, a well-known composer at the time]. He says the Conservatorios have been established at Venice about 200 years, as hospitals. That at first the girls were only taught canto firmo [Gregorian chant], and psalmody; but in process of time, they learned to sing in parts, and, at length joined instruments to the Voices. He says the expense on account of the music is very inconsiderable, there being but 5 or 6 Masters to each of these schools for singing and the several instruments, as the elder girls teach the younger; the Maestro di Cappella [director] only composes and directs; sometimes, indeed, he writes down closes [cadenzas] to suit particular airs, and attends all the rehearsals and public performances.

This morning I went with young Oliver to his Conservatorio of St. Onofrio, and visited all the rooms where the boys practise, sleep, and eat. On the first flight of stairs was a trumpeter, screaming upon his instrument till he was ready to burst; on the second was a french-horn, bellowing in the same manner. In the common practising room there was a *Dutch concert,* consisting of seven or eight harpsichords, more than as many violins, and several voices, all performing different things, and in different keys: other boys were writing in the same room; but it being holiday time, many were absent who usually study and practise there together.

The jumbling them all together in this manner may be convenient for the house, and may teach the boys to attend to their own parts with firmness, whatever else may be going forward at the same time; it may likewise give them force, by obliging them to play loud in order to hear themselves; but in the midst of such jargon, and continued dissonance, it is wholly impossible to give any kind of polish or finishing to their performance; hence the slovenly coarseness so remarkable in their public exhibitions; and the total want of taste, neatness, and expression in all these young musicians, till they have acquired them elsewhere.

The beds, which are in the same room, serve as seats for the harpsichords and other instruments. Out of thirty or forty boys who were practising, I could discover but two that were playing the same piece: some of those who were practising on the violin seemed to have a great deal of hand. The violoncellos practise in another room: and the flutes, oboes, and other wind instruments, in a third, except the trumpets and horns, which are obliged to fag [labor] either on the stairs, or on the top of the house.

There are in this college sixteen young *castrati* [see next selection], and these live up stairs, by themselves, in warmer apartments than the other boys, for fear of colds, which might not only render their delicate voices unfit for exercise at present, but hazard the entire loss of them for ever.

The only vacation in these schools, in the whole year, is in autumn, and that for a few days only: during the winter, the boys rise two hours before it is light, from which time they continue their exercise, an hour and a half at dinner excepted, till eight o'clock at night; and this constant perseverance, for a number of years, with genius and good teaching, must produce great musicians.

Percy A. Scholes (ed.), *Dr. Burney's Musical Tours in Europe* (London: Oxford University Press, 1959), I, 112, 113–15, 121, 269–70.

62

Castrato Singers

The leading male roles of Italian heroic opera in the seventeenth and eighteenth centuries were sung by men with powerful soprano and contralto voices. They had been operated on before puberty, so that they retained their childish voices as grown men. This inhuman custom did not shock most opera lovers, although there were moralists, especially outside of Italy, who found it objectionable. (On the other hand, it should be remembered that even worse things, such as public torture and executions, were still widely accepted at the time.) Because the operation was forbidden by law throughout Italy, foreign travelers were understandably curious to know where all the castratos (or *musici,* as the Italians called them) actually came from. Charles Burney (whom we met in the previous reading and will often meet again) was just such an inquisitive traveler.

I enquired throughout Italy at what place boys were chiefly qualified for singing by castration, but could get no certain intelligence. I was told at Milan that it was at Venice; at Venice, that it was at Bologna; but at Bologna the fact was denied, and I was referred to Florence; from Florence to Rome, and from Rome I was sent to Naples. The operation most certainly is against law in all these places, as well as against nature; and all the Italians are so much ashamed of it, that in every province they transfer it to some other.

However, with respect to the Conservatorios at Naples, Mr. Jemineau, the British consul, who has so long resided there, and who has made very particular enquiries, assured me, and his account was confirmed by Dr. Cirillo, an eminent and learned Neapolitan physician, that this practice is absolutely forbidden in the Conservatorios, and that the young *Castrati* came from Lecce in Puglia; but, before the operation is performed, they are brought to a Conservatorio to be tried as to the probability of voice, and then are taken home by their parents for this barbarous purpose. It is said, however, to be death by the laws to all those who perform the operation, and excommunication to every one concerned in it, unless it be done, as is often pretended, upon account of some disorders which may be supposed to require it, and with the consent of the boy. And there are instances of its being done even at the request of the boy himself, as was the case of the Grassetto at Rome.

But as to their previous trials of the voice, it is my opinion that the cruel operation is but too frequently performed without trial, or at least without sufficient proofs of an improvable voice; otherwise such numbers could never be found in every great town throughout Italy, without any voice at all, or at least without one sufficient to compensate such a loss. Indeed all the *musici* in the churches at present are made up of the refuse of the opera houses, and it is very rare to meet with a tolerable voice upon the establishment in any church throughout Italy. The *virtuosi* who sing there occasionally, upon great festivals only, are usually strangers, and paid by the time.

Percy A. Scholes, (ed.), *Dr Burney's Musical Tours in Europe* (London: Oxford University Press, 1959), I, 247–48.

Obviously, only very few castratos ever became operatic stars. And when they did, they generally behaved as pompously as any self-important star would, thus furnishing humorists with plenty of subject matter for jokes and satirical writings. Some castratos, however, were men of considerable culture and musical genius. The greatest of them by all accounts was Carlo Broschi, called "Farinelli" (1705–82), counselor to two Spanish kings and intimate friend of Italy's greatest poet at the time, Pietro Metastasio (1698–1782). Burney met him in his retirement, and gave his biography as follows:

Farinelli was born at Naples in 1705; he had his first musical education from his father, Signor Broschi, and afterwards was under [Nicola] Porpora [a celebrated composer,

Carlo Broschi, Known as Farinelli. The greatest male soprano of his time. *National Museum of Art, Bucharest, Romania / Art Resource, NY.*

and teacher of Haydn, among others], who travelled with him; he was seventeen when he left that city to go to Rome, where, during the run of an opera, there was a struggle every night between him and a famous player on the trumpet, in a song accompanied by that instrument: this, at first, seemed amicable and merely sportive, till the audience began to interest themselves in the contest, and to take different sides: after severally swelling out a note, in which each manifested the power of his lungs, and tried to rival the other in brilliancy and force, they had both a swell and a shake together, by thirds, which was continued so long, while the audience eagerly waited the event, that both seemed to be exhausted; and, in fact, the trumpeter, wholly spent, gave it up, thinking, however, his antagonist as much tired as himself, and that it would be a drawn battle; when Farinelli with a smile on his countenance, shewing he had only been sporting with him all this time, broke out all at once in the same breath, with fresh vigour, and not only swelled and shook the note, but ran the most rapid and difficult divisions [i.e., passages], and was at last silenced only by the acclamations of the audience. From this period may be dated that superiority which he ever maintained over all his contemporaries.

From Rome he went to Bologna. From thence he went to Venice, and from Venice to Vienna; in all which cities his powers were regarded as miraculous; but he told me, that at Vienna, where he was three different times, and where he received great honours from the Emperor Charles VI, an admonition from that prince was of more service to him than all the precepts of his masters, or examples of his competitors for fame: his Imperial Majesty condescended to tell him one day, with great mildness and affability, that in his singing, he neither *moved* nor *stood still* like any other mortal; all was supernatural. 'Those gigantic strides, said he; those never-ending notes and passages, *ces notes qui ne finissent jamais,* only surprise, and it is now time for you to please; you are too lavish of the gifts with which nature has endowed you; if you wish to reach the heart, you must take a more plain and simple road.' These few words brought about an entire change in his manner of singing; from this time he mixed the pathetic with the spirited, the simple with the sublime, and, by these means, delighted as well as astonished every hearer.

In the year 1734, he came to England, where every one knows who heard, or has heard of him, what an effect his surprising talents had upon the audience: it was ecstasy! rapture! enchantment!

On his arrival here, at the first private rehearsal at Cuzzoni's apartments [Cuzzoni was the great prima donna playing opposite him that season], Lord Cooper, then the principal manager of the opera under Porpora, observing that the band did not follow him, but were all gaping with wonder, as if thunder-struck, desired them to be attentive; when they all confessed, that they were unable to keep pace with him: having not only been disabled by astonishment, but overpowered by his talents.

In the famous air *Son qual Nave,* which was composed by his brother, the first note he sung was taken with such delicacy, swelled by minute degrees to such an amazing volume, and afterwards diminished in the same manner to a mere point, that it was applauded for full five minutes. After this he set off with such brilliancy and rapidity of execution, that it was difficult for the violins of those days to keep pace with him. In short, he was to all other singers as superior as the famous horse Childers was to all other running-horses; but it was not only in speed that he excelled, for he had now every excellence of every great singer united. In his voice, strength, sweetness, and compass; and in his style, the tender, the graceful, and the rapid. Indeed he possessed such powers as never met before, or since, in any one human being; powers that were irresistible, and which must have subdued every hearer; the learned and the ignorant, the friend and the foe.

With these talents he went into Spain in the year 1737, with a full design to return to England; but the first day he performed before the king and queen of Spain, it was determined that he should be taken into the services of the court, to which he was ever after wholly appropriated, not being once suffered to sing again in public. A pension was then settled on him of upwards of £2000 sterling a year.

He told me, that for the first ten years of his residence at the court of Spain, during the life of Philip the Vth, he sung every night to that monarch the same four airs.

When the present king of Spain [Charles III] ascended the throne, he was obliged to quit that kingdom, but a good pension was still continued, and he was allowed to bring away all his effects.

After visiting Naples, the place of his nativity, he settled at Bologna in 1761, in the environs of which city he built himself a splendid mansion, which in Italy is called a palazzo. Here he resided the rest of his life, in the true enjoyment of affluent leisure; respected by the inhabitants of Bologna; visited by illustrious travellers; and still enjoying the smiles of fortune, though denied the blandishments of a court. This extraordinary musician, and worthy man, died in 1782.

Scholes, *Dr. Burney,* I, 153–55; and Charles Burney, *A General History of Music* ed. Frank Mercer (New York: Dover Publications, Inc., 1957), II, 790, 817.

63

The Conventions of the Opera Seria

The dominant form of Italian opera, as it developed through exposure to the realities of public taste in the later seventeenth century, evolved a whole body of conventions that were felt to be inviolable if the singers, and therefore the operas, were to succeed. And since this *opera seria* ("serious opera," in that it dealt with noble, if stereotyped, heroes and heroines) was the only living, popular form of drama in Italy from about 1700 to 1750, even the best dramatists, such as Apostolo Zeno (1668–1750) and Pietro Metastasio (see p. 191), adhered closely to its conventions, or "rules," in writing their librettos. These "rules" were absurd enough (if seen from a purely dramatic point of view, divorced from the singing) to provoke much criticism and laughter. Here is an amusing attack upon them from the reminiscences of Carlo Goldoni (1707–93), who began his career unsuccessfully as an *opera seria* librettist, only to become, in his later years, Italy's first really popular playwright as well as a favorite librettist of comic operas. The year was 1732. Goldoni had just been admitted to the bar in his native Venice; but, finding no clients, he spent his time composing a *dramma per musica* (or serious libretto) entitled *Amalasunta.* Soon he found himself so deeply in debt that he had to flee Venice.

But where to, with what means, and what was I to do outside of Venice? All my hopes were founded on my *Amalasunta.* I decided to take it to Milan, thinking that the impresarios of the famous Theater would pay me well for it, would commission me to write more, and that in a short while I should have obtained credit and made my fortune. It happened to be the Carnival season [when I arrived there], and the Theater was presenting Metastasio's *Demofoonte,* and the principal part in the Drama was being played by the celebrated [castrato] Caffariello, whom I had met in Venice. The Director and composer of the Ballets was Signor Gaetan Grossa-Testa. I knew this excellent man and his kind Spouse, Signora Maria; so that, through these three acquaintances and the merits of my Drama, I hoped the Impresarios would accept it, and pay me handsomely for it. Therefore, having chosen a Friday, when there are no performances at the Theater, I paid a visit to that expert Ballerina and found there, besides her Husband, Caffariello and some others of her acquaintance, among them the Milanese Nobleman Count Prata, a great connoisseur of the Theater and amateur of music and theatrical poetry. When I made my wish known to them, they all offered to lend me their support; but they wisely suggested that, before exposing the Drama to the judgment of the impresarios, it would be well to expose it to that of my friends. Since there was nothing I wished for more eagerly than to read my Composition, I pulled it out of my pocket, and begged them to give me their attention. These listeners were neither erudite nor learned; but, being schooled by practice, and finding that my Drama did not accord with the rules, they began to grow weary. Some yawned, others whispered among themselves, and one Castrato, who played the smallest role in *Demofoonte,* took a sheet of music and began singing in an undertone. Afire with enthusiasm and anger, I now declaimed louder to oblige them to listen more attentively, but this only made some of them laugh and others grow impatient, and it vexed the Lady of the house, who urged them, in vain, to be silent. At last, with the kindest and most civil apologies, she begged me to save the rest for another occasion. I thanked her for her courtesy, but being piqued, especially with the Castratos, made ready to leave at once. Count Prata kindly requested me to accompany him to another room, and obliged me to read him the rest. I did so the more willingly, in that I hoped his approval might render me the justice I had been denied by the rudeness of the others. He listened to the whole Work patiently; and this, approximately, is what he said to me when I had finished:

"Your Work, if it were written differently, might make a good Tragedy; but the *Dramma per musica,* in itself an imperfect [type of] Composition, has been subjected by custom to certain rules—contrary, it is true, to those of Aristotle, Horace, and all who have treated of Poetics, but necessary if it is to serve the Music, the Actors, and the Composers. The profound Apostolo Zeno, the mellifluous, elegant, most learned Metastasio have conformed to those rules, and what might seem a fault in a regular Tragedy becomes a thing of beauty in a *Dramma per musica.* Read the two above-mentioned Authors attentively, and you will gain some notion as to the nature of the Drama we are discussing, and you will mark its rules. I will indicate some of the main ones, whose absence disgusted the Castratos who were listening to you. The leading male soprano, the leading lady, and the tenor, who are the principal Actors of the Drama, must each sing five arias: one *pathetic,* one *virtuosic,* one *speech-like,* one *of mixed character,* and one *brilliant.* The second male and second female must each have four, and the last male three, and a seventh character the same number, should the Work require him; for (by-the-bye) there cannot be more than six or seven characters in it, and you have nine in your Drama. The seconds are always demanding that they, too, be given *pathetic arias,* but the firsts will not hear of it, and if the Scene itself is pathetic, their aria can only be, at the very most, *of mixed character.* The principal Actors' fifteen arias must be so distributed that no two of the *same color* shall follow upon each other's heels, and the other Actors' arias serve to provide the *chiaroscuro* [i.e., the contrast]. You make a character sing and then remain onstage, and this is against the *rules.* On the other hand, you allow a principal Actor to exit without singing an aria, and this again is against the *rules.* You have only three *Scene changes* in your Drama, whereas six or seven are required. The third Act of your Drama is the best in the Work, but this too is against the *rules …*"

I could contain myself no longer; I rose to my feet with unintentional vehemence, apologized, thanked him for his friendly admonishments, and concluded by saying that, as I was horrified by the *rules* of the Drama, I was quite determined never to write one again. In taking my leave of the Nobleman I begged him, as a friend of the House, to have me shown out so that I should not need to re-enter the parlor. This he did. I returned to my hotel, ordered a fire, and with unabated bitterness burnt my *Amalasunta* piecemeal.

Carlo Goldoni, *Tutte le opere,* ed. G. Ortolani (Milan: Mondadori, 1935–56), 1, 682, 687–89. Trans. P. W.

64

Opera Audiences in Eighteenth-Century Italy

The San Carlo opera house, built with astounding speed within seven months in 1737 and still functioning today, was the showplace of Italian opera in the kingdom of Naples. The behavior of Italian opera audiences was a source of wonderment to foreign visitors (see p. 199 for further details); the present description is from a little-known book by Samuel Sharp, a first-rate surgeon (though he was unable to keep Handel from going blind) and, like so many Englishmen of his time, an accomplished amateur musician.

Naples, Nov. 1765

Sir,

A Stranger, upon his arrival in so large and celebrated a city as *Naples,* generally makes the publick spectacles his first pursuit. These consist of the King's Theatre, where the serious Opera is performed, and of two smaller theatres, called *Teatro Nuovo,* and the *Teatro dei Fiorentini,* where they exhibit burlettas [i.e., comic operas] only. There is also a little dirty kind of a play-house, where they perform a comedy every night, though the Drama has so little encouragement at *Naples,* that their comedies are seldom frequented by any of the gentry.

The King's Theatre, upon the first view, is, perhaps, almost as remarkable an object as any a man sees in his travels: I not only speak from my own feeling, but the declaration of every foreigner here. The amazing extent of the stage, with the prodigious circumference of the boxes, and height of the ceiling, produce a marvellous effect on the mind, for a few moments; but the instant the Opera opens, a spectator laments this striking sight. He immediately perceives this structure does not gratify the ear, how much soever it may the eye. The voices are drowned in this immensity of space, and even the orchestra itself, though a numerous band, lies under a disadvantage: It is true, some of the first singers may be heard, yet, upon the whole, it must be admitted, that the house is better contrived to see, than to hear an Opera. There are some who contend, that the singers might be very well heard, if the audience was more silent; but it is so much the fashion at *Naples,* and, indeed, through all *Italy,* to consider the Opera as a

An Opera Seria in Progress. The theater is the Teatro Regio in Turin, the date 1740, but the situation is characteristic of any large opera house in eighteenth-century Italy. On stage, some of the principal singers: the heroine weeping (her train held by two pages), the hero (guarded by four soldiers) kneeling and about to sing an "aria in chains" (one of the standard types of aria) to his captor, who dominates the scene. The costumes are operatic "Roman." In the pit, two harpsichordists: at the left the composer (in the picture, Francesco Feo), his eyes on the singers, whom it is his function to direct; at the right, the local "maestro al cembalo," coordinating the instrumental playing (note the thorough bass contingents grouped around both harpsichords, and, at the far left, the two French horn players brought in for this scene). The members of the audience are just as busy as the performers, though in a myriad different ways that deserve close examination. Through all this, oranges and liquid refreshment are being offered for sale. (Oil painting by Pietro Domenico Olivero. The opera being performed is Feo's *Arsace*.) *Turin, Museo Civico.*

place of rendezvous and visiting, that they do not seem in the least to attend to the musick, but laugh and talk through the whole performance, without any restraint; and, it may be imagined, that an assembly of so many hundreds conversing together so loudly, must entirely cover the voices of the singers.

Notwithstanding the amazing noisiness of the audience, during the whole performance of the Opera, the moment the dances begin, there is a universal silence, which continues so long as the dances continue. Witty people, therefore, never fail to tell me, the *Neapolitans* go to *see*, not to *hear* an Opera. A stranger, who has a little compassion in his breast, feels for the poor singers, who are treated with so much indifference and contempt: He almost wonders that they can submit to so gross an affront; and I find, by their own confession, that however accustomed they be to it, the mortification is always dreadful, and they are eager to declare how happy they are when they sing in a country where more attention is paid to their talents.

The *Neapolitan* quality rarely dine or sup with one another, and many of them hardly ever visit, but at the Opera; on this account they seldom absent themselves, though the Opera be played three nights successively, and it be the same Opera, without any change, during ten or twelve weeks. It is customary for Gentlemen to run about from box to box, betwixt the acts, and even in the midst of the performance; but the Ladies, after they are seated, never quit their box the whole evening. It is the fashion to make appointments for such and such nights. A Lady receives visitors in her box one night, and they remain with her the whole Opera; another night she returns the visit in the same manner. In the intervals of the acts, principally betwixt the first and second, the proprietor of the box regales her company with iced fruits and sweet meats.

Besides the indulgence of a loud conversation, they sometimes form themselves into card parties; but, I believe, this custom does not prevail so much at present, as it did formerly, for I have never seen more than two or three boxes so occupied, in the same night.

The men in the pit do not, upon the whole, make a good figure; for though there are many officers, who are well drest, yet they and the Gentlemen are much the smaller portion of the company there. There is a vulgar set of men who frequent the pit, and another set still more vulgar, who pay nothing for their entrance, such as the upper servants of the Ladies who have boxes, the upper servants of ambassadors, and sometimes, for a small fee to the door-keepers, those servants introduce their friends. It is not to be omitted, amongst the objections to the immense largeness of the house and stage, that, in windy weather, you would imagine yourself in the streets, the wind blows so hard both in the pit and boxes; and this seldom happens without causing colds and fevers. The impressario, or manager, is bound to very bad terms, so that his profits are inconsiderable, and sometimes he is a loser. You will wonder how I became possessed of these particulars; accident threw them in my way, and you may depend on their authenticity.

Samuel Sharp, *Letters from Italy*, 3rd ed. (London, 1767), 77–79, 82–84, 92–93.

65

Domenico Scarlatti at the Harpsichord

Burney, in his *General History of Music,* has preserved for us this rare bit of oral history—an account of the first meeting between a talented young English musician, Thomas Roseingrave (1690–1766), and the only slightly older master harpsichordist

Domenico Scarlatti (1685–1757), who at the time had just completed his studies with the famous composer Francesco Gasparini. In later years, Roseingrave was to become a champion of Scarlatti's harpsichord music in England.

Thomas, being regarded as a young man of uncommon dispositions for the study of his art, was honoured by the chapter of St. Patrick's [in Dublin] with a pension, to enable him to travel for improvement; and about the year 1710 he set off for Italy. Being arrived at Venice in his way to Rome, as he himself told me, he was invited, as a stranger and a virtuoso, to an academia [i.e., a concert, see p. 179] at the house of a nobleman, where, among others, he was requested to sit down to the harpsichord and favour the company with a toccata, as a specimen *della sua virtù* [of his ability]. And, says he, "finding myself rather better in courage and finger than usual, I exerted myself, my dear friend, and fancied, by the applause I received, that my performance had made some impression on the company." After a cantata had been sung by a scholar of Fr. Gasparini, who was there to accompany her, a grave young man dressed in black and in a black wig, who had stood in one corner of the room, very quiet and attentive while Roseingrave played, being asked to sit down to the harpsichord, when he began to play, Rosy said, he thought ten hundred d[evi]ls had been at the instrument; he never had heard such passages of execution and effect before. The performance so far surpassed his own, and every degree of perfection to which he thought it possible he should ever arrive, that, if he had been in sight of any instrument with which to have done the deed, he should have cut off his own fingers. Upon enquiring the name of this extraordinary performer, he was told that it was Domenico Scarlatti, son of the celebrated Cavalier Alessandro Scarlatti [1660–1725; outstanding composer of opera]. Roseingrave declared he did not touch an instrument himself for a month; after this rencontre, however, he became very intimate with the young Scarlatti, followed him to Rome and Naples, and hardly ever quitted him while he remained in Italy.

Charles Burney, *A General History of Music,* ed. Frank Mercer (New York: Dover Publications, Inc., 1957), II, 704.

66

A Traveler's Impressions of Vivaldi

The following excerpts are taken from the travel diaries of a young German law student, J. F. A. von Uffenbach, who in later years became a great patron of music and musicians in his native Frankfurt. Soon after arriving in Venice, he visited the city's largest opera house: unfortunately, like most foreigners, he chose a parterre seat, not knowing that it was an old Venetian custom for the public in the loges to take aim and spit on the people below. The next time Uffenbach went to an opera he was, as we shall see, a wiser man; and it was on this occasion that he first saw and heard Vivaldi, with whom he later became personally acquainted. These diary entries are among the very few first-hand accounts we have of the composer, and they show him in several of his manifold activities—as opera manager, opera composer, violin virtuoso, violin teacher, and composer (and salesman) of concerti grossi. When we remember that he also rehearsed and directed the regular concerts at one of Venice's famous conservatories (see p. 188), we will have some idea of how busy a composer could be in those days.

Venice, February 4th, 1715. I remained [at the masked ball] until it was time to go to the opera, then went with several acquaintances to the St. Angelo theater, which is smaller and not so elegant as the one I described earlier. The manager of this theater is the famous Vivaldi, who was also the composer of the opera, which was very good indeed and a fine spectacle too; the machines, however, were not as sumptuous as those at the other theater, and the orchestra was not as large, but well worth hearing nevertheless. Fearing lest we should be mistreated and spat upon as we were the first time, we took an inexpensive loge and proceeded to avenge ourselves upon those in the parterre according to local custom, just as had been done to us the last time, even though I had thought it utterly impossible for me to do this. Towards the end [of the opera], Vivaldi played an admirable solo to accompany an aria, at the conclusion of which he added an improvisation that really frightened me, for I doubt anything like it was ever done before, or ever will be again: he came to within a hairsbreadth of the bridge, leaving no room for the bow, and this on all 4 strings, with imitations and at an incredible speed. He astonished everyone with this, although to say it touched me would not be true, because it was not as agreeable to listen to as it was cunningly contrived.

Wednesday, March 6th, 1715. Vivaldi, the famous composer and violin player, came to see me, for I had repeatedly left word at his house requesting him to do so. I had spoken of certain concerti grossi which I wished to obtain and had ordered them from him; and I had also sent him (since he belongs to the musical tribe) several bottles of wine. And so he let me hear his very difficult and quite inimitable improvisations on the violin; and I was compelled to admire his dexterity the more at close quarters, although I saw quite clearly that, while he played extra difficult and colorful things, he did so with no great charm or tunefulness.

Saturday, March 9th, 1715. Vivaldi came to see me this afternoon and brought me what I had ordered, namely 10 concerti grossi, some of which, as he said, he had composed expressly for me; and so that I might hear them better, he wished to teach them to me at once and come to see me from time to time; and so we made a beginning today. [As it happens, Uffenbach left Venice a few days later, or we might have had a fascinating record of Vivaldi's teaching.]

Eberhard Preussner, *Die musikalischen Reisen des Herrn von Uffenbach* (Kassel: Bärenreiter-Verlag, 1949), 67, 71. Trans. P. W.

67

Couperin on His *Pièces de Clavecin*

François Couperin's harpsichord pieces are often regarded as prime examples of Rococo style, in which the heroic dimensions of the Baroque were cut down to a more human scale, and where a graceful decorativeness and sweet intimacy of expression were prized above all. Couperin's preface to his first book of *Pièces de clavecin* (Paris, 1713) aptly reflects these concerns in its insistence on expressive playing even on the refractory harpsichord: it is better to be moved than to be astonished. Vivaldi (see the preceding selection) might not have agreed.

I found it impossible to satisfy the public's wishes sooner by presenting them with my engraved pieces: I hope they will not suspect me of having affected the delay in order to increase their curiosity, and trust they will forgive the slowness of my labor for precision's sake. Everyone knows it is in the author's best interest to issue a correct edition of his works, when these have been so fortunate as to find favor: for, while flattered by the applause of connoisseurs, he can only be pained by the ignorance and mistakes of the copyists—a common fate of sought-after manuscripts.

I should have liked to busy myself long ago with the printing of my pieces. Yet some of the occupations that prevented me from doing so have been too honorable for me to permit me to complain of them; for the past twenty years I have had the honor to belong to the King and to instruct, nearly at the same time, my lord the Dauphin-Duke of Burgundy and six Princes or Princesses of the Royal Family: these occupations, those in Paris, and several illnesses must be my reasons for not finding time to compose a greater number of pieces, since seventy appear in this book and I propose to issue a second volume at the end of the year. In composing all these pieces I have always had an object, prompted by various circumstances; thus the Titles correspond to the ideas I had, which I trust I may be exempted from explaining: yet, as among these Titles some will appear to flatter me [i.e., those bearing the names of noble patrons], it should be remarked that the pieces thus inscribed are, as it were, portraits that have sometimes been found to be reasonably good likenesses under my hands, and that the greater part of those advantageous Titles were intended for the gracious originals I have tried to portray, rather than for my copies of them. This first Book has cost more than a year's labor; I have spared neither expense nor pains on it; and only that extreme care can account for the intelligence and accuracy that will be seen in the engraving.

I have included all the necessary embellishments. I have observed the just value of the beats and notes in the vertical alignment; and according to the abilities and age of individuals, there will be found pieces of varying difficulty, within the reach of excellent, middling, and weaker hands. Experience has taught me that vigorous hands, able to execute the quickest, lightest things, are not alway the most successful in tender and sensitive pieces, and I will candidly confess that I like that which stirs my feelings much better than that which astonishes me.

The Harpsichord is perfect as to its compass and is brilliant in itself; but as it is impossible to swell or diminish its tones, I shall always be thankful to those who, by means of infinite artistry borne up by good taste, shall succeed in making the instrument capable of expression: that was my ancestors' endeavor, apart from the good workmanship of their compositions: I have attempted to perfect their discoveries: their works continue to be favored by persons of exquisite taste.

As for my pieces, their novel and diversified character has caused them to be favorably received by the world; and I hope that those which I now issue for the first time will enjoy the same success as those which are familiar.

Œuvres complètes de François Couperin, ed. Maurice Cauchie, II (Paris: Éditions de l'Oiseau Lyre, 1932), 9–11. Trans. P. W.

68

The Piano Is Invented

Most musical instruments evolved gradually over the ages. The piano (short for "pianoforte," or "soft-loud") was invented in 1709, or possibly a year or two earlier, by Bartolomeo Cristofori (1655–1731), instrument maker and, later, curator of instruments to the Grand Dukes of Tuscany. His workshop was most probably in the Uffizi Palace in Florence. The invention was announced and described in 1711 by the scholar and poet Scipione Maffei; yet, despite the importance of this publication (and of a German translation, published in 1725), the new instrument gained very little ground in the following years (see C. P. E. Bach's mention of it on p. 228). No doubt the technique of playing it must have seemed unnecessarily treacherous to performers who were used to controlling the duration of notes, but not their volume. It was not until the last decades of the eighteenth century, when shifting dynamics became an essential part of musical expression, that the piano came into its own. And by then Cristofori had been forgotten. The first half of Maffei's article follows. The rest is devoted to a minute description of the new instrument's mechanism, complete with diagram (see the illustration).

New Invention of a Harpsichord with the *Piano* and the *Forte;* Also Some Remarks upon Musical Instruments

If the value of inventions is to be measured by the novelty and the difficulty, that of which we are now to give an account is certainly not inferior to any that has been discovered for a long time. It is known to every one who delights in music that one of the principal means by which the skillful in that art derive the secret of especially delighting those who listen is the piano and forte in the theme and its response, or in the gradual diminution of tone, little by little, and then returning suddenly to a loud manner; which artifice is frequently used, and with marvelous effect, in the great concerts of Rome, to the incredible delight of such as enjoy the perfection of this art. Now, of this diversity and alteration of tone, in which instruments played by the bow especially excel, the harpsichord is entirely deprived, and it would have been thought a vain endeavor to propose to make it so that it should participate in this power. Nevertheless, so bold an invention has been no less happily conceived than executed in Florence, by Signor BARTOLOMMEO CRISTOFALI [*sic*] of Padua, harpsichordist in the service of the most serene Prince of Tuscany. He has already made three, of the usual size of other harpsichords, and they have all succeeded to perfection. The production of greater or less sound depends on the degree of power with which the player presses on the keys, by regulating which, not only the piano and forte are heard, but also the gradations and diversity of the sound, as in a violoncello. Some professors [i.e., professionals] have not given to this invention all the praise it deserves; because, in the first place, they did not see how much ingenuity was required to overcome the difficulty, and what marvelous delicacy of hand was required to adjust it with so much nicety; and, secondly, because it appeared to them that the tone of such an instrument was more soft and less distinct than the ordinary ones; but this is a feeling that arises upon first placing one's hands upon it, because we are accustomed to the silvery tone of other

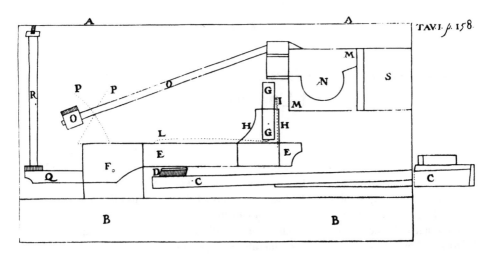

The First Piano. This diagram accompanied Scipione Maffei's account of Cristofori's invention in the *Giornale de' letterati d'Italia,* V (1711), 158.

harpsichords; but in a short time the ear so adapts itself, and becomes so fond of it, that it never tires of it, and the common harpsichord no longer pleases; and we must add that it sounds yet more sweet at some distance. It has further been objected to this instrument that it has not a powerful tone, and not quite so loud as other harpsichords. To this may be answered, first, that it has more power than they imagine, if anyone who wishes and knows how to use it will strike the keys briskly; and, secondly, that one should consider things for what they are, and not expect the same means to be employed to a different end.

This is properly a chamber instrument and is therefore not suitable for church music or for a large stage. How many instruments are there, used on such occasions, which nevertheless are esteemed among the most agreeable? It is certain that, to accompany a singer and to support another instrument, or even in a moderate consort, it succeeds perfectly; although this is not its principal intention, but rather to be played alone, like the lute, the harp, viols of six strings, and other most sweet instruments. But, indeed, the greatest cause of opposition which this new instrument has encountered is the general want of knowledge of how, at first, to play it; because it is not sufficient to know how to play perfectly upon the ordinary keyboard instruments, but, being a new instrument, it requires a person who, understanding its capabilities, shall have devoted some particular study to it, so as to regulate the different amounts of pressure required on the keys, the delicate nuances, the time, the place, as well as to choose suitable, delicate pieces for it, especially to differentiate and lead the parts, that the subject may be heard distinctly in each.

Edward F. Rimbault, *The Pianoforte, Its Origin, Progress, & Construction* ... (London, 1860), 95–97.

69

Addison and Steele Poke Fun at Handel's First London Opera

Opera was always an easy target for men of letters (see St.-Évremond, p. 171). To be sure, much of the criticism was prompted by envy over opera's hold on audiences. In the case of Joseph Addison, who, with Richard Steele, founded the *Spectator* in 1711, there was also some personal bitterness: he had been unsuccessful with his own attempt at an English libretto. And so when Handel produced his first London opera, *Rinaldo,* with the great castrato Nicolini in the title role, and fashionable London capitulated to the charms of Italian opera, Addison and Steele were ready to contribute their bit to the ever-growing literature of operatic satire.

From the Spectator, March 6, 1711:

An Opera may be allowed to be extravagantly lavish in its Decorations, as its only Design is to gratify the Senses, and keep up an indolent Attention in the Audience. Common Sense however requires, that there should be nothing in the Scenes and Machines which may appear Childish and Absurd. How would the Wits of King *Charles's* Time have laughed to have seen *Nicolini* exposed to a Tempest in Robes and Ermine, and sailing in an open Boat upon a Sea of Paste-Board?

As I was walking in the Streets about a Fortnight ago, I saw an ordinary Fellow carrying a Cage full of little Birds upon his Shoulder; and, as I was wondering with my self what Use he would put them to, he was met very luckily by an Acquaintance, who had the same Curiosity. Upon his asking him what he had upon his Shoulder, he told him, that he had been buying Sparrows for the Opera. Sparrows for the Opera, says his Friend, licking his Lips, what,? are they to be roasted? No, no, says the other, they are to enter towards the end of the first Act, and to fly about the Stage.

This strange Dialogue awakened my Curiosity so far, that I immediately bought [the libretto of] the Opera, by which means I perceived that the Sparrows were to act the part of Singing Birds in a delightful Grove: though upon nearer Enquiry I found the Sparrows put [a] Trick upon the Audience; for, though they flew in Sight, the Musick proceeded from a Consort of Flageolets and Birdcalls which was planted behind the Scenes. The Opera of *Rinaldo* is filled with Thunder and Lightning, Illuminations, and Fireworks; which the Audience may look upon without catching Cold, and indeed without much Danger of being burnt; for there are several Engines filled with Water, and ready to play at a Minute's Warning, in case any such Accident should happen. However, as I have a very great Friendship for the Owner of this Theatre, I hope that he has been wise enough to *insure* his House before he would let this Opera be acted in it.

I shall give you a Taste of the [librettist's] Italian, from the first Lines of his Preface. *Behold, gentle Reader, the Birth of a few Evenings, which tho' it be* [born in] *the Night, is not the Abortive of Darkness, but will make itself known to be the Son of* Apollo, *with a certain Ray of Parnassus.* He afterwards proceeds to call Seignor *Hendel* the *Orpheus* of our Age, and to acquaint us, in the same Sublimity of Stile, that he Composed this Opera in a Fortnight. Such are the Wits, to whose Tastes we so ambitiously conform our selves.

But to return to the Sparrows; there have been so many Flights of them let loose in this Opera, that it is feared the House will never get rid of them; and that in other Plays they may make their Entrance in very wrong and improper Scenes besides the Inconveniences which the Heads of the Audience may sometimes suffer from them.

C. [Joseph Addison]

From the Spectator, March 16, 1711:

The Undertakers at the *Hay-Market* [Theatre], having raised too great an Expectation in their printed Opera [libretto], very much disappoint their Audience on the Stage.

The King of *Jerusalem* is obliged to come from the City on foot, instead of being drawn in a triumphant Chariot by white Horses, as my Opera-Book had promised me; and thus while I expected *Armida*'s Dragons should rush forward towards *Argantes,* I found the Hero was obliged to go to *Armida,* and hand her out of her Coach. We had also but a very short Allowance of Thunder and Lightning; th' I cannot in this Place omit doing Justice to the Boy who had the Direction of the Two painted Dragons, and made them spit Fire and Smoke: He flash'd out his Rasin [resin candle] in such just Proportions and in such due Time, that I could not forbear conceiving Hopes of his being one Day a most excellent Player. I saw indeed but Two things wanting to render his whole Action compleat, I mean the keeping his Head a little lower, and hiding his Candle.

The Sparrows and Chaffinches at the Hay-Market fly as yet very irregularly over the Stage; and instead of perching on the Trees and performing their Parts, these young Actors either get into the Galleries or put out the Candles.

As to the Mechanism and the Scenary [*sic*] at the *Hay-Market* the Undertakers forgetting to change their Side-Scenes, we were presented with a Prospect of the Ocean in the midst of a delightful Grove; and tho' the Gentlemen on the Stage had very much contributed to the Beauty of the Grove by walking up and down between the Trees, I must own I was not a little astonished to see a well-dressed young Fellow, in a full-bottom'd Wig, appear in the midst of the Sea, and without any visible Concern taking Snuff.

I am, &c.
R. [Sir Richard Steele]

Otto Erich Deutsch, *Handel: A Documentary Biography* (London: A. & C. Black, 1955), 35–37.

70

Some Contemporary Documents Relating to Handel's Oratorios

The following bits and pieces from O. E. Deutsch's admirable *Handel: A Documentary Biography* have been chosen to show how Handel's oratorios were presented to the public and how they were received. It was from the very beginning a ticklish question, how to present a sacred story in the profane setting of a public theater or opera house. There is a story, not documented, that the Bishop of London would not allow Handel's first oratorio, *Esther,* to be staged in costume and acted. Whether that story is true or not, Handel took every precaution not to offend the more conservative element in his audience. Here is the announcement of the first public performance of *Esther* under the composer's own direction (from the *Daily Journal,* 19 April 1732):

By *His* MAJESTY'S *Command.*

At the King's Theatre in the Hay-Market, on Tuesday the 2d Day of May, will be performed, *The Sacred Story* of ESTHER: an *Oratorio* in *English.* Formerly composed by Mr. *Handel,* and now revised by him, with several Additions, and to be performed by a great Number of the best Voices and Instruments.

N.B. There will be no Action on the Stage, but the House will be fitted up in a decent Manner, for the Audience. The Musick [i.e., musicians] to be disposed after the Manner of the Coronation Service [in a semicircle].

Tickets to be delivered at the Office of the Opera house, at the usual prices.

Concert presentation, with no acting, became the rule for all of Handel's oratorios. Even so, as we shall see, there were objections on religious grounds. Meanwhile here is a glimpse of the great man at work on one of his greatest oratorios, *Saul.* The report is from a letter by his none-too-respectful librettist, Charles Jennens.

Queen's Square, London, 19 September 1738

Mr. Handel's head is more full of maggots than ever. I found yesterday in his room a very queer instrument which he calls carillon. 'Tis played upon with keys like a Harpsichord and with this Cyclopean instrument he designs to make poor Saul stark mad. His second maggot is an organ of £500 price which (because he is overstocked with money) he has bespoke of one Moss of Barnet. This organ, he says, is so constructed that as he sits at it he has a better command of his performers than he used to have, and he is highly delighted to think with what exactness his Oratorio will be performed by the help of this organ; so that for the future instead of beating time at his oratorios, he is to sit at the organ all the time with his back to the Audience. I could tell you more of his maggots: but it grows late and I must defer the rest till I write next, by which time, I doubt not, more new ones will breed in his Brain.

The remark about money is sarcastic—Handel had to work very hard for his living. Both "maggots" were in fact brilliant inspirations. The use of the carillon in *Saul* gives the scoring a surprisingly exotic touch, perfectly in keeping with the Biblical story. And the specially designed organ enabled Handel to accompany and at the same time direct the music without rising from his seat. There was more laughter at his expense when it became known in fashionable London that he had applied to the King's Master of the Ordnance for a pair of the biggest kettledrums in existence; a nobleman (Lord Wentworth) mentioned it in a letter to his father:

London, January 13, 1739

I hear Mr. Handell has borrow'd of the Duke of Argylle a pair of the largest kettle-drums in the Tower, so to be sure it will be most excessive noisy with a bad set of singers; I doubt it will not retrieve his former losses.

Yet the "Dead March" in *Saul* (in which the kettledrums have a large part) became one of Handel's most popular compositions. The first performance of *Saul* was soon followed by that of another one of Handel's greatest works, *Israel in Egypt*. An enthusiastic letter from an unknown writer to the editor of the *London Daily Post* touches on two important themes: the English public's sense of identification with the Jews of the Old Testament (which contributed to the success of several of Handel's oratorios) and the problem of sacred subject matter presented in profane surroundings. There is also mention, at the end, of some difficulties that seem to have accompanied Handel's performances quite often, namely, poor singing and a noisy audience—in other words, an audience behaving as if it were attending an opera.

Wednesday Morning, April 18, 1739

Sir,

I Beg Leave, by your Paper, to congratulate, not Mr. Handel, but the Town, upon the Appearance there was last Night at *Israel in Egypt*. The Glory of one Man, on this Occasion, is but of small Importance, in Comparison with that of so numerous an Assembly. What a glorious Spectacle! to see a crowded Audience of the first Quality of a Nation, headed by the Heir apparent of their Sovereign's Crown, sitting enchanted at Sounds, that at the same time express'd in so sublime a manner the Praises of the Deity itself, and did such Honour to the Faculties of human Nature, in first *creating* those Sounds, if I may so speak; and in the next Place, being able to be so highly delighted with them. *Did such a Taste prevail universally in a People, that People might expect on a like Occasion* [as that described in the oratorio, i.e., Israel's bondage in Egypt], *if such Occasion should ever happen to them, the same* Deliverance *as those Praises celebrate; and Protestant, free, virtuous, united, Christian England, need little fear, at any time hereafter, the whole Force of slavish, bigotted, united, unchristian Popery, risen up against her, should such a Conjuncture ever hereafter happen.*

The Theatre, on this occasion, ought to be enter'd with more Solemnity than a Church; inasmuch, as the Entertainment you go to is really in itself the noblest

Adoration and Homage paid to the Deity that ever was in one. So sublime an Act of Devotion as this *Representation* carries in it, to a Heart and Ear duly tuned for it, would consecrate even Hell itself.—It is the Action that is done in it, that hallows the Place, and not the Place the Action.

I can't conclude, Sir, without great Concern at the Disadvantage so great a Master labours under, with respect to the many of his *Vocal Instruments,* which fall so vastly short in being able to do due Justice to what they perform; and which, if executed in a manner worthy of it, would receive so great Advantage. This Consideration will make a human[e] Mind serious, where a lighter Mind would be otherwise affected [i.e., would be amused at the bad singing, as so many Londoners in fact were]. I shall conclude with this Maxim, "That in Publick Entertainments every one should come with a reasonable Desire of being entertain'd themselves, or with the polite Resolution, no ways to interrupt the Entertainment of others. And that to have a Truce with Dissipation, and noisy Discourse, and to forbear that silly Affectation of beating Time aloud on such an Occasion, is, indeed, in Appearance, a great Compliment paid to the divine Author of so sacred an Entertainment, and to the rest of the Company near them; but at the same time, in reality, a much greater Respect paid to themselves."

I am, Sir, &c.
R.W.

The unknown writer's wishes with regard to "proper" behavior at oratorio performances were eventually fulfilled, and performances of Handel's oratorios became a national British institution of nearly unbearable seriousness not long after Handel's death. Meanwhile the fashionable set, accustomed to Italian opera stars, poked fun at the oratorio singers—for example, Horace Walpole, in a letter of 3 March 1743:

The Oratorios thrive abundantly—for my part, they give me an idea of heaven, where everybody is to sing whether they have voices or not.

Messiah received its first performance, under Handel's direction, on 13 April 1742, in Dublin. It was a great success, as the following newspaper extracts show.

From the *Dublin News-Letter,* April 10:

Yesterday Morning, at the Musick Hall there was a public Rehearsal of the Messiah, Mr. Handel's new sacred Oratorio, which in the opinion of the best Judges, far surpasses anything of that Nature, which has been performed in this or any other Kingdom. The elegant Entertainment was conducted in the most regular Manner, and to the entire satisfaction of the most crowded and polite Assembly.

From the *Dublin Journal,* April 17:

On Tuesday last Mr. Handel's Sacred Grand Oratorio, the MESSIAH, was performed at the New Musick-Hall in Fishamble-street; the best Judges allowed it to be the most finished piece of Musick. Words are wanting to express the exquisite Delight it afforded to the admiring crowded Audience. The Sublime, the Grand, and the Tender, adapted to the most elevated, majestick and moving Words, conspired to transport and charm the ravished Heart and Ear.

Here, finally, is a brief but vivid description of a Handel performance taken from a letter of a French visitor, Madame Fiquet, to her sister. Handel was sixty-five years old now.

London, April 15, 1750

The Oratorio, or pious concert, pleases us highly. HANDEL is the soul of it: when he makes his appearance, two wax lights are carried before him, which are laid upon his organ. Amidst a loud clapping of hands he seats himself, and the whole band of music strikes up exactly at the same moment. At the interludes he plays concertos of his own composition, either alone or accompanied by the orchestra. These are equally admirable for the harmony and the execution. The *Italian* opera, in three acts, gives us much less pleasure.

Otto Eric Deutsch, *Handel: A Documentary Biography* (London: A. & C. Black, 1955), 288–89, 465–66, 472, 481–83, 561, 544–45, 546, 686.

71

Bach's Duties and Obligations at Leipzig

Before taking over the position he was to occupy for the last twenty-seven years of his life, Bach had to sign an agreement that itemized his various duties and obligations. The document is of interest not only because it concerns a very great composer, but also for the light it sheds on the relationship between composer and patron (in this instance the Town Council of Leipzig) in the pre-Revolutionary era.

Their worships, the Council of this town of Leipzig, having accepted me to be Cantor of the School of St. Thomas, they have required of me an agreement as to certain points, namely:

1. That I should set a bright and good example to the boys by a sober and secluded life, attend school, diligently and faithfully instruct the boys.

2. And bring the music in the two chief churches of this town into good repute to the best of my ability.

3. Show all respect and obedience to their worships the Council, and defend and promote their honor and reputation to the utmost, and in all places; also, if a member of the Council requires the boys for a musical performance, unhesitatingly to obey, and besides this, never allow them to travel into the country for funerals or weddings without the fore-knowledge and consent of the burgomaster in office, and the governors of the school.

4. Give due obedience to the inspectors and governors of the school in all they command in the name of the Worshipful Council.

5. Admit no boys into the school who have not already the elements of music or who have no aptitude for being instructed therein, nor without the knowledge and leave of the inspectors and governors.

St. Thomas's, Leipzig, *c.* **1735.** The School, where Bach taught and lived with his family, may be seen at the end of the square, at right angle to the church. (Engraving by J. G. Schreiber.)

6. To the end that the churches may not be at unnecessary expense I should diligently instruct the boys not merely in vocal but in instrumental music.

7. To the end that good order may prevail in those churches I should so arrange the music that it may not last too long, and also in such wise as that it may not be operatic, but incite the hearers to devotion.

8. Supply good scholars to the New Church.

9. Treat the boys kindly and considerately, or, if they will not obey, punish such in moderation or report them to the authority.

10. Faithfully carry out instruction in the school and whatever else it is my duty to do.

11. And what I am unable to teach myself I am to cause to be taught by some other competent person without cost or help from their worships the Council, or from the school.

12. That I should not quit the town without leave from the burgomaster in office.

13. Should follow the funeral processions with the boys, as is customary, as often as possible.

14. And take no office under the University without the consent of their worships.

And to all this I hereby pledge myself, and faithfully to fulfill all this as is here set down, under pain of losing my place if I act against it, in witness of which I have signed this duplicate bond, and sealed it with my seal.

Johann Sebastian Bach

Given in Leipzig, May 5, 1723

Philipp Spitta, *Johann Sebastian Bach,* trans. C. Bell and J. A. Fuller-Maitland, III (London, 1885), 301–302.

72

Bach Remembered by His Son

Carl Philipp Emanuel Bach (1714–88), the most famous of J. S. Bach's composer sons, contributed much valuable information to the first full-length biography of his father, written by J. N. Forkel. The following details are from a letter to Forkel dated 1774.

He understood the whole building of organs in the highest degree. Organists were terrified when he sat down to play on their organs and drew the stops in his own manner, for they thought that the effect could not be good as he was planning it; but then they heard an effect that astounded them. (These sciences perished with him.) The first thing he would do in trying an organ was this: he would say, in fun, "Above all I must know whether the organ has good lungs," and, to find out, he would draw out every speaking stop, and play in the fullest and richest possible texture. At this the organ builders would often grow quite pale with fright. The exact tuning of his harpsichords as well as of the whole orchestra had his greatest attention. No one could tune and quill his harpsichords to please him. He did everything himself. The placing of an orchestra he understood perfectly. He made good use of any space. He grasped the sound properties of any place at first glance. A remarkable illustration of that fact is the following: He came to Berlin to visit me; I showed him the new opera house. He perceived at once its virtues and defects (that is, as regards the sound of music in it). I showed him the great dining hall. He looked at the ceiling, and without further investigation made the statement that the architect had here accomplished a remarkable feat, without intending to do so, and without anyone's knowing about it: namely, that if someone went to one corner of the oblong-shaped hall and whispered a few words very softly upwards against the wall, a person standing in the corner diagonally opposite, with his face to the wall, would hear quite distinctly what was said, while between them, and in the other parts of the room, no one would hear a sound. A feat of architecture hitherto very rare and much admired! This effect was brought about by the arches in the vaulted ceiling, which he saw at once. He heard the slightest wrong note even in the largest combinations. As the greatest expert and judge of harmony, he liked best to play the viola, with appropriate loudness and softness.

In his youth, and until the approach of old age, he played the violin cleanly and penetratingly, and thus kept the orchestra in better order than he could have done with the harpsichord [a reference to the two methods of directing ensembles before the advent of conductors]. When he listened to a rich and many-voiced fugue, he could soon say, after the first entries of the subjects, what contrapuntal devices it would be possible to apply, and which of them the composer by rights ought to apply, and on such occasions, when I was standing next to him, and he had voiced his surmises to me, he would joyfully nudge me when his expectations were fulfilled. He had a good penetrating voice of wide range and a good manner of singing. In counterpoints and fugues no one was as happy as he in all kinds of taste and figuration, and variety of ideas in general.

73

Bach's Obituary

The most extensive account of Bach's life and work to be published during the eighteenth century was the obituary prepared by C. P. E. Bach with the help of J. F. Agricola, one of his father's pupils, and published in 1754 in the *Musikalische Bibliothek,* a periodical put out by another former Bach pupil, Lorenz Mizler. In addition to what is given below, the obituary contained genealogical data, lists of works both published (mainly keyboard music) and unpublished (the vast bulk of Bach's output), and many more anecdotes, some of them rather heavy-handed in their partisanship: Bach had been a church musician in the traditional Lutheran mold, whose relatively placid career had never taken him far from home. As a result, he had never won the fame that Handel, Scarlatti, and perhaps a dozen lesser composers had enjoyed. His son and pupil evidently felt this needed explaining.

OBITUARY

of

The World-Famous Organist, Mr. Johann Sebastian Bach,

Royal Polish and Electoral Saxon Court Composer,

and Music Director in Leipzig

Johann Sebastian Bach belongs to a family that seems to have received a love and aptitude for music as a gift of Nature to all its members in common. So much is certain, that Veit Bach, the founder of the family, and all his descendants, even to the present seventh generation, have been devoted to music, and all save perhaps a very few have made it their profession. It would be a matter for astonishment that such excellent men should be so little known outside their native land if one did not remember that these honest Thuringians were so well satisfied with their native land and with their station in life that they did not even dare to wander far to seek their fortune. They gladly preferred the approval of the rulers in whose domains they were born, and the approval of a throng of their faithful countrymen, who were close at hand, to the uncertain manifestations of praise that they might gather, at great pains and expense, from a few (perhaps even envious) foreigners.

Johann Sebastian was not yet ten years old when he found himself bereft of his parents by death. He betook himself to Ohrdruff, where his eldest brother Johann Christoph was organist, and under this brother's guidance he laid the foundations for his playing of the clavier. Afterwards Johann Sebastian betook himself to the Michaels-Gymnasium in Lüneburg. From there he journeyed now and again to Hamburg, to hear the then famous organist of the Church of St. Catharina, Johann Adam Reincken [1643–1722]. And here, too, he had the opportunity to go and listen to a then famous band kept by the Duke of Celle, and consisting for the most part of Frenchmen; thus he acquired a thorough grounding in the French taste, which, in those regions, was at the time something quite new.

In the year 1703 he came to Weimar, and there became a musician of the Court. The next year he received the post of organist in the New Church in Arnstadt. Here he really showed the first fruits of his application to the art of organ playing, and to composition, which he had learned chiefly by the observation of the works of the most famous and proficient composers of his day and by the fruits of his own reflection upon them. In the art of the organ he took the works of [Nikolaus] Bruhns [1665–97], Reincken, [Dietrich] Buxtehude [c. 1637–1707], and several good French organists as models. While he was in Arnstadt he was once moved by the particularly strong desire to hear as many good organists as he could, so he undertook a journey, on foot, to Lübeck, in order to listen to Buxtehude, the famous organist of the Church of St. Mary. There he tarried, not without profit, for almost a quarter of a year, and then returned to Arnstadt.

In the year 1707 he was called as organist to the Church of St. Blasius in Mühlhausen. But this town was not to have the pleasure of holding him long. For in the following year, 1708, he undertook a journey to Weimar, had the opportunity to be heard by the reigning Duke, and was offered the post of Chamber and Court Organist in Weimar, of which post he immediately took possession. The pleasure His Grace took in his playing fired him with the desire to try every possible artistry in his treatment of the organ. Here, too, he wrote most of his organ works.

The year 1717 gave our already famous Bach a new opportunity to achieve still further honor; the reigning Prince Leopold of Anhalt-Cöthen, a great connoisseur and amateur of music, called him to be his Capellmeister. He entered forthwith upon the duties of this post, which he filled for almost six years, to the greatest pleasure of his gracious Prince. During this time, about the year 1722, he made a journey to Hamburg and was heard for more than two hours on the fine organ of the St. Catharina Church before the Magistrate and many other distinguished persons of the town, to their general astonishment. The aged organist Reincken, who at that time was nearly a hundred years old [in fact he was only 78], listened to him with particular pleasure. Bach, at the request of those present, performed extempore the chorale *By the Waters of Babylon* at great length (for almost half an hour) and in different ways, just as the better organists of Hamburg in the past had been used to do at the Saturday Vespers. Particularly on this, Reincken made Bach the following compliment: "I thought that this art was dead, but I see that in you it still lives."

The Town of Leipzig chose our Bach in the year 1723 as its Music Director and Cantor at the Thomas-Schule. Not long thereafter, the Duke of Weissenfels appointed him to be his Capellmeister; and in the year 1736 he was named Royal Polish and Electoral Saxon Court Composer, that is, after he had let himself be heard variously at Dresden, playing the organ publicly and with great success before the Court and the connoisseurs of music of that city.

In the year 1747, he made a journey to Berlin and on this occasion had the opportunity of being heard at Potsdam by His Majesty the King of Prussia [Frederick the Great—see p. 258]. His Majesty himself played him a theme for a fugue, which he at once developed, to the particular pleasure of the Monarch, on the pianoforte. Hereupon His Majesty demanded to hear a fugue with six voices, which command he also fulfilled, to the astonishment of the King and the musicians there present, using a theme of his own. After his return to Leipzig, he set down on paper a three-voiced and a six-voiced so-called *ricercar* together with several other intricate little pieces, all on the very theme that had been given him by His Majesty, and this [the *Musical Offering*] he dedicated, engraved on copper, to the King.

His naturally somewhat weak eyesight, further weakened by his unheard-of zeal in studying, which made him, particularly in his youth, sit at work the whole night through, led, in his last years, to an eye disease. He wished to rid himself of this by an operation, partly out of a desire to be of further service to God and his neighbor with his other spiritual and bodily powers, which were still very vigorous, and partly on the advice of some of his friends, who placed great confidence in an oculist who had recently arrived in Leipzig. But the operation, although it had to be repeated, turned out very badly. Not only could he no longer use his eyes, but his whole system, which was otherwise thoroughly healthy, was completely overthrown by the operation and by the addition of harmful medicaments and other things, so that, thereafter, he was almost continuously ill for full half a year. Ten days before his death his eyes suddenly seemed better, so that one morning he could see quite well again and could also again endure the light. But a few hours later he suffered a stroke; and this was followed by a raging fever, as a victim of which, despite every possible care given him by two of the most skillful physicians of Leipzig, on the 28th of July, 1750, a little after a quarter to nine in the evening, in the sixty-sixth year of his life, he quietly and peacefully, by the merit of his Redeemer, departed this life. This is the brief description of the life of a man who contributed quite exceptionally to the honor of music, of his fatherland, and of his family.

If ever a composer showed polyphony in its greatest strength, it was certainly our late lamented Bach. If ever a musician employed the most hidden secrets of harmony with the most skilled artistry, it was certainly our Bach. No one ever showed so many ingenious and unusual ideas as he in elaborate pieces such as ordinarily seem dry exercises in craftsmanship. His melodies were strange, but always varied, rich in invention, and resembling those of no other composer. His serious temperament drew him by preference to music that was serious, elaborate, and profound; but he could also, when the occasion demanded, adjust himself, especially in playing, to a light and more humorous way of thought. His constant practice in the working out of polyphonic pieces had given his eye such facility that even in the largest scores he could take in all the simultaneously sounding parts at a glance. His hearing was so fine that he was able to detect the slightest error even in the largest ensembles. It is but a pity that it was only seldom he had the good fortune of finding a body of such performers as could have spared him unpleasant discoveries of this nature. In conducting he was very accurate, and of the tempo, which he generally took very lively, he was uncommonly sure.

So long as we can be offered in contradiction no more than the mere suggestion of the possible existence of better organists and clavier players, so long we cannot be blamed if we are bold enough to declare that our Bach was the greatest organist and clavier player that we have ever had. It may be that many a famous man has accomplished much in polyphony upon this instrument; is he therefore just as skillful, in both hands and feet—just as skillful as Bach was? This doubt will not be considered unfounded by anyone who ever had the pleasure of hearing both him and others and is not carried away by prejudice. And anyone who looks at Bach's organ and clavier pieces, which, as is generally known, he himself performed with the greatest perfection, will also not find much to object to in the sentence above. How strange, how new, how expressive, how beautiful were his ideas in improvising! How perfectly he realized them! All his fingers were equally skillful; all were equally capable of the most perfect accuracy in performance. He had devised for himself so convenient a system of fingering that it was not hard for him to conquer the greatest difficulties with the most flowing facility. Before him, the most famous clavier players in Germany and other lands had used the thumb but little. All the better did he know how to use it. With his two feet, he could play things on the pedals which many not unskillful clavier players would find it bitter enough to have to play with five fingers. He not only understood the art of playing the organ, of combining the various stops of that instrument in the most skillful manner, and of displaying each stop according to its character in the greatest perfection, but he also knew the construction of organs from one end to the other. Of his moral character, those may speak who enjoyed association and friendship with him and were witnesses to his uprightness towards God and his neighbor.

Hans T. David and Arthur Mendel (eds.), *The Bach Reader: A Life of Johann Sebastian Bach in Letters and Documents,* rev. ed. (New York: W. W. Norton & Company, Inc., 1966), 215–24. Reprinted by permission of W. W. Norton & Company, Inc. Copyright © 1966, 1945 by W. W. Norton & Company, Inc.

PART FIVE

The Pre-Classical Period

74

The Cult of the Natural

A swing away from "reason" and back to "the ear" can be seen when writers on music begin to emphasize "naturalness" as the highest aesthetic ideal, and to find fault with too much technical complexity or too heroic a tone or sentiment. Bach had some difficulty with proponents of this idea, and was notoriously criticized in print by some for the very attributes we prize most in his music today. Johann David Heinichen (1683–1729) included a little disquisition on "good taste" (rather than reason) as the ultimate arbiter of things musical as a footnote to his thorough-bass manual *Der General-Bass in der Composition* (1728). Here an incipient hostility towards "learned" music (such as Bach's) may be detected.

If experience is needed in any art or science, it is certainly needed in music. In this applied art, we must first of all gain experience, either at home (provided opportunities are plentiful) or abroad. But why must we seek experience? I will give you one little word that encompasses the three basic requirements in music (talent, knowledge, and experience) and its heart and its outer limits as well, and all in four letters: *Goût*. Through application, talent, and experience, a composer needs to acquire above all an exceptional sense of taste in music. An experienced musician need not be told the meaning of *Goût, Gusto,* or good taste; but to describe its essential characteristics is as difficult as describing the essence of the soul. One could even say that good taste is the soul of music, which it enlivens even as it gives pleasure to the senses. The distinguishing feature of a composer with good taste is simply the skill with which he makes music pleasing to and beloved by the general, educated public; in other words, the skills by which he pleases our ear and moves our sensibilities. Specifically, this is achieved by an ever-dominating *cantabile* [singing melody], suitable and affecting accompaniments, changing harmonies that refresh the ear, and other methods gained from experience, which frequently may look poor on paper. An exceptional sense of taste is the philosopher's stone and principal musical mystery by means of which the emotions are unlocked and the senses won over. For the inventions of even the richest natural gift or talent can only be compared to crude gold and silver dross that must first be purified by the fire of experience before it can be pressed into a solid ingot—I mean into a finely developed and reliable sense of taste.

George Buelow, *Thorough-Bass Accompaniment according to Johann David Heinichen* (Berkeley: University of California Press, 1966), 273–74.

> Johann Adolph Scheibe (1708–76) waged war on behalf of the "natural" in his journal *Der critische Musicus,* which appeared from 1737 to 1740. One easily sees that his arguments are loaded and circular, for the "nature" Scheibe holds up as a model is no longer speech (Plato), or "movements of the spirit" (Descartes), but simply what pleases Scheibe, or, in Heinichen's phrase, what pleases the "general, educated public."

True art always seeks that which is natural, while too much art exceeds nature, leading one into bombast and confusion. Even public speakers and poets are careful to avoid too much art just as they seek to avoid what is common, flat, and vulgar. Although it takes great effort and patience to write artfully, all one gets for one's pains is that one exceeds nature and consequently becomes disordered, unnatural, and confused. When has anyone ever been moved or convinced by something unnatural? When has such a thing expressed emotions and captivated the listener? Excessive art and unnatural contrivance have never been known to advance the sciences that concern the soul and arouse within us those tender feelings which, being a pleasant product of reason, distinguish us from the unreasoning animals.

Art must imitate nature. As soon as this imitation is exceeded, however, art is to be condemned. It is not art that endows nature with beauty but nature that endows art. Nature already possesses everything of merit and need borrow no rouge from art. The more extravagant art becomes, the further it goes along its own way, the more it alienates itself from nature. It is therefore a fact that too much art obscures true beauty.

> At his most acerbic, Scheibe reads like a humanist of 150 years before, carrying on a one-man anti-counterpoint crusade. The critic is, however, a good witness to the style changes taking place around him.

In the past, the style of concerted music was altogether unlike today's. In melody, in harmony, and in form it differed greatly from what is being written now. Melody was neither as free nor as natural, and consequently less lively and flowing. More attention was paid to working out a full texture. Music thus artificially and laboriously fashioned could not hope to embody the affections the way today's music does. It was neither as pleasant nor as moving and expressive. Owing to the polyphonic texture, contrivance gained the upper hand over nature. Melody, that is to say pure song, was suppressed and such music was unable to achieve that degree of expression which is the specialty of today's music. Composers of the past who strove to exhibit their skill at counterpoint had to find room for all kinds of devices; their music was laced through with fugues, canons, and similarly artificial imitative procedures. The instruments weaved in and out and lost themselves amid incessant suspensions. How could a free and intelligible melody find employment under such conditions?

But now consider the music of today. We certainly find different qualities. By striving for a flowing, expressive, lively melody, the only kind that can call nature its mother, composers achieve very different effects, much to be preferred over those of old. Even though a few particularly serious works may still contain severely contra-puntal sections, even extensive passages of imitation, the overall form of the work and the way its sections succeed one another show that everything is geared towards emphasizing the melody and bringing out its natural beauty, emotion, and dignity. Through melody one can arouse and express all sorts of affections and passions, which proves that melody is the primary and most worthy element in music and is to be preferred to harmony [i.e., counterpoint]. Any attempt to give harmony the place of honor that belongs to melody alone is doomed to failure.

Imanuel Willheim, "Johann Adolph Scheibe: German Musical Thought in Transition" (Ph.D. dissertation, University of Illinois, 1956), 103–104, 106–107.

75

The Advice and Opinions of an Italian Singing Master

Pier Francesco Tosi (1654–1732), a castrato singer and a man of considerable learning and taste, was the author of one of the earliest primers on the great Italian tradition of singing. By 1723, when he published it, Tosi was a seasoned veteran. He viewed the increasing flamboyance of late Baroque singing with unconcealed disgust and held up the simpler, more affecting style of his youth as a model of perfection. As so often happens in the seesawing history of taste, a later generation, working its way out of the Baroque towards a new simplicity, found Tosi's opinions totally congenial: the English and German translations of his little work, which enjoyed much popularity, date from the 1740s and 1750s, respectively. Note, together with many homely and amusing bits of practical advice, Tosi's insistence on moderation and on naturalness of expression.

After the Scholar has made himself perfect in the Shake [i.e., trill] and the Divisions [i.e., rapid passages], the Master should let him read and pronounce the Words, free from those gross and ridiculous Errors of Orthography, by which many deprive one Word of its double Consonants, adding them instead to another, where they are single.

After having corrected the Pronunciation, let him take Care that the Words be uttered in such a Manner, without any Affectation, that they be distinctly understood, and no one Syllable be lost; for if they are not distinguished, the Singer deprives the Hearer of the greatest Part of that Delight which vocal Musick receives from their Power. If they are not distinguished, the Singer omits Truth from the Art. Finally, if they are not distinguished, there will be no great difference between a human Voice and a Cornet or a Hautboy. Let the modern Master learn to make use of this Advice, for never was it more necessary than at present.

Let him forbid the Scholar to take Breath in the Middle of a Word, because the dividing it in two is an Error intolerable to Nature, which we must imitate, if we would avoid being laugh'd at. In interrupted Movements [i.e., between short phrases], or in long Divisions, it is not so rigorously required, when the one or the other cannot be sung in one Breath.

Let him show, in all Compositions, the proper Place where to take Breath, and without Fatigue; because there are Singers who, to the dismay of the Hearer, labour as if they had an Asthma, taking Breath every Moment with Difficulty, or arriving at the last Notes as if they were breathing their last.

Let him never suffer the Scholar to hold the Musick-Paper, in Singing, before his Face, both that the Sound of the Voice may not be obstructed, and to prevent him from being bashful.

Let him accustom the Scholar to sing often in presence of Persons of Distinction, whether from Birth or Eminence in the Profession, that by gradually losing his Fear, he may acquire an Assurance, but not a Boldness. Assurance is the first-born of Success, and in a Singer becomes a Merit. On the contrary, the Fearful is most unhappy: labouring under the Difficulty of fetching Breath, the Voice is always trembling; he is obliged to lose Time at every Note in order to swallow; he suffers in not being able to take his Ability with him when he leaves his House; he disgusts the Hearer; and he ruins the Compositions in such a Manner, that they cannot be recognized. A timorous Singer is unhappy, like a Prodigal, who is miserably poor.

Let the Master remember, that whosoever does not sing to the utmost Rigour of Time, deserves not the Esteem of the Judicious; therefore let him take Care, when teaching, that there be no Alteration or Diminution in it, if he pretends to teach well, and to make an excellent Scholar.

Let him encourage the Scholar if he improves; let him mortify him, without Beating, if he is persistently obtuse; let him be more rigorous for Negligences; nor let the Scholar ever end a Lesson without having profited something.

An Hour of Application in a Day is not sufficient, even for one of the quickest Apprehension; the Master therefore should consider how much more Time is necessary for one that has not the same Quickness, and how much he is obliged to consult the Capacity of his Scholar. From a mercenary Teacher this necessary Regard is not to be hoped for; expected by other Scholars, tired with the Fatigue, solicited by his Necessities, he thinks the Month is still long; he looks on his Watch, and goes away. If he be but poorly paid for his Teaching—a God-speed to him.

A necessary Exercise is the Study of an agreeable *Portamento* [i.e., connection between notes], without which all Application is vain. Whosoever pretends to obtain it, must hearken more to the Dictates of the Heart, than to those of Art.

Oh! how great a Master is the Heart! Confess it, my beloved Singers, and gratefully own, that you would not have arrived at the highest Rank of the Profession if you had not been its Scholars; own, that in a few Lessons from it, you learned the most beautiful Expressions, the most refin'd Taste, the most noble Action, and the most exquisite Graces: Own (though it hardly be credible) that the Heart corrects the Defects of Nature, since it softens a Voice that's harsh, betters an indifferent one, and perfects a good one: Own, when the Heart sings, you cannot dissemble, nor has Truth a greater Power of persuading: And, lastly, do you convince the World, (what is not in my Power to do) that from the Heart alone you have learn'd that ineffable Sweetness, that so subtily passes from Vein to Vein, till it finds the Soul.

Pier Francesco Tosi, *Observations on the Florid Song; or, Sentiments on the Ancient and Modern Singers,* trans. [J. E.] Galliard, 2nd ed. (London, 1743), 58–65, 157–58, with corrections based on the original Italian text.

76

From Geminiani's Violin Tutor

Francesco Geminiani (1687–1762), a famous violinist and the composer of sonatas and concertos, was an early exponent of the Italian (as against the French) style of violin playing in England. He described it in a violin treatise published in 1751 and consisting of only nine pages of text followed by fifty-one of musical examples. Apart from terse, but most informative, remarks of a technical nature, the text contains some passages, reproduced below, that reveal Geminiani's broader views on music in general and musical performance. These seem decidedly "modern," i.e., they are characteristic of post-Baroque attitudes.

From the Preface

The Intention of Musick is not only to please the Ear, but to express Sentiments, strike the Imagination, affect the Mind, and command the Passions. The Art of playing the Violin consists in giving that Instrument a Tone that shall in a Manner rival the most perfect human Voice; and in executing every Piece with Exactness, Propriety, and Delicacy of Expression according to the true Intention of Musick. But as the imitating the Cock, Cuckoo, Owl, and other Birds; or the Drum, French Horn, and the like; and also sudden Shifts of the Hand from one Extremity of the Finger-board to the other, accompanied with Contortions of the Head and Body, and all other such Tricks rather belong to the Professors of Legerdemain and Posture-masters than to the Art of Musick, the Lovers of that Art are not to expect to find any thing of that Sort in this Book. But I flatter myself they will find in it whatever is Necessary for the Institution of a just and regular Performer on the Violin.

On Ornaments

Example XVIII contains all the Ornaments of Expression, necessary to the playing in a good Taste.

What is commonly call'd good Taste in singing and playing, has been thought for some Years past to destroy the true Melody, and the intention of their Composers. It is supposed by many that a real good Taste cannot possibly be acquired by any Rules of Art; it being a peculiar Gift of Nature, indulged only to those who have naturally a good Ear: And as most flatter themselves to have this Perfection, hence it happens that he who sings or plays, thinks of nothing so much as to make continually some favourite Passages or Graces, believing that by this Means he shall be thought to be a good Performer, not perceiving that playing in good Taste doth not consist of frequent Passages, but in expressing with Strength and Delicacy the Intention of the Composer. This Expression is what everyone should endeavour to acquire, and it may easily be obtained by any Person, who is not too fond of his own Opinion, and doth not obstinately resist the Force of true Evidence. I would not however have it supposed that I deny the powerful Effects of a good Ear; as I have found in several Instances how great its Force is: I only assert that certain Rules of Art are necessary for a moderate Genius, and may improve and perfect a good one.

Geminiani proceeds to list some of the main "graces" and expressive devices that will enliven performance according to the requirements of "taste" and without the exaggerations of the older style. He attempts to describe their effect, so that they may be used with "propriety." For example:

The turn'd Shake [trill with concluding turn] being made quick and long is fit to express Gaiety; but if you make it short, and continue the Length of the Note plain and soft, it may then express some of the more tender Passions.

The Superior Appoggiatura [i.e., accented dissonance] is supposed to express Love, Affection, Pleasure, &c.

Of Holding a Note

It is necessary to use this often; for were we to make Beats and Shakes continually without sometimes suffering the pure Note to be heard, the Melody would be too much diversified.

Of Piano and Forte

They are both extremely necessary to express the Intention of the Melody; and as all good musick should be composed in Imitation of a Discourse, these two Ornaments are designed to produce the same Effects that an Orator does by raising and falling his Voice.

Of the Beat [i.e., mordent]

This is proper to express several Passions; as for Example, if it be perform'd with Strength, and continued long, it expresses Fury, Anger, Resolution, &c. If it be play'd less strong and shorter, it expresses Mirth, Satisfaction, &c. But if you play it quite soft, and swell the Note, it may then denote Horror, Fear, Grief, Lamentation, &c. By making it short and swelling the Note gently, it may express Affection and Pleasure.

Of the Close Shake [i.e., vibrato]

This cannot possibly be described by Notes as in former Examples. To perform it, you must press the Finger strongly upon the String of the Instrument, and move the Wrist in and out slowly and equally; when it is long continued, swelling the Sound by Degrees, drawing the Bow nearer to the Bridge, and ending it very strong, it may express Majesty, Dignity, &c. But making it shorter, lower and softer, it may denote Affliction, Fear, &c. and when it is made on short Notes, it only contributes to make their Sound more agreeable and for this Reason it should be made use of as often as possible.

Geminiani's parting advice, with its emphasis on sentiment and inspiration, was very much a sign of the times.

Men of purblind Understandings, and half Ideas may perhaps ask, is it possible to give Meaning and Expression to Wood and Wire; or to bestow upon them the Power of raising and soothing the Passions of rational Beings? But whenever I hear such a Question put, whether for the Sake of Information, or to convey Ridicule, I shall make no Difficulty to answer in the Affirmative, and without searching over-deeply into the Cause, shall think it sufficient to appeal to the Effect. Even in common Speech a Difference of Tone gives the same Word a different Meaning. And with Regard to musical Performances, Experience has shown that the Imagination of the Hearer is in general so much at the Disposal of the Master, that by the Help of Variations, Movements, Intervals and Modulation he may almost stamp what Impression on the Mind he pleases.

These extraordinary Emotions are indeed most easily excited when accompany'd with Words; and I would besides advise, as well the Composer as the Performer, who is ambitious to inspire his Audience, to be first inspired himself; which he cannot fail to be if he chooses a Work of Genius, if he makes himself thoroughly acquainted with all its Beauties; and if while his Imagination is warm and glowing he pours the same exalted Spirit into his own Performance.

Francesco Geminiani, *The Art of Playing on the Violin* (London, 1751), 1, 6–8.

77

From Quantz's Treatise on Flute Playing

Johann Joachim Quantz (1697–1773), Frederick the Great's flute teacher and composer in residence (see Burney's thumbnail sketch of him, p. 258), published his famous flute treatise in 1752. Far from limiting himself to technicalities pertaining to the flute, he branched out to all matters involving musical education and performance, doubtless providing the inspiration for two slightly later treatises, C. P. E. Bach's on keyboard performance (see p. 227) and Leopold Mozart's on the violin.

From Chapter XI, "Of Good Execution in General in Singing and Playing"

Reason teaches us that if in speaking we demand something from someone, we must make use of such expressions as the other understands. Now music is nothing but an artificial language through which we seek to acquaint the listener with our *musical* ideas. If we execute these ideas in an obscure and bizarre manner which is incomprehensible to the listener and arouses no feeling, of what use are our perpetual efforts to be thought learned? If we were to demand that all our listeners be connoisseurs and musical scholars, their number would not be very great; we would have to seek them out one at a time among the professional musicians. And from the latter it would be most unwise to hope for many benefits. For they could do no more than acquaint the amateurs with the skill of the performer by their approval. Yet how rare and unlikely this is! The majority are so carried away by passion, and particularly by envy, that they are neither able to perceive the merits of their equals, nor willing to make them known to others. If, on the other hand, every amateur knew as much as the professional should know, there again would be no advantage, since there would be little or no further need of the professional artist. Thus it is most important that the professional musician seek to play each piece distinctly, and with such expression that it becomes intelligible to both the learned and the unlearned, and hence may please them both.

"Both the learned and the unlearned": Quantz considers it a professional musician's obligation to please *everybody,* not merely an élite; and he even gives shrewd advice on how to cope with a predominantly uncultivated audience (below: play a little faster). In this he is motivated not merely by opportunism but also, importantly, by a benign humanitarianism typical of the Enlightenment. Note, in this connection, the frequent injunctions to enter into the spirit of the music: "For that which does not come from the heart does not easily reach the heart." The musician's gift to his listeners must be genuinely felt—it is a theme that recurs in virtually every one of these pre-Classical selections in some form or other, and it will survive well into the nineteenth century. In the following discussions of fast (allegro) and slow (adagio) music, Quantz is referring to the movements of concertos for flute and orchestra. It will be well to notice that the Baroque unity of the "affection" within a single piece (compare p. 184) is now replaced by a succession of alternating moods: a decisive break!

From Chapter XII, "Of the Manner of Playing the Allegro"

The passions change frequently in the Allegro just as in the Adagio. The performer must therefore seek to transport himself into each of these passions, and to express it suitably. Hence it is necessary to investigate whether the piece to be played consists entirely of gay ideas, or whether these are joined to others of a different kind.

From Chapter XIV, "Of the Manner of Playing the Adagio"

The Adagio ordinarily affords persons who are simple amateurs of music [i.e., nonprofessional music lovers] the least pleasure. There are even some professional musicians who, lacking the necessary feeling and insight, are gratified to see the end of the Adagio arrive. Yet a true musician may distinguish himself by the manner in which he plays the Adagio, may greatly please true connoisseurs and sensitive and feeling amateurs, and may demonstrate his skill to those who know composition. Since it does remain a stumbling block, however, intelligent musicians will, without my advice, accommodate themselves to their listeners and to the amateurs, not only to earn more easily the respect befitting their skill, but also to ingratiate themselves.

To play an Adagio well, you must enter as much as possible into a calm and almost melancholy mood, so that you execute what you have to play in the same state of mind as that in which the composer wrote it. A true Adagio must resemble a flattering petition. For just as anyone who wishes to request something from a person to whom he owes particular respect will scarcely achieve his object with bold and impudent threats, so here you will scarcely engage, soften, and touch your listeners with a bold and bizarre manner of playing. For that which does not come from the heart does not easily reach the heart.

From Chapter XV, "Of Cadenzas"

By the word cadenza I understand here that extempore embellishment created, according to the fancy and pleasure of the performer, by a solo part at the close of a piece on the penultimate note of the bass, that is, the fifth of the key of the piece [nowadays called the dominant].

Whether cadenzas were at first formed according to specific rules, or whether they were simply invented by a few skillful people extemporaneously and without rules, I do not know. I believe the latter, since more than twenty years ago the composers in Italy were already fighting against the abuses committed so abundantly in this respect by mediocre singers in operas.

The object of the cadenza is simply to surprise the listener unexpectedly once more at the end of the piece, and to leave behind a special impression in his heart.

Regular meter is seldom observed, and indeed should not be observed, in cadenzas. They should consist of detached ideas rather than a sustained melody, as long as they conform to the preceding expression of the passions.

From Chapter XVI, "What a Flutist Must Observe If He Plays in Public Concerts"

If the flutist who wishes to be heard publicly is timorous, and as yet unaccustomed to playing in the presence of many people, he must try while playing to direct his attention only to the notes before him, never turning his eyes to those present, since this distracts his thoughts, and destroys his composure. He should not undertake pieces which are so difficult that he has had no success with them in his individual practice, but should rather keep to those which he can play fluently. Fear causes an ebullition of the blood, which disturbs the regular action of the lungs, and which likewise warms the tongue and fingers. From this a most obstructive trembling of the limbs arises in playing, and as a result the flute player will be unable to produce extended passage-work in one breath, or other specially difficult feats, as well as he does in a tranquil state of mind. In such circumstances, and especially in warm weather, it also may happen that he perspires about the mouth, and the flute in consequence does not remain lying securely in the proper place, but slips downwards, so that the mouth-hole is too much covered, and the tone, if not lacking altogether, is at least too weak. Quickly to remedy this last evil, let the flutist wipe his mouth and the flute clean, then touch his hair or wig and rub the fine powder clinging to his finger upon his mouth. In this way the pores are stopped, and he can continue playing without great hindrance.

Anyone who wishes to be heard publicly must consider his listeners well, especially those whom it is most important that he please. He must consider whether or not they are connoisseurs. Before connoisseurs he can play something a little more elaborate, in which he has the opportunity to show his skill in both the Allegro and the Adagio. But before pure amateurs, who understand nothing of music, he will do better to produce those pieces in which the melody is brilliant and pleasing. To avoid boring such amateurs, he may also take the Adagio a little more quickly than usual.

If someone requests him to play, let him do so at once, without grimaces or false modesty. And when he has finished his piece, he should not insist upon playing more than is demanded of him, lest we must beg him as many times to cease as we had to beg him to begin, a common reproach made against virtuosos.

> Quantz now methodically addresses himself to the body of musicians whose task is to accompany the flutist: the orchestra. In the absence of orchestral conductors (who only began to appear in the nineteenth century), concertos and, later, symphonies were normally led by the principal violinist.

From Chapter XVII, Section 1, "Of the Qualities of a Leader of an Orchestra"

Whether a leader plays this or that instrument may be of no importance. Since, however, the violin is absolutely indispensable in the accompanying body, and is also more penetrating than any of the other instruments most used for accompanying, it is better if he does play the violin. Yet there is no urgent necessity that he demonstrate his ability to perform unusually difficult feats upon his instrument; this may be left to those who seek to distinguish themselves only through the delicacy of their playing, of whom there are sufficient numbers. If, however, a leader does possess this talent, he deserves so much the greater honor.

The leader must frequently direct his eyes and ears both to the performer of the principal part and to the accompanists, in case it is necessary to accommodate the one and keep the others in order. The leader must judge from the execution of the soloist whether the latter would prefer what he is playing to go either faster or slower, so that the others may be guided smoothly to the correct tempo.

> The Baroque practice of backing up ensembles with the thorough bass showed no signs of dying at this date. Quantz's advice to keyboard (clavier) players is useful to an understanding of a tradition that was soon to become obsolete.

From Chapter XVII, Section 6, "Of the Clavier Player in Particular"

Since the art of accompanying well is part of the design of this work, I wish, with the permission of my lords the clavier players, to make a few remarks on that subject here, leaving the rest to the further consideration of each able and experienced clavier player.

It is possible that a player who has an exhaustive knowledge of thorough bass may nevertheless be only a poor accompanist. Thorough bass requires that the parts which the player adds extemporaneously above the bass, in conformity with the figures, be performed according to the rules, and as if they were written out on paper. The art of accompanying requires both this and much else besides.

A piece with full harmony, accompanied by a large body of instruments, also requires a full and strong clavier accompaniment. A concerto executed by a few instruments already requires some moderation in this respect, particularly in the solo passages. You must then pay attention to whether these passages are accompanied by the bass alone or by additional instruments; whether the solo part plays softly or loud, in the low or high register; whether it has a sustained and singing melody, leaps or passage-work to execute; whether the passage-work is played quietly or with fire; whether the passage-work remains consonant or becomes dissonant in order to modulate to a new key; whether the bass moves slowly or quickly beneath the passage-work; whether the quick notes of the bass are written in steps or in leaps, or whether four or eight notes appear under the same pitch; whether rests or long and short notes are intermingled; whether the piece is an Allegretto, Allegro, or Presto, the first of which must be played seriously in pieces for instruments, the second in a lively manner, and the third fleetingly and playfully; or whether it is an Adagio assai, Grave, Mesto, Cantabile, Arioso, Andante, Larghetto, Siciliano, Spiritoso, or so forth, each of which requires a special execution both in the principal part and in the accompaniment. If each person observes these matters properly, the piece will produce the desired effect upon the listeners.

> In the following passage, Quantz casts a glance at German music past and present, and is encouraged to hope that some day it might be as highly regarded as French and Italian. Both that hope and his preference for a cosmopolitan, rather than national, style were destined to be realized very soon.

From Chapter XVIII, "How a Musician and a Musical Composition Are to Be Judged"

Bad as the style of German singers and instrumentalists appears to have been in former times (despite the thorough insight of the German composers into harmony), it did gradually take on a new aspect. Even if it cannot be said that the Germans have produced an individual style entirely different from that of other nations, they are all the more capable in taking whatever they like from another style, and they know how to make use of the good things in all types of foreign music.

Towards the middle of the last century there were already some celebrated persons who began to effect the improvement of musical style, partly by visiting and profiting from Italy and France themselves, partly by imitating the works and the taste of these meritorious foreign lands. The organ and harpsichord players, especially *Froberger* [1616–67] and after him *Pachelbel* [1653–1706] among the latter, and *Reincken, Buxtehude, Bruhns,* and some others among the former [see p. 213], wrote almost the first very tasteful instrumental pieces of their time for their instruments. In particular *the art of playing the organ,* inherited in large part from the Netherlanders, had already been carried a long way at about this time by the able men enumerated above and by some others. Finally the admirable *Johann Sebastian Bach* in more recent times brought it to its greatest perfection. We should hope that, with his death, it will not suffer decay or ruin because of the small number of those who apply themselves to it.

If one has the necessary discernment to choose the best from the styles of different countries, a *mixed style* results that, without overstepping the bounds of modesty, could well be called *the German style,* not only because the Germans came upon it first, but because it has already been established at different places in Germany for many years, flourishes still, and displeases in neither Italy nor France, nor in other lands.

A style of music that is received and approved by many peoples, and not just by a single land, a single province, or a particular nation, must, if it is also founded on sound judgment and healthy feeling, be the very best.

Johann Joachim Quantz, *On Playing the Flute,* trans. Edward R. Reilly (London: Faber and Faber, 1966), 120–21, 133, 162, 163, 179, 180, 185, 198–99, 200, 203, 207–208, 209, 251–52, 338–39, 341, 342. Copyright © 1966 by Faber and Faber Ltd. Reprinted by permission of Faber and Faber Ltd. and Macmillan Publishing Company.

78

Carl Philipp Emanuel Bach on Playing Keyboard Instruments

We have already met C. P. E. Bach as chronicler of his father's life (see page 211). Actually, in his own right he was far better known in his lifetime than his father had ever been. His expressive keyboard works, especially, were widely admired and exerted a notable influence—for example, on Beethoven. The following excerpts, selected as much for their commonsense practicality as for what they reveal concerning

C. P. E. Bach's attitudes and ideals, are from his well-known *Essay on the Correct Manner of Playing the Clavier* (1753).

Though the clavier has many excellent qualities, it is fraught with as many difficulties. Its perfection could easily be demonstrated, were it necessary to do so, for it incorporates those properties which other instruments possess but singly; for it is capable of producing a full harmony, where three, four, or more instruments would ordinarily be needed; and has other advantages besides. But then, who is not aware of all the demands made on the clavier? It is not enough that a player on the clavier should satisfy the expectations we rightly have of any instrumentalist, that is, that he be able to perform a piece composed for his instrument according to the rules of good execution. He must, besides, extemporize in a variety of manners; work up a given composition on the spot, observing the strictest rules of harmony and melody; play with equal ease in all the keys, transpose unhesitatingly and faultlessly, play anything whatsoever at sight, whether composed specially for his instrument or not; he must have a total command of the science of the thorough bass and be able to execute it in a variety of ways, often contradictory: now in many parts, now in few, now in strict harmony, now elegantly, from bass parts that may be insufficiently or overabundantly furnished with figures, or not at all, or incorrectly; he must sometimes extract the thorough bass, and so strengthen the concordance, from full scores in which the basses are unfigured or, often indeed, pause altogether, one of the other parts serving as foundation to the harmony. And who can count all the other requirements? This, furthermore, must for the most part be accomplished on an unfamiliar instrument; and whether the latter is good or bad, in suitable condition or not, is immaterial: excuses are often out of place. On the contrary, the commonest expectation is that the clavier player shall oblige with some improvisations, no one troubling to inquire whether he is sufficiently inspired at the moment or offering him the use of a proper instrument to stimulate, or preserve, his inclination.

These demands notwithstanding, the clavier always, and justifiably, attracts its devotees. Its difficulty is not sufficient to deter those who would learn to play upon an instrument whose extraordinary charms are ample reward for the time and trouble spent on it. Not every devotee, moreover, is duty-bound to satisfy all of its demands. He will do so to the extent he pleases and his natural gifts allow.

Apart from the many types of clavier that have remained unknown because of their shortcomings or have yet to gain universal acceptance, two principal types, namely the harpsichords and clavichords, have until now met with the greatest approval. The former are generally employed in ampler settings, the latter in playing solos. The newer forte-pianos [i.e., pianos], when well-made and of stout construction, have many advantages, though their handling does need to be specially worked out and is not devoid of difficulties. They do well in solos and in music that is not too heavily scored. I, however, believe a good clavichord, except that it has a weaker sound, can match all their beauties; it has, moreover, the advantage of the vibrato and the sustaining of tones, for I can always press a note down again after playing it. The clavichord, therefore, is the instrument on which a player's competence can most accurately be judged.

The clavier player must sit opposite the middle of the keyboard, so that he may play the highest and the lowest notes with equal ease.

He will be sitting at the proper height when his forearms slope down ever so little towards the keyboard.

We play with curved fingers and relaxed muscles; the less these conditions are met, the more it will be necessary to fix the mind on them. Stiffness hinders all movement, especially the ability quickly to expand and contract the hands, which is a constant requirement.

Through practice and diligence, the use of the fingers becomes, indeed must become, so mechanical at last that, no further thought being needed in that direction, we are free to devote our attention to the expression of more important matters.

No one, surely, has ever questioned the need for embellishments, witness their presence everywhere in great profusion. It is nonetheless certain that they are indispensable, if we but pause to reflect on their usefulness. They connect notes; animate them; lend them, in case of need, a peculiar emphasis and weight; make them pleasing and, consequently, attract special attention; they help to reveal the music's content—whether it is sad or gay, or whatever, embellishments always contribute their share to the effect; they form a considerable part of both the opportunity and the substance of good playing; by their aid, a middling composition may be improved, where, on the other hand, the best melody must seem empty and plain in their absence, and the clearest content turgid.

Great, therefore, is the value of embellishments; but just as great can be their harm, if wrong embellishments are chosen or the right ones awkwardly applied, out of context and in unbecoming profusion.

That is why those [composers] who have clearly marked the appropriate embellishments in their pieces have always been prudent, not abandoning their things to the whims of awkward performers.

Here, again, we must do justice to the French, who are specially meticulous in marking their pieces. In Germany, the greatest masters of our instrument have proceeded in similar fashion, if not so lavishly; and who knows but that, through their judicious selection and restraint in embellishing, they might not have been the cause why the French do not now, as formerly, burden every note with such adornments, rendering obscure the necessary distinctness and noble simplicity of the melody.

I believe that, with the clavier as with other instruments, the best style of performance is that which succeeds in uniting the neatness and brilliance of the French style with the seductiveness of the Italian manner of singing. The Germans are particularly disposed to this, provided they stay free of prejudice. I also believe, following the dictum of a certain great man [i.e., Johann Sebastian Bach], that, though one style may on the whole be better than another, there is nevertheless something of particular value in each and that no style is so perfect that it will not suffer any additions. Through these additions and refinements we have progressed up to this point, and we shall progress even farther; but this will never come about if we pursue and, so to say, worship only one style; on the contrary, we must utilize all that is good, no matter where we may find it.

And so, since the embellishments and the manner of their application contribute eminently to good taste, we must neither be too changeable, adopting every new embellishment uncritically and instantaneously, from no matter what source; nor must we be so partial to ourselves and to our own taste as to refuse stubbornly to adopt all things foreign. To be sure, a close inspection should always be the rule before we adopt anything foreign, and it can be that, because of imported unnatural innovations, good taste will in time become as rare a thing as knowledge. Still, if not the first, we should also not be the last to take up certain new embellishments, or we may fall behind the fashion. And if at first we may not find them entirely to our liking, it is no great matter. New things, though at times enticing, may sometimes strike us as repugnant. The latter circumstance is often evidence of a thing's true worth, for it may well prove to be more enduring in the long run than other things, which become inordinately popular at once. These are generally so overused that they soon become abominations.

It is indisputably a prejudice to think that a clavier player's strength lies merely in his speed. Let him have the nimblest fingers, possess trills both simple and double, have mastery over the art of fingering, be able to play impeccably at sight, regardless of the clefs a piece might contain, transpose everything with tolerable ease on the spur of the moment, span tenths, nay twelfths [at the keyboard], be able to execute runs and cross-leaps of all sorts, and much more; yet despite all these attainments, he may still not make a clear, a pleasing, a moving performer. Experience teaches us all too often that the sharpshooters and speedy professional players are the least likely to possess those virtues, that their fingers can provoke wonderment on a listener's face but can provide no occupation for his responsive soul. A mere sharpshooter ought not to lay claim to the true merits of one who is capable of causing the ear (rather than the face) and the heart (rather than the ear) to be gently affected, to be transported hither and yon at will.

But what constitutes a good performance? Just this: the ability, by means of singing or playing, to make musical ideas perceptible to the ear in accordance with their true content and affection.

We must play from the soul, not like trained birds.

One should miss no opportunity of hearing capable singers; from this one learns to think in terms of song. And it is a good idea to sing musical themes to oneself in order to find out how they should be played; this will in any case be more useful than relying on long-winded books and tracts, in which all the talk is of Nature, Taste, Song, Melody, notwithstanding the fact that their authors are often incapable of composing two notes naturally, tastefully, songfully or melodiously, since they attribute all those gifts and qualities to this and that according to their whims, but mostly injudiciously.

Since a musician cannot move us unless he himself is moved, it follows that he must be capable of entering into all the affections which he wishes to arouse in his listeners; he communicates his own feelings to them and thus most effectively moves them to sympathy. In languid and sad passages he becomes languid and sad. We see and hear it. The same will also be true of vigorous, merry, and other sorts of musical themes, as he enters into those affections. Hardly has he stilled one than he awakens another; therefore, he is constantly changing affections. He will fulfill this function in all pieces that have been composed expressively, whether they are his own or someone else's; in the latter instance he must feel within himself the very emotions which moved the author as he composed the piece. That all this can be done with an impassive countenance will only be asserted by those whose insensibility obliges them to sit at their instruments like engraved portraits. Ugly faces, to be sure, are unmannerly and detracting; but suitable expressions are useful, in that they help to reveal our intentions to the listener.

Since nature has wisely endowed music with so much variety, in order that every man may take his share of it, it is therefore a musician's obligation, within the limits of his ability, to satisfy every sort of listener.

C. P. E. Bach, *Versuch über die wahre Art das Clavier zu spielen* (Berlin, 1753), Introduction (unpaginated), 8–9, 18, 20, 51–52, 60–61, 115, 117, 119, 121–23. Trans. P. W.

79

The Rise of the Italian Comic Opera Style

The realistic treatment of comic situations and characters in opera was the last major contribution of the Italians to European music: apart from its purely operatic conse-quences, it led indirectly to the dramatic instrumental style of the Classical period, to the style of Haydn and Mozart, and maybe even Beethoven. Comic operas had been few and far between in the seventeenth century. Comic scenes, however, involving servants, old men and women, or peasants, had been a regular feature of the serious operas, where they served as comic relief, much as in the Shakespeare tragedies. In the early eighteenth century, these comic scenes were gradually abandoned, in deference to a new, rationalistic sense of dramatic propriety. Then, beginning in Venice in 1706, the singers of those comic roles took to entertaining the public between the acts of serious operas; these intermezzos, or interludes, usually involved two characters (a third sometimes mimed his part) in a kind of mini-opera that had its own plot, entirely independent of the evening's major production. The vogue for intermezzos soon spread to the rest of Italy and eventually to the rest of Europe, only to give way to a more lasting vogue, that of the full-length comic opera, by the mid-century. The best-known of all the intermezzos is without doubt *La serva padrona* (*The Maid Who Would Be Mistress*, Naples 1733) by Giovanni Battista Pergolesi (1710–36). In the opening extract given below, we meet all the characters: Uberto (bass), an old bachelor; Serpina (soprano), his pretty maid who eventually becomes his wife; and Vespone (the mime), his manservant.

Antechamber.
UBERTO, *not fully dressed, discovered pacing up and down; then enter his servant* VESPONE, *who never speaks.*

ARIA

UBERTO:

To wait and not be met,
Aspettare e non venire,
To lie in bed and fret,
stare a letto e non dormire,
To serve those who forget,
ben servire e non gradire,
Are matters of regret.
son tre cose da morire.

RECITATIVE

What a calamity for me!
Questa è per me disgrazia!
I have been waiting for three hours, and my maid
Son tre ore che aspetto, e la mia serva
Will not favor me with a cup of chocolate;
portarmi il cioccolate non fa grazia;

A Comic Opera Performance. According to an unconfirmed tradition, the composer (sitting at the harpsichord) is Haydn and the theater that of Prince Esterházy. *Munich, Deutsches Theatermuseum.*

And I'll be late going out.
ed io d'uscire ho fretta.
My sainted patience! Now I do see
Oh flemma benedetta! Or sílo vedo
That, by being so good to her,
che, per esser sí buono con costei,
I've brought down all these ills upon myself.
la causa son di tutti i mali miei.
[*Calls into the wings.*]
Serpina! (She'll be here tomorrow!)
Serpina! Vien dimani!
[*To* VESPONE.]
And you too, what are you doing?
E tu altro, che fai?
Why do you stand there like a puppet?
A che qui te ne stai come un balocco?
[VESPONE *tries to excuse himself.*]
Hey? What do you say? Go, fool! Run, break
Come? che dici? Eh, sciocco! corri, ròmpiti
Your neck, quickly, hurry,
presto il collo, sollecita,
See what's the matter.
vedi che fu.
[*Exit* VESPONE.]

        A fine thing! I brought up
        Gran fatto! Io m'ho cresciuta
This maid, a mere child,
questa serva piccina,
Fondled her, kept her
le ho fatto di carezze, l'ho tenuta
As if she'd been my own daughter; and now
come mia figlia fosse; ed ella ha preso
She's full of arrogance,
perciò tanta arroganza,
So proud and uppish,
fatta è sí superbina,
That at last the maid will be mistress.
che alfin di serva diverrà padrona.
But I'll assert myself in time.
Ma bisogna risolversi in buon'ora.
Meanwhile that other blockhead's gone to sleep!
E quell'altro babbion vi è morto ancora!
[*Enter* SERPINA *arguing with* VESPONE.]

SERPINA: Have you finished? Do I need
            L'hai finita? ho bisogno
            To be scolded by you? Quite so! It's not convenient,
            che tu mi sgridi? E pure! Io non sto comoda,

I tell you.
ti dissi.

UBERTO: (Good!)
                    Brava!

SERPINA: Not done? If the master
                         E torna! Se 'l padrone
Is pressed for time, I'm not, d'you hear?
ha fretta, non ne ho io: il sai?

UBERTO: (Excellent!)
                                   Bravissima!

SERPINA: What, again? Oh, you are seriously
Di nuovo? Oh, tu da senno
Beginning to try my patience,
vai stuzzicando la pazienza mia,
And you are begging me to come to blows!
e vuoi che un par di schiaffi alfin ti dia!
[*And she hurls herself at* VESPONE, *who rushes to* UBERTO *for cover.*]

UBERTO: Whoa! What's all this?
Olà! dove si sta?
Whoa, Serpina, won't you stop it?
Olà, Serpina, non ti vuoi fermare?

SERPINA: Let me teach
Lasciatemi insegnare
Good manners to this rascal ...
le creanze a quel birbo ...

UBERTO: But in your master's presence ...
Ma in presenza del padrone ...

SERPINA: And so,
                         Adunque,
Because I am a maid, am I to be overcome,
perché io son serva, ho ad esser sopraffatta,
Am I to be mistreated?
ho ad esser maltrattata?
No, sir, I insist on being respected,
No, signore, voglio esser rispettata,
I insist on being revered, as if I were
voglio esser riverita, come fossi
Mistress, archmistress, mistress extraordinary.
padrona, arcipadrona, padronissima.

UBERTO: What the devil ails your illustrious Ladyship?
Che diavol ha Vossignoria illustrissima?
Let's hear, what happened?
Sentiam, che fu?

SERPINA: This upstart ...
                         Cotesto impertinente ...

[VESPONE *attempts to reply.*]

UBERTO: Be quiet, you! [*To* VESPONE.
Queto tu!

SERPINA: Came to me ...
Venne a me ...

[VESPONE *as above.*]

UBERTO: Quiet, I say! [*To* VESPONE.
Queto, ti ho detto!

SERPINA: And with the most improper manners ...
E con modi sí impropri ...
[VESPONE *as above.*]

UBERTO: Quiet, quiet, a pox on you! [*To* VESPONE, *becoming angry.*
Queto, queto, che sii tu maledetto!

SERPINA: But you'll pay for this! [*Threatening* VESPONE.
Ma me la pagherai!

UBERTO: I sent this man to you.
Io costui t'inviai.

SERPINA: What for?
Ed a che fare?

UBERTO: What for? Did I not ask you
A che far? non ti ho chiesto
For a cup of chocolate?
il cioccolate, io?

SERPINA: Well; and what then?
Ben: che per questo?

UBERTO: And am I to waste away waiting
E m'have ad uscir l'anima aspettando
For it to be brought in?
che mi si porti?

SERPINA: And when
E quando
Do you wish to have it?
voi prenderlo dovete?

UBERTO: Now. (When!)
Adesso: quando?

SERPINA: You think this is the right moment? It is time
E vi par ora questa? È tempo ormai
For dinner.
di dover desinare.

UBERTO: And so ...
Adunque ...

SERPINA: And so,
Adunque,
I didn't prepare it;
io già nol preparai;
You will have to do without it,
voi di men ne farete,

My master dear, and be content.
padron mio dolce, e ve n'acqueterete.

UBERTO: Vespone, now that I have taken
Vespone, ora che ho preso
My chocolate,
il cioccolate già,
Wish me good cheer, good health.
dimmi: Buon pro vi faccia, sanità.
[VESPONE *laughs.*]

SERPINA: What is that jackass laughing at?
Di che ride quell'asino?

UBERTO: At me, for I'm as patient as a brute.
Di me, che ho più flemma di una bestia.
But I will not be a brute,
Ma io bestia non sarò,
I'll be patient no more,
più flemma non avrò,
I will cast off the yoke,
il giogo scuoterò,
And I'll do at last what I've never done before.
e quel che non ho fatto alfin farò.

ARIA

Forever brawling,
Sempre in contrasti
That's all you do.
con te si sta.
And here and there,
E qua e là,
And down and up,
e giú e su,
And no and yes:
e no e sí:
That is enough now,
or questo basti,
It's got to stop.
finir si può.
What are you thinking?
Ma che ti pare?
Am I to expire?
ho io a crepare?
No, sir, I'll not!
Signor mio, no!
But you will rue
Però dovrai
With endless tears
per sempre piangere

Your sorry plight;
la tua disgrazia;
And then you'll say,
e allor dirai
"It serves me right."
che ben ti sta.
     What say you now? [*To* VESPONE.
     Che dici tu?
Is it not so?
Non è così?
Go to it, go!
Ma cosi va!
Forever brawling ... [*Etc.*, da capo
Sempre in contrasti ...

Benedetto Croce, *I teatri di Napoli dal Rinascimento alla fine del secolo decimottaco*, 4th ed. (Bari: Laterza, 1947), 311–14. Trans. P. W.

The Italian comic opera style was received with pleasure by audiences everywhere because it gave musical expression to many of the new attitudes of the Enlightenment. In Paris, the capital of the Enlightenment and home of its chief Philosophers, *La serva padrona* and some other intermezzos, as well as one full-length comic opera, provoked a celebrated paper war: the "War of the Buffoons." An Italian troupe had brought these works to the Paris Opera, where they produced them (alternating with the regular performances of French operas, mostly serious) between 1752 and 1754. The Philosophers welcomed them as ideal examples of the naturalness and simplicity they sought in works of art and used them as fresh weapons in the dreary old squabble on the relative merits of Italian and French music. The defenders of French music were quick to answer, and pamphlet followed pamphlet, satire followed satire, while at the Opera the antagonists gathered at opposite sides of the theater, vociferously cheering and condemning the Italian or French productions. By 1753 tempers seemed to have cooled somewhat; then Rousseau launched his inflammatory *Letter on French Music*, in which he demonstrated to his own satisfaction that the French could have no music at all (this despite the success of his own French comic opera, *The Village Soothsayer*), and the debate flared up once more. Only the departure of the Italian "Buffoons" put an end to it. Their effect on French music was limited, though the new *opéra comique* undoubtedly received a strong impulse from the music of the Italians. As for French literature, it was enriched by several thousand extra pages, of which the following excerpt is a modest sample. Written in 1752 by the famous Baron d'Holbach (1723–89), a leading patron and expounder of the enlightened philosophy, it was possibly the first pamphlet, the opening salvo, in this paper war.

Letter to a Lady of a Certain Age, on the Present State of the Opera

Madam,

It was a foreboding, there can be little doubt of it, that caused you to leave a City in which the strangest extravagances were about to occur. How fortunate for you that you did not have to witness them! And how sad for me to be destined, by your command, to acquaint you with calamities which, I sense it already, will move you so deeply! Hear me, Madam, and shudder. The times you had foretold are upon us. We have seen, to the everlasting shame of our Nation and century, the *august* Théâtre de l'Opéra profaned by unworthy Mountebanks. Yes, Madam, that grave, venerable spectacle, from which the immortal Lully, its founder, seemed to have exerted every possible care to banish senseless laughter and indecent gaiety, has been abandoned to Strollers from beyond the Alps: its *dignity* has been debased by the most burlesque performances, by the giddiest music: a noisy joviality and immoderate outbursts have rent the veil of that Temple, replacing the noble and majestic composure, the judicious and measured applause of the admirers of Campra, Mouret, and Destouches [fashionable French composers of the previous generation]. O what times! O what habits!

It was left to our own days, these days of depravity, bad taste, and dizziness, to disconcert the grave countenances that had so long set the tone at our Lyric Theater.

They are laughing at the Opéra, splitting their sides with laughter!

Frenchmen have abandoned the music of their forefathers; they are flocking to productions that are monstrous, which we cannot even conceive; they pretend to discover new beauties there each day. Such fanaticism has never been seen before. Three miserable intermezzos have been fascinating the Public for three months and have been applauded more at their fiftieth performance than at their first. I should never have finished were I obliged to describe you all the follies I see and all the blasphemies I hear at the performances of these intermezzos. "It is," say our modern Enthusiasts, "a dialogued music without equal. The tunes have a simplicity, elegance, and expressiveness the likes of which we never heard before; they would suffice alone to convey the meaning of the words. The tone of nature is there, always rendered with power and truth, and often at those very moments when it would seem least likely of being captured. The accompaniments are of a sort that stimulates the attention, contributes to the expression, and supports the voices without overwhelming them. There are refinements here which our own imbeciles never dreamt their art was capable of ... And what, after all, can such epithets as *Mountebanks, Buffoons* signify when applied to Comedians who, with the utmost delicacy, give expression to passions common to all humanity and who present them from the most striking angles? Someone, a better judge of these extraordinary portrayals, said, 'It is life itself; and, at the same time, these melodies are divine!' Is there anything more astonishing than the long-lived dogmatism with which our grandparents admired the dullest compositions—but, after all, they only admired them because they knew of none better—they came here, the dear old people, to amuse themselves, and were bored. They cried out (yawning all the while), 'Ah, how beautiful that is!' and we should have continued to mistake Boredom for *Dignity,* had not these Italians, who are so contrary to our pompous and lethargic harmony, come and torn the blindfold from our eyes and taught us that music is capable of variety, of character, of expression, and of playfulness; that it can be tender without insipidity, natural without monotony, gay without triviality, numerous without confusion. What duets *we* have! And what duets are those in the *Giocatore* [*The Gamester,* by Orlandini] and the *Serva padrona!* There's more genius in only one of these pieces than in all our immense compilations of notes. Let us at long last shake off the yoke of national prejudice, and let us not blush to yield to accents that have charmed all Europe. After the lessons we have received, it would be most surprising if we were to return to a Gothic, barbarous music which for too long has been the occasion of our boredom and the derision of Foreigners."

Such, Madam, are the horrors you would be obliged to hear were you in my shoes. But if our Enthusiasts crave for originals, why do they not leave us to the peaceful enjoyment of our own music, which, as all the world allows, is a most original thing? Let those Foreigners who accuse us of frivolity but listen (if they dare) to the productions of our Composers, then let them blush at their slander. Italian music has enslaved all other Nations; well, so much the better; we will be the more honored for having constantly resisted a flood which has carried off so many barbarians.

Denise Launay (ed.), *La Querelle des Bouffons* (Geneva: Editions Minkoff, 1973), 121–22, 123–25, 126. Trans. P. W.

The full-length Italian comic opera of the eighteenth century was derived neither from the rare seventeenth-century specimens nor from the intermezzos but from the highly popular and realistic dialect operas that were given at the smaller theaters of Naples, beginning in 1709. The type moved north gradually: it reached Rome (having dropped the dialect for normal Italian) in the 1730s, the northern Italian cities in the 1740s, and by the 1750s was rivaling the *opera seria* in popularity, soon overtaking it and establishing itself as the dominant type both in Italy and abroad for the rest of the century. Here is a little-known, slightly skeptical, but penetrating appraisal of this new phenomenon by one of Germany's most talented musical critics, Johann Adam Hiller 1728–1804, who, as a composer, was one of the founders of the German comic opera, or *singspiel*. What makes this extract especially valuable is Hiller's recognition that the comic opera style had reached out far beyond the theater and crucially influenced the new instrumental genres.

A few more words regarding the comic opera. Everyone knows that it is the dominant fashion today, at least in Italy. Though the plot of these pieces is often miserable enough, yet the characters are so deftly caricatured and their actions so overdone that it is quite impossible to refrain from laughing. There's no denying that a special genius is required to give such things their proper musical expression. It was Pergolesi, with his *Serva padrona,* who, to a certain extent, set the tone; [Baldassare] Galuppi, [Gioacchino] Cocchi, and others followed suit and were even more comical than Pergolesi. Now [Nicolò] Piccinni dominates the comic stage and seems, through the great quantity of his operas, to be nearly exhausting the possibilities of innovation in that department. Not so simple melodically as Pergolesi, less comical than Galuppi and Cocchi, he seems more inclined to the naïve and tender. He has pieces as touching as any we might hope to hear in a serious opera, at least in one by an Italian. Lest it should be thought that the serious opera is quite forgotten, the Italians now never fail to introduce, in their comic operas, a pair of serious characters who would prompt as much yawning as the others do laughter, were it not that their somewhat better style of singing attracts a modicum of attention. The singers of comic opera are ordinarily mediocre, often quite bad, and if Italy continues on her present path, it will be a sign that good singers no longer abound there or will soon begin to grow scarce. Comic opera is not precisely the best school for singers; but it has become much the best for today's composers. Symphonies, concertos, trios, sonatas—all, nowadays, borrow something of its style, and there would be nothing to object to here, if only the low elements in it and the poor taste could always be avoided with success.

Wöchentliche Nachrichten und Anmerkungen, die Musik betreffend, III, 8 (22 August 1768), 62. Trans. P. W.

80

From Rousseau's *Dictionary of Music*

The musical articles in the great French Encyclopedia, written in some haste to meet the deadlines, were the work of Jean-Jacques Rousseau. Later he revised them and made them the basis of his famous *Dictionary of Music* (Geneva, 1767), a fascinating source of French eighteenth-century musical lore as well as an infallible guide to the mind of that crabbed genius, who could rarely give a merely objective explanation of anything. The following entries have been selected for the flashes of insight they reveal (countless others could have been chosen to show Rousseau's narrow-mindedness and partisanship). Here and there we glimpse early signs of what will at a later date be defined as "Romanticism": as everyone knows, Rousseau was one of its great precursors.

Composer

He who composes music or forms the rules of composition. See, under the word COMPOSITION, the detail of knowledge necessary for the art of composing. It is not yet enough to fashion a true composer. All the science in the world is not sufficient without a genius to animate it. Whatever efforts we may make, whatever acquisitions we may have, we must still be born to the art, otherwise our works can never mount above the insipid. It is with the composer as with the poet. Nature herself must have form'd him so. What I would express by genius is by no means that strange capricious taste which spreads on all sides uncouth and idle difficulties, which knows not how to ornament its harmony but by dint of dissonances, contrasts, and confusion. 'Tis an inward flame which burns, torments the composer spite of himself, which continually inspires him with airs new and always agreeable, with expressions lively, natural, and which touch the heart, with a harmony pure, affecting, majestic, which strengthens and adorns the air, but does not overwhelm it.

Imitation

Dramatic or theatrical music contributes to imitation, as well as poetry and painting: 'tis to this common principle that all the fine arts are connected, as Monsieur le Batteux has demonstrated. But this imitation has not the same extent for all. All that the imagination can represent to itself lies within the domain of poetry. Painting, which does not offer its pictures to the imagination but to the sense, and to one sense alone, paints only objects that can be seen. Music would appear to have the same bounds, in regard to the sense of hearing; however it paints all, even the objects that are only visible: by a magic almost inconceivable, it seems to place the eye in the ear, and the greatest marvel of an art which operates only by means of movement is to be able to form from it even the image of repose. Night, sleep, solitude, and silence enter into the number of the great paintings of music. We know that noise can produce the effect of silence, and silence the effect of noise; as when we slumber at an even and monotonous reading and awaken at the instant that it ceases. But music acts more intimately upon us in exciting, by one sense, affections similar to those which may be excited by another; and, as the connection cannot be sensible unless the impression is strong, so painting, stript of that force, cannot render to music the imitations which that draws from it. Let all nature be in a slumber, he that contemplates it, sleeps not; and the art of the musician consists in substituting, for the insensible image of the object, that of the movements which its presence excites in the heart of the contemplator. He will not only agitate the sea, animate the flame of a conflagration, make rivulets flow, the rain fall, and torrents swell; but he will paint the horrors of a hideous desert, darken the walls of a subterranean dungeon, calm the tempest, render the air tranquil and serene, and spread, from the orchestra, a new and pleasing freshness through the woodlands. He will not represent these things directly; but he will excite in the soul the same movements which we feel in seeing them.

Recitative

Amongst the Greeks, all their poetry was in recitative, because, the language being melodious, it was sufficient to add to it the cadence of the metre and the sustained recitation to render this recitation entirely musical; from whence it comes that those who versified called it *singing*. This custom, having ridiculously passed into other languages, still causes poets to say, *I sing*, when there is no singing in the case. The Greeks could sing in speaking; but amongst us we must either sing or speak; we cannot do both at the same time. 'Tis this very distinction which has rendered the recitative necessary for us. The music predominates too much in our airs; the poetry is almost forgotten. Our lyric dramas are too much sung to be so always. An opera which should be only an unbroken sequence of airs would tire almost as much as a whole single air of the same length. We must divide and separate the airs by words; but these words should be modified by music. The ideas should change, but the language must continue the same. This language being once given, to change it in the course of a piece would be to speak half French, half German. The passage from speech to song, and reciprocally, is too unequal; it shocks the ear and verisimilitude at the same time: two interlocutors should speak or sing; they cannot do alternatively one and the other. Now the recitative is the means of uniting song and words; it is that which separates and distinguishes the airs, which rests the ear, astonished at what preceded, and disposes it to taste what follows: in sum, 'tis by the assistance of the recitative that what is only dialogue, recital, narration in the drama may be rendered without going out of the given language, and without displacing the eloquence of the airs.

> In the following, Rousseau describes pretty accurately, as to their external forms, the French overture and the Italian, which, given his commitment to the Italian cause versus the French, he of course prefers. It should be noted (Rousseau ignored this) that the Italian overture in three movements (fast, slow, fast) had by this time spawned a new sort of musical entertainment, away from the opera house: the symphony. (Concerning the "first stroke of the fiddle-stick," on which the French apparently prided themselves already in Lully's day, see Mozart's equally derisive comments, p. 265.)

Overture

Symphonic piece which one endeavours to make splendid, imposing, harmonious, and which serves as an introduction to operas and other lyric dramas of a certain length.

The overtures of the French operas are almost all modeled on those of Lully. They are composed of a slow piece called *grave,* which is generally played twice, and of a tripping section called *gaie,* which is commonly fugued: several of these sections return to the *grave* at their conclusion as well.

There was a time when the French overtures served as a model for all Europe. Not sixty years ago they were being sent for in Italy to be placed at the head of their operas. I have even seen several ancient Italian operas written with an overture of Lully at their head. This is what the Italians at present deny, since the whole has had such a change; but, nevertheless, the fact is very certain.

Instrumental music having made astonishing progress in the last forty years or so, the old overtures, made for players who were little skilled in managing their instruments, were very soon left to the French, and at first only their general outline was preserved. But the Italians were not slow in freeing themselves from that encumbrance, and they at present distribute their overtures in another manner. They begin by a striking, lively piece in double or common time; then they give an *Andante à demi-jeu* [i.e., softly] in which they aim at displaying all the graces of lovely singing; and they conclude with a brilliant *Allegro,* generally in triple time.

The reason they give for this distribution is that in a numerous assembly, where the spectators make great noise, it is necessary at first to persuade them to silence and arrest their attention by means of a glittering, striking beginning. They say that the *grave* of our overtures is neither heard nor listened to by anyone; and that our first stroke of the fiddle-stick, which we boast of with so great emphasis, less noisy than the tuning of instruments which precedes it, and with which it is confused, is more suitable for persuading the audience to slumber than attention. They add, that after having rendered the spectator attentive, it is necessary that he should be interested with less noise by an agreeable and flattering air, which may dispose him to the tenderness with which he is to be inspired; and lastly, to conclude the Overture with a piece of a different character which, contrasting with the beginning of the drama, may, by its loud end, mark the silence which the actor, at his entrance on the stage, requires of the spectators.

Taste

Genius creates, but taste selects: and a too abundant genius is often in want of a severe censor to prevent it from abusing its valuable riches. One can do great things without taste; but it is taste which makes them interesting. It is taste which makes the composer catch the ideas of the poet; it is taste which makes the performer catch the ideas of the composer; it is taste which furnishes to each whatever may adorn and enliven their subject; and it is taste which gives the listener the perception of all these agreements. Yet taste is not sensibility. It is possible to have much taste, with a frigid soul; and a man transported with things really passionate is little touched by merely graceful things. It seems that taste attaches itself rather to the smaller expressions, and sensibility to the greater.

Jean-Jacques Rousseau, *A Complete Dictionary of Music,* trans. William Waring, 2nd. ed. (London, 1779). Corrected and revised on the basis of the French original.

PART SIX

The Classical Period

81

A Side Trip into Aesthetics

The latter part of the eighteenth century witnessed a momentous development in musical thought. The grip of the imitation theory founded on Plato and Aristotle, which had held firm sway since the late Renaissance and had been a crucial factor in bringing about the birth of the Baroque, was decisively broken, and in its place there emerged a theory of music as "expression," which was to remain dominant into the twentieth century (and in some quarters, up to the present). This new view was intimately bound up with the style changes that led to the dissolution of Baroque music and the establishment of the periods in music history that we now term the Classic and the-Romantic. The imitation theory, in which music took its place alongside all the other arts as a medium for the stylized representation of reality, was chiefly associated with vocal music. In its earlier manifestations it had fathered the recitative and, through it, the opera, and later it had been responsible for the formulation of the "doctrine of affections" of the late Baroque. The first major challenge to its authority came from the stream of "abstract" instrumental sonatas and concertos that originated among the violinists of Italy and turned into a veritable flood by the early eighteenth century. This music did not fit at all into the categories of imitation, and caused a great consternation among the upholders of the older doctrine, among whom the ever-rationalistic French were loudest. The classic expression of this consternation was given by Rousseau, who took the opportunity of railing against this "meaningless" instrumental music in his *Dictionnaire de musique*.

Sonata

Nowadays, when instrumental music is the most important branch of the art, *sonatas* are extremely fashionable, along with *Symphonie* [that is, instrumental compositions generally] of all kinds. Vocal music is hardly anything but an accessory to it, and song merely accompanies its accompaniment. We have adopted this poor taste from those who, wishing to introduce the manner of Italian music in a language alien to it, have forced us to try to do with instruments what we cannot accomplish with our voices.

I dare predict that so unnatural a taste will not last. Purely harmonic music [i.e., without text] is short on substance; in order to be continually pleasing and avoid boredom, music must raise itself to the level of the imitative arts; but its imitation is not always immediate like that of poetry or painting; the word is the means through which music most frequently determines the object whose image it offers us, and it is by means of sounds in conjunction with the human voice that this image awakens at the bottom of our hearts the sentiment it is its purpose to produce. Who does not sense how far pure *Symphonie,* in which nothing is sought but instrumental brilliance, is from such an effect? Can all the violinistic fireworks of M. Mondonville [1711–72, foremost French violinist and director of the Concert Spirituel] evoke in me the tenderness the voice of a great singer produces in two notes? *Symphonie* can enliven song and add to its expressiveness, but it cannot supplant it. In order to know what all these heaps of sonatas mean, one would have to follow the example of the inept painter who must label his figures: *this is a tree, this is a man, this is a horse.* I shall never forget the sally of the celebrated Fontenelle [1657–1757, French academician], who, finding himself overburdened with these interminable *Symphonies,* cried out in a fit of impatience, "*Sonate, que me veux-tu?* [Sonata, what do you want of me?]."

Jean-Jacques Rousseau, *Dictionnaire de musique* (Paris, 1768), 451–52. Trans. R. T.

> Even before Rousseau wrote these lines, however, there had appeared in England what was to prove a very influential little book: *An Essay on Musical Expression* (1752, revised in 1753) by the organist, composer, and impresario Charles Avison (1709–70). Avison rejected (or to be more precise, ignored) the imitation theory of music except insofar as it involved "sounds and motions." In so doing, he restricted musical imitation to the fairly paltry level of "madrigalism," and viewed the true aim of music as something quite unrelated to imitation: the direct "raising" or exciting of the passions in the listener. This could be accomplished by "air and harmony" well enough without any pretense at imitation. It was this that Corelli (and Geminiani, his pupil residing in England) did so effectively in their music. In Avison's formulation, music acted directly on the emotions and seemed to bypass the intellect. This idea was anathema not only to the French, but also to British rationalists, some of whom went to the trouble of publishing rebuttals to Avison's *Essay.*

Expression arises from a combination of *Air* and *Harmony;* and is no other than a strong and proper application of them to the intended subject.

From this definition it will plainly appear, that Air and Harmony are never to be deserted for the sake of Expression: because Expression is founded on them. And if we should attempt any thing in defiance of these, it would cease to be *Musical Expression.* Still less can the horrid dissonance of cat-calls deserve this appellation, though the Expression or Imitation be ever so strong and natural.

And, as dissonance and shocking sounds cannot be called Musical Expression, so neither do I think, can mere Imitation of several other things be entitled to this name, which, however, among the generality of mankind hath often obtained it. Thus the gradual rising or falling of the notes in a long succession, is often used to denote ascent or descent; broken intervals, to denote an interrupted motion; a number of quick divisions [flurries of rapid notes], to describe swiftness or flying; sounds resembling laughter, to describe laughter; with a number of other contrivances of a parallel kind, which it is needless here to mention. Now all these I should choose to style Imitation, rather than Expression; because, it seems to me, that their tendency is rather to fix the hearer's attention on the similitude between the sounds and the thing which they describe, and thereby to excite a reflex act of understanding, than to affect the heart and raise the passions of the soul.

Here then we see a defect or impropriety, similar to those which have been above observed to arise from a too particular attachment either to the modulation or harmony. For as in the first case, the master often attaches himself so strongly to the beauty of *Air* or modulation [i.e., melody], as to neglect the Harmony; and in the second case, pursues his Harmony or Fugues so as to destroy the beauty of modulation; so in this third case, for the sake of a forced, and (if I may so speak) an unmeaning Imitation, he neglects both Air and Harmony, on which alone true Musical Expression can be founded.

This distinction seems more worthy our notice at present, because some very eminent composers have attached themselves chiefly to the method here mentioned; and seem to think they have exhausted all the depths of Expression, by a dextrous Imitation of the meaning of a few particular words, that occur in the hymns or songs which they set to music. Thus, were one of these gentlemen to express the following words of Milton:

> Their Songs
> *Divide* the Night, and *lift* our Thoughts to Heav'n.

It is highly probable, that upon the word *divide,* he would run a *division* of half a dozen bars; and on the subsequent part of the sentence, he would not think he had done the poet justice, or *risen* to that *Height* of sublimity which he ought to express, till he had climbed up to the very top of his instrument, or at least as far as a human voice could follow him. And this would pass with a great part of mankind for Musical Expression, instead of that noble mixture of solemn Air and various Harmony, which indeed elevates our thoughts, and gives that exquisite pleasure which none but true lovers of Harmony can feel.

Were it necessary I might easily prove, upon general principles, that what I now advance concerning musical Imitation is strictly just; both, because Music as an Imitative Art has *very confined powers,* and because when it is an ally to poetry (which it ought always to be when it exerts its mimetic faculty) it obtains its end *by raising correspondent Affections* in the soul with those which ought to result from the genius of the poem. I shall content myself in this place, with adding two or three practical observations by way of corollary to this theory.

First, as music passing to the mind through the organ of the ear, can imitate only by *Sounds and Motions,* it seems reasonable, that when *Sounds* only are the objects of Imitation, the composer ought to throw the mimetic part entirely amongst the accompanying *Instruments;* because, it is probable, that the Imitation will be too powerful in the *voice* which alone ought to be engaged in *Expression* alone; or, in other words, in raising correspondent Affections with the part. Indeed, in some cases, Expression will coincide with Imitation, and may then be admitted universally: as in such *Chromatic Strains* as are mimetic of the Grief and Anguish of the human voice. But to the Imitation of sounds in the natural or inanimate world, this, I believe, may be applied as a general Rule.

Secondly, when music imitates *Motions,* the rhythm, and cast of the Air, will generally require, that both the vocal and instrumental parts coincide in their Imitation. But then, be it observed, that the composer ought always to be more cautious and reserved when he applies this faculty of music to *Motion,* than when he applies it to Sound, and the reason is obvious: the intervals in music are not so strictly similar to animate or inanimate motions, as its tones are to animate or inanimate sounds. Notes ascending or descending by large intervals, are not so like the stalking of a giant, as a flow of even notes are to the murmuring of a stream; and little jiggish slurs are less like the nod of Alexander, than certain shakes and trills are to the voice of the nightingale.

Thirdly, as music can only imitate motions and sounds, and in the *Motions* only imperfectly, it will follow, that musical Imitation ought never to be employed in representing objects, of which motion or sound are not the principal constituents. Thus, to light, or lightning, we annex the property of celerity of motion; yet, it will not follow from thence, that an extremely swift progression of notes will raise the idea of either one or the other; because as we said, the Imitation must be, in these cases, very partial. Again, it is one property of frost to make persons shake and tremble; yet, a tremulous movement of semitones, will never give the true idea of frost: though, perhaps, they may of a trembling person.

Fourthly, as the aim of music is to affect the passions in a pleasing manner, and as it uses melody and harmony to obtain that end, its Imitation must never be employed on *ungraceful Motions,* or *disagreeable Sounds;* because in the one case, it must injure the *Melody* of the Air, and in the other, the *Harmony* of the accompaniment; and, in both cases, must lose its intent of affecting the passions *pleasingly.*

Fifthly, as Imitation is only so far of use in music, as when it aids the expression; as it is only analogous to poetic Imitation, *when Poetry imitates* through mere natural media, so it should only be employed in the same manner. To make the sound echo to the sense in descriptive lyric, and perhaps, in the cooler parts of epic poetry is often a great beauty; but should the tragic poet labor at showing this art in his most distressful speeches, I suppose he would rather flatten than inspirit his drama. In like manner, the musical composer, who catches at every particular epithet or metaphor that the part affords him, to show his imitative power, will never fail to hurt the true aim of his composition, and will always prove the more deficient in proportion as his author is more pathetic or sublime.

What then is the composer, who would aim at true musical Expression, to perform? I answer, he is to blend such an happy mixture of Air and Harmony, as will affect us most strongly with the Passions or Affections which the poet intends to raise; and that, on this account, he is not principally to dwell on particular words in the way of Imitation, but to comprehend the poet's general drift or intention, and this too for his Airs and Harmony, either by Imitation (so far as Imitation may be proper to this end) or by any other means. But this I must still add, that if he attempts to raise the passions by Imitation, it must be such a temperate and chastised Imitation, as rather brings the object before the hearer, than such a one as induces him to form a comparison between the object and the sound. For, in this last case, his attention will be turned entirely on the composer's art, which must effectually check the passion. The power of music is, in this respect, parallel to the power of eloquence: if it works at all, it must work in a secret and unsuspected manner. In either case, a pompous display of art will destroy its own intentions: on which account, one of the best general rules, perhaps, that can be given for musical Expression, is that which gives rise to the pathetic in every other art, *an unaffected strain of nature and simplicity.*

Charles Avison, *An Essay on Musical Expression* (London, 1753), Chap. 3 ("On Musical Expression, so far as it relates to the Composer"), condensed.

> Avison's line of thought took hold (and is much echoed in the works of the nineteenth-century formalist and anti-Wagnerian Eduard Hanslick). One of his early followers was the Scottish poet and philosopher James Beattie (1735–1803), whose *Essay on Poetry and Music, as They Affect the Mind* (1762; published in 1778) contains a remarkable passage in which the pleasures of music are described in "absolute" terms, and training is advocated ("music appreciation"!) to sharpen the purely musical responses of listeners. Later in his book, it is true, Beattie claims vocal music to be superior to instrumental in "expression" (as we might expect from a poet), but his implicit recognition that the pleasures of musical sounds and the "meaning" of music are closely related makes Beattie a very "modern" musical thinker.

How Are the Pleasures We Derive from Music to Be Accounted For?

It was said, that certain melodies and harmonies have an *aptitude* to raise certain passions, affections, and sentiments, in the human soul. Let us now inquire a little into the nature of this *aptitude;* by endeavouring, from acknowledged principles of the human constitution, to explain the cause of that pleasure which mankind derives from music. I am well aware of the delicacy of the argument, and of my inability to do it justice; and therefore I promise no complete investigation, nor indeed anything more than a few cursory remarks. As I have no theory to support, and as this topic, though it may amuse, is not of any great utility, I shall be neither positive in my assertions, nor abstruse in my reasoning.

The vulgar distinguish between the sense of hearing, and that faculty by which we receive pleasure from music, and which is commonly called a *musical ear.* Everybody knows, that to hear, and to have a relish for melody, are two different things; and that many persons have the first in perfection, who are destituted of the last. The last is indeed, like the first, a gift of nature; and may, like other natural gifts, languish if neglected, and improve exceedingly if exercised. And though every person who hears, might no doubt, by instruction and long experience, be made sensible of the musical properties of sound, so far as to be in some measure gratified with good music and disgusted with bad; yet both his pain and his pleasure would be very different in kind and degree, from that which is conveyed by a true musical ear.

I. Does not part of the pleasure, both of melody and of harmony, arise from the very nature of the notes that compose it? Certain inarticulate sounds, especially when continued, produce very pleasing effects on the mind. They seem to withdraw the attention from the more tumultuous concerns of life, and, without agitating the soul, to pour gradually upon it a train of softer ideas, that sometimes lull and soothe the faculties, and sometimes quicken sensibility, and stimulate the imagination.

II. Some notes, when sounded together, have an agreeable, and others a disagreeable effect. The former are *concords,* the latter *discords.* Musicians have taken pains to discover the principles on which concords and discords are to be so arranged as to produce the best effect; and have thus brought the whole art of harmony within the compass of a certain number of rules, some of which are more, and others less indispensable. These rules admit not of demonstrative proof: for though some of them may be inferred by rational deduction from the very nature of sound, yet the supreme judge of their propriety is the human ear.

But Natural sensibility is not taste, though it be necessary to it. A painter discovers both blemish and beauties in a picture, in which an ordinary eye can perceive neither. In poetical language, and in the arrangement and choice of words, there are many niceties, whereof they only are conscious who have practised versification, as well as studied the works of poets, and rules of the art. In like manner, harmony must be studied a little in its principles by every person who would acquire a true relish for it; and nothing but practice will ever give that quickness to his ear which is necessary to enable him to enter with adequate satisfaction, or rational dislike, into the merits or demerits of a musical performance. When once he can attend to the progress, relations, and dependencies, of the several parts; and remember the past, and anticipate the future, at the same time he perceives the present: so as to be sensible of the skill of the composer, and dexterity of the performer;—a regular concerto, well executed, will yield him high entertainment, even though its regularity be its principal recommendation. The pleasure which an untutored hearer derives from it is far inferior: and yet there is something in harmony that pleases, and in dissonance that offends, every ear; and were a piece to be played consisting wholly of discords, or put together without any regard to rule, I believe no person whatever would listen to it without great disgust.

James Beattie, *An Essay on Poetry and Music, as They Affect the Mind* (Edinburgh, 1778), 128–29, 133–36.

The classicist Thomas Twining directly continued and refined the argument in a book of 1789. For him and (as we see from his quotation) for Dr. Burney, the issue of musical imitation was dead. Twining went further than anyone had yet gone in asserting that the very indefiniteness of musical impressions was a positive attribute. To see pleasure in indefiniteness is a mark of incipient Romanticism in a philosopher, but of course lay audiences had been listening to music that way for years. The institution of public concerts had been the greatest stimulus of all to the development of complex, large-scale instrumental forms, most notably the Classical symphony, which was to reach its apogee a few years after Twining wrote, and in his very city, with Joseph Haydn's triumphant visits (see page 266). Twining returns us to the starting point of this aesthetic inquiry with a stinging answer to Rousseau.

On the Different Senses of the Word Imitative, as Applied by the Ancients, and by the Moderns

The whole power of music may be reduced, I think, to three distinct effects; upon the *ear,* the *passions,* and the *imagination:* in other words, it may be considered as simply delighting the *sense,* as raising *emotions,* or, as raising *ideas.* The two last of these effects constitute the whole of what is called the *expressive* power of music; and in these only we are to look for anything that can be called *imitation.* Music can be said to imitate, no farther than as it *expresses* something. As far as its effect is merely physical, and confined to the ear, it gives a simple original pleasure; it expresses nothing, it *refers* to nothing; it is no more imitative than the smell of a rose, or the flavor of a pineapple.

Music is capable of raising ideas through the medium of those *emotions* which it raises *immediately.* But this is an effect so delicate and uncertain—so dependent on the fancy, the sensibility, the musical experience, and even the temporary disposition, of the *hearer,* that to call it *imitation,* is surely going beyond the bounds of all reasonable analogy. Music, here, is not *imitative,* but if I may hazard the expression, merely *suggestive.* But, whatever we may call it, this I will venture to say: that in the *best* instrumental music, expressively *performed,* the very indecision itself of the expression, leaving the hearer to the free operation of his emotion upon his *fancy,* and, as it were, to the free *choice* of such ideas as are, to *him,* most adapted to react upon and heighten the emotion which occasioned them, produces a pleasure, which nobody, I believe, who is able to feel it, will deny to be one of the most delicious that music is capable of affording. But far the greater part even of those who have an ear for music, have *only* an *ear;* and to *them* this pleasure is unknown. The complaint, so common, of the separation of poetry and music, and of the total want of meaning and expression in *instrumental* music, was never, I believe, the complaint of a man of true musical feeling: and it might, perhaps, be not unfairly concluded, that Aristotle, who expressly allows that "Music, even *without words, has expression,*" was more of a musician than his master Plato, who is fond of railing at instrumental music, and asks with Fontenelle, *"Sonate, que me veux-tu?"* I would by no means be understood to deny, that there is now, and has been at all times, much unmeaning trash composed for instruments, that would justly provoke such a question. I mean only to say, what has been said for me by a superior judge and master of the art:

> There is some kind even of instrumental music, so divinely composed, and so expressively performed, that it wants no words to explain its meaning: it is itself the language of the heart and of passion, and speaks more to both in a few notes, than any other language composed of clashing consonants, and insipid vowels, can do in as many thousand. [Burney, A *General History* (see p. 257) I, 85.]

The notion, that painting, poetry and music are all *Arts of Imitation,* certainly tends to produce, and has produced, much confusion. That they all, in *some* sense of the word, *or other,* imitate, cannot be denied; but the senses of the word when applied to poetry, or music, are so different both from each other, and from that in which it is applied to painting, sculpture, and the arts of design in general—the only arts that are *obviously* and *essentially* imitative—that when we include them all, without distinction, under the same general denomination of *Imitative Arts,* we seem to defeat the only useful purpose of all classing and arrangement; and, instead of producing order and method in our ideas, produce only embarrassment and confusion.

Thomas Twining, *Aristotle's Treatise on Poetry, Translated: with Notes on the Translation, and on the Original: and Two Dissertations, on Poetical, and Musical, Imitation,* 2nd ed. (London, 1812), 66, 73–75, 92–93.

The famous economist and philosopher Adam Smith (1712–90), no longer inclined even to expect music to "raise the passions," voices a fully formed musical "absolutism." As an object of intellectual contemplation, music for Smith can stand entirely on its own: he is among the first aestheticians so to view the art. His description of musical understanding, moreover, is one to which the modern listener might well aspire.

If instrumental music can seldom be said to be properly imitative, even when it is employed to support the imitation of some other art, it is commonly still less so when it is employed alone. Why should it embarrass its melody and harmony, or constrain its time and measure, by attempting an imitation which, without the accompaniment of some other art to explain and interpret its meaning, nobody is likely to understand? In the most approved instrumental music, accordingly, in the overtures of Handel and the concertos of Corelli, there is little or no imitation, and where there is any, it is the source of but a very small part of the merit of those compositions. Without any imitation, instrumental music can produce very considerable effects; though its powers over the heart and affections are, no doubt, much inferior to those of vocal music, it has, however, considerable powers; by the sweetness of its sounds it awakens agreeably, and calls upon the attention; by their connection and affinity it naturally detains the attention, which follows easily a series of agreeable sounds, which have all a certain relation both to a common, fundamental, or leading note, called the key note; and to a certain succession or combination of notes, called the subject of the song or composition. By means of this relation each foregoing sound seems to introduce, and as it were prepare the mind for the following: by its rhythms, by its time and measure, it disposes that succession of sounds into a certain arrangement, which renders the whole more easy to be comprehended and remembered. Time and measure are to instrumental music what order and method are to discourse; they break it into proper parts and division, by which we are enabled both to remember better what is gone before, and frequently to foresee somewhat of what is to come after: we frequently foresee the return of a period which we know must correspond to another which we remember to have gone before; and, according to the saying of an ancient philosopher and musician, the enjoyment of music arises partly from memory and partly from foresight. When the measure, after having been continued so long as to satisfy us, changes to another, that variety, which thus disappoints, becomes more agreeable to us than the uniformity which would have gratified our expectation: but without this order and method we could remember very little of what had gone before, and we could foresee still less of what was to come after; and the whole enjoyment of music would be equal to little more than the effect of the particular sounds which rung in our ears at a very particular instant. By means of this order and method it is, during the progress of the entertainment, equal to the effect of all that we remember, and of all that we foresee; and at the conclusion, to the combined and accumulated effect of all the different parts of which the whole was composed.

A well-composed concerto of instrumental music, by the number and variety of the instruments, by the variety of the parts which are performed by them, and the perfect concord or correspondence of all these different parts; by the exact harmony or coincidence of all the different sounds which are heard at the same time, and by that happy variety of measure which regulates the succession of those which are heard at different times, presents an object so agreeable, so great, so various, and so interesting, that alone, and without suggesting any other object, either by imitation or otherwise, it can occupy, and as it were fill up completely the whole capacity of the mind, so as to leave no part of its attention vacant for thinking of anything else. In the contemplation of that immense variety of agreeable and melodious sounds, arranged and digested, both in their coincidence and in their succession, into so complete and regular a system, the mind in reality enjoys not only a very great sensual, but a very high intellectual, pleasure, not unlike that which it derives from the contemplation of a great system in any other science. A full concerto of such instrumental music, not only does not require, but it does not admit of any accompaniment. A song or a dance, by demanding an attention which we have not to spare, would disturb, instead of heightening, the effect of the music; they may often very properly succeed, but they cannot accompany it. Music seldom means to tell any particular story, or to imitate any particular event, or in general to suggest any particular object, distinct from that combination of sounds of which itself is composed. Its meaning, therefore, may be said to be complete in itself, and to require no interpreters to explain it. What is called the subject of such music is merely, as has already been said, a certain leading combination of notes, to which it frequently returns, and to which all its digressions and variations bear a certain affinity. It is altogether different from what is called the subject of a poem or a picture, which is always something which is not either in the poem or in the picture, or something quite distinct from that combination, either of words on the one hand, or of colors on the other, of which they are respectively composed. The subject of a composition of instrumental music is a part of that composition: the subject of a poem or picture is no part of either.

Adam Smith, *Essays on Philosophical Subjects* (Dublin, 1795), 232–36.

Finally, the great philosopher Immanuel Kant (1724–1804) offered, in his *Critique of Judgment* (1790), a hierarchy of the arts that reflected, in the case of music, the new "enlightened" view of it as an autonomous and nonconceptual art. The passage is a curious one: at the end, Kant suddenly drops his stance as transcendental thinker and reveals himself to be an ordinary mortal, not overly sympathetic to the "art of tone," especially when performed by his neighbors.

After poetry, if we are to deal with charm and mental movement, I would place that art which comes nearest to the art of speech and can very naturally be united with it, viz., *the art of tone*. As melody is, as it were, a universal language of sensations intelligible to every man, the art of tone employs it by itself alone in its full force, viz., as a language of the affections, and thus communicates universally, according to the laws of association, the aesthetical ideas naturally combined therewith. This can be brought mathematically under certain rules, because it rests in the case of tones on the relation between the number of vibrations of the air in the same time, so far as these tones are combined simultaneously or successively. But in the charm and mental movement produced by music, mathematics has certainly not the slightest share. It is only the indispensable condition of that proportion of the impressions in their combination and in their alternation by which it becomes possible to gather them together and prevent them from destroying each other, and to harmonize them so as to produce a continual movement and animation of the mind, by means of affections consonant therewith, and thus a delightful personal enjoyment.

If, on the other hand, we estimate the worth of the beautiful arts by the culture they supply to the mind and take as a standard the expansion of the faculties which must concur in the judgment for cognition, music will have the lowest place among them (as it has perhaps the highest among those arts which are valued for their pleasantness), because it merely plays with sensations.

Besides, there attaches to music a certain want of civility from the fact that, chiefly from the character of its instruments, it extends its influence further than is desired (in the neighborhood), and so as it were obtrudes itself and does violence to the freedom of others who are not of the musical company. The arts which appeal to the eyes do not do this, for we need only turn our eyes away if we wish to avoid being impressed. The case of music is almost like that of the delight derived from a smell that diffuses itself widely.

The man who pulls his perfumed handkerchief out of his pocket attracts the attention of all around him, even against their will, and he forces them, if they are to breathe at all, to enjoy the scent; hence this habit has gone out of fashion. Those who recommend the singing of spiritual songs at family prayers do not consider that they inflict a great hardship upon the public by such *noisy* (and therefore in general pharisaical) devotions, for they force the neighbors either to sing with them or to abandon their meditations.

Immanuel Kant, *Critique of Judgment,* trans. J. H. Bernard, Hafner Library of Classics, XIV (New York: Hafner Publishing Co., 1951), 170–74.

82

Haydn's Duties in the Service of Prince Esterházy

The terms of the contract entered into by Haydn with his very eminent employer in 1761 give a fair representation of the manifold duties of an eighteenth-century composer attached to an aristocratic court. Specifically with regard to Haydn's career it may be noted, first, that he succeeded to the title of a full *Capellmeister* (music director) upon the death of his predecessor in 1766, and, second, that he soon must have obtained a release from the restrictions in clause 4 that forbade him to sell his music elsewhere, since for the greater part of his life, once he became well known, he derived a considerable income from the publication of his music. Still, he did wear the court uniform, and his duties were indeed numerous and heavy until he was pensioned some thirty years later.

This day (according to the date hereto appended) Joseph Heyden [*sic*], native of Rohrau in Austria, is accepted and appointed Vice-Capellmeister in the service of his Serene Highness Paul Anton, Prince of the Holy Roman Empire, of Esterháza and Galantha, etc. etc., subject to conditions here following:

1. Whereas the Capellmeister at Eisenstadt, namely Gregorius Werner, having devoted many years of true and faithful service to the princely house, is now, on account of his great age and infirmities, unfit to perform the duties incumbent on him, it is hereby declared that the said Gregorius Werner, in consideration of his long services, shall retain the post of Capellmeister, and the said Joseph Heyden as Vice-Capellmeister shall, so far as regards the music of the choir, be subordinate to the Capellmeister and receive his instructions. But in everything else relating to musical performances, and in all that concerns the orchestra, the Vice-Capellmeister shall have the sole direction.

2. The said Joseph Heyden shall be considered and treated as a member of the household. Therefore his Serene Highness is graciously pleased to place confidence in his conducting himself as becomes an honorable official of a princely house. He must be temperate, not showing himself overbearing towards his musicians, but mild and lenient, straightforward and composed. It is especially to be observed that when the orchestra shall be summoned to perform before company, the Vice-Capellmeister and

all the musicians shall appear in uniform, and the said Joseph Heyden shall take care that he and all the members of his orchestra follow the instructions given, and appear in white stockings, white linen, powdered, and with either a pigtail or a tiewig.

3. Whereas the other musicians are referred for directions to the said Vice-Capellmeister, he shall therefore take the more care to conduct himself in an exemplary manner, abstaining from undue familiarity and from vulgarity in eating, drinking, and conversation, not dispensing with the respect due to him, but acting uprightly and influencing his subordinates to preserve such harmony as is becoming in them, remembering how displeasing the consequences of any discord or dispute would be to his Serene Highness.

4. The said Vice-Capellmeister shall be under obligation to compose such music as his Serene Highness may command, and neither to communicate such compositions to any other person, nor to allow them to be copied, but he shall retain them for the absolute use of his Highness, and not compose for any other person without the knowledge and permission of his Highness.

5. The said Joseph Heyden shall appear daily in the antechamber before and after midday, and inquire whether his Highness is pleased to order a performance of the orchestra. On receipt of his orders he shall communicate them to the other musicians, and take care to be punctual at the appointed time, and to ensure punctuality in his subordinates, making a note of those who arrive late or absent themselves altogether.

6. Should any quarrel or cause of complaint arise, the Vice-Capellmeister shall endeavor to arrange it in order that his Serene Highness may not be incommoded with trifling disputes; but should any more serious difficulty occur, which the said Joseph Heyden is unable to set right, his Serene Highness must then be respectfully called upon to decide the matter.

7. The said Vice-Capellmeister shall take careful charge of all music and musical instruments, and be responsible for any injury that may occur to them from carelessness or neglect.

8. The said Joseph Heyden shall be obliged to instruct the female vocalists, in order that they may not forget in the country what they have been taught with much trouble and expense in Vienna, and, as the said Vice-Capellmeister is proficient on various instruments, he shall take care himself to practice on all that he is acquainted with.

9. A copy of this agreement and instructions shall be given to the said Vice-Capellmeister and his subordinates, in order that he may be able to hold them to their obligations therein laid down.

10. It is considered unnecessary to detail the services required of the said Joseph Heyden, more particularly since his Serene Highness is pleased to hope that he will of his own free will strictly observe not only these regulations, but all others that may from time to time be made by his Highness, and that he will place the orchestra on such a footing, and in such good order, that he may bring honor upon himself and deserve the further favor of the prince his master, who thus confides in his zeal and discretion.

11. A yearly salary of four hundred florins to be received in quarterly payments is hereby bestowed by his Serene Highness upon the said Vice-Capellmeister.

12. In addition, the said Joseph Heyden shall board at the officers' table, or receive a half-gulden per day in lieu thereof.

13. Finally, this agreement shall hold good for at least three years from May 1, 1761, with the further condition that if at the conclusion of this term the said Joseph Heyden shall desire to seek his fortune elsewhere, he shall give his Highness six months' previous notice, that is at the beginning of the third mid-year.

14. His Serene Highness undertakes to keep Joseph Heyden in his service during this time and, should he be satisfied with him, he may look forward to being appointed a full Capellmeister. This, however, must not be understood to deprive his Serene Highness of the right to dismiss the said Joseph Heyden at the expiration of the term, should he see fit to do so.

In witness whereof, duplicate copies of this document have been drawn up and exchanged.

Given at Vienna this first day of May, 1761.

(signed) Joseph Haydn

Karl Geiringer, *Haydn: A Creative Life in Music* (New York: W. W. Norton & Company, Inc., 1946), 52–54. Reprinted by permission of W. W. Norton & Company, Inc., and George Allen & Unwin Ltd. Copyright © 1946 by W. W. Norton & Company, Inc. Copyright renewed 1974.

83

Gluck's Operatic Manifesto

The score of Gluck's second "reform" opera, *Alceste,* was published in Vienna in 1769 with a dedicatory letter addressed to Leopold, Grand Duke of Tuscany and future Holy Roman Emperor. In this letter Gluck (or more accurately his librettist Ranieri Calzabigi) attacked some of the traditional conventions of the *opera seria* in what has long been regarded as the most important manifesto of his "reform." But we prefer to use quotation marks around that word, first, because, while Gluck's "reform" operas were indeed different from the usual product of the time, they remained without influence, at least on Italian opera; and secondly, because the Gluck–Calzabigi reformist ideas were by no means original with them, but had been common currency among French and Italian writers from at least the beginning of the century. Furthermore, the "da capo aria," with its two sections, the first of which was repeated and embellished at the end, was on its way out by the late 1760s. But the well-known document remains a caustic example of operatic criticism; and the ideals expounded at the end of our excerpt are characteristic of the early Classical period.

When I set to work on the music of *Alceste,* I determined to divest it entirely of all those abuses (introduced either by the uncomprehending vanity of the Singers or by the Composers' excessive wish to please) which have so long disfigured the Italian Opera and have made of the grandest and loveliest of all spectacles the silliest and the most tedious.

I proposed to restrict the music to its true function of serving the poem in the expression and in the situations of the story without interrupting the action or cooling it down with useless, superfluous ornaments; for I am inclined to believe it should be as lively coloring and a well-chosen assortment of lights and shadows are to a correct, well-proportioned drawing, animating its forms without altering their contours.

Therefore, I have not seen fit to arrest an actor in the heat of dialogue to make him wait out a tedious *ritornello* [orchestral introduction], or to stop him in mid-word over a favorable vowel, or to show off the nimbleness of his fine voice by means of a lengthy passage, or to purchase time with the Orchestra while he took breath for a cadenza. I have not deemed it necessary to hurry through the second stanza of an aria, though it be the more impassioned and significant, in order to have the leisure to repeat four times the words of the first; or to end an aria at a point where its sense may well be incomplete, in order to give the singer an opportunity to display his whimsical capacity to vary a passage in so many different ways; in short, I have endeavored to banish all those abuses against which common sense and reason have for so long cried out in vain.

It occurred to me that the overture ought to prepare the audience for the events to be presented, that it ought, so to speak, to set the theme; that the intervention of instrumental music ought to be determined by and reflect the interests and the passion [of the moment] and not cause the dialogue to be so forcibly split up into recitatives and arias, nor make mincemeat of sentences or interrupt inopportunely the impetus and warmth of the action.

I further imagined that my greatest labor should consist in the search for a beautiful simplicity; and I have avoided making a display of difficulties at the expense of clarity; I have not underrated the discovery of certain innovations, provided always they were offered naturally by the situation and the expression; nor is there a hallowed rule I have not willingly sacrificed for the sake of the [intended] effect.

These are my principles. By good fortune, the libretto lent itself marvelously well to my design, for in it the celebrated author had imagined a novel plan for the drama, substituting for florid descriptions, for superfluous metaphors, and for cold, sententious morality the language of the heart, strong passions, interesting situations, and a constantly varying spectacle. Success has borne out my maxims, and the universal approbation of so enlightened a city [Vienna] has plainly shown that simplicity, truth, and naturalness are the great principles of the Beautiful in all productions of art.

Andrea Della Corte (ed.), *Antologia della storia della musica,* 4th ed. (Turin: G. B. Pavia & Co., 1954), 229–30. Trans. P. W.

84

"Folk Song": A New Name for Something Very Old

It was Johann Gottfried Herder (1744–1803) who in 1773 coined the German word "Volkslied," which was gradually and reluctantly adopted into English as "folk song" but still not given a separate entry in the *Oxford English Dictionary* of 1933 or in the *New Grove Dictionary of Music and Musicians* of 2001. This reluctance is no doubt due to differences between German culture and that of most other Western countries. Collecting and publishing orally transmitted tales, ballads, lyrical poetry, and tunes was certainly not unique to Germany; in fact, the early impulse came from Scotland and

England and was taken up elsewhere in Europe, particularly in the Scandinavian countries. But it was Herder who pursued this endeavor with an ultimately ethical purpose, that of giving his contemporaries the wholesome nourishment of their ancestors' unadorned poetry and song at a time when the lower classes were cut off from their own traditions and the upper classes indulged in fashionable, refined works of art. The morally uplifting implication thus accorded to the folk song was to prove a determining influence in the development of the German art song (the *Lied*) from its beginnings down to Brahms and Mahler. To further emphasize its ethical values, Herder prefaced his second collection of *Volkslieder* (1778–79) with a set of quotations from earlier authors intended to round out and support his argument. He translated all the foreign quotations into German and entitled them "Testimonials to the Folk Song," though several, which were plucked out of context, were not originally intended as such:

> A violet in the youth of primy nature,
> Forward, not permanent, sweet, not lasting,
> The perfume and suppliance of a minute—

Shakespeare's Hamlet [I, iii, 6–10]

Popular and purely natural poetry has naïveties and graces with which it can be compared to the principal beauty of poetry which has been perfected by art.

Montaigne, Bk. 1, chap. 14

> Flowers worthy of Paradise, which not nice Art
> In beds and curious knots, but Nature boon
> Poured forth profuse on hill, and dale, and plain.

Milton [*Paradise Lost, Bk. IV, 241–43*]

I never heard the old Song of *Percy* and *Duglas,* that I founde not my heart mooved more than with a Trumpet; and yet is it sung but by some blinde Crowder, with no rougher voice, then rude style— — —

Philip Sidney [*The Defence of Poesy*]

An ordinary song or ballad, that is the delight of the common people, cannot fail to please all such readers as are not unqualified for the entertainment by their affectation or ignorance; and the reason is plain, because the same paintings of nature which recommend it to the most ordinary reader, will appear beautiful to the most refined.

Addison, Spectator, No. 70

After so many references to English literature, it is not surprising to find Herder making a direct connection between the cultivation of folk songs in the British Isles and Gluck's operatic reform, as reported in 1772 by the composer himself to Burney (see the next reading) and recorded by Burney in *The Present State of Music in Germany, the Netherlands and United Provinces,* which appeared in German soon after the first English edition:

Gluck [during his stay in England in 1745–46] remarked particularly what the audience seemed most to feel; and finding that plainness and simplicity had the greatest effect upon them he has, ever since that time, endeavoured to write for the voice, more in natural tones of the human affections and passions, than to flatter the lovers of deep science or difficult execution. And it may be remarked, that most of his airs in *Orfeo* are as plain and simple as English ballads.

Gluck is simplifying music; and, with unbounded invention and powers for creating capricious difficulties, and decking his melodies with meretricious ornaments, he tries all he can to keep his music chaste and sober.

Burney

Who loves not wine, woman, and song,
He is a fool his whole life long.

Luther

Johann Gottfried Herder, *Volkslieder, Übertragungen, Dichtungen,* ed. Ulrich Gaier, Vol. III of *Werke in zehn Bänden* (Frankfurt am Main: Deutscher Klassiker Verlag, 1990), 69–74, 966–72. Original texts restored and/or trans. P.W.

85

Some General Thoughts on Music by Dr. Burney

Charles Burney (1726–1814), organist, composer, friend of Dr. Johnson, has already furnished us with several illuminating passages culled from his travel journals (*The Present State of Music in France and Italy,* 1771, and *The Present State of Music in Germany, the Netherlands, and United Provinces,* 1773) as well as from the great work that prompted him to undertake those journeys, the four volume *General History of Music,* 1776–89. He loved Italian opera and German instrumental music. Though an ardent admirer of Handel (whom he had known personally), he felt music had reached the peak of perfection in his own time. His views reflect the optimistic outlook of the age of Enlightenment, when reason and common sense still seemed capable of solving every human dilemma, of explaining every obscurity.

Music is an innocent luxury, unnecessary, indeed, to our existence, but a great improvement and gratification of the sense of hearing.

With respect to excellence of Style and Composition, it may perhaps be said that to practised ears the most pleasing Music is such as has the merit of novelty, added to refinement, and ingenious contrivance; and to the ignorant, such as is most familiar and common.

As Music may be defined as the art of pleasing by the succession and combination of agreeable sounds, every hearer has a right to give way to his feelings, and be pleased or dissatisfied without knowledge, experience, or the fiat of critics; but then he has certainly no right to insist on others being pleased or dissatisfied in the same degree. I can very readily forgive the man who admires a different Music from that which pleases me, provided he does not extend his hatred or contempt of my favourite Music to myself, and imagine that on the exclusive admiration of any one style of Music, and a close adherence to it, all wisdom, taste, and virtue depend.

There is a certain portion of enthusiasm connected with a love of the fine arts, which bids defiance to every curb of criticism; and the poetry, painting, or Music that leaves us on the ground, and does not transport us into the regions of the imagination beyond the reach of cold criticism, may be correct, but is devoid of genius and passion.

Charles Burney, *A General History of Music,* ed. Frank Mercer (New York: Dover Publications, Inc., 1957), I, 21, 22; II, 7.

Burney's notions of "enthusiasm" extended to the makeup of musicians themselves. In *The Present State of Music in Germany* he has this to say about the composer J. B. Vanhall (1739–1813):

A little perturbation of the faculties, is a promising circumstance in a young musician, and Mr. V. began his career very auspiciously, by being somewhat flighty. Enthusiasm seems absolutely necessary in all the arts, but particularly in music, which so much depends upon fancy and imagination. A cold, sedate, and wary disposition, but ill suits the professor of such an art; however, when enthusiasm is ungovernable, and impels too frequent and violent efforts, the intellects are endangered. But as insanity in an artist is sometimes nothing more than an ebullition of genius, when that is the case, he may cry out to the physicians who cure him,

—Pol me occidistis, amici,
Non servastis.

["Indeed, you have killed me, friends, not saved me."]

Percy A. Scholes (ed.), *Dr. Burney's Musical Tours in Europe* (London: Oxford University Press, 1959), II, 121.

Here are two more extracts from *A General History of Music:*

What judgment and good taste admire at first hearing, makes no impression on the public in general but by dint of repetition and habitude.

The extraneous, and seemingly forced and affected modulation of the German composers of the present age, is only too much for us, because we have heard too little. Novelty has been acquired, and attention excited, more by learned modulation in Germany, than by new and difficult melody in Italy. We dislike both, perhaps, only because we are not *gradually* arrived at them; and difficult and easy, new and old, depend on the reading, hearing, and knowledge of the critic. The most easy, simple, and natural is new to youth and inexperience, and we grow nice and fastidious by frequently hearing compositions of the first class, exquisitely performed.

Burney, *A General History of Music,* II, 11.

86

Frederick the Great Gives a Concert

King Frederick II of Prussia (1712–86; ruled from 1740) was a brilliant military strategist, an able and tireless administrator, and, intellectually, a devotee of the French Enlightenment. His musical tastes ran to Italian operas as written by his court composers (he assisted them by furnishing dramatic subjects) and to compositions for the flute as performed by himself. As a composer he is credited with writing 121 sonatas and four concertos for the flute, as well as some opera arias. But his chief supplier of flute music was his teacher, the eminent Johann Joachim Quantz (see page 223). The following eyewitness account is taken from Burney's *The Present State of Music in Germany, the Netherlands, and United Provinces.*

Thursday, October 1st [1772]

As some readers may, perhaps, be curious to know in what manner his majesty spends his time each day, at Sans-Souci, I shall here present them with a detail of that regular disposition of it, to which he has strictly adhered, during peace, ever since he began his reign: indeed, the evolutions of his soldiers, on the parade, cannot be more exact than his own diurnal motions.

His majesty's hour of rising, is constantly at four o'clock in the morning, during summer, and at five in winter; and from that time till nine, when his ministers of different departments attend him, he is employed in reading letters, and answering them in the margin. He then drinks one dish of coffee, and proceeds to business with his ministers, who come full fraught with doubts, difficulties, documents, petitions, and other papers, to read. With these he spends two hours, and then exercises his own regiment on the parade, in the same manner as the youngest colonel in his service.

At twelve o'clock he dines. His dinner is long, and generally with twelve or fourteen persons; after this he gives an hour to artists and projectors: then reads and signs the letters, written by his secretaries, from the marginal notes which he had made in the morning. When this is over, he thinks the *business* of the day is accomplished; the rest is given to amusement; after his evening concert, he gives some time to conversation, if disposed for it, and his courtiers in waiting constantly attend for that purpose; but whether that is the case or not, he has a lecturer to read to him, every evening, titles and extracts of new books, among which he marks such as he wishes to have purchased for his library, or to read in his cabinet. In this manner, when not employed in the field, reviewing his troops, or in travelling, he spends his time: always retiring at ten o'clock after which, however, he frequently reads, writes, or composes music for his flute, before he goes to bed.

I was carried [to Sans-Souci] between five and six o'clock in the evening, by an officer of the household, a privileged person, otherwise it would have been impossible for a stranger, like myself, to gain admission into a palace where the king resides; and even with my well-known guide, I underwent a severe examination, not only at going out of the gates at Potsdam, but at every door of the palace. When we arrived at the vestibule, we were met by M. de Catt, lecturer to his majesty, and member of the royal academy, to whom I had been furnished with a letter, who very politely attended my conductor and me the whole evening.

I was carried to one of the interior apartments of the palace, in which the gentlemen of the king's band were waiting for his commands. This apartment was contiguous to the concert-room, where I could distinctly hear his majesty practising *Solfeggi* [i.e., exercises] on the flute, and exercising himself in difficult passages, previous to his calling in the band. Here I met with M. Benda [a famous violinist and composer attached to Frederick's court], who was so obliging as to introduce me to M. Quantz.

The figure of this Veteran Musician, is of an uncommon size:

> The son of Hercules he justly seems,
> By his broad shoulders, and gigantic limbs;

and he appears to enjoy an uncommon portion of health and vigour, for a person arrived at his 76th year. We soon began a musical conversation; he told me, that his majesty and scholar played no other concertos than those which he had expressly composed for his use, which amounted to 300, and these he performed in rotation. This exclusive attachment to the productions of his old master, may appear somewhat contracted; however, it implies a constancy of disposition, but rarely to be found among princes.

These reflections, which occurred to me while I was conversing with M. Quantz, were interrupted by the arrival of a messenger from the king, commanding the gentlemen of his band to attend him in the next room.

The concert began by a German-flute concerto, in which his majesty executed the solo parts with great precision; his *embouchure* was clear and even, his finger brilliant, and his taste pure and simple. I was much pleased, and even surprised with the neatness of his execution in the *allegros,* as well as by his expression and feeling in the *adagio;* in short, his performance surpassed, in many particulars, any thing I had ever heard among *Dilettanti,* or even professors. His majesty played three long and difficult concertos successively, and all with equal perfection.

M. Quantz bore no other part in the performance of the concertos of to-night than to give the time with the motion of his hand, at the beginning of each movement, except now and then to cry out *bravo!* to his royal scholar, at the end of the solo parts and closes; which seems to be a privilege allowed to no other musician of the band. The cadences [here both "closes" and "cadences" = cadenzas] which his majesty made, were good, but very long and studied. It is easy to discover that these concertos were composed at a time when he did not so frequently require an opportunity of breathing as at present; for in some of the divisions [rapid passages], which were very long and difficult, as well as in the closes, he was obliged to take his breath, contrary to rule, before the passages were finished.

After these three concertos were played, the concert of the night ended, and I returned to Potsdam; but not without undergoing the same interrogatories from all the sentinels, as I had done in my way to Sans-Souci.

Percy A. Scholes (ed.), *Dr. Burney's Musical Tours in Europe* (London: Oxford University Press, 1959), II, 180–82.

87

The Young Mozart as a Scientific Curiosity

Mozart's father traveled far and wide with his precocious son and somewhat older daughter, determined to make the most of their talent while they were still young and, therefore, box-office sensations. While in London in 1765, Mozart (then nine years

Leopold, Wolfgang, and Marianne Mozart in Paris in 1764. Engraving after a water color by Louis Carrogis (known as Carmontelle, 1716–1806). It was clearly intended for publicity purposes. An earlier, more realistic version exists, in which Mozart's face is less cherubic and his legs are considerably longer; understandably, no engraving was ever made of that picture.

old) was made the object of scientific scrutiny by Daines Barrington, a Fellow of the Royal Society, who later sent in an official report to its Secretary. The report (excerpts of which appear below) was eventually read at a meeting and published in the Society's *Philosophical Transactions*. Like a true scientist, Barrington obtained a copy of Mozart's birth date from the parish register in Salzburg and so was able to satisfy himself that he had not been examining a dwarf.

Account of a Very Remarkable Young Musician

SIR,

If I was to send you a well attested account of a boy who measured seven feet in height, when he was not more than eight years of age, it might be considered as not undeserving the notice of the Royal Society.

The instance which I now desire you will communicate to that learned body, of as early an exertion of most extraordinary musical talents, seems perhaps equally to claim their attention.

Joannes Chrysostomus Wolfgangus Theophilus Mozart, was born at Saltzbourg, on the 17th [really the 27th] of January, 1756.

I have been informed by a most able musician and composer, that he frequently saw him at Vienna, when he was little more than four years old.

By this time he not only was capable of executing lessons on his favourite instrument the harpsichord, but composed in an easy stile and taste, which were much approved of.

His extraordinary musical talents soon reached the ears of the present empress dowager, who used to place him upon her knees whilst he played on the harpsichord.

This notice taken of him by so great a personage, together with a certain consciousness of his most singular abilities, had much emboldened the little musician. Being therefore the next year at one of the German courts, where the elector encouraged him, by saying, that he had nothing to fear from his august presence, little Mozart immediately sat down with great confidence to his harpsichord, informing his highness, that he had played before the empress.

At seven years of age his father carried him to Paris, where he so distinguished himself by his compositions, that an engraving was made of him.

The father and sister who are introduced in this print, are excessively like their portraits, as is also little Mozart, who is stiled "Compositeur et Maître de Musique, agé de sept ans."

After the name of the engraver, follows the date, which is in 1764: Mozart was therefore at this time in the eighth year of his age.

Upon leaving Paris, he came over to England, where he continued more than a year. As during this time I was witness of his most extraordinary abilities as a musician, both at some publick concerts, and likewise by having been alone with him for a considerable time at his father's house; I send you the following account, amazing and incredible almost as it may appear.

I carried him a manuscript duet, which was composed by an English gentleman to some favourite words in Metastasio's opera of Demofoonte.

The whole score was in five parts, viz. accompaniments for a first and second violin, the two vocal parts, and a bass.

My intention in carrying with me this manuscript composition, was to have an irrefragable proof of his abilities, as a player at sight, it being absolutely impossible that he could have ever seen the music before.

The score was no sooner put upon his desk, than he began to play the symphony [i.e., the orchestral introduction] in a most masterly manner, as well as in the time and stile which corresponded with the intention of the composer.

I mention this circumstance, because the greatest masters often fail in these particulars on the first trial.

The symphony ended, he took the upper [vocal] part, leaving the under one to his father.

His voice in the tone of it was thin and infantine, but nothing could exceed the masterly manner in which he sung.

His father, who took the under part in this duet, was once or twice out, though the passages were not more difficult than those in the upper one; on which occasions the son looked back with some anger pointing out to him his mistakes, and setting him right.

He not only however did complete justice to the duet, by singing his own part in the truest taste, and with the greatest precision: he also threw in the accompaniments of the two violins, wherever they were most necessary, and produced the best effects.

It is well known that none but the most capital musicians are capable of accompanying in this superior stile.

> Barrington next asked Mozart to improvise a love song and a song of rage, "such as might be proper for the opera stage." He did both extremely well, and by the middle of the second song "he had worked himself up to such a pitch, that he beat his harpsichord like a person possessed, rising sometimes in his chair."

After this he played a difficult lesson [a sonata], which he had finished [composing] a day or two before: his execution was amazing, considering that his little fingers could scarcely reach a fifth on the harpsichord.

His astonishing readiness, however, did not arise merely from great practice; he had a thorough knowledge of the fundamental principles of composition, as, upon producing a treble [i.e., a melody], he immediately wrote a bass under it, which, when tried, had very good effect.

The facts which I have been mentioning I was myself an eye witness of; to which I must add, that I have been informed by two or three able musicians, when [John Christian] Bach the celebrated composer had begun a fugue and left off abruptly, that little Mozart hath immediately taken it up, and worked it after a most masterly manner.

Witness as I was myself of most of these extraordinary facts, I must own that I could not help suspecting his father imposed with regard to the real age of the boy, though he had not only a most childish appearance, but likewise had all the actions of that stage of life.

For example, whilst he was playing to me, a favourite cat came in, upon which he immediately left his harpsichord, nor could we bring him back for a considerable time.

He would also sometimes run about the room with a stick between his legs by way of a horse.

O. E. Deutsch (ed.), *Mozart: Die Dokumente seines Lebens (Neue Ausgabe sämtlicher Werke*, Ser. X/34 [Kassel: Bärenreiter, 1961]), 86–90.

88

From Mozart's Letters

During his stay in Paris in 1778, Mozart made the acquaintance of a musical noble-man, the Duc de Guines, who commissioned him to write the Concerto for Flute and Harp, K. 299. In a letter to his father, Mozart describes his amusing attempts to get the nobleman's inhibited daughter to compose an original tune. His father, commenting on the situation, reminded him quite sensibly that one could not expect a student to put down original ideas at the fourth lesson and added, "Do you think everybody has your genius?"

Paris, 14 May 1778

I believe I already wrote you in my last letter that the Duc de Guines, whose Daughter is my Pupil in Composition, plays the flute surpassingly well, and she the Harp magnificently; she has a great deal of Talent, and genius, and in particular an incomparable memory, for she plays all her pieces by heart—200 of them, in fact. But she seriously doubts whether she also has any genius for Composition—especially with regard to thoughts—ideas; but her father (who, between ourselves, dotes on her a little too much) says she most certainly has ideas; that it's just bashfulness—that she just lacks self-confidence. Well, we shall see. If she gets no ideas or thoughts (for at the moment she hasn't any at all), then there is no help for it—goodness knows I cannot give her any. It is not her father's intention to make a great Composer of her; she need not (he said) write any operas, any arias, any Concertos, any Symphonies, but merely grand Sonatas for her instrument and mine. I gave her her 4th Lesson today, and I'm tolerably pleased with her where the Rules of Composition and part writing are concerned—she set me a pretty good Bass part under the first Minuet I wrote down for her. Now she's already begun to write in 3 parts. It is going quite well, but she is soon Bored; only I cannot help it, I cannot possibly move on: it's too early, even if the genius were really there, but unfortunately it is not—it will all have to be done artificially.

She has no ideas at all. Nothing will come. I have Tried all kinds of things with her; among others, it occurred to me to write down quite a simple Minuet and see whether she might not be able to make a variation on it. Well, that was of no use. Now then, thought I, she just doesn't know how to go about it—and so I began a variation, just on the first bar, and told her to go on in the same vein and to stick to the idea; this, at last, went pretty well. When she had finished, I asked her to be so good as to begin something herself—just the top part, a Melody. Well, she brooded for a whole quarter of an hour—and nothing came. So then I wrote down 4 bars of a Minuet and said, "Just see what an Ass I am! Here I've begun a Minuet and can't even finish the first part of it! Do be so Kind as to complete it for me." This she believed to be impossible. Finally, after much effort, something was brought forth; I was glad indeed that for once something had come.

Piero Weiss (ed.), Letters of Composers Through Six Centuries (Philadelphia: Chilton Books, 1967), 125–26.

While in Paris, Mozart was commissioned to write a symphony for the so-called Concert Spirituel (see p. 176). In the following letter to his father, he has been describing the afternoons he and his friend Anton Raaff (a well-known tenor) have been spending at the house of a German diplomat:

---

12 June 1778

Today I brought along the new Symphony, which I have just completed and which will open the Concert Spirituel on Corpus Christi. They both liked it extremely well. I am very pleased with it myself. Whether or not it will be a success, however, I can't say—nor, to tell the truth, do I really care. For, who will not like it?—I'll wager it will please the *few* sensible Frenchmen there; as for fools, I cannot view it as a calamity if they don't like it. But I have hopes that even Donkeys will find in it something to please them; what's more, I haven't forgotten the First Stroke of the Bow!—and that's quite enough.

The fuss these blockheads make about it! What the devil! *I* can't make out the difference—they all begin together—just as they do in other towns. It's too ridiculous. Raaff has told me a story on the subject—it happened to [the composer] dall'Abaco in Munich, or somewhere. A Frenchman asked him:

"Monsieur, have you been to Paris?"

"Oui."

"Have you attended the Concert Spirituel?"

"Oui."

"What think you of the First Stroke of the Bow? Have you heard the First Stroke of the Bow?"

"*Oui*, I have heard the first stroke and the last."

"The last? What d'you mean, the last?"

"*Mais oui*, the first and the last. And I liked the last even better."

I must close now.

The symphony, K. 297 (300a), was performed six days later, on June 18. Here is Mozart's account of the event to his father:

---

3 July 1778

It was performed to general applause on Corpus Christi; and the "Courrier de l'Europe," so I hear, has printed a notice on it, which makes it an exceptional success. I was very upset at the Rehearsal, for I had not heard such miserable playing in all my Days; you cannot imagine how they twice stumbled through the Symphony without stopping, and scratching all the while.—I was really quite upset.—I should have liked to Rehearse it once more, but as they always Rehearse so many things, there was no time for it; and so I went to bed with a heavy heart and in a dissatisfied and angry frame of mind. The next day I resolved not to attend the Concert; but the weather turning fine in the evening, I finally decided to go—determined, however, that if things went as badly as they had at the Rehearsal, I should certainly go up to the stage, snatch the violin from Mr. La Houssaye (the leader of the orchestra), and conduct myself.

I prayed God that it might go well—it is all for his greater honor and glory—and lo and behold, the Symphony began. Raaff stood next to me. Just in the middle of the first Allegro [movement] there was a Passage I was sure would please. All the listeners went into raptures over it—applauded heartily. But as, when I wrote it, I was quite aware of its Effect, I introduced it once more towards the end—and it was applauded all over again. The Andante [movement] pleased them too, but the last Allegro even better. I had heard that final Allegros, here, must begin in the same way as the first ones, all the instruments playing together, mostly in unison. I began mine with nothing but the 1st and 2nd violins playing softly for 8 bars—then there is a sudden *forte*. Consequently, the listeners (just as I had anticipated) all went "Sh!" in the soft passage—then came the sudden *forte*—and no sooner did they hear the *forte* than they all clapped their hands. I was so glad, that, the minute the Symphony was finished, I went to the Palais Royal, ordered a good ice cream, said my Rosary as I had vowed to do, and went home.

W. A. Bauer and O. E. Deutsch (eds.), *Mozart: Briefe und Aufzeichnungen,* II (Kassel: Bärenreiter, 1962), 378–79, 388–89. Trans. P. W.

89

Haydn's Reception in London

Haydn's two visits to England late in his career (1791–92, 1794–95) represent a bright culminating point in the story of the man's life; and since his last, and greatest, symphonies were composed to be performed in London (six for the first visit, six for the last), Haydn's connection with England also forms a vital chapter in the history of the symphony. In the present context we may, perhaps, concentrate on yet a third aspect of those visits: the emergence of the veteran composer (he was fifty-eight years old when he first went to London) from an appreciative, yet still essentially feudal society (see his original contract with his patron, p. 252) into the glare of public recognition of England's far more modern society. The aristocracy, to be sure, gave him a warm welcome. But it was his personal appearances at crowded concerts and the endless stream of rapturous prose—and verse—published in the daily papers that made this such an unusual experience for him. Concerts and newspapers were, of course, symbols of the importance of the middle class, which, on the European continent, even at this late date, had not yet acquired a comparable position. Our first excerpt is taken from a lengthy poem (doggerel, really) written—and published—by Charles Burney soon after Haydn's first arrival, in 1791. The fourth stanza is particularly noteworthy for its recognition of Germany's new-won hegemony in the realm of instrumental music—a preeminence for which Haydn was chiefly responsible.

Verses on the Arrival of *Haydn* in England   PRICE ONE SHILLING

Music! The Calm of life, the cordial bowl,
Which anxious care can banish from the soul,
Affliction soothe, and elevate the mind,
And all its sordid manacles unbind,
Can snatch us from life's incidental pains,
And "wrap us in Elysium with its strains!"
To cultivated ears, this fav'rite art
No new *delight was able to impart;*
No Eagle flights its votaries durst essay,
But hopp'd, like little birds, from spray to spray.
At length great HAYDN'S new and varied strains
Of habit and indiff'rence broke the chains;
Rous'd to attention the long torpid sense,
With all that pleasing wonder could dispense.
Whene'er Parnassus' height he meant to climb,
Whether the grand, pathetic, or sublime,
The simply graceful, or the comic vein,
The theme suggested, or enrich'd the strain,
From melting sorrow to gay jubilation,
Whate'er his pen produc'd was Inspiration!

Haydn! Great Sovereign of the tuneful art!
Thy works alone supply an ample chart
Of all the mountains, seas, and fertile plains,
Within the compass of its wide domains.—
Is there an Artist of the present day
Untaught by thee to think, as well as play?
Whose hand thy science has not well supplied?
Whose hand thy labours have not fortified?—

Thy style has gain'd disciples, converts, friends,
As far as Music's thrilling power extends.
Nor has great Newton more to satisfaction
Demonstrated the influence of Attraction.
And though to Italy of right belong
The undisputed sovereignty of *Song:*
Yet ev'ry nation of the earth must now
To Germany pre-eminence allow
For instrumental *powers, unknown before*
Thy happy flights had taught her sons to soar.

Welcome, great Master! to our favour'd Isle,
Already partial to thy name and style;
Long may thy fountain of invention run
In streams as rapid as at first begun;
While skill for each fantastic whim provides,

> And certain science ev'ry current guides!
> Oh, may thy days, from human suff'rings free,
> Be blest with glory and felicity!
> With full fruition, to a distant hour,
> Of all thy magic and creative pow'r!
> Blest in thyself, with rectitude of mind;
> And blessing, with thy talents, all mankind!

The concerts at which Haydn presented his symphonies (which the British at this time persisted in calling "Overtures" or "Grand Overtures"), marking the time and accompanying them from the harpsichord or piano, were faithfully described and reported on by several of the London dailies. Here are some excerpts. After the first concert (11 March 1791):

The First Concert under the auspices of HAYDN was last night, and never, perhaps, was there a richer musical treat.

It is not wonderful that to souls capable of being touched by music, HAYDN should be an object of homage, and even of idolatry; for like our own SHAKSPEARE, he moves and governs the passions at will.

His *new Grand Overture* was pronounced by every scientific ear to be a most wonderful composition; but the first movement in particular rises in grandeur of subject, and in the rich variety of *air* and passion, beyond any even of his own productions. The *Overture* has four movements—An Allegro—Andante—Minuet—and Rondo. They are all beautiful, but the first is pre-eminent in every charm, and the Band performed it with admirable correctness.

We were happy to see the Concert so well attended the first Night; for we cannot suppress our very anxious hopes, that the first musical genius of the age may be induced, by our liberal welcome, to take up his residence in England.

The symphony performed at that first concert was, according to Haydn scholar H. C. Robbins Landon, the "Oxford" Symphony, no. 92 (Haydn presented it at Oxford later that year, when he was awarded the honorary degree of Doctor of Music). Here, next, are comments on the first performance of Symphony no. 94, known as the "Surprise," after the sudden crash in the slow movement, which, as we can see, caused quite a flutter the first time it was heard (23 March 1792):

Act 2d [i.e., the second half of the program] opened with a first performance of the GRAND OVERTURE composed by HAYDN for that evening.

The Second Movement was equal to the happiest of this great Master's conceptions. The surprise might not be unaptly likened to the situation of a beautiful Shepherdess who, lulled to slumber by the murmur of a distant Waterfall, starts alarmed by the unexpected firing of a fowling-piece. The flute obligato was delicious.

The "Clock" Symphony, no. 101, was completed during Haydn's second visit and first performed on 3 March 1794:

As usual the most delicious part of the entertainment was a new grand Overture by HAYDN; the inexhaustible, the wonderful, the sublime HAYDN! The first two movements were encored; and the character that pervaded the whole composition was heartfelt joy. Every new Overture he writes, we fear, till it is heard, he can only repeat himself; and we are every time mistaken. Nothing can be more original than the subject of the first movement; and having found a happy subject, no man knows like HAYDN how to produce incessant variety, without once departing from it. The management of the accompaniments of the andante, though perfectly simple, was masterly; and we never heard a more charming effect than was produced by the trio to the minuet.—It was HAYDN; what can we, what need we say more?

> The "Military" Symphony (no. 100) was first performed on 31 March 1794, and again on April 7. It became Haydn's most popular symphony, thanks to the effect created by the second movement:

Another new Symphony, by Haydn, was performed for the second time; and the middle movement was again received with absolute shouts of applause. Encore! encore! encore! resounded from every seat: the Ladies themselves could not forbear. It is the advancing to battle; and the march of men, the sounding of the charge, the thundering of the onset, the clash of arms, the groans of the wounded, and what may well be called the hellish roar of war increased to a climax of horrid sublimity! which, if others can conceive, he alone can execute; at least he alone hitherto has effected these wonders.

H. C. Robbins Landon, *Haydn: Chronicle and Works*, III: *Haydn in England* (Bloomington, Ind.: Indiana University Press, 1976), 32–35, 49–50, 150, 241, 247.

90

Sonata Form and the Symphony Described by a Contemporary of Haydn

Augustus Frederic Christopher Kollmann (1756–1829) was a German-born, German-trained musician who plied his trade as organist and chapel master in England from 1782 until his death. He was also the author of a number of respectable technical treatises in the language of his adopted country. These culminated in 1799 with *An Essay on Practical Musical Composition*, which gives detailed instructions for composition in the older strict forms (fugue, canon) and somewhat more general ones for the more modern symphony, sonata, and concerto. At the beginning of our excerpt, Kollmann addresses himself to what today is generally referred to as "sonata form"—i.e., the form of "long movements" (typically, but not exclusively, the first) in symphonies and sonatas. In keeping with the views of his time, he sees the sonata form as a kind of expanded two-part ("binary") form and describes it solely according to its modulations. Later writers (beginning with Carl Czerny in the nineteenth century) have viewed the form as a three-part ("ternary") design to be described according to the progress of its themes (the familiar complex of Bithematic Exposition—Development—Recapitulation). The nineteenth-century view has always made it necessary to regard some of the ripest Classical symphonies (Haydn's "London,"

Beethoven's "Eroica") as somehow irregular or deviant, which is not the case if the older description is applied. Kollmann in fact tells us he has been influenced directly, in his description of form in general and of symphonies in particular, by the example of Haydn's late works, so recently presented to London audiences (see the preceding selection).

Modulation of a Piece

In its *outlines*, a long movement is generally divided into *two sections*. The first, when the piece is in major, ends in the fifth of the scale [i.e., the dominant], and the second in the key; but when the piece is in minor, the first section generally ends in the third of the scale [i.e., the relative major], and the second in the key. These two sections are either separated by a *double bar* or *repeat*, or not distinguished by any particular mark; which latter commonly is the case in concertos or those pieces which would become too long by a repetition. But though pieces are not calculated for a repetition, the above distinction of two sections is required in them, if they shall create an expectation at the beginning, and give a satisfaction at the end; without which they cannot be truly entertaining.

In regard to *other particulars*, the said two sections admit, besides a regular setting out, and a return, *three sorts of elaboration*, all of which may be distributed in the following manner, viz.:

Each *section*, may be divided into two *subsections;* which in the whole makes *four* subsections.

The *first* subsection must contain the setting out from the key towards its fifth in major, or third in minor; and it may end with the chord of the key note or its fifth, but the latter is better. The *second* subsection comprehends a first sort of elaboration, consisting of a more natural modulation than that of the third subsection; it may be confined to the fifth or third of the key only, or also touch on some related, or even non-related keys if only no formal digression is made to any key but the said fifth in major, or third in minor. The *third* subsection or beginning of the second section, comprehends a second sort of elaboration, consisting of digressions to all those keys and modes which shall be introduced besides that of the fifth (or third); and being the place for those abrupt modulations, or enharmonic changes, which the piece admits or requires. The *fourth* subsection contains the return to the key, with a third sort of elaboration, similar to that of the first subsection.

The above is the plan of modulation, which will be found attended to in most sonatas, symphonies, and concertos, as well as elaborate airs and choruses, of all great Composers, because it is the most reasonable one, and the most adapted to the nature of our attention, and our feeling, hitherto known. But it may be *varied* almost to the infinite. For, the different sections and subsections of a piece may be of any reasonable variety of length, and the said sorts of modulation and elaboration may be diversified without end, as it also appears from the composition of great Composers, and will require no demonstration.

In pieces of *three* and *more* movements, the first and last should be set in the same *key*, to preserve the impression of one and the same piece, but they may be different in *mode* [i.e., minor and major], the same as in those of *two* movements. And the one or more movements between the first and last, may be set in any variety of related keys and modes; which a judicious fancy can suggest. Fine examples of pieces of *four* movements are most of *Haydn's* Symphonies.

Of Free Symphonies

Under this denomination I comprehend all those Symphonies which have *no prescribed* [i.e., programmatic] Character; though I have said before that every Musical Piece ought to have *some* general character.

They may be used either to precede a Concert or Theatrical Piece like an Overture, or to fill up some intervals between the said pieces; or also on any other occasion.

They may be written of any reasonable *Length,* like Sonatas, and consist of the same Number and Variety of *Movements* as Sonatas, from which they differ chiefly in that they are calculated to be performed by *more than one Performer* to each part, that is, by an *Orchestra.* But *Haydn's* Symphonies generally consist of *four* Movements, viz: an Allegro; an Adagio; a Menuetto; and a Presto; or some other Movement similar to these. In most of his latter Symphonies that Author also begins with a short Adagio before the first Allegro, which serves to prepare the hearers for the piece to which it is an introduction, and heightens the effect of its beginning. Here I refer to *Haydn's* twelve Symphonies lately published by Mr. *Salomon.*

When a Symphony is to be written for an Orchestra, there ought to be considered: first, the construction of its *Subjects* [i.e., themes]; secondly, the distribution of its *Harmony* between the different instruments.

If a Symphony for an Orchestra shall not be imperfect, its principal *Subjects* ought to be of such a nature, that all Instruments can *execute* them, or at least *join* in them in the principal Key. If this role is not attended to, a Symphony cannot answer the purpose of employing the whole Orchestra to advantage; and *Haydn* will be found very particular in attending to this rule, for the subjects of most of his best Symphonies are not only calculated for the Horn and Trumpet, but even for the Kettle Drums, of which the beginning of No. I of the twelve mentioned above [i.e., Symphony no. 97 in C major], may serve for an Example.

Augustus F. C. Kollmann, *An Essay on Practical Musical Composition* (London, 1799), 5–7, 16–17.

91

A Musical Episode of the French Revolution

The effects of the French Revolution on European music were as vast and immeasurable as its effects on European life generally. Its most immediate and measurable effects form part of French, and more particularly Parisian, musical history. For example, when the Royal Guard became the National Guard, its musicians found themselves unprovided for by the new statutes; after various vicissitudes, and after merging with the erstwhile Royal School of Singing and Declamation, they became the faculty of a new, municipal "free music school"; the National Convention made it a government institution in 1793 and renamed it "Conservatoire" in 1795. Thus one of France's most famous and important musical institutions was a direct offspring of the Revolution. Understandably, its members were among the most ardent supporters of the new order. And since music, in turn, had an impact on the course of events, it is fair to say that Gossec, Lesueur, Méhul, and the rest of the composer–teachers of that early National Institute of Music fought in the front ranks on the side of liberty and equality. An instance of this follows. At the height of the Reign of Terror, Robespierre (in opposition to both the extreme atheist position and orthodox Catholicism) established by decree the cult of the Supreme Being and appointed 20 *Prairial*, year II (i.e., 8 June 1794), as the day on which the first Festival of the Supreme Being would be celebrated. The painter Jacques Louis David, entrusted with the arrangements, decided that twenty-four hundred representatives of the various Parisian "sections" should sing atop an artificial "mountain" and that "the whole people" should join in the singing. There was to be a new hymn as well as the "Marseillaise" decked out with a new, appropriate text. Who but the members of the Institute of Music could be entrusted with the task of teaching half of Paris to sing the new music? The Institute (whose director, Bernard Sarrette, had narrowly escaped the guillotine a couple of months earlier) hastened to offer its services to the dread Committee of Public Safety in the terms given below. And on 19 *Prairial*, from 7 to "well after 10" at night, France's most distinguished composers were seen in every "section" of the city, violin or flute in hand, teaching the people of Paris to sing in tune. The Festival of the Supreme Being proved to be the most impressive, if not the most spontaneous, of the French Revolution's many public ceremonies.

Representatives of the people:

The National Convention, in decreeing festivals worthy of the people's majesty, has called on all the arts to contribute to their magnificence.

Music, by virtue of the special character it stamps on them, plays too important a part in the celebration of these festivals for the National Institute not to be penetrated with a sense of the sublime duties it must carry out.

Not only is it mindful of the riches which the art of music must bring to these festivals, and the scholar musicians it must form for every part of the Republic; there is yet a more honorable function to which it pledges itself: that is, to transmit to the people the music of the hymns which shall have been chosen to be consecrated at the public festivals.

The void left by the suppression of fanaticism's rites must be filled by the songs of liberty, and the people must, with its accents, increase the solemnity of the festivals dedicated to the virtues honored by the Republic.

Simple songs shall be composed; the members of the Institute shall betake themselves to each district, to the primary schools: the people, and its most interesting portion, the hope of the fatherland, shall there learn the hymns that are to be performed at the festivals.

Thus shall the free French people prove to enslaved Germany and Italy that they, too, possess genius in this art, but that they dedicate it solely to songs of liberty.

In the School of Martial Arts, young patriots shall be drilled by the Institute in warlike songs: these will impart fresh vigor to their enthusiasm for liberty, love of equality, and severe character of pure republicanism.

Let the despots tremble: more than once has a national song, sounded in battle, caused Frenchmen to redouble their valorous efforts; and the courage that shattered the tyrant's throne was nurtured by the songs of the people.

The accents of liberty always precede its banners.
In the name of the National Institute of Music:

LESUEUR, composer; MÉHUL, composer; GOSSEC, composer; DALAYRAC, composer; SARRETTE; CATEL, composer; P. RODE, violinist; DEVIENNE, composer; HERMANN, harpsichordist; LEFÈVRE, clarinetist; OZI, bassoonist; VENY, secretary; BUCH, horn player; SALLANTIN, oboist; L. JADIN, composer; MATHIEU, serpent player; HUGOT, flutist; LEVASSEUR, violoncellist; F. DUVERNOY, horn player; BLASIUS, violinist.

Julien Tiersot, *Les Fêtes et les chants de la révolution française* (Paris: Hachette & Cie., 1908), 150–51. Trans. P.W.

92

Vienna, 1800

Musical conditions in the fabled capital—where Mozart had died nine years before in comparative neglect, where Haydn was living out his last creative years in honor, where Beethoven's brilliant career was in the ascendant—are graphically described here by the correspondent of the leading German musical journal, and it does not seem at all necessary to qualify his words or to warn modern readers of any exaggerations or distortions: his report is quite objective, as anyone acquainted with the lives of the three masters can testify. Indeed, the part of the article dealing with Beethoven's first concert of his own works (which included the first performance of his Symphony no. 1) will be familiar to readers of his biography. Less familiar, perhaps, will be the description of the general decay of musical standards that went with the decline of aristocratic patronage, or of the rise of trivial "salon music" that attended the rise of the bourgeoisie. For that reason, the article has been quoted at some length. (We should note that when the writer is discussing the "direction" of an orchestra, he does not yet mean conducting with a baton, but rather the traditional leadership by a violinist–concertmaster—see the comments by Quantz, p. 225, and the extract from Spohr's autobiography, p. 293.)

A SKETCH OF THE PRINCIPAL FEATURES OF CONTEMPORARY MUSICAL LIFE IN VIENNA
Theater Music
It is in this field, as everybody knows, that instead of attaining perfection, music has in many respects suffered harm. The administration [of the theaters] cannot possibly escape the reproach of having repeatedly misused both art and artists.

Italian Opera
[After appraising the leading singers, the writer continues:] The rest of the Italian singers are less remarkable. The orchestra has no lack of estimable players, but it lacks good will, unanimity, and dedication to the art. Such selfless dedication seems quite

foreign to them, and often the orchestra is not, as the saying goes, together. One might wish that the gentlemen who play the double bass were somewhat less easy-going. In very loud passages, we hear rather a buzzing and a rumbling than a clear penetrating bass-tone (which would greatly enhance the general effect). Herr Conti, the director, is obviously unequal to his task. It often happens that half the orchestra is made up of substitutes sent in by these gentlemen while they are pursuing some other engagement or their own pleasure: the effect of this we leave to the reader's imagination. The selection of the operas is poor indeed: the recognized older ones are neglected in favor of the newer ones which, taken as a whole, can please no connoisseur. These are sent for from Italy, mostly at the request of some member of the company who has taken a fancy to a role in them, or even to a single, brilliant aria. Many operas are performed which are clearly seen to be failures at the first rehearsal.

German Opera

In every respect, the German opera falls short of the expectations we might with reason entertain of it in Germany's greatest city, her imperial capital! Its orchestra has far fewer worthy subjects than the Italian opera's: the pay is too low. And yet we often have far better performances of Haydn's symphonies or even, on occasion, of a Mozart opera by this orchestra than by the other; and this, to a large extent, redounds to the credit of its worthy director, Herr Paul Wranitzky.

Public Concerts

There are no regular concerts here, except the yearly four established for the benefit of the Fund for Musicians' Widows. These, in the past, were often quite inferior; but now that P. Wranitzky is the Secretary we have had, for example, [the oratorios] *The Seven Last Words* and *The Creation* by Haydn, who took part in the performances, thanks to W.'s good offices. At the performance of *The Creation,* the orchestra numbered almost 200 strong and consisted in the main of the most skillful individuals. It was truly an *excellent* performance. If only the theater had been built to better advantage, the effect would have been quite extraordinary, for it is a work expertly calculated to produce great effects. *The Creation* is at present the great favorite hereabouts and brings in the most money—a consideration of some moment, and rightly so, in the case of charitable causes. There are, in addition, twelve morning concerts at the Augarten, called the Amateur-Concerts.

Incidental concerts by traveling artists are relatively scarce, because the theater administration rarely lets out the theater for anything but a considerable sum. There is, in any case, not much to be gained by them. I will mention only a few of this year's concerts. Herr Simon was granted the use of the theater for a high fee; but he hardly deserved it, for he is to be counted amongst the most mediocre oboists. His concerto is beneath all criticism. Madame Plomer Salvini gave a concert at 1 ducat the ticket: she enjoyed, it seems, much support from the nobility. Her voice has a wide range, but she herself is still quite a novice in the art. She often sings out of tune; her wild *roulades* often do not match the harmony, etc. The Polonaise, which happened to be her worst offering, was encored, while the lovely Haydn symphonies, which were very well performed, went all but unnoticed.—Herr Punto, the well-known master of the French horn, was granted the theater and astounded everyone with his artistry. Herr Beethoven was good enough to provide him with a sonata for pianoforte and horn, and it was splendid. It did one good to hear Herr Punto in a good composition, for his own concertos are not exactly significant, indeed they are now and again quite bizarre.—At length Herr Beethoven, too, was granted the use of the theater, and this, truly, proved to be the most interesting concert we have had in a long while. He played a new concerto of his own composition, which contained many beautiful things—especially the first two movements. Then a Septet of his, written with much taste and invention, was produced. Next he improvised in a masterly fashion, and at the end we had a symphony of his own composition which displayed great artistry, innovation, and wealth of ideas; except that the winds were overused, so that it was rather music for band than for the whole orchestra. The Italian orchestra distinguished itself mainly to its discredit on this occasion. First—directorial squabbles! Beethoven rightly thought he should entrust the direction not to Herr Conti, indeed to nobody but Herr Wranitzky. Under the latter, however, those gentlemen refused to perform. The above-mentioned failings of the orchestra thus became even more evident, for B.'s work is hard to play. In the accompaniments they did not trouble to pay close attention to the solo player—no trace, therefore, of following the train of his impressions or of similar matters. In the second movement of the symphony they made themselves so comfortable that, despite all beating of time, not a spark could be obtained, especially from the winds. To what avail, given such behavior, is all their agility—a quality we would not wish to deny the majority of the society's members? What significant effect can even the most remarkable composition produce under such circumstances? Who will discover and teach us the magic word that will make an end of convenience, of personal and other petty considerations, that will instill life, spirituality, ardor for the art itself? Perhaps matters are not much better in other great cities; but it is precisely when we consider how much—how *very* much, in every respect, could be accomplished in this wealthy imperial city, with its love of music and capable practitioners, if only we *willed* it so, that we must be heartsick and must complain, and wish, and blame those who are responsible.

All in all, concerts are not too popular here; hence, many a deserving artist is obliged to suffer, unless he enjoys strong patronage.

Regular private concert series of importance have ceased to exist altogether. Even the worthy Baron van Swieten [an important patron of Mozart, Haydn, and Beethoven], thanks to whom alone we occasionally would hear an oratorio by Hasse [1699–1783, the leading composer of serious opera in the mid-eighteenth century] or Handel, has given us nothing this year. As everybody knows, he is the author of the words in *The Creation* and in *The Seasons,* which Haydn is now setting to music.

Amateurism

There cannot be many cities in which musical amateurism is as widespread as it is here. Everybody plays, everybody takes music lessons. It goes without saying that, given the multitude, we have some excellent dilettanti; however, they are not as common as they were formerly. Music is rated as too easy a thing, something to be acquired incidentally, and one's capacity in it is generally overestimated, though in the end, of course, the word *dilettante* is offered as an excuse and the whole affair is taken in a spirit of gallantry and *bon ton.* Yet, truly, the genuine connoisseurs and friends of music—music *as art,* that is—are more numerous here than strangers seem to think. The reason why they are so little bruited abroad may well be that they themselves make so little noise, preferring to worship and enjoy their idol unobtrusively. So-called "private concerts" (music in well-to-do homes) are legion here all winter long. Not a name-day, not a birthday goes by without a musical performance. To be sure, very little can be said about these performances; nothing at all, if we are required to keep a straight face. They are all pretty much the same: behold their true likeness! First, a quartet or a symphony (deemed, at bottom, a necessary evil—you must begin with *something*!) and it is drowned in conversation. Then come the young ladies, one after the other. Each one opens up her pianoforte sonata—if possible, not without a certain gracefulness and charm—and proceeds to rattle it off, hit or miss. Then come others, and they sing arias from the latest operas in exactly the same fashion. The thing gives pleasure—and why should it not? And who can find fault with it, so long as it is regarded simply as a family entertainment? Only we mustn't consider it as a contribution to art, nor the fair participants, despite their guests' compliments, as artists. On the contrary, it is this universal, easy amateurism—as well as the myriads of little concerts with their ready-made music—that has ruined taste and caused a sense for better things to slumber.

It should be added that the fate of traveling virtuosos is in the hands of these amateurs, who often make up for their want of knowledge with ardent displays of partisanship. If the stranger fails to put in an appearance at every reception, to flatter, to discover and praise talent in everyone, etc., then he must possess the *greatest* reputation if he is to survive in spite of such omissions. Should he be struck with a notion of settling in Vienna, he would soon find the body of musicians his enemies. The standard by which virtuosos are judged is high (and rightly so, for we have known so many among the very greatest); yet the setting at naught of those who fall short of that standard is discouraging, the more so because then not one of our local practicing musicians can wholly escape condemnation—at least among the violinists; only, perhaps, Beethoven and [Joseph] Wölfl [Beethoven's early rival in Vienna], and they are pianists.

The Outlook for Artists

From the preceding it follows that the outlook for traveling artists is not good; and we have explained why. As for the artists here—: all the well-to-do and wealthy houses that once had their own orchestras have dismissed them. A player in the theater orchestra can expect to make from 200 to 300 gulden. Without steady employment, only a pianoforte player may perhaps earn a decent livelihood—and even so, he must possess enough self-denial to serve willingly the houses that support him, furthermore to give lessons morning, noon, and night. The violinists are in the worst position of all; they are expected to play for nothing, since 10 dilettanti can readily be found who will do so with great pleasure, ably or otherwise. Paid private concerts are rare; and if one is set up, the musician, for a variety of reasons, profits little. Music lessons are not nearly as profitable as they once were, since dilettanti can always be had for trifling fees; the same may be said for quartet performances, once such a lucrative activity for musicians. In the society of well-to-do bourgeois or aristocratic houses, the musician today is less respected than ever before, and indeed often humiliated; to be sure, many of our musicians have themselves brought about this painful situation through their lack of culture, rough manners, debauched living, etc. But, just as there are exceptions in this amongst the musicians, so are there worthy houses to which the above complaints do not apply.

Allgemeine musikalische Zeitung, III (1800), cols. 41–50, 65–68. Trans. P. W.

93

Beethoven's Heiligenstadt Testament

This famous document, drafted in the form of a testament addressed to his two brothers, was found among Beethoven's effects when he died. It had been written twenty-five years earlier in the village of Heiligenstadt, on the outskirts of Vienna, at the most critical moment in the composer's life, when he had had to face the fact that his deafness was progressive and, probably, incurable.

For my brothers Carl and [Johann] Beethoven.

O ye men who think or declare that I am hostile stubborn or Misanthropic, how you wrong me you do not know the secret motive of what seems thus to you, from Childhood my Heart and Mind were inclined to the Gentle Feeling of goodwill, indeed I was ever disposed to accomplish great Feats, but only reflect that for the last 6 years an incurable condition has seized me, worsened by senseless physicians, cheated from year to year in the Hope of improvement, finally compelled to the prospect of a *lasting Ailment* (whose Curing may perhaps take years or indeed be impossible). Born with a fiery Lively Temperament susceptible even to the Diversions of Society, I soon had to keep to myself, pass my life in solitude, if I attempted from time to time to rise above all this, o how harshly then was I repulsed by the doubly sad Experience of my bad Hearing, yet I could not say to People: speak louder, shout, for I am deaf, alas how could I then acknowledge the Weakness of *a Faculty* which ought to be more perfect in me than in others, a Faculty I once had to the highest degree of Perfection, such Perfection as only few of my Calling surely have or have had—o I cannot do it. Therefore forgive me if you see me withdrawing when I should gladly join you. My misfortune afflicts me doubly, since it causes me to be misunderstood. Diversion in Human Society, civilized Conversation, mutual Effusions cannot take place for me. All but alone, I enter society no more than is required by the most urgent Necessity. I must live like a Banished man; if I approach a company, a hot anxiety invades me, because I am afraid of being exposed to the Danger of letting my Condition be noticed—and thus has it been this half-year too, which I have spent in the country, my wise Physician having ordered me to spare my Hearing as much as possible. He nearly met my present Disposition, even though I have sometimes let myself be led astray by an Urge for Society. But what Mortification if someone stood beside me and heard a flute from afar and *I* heard *nothing;* or someone *heard a Shepherd Singing,* and I heard nothing. Such Happenings brought me close to Despair; I was not far from ending my own life—only Art, only art held me back. Ah, it seemed impossible to me that I should leave the world before I had produced all that I felt I might, and so I spared this wretched life—truly wretched; a body so susceptible that a somewhat rapid change can take me from the Best Condition to the worst. *Patience*—so now I must choose Her for my guide, I have done so—I hope that my decision to

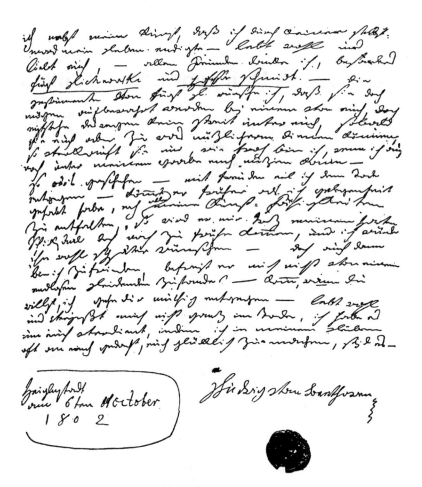

A Page from Beethoven's Heiligenstadt Testament. Dated 6 October 1802, signed, and sealed; but four days later Beethoven added a heartrending postscript. *Hamburg, Staats- und Universitätsbibliothek.*

persevere may endure until it please the inexorable Fates to break the Thread; perhaps I will improve, perhaps not. I am resigned—to be forced already in my 28th year to become a Philosopher is not easy, and harder for an Artist than for anyone else. Deity, thou lookest down into my innermost being; thou knowest it, thou seest that charity and benevolence dwell within,—o Men, when you read this some day, think then that you have wronged me, and let any unhappy man console himself by finding another one like himself, one who, despite Nature's Impediments, yet did what was in his Power to do to be admitted to the Ranks of worthy Artists and Men. And so it is done—I hasten with joy towards my Death—should it come before I have had an Opportunity to disclose all my Artistic Capacities, then it shall still have come too soon despite my Hard Destiny, and I should indeed wish it came later—yet even then am I content. Does it not free me from an endless Suffering State? Come *when* you will, I'll meet you bravely—farewell and do not wholly forget me in Death. I have deserved it of you, for in Life I thought of you often, in order to make you happy, so may you be—

Ludwig van Beethoven

Heiligenstadt
6th October
1802

Heiligenstadt 10th October *1802* and so I bid you farewell—and sadly too—yes the cherished Hope—which I brought here with me, that I might be cured at least up to a Point—it must abandon me completely now, as Autumn Leaves fall away, wither; so has—it too wilted for me, I go from here—much as I came—even the High Courage—that often inspired me during the Lovely Days of Summer—has vanished—o Providence—grant me one day of pure *Joy*—the inner reverberation of true Joy has so long been a stranger to me—o when—o when, o Deity—may I feel it once more in the Temple of Nature and Mankind,— Never?—no—o it would be too hard.

Piero Weiss (ed.), *Letters of Composers Through Six Centuries* (Philadelphia: Chilton Books, 1967), 167–69.

94

The First Reactions to Beethoven's "Eroica" Symphony

Beethoven's Third Symphony (the "Eroica") represented a wilful break with tradition to those who knew him only through the first two symphonies and some other, earlier works. The sheer length of the "Eroica" (about twice the length of normal symphonies) was in itself bewildering. Here is a review of its first public performance, on 7 April 1805, by the Vienna correspondent of a German literary journal (*Der Freymüthige*).

Some, Beethoven's particular friends, assert that it is just this symphony which is his masterpiece, that this is the true style for high-class music, and that if it does not please now, it is because the public is not cultured enough, artistically, to grasp all these lofty beauties; after a few thousand years have passed it will not fail of its effect. Another faction denies that the work has any artistic value and professes to see in it an untamed striving for singularity which has failed, however, to achieve in any of its parts beauty or true sublimity and power. By means of strange modulations and violent transitions, by combining the most heterogeneous elements, as for instance when a pastoral in the largest style is ripped up by the basses, by three horns, etc., a certain undesirable originality may be achieved without much trouble; but genius proclaims itself not in the unusual and the fantastic, but in the beautiful and the sublime. Beethoven himself proved the correctness of this axiom in his earlier works. The third party, a very small one, stands midway between the others—it admits that the symphony contains many beauties, but concedes that the connection is often disrupted entirely, and that the inordinate length of this longest, and perhaps most difficult of all symphonies wearies even the cognoscenti, and is unendurable to the mere music lover; it wishes that Herr v. B. would employ his acknowledgedly great talents in giving us works like his symphonies in C and D, his ingratiating Septet in E flat, the intellectual Quintet in D [C?] and others of his early compositions that have placed B. forever in the ranks of the foremost instrumental composers. It fears, however, that if Beethoven continues on his present path both he and the public will be the sufferers. His music could soon reach the point where one would derive no pleasure from it, unless well trained in the rules and difficulties of the art, but rather would leave the concert hall with an unpleasant feeling of fatigue from having been crushed by a mass of unconnected and overloaded ideas and a continuing tumult by all the instruments. The public and Herr van Beethoven, who conducted, were not satisfied with each other on this evening; the public thought the symphony too heavy, too long, and himself too discourteous, because he did not nod his head in recognition of the applause which came from a portion of the audience. On the contrary, Beethoven found that the applause was not strong enough.

Elliot Forbes (ed.), *Thayer's Life of Beethoven*, rev. ed. (Princeton: Princeton University Press, 1967), 376.

95

A Contemporary Portrait of Beethoven

The following description of Beethoven's character and personal circumstances appeared in 1823, at the end of a biographical article in the London musical periodical *The Harmonicon*.

[Beethoven] has secured a name, and reached a height of renown, to which no other author, Handel, Haydn, and Mozart excepted, has attained. For though Rossini's name is, at the present instant, more often pronounced than that of any other composer, yet his works, so far as they now extend, are not likely to confer on him a lasting reputation equal to that which the great German musicians have permanently gained.

Beethoven is as original and independent in his general modes of thinking as he is in his musical productions. A decided enemy to flattery, and an utter stranger to every thing dishonourable, he disdains to court the favour of every one, however wealthy or exalted in rank. The consciousness of his talents not being duly rewarded too frequently makes him vent his complaints in the bitterest terms, and against individuals who, from their high station, have the power to obstruct his success in life. Thus he has for years resided in Vienna in open hostility with many, and in friendship only with the few whom the admiration of his great genius will not allow to take offence, either at the singularities of his manners, or at the ill-judged candour with which he declares his opinion both of persons and things. Till very lately he had hardly any other income than what his compositions procured him; and consequently he has too often lived in circumstances very unworthy of so great a genius. This, together with an increase of difficulties and of invidious enemies, determined him, in 1809, to accept an offer of the situation of *maestro di cappella* to the new Westphalian court of Jerome Buonaparte. His intention was made known to the Archduke Rudolph, and the Princes Lobkowitz and Kinsky, and fortunately for the honour of Vienna and of Austria those personages induced him to alter his resolution. In terms at once the most flattering and the most delicate, they had a deed drawn up, by which they settled on him an annuity of 4000 florins. The only conditions attached to this pension were, that he should reside in Vienna, or some other part of Austria-Proper, and not undertake any journey into foreign countries without the consent of his patrons. The issue of the late war has sufficiently proved how judiciously he acted in declining the offers of the court of Westphalia. We are sorry to be obliged to add that, from a variety of untoward circumstances, the greater portion of this pension has been for a considerable time past discontinued. Prince Lobkowitz, who is since dead, was so utterly ruined, that his palace in Vienna is now converted into a hotel. Prince Kinsky was killed at the beginning of the last war with France, and the Archduke Rudolph is now, therefore, his only remaining protection.

We have been assured that he has always expressed a great wish to see foreign countries, and particularly England, but it does not appear that he has ever made any application for leave of absence for such a purpose; though, under present circumstances, but few difficulties could be expected to present themselves on this point. Some few years back he was applied to by the Philharmonic Society of London to visit England, and the conditions were not only fully agreed upon, but he had actually begun to make preparations for his journey. Notwithstanding which, he had not the courage to carry his intentions into execution, and it is hardly now to be expected that he will ever cross the seas, and give the peoples of these kingdoms an opportunity of paying him that homage which his vast talents would assuredly command from a liberal and enlightened nation.

It may, however, be doubted whether his presence would add, either here or elsewhere, to his celebrity. His extreme reserve towards strangers, which is carried to such excess as to render it painful for his most intimate friends to witness, prevents him from displaying those excellent qualities which, under a forbidding exterior, he is known to possess. And yet such are the contrasts that meet in his character, that occasionally his warmth of manners, together with his total want of reserve in offering his opinion of others, tend to estrange him much from the prescribed forms of society. Add to all this that deplorable calamity, the greatest that could befall a man of his profession, his extreme deafness, which we are assured is now so great as to amount to a total privation of hearing. Those who visit him are obliged to write down what they have to communicate. To this cause may be traced many of the peculiarities visible in his later compositions. [This was for a long time a commonly held opinion with regard to Beethoven's more difficult late works.]—This calamity has also the effect of rendering him dreadfully suspicious, so that no conversation can pass in his presence without his imagining himself the subject of it: a weakness which is the usual attendant on deafness. It should, however, be here mentioned that, notwithstanding his foibles, which far more frequently belong to great than to ordinary minds, his character as a man and a citizen ranks deservedly high. Though his eccentricity leads him to deviate from ordinary rules in the smaller affairs of life, yet his high feeling of truth and justice has produced a rectitude in his moral conduct which ensures him the esteem of every honourable man. Though his early education was neglected, yet he has made up for the deficiency by subsequent diligence and industry, so that we are assured by those who know him well that his knowledge of German literature is very respectable, and that he is a very tolerable proficient in Italian, though of French he knows but little. Whenever he can be induced to throw off his natural reserve, his conversation becomes extremely animated, full of interesting anecdote, and replete with original remarks on men and manners.

The last account we hear of this great man is that he has just completed a new grand mass [the *Missa Solemnis*]. The dark tone of his mind is in unison with that solemn style which the services of the church demand; and the gigantic harmony he knows so well how to wield enables him to excite feelings of the awful and sublime in a manner that none living can attempt to rival.

The Harmonicon, I (1823), 156.

96

The First Performance of Beethoven's Ninth Symphony

When, in February 1824, word got out in Vienna that Beethoven had made inquiries whether his new symphony and Mass might receive their first performance in Berlin, a group of aristocrats, colleagues, and music publishers addressed a long, flowery letter to him, begging him to have the event take place in Vienna. It was published in two leading journals; what follows is a much-shortened version:

To Herr Ludwig van Beethoven.

Out of the wide circle of reverent admirers surrounding your genius in this your second native city, there approach you today a small number of the disciples and lovers of art to give expression to long-felt wishes, timidly to prefer a long-suppressed request.

It is the wish of those of our countrymen who reverence art to which we desire more especially to give expression; for although Beethoven's name and creations belong to all contemporaneous humanity and every country which opens a susceptible bosom to art, it is Austria which is best entitled to claim him as her own. Among her inhabitants appreciation for the great and immortal works which Mozart and Haydn created for all time within the lap of their homes still lives, and they are conscious with joyous pride that the sacred triad in which these names and yours glow as the symbol of the highest within the spiritual realm of tones, sprang from the soil of their fatherland. All the more painful must it have been for you to feel that a foreign power has invaded this royal citadel of the noblest, that above the mounds of the dead and around the dwelling place of the only survivor of the band, phantoms are leading the dance who can boast of no kinship with the princely spirits of those royal houses; that shallowness is beclouding and dissipating appreciation for the pure and eternally beautiful.

Do not withhold longer from the popular enjoyment, do not keep longer from the oppressed sense of that which is great and perfect, a performance of the latest masterworks of your hand.

Need we tell you with what regret your retirement from public life has filled us? Need we assure you that at a time when all glances were hopefully turned towards you, all perceived with sorrow that *the one* whom all of us are compelled to acknowledge as foremost among living men in his domain, looked on in silence as foreign art took possession of German soil, the seat of honor of the German muse, while German works gave pleasure only by echoing the favorite tunes of foreigners and, where the most excellent had lived and labored, a second childhood of taste threatens to follow the Golden Age of Art?

Alexander Wheelock Thayer, *The Life of Ludwig van Beethoven,* ed. H. E. Krehbiel (New York: The Beethoven Association, 1921), III, 153–54.

The letter succeeded in its immediate intent, but let us not overlook its broader significance: its adherence to a new and, as it turned out, enduring myth of "pure and eternally beautiful" German music battling against the invasive "shallowness" of inferior foreign "tunes." For "foreign," here, we must of course read "Italian": Rossini (see p. 286) had taken the city by storm two years earlier. And while the letter is quite right about Beethoven's international reputation, it also testifies to where the money was going in the 1820s. Now let us draw once again on the London *Harmonicon* for a description of one of the most celebrated concerts in history:

Beethoven, having for some time past continued to withdraw himself more and more from public notice and to shut out the world, really seemed desirous of living only amidst the creations of his own fancy; a meeting therefore of some patrons and amateurs of the art was assembled in Vienna, when [an] address was drawn up; which being presented to this great, but singular man, was attended with the results that were so anxiously desired.

Accordingly, on the 7th of May, a grand musical performance took place at the Kärnthnerthor Theatre. The leaders of the music were Kapellmeister Umlauf and M. Schuppanzigh, and the great Composer himself assisted on the occasion. He took his place at the side of the principal leader, and, with his original score before him, indicated the different movements and determined the precise manner in which they were to be given; for, unfortunately, the state of his hearing prevented him from doing more. The theatre was crowded to excess, and the sensation caused by the appearance of this great man was of a kind that is more easy to imagine than to describe. The arrangement of the pieces performed was as follows: 1st, Beethoven's Grand Overture in C major ["The Consecration of the House"]; 2nd, Three Grand Hymns, with solo and chorus parts, from his new Mass, never before performed [the *Missa Solemnis*]; 3rd, A grand New Symphony, with a finale, in which are introduced a solo and chorus part, from Schiller's *Lied an die Freude* (Song of Joy). This also was performed for the first time, and is Beethoven's last composition.—We shall offer a few observations on each of these in the order of their performance.

After lengthy, appreciative comments on the overture and on the three pieces from the *Missa Solemnis,* the report continues:

With respect to the new symphony, it may, without fear, stand a competition with its eight sister-works, by none of which is the fame of its beauty likely to be eclipsed; it is evidently of the same family, though its characteristic features are different. The opening passage is a bold *allegro,* in D minor, full of rich invention and of athletic power; from the first chord till the gradual unfolding of the colossal theme, expectation is constantly kept alive and never disappointed. To give a skeleton of this composition would be scarcely practicable and, after all, would convey but a very faint idea of the body; we shall therefore only touch upon some of the more prominent features, among which is a *scherzo* movement (D minor) full of playful gaiety, and in which all the instruments seem to contend with each other in the whim and sportiveness of the passage;— and a brilliant march in the vivid major mode forms a delightful contrast with the passages by which it is introduced. Whoever has imagined, in hearing the *andante* of the 7th symphony, that nothing could ever equal, not to say surpass it, has but to hear the movement of the same kind in the present composition in order to change his sentiments. In truth, the movement is altogether divine, the interchanges and combinations of the motifs are surprising, the tasteful conduct of the whole is easy and natural, and in the midst of the rich exuberance of the subject the simplicity that prevails throughout is truly admirable. But it is in the finale that the genius of this great master shines forth most conspicuously. We are here in an ingenious manner presented with a return of all the subjects in short and brilliant passages, and which, as in a mirror, reflect the features of the whole. After this, a singular kind of recitative by the contra-basses introduces a *crescendo* passage of overwhelming effect, which is answered by [a solo singer and] a chorus of voices that bursts unexpectedly in, and produces an entirely new and extraordinary result. The passages from Schiller's "Song of Joy" are made admirably expressive of the sentiments which the poet intended to convey and are in perfect keeping with the tone and character of the whole of this wonderful composition. Critics have remarked of the finale that it requires to be heard frequently in order to be duly appreciated.

At the conclusion of the concert, Beethoven was unanimously called forward. [Witnesses to the event report that he had to be turned around to *see* the public's acclamation, because he could not hear it.] He modestly saluted the audience and retired amidst the loudest expressions of enthusiasm. Yet the feeling of joy was tempered by an universal regret, to see so gifted an individual labouring under an infliction, the most cruel that could befall an artist in that profession for which nature had destined him. We have no doubt but the master will consider this as one of the proudest days in his existence, and it is to be hoped that the testimony of general feeling which he has witnessed will tend to soothe his spirit, to soften down some of its asperities, and to convince him that he stands upon a pinnacle, far above the reach of envy and every malignant passion.

The Harmonicon, II (1824), 178, 180–81.

PART SEVEN

The Later Nineteenth Century: Romanticism and Other Preoccupations

97

Music as a Proper Occupation for the British Female

Readers of Jane Austen, Dickens, Thackeray, and the other British novelists of the nineteenth century will remember the many occasions on which some lovely young lady showed her accomplishment "upon the piano-forte" to the delight of her admirers. Here is an early testimonial to this peculiarly British phenomenon, along with suitable moral comments, from a strange three-volume work by one A. Burgh, A.M. It forms the Preface.

Among the various refinements of the present enlightened age, the Science of Music appears, in an eminent degree, to have attracted the attention, not only of the exalted and affluent, but to have insinuated itself into the social enjoyments of every rank in Society.

In the modern System of Female Education, this fascinating accomplishment is very generally considered, as an indispensable requisite; and the Daughters of Mechanics, even in humble stations, would fancy themselves extremely ill-treated, were they debarred the Indulgence of a piano-forte.

Whether this passion be indulged to excess—whether it be a *musicomania*, or an innocent recreation, under the guidance of Reason and Discretion—it is not the business of this Publication to discuss.

The Author of the following Sheets is strongly impressed with the idea, that Music is not only a harmless amusement; but, if properly directed, capable of being eminently beneficial to his fair Countrywomen. In many instances, it may be the means of preventing that vacuity of mind, which is too frequently the parent of libertinism; of precluding the intrusion of idle and dangerous imaginations; and, more particularly among the Daughters of ease and opulence, by occupying a considerable portion of time, may prove an antidote to the poison insidiously administered by the innumerable licentious Novels, which are hourly sapping the foundations of every moral and religious principle.

As practical Musicians, the British Female Dilettanti are universally acknowledged, not only to have rivalled, but to have surpassed, in their exquisite execution upon keyed Instruments, all their continental competitors.

To these, it is presumed, that a concise, and, perhaps, entertaining History of a Science, in which they so eminently excel, may not be unacceptable.

A. Burgh, *Anecdotes of Music, Historical and Biographical, in a Series of Letters from a Gentleman to his Daughter* (London, 1814), I, v–vii.

98

Leigh Hunt on Rossini

Leigh Hunt (1784–1859), the essayist, poet, journalist, and friend of Lamb, Shelley, Keats, Byron, was surprisingly knowledgeable and perceptive on musical questions. It is a pleasure to find the Rossini craze, which swept all of Europe in the years following the Napoleonic wars, recorded by his fluent pen in a letter from Italy to his friend Vincent Novello, the English organist and music editor. The second extract, written five years later, is a remarkably calm estimate of the composer, whom he does not hesitate to classify a "genius," with qualifications.

March, 1823

MY DEAR N.:

You ask me to tell you a world of things about Italian composers, singers, etc. Alas! my dear N. I may truly say to you that, for music, you must "look at home"— at least, as far as my own experience goes. But I will tell you one thing which, albeit you are of Italian origin, will mortify you to hear, namely, that Mozart is nothing in Italy, and Rossini everything. Nobody ever says anything of Mozart since "Figaro" (tell it not in Gothland!) *was hissed at Florence.* His name appears to be suppressed by agreement, while Rossini is talked of, written of, copied, sung, hummed, whistled, and demi-semi-quavered from morning to night. If there is a portrait in a shop-window, it is Rossini's. If you hear a song in the street, it is Rossini's. If you go to a music-shop to have something copied—"An air of Rossini's?"

There is one blind beggar who seems an enthusiast for Rossini. Imagine a sturdy-looking fellow in rags, laying his hot face against his fiddle, rolling his blind eyeballs against the sunshine, and vociferating, with all the true open mouth and syllabical particularity of the Italians, a part of one of the duets of that lively master. His companion, having his eyesight and being, therefore, not so vivacious, sings his part with sedate vigor; though even when the former is singing a solo, I have heard him throw in some unisons at intervals, as if his help were equally wanting to the blind man, vocal as well as corporeal.

Mary Cowden-Clarke, "Leigh Hunt," *Century Illustrated Monthly Magazine,* XXIII (March 1882), n.s. 1, 708–709.

We fear it is a little out of the scientific pale to think Rossini a man of genius; but we confess, with all our preference for such writers as Mozart, with whom indeed he is not to be compared, we do hold that opinion of the lively Italian. There is genius of many kinds; and of kinds very remote from one another, even in rank. The greatest genius is so great a thing, that another may be infinitely less, and yet of the stock. Now Rossini, in music, is the genius of sheer animal spirits. It is a species as inferior to that of Mozart, as the cleverness of a smart boy is to that of a man of sentiment; but it is genius nevertheless. It is rare, effective, and a part of the possessor's character:—we mean, that like all persons who really effect anything beyond the common, it belongs and is peculiar to him, like the invisible genius that was supposed of old to wait upon individuals. "He hath a devil," as Cowley's friend used to cry out when he read Virgil; and a merry devil it is, and graceful withal. It is a pity he has written so many common-places; so many bars full of mere chatter; and overtures so full of cant and puffing. But this exuberance appears to be a constituent part of him. It is the hey-day in his blood; and perhaps we could no more have the good things without it, than some men of wit can talk well without a bottle of wine and in the midst of a great deal of nonsense. Now and then he gives us something worthy of the most popular names of his country. Sometimes he is not deficient even in tenderness, as in one or two airs in his *Othello;* but it is [in] his liveliest operas, such as the *Barbiere di Siviglia* and the *Italiana in Algeri* that he shines. His mobs make some of the pleasantest riots conceivable; his more gentlemanly proceedings, his bows and compliments, are full of address and elegance; and he is a prodigious hand at a piece of pretension or foppery. Not to see into his merit in these cases, surely implies only, that there is a want of animal spirits on the part of the observer.

The Companion, II (16 January 1828), 14–15.

99

Schubert Remembered by a Friend

The first full-length biography of Schubert appeared in 1865 (the same year that saw the first performance of the Unfinished Symphony), or thirty-seven years after the composer's death. Schubert's brief career (he composed a vast amount of music within a span of little more than sixteen years) went virtually unnoticed by the world at large. It has been argued that his premature death deprived him of the recognition he would doubtless have gained, in time. But, as the following reminiscences by his close friend Josef von Spaun help to make clear, the comparative neglect was at least partly due to Schubert's own set of values, which were typical of the new, Romantic generation: his art meant everything to him; and the requirements for self-advancement (impressing the fashionable world, appearing in public, and so forth) pained him. What a difference from the values of the Enlightenment, when the artist's highest aspiration was "to please." The notes from which the following extracts are taken were written in 1858.

[When Schubert was about eleven years old] I once found him alone in the music room [at school,] sitting at the piano which, with his little hands, he already played quite nicely. He was just trying through a Mozart sonata, and said that he liked it very much but that he found Mozart very difficult to play well. At my request and aware of my sympathy, he played me a minuet of his own invention. He was shy about it and blushed, but my approval pleased him. He told me that secretly he often wrote down his thoughts in music, but his father must not know about it, as he was dead against his devoting himself to music. After that I used to slip manuscript paper into his hands from time to time.

During the first days of September 1809 I left Vienna to start my career. At the end of March 1811 my fate took me back to Vienna. In 1812 he composed twelve minuets and trios, which were of extraordinary beauty.

About this time people began to pay attention to his talent. The old Court organist Ruzicka was engaged to give Schubert lessons in thorough bass. After only the second lesson the worthy old man, quite stirred by emotion, said to me in Schubert's presence: "I can teach him nothing, he has learnt it from God himself."

Now the barriers had fallen. The father recognized his son's great talent and let him have his own way, and now began the series of his songs and sonatas. Some quartets, too, date from this early period.

One day when he sang me some little songs [he had composed to poetry] by Klopstock, and I was utterly delighted with them, he looked me frankly in the eyes and said, "Do you really think something will come of me?" I embraced him and said, "You have done much already and time will enable you to do much more and great things too." Then he said quite humbly: "Secretly, in my heart of hearts, I still hope to be able to make something out of myself, but who can do anything after Beethoven?"

Greatly as the circle now increased of those who admired Schubert's extraordinary talents and bestowed the greatest applause on his songs, he nevertheless remained without any substantial provision, and his position was a truly depressing one. No publisher could be found who would have dared to risk even a little for his magnificent creations. He remained for years a victim of money troubles, indeed he who was so rich in melodies could not even afford the rent for the hire of a piano. Yet the difficulties of his position did not check his industry in the least; he had to sing and compose, it was his life.

He ought to have given piano lessons in order to make a living, but that was a bitter task for him. In the morning he felt the urge to compose, and in the afternoon he wanted to rest and, in summer, go out of doors.

Finally, at the instigation of some kind friends, an edition of the "Erlkönig" was brought out at their own expense. The undertaking was a great success and yielded Schubert a not inconsiderable profit as the first fruit of his talent. Now the spell was broken and the publishers gradually accepted his compositions, but the modest Schubert (who, in money matters, was an absolute child) was satisfied with whatever they gave him, and so he still could not even earn the barest necessities of existence.

Once when he was invited, with Baron Schönstein [who had an excellent tenor voice], to a princely house in order to perform his songs before a very aristocratic audience, the enraptured audience surrounded Baron Schönstein with the most ardent appreciation and with congratulations on his performance. But when no one showed any sign of granting so much as a look or a word to the composer sitting at the piano, the noble hostess, Princess K[insky], tried to make up for this neglect and greeted Schubert with the highest praise, at the same time suggesting that he overlook the fact that the audience, quite carried away by the singer, complimented only him. Schubert replied that he thanked the Princess very much but she was not to bother herself in the least about him, he was quite used to not being noticed, indeed he was really very glad of it, as it caused him less embarrassment.

Many people thought, and perhaps still think, that Schubert was a dull fellow with no feeling, but those who knew him better know how deeply his creations affected him and that they were conceived in suffering. Anyone who has seen him of a morning occupied with composition, aglow, with his eyes shining and even his speech changed, like a sleepwalker, will never forget the impression. And how could he have written these songs without being stirred to the depths by them! In the afternoon he was admittedly another person, but he was gentle and deeply sensitive, only he did not like to show his feelings but preferred to keep them to himself.

Schubert did not get the recognition he deserved in Vienna. The great majority of people remained, and still remain, uninterested.

Nor are his songs suited to the concert hall or stage. The listener, too, must have a feeling for the poem and enjoy the lovely song together with it; in a word, the public must he quite a different one from that which fills the theatres and concert halls.

When publishers told him that people found the accompaniment to his songs too hard and the keys often so difficult, and that, in his own interest, he ought to pay attention to this, he always replied that he could not write differently and that anyone who could not play his compositions should leave them alone, and a person to whom one key was not as easy as another was, anyhow, not in the least musical.

Schubert's music must either be performed well or not at all.

His incredible wealth of melody remains a treasure for all time, and musicians yet unborn will gather spoils from this rich mine. In the span of time he was vouchsafed he wrote 600 songs, of which no one is like another, so rich was he in melodies.

Schubert was an affectionate son and brother, and a loyal friend. He was a kind, generous, good man.

May he rest in peace, and thanks be to him for having beautified the lives of his friends by his creations!

O. E. Deutsch (ed.), *Schubert: Memoirs by his Friends* (London: A. & C. Black, 1958), 126–27, 127–28, 133, 134, 135, 140–41. Reprinted by permission.

100

Paganini, the Spectacular Virtuoso

A "virtuoso" was, originally, a highly accomplished musician, but by the nineteenth century the term had become restricted to performers, both vocal and instrumental, whose technical accomplishments were so pronounced as to dazzle the public. Virtuoso singers, of course, had been the mainstay of Italian opera almost from its beginnings. Virtuoso instrumentalists, on the other hand, really came into their own in the nineteenth century, with the spread of public concerts designed to cater to the vast new middle-class audiences. Niccolò Paganini (1782–1840), the greatest violin virtuoso of the century, emerged from his native Italy in 1828. Beginning in Vienna,

The Debut of Paganini in London. Friday, 3 June 1831, at the King's Theatre. (Drawing by D. Maclise.) ©*Victoria and Albert Museum / Art Resource, NY.*

where he created a sensation, he eventually took all of Europe by storm, leaving his audiences openmouthed at the unprecedented effects he produced on his instrument. "Unfortunately," wrote the Vienna correspondent of *The Harmonicon*, "the worst parts of his performance seemed to call forth the loudest applause, such, for instance, as his imitation of bells, his laborious performance upon a single string, &c., all of which, in the eyes of the true amateur, savour more of charlatanism than of the legitimate objects of art." The demonic command, however, with which Paganini summoned forth whatever he wished from his violin had an enormous impact on the imagination of some young composers who were soon to make a name for themselves. "Paganini," wrote Schumann in 1832, "represents the turning-point of virtuosity." And Liszt, in a letter of the same year, exclaimed: "What a man, what a violinist, what an artist! God, what sufferings, what misery, what tortures in those four strings! And his expressiveness, his phrasing, his soul!!" Leigh Hunt (see p. 286), writing as theater critic for *The Tatler* in London, presents a vivid, admirably balanced picture of a typical Paganini concert, seen as both a musical and social phenomenon.

June 23, 1831   *King's Theatre*

Signor Paganini favoured the public with his "fifth and last concert at this theatre," last night, but not, it seems, with his fifth and last appearance; for he is to play this evening for the benefit of [the bass singer] Lablache, besides the four other performances, we suppose, which he is to be prevailed upon to bestow upon us, and the forty elsewhere. Well: the public are accustomed to these managerial tricks, and ought to be prepared for them; which does not seem to have been the case with some persons last night, by their hissing at the commencement of the benefit. Besides, Paganini is fine enough to make the public wish to hear him again and again, at some little expence to the perfection of his *morale*. Whether he would not be finer still if his proceedings were as straight-forward as his bow is a question of refinement, which it may be hard to urge in a matter of violin-playing.

Let us not belie the effect however which this extraordinary player had upon us last night. To begin with the beginning, he had a magnificent house. We thought at first we were literally going to *hear* him, without seeing his face; for the house was crammed at so early an hour that, on entering it, we found ourselves fixed on the lowest of the pit stairs. It was amusing to see the persons who carne in after us. Some, as they cast up their eyes, gaped amazement at the huge mass of faces presented in all quarters of the house; others looked angry; others ashamed and cast a glance around them to see what was thought of them; some gallantly smiled, and resolved to make the best of it. One man exclaimed, with unsophisticated astonishment, "Christ Jesus!" and an Italian whispered in a half execrating tone, "Oh, Dio!"

Meantime we heard some interesting conversation around us. We had been told, as a striking instance of the effect that Paganini has produced upon the English musical world, that one eminent musician declared he could not sleep the first night of his performance for thinking of him, but that he got up and walked about his room. A gentleman present last night was telling his friends that another celebrated player swore that he would have given a thousand guineas to keep the Italian out of the country, he had put everybody at such an immeasurable distance. These candid confessions, it seems, are made in perfect good-humour, and therefore do honour to the gentlemen concerned. Envy is lost in admiration.

The performances commenced with Haydn's beautiful symphony, No. 9 [i.e., no. 102], the fine, touching exordium of which, full of a kind of hushing meaning, appeared admirably adapted to be the harbinger of the evening's wonder. A duet between [the singers] Santini and Curioni followed; and then, after a due interval, came in Signor Paganini, and "brought the house down" with applause.

As it was the first time we had seen the great player, except in the criticisms of our musical friends, which had rendered us doubly curious, we looked up with interest at him from our abysm in the pit. A lucky interval between a gentleman's head and a lady's bonnet favoured our endeavour, and there we beheld the long, pale face of the musical marvel, hung, as it were, in the light, and looking as strange as need be. He made divers uncouth obeisances, and then put himself in a masterly attitude for his work, his manner being as firm and full of conscious power when he puts the bow to the instrument as it is otherwise when he is not playing. We thought he did not look so old as he is said to be; but he is long-faced and haggard, with strongly-marked prominent features, wears his black hair flowing on his neck like an enthusiast, has a coat of ancient cut which astonishes Fop's Alley; in short, is very like the picture of him in the shops. He is like a great old boy, who has done nothing but play the violin all his life, and knows as much about that as he does little of conventional manners. His face at the same time has much less expression than might be looked for. At first it seemed little better than a mask; with a fastidious, dreary expression, as if inclined to despise his music and go to sleep. And such was his countenance for a great part of the evening. His fervour was in his hands and bow. Towards the close of the performances, he waxed more enthusiastic in appearance, gave way to some uncouth bodily movement from side to side, and seemed to be getting into his violin. Occasionally also he put back his hair. When he makes his acknowledgments, he bows like a camel, and grins like a goblin or a mountain-goat.

His playing is indeed marvellous. What other players can do well, he does a hundred times better. We never heard such playing before; nor had we imagined it. His bow perfectly talks. It remonstrates, supplicates, answers, holds a dialogue. It would be the easiest thing in the world to put words to his music. We are sure that with a given subject, or even without it, Paganini's best playing could be construed into discourse by any imaginative person.

Last night he began a composition of his own (very good, by the way)—an *Allegro Maestoso* movement (majestically cheerful) with singular force and precision. Precision is not the proper word; it was a sort of peremptoriness and dash. He did not put his bow to the strings, nor lay it upon them; he struck them, as you might imagine a Greek to have done when he used his plectrum, and "smote the sounding shell." He then fell into a tender strain, till the strings, when he touched them, appeared to shiver with pleasure. Then he gave us a sort of minute warbling, as if half a dozen humming birds were singing at the tops of their voices, the highest notes sometimes leaping off and shivering like sprinkles of water; then he descended with wonderful force and gravity into the bass; then he would commence a strain of earnest feeling or entreaty, with notes of the greatest solidity, yet full of trembling emotion; and then again he would leap to a height beyond all height, with notes of desperate minuteness, then flash down in a set of headlong harmonies, sharp and brilliant as the edges of swords; then warble again with inconceivable beauty and remoteness, as if he was a ventriloquizing-bird; and finally, besides his usual wonderful staccatos in ordinary, he would suddenly throw handfuls, as it were, of staccatoed notes, in distinct and repeated showers over his violin, small and pungent as the tips of pins.

In a word, we never heard anything like *any* part of his performance, much less the least marvel we have been speaking of. The people sit astonished, venting themselves in whispers of "Wonderful!"—"Good God!"—and other unusual symptoms of English amazement; and when the applause comes, some of them take an opportunity of laughing, out of pure inability to express their feelings otherwise.

June 25, 1831

Our wizard's *Allegro Maestoso* was succeeded by an *"Adagio Flebile con Senti-mento"*—a composition with a very "particular fellow" of a title, by which we are to understand a strain of pathos amounting to the lachrymose, and disclosing a deep perception of the delicacy of that matter. If we are inclined to doubt the perfection of Signor Paganini's playing it would be upon this point. He has a great deal more feeling than is usually shewn by players of extreme execution: his supplication in particular is admirable; he is fervent and imploring; you would think his violin *was on its knees;* the very first note he draws, in movements of this character, is the fullest, the gravest, the most forcible, and the most impassioned we ever heard; it is wonderfully in earnest. And yet, though there is a feeling of this kind throughout, and we never heard notes so touching accompanied with such admirable execution, we cannot help thinking that we miss, both in the style and in the composition, that perfection of simplicity, and of unconsciousness of every-thing but the object of its passion or admiration, which is perhaps incompatible with these exhibitions of art.

Upon the whole, our experience of the playing of this wonderful person has not only added to our stock of extraordinary and delightful recollections, but it has done our memories another great good, in opening afresh the world of ancient Greek music and convincing us of the truth of all that is said of its marvellous effects. To hear Paganini, and to see him playing on that bit of wood with a bit of catgut, is to convince us that the Greeks might really have done the wonders attributed to them with their shells and quills. What if he is but a poor player to the least of them? For now that we see what such instruments can do, there is no knowing how much they can do beyond it.

But even after what we have heard, how are we to endure hereafter our old violins and their players? How can we consent to hear them? How crude they will sound, how uninformed, how like a cheat! When the Italian goes away, violin-playing goes with him, unless some disciple of his should arise among us and detain a semblance of his instrument. As it is, the most masterly performers, hitherto so accounted, must consent to begin again, and be little boys in his school.

L. H. Houtchens and C. W. Houtchens (eds.), *Leigh Hunt's Dramatic Criticism: 1808–1831* (New York: Columbia University Press, 1949), 270–74, 275–76.

101

The Virtuoso Conductor

Conditions of orchestral execution, in the early nineteenth century often deplorable (see pp. 274–75), greatly improved under pressure of the ever-increasing demands made by composers of complex and colorful Romantic scores. A necessary part of that improvement was the introduction of orchestral conducting in the modern sense. This was pioneered by such German composer-performers as Beethoven and especially Carl Maria von Weber (1786–1826), and soon spread to other musical centers. In his autobiography, the German violinist and composer Louis Spohr (1784–1859) claimed to have been the first to conduct an orchestra in England (where conservatism in matters of orchestral performance had already disconcerted Haydn), during a guest appearance with the London Philharmonic Society in 1820. His description of the revolutionary effect of this innovation is vivid:

Meanwhile my turn had come to direct one of the Philharmonic concerts, and I created no less sensation than with my solo play. It was at that time still the custom there that when symphonies and overtures were performed, the pianist had the score before him, not exactly to conduct from it, but only to read after and to play in with the orchestra at pleasure, which when it was heard, had a very bad effect. The real conductor was the first violin, who gave the *tempi,* and now and then when the orchestra began to falter gave the beat with the bow of his violin. So numerous an orchestra, standing so far apart from each other as that of the Philharmonic, could not possibly go exactly together, and in spite of the excellence of the individual members, the *ensemble* was much worse than we are accustomed to in Germany. I had therefore resolved when my turn came to direct, to make an attempt to remedy this defective system. Fortunately at the morning rehearsal on the day when I was to conduct the concert, Mr. *Ries* [1784–1838, a former pupil of Beethoven's] took the place at the Piano, and he readily assented to give up the score to me and to remain wholly excluded from all participation in the performance. I then took my stand with the score at a separate music desk in front of the orchestra, drew my directing baton from my coat pocket and gave the signal to begin. Quite alarmed at such a novel procedure, some of the directors would have protested against it; but when I besought them to grant me at least one trial, they became pacified. The symphonies and overtures that were to be rehearsed were well known to me, and in Germany I had already directed at their performance. I therefore could not only give the tempi in a very decisive manner, but indicated also to the wind instruments and horns all their entries, which ensured to them a confidence such as hitherto they had not known there. I also took the liberty, when the execution did not satisfy me, to stop, and in a very polite but earnest manner to remark upon the manner of execution, which remarks Mr. *Ries* at my request interpreted to the orchestra. Incited thereby to more than usual attention, and conducted with certainty by the visible manner of giving the time, they played with a spirit and a correctness such as till then they had never been heard to play with. Surprised and inspired by this result the orchestra immediately after the first part of the symphony, expressed aloud its collective assent to the new mode of conducting, and thereby overruled all further opposition on the part of the directors. In the vocal pieces also, the conducting of which I assumed at the request of Mr. *Ries,* particularly in the recitative, the leading with the baton, after I had explained the meaning of my movements, was completely successful, and the singers repeatedly expressed to me their satisfaction for the precision with which the orchestra now followed them.

The result in the evening was still more brilliant than I could have hoped for. It is true, the audience were at first startled by the novelty, and were seen whispering together; but when the music began and the orchestra executed the well-known symphony with unusual power and precision, the general approbation was shown immediately on the conclusion of the first part by a long-sustained clapping of hands. The triumph of the baton as time-giver was decisive, and no one was seen any more seated at the piano during the performance of symphonies and overtures.

Louis Spohr's Autobiography, Translated from the German (London, 1865), II, 81–82.

102

The State of Music in Italy in 1830

In the nineteenth century, Italian music came to mean opera and nothing else. Even so, opera in the years between the brilliant successes of Rossini and the rise of Italy's greatest operatic master, Giuseppe Verdi, presented a bleak aspect to thoughtful observers. Bellini, it is true, and Donizetti helped to fill the void, especially after they settled in Paris. Meanwhile Italian music appeared to languish. Here is an un-usually gloomy report from the Milan correspondent of *The Harmonicon,* writing in 1831 on the preceding operatic season. To be sure, his view of musical conditions in the previous century is tinged with nostalgia.

The last season has been, throughout the whole of Italy, a season of failures: not a single opera has obtained anything like distinguished success; and while few have survived, still fewer have merited to survive, even three or four representations. How is this? Has Italy, once the fruitful mother of great composers, lost for ever her fecundity? Has the genius of composition fled from the sunny regions of the Arno, Po, and Tiber, and taken up her abode on the sterner banks of the Danube, the Rhine, and the Elbe? We fear it is so; and still further, we fear her return to her once favoured country, if she ever do return, will be long delayed. Music in Italy is now feeling, to the full extent, the effects of the French Revolution. Let no one smile, and say the cause quoted is infinitely too important for the effect traced to it. Before 1796, the Conservatorios, the Cathe-drals, the rich monasteries formed asylums which supplied a host of learned musicians with situations which relieved them from any immediate pecuniary cares, and allowed of their giving the due *limae labor* [finishing touches] to their compositions before they were subjected to the public ordeal. In short, the composers of the eighteenth century, having these honorary retreats, could afford to write for fame rather than money, and to keep back their works till reiterated correction and polish had rendered them secure of reputation. These were the schools which educated, and the retreats which nourished, the [famous eighteenth-century composers, the] Paisiellos, Cimarosas, Jomellis, and in fact the almost endless roll of great composers who flourished in the last age. The invasion of Italy by the armies of republican France, in 1796, followed as it was by an almost total destruction of the power, and dissipation of the riches of the Church; by the suppression of monasteries and hospitals, and the sale of the lands destined for their support, destroyed at once the schools which educated the young, and the retreats which fostered the adult musician. The effect of this was not immediate: many com-posers, formed under the old school, still remained; and just as the last of them were dropping off, Rossini suddenly arose, and for several years filled all Europe with his energy and glitter. For some time his compositions, continually resorted to when those of other writers failed, concealed the real dearth of musical talent; but now that constant repetition has rendered even Rossini's operas unattractive, we awake to a perfect sense of the nothingness of [today's leading composers,] the Mercadantes, the Pavesis, Pacinis, &c. &c., who have followed and imitated him.

If we flatter ourselves that the failures of the last season have been merely accidental, we shall be much deceived; the seasons of 1828 and 1829 were quite as bad; and of all the operas produced in 1827, two only survive.

The Harmonicon, IX (1831), 253.

103

From the Writings of Berlioz

The decay of absolutism on the European continent spelled the end of artistic patronage on the part of the aristocracy and the church. The broad middle-class public now replaced the traditional élite: it attended concerts and the opera, it purchased printed music, it was swayed by the opinions of newspaper reviewers. Italian opera composers never noticed the difference: they had been addressing the broadest public for two hundred years and continued to do so in the nineteenth century. Brilliant virtuosos and agreeable "salon" composers knew how to keep in fashion, and they thrived. But the young Romantic composers, who sought to express their innermost feelings through their art, found themselves ignored by the public and the press. It is no wonder, then, that so many of them, from Weber (see p. 294) to Wolf (1860–1903), decided to take up arms against the prevailing situation and entered the battlefield as newspaper critics and authors of pamphlets and books, each according to his temperament and his individual experience of life. Among the great composers of the nineteenth century, Berlioz, Schumann, Liszt, and Wagner stand out as energetic, crusading writers, bent on elevating the public's taste and reforming the musical life of Europe. Our opening selection first appeared in Berlioz's *Musical Travels in Germany and Italy* (1844). Though it purports to give a definition of music and its constituent parts in the objective style of an encyclopedia entry, it soon reveals itself as something quite different—a Romantic's glorification of the power of music. In his documentation of the effects of music on susceptible people (including himself), Berlioz slips easily into a style reminiscent of medical books, reminding us that his father was a doctor and that he himself had, for a time, been an unwilling medical student. His contempt for all the durable old legends about ancient music and his claim on behalf of the equal if not superior powers of modern music show that Berlioz (like many French Romantics) was heir to the melioristic views of the Enlightenment, which in many other ways he (and they) despised.

Music

Music, the art of moving intelligent human beings, endowed with special, well-trained organs, by means of combinations of sounds. To define music thus is to admit that we do not consider it, as the saying goes, *fit for everyone*. Whatever its conditions, whatever means it may have employed in the past, whether simple or compound, gentle or vigorous, it has always been apparent to the impartial observer that, a great number of individuals being incapable of feeling and understanding its power, *they were not fit for music* and, consequently, *music was not fit for them.*

Music is both a sentiment and a science; it requires of its practitioner, whether he be a performer or a composer, natural inspiration and skills that can only be acquired through prolonged studies and profound thought. The union of knowledge and inspiration constitutes art. Lacking these conditions, therefore, a musician can only be an incomplete artist, if indeed he deserves the title of artist.

What we call *music* is a new art, in the sense that it most probably bears very little resemblance to what the ancient civilized peoples meant by that term.

What the art of sounds was then we know but very imperfectly. Some isolated facts, told possibly in an exaggerated manner of the kind we witness daily; the bloated or totally absurd ideas of certain philosophers—sometimes, too, false interpretations of their writings; these would tend to attribute to ancient music an immense power and a moral influence so great as to oblige legislators, in the interest of the people, to fix its course and regulate its use. Disregarding for the moment the reasons why the truth in this regard may have been altered, and admitting that the music of the Greeks may indeed have produced extraordinary impressions on certain individuals, this fact would still not in the least constitute a proof that their musical art had reached a high degree of perfection.

Simply by glancing around it would be easy to cite incontrovertible facts in favor of the power of our own music—facts whose worth would at least equal that of the doubtful anecdotes of ancient historians. How often, at performances of the masterpieces of our great composers, have we seen listeners overcome by the most violent spasms, crying and laughing at the same time, and manifesting all the symptoms of delirium and fever! A young musician from Provence, overcome by the impassioned feelings aroused in him by Spontini's [opera] *La Vestale,* could not bear the thought of returning to our prosaic world after leaving the poetic heaven that had just been revealed to him; he forewarned his friends by letter of his intention, and after hearing once more the masterpiece that was the object of his ecstatic admiration, thinking rightly that he had attained the maximum share of happiness allotted to man on earth, one evening, at the entrance to the [Paris] opera house, he blew out his brains.

The famous singer Mme. Malibran, upon hearing for the first time, at the Conservatoire, Beethoven's C-minor symphony, was seized by such strong convulsions that she had to be helped out of the concert room. Dozens of times we have seen serious men finding themselves obliged to leave in order to hide the violence of their emotions from the public gaze. As for the feelings which the present author personally derives from music, he affirms that nothing in the world could convey an exact notion of them to one who has never experienced the like. Leaving aside the moral influences which this art has developed in him, and to cite only the impressions received and the effects experienced at the very moment of the performance of works he admires, here is what he can say in all candor: Upon hearing certain pieces of music, my vital forces seem at first to double in strength; I feel a delicious pleasure in which the reasoning faculty has no share; the habit of analysis arises spontaneously later and brings forth admiration; emotion, increasing proportionately with the energy or loftiness of the composer's inspiration, soon produces a strange commotion in my circulation; my arteries throb violently; tears, which ordinarily signal the end of the paroxysm, often only indicate an advancing condition that is far from having reached its peak. In such cases, there are spasmodic muscular contractions, a trembling of all the limbs, a *total numbness of feet and hands,* a partial paralysis of the optical and auditory nerves; I cannot see, I barely hear; vertigo ... a half-swoon ... One may well imagine that feelings heightened to such a degree represent a rare occurrence and that, besides, they are counterbalanced by a vigorous contrast, namely, that of the *negative musical effect* which produces the opposite of admiration and pleasure. There is no music more apt to arouse me in this sense than that whose principal fault seems to me to be platitude conjoined with falseness of expression. Then I blush as if in shame; a genuine sense of indignation invades me; anyone seeing me might suppose I had just suffered an insult of the kind that can never be forgiven; to dispel the impression, there is a general upsurge, my entire organism makes efforts at excretion analogous to the effort of vomiting when the stomach wants to reject a nauseating liquid. It is disgust and hatred carried to their extreme limits; such music exasperates me, and I vomit it from all my pores.

Doubtless the habit of disguising or mastering my sentiments rarely permits them to appear in their true light; and if on occasion, from the days of my youth, I have chanced to give them full rein, it is because I lacked the time to reflect: I was taken unawares.

Modern music, therefore, as to power, has no cause to envy the music of the ancients.

Hector Berlioz, *À travers Chants* (Paris, 1862), 1–4, 5–7. Trans. P. W.

Sharp satire and wit, mingled with considerable bitterness, characterize much of Berlioz's writing. In the following extract (from his *Memoirs*), however, the crass indifference of the billiard player serves only as a comic foil to the exaltation of Berlioz and one other person.

That evening I had dragged to the [Paris] opera one of my friends, a perfect stranger to all the arts but billiards, whom I wished nevertheless to convert forcibly to music. The sorrows of Antigone and her father [in the opera *Oedipus* by Sacchini] were not such as to move him very deeply. And so, after the first act, despairing of my friend, I left him and moved up to a seat in front of him, in order not to be upset by his coolness. As if to make his impassiveness even more glaring, fate had seated to his right a spectator who was as impressionable as he himself was indifferent. I soon grew aware of this. [The singer] Dérivis had just delivered himself with fine effect of the famous recitative:

> My son! Ah, no! my son no more!
> Go! My hatred is too vehement!

Absorbed though I was by this lovely scene, so natural and full of antique feeling, I could not help overhearing the dialogue that had begun behind me, between my young friend, who was peeling an orange, and the stranger beside him, who was visibly shaken:

"Good Heavens, sir, calm down."

"No! It is too much! It's overwhelming! Crushing!"

"But, sir, you really mustn't let it *affect* you so. You will make yourself sick."

"No, let me be.—Oh!"

"Come, come, sir, cheer up! *After all, it's only a show!* May I offer you a slice of my orange?"

"Ah! Sublime!"

"It's imported from Malta."

"A heavenly work of art!"

"Please accept it."

"Ah, sir, what a piece of music!"

"Yes, it's pretty."

During this dissonant conversation the opera had progressed through the reconciliation scene to the lovely trio *"O joyful moment!"*; the penetrating sweetness of that simple melody had now seized me too; and I began to weep, covering my face with my hands, like a man overcome with grief. No sooner had the trio ended than two muscular arms lifted me off my chair, clasping my chest so tightly that I thought my bones would break; it was the stranger: unable to contain his emotion, and noticing that, of all those around him, I was the only one who shared it, he embraced me fervently and cried out in a fitful voice: "By *God*, sir, how beautiful it is!!!" Not in the least surprised, my face crisscrossed by tears, I asked:

"Are you a musician?"

"No, but I feel music as deeply as any man."

"Well, it is all the same; let me shake your hand. Gad, sir, you are a splendid fellow!"

Whereupon, perfectly undisturbed by the mirth of the spectators who had gathered around us and by the dumbfounded expression on the face of my orange-eating friend, we exchanged some words in an undertone; I told him my name, he told me his (it was Le Tessier—I never saw him again) and his profession. He was an engineer! A mathematician!! What the devil! Sensitivity lurks in the oddest nooks!

Mémoires de Hector Berlioz (Paris: Calmann-Lévy, n.d. [1910?]), I, 80–82. Trans. P. W.

"Thunderclaps occasionally follow one another in the life of an artist," writes Berlioz in Chap. 20 of his *Memoirs*, "as rapidly as during certain storms in which the clouds, replete with electric fluid, seem to toss the lightning back and forth and to breathe the hurricane. I had hardly experienced two apparitions—Shakespeare and Weber—when, at another point in the horizon, I saw the immense Beethoven rise up. The impact on me was nearly comparable to that which I had felt with Shakespeare. He opened up for me a new world in music, just as the poet had revealed to me a new universe in poetry." In article after article, review after review, Berlioz was to champion the cause of Beethoven's music. Beethoven, to him, stood for all that mattered and, just as important, *against* all that was trivial in music. Here, in a report sent to his paper from London in 1851, his devotion to the master appears mingled with light touches of social satire and humor.

The Beethoven Room

I must still acquaint you with *The Beethoven Quartet Society*. This has as its sole aim the performance at regular intervals, and in pretty close succession, of Beethoven's quartets. Each evening's program contains three of them—nothing less, nothing more. Usually they are selected from the three different manners of the author; and it is always the last, in the third manner (from the period of Beethoven's supposedly incomprehensible compositions), which excites the greatest enthusiasm. Then you may see Englishmen follow with their eye, in little pocket scores printed in London for that purpose, the capricious flight of the master's thoughts; which might be considered proof that several among them have some rudimentary knowledge of score reading. But I feel a certain skepticism regarding the science of these devourers, ever since I surprised one of them (I was peering over his shoulder) with his eyes fixed on page 4, while the performers were on page 6. This music lover no doubt belonged to the same school as the king of Spain whose passion it was to play the first fiddle in Boccherini's quintets and who, always falling behind the other performers, used to say to them, when the confusion grew too serious, "Keep going, I'll catch up with you!"

The meeting place of the *Beethoven Quartet Society* is known as the *Beethoven Room*. For a time I inhabited an apartment in the same house with it. The hall, seating two hundred and fifty persons at most, is for that reason often rented out for concerts intended for small audiences; there are many such. Now, since my apartment door opened on the staircase leading to the hall, I had only to keep it open in order to hear everything that was performed there. One evening I hear Beethoven's C-minor trio resounding ... I fling open my door ... Come in, come in, and welcome, proud melody!... God! How noble and beautiful!... Where, then, did Beethoven discover these countless phrases, each more poetically characterized than the other, all of them different, all of them original, not even sharing that family air one recognizes in the works of great masters renowned for their fecundity? And what ingenious developments! What unforeseen motions!... How he soars, this indefatigable eagle! How he glides, poised in his harmonious heaven!... Now he plunges down, loses himself in it, rises, descends again, disappears ... then he returns to his starting point, his eye glinting brighter, his wing beating more vigorously, disdaining repose, quivering, inebriated with infinity ... Very well performed! I wonder who played the piano part so well?... My servant informs me it was an Englishwoman. A true talent, I must say!... Oh dear! What's this? A prima donna's grand aria?... John! *Shut the door!* Quick, quick. Ah! Miserable woman! I hear her still. Shut the second door, the third; is there a fourth?... At last ... I breathe again ...

Hector Berlioz, *Beethoven*, ed. J.-G. Prod'homme (Paris: Corrêa, 1941), 141–44. Trans. P. W.

104

The Program of the *Symphonie Fantastique*

Although by the nineteenth century "program music" (i.e., instrumental music embodying extramusical content of one kind or another) was anything but new, one school of Romantic composers attached an unprecedented importance to it. It became in their eyes the highest form of music, for it was the kind best suited to their ideal of self-expression. The use of an extramusical program also gave license to all kinds of coloristic effects of harmony and orchestration, and thus furthered the tendency towards technical experimentation in the name of "originality"—something that went hand in hand with the Romantic exaltation of self. The best possible example of the new status of program music is one that has remained famous to this day— Berlioz's *Symphonie Fantastique* (1830), in which the composer sought to give expression to the passion for Harriet Smithson (an Irish Shakespearean actress who later became his wife) that possessed him at the time of its writing. Rather than a literal autobiography in tones, the *Symphonie Fantastique* is a kind of five-act drama of nightmares and hallucinations (to a Romantic like Berlioz, a higher reality than that of the senses). The Program of the symphony, which Berlioz wished to have distributed to audiences to prepare them to understand the work—and which many in the Victorian era understandably found shocking—must be regarded not simply as an explanation but as in some sense a part of the composition.

Note

It has been the composer's goal to develop different situations in the life of an artist, insofar as they are susceptible of musical treatment. The plot of the instrumental drama, lacking the help of the spoken word, needs to be presented beforehand. The following program* must accordingly be viewed as the spoken text of an opera [e.g., of a French *opéra comique,* where spoken dialogue was used instead of recitative], serving to introduce musical pieces whose character and expression it motivates.

First Part: Daydreams—Passions

The author imagines that a young musician, affected by the moral malady which a famous writer calls *le vague des passions* [i.e., seemingly rootless emotions], sees for the first time a woman who possesses all the charms of the ideal being he had fancied in his dreams, and falls hopelessly in love. Through a singular oddity, the image of the beloved never presents itself to the artist's imagination except tied to a musical idea, in which he perceives a certain impassioned quality, though noble and shy, as he imagines the object of his love to be.

This musical reflection and its model pursue him incessantly like a double *idée fixe* [obsession]. This is why the melody that opens the first *allegro* reappears constantly in all the other movements of the symphony. The passage from that state of dispirited daydreaming, occasionally interrupted by baseless transports of joy, to one of delirious passion, with its gusts of fury, of jealousy, its relapses into tenderness, its tears, its religious consolations, forms the subject of the first movement.

Second Part: A Ball

The artist finds himself in the most diverse situations of daily life: amid *the tumult of a festivity,* in the peaceful contemplation of the beauties of nature. But everywhere, whether in the town or in the fields, the image of the beloved obtrudes on him, bringing trouble to his spirit.

Third Part: Country Scene

Finding himself in the country one evening, he hears two shepherds playing a *ranz de vaches* [an Alpine cattle-call] in dialogue, far away; this pastoral duet, the scenery, the

---

*The distribution of this program to the audience, at concerts in which this symphony is to be played, is indispensable for the complete understanding of the work's dramatic plan [Berlioz's footnote].

Berlioz Conducts a Benefit Concert. The legend reads: ARTILLERY CON-
CERT. LUCKILY THE HALL IS SOLIDLY BUILT, IT RESISTS. The illustration
is taken from a highly successful satirical novel, *Jérôme Paturot à la recherche d'une
position sociale* by Louis Reybaud (1st illustrated ed., Paris, 1846). Berlioz is not
mentioned by name, but the several pages of description (pp. 203–205), including
comments on his propensity for "setting public and private life to music," leave no
doubt as to his identity; neither, of course, does the portrait. (Artist: J.-J. Grandville.)

slight murmuring of the trees gently swayed by the wind, some recently formed grounds for hope—everything contributes to bringing an unaccustomed calm to his heart and a brighter color to his thoughts. He thinks of his loneliness; he hopes soon not to be alone any more ... But what if she were deceiving him?... This mixture of hope and fear, these visions of happiness troubled by dark forebodings, form the subject of the *adagio*. In the end, one of the shepherds resumes the *ranz de vaches;* the other no longer answers ... Distant sound of thunder ... solitude ... silence ...

Fourth Part: March to the Scaffold

Having become convinced that his love is not returned, the artist poisons himself with opium. The dose of narcotic, too weak to kill him, plunges him into a sleep beset with the most horrible visions. He dreams he has murdered the one he loved; he has been sentenced, is being led to the scaffold, is *witnessing his own execution*. The procession moves forward to the sounds of a march now somber and ferocious, now brilliant and stately, during which the muffled noise of heavy footsteps follows without transition upon the noisiest outbursts. At the end of the march, the first four measures of the *idée fixe* reappear like a last thought of love interrupted by the fatal blow.

Fifth Part: Dream of a Sabbath Night

He sees himself at the sabbath, surrounded by a hideous crowd of spirits, sorcerers, monsters of every kind, assembled for his funeral. Strange noises, moans, bursts of laughter, distant cries to which other cries apparently respond. The beloved melody reappears again, but it has lost its noble and shy quality; now it is only a vile dance tune, trivial and grotesque; it is she, arriving at the sabbath ... Roar of joy at her arrival ... She joins the diabolic orgy ... Funeral knell, ludicrous parody of the *Dies irae,** sabbath round dance. The sabbath round dance and the *Dies irae* combined.

Hector Berlioz, *New Edition of the Complete Works*, XVI (Kassel: Bärenreiter, 1972), 3–4. Trans. P. W.

105

From the Writings of Schumann

Criticism, according to Matthew Arnold, is "a disinterested endeavour to learn and propagate the best that is known and thought in the world." Elsewhere he says it is an attempt "to see the object as in itself it really is." Schumann's poetic—sometimes even purposely mystifying—approach to musical journalism may mislead a casual reader into not taking him quite seriously. That would be a mistake, for Schumann, more than any other composer-writer, fulfilled Arnold's high requirements: he was disinterested, idealistic, deeply intuitive, and, as it has turned out, rarely wrong. In 1852, not long

---

*Hymn sung at the funeral rites of the Catholic Church [Berlioz's footnote].

before his final illness, Schumann set to work collecting his criticisms (most of which had appeared in his own journal, the *Neue Zeitschrift für Musik,* from 1834 to 1844) into a more permanent shape, "as a remembrance of that time and also of myself; for they present a living mirror-image of those stirring days and may give many a younger artist some instructive hints on things I've learnt and experienced" (letter of 3 June 1852). Elsewhere (letter of 11 July 1853) he says, "I do not care to earn a fortune with [this book]; I should like to leave behind me a remembrance of myself—if I may say so, the text (as it were) to my creative work." And, considering how autobiographical much of his music is, Schumann's critical writings do bear some such relationship to his musical compositions.

BY WAY OF INTRODUCTION

Towards the end of the year 1833, a number of musicians—most of them young—met together almost as if by accident every evening in Leipzig; they met for convivial reasons, but at least as much, too, for the exchange of ideas on the Art that was meat and drink to them—music. It cannot be said that Germany's musical situation at the time was very satisfactory. The stage was still dominated by Rossini, the piano nearly exclusively by [the fashionable composers] Herz and Hünten. And yet but a few years had passed since Beethoven, Weber, and Schubert had dwelt among us. True, Mendelssohn's star was in the ascendant, and wondrous things were being said of a young Pole, Chopin—but their influence was not deeply felt till later. Then, one day, a thought occurred to the young hotheads: "Let us not look idly on, let us take matters in hand, so that the situation may improve, so that the poetry of art may once again be held in high esteem!" Thus were born the first numbers of a new musical periodical. But the joy of close collaboration did not last long in this society of young talents. Death robbed it of one of its most valuable members, Ludwig Schunke. Some of the others left Leipzig altogether at different times. The undertaking was on the point of being dissolved. Then one of them, in fact the group's musical dreamer, who until then had whiled his life away at the piano far more than among books, decided to assume the editorship himself and led the journal for upwards of ten years, to 1844. This was the origin of a series of essays, a selection from which is collected here. The majority of the opinions given there are still held by him today. What, in hope and fear, he expressed regarding many an artist and artistic event has come true in the course of time.

There remains to be mentioned a League that was a more than secret one, since it only existed in the head of its founder: the *League of David* [*Davidsbund*]. It appeared not unsuitable to imagine contrasting artistic personalities in order to express different views of art; the principal figures were *Florestan* and *Eusebius,* between whom Master *Raro* stood as mediator. This Davidite society wound like a red thread through the periodical, binding together fact and fiction in a fanciful way. Later these comrades, who had been received not unkindly by the paper's readers, disappeared altogether from its pages.

Robert Schumann, *Gesammelte Schriften über Musik und Musiker* (Leipzig, 1854), I, iii–v. Trans. P. W.

Schumann's first published article appeared in the leading German musical periodical, the *Allgemeine musikalische Zeitung,* in 1831—three years, that is, before he founded his own periodical. The article is famous for having introduced the then-unknown Chopin to the German public; and it marks the first appearance of Schumann's imaginary Davidites, chief among them Eusebius, Florestan, and Master Raro. It should be pointed out, for the benefit of those who are not acquainted with these characters' musical incarnations (as in Schumann's *Carnaval*, op. 9), that the League of David's ultimate mission was to slay the Philistines. Who were the Philistines? Why, the fashionable mass producers of trivial music and the thousands upon thousands of unthinking concert and opera goers who applauded their efforts. Against such overwhelming numbers only a secret League could hope to prevail.

AN OPUS 2

Eusebius recently came softly into the room. You know the ironic smile on that pale face; it is meant to awaken your curiosity. I was sitting at the piano with Florestan. Florestan, as you know, is one of those rare musical natures who seem to anticipate all that is imminent, new, or out of the ordinary. Yet today there was a surprise in store for him. With the words, "Hats off, gentlemen, a genius!" Eusebius produced a piece of music. He would not let us see the title. I turned the pages idly; this veiled enjoyment of soundless music has something magical about it. Besides, it seems to me that each composer has his own individual note-patterns, recognizable to the eye: Beethoven looks different from Mozart, on paper. But now it seemed to me as if strange eyes, flower eyes, basilisk eyes, peacock eyes, maiden eyes were peeping up at me most wondrously; some parts seemed clearer—I thought I could detect Mozart's "Là ci darem la mano" [from *Don Giovanni*] entwined through a hundred chords. "Now play it," said Florestan.—Eusebius obliged; and we listened, huddled in the recesses of a window. Eusebius played as in a rapture and conjured forth countless images drawn from palpitating life; it was as if the rapture of the moment had lent his fingers powers beyond the ordinary. Florestan's approval, of course, consisted (apart from a blissful smile) of nothing more than the remark that the variations might have been composed by Beethoven or Franz Schubert, had they been piano virtuosos. But then he turned to the title page and read nothing but:

"Là ci darem la mano, Variations for the Piano
by Frédéric Chopin, Opus 2."

Surprised, we both exclaimed, "An Opus 2!" And everyone's face fairly glowed with astonishment. Apart from sundry and various exclamations, little could be made out but: "Well, here's something worthwhile again—Chopin—I've never heard of him—in any case a genius."—I cannot describe the scene. Heated by the wine, by Chopin, by our discussion, we repaired to Master Raro, who burst out laughing and displayed very little curiosity concerning the Opus 2, "for," said he, "I know you well enough, and your enthusiasm for the latest fashions; well, well, bring your Chopin to me." We promised to do so the next day. Eusebius soon bade us quietly good-night, and I remained with Master Raro for a while; Florestan, who has been homeless recently, flew through the moonlit street towards my house. At about midnight I found him in my room, lying on the sofa with his eyes shut. "Chopin's variations," he began, as if in a trance, "are still running through my head; to be sure," he went on, "it is all very dramatic and altogether Chopin-like … " [Here follows a detailed, though very fanciful, appreciation of this very early work, which, today, is rarely performed.]

"My very dear Florestan," said I, "these private feelings may be praiseworthy, though they are somewhat subjective; but though Chopin hardly needs to exert himself to follow his inspiration, I nevertheless bow to his genius, his aspiration, his mastery!"

Ibid., 3–5, 7.

Schumann was not inclined by temperament to organize his views on the aesthetics—and ethics—of music into a formal system. Yet a perfectly coherent outlook emerges, cumulatively, from a reading of his collected writings. Schumann's nearest approach to a direct statement of his views will be found, characteristically enough, in some sets of unrelated aphorisms he published occasionally, from which the following have been selected.

APHORISMS

I have no liking for those whose life is not in unison with their works.

Fl.[orestan]

Music speaks the most universal of languages, one by which the soul is freely, yet *indefinably* moved; but it is then at home.

Reviewers: Music extracts love-calls from nightingales, yelps from pug-dogs.

It is a sign of the extraordinary that it is not always grasped at once; the majority are inclined to superficial things, such as virtuoso music.

E.[usebius]

Let the artist preserve his balance in life; else his position becomes difficult.

In every child there is a wondrous depth.

Genius: We forgive the diamond its sharp edges; it is very costly to round them off.

Fl.

It is not a good thing to have acquired too great a facility in any skill.

Raro

There is spirit in all new things.

Eusebius

The first conception is always the most natural one and the best. Reason errs, feeling does not.

Raro

Talent labors, genius creates.

Fl.

The educated musician may study a Madonna by Raphael, the painter a Mozart symphony with equal advantage. Yet more: to the sculptor every actor is a motionless statue, to the actor the sculptor's works come alive; the painter sees a poem as a picture, the musician transforms paintings into tones.

E.

The aesthetics of one art is that of the others too; only the materials differ.

Fl.

That a distinct Romantic school can form itself in music, which is itself Romantic, is
difficult to believe.

Fl.

People say, "It pleased," or "It did not please." As if there were nothing higher than to
please people!

To cast light into the depths of the human heart—the artist's mission!

The laws of morality are also those of art.

Ibid., 29–43, *passim;* IV, 278, 303.

> Schumann withdrew as editor of the *Neue Zeitschrift für Musik* in 1844 and only
> seldom contributed to its pages thereafter. But his last contribution, which was printed
> on its front page late in 1853, caused a tremendous stir. Apart from its bold tone of
> prophecy concerning a totally unknown young composer, Johannes Brahms, the
> article came at a moment when Germany's musicians were splitting over the issue
> of the "music of the future" (see p. 324), towards which Schumann was known to be
> cool. Hence the intense reactions, both friendly and skeptical, that greeted the article.
> Brahms's name became well known overnight, and, as it happened, Brahms himself
> eventually became the titular, if inactive, leader of the opponents of the "musicians of
> the future."

NEW PATHS

Years have gone by—nearly as many as I devoted to editing these pages, namely ten—
since I last let myself be heard on this terrain so rich in memories. Often, in spite of
strenuous productive activity, have I felt so impelled: several new, remarkable talents
have appeared, a new force in music seemed to announce itself, manifested by many of
the upward-striving artists of recent times, even if their productions are only known to a
narrower circle. In following the paths of these elect with the greatest sympathy, I felt
that, after such a beginning, there should and would suddenly appear one destined to
give utterance to the highest expression of our time in an ideal way, one who should
reveal to us his mastery not gradually, but who should spring, like Minerva, fully armed
from the head of Jupiter. And he has come, a youth at whose cradle graces and heroes
kept watch. His name is *Johannes Brahms,* he has come from Hamburg, working there
in tranquil obscurity but instructed by an outstanding, enthusiastic teacher in the most
difficult statutes of the art, and recommended to me shortly before by a respected,
celebrated Master [the violinist Joseph Joachim]. He possessed, even in outward
appearance, all the signs that announce: he is a chosen one. Sitting at the piano he
began to unveil wondrous regions. We were drawn into ever more enchanted circles.
To this was added an inspired way of playing that transformed the piano into an
orchestra of lamenting and rejoicing voices. He played sonatas, or rather disguised
symphonies, songs whose poetry would be understood without knowing their words,
although a profound vocal melody threads through them all, single piano pieces, some
of demonic nature and in the shapeliest form, then sonatas for violin and piano, string
quartets—each so different from the others that they appeared to gush from different
sources. And then it seemed as if he united them all as a stream pouring down a
waterfall, bearing a serene rainbow above its plunging waves; and butterflies played
along its banks accompanied by the voices of nightingales.

If he will plant his magic wand where the massed forces of chorus and orchestra will lend him their power, then even more wondrous glimpses into the world of the spirit still await us. May the highest genius prompt him where expectation waits for him, for another genius, that of modesty, lives in him. His colleagues greet him upon his entry into the world, where wounds perhaps await him, but also laurels and palms; we welcome him as a doughty contender.

At all times there rules a sacred bond of kindred spirits. Tighten your circle, ye who belong together, that the truth of art may shine ever brighter, spreading joy and abundance everywhere.

R. S.

Robert Schumann, *Gesammelte Schriften über Musik und Musiker,* ed. Martin Kreisig (Leipzig: Breitkopf & Härtel, 1914), II, 301–302. Trans. P. W.

106

Liszt, the All-Conquering Pianist

Almost exactly ten years after Paganini emerged from obscurity by appearing in a series of concerts in Vienna, Liszt created a similar sensation in the Austrian capital and embarked on an equally memorable career as a traveling virtuoso. Here are excerpts from the report sent in by the Viennese correspondent of Germany's leading musical journal, the *Allgemeine musikalische Zeitung,* published in May 1838.

Vienna, end of April.—Unusual events require an extraordinary report. The present one is prompted by the wholly unexpected arrival of the famous pianist Franz Liszt, whom Vienna had not seen since his 12th year and who, like a *Deus ex machina* [i.e., an unhoped-for savior], came to us quite suddenly from the slopes of the Apennines [he had spent the winter in Italy].

We have now heard him, the strange wonder, whom the superstition of past ages, possessed by the delusion that such things could never be done without the help of the Evil One, would undoubtedly have condemned without mercy to the stake—we have heard him, and seen him too, which, of course, makes a part of the affair. Just look at the pale, slender youth in his clothes that signal the nonconformist; the long, sleek, drooping hair, the thin arms, the small, delicately formed hands; the almost gloomy and yet childlike pleasant face—those features so strongly stamped and full of meaning, in this respect reminding one of Paganini, who, indeed, has been his model of hitherto undreamt-of virtuosity and technical brilliance from the very first moment he heard him and was swept away.

Liszt introduced himself with Weber's *Konzertstück* in F minor. Karl Maria [von Weber] himself played us this beautiful and strongly conceived composition about twenty years ago; his hearers were indifferent if not cold. Several pianists of both sexes had ventured on it at different times [with no better success]. This notorious fact was not unknown to our worthy guest; but he wished, as he himself put it, to bring that glorious master's favorite child into honor among the Viennese. And it came to

Franz Liszt Exerts His Spell on the Ladies in the Audience. A caricature of the 1840s. (From the periodical *Berlin, wie es ist ... und trinkt,* no. 14.)

pass! No one imagined he was listening to the oft-heard piece; the notes, to be sure, were the same, perhaps not one more or less—yet how infinitely different! Through a quite personal method of fingering, in which the thumb assumes a wide variety of functions, through a technique cultivated to the point of perfection, through a touch which he is capable of shading through all conceivable degrees, from the softest breath to the most overwhelming thunderstorm, he brings forth the most stupendous effects; yes, even effects of detail which one would not think of expecting of the instrument. The introductory Largo was performed with melancholy pathos, with passionate feeling, speaking to the inmost heart; every note a complaint of the oppressed spirit, a sigh of the troubled, anguished soul. The tempo of the first and final allegros he urged on in such a manner that one trembled for the outcome—but how needlessly! For the pining David became a gigantic Goliath; and, to the contrary, his lavishly expended energies seemed steadily to augment, and the flood of tones poured forth in one stream, yet never at the cost of intelligibility, to the last chord, with which were mingled cheers of acclamation that threatened never to end, and for which the expression "enthusiastic" is only an empty unmeaning sound. When, in the magnificent March, the orchestra gradually swelled to *fortissimo,* and the mighty one thundered in imperiously, penetrating the massed instruments victoriously—a tamer of the waves, to whom the watery element pays obeisance, here already the thunderous applause knew no bounds; and such a tribute of recognition must have affected the virtuoso deeply, accustomed though he was to homage [in France and England], for hot tears rolled down his cheeks.

The arrival of this phenomenon amongst pianists was so unexpected, and his stay is of so short duration, that the longing to hear and admire him is quite pardonable. And so, invitation upon invitation from the highest nobility and most distinguished families press and cross each other daily, nay hourly; and the modest, unassuming artist, doubly amiable by his obliging courtesy, which can refuse no one anything, is quite out of breath; at times, indeed, he would need to divide himself in two.

Who can doubt that this meteor has set in motion all the ready pens of the imperial city? [The painter Josef] Kriehuber has lithographed him to the life. But the most characteristic of his portraits was done by [Moritz] Saphir, who, to be sure, is not a professional musician, but a poet.

"Liszt," said he, "knows no rule, no form, no law; he creates them all himself! He remains an inexplicable phenomenon, a compound of such heterogeneous, strangely mixed materials, that an analysis would inevitably destroy what lends the highest charm, the individual enchantment: namely, the inscrutable secret of this chemical mixture of genial coquetry and childlike simplicity, of whimsy and divine nobleness.

"After the concert, he stands there like a conqueror on the field of battle, like a hero in the lists; vanquished pianos lie about him, broken strings flutter as trophies and flags of truce, frightened instruments flee in their terror into distant corners, the hearers look at each other in mute astonishment as after a storm from a clear sky, as after thunder and lightning mingled with a shower of blossoms and buds and dazzling rainbows; and he the Prometheus, who creates a form from every note, a magnetizer who conjures the electric fluid from every key, a gnome, an amiable monster, who now treats his beloved, the piano, tenderly, then tyranically; caresses, pouts, scolds, strikes, drags by the hair, and then, all the more fervently, with all the fire and glow of love, throws his arms around her with a shout, and away with her through all space; he stands there, bowing his head, leaning languidly on a chair, with a strange smile, like an exclamation mark after the outburst of universal admiration: this is Franz Liszt!"

Lina Ramann, *Franz Liszt, Artist and Man,* trans. E. Cowdery (London, 1882), II, 315–18. Corrections based on the original source.

107

From the Writings of Liszt

Liszt was in his twenties (and very much under the influence of Saint-Simonian socialism and the religious ideas of the unorthodox reformer Lamennais) when he published a series of articles in the *Gazette musicale de Paris* under the title "Concerning the Situation of Artists and Their Condition in Society." The following extract (from the article of 30 August 1835) points up the unbroken line that connects Rousseau and the French Revolution to some of the socio-religious ideals of the Romantics. (Note the close resemblance between Liszt's program and that of the founders of the Conservatoire, p. 271.)

Gods depart, kings depart, but God remains, and the peoples rise. Let us then not despair of art.

According to a law passed by the Chamber of Deputies in 1834, music will soon be taught in the schools. We rejoice at this sign of progress and accept it as a pledge of even vaster progress, whose influence on the masses will appear all but miraculous.

We allude to the regeneration of *religious music.*

Although the term is normally restricted to music performed in church during the divine service, I take it here in its wider sense.

In the days when worship expressed and at the same time satisfied the people's beliefs, needs, and sympathies, when men and women sought and found in their churches an altar before which they could kneel, a pulpit that nourished their spirits, a spectacle that entertained and elevated their senses piously, religious music could afford to confine itself within the holy precincts, could be content merely to accompany the splendors of the Catholic liturgy.

Today, when the altar is cracked and tumbling, today, when pulpit and ceremonies have become objects of doubt and derision, art must emerge from the temple, must spread out and accomplish its far-reaching evolution outside.

As before, and to an even greater degree, music must seek out the PEOPLE and GOD, go from one to the other; improve, moralize, console man, bless and glorify God.

Now, to accomplish this, the creation of a *new music* is imminent; essentially religious, strong, and effective, this music, which for want of a better name we will call *humanitarian,* will embrace within its colossal dimensions both the THEATER and the CHURCH. It will be both dramatic and sacred, splendid and simple, pathetic and solemn, fiery and unruly, tempestuous and calm, serene and tender.

The *Marseillaise*—which better than Hindu, Chinese, and Greek myths, has *proved* the effectiveness of music—the *Marseillaise* and the other fine songs of the Revolution have been its terrible and glorious precursors.

Yes, we do not doubt it: soon we shall hear the fields, hamlets, villages, suburbs, workshops, and cities resound to national, moral, political, religious songs, canticles, airs, and anthems *made* for the people, *taught* to the people, *sung* by tillers of the soil, artisans, laborers, the boys and girls, the men and women of the *people.*

All great artists, the poets and the musicians, will furnish their quota to the constantly enriched popular repertory. The state will distribute honors, public rewards, to those who have won three general competitions; and *all classes of society,* finally, will merge in a common religious sentiment, grand and sublime.

And art shall say, "Let there be light."

May it come, may it come, therefore, this glorious era in which art shall fulfill itself by developing in all its aspects and rise to the highest level by uniting mankind in brotherhood by means of rapturous wonders. May the time come when the artist's inspiration shall no longer be as bitter, elusive water reached after much effort beneath sterile sands, when instead it shall pour out as an inexhaustible, life-giving stream. May it, oh may it come, the hour of deliverance when poet and musician shall no longer say "the public"—but the PEOPLE and GOD!

Jean Chantavoine (ed.), *Fr. Liszt: Pages romantiques* (Paris: F. Alcan, 1912), 65–67, Trans. P. W.

Liszt's pen portrait of the Irish pianist and composer John Field (1782–1837) and his works is a repository of many of the tenets of Romanticism in music. The artist's idealism; his complete individuality and indifference to public acclaim; the exaltation of spontaneous feeling over form, its supposed enemy; music as a magic conveyance to an "inner world" of subjective reverie—these were the ideas that reigned in the salons and the garrets of the early nineteenth century, and Liszt (or probably his ghost writer, Princess Wittgenstein) recaptured them well in retrospect, some two decades after Field's death. The prose itself calls for comment: poetic, evocative, full (perhaps overfull) of imagery, it seeks to recreate the feelings it describes. Here is the Romantic conviction of the underlying unity of the arts confirmed from the other end—it was an age not only of "literary music," but of musical writing as well. We should add, too, that Liszt was as little concerned with objective matters as was his subject. The history of the "character piece" for piano did not begin with Field, and the view of his effortlessly spontaneous creative process is no doubt exaggerated. For a more realistic account of a Romantic genius at work, see George Sand on Chopin (next reading).

John Field and His Nocturnes

Alongside so much that has long since grown old, the Nocturnes of Field have retained their youth. Forty years and more have passed over them and still they exude a balmy freshness, still they give off their sweet perfume. Where else but in Field will we find an innocence so perfect and incomparable? No one after him has been able to recreate the charms of his language—a language as coaxing as a tearful look, as lulling as the even back-and-forth of a rocking boat or a swinging hammock, whose languorously easeful movements persuade us that we hear the sweetest of breezes whispering all around us.

No one since has achieved these Aeolian-harp sounds hanging like half-sighs in the air, which, softly plaintive, lose themselves in blissful pain. No one has dared venture to create anything like them, least of all those who were privy to Field's own playing, or rather, dreaming, when he would give himself up entirely to the inspiration of the moment. He did not restrict himself then to the notes he had earlier prescribed, but festooned his melodies anew with uninterrupted arabesques and garlands. Although he ever-resourcefully decorated them with new bouquets that fell on them like a rain of flowers, the melodies never disappeared beneath the ornaments, whose languorous billows and exquisitely graceful tracery veiled them but never covered them up. With what inexhaustible richness he varied the repetitions! With what rare felicity he could twist his thoughts, without ever losing their thread in the network of his fancies!

If there is anything whose secret it would be vain to investigate (unless by a special favor Nature had confided it to our talent), it is the chaste grace of purity, the charm of a naive, innate ingenuity—qualities which one either possesses as Nature's dowry or not at all. Field was endowed with them. They lent his creations a magic over which time can have no power. Their form will never grow old, for it accords perfectly with his feeling, which belongs not to the category of transitory, passing moods engendered by the moment, but to that pure exaltation which has a permanent hold over the heart of man. Unlike the beauties of Nature, and unlike those sweet moods which belong to the morning of one's life, when the shining prisms of feeling are as yet unclouded by the shadows of reflection, these feelings endure; they are forever the same. So we may never dream of taking these works as a model, of patterning our own works after them. Without a wholly unique impulse their effects are unattainable. They cannot be found unless one seeks them not. Vain would be any attempt to analyze the charms of their spontaneity.

In writing as in playing, in the one as in the other, Field was intent only on expressing his inner feelings for his own gratification. It would be impossible to imagine a more unabashed indifference to the public than his. He enchanted his public without knowing it or wishing it. His nearly immobile posture, his expressionless face did not attract notice. His glance did not rove. His playing flowed on, peaceful and limpid. His fingers glided over the keys and the sounds they evoked seemed to follow one another in a curling wake. Withal, it is not hard to see that he was his own chief audience. His calm was all but sleepy, and could be neither disturbed nor affected by thoughts of the impression his playing made on his hearers. No haste, no excess, whether in deportment, in phrasing, or in tempo ever broke the melodious reverie that filled the atmosphere with an exquisite aura that seemed to whisper love-drunk melodies, impressions of sweetest bliss, and delightful murmurs, *mezza voce,* all around us.

Art was for him in itself sufficient reward for any sacrifice. Anything over and above that—positions he might be appointed to, the reputation that might surround him, the success and longevity of his composition—all this did not concern him. Field sang for himself alone. To please himself was all he asked of music. But it is directly to this total disregard of anything that aims merely at effect that we owe the first attempts—and what perfect ones!—to infuse the piano with feelings and dreams and to free piano music from the constraints imposed until then by regular and "official" form on compositions of all kinds. Before him they all had of necessity to be cast as sonatas or rondos or some such. Field, contrariwise, introduced a genre that belonged to none of these existing categories, in which feeling and melody reigned supreme, and which moved freely, without the fetters and constraints of any preconceived form. He cleared the path for all those offspring which have since appeared sporting names like "Songs Without Words," "Impromptu," "Ballade," and so on, and one can trace to him the origin of all such pieces, which seek to express intimate, subjective emotions. He was the discoverer of these realms; he opened up a field as new as it was propitious for subtle rather than grandiose imaginings, for delicate rather than lyric inspirations.

The name "Nocturne" suits splendidly the pieces Field was inspired so to christen. For from their very first sounds we are immediately transported to those hours when the soul, released from the day's burdens, retreats into itself and soars aloft to secret regions of star and sky. We see it here all airy and winged, hovering like Philomela of old in the scented air over the flowers, rapturously engulfed by Nature.

L. Ramann (ed.), *Gesammelte Schriften von Franz Liszt,* IV (Leipzig, 1882), 263–68. Trans. R. T.

108

Glimpses of Chopin Composing, Playing the Piano

An aura of mystery and of magic surrounded the highly reserved personality of Chopin in his own day, and that aura still surrounds him for us today. By all accounts his music cast a spell on his listeners, and critics spoke of the intensely personal style of Chopin's compositions (see Schumann, p. 305). It is hard to imagine his playing can have been any less so. Yet putting down his inspirations on paper in their final form proved an agonizing process for him according to George Sand, the French novelist and author who shared her life with him for many years:

His creation was spontaneous and miraculous. He found it without seeking it, without foreseeing it. It came on his piano suddenly, complete, sublime, or it sang in his head during a walk, and he was impatient to play it to himself. But then began the most heart-rending labor I ever saw. It was a series of efforts, of irresolutions, and of frettings to seize again certain details of the theme he had heard; what he had conceived as a whole he analyzed too much when wishing to write it, and his regret at not finding it again, in his opinion, clearly defined, threw him into a kind of despair. He shut himself up for whole days, weeping, walking, breaking his pens, repeating and altering a bar a hundred times, writing and erasing it as many times, and recommencing the next day with a minute and desperate perseverance. He spent six weeks over a single page to write it at last as he had noted it down at the very first.

I had for a long time been able to make him consent to trust to this first inspiration. But when he was no longer disposed to believe me, he reproached me gently with having spoiled him and with not being severe enough for him. I tried to amuse him, to take him out for walks; but it was not always possible to prevail upon him to leave that piano which was much oftener his torment than his joy, and by degrees he showed temper when I disturbed him. I dared not insist. Chopin when angry was alarming; and as, with me, he always restrained himself, he seemed almost to choke and die.

Frederick Niecks, *Frederick Chopin as a Man and Musician* (London: Novello, 1902), II, 132.

Carl Mikuli, who studied with Chopin and in later years became a trustworthy transmitter of his master's legacy, remembered:

Chopin played rarely and always unwillingly in public; "exhibitions" of himself were totally repugnant to his nature. Long years of sickliness and nervous irritability did not always permit him the necessary repose, in the concert hall, for displaying untrammeled the full wealth of his resources. In more familiar circles, too, he seldom played anything but his shorter pieces, or occasional fragments from the larger works. Small wonder, therefore, that Chopin the Pianist should fail of general recognition.

Yet Chopin possessed a highly developed technique, giving him complete mastery over the instrument. In all styles of touch the evenness of his scales and passages was unsurpassed—nay, fabulous; under his hands the pianoforte needed to envy neither the violin for its bow nor wind instruments for the living breath. The tones melted one into the other with the liquid effect of beautiful song.

Carl Mikuli, ed., *Chopin's Complete Works for the Piano* (New York: G. Schirmer, Inc., 1916), Introductory Note.

Towards the end of his life, Chopin accepted an invitation to play in Great Britain. An unusually perceptive review of his second London concert by the Scottish journalist George Hogarth appeared on 10 July 1848 in the *Daily News*. (Although he speaks of a "numerous" audience, there were only about 200 people in attendance, at a nobleman's house.)

Monsieur Chopin performed an *Andante sostenuto* and a Scherzo from his Opus 31, a selection from his celebrated studies, a Nocturne and a *Berceuse* and several of his own Preludes, Mazurkas and Waltzes. In these various pieces he showed very strikingly his original genius as a composer and his transcendental powers as a performer. His music is as strongly marked with individual character as that of any master who has ever lived. It is highly finished, new in its harmonies, full of contrapuntal skill and ingenious contrivance; and yet we have never heard music which has so much the air of unpremeditated effusion. The performer seems to abandon himself to the impulses of his fancy and feeling, to indulge in a reverie and to pour out unconsciously, as it were, the thoughts and emotions that pass through his mind.

He accomplishes enormous difficulties, but so quietly, so smoothly and with such constant delicacy and refinement that the listener is not sensible of their real magnitude. It is the exquisite delicacy, with the liquid mellowness of his tone, and the pearly roundness of his passages of rapid articulation which are the peculiar features of his execution, while his music is characterized by freedom of thought, varied expression and a kind of romantic melancholy which seems the natural mood of the artist's mind.

Arthur Hedley, *Chopin* (London: J. M. Dent, 1947), 107.

We will leave the last word to a poet, Heine, who covered the cultural scene in Paris in witty letters to the German press. But when speaking of Chopin, he became serious:

Yes, Chopin must be considered a genius in the full sense of the word; he is not just a virtuoso, he is also a poet, he is able to make evident for us the poetry that lives in his soul, he is a tone-poet, and nothing equals the pleasure he gives us when he sits at the piano and improvises. Then he is neither Polish, nor French, nor German, he reveals then a far higher origin: one realizes then that he comes from the land of Mozart, Raphael, Goethe. His true fatherland is the dream-kingdom of poetry. When he sits at the piano and improvises, I feel as if I were being visited by a man from my beloved country, as if he were telling me the strangest things that have occurred there during my absence ...

Heinrich Heine, *Historisch-kritische Gesamtausgabe der Werke* (Hamburg: Hoffmann und Campe, 1980), XII, 289–90. Trans. P. W.

109

Mendelssohn and Queen Victoria

Buckingham Palace "cozy"? Mendelssohn was a marvelously acute observer, and while he used that word in fun, there is no mistaking the comfortable German middle-class atmosphere that prevailed at the Palace when the Queen was young and her adored husband, Prince Albert, set the tone. We have come a long way since the days when (as in Molière's *Bourgeois gentilhomme*) the middle class tried to ape the ways of the aristocracy. By the 1840s, bourgeois ideals emanated from the thrones of Europe. Indeed, the Victorian era might well be defined as the era in which middle-class ideals became officially enshrined. Mendelssohn, unlike so many of his fellow artists, did not openly rebel against those ideals; in fact his music accorded remarkably well with the tastes of the educated portion of his public, and this guilt by association no doubt contributed to the decline of his reputation in the years following his death. Bourgeois ideals no longer seem to trouble us today, and we are free to enjoy the many delicate and beautiful things Mendelssohn composed. The following is from a letter to his mother dated 19 July 1842.

Buckingham Palace is the only friendly home in England, really cozy, one feels at one's ease in it. Joking aside, Prince Albert had sent word asking me to go to him on Saturday at half past one, so that I might try out his organ before I left; I found him quite alone, and just as we were in the middle of our conversation, in came the Queen, also quite alone, in her house dress. She had to leave for Claremont in an hour, she said—"but gracious me, how very untidy it is here!" she added, noticing that the wind had knocked over all the sheets, separately, from an unbound music book onto the pedals of the organ (which forms a lovely adornment to the room) and into the corners. Saying this, she knelt down and began gathering them together; Prince Albert helped, and I did not lag behind. Then the Prince began to elucidate the stops for me, and meanwhile she said she would put things straight herself. But then I begged that the Prince would rather play for me first—I wished to boast about it in Germany, I said, and so he played me a chorale by heart, with the pedals, so nicely and purely and faultlessly that many an organist might well have profited from it, and the Queen, who had finished her task, sat near and listened, very pleased. I had to play next, and struck up the chorus from my *St. Paul*, "How Lovely are the Messengers." Even before I had finished the first verse, they both chimed in with the chorus in good earnest, and now Prince Albert drew the stops for me ever so skillfully during the whole piece; first he added a flute, then at the forte the full organ, at the D major the whole register, then he made such an excellent diminuendo with the stops, and so on to the end of the piece, and all of this by heart, that I was really quite delighted with it and very happy. Then the Hereditary Prince of Gotha [Prince Albert's older brother] came in and there was more conversation, and the Queen said, among other things, had I composed any new songs, and she enjoys singing the printed ones very much. "You ought to sing one for him," said Prince Albert. She had to be coaxed a bit at first, then she said she'd attempt the "Spring Song" in B-flat major. That is, if it was still here, because all the music had already been packed up for Claremont. Prince Albert went to look for it, but came back: it had already been packed away. "Oh, perhaps one could unpack it again," said I.—"We must send for Lady N. N.," she said (I didn't catch the name). The bell was rung, and the servants ran off, but came back embarrassed, and then the Queen went herself, and while she was out, Prince Albert said to me: "She begs you to accept this present too, as a keepsake," and gave me a little case containing a lovely ring with V. R. 1842 engraved on it, and then the Queen came back and said, "Lady … has driven off and taken all my things along— I really think it is most improper!" (You cannot imagine how this amused me.) Then I said I hoped she wouldn't make me suffer for the incident and would pick something else, and after a short consultation with her husband, he said, "She'll sing you something by Gluck." Meanwhile the Princess of Gotha had also come in, and so we five went through the corridors and rooms till we reached the Queen's sitting room, where a massive rocking horse was standing next to the sofa, and two large bird cages, and pictures on the walls, and beautifully bound books on the tables, and music on the piano. The Duchess of Kent came in, and while they were talking I rummaged a bit among the music books and found there my very first book of songs. So then I naturally asked her to choose something from that rather than the Gluck, and she did so very amiably, and what did she pick? "Lovelier and Lovelier" [composed by Mendelssohn's sister, though published under his name], and sang it in a most charming manner, cleanly, in strict time, and with very nice expression; except that when it goes down to D, she hit D sharp both times, and since both times I gave her D, she took it right the last time, when it ought to have been D sharp, of course. But apart from this oversight it was really most charming, and I've never heard an amateur sing the last long G better, and more purely and naturally. I then had to confess that Fanny had written the song (found it difficult, actually, but pride must have a fall) and asked her to sing me one of my very own too. If I would help her a great deal she'd be happy to, she said, and sang "Leave Off Those Vain Regrets" really quite faultlessly and with wonderfully pleasant feeling and expression. One ought not to pay too many compliments on such occasions, thought I to myself, and merely thanked her very much indeed; but when she said, "Oh, if only I had not been so frightened; I usually have quite a long breath," I praised her thoroughly and with the best conscience in the world; for the passage with the long C, at the end, is exactly what she had done so well, and she had joined the next three notes to it all in the same breath, as you seldom hear it done, and so I was especially amused that she should have carried on about that. And now Prince Albert sang "There's a Tailor," and then he said I really ought to play them something else before I left and suggested as themes the chorale he had played on the organ and the "Tailor." Had I played as usual, then I should have ended by improvising quite dreadfully, since that is what happens to me nearly always when I try very hard to succeed; and then I should have been left with nothing but vexation at the end. But just as if it had been destined that I should keep a really pleasant, happy recollection, free of any annoyance, my improvisation came off exceptionally well; I was quite freshly disposed and played long and enjoyed it myself; needless to say, besides the two themes I also worked in the songs the Queen had sung; but it all went so naturally that I should have liked not to stop at all, and they followed me with so much sympathy and attentiveness that I felt in better spirits there than I ever have when improvising in public. Well, and then she said, "I hope you will visit us in England soon again," and then I retired and saw the lovely chaises waiting below, with the scarlet outriders, and a quarter of an hour later the Palace's flag was lowered, and the papers said "Her Majesty left the Palace at 20 minutes past 3," and I walked [home] through the rain.

Piero Weiss (ed.), *Letters of Composers Through Six Centuries* (Philadelphia: Chilton Books, 1967), 268–70.

110

Verdi's Rise to Solitary Eminence

Abramo Basevi (1818–85) was the author of *Studio sulle opere di Giuseppe Verdi*, the first full-length study of Verdi's operas, published in Florence in 1859. He divided the composer's output into no less than four successive "manners" or style periods, and one wonders how many more he would have discovered in the six great operas yet to come after that date. After analyzing Verdi's first three successes, *Nabucco* (1842), *I Lombardi alla prima crociata* (1843), and *Ernani* (1844), Basevi proceeds to place Verdi in the setting of mid-century Italian opera and finds him standing alone in an otherwise barren musical landscape—the same bleak prospect described already in 1830 by the English correspondent of *The Harmonicon* (see p. 295).

If any doubts remained in the minds of Italians regarding which composer was destined to inherit the legacy of Donizetti and Bellini in the world of music, then surely the success of *Ernani* must have dispelled them altogether. After that opera, Verdi was recognized almost unanimously in Italy as the worthy successor of the aforementioned masters. But the composer was still to write other operas before being equally acclaimed in Europe.

When we consider that, without Verdi, a new Lamartine might exclaim, and perhaps with more justice, that Italy is now *the land of the dead* where music is concerned, we must not only admire, but be grateful to the genius from Busseto, who causes the name of Italy to resound gloriously in the arts throughout the world. The greater the marvel when one considers the swarm of composers who stood in his way on his path to eminence. From 1842 through 1857 there were not less than 641 new operas given in Italy, witness the following table showing the number produced each year:

Year	Operas	Year	Operas
1842	42	1850	27
1843	53	1851	60
1844	35	1852	60
1845	32	1853	52
1846	36	1854	44
1847	29	1855	53
1848[1]	14	1856	40
1849[2]	...	1857	64[3]

[1] The political events [i.e., the ill-fated war of independence in 1848–49] having transformed nearly all musical and theatrical journals, I was unable to record the new operas produced after mid-July.
[2] For the reason given in the preceding note, I leave blank the number of operas. Verdi in this year produced *Luisa Miller*.
[3] In 1858 through September there were already produced 31 new operas.

The greater part of these operas are first or second attempts by young composers; whence one may conjecture the extraordinary number of composers involved. Notwithstanding this abundance of operas and composers, Italy has never been so poor, because never before did she find herself with but one composer. The expression *but one* is not meant to imply that there are no other deserving composers; but only one, today, is able to satisfy the musical tastes of the public, not just in Italy, but in the world. The great Rossini, though a colossus, had nonetheless competitors who shared with him the popular favor. Verdi, instead, has up to now had no rival capable of overshadowing him. And yet, other composers have written beautiful operas, if not as fortunate. [Saverio] Mercadante [1795–1870] and [Giovanni] Pacini [1796–1867], who never laid down their pens, wrote operas that certainly are not without many virtues. Among new composers, a great many can vaunt the most brilliant successes, that is, applause and calls to the stage; but time has been the prompt, inexorable enemy of their work.

Piero Weiss (ed.), *Opera: A History in Documents* (New York: Oxford University Press, 2002), 189–91.

111

From the Writings of Wagner

It is almost as difficult to select short, representative passages from Wagner's volumi-
nous writings as it is to do so from his massively conceived music dramas. The
following two specimens, therefore, must be viewed as mere fragments from a body
of writings too various and complex to be summarized in the space available. The first,
written in 1852, records the decisive step in Wagner's musical development: his break
with operatic tradition. It is, in part, an astonishingly prophetic declaration, since,
though the words of *The Ring of the Nibelung* were completed, Wagner had not yet
written a note of the music!

With *Rienzi,* my intention was still only to write an "opera"; I sought out my materials to
that end, and, concerned only with "operas," I took them from finished poems, which had
been fashioned, even as to their form, with artistic intent. With *The Flying Dutchman*
I entered upon a new path, in that I myself grew to be the artificer of a material that lay
before me only in its simple, unelaborated outline as a folk saga. From then on I was, in
relation to all my dramatic works, first a *poet;* and only as I fully worked out the poem did
I again become a musician. However, I was a poet conscious beforehand of the expressive
capacity to work out his poems *musically;* I had exercised this capacity to the point where
I was fully aware of my ability to use it for the realization of a poetic intention; and not only
could I rely with assurance on the aid of that capacity in drafting poetic sketches, but
I could even, in that knowledge, shape the sketches in accordance with poetic necessity
more freely than if I had shaped them expressly to be set to music. Before [I reached this
stage] I had to master the skill of musical expression, much as one learns a language. But
now I had thoroughly learnt the language of music; I had mastered it like a true mother
tongue; and so I no longer needed to concern myself over formalities of expression in that
which I had to set forth: [expression] stood at my command wholly as I required it, to
communicate a particular view or sensation from inner necessity. But that which is to be
expressed in the language of music consists solely of *emotions* and *sensations:* [the
language of music] expresses altogether, and in full measure, the emotional content of
the elemental human language, independently of our word-language, which has become
purely an informational tool. That which, accordingly, remains inexpressible to absolute
music is the precise identification of the emotion's or sensation's cause, through which
they themselves attain greater definition; the necessary continuation and extension of the
musical language's range of expression consists, then, in acquiring also the capacity to
indicate with recognizable precision the individual, the particular; and this it acquires only
by being wedded to the word-language. But that union will only be successful when the
musical language is linked primarily with that which is congenial and related to it in the
word-language; the bond must occur exactly at *that* point in the word-language where
an irresistible urge towards the expression of true, sensuous emotion makes itself felt.
From what has been said, the content of that which must be expressed by the word and
tone poet becomes self-evident: it is *the purely human, released from all convention.*
    Since, from the above-mentioned turning point in the direction of my art, I have
been guided once and for all by my [poetic] *material,* specifically by material perceived

through music's eye, I could not, in shaping it, proceed otherwise than by gradually and totally abolishing, of necessity, the *operatic form* I had inherited. This operatic form had never in itself been a definite form embracing the whole of the drama, but rather only an arbitrary conglomeration of single, shorter vocal forms which, in their quite accidental arrangement as arias, duets, trios, etc. with choruses and so-called ensemble pieces, actually went to make up the substance of operatic form. In the poetic organization of my materials, I could not possibly any longer be concerned with filling up these ready-made forms, but only, and exclusively, with the emotionally-understood presentation of the drama's subject taken as a whole. In the entire course of the drama I saw no possibility of divisions or distinctions other than the acts, in which the place or the time, or the scenes, in which the characters themselves change.

As I drafted my scenes, I was not in the least constrained, by the nature of the material thus conceived, to have a care for any particular musical form in advance, for the scenes themselves dictated the musical working out as intrinsic and necessary to them. With my ever-increasing sureness of perception in this regard, I could no longer even conceive of interrupting and inhibiting the spontaneous musical form emerging necessarily from the very nature of the scenes with arbitrary external accretions, with the violent implanting of conventional operatic vocal forms. And so, I emphatically did not set out to destroy methodically—say, as a scheming modifier of forms—the aria, duet, or any other operatic form; instead, the omission of that form resulted quite spontaneously from the nature of the material.

Richard Wagner, *Drei Operndichtungen nebst einer Mittheilung an seine Freunde* (Leipzig, 1852), 143–52. Trans. P. W.

> The following program note on the Prelude to *Tristan und Isolde* was first published among Wagner's posthumous writings. It was written about 1860.

An old, primeval love poem, imperishably reborn in ever-new forms and repeated in the poetry of all the languages of medieval Europe, tells us of Tristan and Isolde. For his king the trusty vassal had wooed a maid he dared not tell himself he loved, Isolde; as his master's bride she followed him, powerless to do otherwise than to follow the suitor. The goddess of love, jealous of her suppressed rights, avenged herself: the love potion intended by the prudent mother for the partners in this marriage contracted (as was then the custom) for purely political reasons, the goddess foists on the youthful pair by means of an imaginative oversight; suddenly aflame, they must confess they belong only to each other. No end, now, to the yearning, the desire, the bliss, the suffering of love: world, power, fame, splendor, honor, knighthood, loyalty, friendship—all scattered like an empty dream; one thing alone still living: yearning, yearning, unquenchable, ever-regenerated longing—languishing, thirsting; the only redemption—death, extinction, eternal sleep!

The musician who chose this theme as introduction to his love drama, feeling himself in the presence of the essential, boundless element of music, could have only one concern: how to limit himself, since the theme is inexhaustible. And so he let the insatiable longing well up one time only, but in a long-drawn-out progression, from timid avowal, gentlest attraction, through hesitant sighs, hopes and fears, laments and wishes, joys and torments, up to the mightiest compulsion, the most powerful effort to discover a breach, opening for the heart the way to the sea of endless rapturous love. In vain! Its power spent, the heart sinks back to pine of its desire—unfulfilled desire, since

***Tristan und Isolde:* The End of Act I.** "The curtains are thrown wide apart; the whole ship is crowded with knights and sailors who joyfully wave signals to the shore, which is now seen close at hand, crowned with a castle. Tristan and Isolde remain lost in contemplation of each other, without noticing what is going on about them." Contemporary illustration, on the occasion of the first performance. (*Illustrirte Zeitung,* Vol. XLV [1865].)

fulfillment only sows the seed of fresh desire; till to the faltering eye, in utmost exhaustion, there dawns a glimmer of the most rapturous fulfillment: it is the rapture of dying, of being no more, of ultimate release into that wondrous realm from which we stray the furthest when we strive to penetrate it by the most impetuous force. Shall we call it death? Or is it not night's wonder-world, out of which, as the saga tells us, an ivy and a vine sprang up in locked embrace over Tristan's and Isolde's grave?

Richard Wagner, *Nachgelassene Schriften und Dichtungen* (Leipzig, 1895), 163–64. Trans. P. W.

112

Wagner's Beethoven

Practically every nineteenth-century composer, of whatever aesthetic persuasion, saw Beethoven as his spiritual as well as musical preceptor, and the Ninth Symphony, in particular, cast a long shadow over the music of the entire century. Specific musical resonances from the Ninth crop up time and again in symphonies by Schubert, Brahms, Franck, Bruckner, Mahler, and many others. But the work's significance was profounder yet, fundamentally affecting the most basic aesthetic tenets of many of the century's greatest musicians. Most conspicuous among them was Wagner. In this famous passage from his tract *The Art Work of the Future* (*Das Kunstwerk der Zukunft* [1849]), Wagner practically recreated Beethoven in his own image, casting the Master (as he always called him) in the role of forerunner to his own ideals of the union of all artistic media in a transcendent amalgam (the music drama). The Ninth Symphony, for Wagner, was an irrevocable step along that path. It sounded the death knell of "pure music," and finished off the symphony as a viable independent genre. Along the way, Wagner offers memorable characterizations of the symphonies, beginning with the Fifth, in which Beethoven led up to his momentous break with the past. His description of the Seventh as the "Apotheosis of Dance," in particular, has "stuck." Of course, not everyone shared Wagner's radical view of Beethoven's achievement. It was in fact famously controversial (see Hanslick on Brahms, p. 343). Nor has Wagner's prose won him many friends. Heavily indebted to the style of the German Idealist philosophers (mainly Hegel and Schopenhauer) who provided him with his ideological base, it is convoluted, inflated, occasionally stilted and archaic. But it is nonetheless at the same time impassioned and apocalyptic, and strives for an effect similar to the one Wagner sought to make in his music, too.

What inimitable art did Beethoven employ in his "C-minor Symphony," in order to steer his ship from the ocean of infinite yearning to the haven of fulfillment! He was able to raise the utterance of his music *almost* to a moral resolve, but not to speak aloud that final word; and after every onset of the will, without a moral handhold, we feel tormented by the equal possibility of falling back again to suffering, as of being led to lasting victory. Nay, this falling-back must almost seem to us more "necessary" than the morally ungrounded triumph, which therefore—not being a necessary consummation, but a mere arbitrary gift of grace—has not the power to lift us up and yield to us that "ethical" satisfaction which we demand as outcome of the yearning of the heart.

Who felt more uncontented with this victory than Beethoven himself? Was he lief to win a second of the sort? 'Twas well enough for the brainless herd of imitators, who from glorious "major"-jubilation, after vanquished "minor"-tribulation, prepared themselves unceasing triumphs—but not for the Master, who was called to write upon his works the *world history of music*.

With reverent awe, he shunned to cast himself afresh into that sea of boundless and insatiate yearning. He turned his steps toward the blithesome, life-glad men he spied encamped on breezy meads, along the outskirt of some fragrant wood beneath the sunny heaven; kissing, dancing, frolicking. There in shadow of the trees, amid the rustling of the leaves, beside the tender gossip of the brook, he made a happy pact with Nature; there he felt that he was man, felt all his yearning thrust back deep into his breast before the sovereignty of sweet and blissful *manifestation*. So thankful was he toward this manifestation that, faithfully and in frank humility, he superscribed the separate portions of the tone work, which he built from this idyllic mood [that is, the Sixth Symphony], with the names of those life pictures whose contemplation had aroused it in him: "Reminiscences of Country Life" he called the whole.

But in very deed they were only "Reminiscences"—pictures, and not the direct and physical actuality. Toward this actuality he was impelled with all the force of the artist's inexpungable yearning. To give his tone shapes that same compactness, that directly cognizable and physically sure stability, which he had witnessed with such blessed solace in Nature's own phenomena—this was the soul of the joyous impulse which created for us that glorious work the "Symphony in A major" [i.e., the Seventh]. All tumult, all yearning and storming of the heart become here the blissful insolence of joy, which snatches us away with bacchanalian might and bears us through the roomy space of Nature, through all the streams and seas of life, shouting in glad self-consciousness as we tread throughout the universe the daring measures of this human sphere-dance. This symphony is the *Apotheosis of Dance* herself: it is Dance in her highest aspect, as it were the loftiest deed of bodily motion incorporated in an ideal mold of tone. Melody and Harmony unite around the sturdy bones of Rhythm to firm and fleshy human shapes, which now with giant limbs' agility, and now with soft, elastic pliance, *almost before our very eyes,* close up the supple, teeming ranks; the while now gently, now with daring, now serious, now wanton, now pensive, and again exulting, the deathless strain sounds forth and forth; until, in the last whirl of delight, a kiss of triumph seals the last embrace.

And yet these happy dancers were merely shadowed forth in tones, mere sounds that imitated men! Like a second Prometheus who fashioned men of clay (*Thon*), Beethoven had sought to fashion them in sound (*Ton*). Yet not from *Thon* or *Ton*, but from both substances together, must man, the image of life-giving Zeus, be made. Were Prometheus's moldings only offered to the *eye*, so were those of Beethoven *only* offered to the *ear*. But only *where eye and ear confirm each other's sentience of him, is the whole artistic man at hand.*

But where could Beethoven find *those* men, to whom to stretch out hands across the element of his music? Those men with hearts so broad that he could pour into them the mighty torrent of his harmonic tones? With frames so stoutly fair that his melodic rhythms should *bear* them and not *crush* them?—Alas, from nowhere came to him the brotherly Prometheus who could show to him these men! He needs must gird his loins about, and start *to find out for himself the country of the manhood of the future.*

From the shore of dance he cast himself once more upon that endless sea, from which he had erstwhile found a refuge on this shore; the sea of unallayable heart-yearning. But 'twas in a stoutly built and giant-bolted ship that he embarked upon the stormy voyage; with firm-clenched fist he grasped the mighty helm: he *knew* the journey's goal, and was determined to attain it. No imaginary triumphs would he prepare himself, nor after boldly overcome privations tack back once more to the lazy haven of his home; for he desired to measure out the ocean's bounds, and find the land which needs must lie beyond the waste of waters.

Thus did the Master urge his course through unheard-of possibilities of absolute tone-speech—not by fleetly slipping past them, but by speaking out their utmost syllable from the deepest chambers of his heart—forward to where the mariner begins to sound the sea depth with his plumb; where, above the broadly stretched-forth shingles of the new continent, he touches on the heightening crests of solid ground; where he has now to decide him whether he shall face about toward the bottomless ocean, or cast his anchor on the new-found shore. But it was no madcap love of sea adventure, that had spurred the Master to so far a journey; with might and main he willed to land on this new world, for *it* alone had he set sail. Staunchly he threw his anchor out; and this anchor was *the word*. Yet this word was not that arbitrary and senseless cud which the modish singer chews from side to side, as the gristle of his vocal tone; but the necessary, all-powerful, and all-uniting word into which the full torrent of the heart's emotions may pour its stream; the steadfast haven for the restless wanderer; the light that lightens up the night of endless yearning: the word that the redeemed world-man cries out aloud from the fullness of the world-heart. This was the word which Beethoven set as crown upon the forehead of his tone creation; and this word was—*"Freude!"* (Rejoice!) With this word he cries to men: *"Breast to breast, ye mortal millions! This one kiss to all the world!"*—And *this word* will be the language of the *artwork of the future*.

The last symphony of Beethoven is the redemption of Music from out her own peculiar element into the realm of *universal art*. It is the human evangel of the art of the future. Beyond it no forward step is possible; for upon it the perfect artwork of the future alone can follow, the *universal drama* to which Beethoven has forged for us the key.

Richard Wagner's Prose Works, trans. William Ashton Ellis, I (London, 1895), 123–26.

113

The "Music of the Future" Controversy

"Music of the future," "musicians of the future" were derisory epithets applied by one of the contending sides against the other in the lengthy, confused debate that raged in German musical circles through most of the latter part of the nineteenth century. The assumption by Liszt, Wagner, and their adherents that theirs was the only true way, that the mantle of Beethoven had fallen on their shoulders, and so forth, understandably provoked considerable indignation on the part of those who were not prepared to become converts to the new religion. The harnessing of music to specific ideas outside itself was the main bone of contention on the ideological front; though it is safe to assume that there would have been no debate if the ideas to which music was harnessed by the "musicians of the future" had been less provocative and if the music itself had been conventional, which it decidedly was not. Berlioz's *Symphonie Fantastique* (see p. 300) is a case in point. Adverse reaction to its program was immediate, and extended even to some who, like Schumann, were farsighted enough to appreciate the music. After summarizing Berlioz's program in an otherwise laudatory notice in the *Neue Zeitschrift für Musik* in 1835, Schumann wrote:

Thus the program. All Germany is happy to let him keep it: such signposts always have something unworthy and charlatan-like about them! In any event the five titles would have been enough; word of mouth would have served to hand down the more circumstantial account, which would certainly arouse interest because of the personality of the composer who lived through the events of the symphony himself. In a word, the German, with his delicacy of feeling and his aversion to personal revelation, dislikes having his thoughts so rudely directed; he was already offended that Beethoven should not trust him to divine the sense of the *Pastoral Symphony* without assistance. Men experience a certain timidity before the genius's workshop: they prefer to know nothing about the origins, tools, and secrets of creation, just as Nature herself reveals a certain sensitivity when she covers over her roots with earth. So let the artist lock himself up with his woes; we should experience too many horrors if we could witness the birth of every work of art!

But Berlioz was writing primarily for his French compatriots, who are not greatly impressed by refinements of modesty. I can imagine them, leaflet in hand, reading and applauding their countryman who has depicted it all so well; the music by itself does not interest them.

Whether a listener unfamiliar with the composer's intent would find that the music suggested pictures similar to those he wished to draw, I cannot tell, since I read the program before hearing the music. Once the eye has been led to a given point, the ear no longer judges independently. But if you ask whether music can really do what Berlioz demands of it in his symphony, then try to associate with it different contrasting images.

At first the program spoiled my own enjoyment, my freedom of imagination. But as it receded more and more into the background and my own fancy began to work, I found not only that it was all indeed there, but what is more, that it was almost always embodied in warm, living sound.

Hector Berlioz, *Fantastic Symphony,* ed. Edward T. Cone (New York: W. W. Norton & Co., Inc., 1971), 246–47.

And it comes as no surprise that Mendelssohn, one of the least avant-garde composers of the period (though considered modern enough by many of his contemporaries), should have expressed himself even more fully on the subject in a letter of 1842. Answering a Frenchman who had asked him what some of his famous "Songs Without Words" for piano were about, he wrote:

People talk so much about music, and say so little. I believe anyway that words are not up to the task; and if I ever found out they were, I should end by writing no more music.—People usually complain that music is so ambiguous; that what they are supposed to imagine when they listen to it is so open to question, while everybody understands words. With me it is just the other way around. And not only with regard to whole speeches, but even to single words—they, too, strike me as so ambiguous, so indefinite, so open to misunderstanding, compared to a good piece of music that fills one's soul with a thousand better things than words. What a piece of music that I love tells me are thoughts not too *indefinite,* but too *definite* to be put into words. And so, in all attempts to express those thoughts I find something right, but also in all of them, including yours, something unsatisfactory. But that is not your fault, it is the fault of words, which cannot do better. If you ask me what I was thinking of when I composed it, my answer is: the song exactly as it stands. And if I did have a particular word or particular words in mind, I would not breathe them to anyone, because a word does not mean to one person what it means to the other, because only the song says the same thing to one, awakens the same feeling in him, as in the other—a feeling that cannot be expressed by the same words.

Will you allow this to stand as the answer to your question? It is the only one, at least, that I can give, even though these are nothing but ambiguous words.

Felix Mendelssohn Bartholdy, *Briefe aus den Jahren 1830 bis 1847*, ed. Paul and Carl Mendelssohn Bartholdy, 7th ed. (Leipzig: Hermann Mendelssohn, 1899), Part 2, 229–30. Trans. P. W.

> In 1848 Liszt entered the field of orchestral composition with a long series of programmatic "tone poems" and two full-length program symphonies. Wagner, meanwhile, was outlining the "artwork of the future" in which music would cease to have an independent existence and merge, instead, with drama and the other arts. It seemed to many that the integrity of music was being endangered by Liszt, Wagner, and their militant supporters. Eduard Hanslick (see p. 343), an influential newspaper critic in Vienna and later a friend and staunch supporter of Brahms, published a much-discussed booklet, *On the Beautiful in Music* (1854), which became the breviary of the opposition party. Defining the content of music as "sound-enlivened forms," Hanslick denied it the power of expression; insofar as it attempts to transcend its limits, he argued, it ceases to be music. Thus the battle lines were drawn—between "program music" and "absolute music," between the "music drama" and the opera. On the emotional level, the opposition regarded the "musicians of the future" as artistically indecent, while the latter regarded their opponents as, at best, desiccated academics. Very little of permanent value can be expected from writings engendered in such heated circumstances. We might note, however, that the use of programs did enable musicians like Wagner and Liszt to expand significantly the time scale of their music by synchronizing their compositions to the unfolding of a drama or a narrative. Something of the sort is expressed by Liszt (or perhaps the Princess Wittgenstein, who did much of his writing for him) in an otherwise impossibly wordy article on Berlioz's programmatic symphony *Harold in Italy*.

The purely musical composer, who only values and emphasizes the formal working-out of his material, does not have the capacity to derive new formulations from it or to breathe new vigor into it. For he is not impelled by a spiritual necessity to discover new means, he is not driven and compelled by a glowing passion that demands to break out into the light of day! It is for this reason, too, that those who make use of form solely as a *means of expression*, as a *language* which they shape according to the requirements of ideas to be expressed are peculiarly qualified to enrich it, enlarge it, and make it pliant. The formalists, on the other hand, can do nothing better or cleverer than to adopt, propagate, rearrange, and perhaps work over the others' hard-won achievements.

The program's function is merely to indicate in a preparatory way the states of mind that impelled the composer to create his work, the thoughts he tried to embody in it. It is childishly useless, indeed for the most part quite wrong, to draw up programs after the event and to presume to *explain* the emotional content of an instrumental poem, for in this case words can only destroy the magic, profane the emotions, tear up the gossamer spiritual webs that took on this form, and not another. But then again, a master is the master of his own work and may well have created it under the influence of specific impressions, which he may then wish to bring to the listener's full awareness.

All in all, the pure symphonist takes his listeners with him into ideal regions, which he leaves to one's own imagination to penetrate and adorn. In such cases it is very dangerous for us to regale our neighbor with the scenes and trains of thought to which our imagination draws us. Let, rather, each person silently rejoice in revelations and visions that have no names, no designation. But the poet-symphonist, who takes it upon himself to convey clearly an image distinctly perceived in his own mind, a succession of feelings unambiguously and definitely present in his consciousness— why, pray, should he not strive to be fully understood by the aid of a program?!

In so-called Classical music, the recurrence and thematic development of themes are determined by formal rules that are looked upon as irrevocable, even though its composers never had other guidelines than their own imagination and themselves hit upon those formal patterns which are now propounded as law. In program music, on the other hand, the recurrence, alternation, transformation, and modulation of motifs are determined by their relationship to a poetic conception. Here one theme does not elicit another in accordance with formal requirements, here the motifs are not a result of stereotyped juxtapositions or contrasts of timbres, and the coloring as such does not determine the grouping of ideas. All exclusively musical considerations, though by no means ignored, are subordinated to the incidents of the given subject. Accordingly, the incidents and subject of this symphonic genre require an interest that transcends the technical treatment of the musical material, and indeterminate spiritual impressions are elevated to specific impressions by means of an explicit outline, which the ear apprehends much as the eye takes in a cycle of paintings. The artist who favors this type of artwork enjoys the advantage of being able to link all the affections (which the orchestra can express so powerfully) to a poetic model.

L. Ramann (ed.), *Gesammelte Schriften von Franz Liszt*, IV (Leipzig, 1882), 49–50, 69, Trans. P. W.

Schumann's periodical, the *Neue Zeitschrift für Musik*, had now passed into the hands of a partisan of the "musicians of the future," Franz Brendel, who played a consider-able role in tidying up his faction's battle formation. He organized a grand convention of musicians at Leipzig on June 1–4, 1859, to celebrate the twenty-fifth anniversary of the periodical's founding; from this gathering (at which Liszt and his retinue of supporters figured prominently) evolved the German Musical Society (Allgemeiner Deutscher Musikverein), which for many years furthered the interests of the "music of the future." Interestingly enough, in his inaugural address to that convention, Brendel attempted to dispose of the unwelcome epithet once and for all:

In this connection, an apparently inconsequential matter, the term "Music of the Future," becomes important. To be sure, the term is fairly neutral in itself; but it gains in importance in that it is made a *party slogan. I would, therefore, propose and move that this name be dropped.* You are aware that the term is in itself nonsensical— indeed, I have dealt with the subject in our periodical. Wagner called the union of the arts the "Artwork of the Future." By this he means a fusion of the arts, in which each art gives up a part of its independence in order to be dissolved into a greater whole. Each single art, consequently, ceases to be independent in this sense. But those who speak of "Music of the Future" make a specialty, music, independent again, contradicting the underlying concept—in other words, effecting the opposite of what was intended.

But this is only the first half of my motion. The other part is, to set up a new name for the one we have dropped.

I therefore take the liberty of suggesting a new name, while begging you to examine it and, should it meet with your approval, adopt it. The name I propose is: *Neo-German School,* or *New German School.* Perhaps you will be surprised by such a name, since it must be understood to include two non-German masters [i.e., Berlioz and Liszt]. Yet permit me a few remarks in order to dispel any bewilderment. There is no need to waste words over the aptness of the name I propose in the case of one member of the triumvirate that represents the Music of the Future—R. Wagner. It was he, after all, who, on the traces of Beethoven, Weber, and some few others, for the first time realized most splendidly the ideal of a purely German opera, as against the Italian-French-German trend represented by Gluck, Mozart, and others. The matter becomes more complex if we are to include the two foreign masters under this denomination. To be sure, it is common knowledge that they, too, took Beethoven as their point of departure and so are German as to their origins. [Berlioz, though thus adopted, maintained his lonely independence; indeed in 1860 he published his position on the "music of the future": "non credo"!]

The birthplace cannot be considered decisive in matters of the spirit. The two artists would never have become what they are today had they not from the first drawn nourishment from the German spirit and grown strong with it. Therefore, too, Germany must of necessity be the true homeland of their works, and it is in this sense that I suggested the denomination *Neo-German School* for the entire post-Beethoven development. We thus gain both in clarity as to grouping and in simplicity and meaningfulness as to the name. Protestant church music up to and including Bach and Handel has long been known as the Old German School. The Italian-influenced epoch of the Viennese masters is the period of Classicism, of the equal supremacy of idealism and realism. Beethoven once more clasps hands with the specifically Germanic North and inaugurates the Neo-German School.

Neue Zeitschrift für Musik, L (1859), 271–72. Trans. P. W.

> Drivel of this sort was to Brahms as a red rag is to a bull. He despised the publicists of the Lisztian party, and the terms he used in describing Liszt's music (in private correspondence) are, shall we say, blunt and unequivocal. For the first and only time in his life he entered the world of public debate, instigating a solemn declaration that he and his friend Joseph Joachim, the great violinist, circulated privately in an attempt to gather an impressive number of signatures among musicians opposed to Liszt and Brendel. Unfortunately, someone slipped the text to a Berlin newspaper before it was ready for publication, with the result that it appeared over the signatures of only Brahms, Joachim, and two others, who were promptly made the objects of ridicule by their opponents. After this, Brahms again confined his remarks to private conversation and correspondence. Here is the text of the unfortunate declaration, and with this we take leave of the great debate:

The undersigned have for long past followed with regret the activities of a certain party whose organ is Brendel's *Zeitschrift für Musik.*

The said periodical constantly disseminates the opinion that seriously striving musicians are fundamentally in accord with the tendencies it champions and recognize the compositions of the leaders of this movement as works of artistic value; and that, in general, and especially in North Germany, the controversy for and against the so-called "Music of the Future" has already been fought out, and settled in its favor.

The undersigned consider it their duty to protest against such a distortion of the facts, and declare that, so far as they themselves are concerned, they do not recognize the principles which find expression in Brendel's *Zeitschrift*, and can only deplore or condemn as contrary to the most fundamental essence of music the productions of the leaders and disciples of the so-called "Neo-German" School, some of whom put these principles into practice, while others keep trying to impose the establishment of more and more novel and preposterous theories.

JOHANNES BRAHMS. JOSEPH JOACHIM. JULIUS OTTO GRIMM.
BERNHARD SCHOLZ.

Walter Niemann, *Brahms,* trans. C. A. Phillips (New York: Tudor Publishing Co., 1929), 77–78.

114

P. T. Barnum Brings the Swedish Nightingale to America

Jenny Lind (1820–87), the great Swedish soprano, was famous not only for her lovely voice but for her sincere artistry and personality, which won her the friendship and respect of such composers as Mendelssohn and Schumann. Phineas T. Barnum (1810–91), founder of "The Greatest Show on Earth" and promoter extraordinary, was a genius in his own right. His management of Jenny Lind's American tour in 1850–51, while comical in many ways (and Berlioz satirized it mercilessly in his *Evenings with the Orchestra*), is nevertheless significant historically, because it points dramatically to the new, audience-oriented economics of music in which the star performer, rather than the composer, reaps the greatest rewards. The extract is taken from Barnum's autobiography.

It was in October 1849, that I conceived the idea of bringing Jenny Lind to this country. I had never heard her sing, inasmuch as she arrived in London a few weeks after I left that city with General Tom Thumb [the famous dwarf]. Her reputation, however, was sufficient for me.

Reflecting that very much would depend upon the manner in which she should be brought before the public, I saw that my task would be an exceedingly arduous one. "The public" is a very strange animal, and although a good knowledge of human nature will generally lead a caterer of amusements to hit the people, they are fickle, and ofttimes perverse. But I had marked the "divine Jenny" as a sure card.

I was at my Museum in Philadelphia when [my agent telegraphed] that he had signed an engagement with Jenny Lind, by which she was to commence her concerts in America in the following September.

The next morning I started for New York. On arriving at Princeton we met the New York cars, and purchasing the morning papers, I was surprised to find in them a full account of my engagement with Jenny Lind. Anxious to learn how this communication would strike the public mind, I informed the conductor, whom I well knew, that I had made an engagement with Jenny Lind, and that she would surely visit this country in the following August.

"Jenny Lind! Is she a dancer?" asked the conductor.

I informed him who and what she was, but his question chilled me as if his words were ice. Really, thought I, if this is all that a man in the capacity of a railroad conductor between Philadelphia and New York knows of the greatest songstress in the world, I am not sure that six months will be too long a time for me to occupy in enlightening the public in regard to her merits.

I then began to prepare the public mind, through the newspapers, for the reception of the great songstress. How effectually this was done, is still within the remembrance of the American public.

A few minutes before twelve o'clock, on Sunday morning [1 September 1850], the [steamship] Atlantic hove in sight.

Thousands of persons covered the shipping and piers [of New York harbor], and other thousands had congregated on the wharf at Canal Street, to see her. The wildest enthusiasm prevailed as the steamer approached the dock. So great was the rush on a sloop near the steamer's berth, that one man, in his zeal to obtain a good view, accidentally tumbled overboard, amid the shouts of those near him. Miss Lind witnessed this incident, and was much alarmed. He was, however, soon rescued, after taking to himself a cold duck instead of securing a view of the Nightingale. A bower of green trees, decorated with beautiful flags, was discovered on the wharf, together with two triumphal arches, on one of which was inscribed, "Welcome, Jenny Lind!" The second was surmounted by the American eagle, and bore the inscription, "Welcome to America!" These decorations were not produced by magic, and I do not know that I can reasonably find fault with those who suspected I had a hand in their erection. My private carriage was in waiting, and Jenny Lind was escorted to it by Captain West. The rest of the musical party entered the carriage, and mounting the box at the driver's side, I directed him to the Irving House. I took that seat as a legitimate advertisement, and my presence on the outside of the carriage aided those who filled the windows and sidewalks along the whole route, in coming to the conclusion that Jenny Lind had arrived.

A reference to the journals of that day will show, that never before had there been such enthusiasm in the City of New York, or indeed in America. Within ten minutes after our arrival at the Irving House, not less than twenty thousand persons had congregated around the entrance in Broadway, nor was the number diminished before nine o'clock in the evening.

At twelve o'clock that night, she was serenaded by the New York Musical Fund Society, numbering, on that occasion, two hundred musicians. They were escorted to the Irving House by about three hundred firemen, in their red shirts, bearing torches. There was a far greater throng in the streets than there was even during the day. The calls for Jenny Lind were so vehement that I led her through a window to the balcony. The loud cheers from the crowds lasted for several minutes, before the serenade was permitted to proceed again.

I have given the merest sketch of but a portion of the incidents of Jenny Lind's first day in America. For weeks afterwards the excitement was unabated. Songs, quadrilles and polkas were dedicated to her, and poets sung in her praise. We had Jenny Lind gloves, Jenny Lind bonnets, Jenny Lind riding hats, Jenny Lind shawls, mantillas, robes, chairs, sofas, pianos—in fact, every thing was Jenny Lind. Her movements were constantly watched, and the moment her carriage appeared at the door, it was surrounded by multitudes, eager to catch a glimpse of the Swedish Nightingale.

My arrangements of the concert room were very complete. In order to prevent confusion, the doors [of Castle Garden] were opened at five o'clock, while the concert did not commence until eight. The consequence was, that although about five thousand persons were present at the first concert, their entrance was marked with as much order and quiet as was ever witnessed in the assembling of a congregation at church.

The reception of Jenny Lind on her first appearance, in point of enthusiasm, was probably never before equalled in the world. As Mr. [Julius] Benedict [the composer and conductor] led her towards the foot-lights, the entire audience rose to their feet and welcomed her with three cheers, accompanied by the waving of thousands of hats and handkerchiefs. This was by far the largest audience to which Jenny Lind had ever sung. She was evidently much agitated, but the orchestra commenced, and before she had sung a dozen notes of "Casta Diva" [from Bellini's opera *Norma*], she began to recover her self-possession, and long before the *scena* was concluded, she was as calm as if she was in her own drawing-room. Towards the last portion of the *cavatina*, the audience were so completely carried away by their feelings, that the remainder of the air was drowned in a perfect tempest of acclamation. Enthusiasm had been wrought to its highest pitch, but the musical powers of Jenny Lind exceeded all the brilliant anticipations which had been formed, and her triumph was complete. At the conclusion of the concert Jenny Lind was loudly called for, and was obliged to appear three times before the audience could be satisfied. They then called vociferously for "Barnum," and I reluctantly [!] responded to their demand.

P. T. Barnum, *Struggles and Triumphs; or, Forty Years' Recollections* (Buffalo, 1873), 271–99, *passim*.

115

Smetana and the Czech National Style

Bedřich Smetana, the composer of the symphonic cycle *My Country*, the folk opera *The Bartered Bride*, and many other works that incorporate the spirit of Czech folk music, arrived only gradually at a consciousness of his Czech identity and mission. If one is to believe the following reminiscence, recorded by V. J. Novotný (a composer and writer), the decisive moment occurred during a visit of Smetana to Liszt in 1857.

I can see him now, eyes flashing as he told us how the idea of creating an independent Czech musical style began to mature in him for the first time.

It was in Weimar. The celebrated master Liszt had come to know Smetana from twelve character pieces for the piano which had then appeared in Leipzig. He conceived a great liking for our modest artist and invited him to come to Weimar, where he [Liszt] lived like a King of Music amid a select circle of artists from all parts of the world. Naturally, in such a heterogeneous circle of musical brains much wrangling went on about the most varied questions, directly or indirectly connected with art.

One of these musical disputes was to have a decisive influence on Smetana's entire further musical creation.

In the Weimar music circle of that time there was, apart from Smetana, the well-known Viennese composer Herbeck, who was a confirmed enemy of everything Czech. They fell to discussing what various nations had done in the great sphere of music, and Herbeck began, pointedly and maliciously, to attack the honor of the Czech nation. "What have you achieved up to now," he scoffed, turning to Smetana. "All that Bohemia can bring forth is fiddlers, mere performing musicians who can brag only of their perfection in craftsmanship, in the purely mechanical side of music, whereas on the real artist's path of truth and beauty your creative strength dwindles; indeed hitherto you have not done anything for the development and progress of musical art, for you have not a single composition to show which is so purely Czech as to adorn and enrich European music literature by virtue of its characteristic originality."

These words seared Smetana's soul like a shaft of lightning, for in this accusation directed against our musical art at the beginning of our century there was, unhappily, more than a grain of truth. It is generally known that our country has always supplied all military bands and theater orchestras with musicians, who as mere musicians had always occupied a menial position in relation to those creative spirits whose compositions they performed. They greatly predominated over the small number of composers endowed with the creative spirit who, born in the Czech lands, strayed abroad and there, as time went on, became absolutely estranged from the Czech spirit; as mere followers of outstanding masters of differing schools, they could not, of course, contribute to new developments in music, nor to any reform in a Czech sense—indeed they did not wish to, since at that time their national awareness had not yet been awakened. Music was still cosmopolitan. The classics and, after them, the romantics held unlimited sway over all educated nations. Modern musical art has shaken off this colorless cosmopolitanism and has raised national music to new heights by reaching out for elements characteristic in national music.

All this Smetana knew very well. He felt the burning truth of much of what his opponent said; it was very difficult to answer this. Smetana pointed to the older composers of Czech origin, above all Mysliveček.

"What sort of Czech was he," laughed Herbeck; "under the name of Venatorini he wrote operas in typical Italian style to Italian words!"

"And what about Tomášek," Smetana rallied. "Surely we all know," Herbeck retaliated, "that he imitated Mozart, a German master—in everything, down to the smallest detail."

Nothing was left to Smetana but to fall back on the outstanding musical talent of the Czech people which was the first to recognize and celebrate the epoch-making work of that great master, Mozart.

"Yes, yes, Smetana is right. Mozart wrote *Don Giovanni* for his beloved Prague," came the cry from other artists in the company. This so roused the choleric Herbeck that he shouted: "Bah, Prague has gnawed that old Mozart bone long enough!"

Smetana shot up as though stung by a snake, righteous anger flashing in his eyes. At that moment, however, Liszt, who had followed the quarrel with a quiet smile, bent slightly forward, took a bundle of music from the table, and with the words: "Allow me, gentlemen, to play you the latest, purely Czech music," sat down at the piano. In his enchanting, brilliant style he played through the first book of Smetana's character pieces.

After he had played the compositions, Liszt took Smetana, who was moved to tears, by the hand and with the words "here is a composer with a genuine Czech heart, an artist by the grace of God," he took leave of the company. Herbeck sobered down and holding out his hand to Smetana asked his forgiveness.

It was already late when the artists separated in a strange mood. But on the way home, Smetana turned moist eyes to the starry heaven, raised his hand, and deeply moved swore in his heart the greatest oath: that he would dedicate his entire life to his nation, to the tireless service of his country's art. And he remained true to his oath even during the most trying periods of his life, to the last flickerings of his spirit, to the last breath.

František Bartoš (ed.), *Bedřich Smetana: Letters and Reminiscences,* trans. Daphne Rusbridge (Prague: Artia, 1955), 45–47. Reprinted by permission.

116

The "New Russian School"

One of the most vigorous statements on behalf of artistic nationalism in the late nineteenth century is the essay "Our Music," which, along with essays on literature, painting, and architecture, formed a part of the encyclopedic survey *Twenty-five Years of Russian Art* (1882) by Vladimir Vasilievich Stasov (1824–1906). The author, a librarian by vocation, has won an enduring place in the history of Russian letters as an untiring champion of and spokesman for native talent. More a publicist than a critic or historian, Stasov communicates a heady atmosphere of artistic ferment in his enthusiastic, opinionated, and outrageously partisan writings. It is his very partisanship, however, that makes him so valuable a witness. Through him we may truly see the "New Russian School" of composers through their own eyes. And in a curious way, perhaps the most revealing aspect of the introductory section of Stasov's essay, given below, is the almost comically one-sided view it presents of the West and of the German-dominated "traditions" that composers at the peripheries of Europe (many of whom, especially in Russia, were self-taught amateurs, at least at first) so resented and so urgently felt the need to resist. The seriously distorted portrayal of Beethoven as the originator of program music is typical of the way nineteenth-century musicians and writers tried to see in Beethoven the founding father of whatever they held dear (see, for example, the "Neo-Germans," p. 327).

What are the forces that have molded the specific features of the New Russian School? What factors are responsible for its unique outlook and its peculiar characteristics?

Such a force and factor, above all, was the absence of preconception and blind faith. Beginning with [Mikhail Ivanovich] Glinka [1804–57] the Russian school of composers has been distinguished by its complete independence of thought and skepticism towards musical creations of the past. Recognized authorities have never existed for it. Our musicians need to verify everything for themselves according to their own lights, and only then will they acknowledge greatness in a composer and significance in his works. Such independence of thought is only too rarely encountered even now among

European musicians, and was even more unusual fifty years ago. Only a few—Schumann, for example—dared apply an independent critical judgment to universally recognized and idolized celebrities; the majority of Western musicians blindly believe in all authorities and share all the tastes and prejudices of the crowd. The musicians of the New Russian School, on the other hand, are terribly "disrespectful." They will give credence to no tradition until they have themselves been persuaded of the value of that which they are supposed to esteem.

Further along this line, the best Russian musicians beginning with Glinka have never set much store by academic training and have never regarded it with the servility and the superstitious veneration with which it is regarded even now in many parts of Europe. It would be absurd to reject scientific knowledge in any field, music included. It is just that the musicians of the New Russian School, unfettered by the long chain of European scholastic traditions in the form of a historical legacy from past centuries, can look learning bravely in the eye. They respect it; they avail themselves of its benefits, but without excess and without genuflections. They reject all dry academicism and pedantry, reject the gymnastic exercises to which thousands in Europe attach so much importance, and do not believe it necessary to vegetate long years over ritualistic mysteries. This attitude toward the alleged "wisdom of the ages," so honored by music schools, has saved the Russian school from creating pedantic or routine works—there simply are none of this kind in the output of the New Russian School. And this is one of its major points of difference from older European schools.

Another important feature characterizes our new school: its striving for national character. This began with Glinka and has continued unabated up to the present. Such a striving cannot be found in any other European school. The historical and cultural conditions of other nations have been such that folk song—the expression of the spontaneous, unaffected musicality of the people—has long since all but vanished in most civilized countries. Who in the nineteenth century knows or hears French, German, Italian, or English folk songs? They of course once existed and were at one time in general use, but over them passed the leveling scythe of European culture, so inimical to all that is at the root of popular life, so that now it takes the efforts of musical archaeologists or inquisitive travelers to seek out the remnants of old folk songs in remote provincial corners. In our country it is an altogether different story. Folk songs fill the air everywhere to this day. Every peasant, every carpenter, every stonemason, janitor, and driver; every peasant woman, every washerwoman and cook, every nurse and wetnurse—they all bring folk songs from their native villages to St. Petersburg, to Moscow, or any other city, and you hear them the whole year round. They surround us everywhere, all the time. A working man or woman in Russia today, just as it was a thousand years ago, never does his or her work except while singing a whole series of songs. The Russian soldier goes into battle with a folk song on his lips. These songs are our birthright: we need no archaeologist's help to learn them and love them. And therefore every Russian born with a creative musical spirit is brought up from his first days in a profoundly national musical environment. And it so happens, moreover, that almost all the most significant Russian musicians (Glinka, Dargomyzhsky, Musorgsky, Balakirev, Rimsky-Korsakov) were born not in urban centers, but in the midst of Russia, in provincial towns or on their fathers' estates, and it was there that they spent their early youth. Others spent much of their youth in the provinces, in frequent and close contact with folk songs and folk singing. Their first and most profound musical impressions were national. If for a long time we had no art music of our own, it was strictly on account of the unfavorable conditions that existed in Russia in the eighteenth and nineteenth centuries, when all that was native was trampled in the mud. But no sooner had times changed a bit, no sooner had talk of native things arisen in life and in literature, no sooner had interest in them been rekindled, than talented individuals immediately appeared on the scene ready to create music in the idioms most congenial and most dear to them, that is, in Russian folk idioms. There can be no doubt that European composers (at least the strongest and most talented among them) would very likely have taken the same path as ours have taken since Glinka, but that path was no longer open to them. Clear proof of this is the eagerness with which they have seized upon other national idioms, even ones foreign to them, and even on the merest shreds of themes. Only recall, for example, how Beethoven tried on more than one occasion to use Russian folk songs as themes, or Franz Schubert used Slovak, or Liszt Hungarian. But, withal, they did not create Russian, Slovak, or Hungarian music. For music is more than just themes. In order to be national, to express the soul and spirit of a nation, music must partake of the very roots of the life of a people. And neither Beethoven, nor Schubert, nor Liszt partook in the slightest of national life but only selected a few precious gems that had been preserved by this or that people and mounted these beautiful, fresh, ever-young and sparkling creations in the kind of setting that was typical of European art music. They never immersed themselves in the world to which these elegant fragments belonged, and upon which they had come quite by accident. They merely played with them, admired their beauty, and displayed them in the brilliant light of their talent. To the lot of Russian composers fell a wholly different set of circumstances. They were not outsiders, they were "at home" in that world from which our folk melodies—and for that matter, all Slavic melodies—stem, and therefore they are equipped to deploy them with a free hand and to let them flourish full strength in their true coloring, form, and character.

Along with the national Russian element, there is another by which the New Russian School is distinguished. This is the Oriental element. Nowhere else in Europe does it play so conspicuous a role as it does among our musicians. For a long time now no truly talented European architect, sculptor, or painter has failed to attempt to reproduce the unique forms of the East. Only musicians up to now have lagged behind their creative counterparts in the other arts. The few attempts made by Mozart, Beethoven, Weber, and a few others who wrote pieces "alla turca," to create something in the Oriental vein, have testified to the interest their authors have had in the East, but also to their lack of success. Félicien David [1810–76, French composer] actually spent some time in the East and introduced a few genuine Oriental melodies into his symphonic ode *Le Désert,* even occasionally capturing a genuine Oriental flavor. But he was not very talented and produced nothing of lasting importance. It is a different matter with the musicians of the New Russian School. Some of them have actually seen the East (Glinka and Balakirev, who spent time in the Caucasus), while others, though they never went there, were surrounded all their lives with impressions of the Orient and therefore reproduced them distinctly and vividly. In this they have shared the general Russian attraction for all things Eastern. And this is hardly surprising, since so much that is Eastern has joined the mainstream of Russian life and lent it such a special, characteristic coloring. To see in this only a strange whim or caprice on the part of Russian composers (as our music critics have often done) is absurdly shortsighted.

Finally, one more feature strongly characterizes the musicians of the New Russian School, and that is their extreme inclination toward "program music." Glinka wrote to his friend [Nestor] Kukolnik [1809–68, poet and dramatist] from Paris in April, 1845, of his sudden intention of writing a few "Fantaisies pittoresques" for orchestra. This was the origin of his *Jota Aragonesa, Night in Madrid,* and a bit later, of *Kamarinskaya.* These works were not only excellent in themselves, but extremely significant in that they were the prototypes of program music in Russia. In writing them Glinka followed the general trend of the time, which had manifested itself first in Beethoven, then in Weber, Berlioz, and Mendelssohn, and later still in all the most significant recent composers—Liszt, Wagner, and the rest. Of course, the programmatic content in the works of these composers varies in definiteness. With some it takes a rather nebulous, embryonic form, while with others it is more concrete and sharply defined. But that it exists in the works of all of them there can be no doubt. What are most of Beethoven's overtures (*Leonora, Coriolanus, Egmont,* etc.), what are certain movements of his late quartets and many of his sonatas, what are all his symphonies (beginning with the third) if not "program music," on more or less easily guessed subjects? In some cases Beethoven himself has aided our understanding by means of inscriptions: *Sinfonia eroica, Pastoral* symphony, "Storm," "Song of Thanksgiving for his Recovery, in the Lydian Mode," and so on. In other cases he gave information about otherwise unmentioned programs in conversation with his companions: thus, for example, he referred to the opening theme of the first movement of his Fifth Symphony one day as "Fate knocking at the door." In still other cases one can easily guess the subject Beethoven took as his program: thus, in the finales of the Seventh and Eighth Symphonies the sounds of war are clearly heard [!], and in the Allegretto of the Seventh Symphony it is not hard to discern a procession. The overtures of Weber, Mendelssohn, and Berlioz are also "programmatic"—all of this music is far removed from the "absolute" music of bygone times. Glinka followed this path in his instrumental works. As he put it in the letter to Kukolnik cited above: "For my imagination to run freely I need a text or else positive data of some kind."

What Glinka began has been continued by his successors and adherents. Practically without exception Russian symphonic music is programmatic. One cannot help noticing that the inclination toward program music is much stronger with us than almost anywhere else in Europe.

V. V. Stasov, *Izbrannïye sochineniya* (Moscow: Iskusstvo, 1952), II, 523–29. Trans. R. T.

117

Musorgsky, a Musical Realist

Certainly the most original composer in the New Russian School was Modest Musorgsky (1839–81). And certainly, too, he was the most extreme and uncompromising in his artistic views, as an enthusiastic adherent of the "Realist" ideals that gained much currency among the progressive intellectuals of mid-nineteenth-century Russia and France. Firmly convinced that art must mirror the conditions of real life so as to enlighten and teach, Musorgsky cast himself rather self-consciously in the role of reformer of vocal music, and in his preoccupation with speech-derived recitative unwittingly repeated many of the ideas and pronouncements of the Renaissance humanists who attended the birth of opera (see p. 139). The stylistic characteristics of Realist art can be defined as including: "low" subjects, objectively treated; preoccupation with minute detail hand in hand with a casual attitude toward overall form; and the attempt to impart intimate emotions in a vivid manner. Musorgsky notably embodied these traits in his songs and in his historical operas *Boris Godunov* and *Khovanshchina*. And his writings—mostly letters not meant for publication and therefore somewhat uncouth in expression—are liberally sprinkled with the slogans and emblems of his musical beliefs, as in the sampling below.

To Ludmila Shestakova, 30 July 1868

I am keeping an eye out for characteristic peasant women and typical peasant men—they might come in handy. The Russian personality teems with so much that is fresh and untouched by art, oh so much! And so rich, so splendid ... A small fraction of what life has imparted to me I have embodied in musical images for those dear to me; I have communicated my thoughts to them. If God grants me life and strength, I shall communicate mightily. Here is what I would like: that my characters should speak on stage like living people, but at the same time, that the force and style of their intoning, supported by the orchestra (which provides a musical framework for their speech), should hit the mark, that is, that my music should be an artistic reproduction of human speech in all its subtlest shadings; that is, *the sounds of human speech,* as the outward manifestation of thoughts and feelings, should, without forcing or exaggeration, become *music*—truthful, accurate, *and yet* (read: which means) artistic, highly artistic. There you have the ideal towards which I am striving.

To Nikolai Rimsky-Korsakov, 30 July 1868

Whatever speech I hear, whoever is speaking (and most important, whatever is being said), in my mind the musical embodiment of that speech takes shape.

To Rimsky-Korsakov, 15 August 1868

And another thing about *symphonic development:* I tell you, our cold *kvass* soup is a horror to the Germans, and yet we eat it with pleasure. And their cold cherry soup is a horror to us, and yet it sends a German into ecstasy. In short, *symphonic development in the technical sense* is just like German philosophy—all worked out and systematized. And lately that philosophy has been overturned by the English psychologists. When a German thinks, he *reasons* his way to a *conclusion.* Our Russian brother, on the other hand, starts with the conclusion and then might amuse himself with reasoning. That's all I have to say to you about symphonic development. Just keep one thing in mind: the creative act carries within itself its own aesthetic laws. Their verification is inner criticism; their application is the artist's instinct. Without these there is no creative artist; if there is a creative artist, then these will be present, and the artist is a law unto himself. When an artist revises, it means he is dissatisfied. When he revises although satisfied, or worse, adds to what already satisfies, he is *germanizing,* chewing over what has been said. We are not cud-chewers, but omnivores.

To V. V. Stasov, 18 October 1872

The artistic depiction of beauty alone, in the material sense of the word, is coarse childishness, the babyhood of art. *The subtlest aspects of human nature* and of *humanity as a whole,* the persistent exploration of these uncharted regions and their conquest—that is the true mission of an artist. "To new shores!"—fearlessly, through storms and shallows and treacherous reefs, "to new shores!"

Autobiographical sketch, June 1880

By virtue of the nature of his compositions and his musical views, Musorgsky belongs to no existing musical school. The formula of his artistic *profession de foi:* art is a means of communication with people, not an end in itself. This guiding principle has determined all his creative activity. Proceeding from the conviction that human speech is governed by strictly musical laws, he looks upon the task of musical art as one of reproducing in musical tones not only qualities of feeling, but chiefly qualities of human speech. Acknowledging as law-givers in the realm of art only such artist–reformers as Palestrina, Bach, Gluck, Beethoven, Berlioz, and Liszt, he does not regard even their laws as immutable, but as subject to transformation and to progress, like everything else in man's spiritual world.

Modest Petrovich Musorgsky, *Literaturnoye naslediye,* I (Moscow: Muzïka, 1971), 100, 102, 106–07, 141, 270. Trans. R. T.

118

Chaikovsky on Inspiration and Self-Expression

The name of Pyotr Ilyich Chaikovsky (1840–93) is synonymous with late Romantic musical subjectivism. No nineteenth-century composer was more convinced, not only of the possibility, but of the necessity of intimate personal disclosure through music. He viewed his art as a kind of autobiography or confession, and gave this belief a famous expression in the letter below, which concerns his Fourth Symphony. It is addressed to the composer's patroness, Nadezhda Filaretovna von Meck, a wealthy widow who supported him for years and with whom he carried on a mammoth correspondence, but whom—according to her express stipulation—he never met face to face. As for the rather neurotically self-pitying "program" Chaikovsky describes as lying behind his symphony—reminiscent and undoubtedly influenced both by the program of the *Symphonie Fantastique* (see p. 300) and by Beethoven's Fifth as it was popularly viewed—one suspects that it was to some extent manufactured *ex post facto* to please his correspondent (which, however, is not to deny the essential sincerity of the letter as a whole). Particularly forced is the description of the third movement, a delightful orchestral showpiece of a scherzo. We should add that Chaikovsky held aloof from the New Russian School described by Stasov (see p. 333). The issue that divided them was not nationalism (contrary to popular opinion) but professionalism. Chaikovsky was a graduate of Russia's first conservatory of music, and did not share the fear of tradition and of the European mainstream that gripped many of his musical countrymen. (N.B. Since the letter was written in Italy, it carries two dates: the earlier one is that of the Julian calendar used in Russia until 1918, and the later one is that of the Gregorian calendar, by then in use throughout the rest of Europe and America.)

Florence, $\frac{1\ March}{17\ Feb.}$ 1878

Your letter today gave me such joy, my precious Nadezhda Filaretovna! What boundless joy that my symphony pleased you and that, listening, you experienced the same feelings that filled me when I wrote, and that my symphony has touched your heart.

You ask whether the symphony has a definite program. Usually when I am asked this question about a symphonic work I answer, "None at all!" And in truth, it is a hard question to answer. How shall I convey those vague sensations one goes through as one composes an instrumental work without a definite subject? It is a purely lyrical process. It is a musical cleansing of the soul, which boils over with an accumulation that naturally seeks its outlet in tones, just as a lyric poet will express himself in verse. The difference is only that music possesses an infinitely more powerful and more subtle language for expressing the myriad shifts and shades of our spiritual life. The kernel of a new work usually appears suddenly, in the most unexpected fashion. If the soil is fertile, that is if one is disposed to work, this kernel will sprout roots with irrepressible strength and speed, will break through the ground, will put forth branches, leaves, twigs, and, finally, blossoms. I cannot define the creative process except by this analogy. The whole difficulty lies in getting that kernel to appear and making sure that it lands amid favorable conditions. All the rest takes care of itself. It would be useless to try and put into words for you the boundless delight that seizes me when the main idea has come and when it begins to assume definite shape. You forget everything, you become a madman for all practical purposes, all your insides quiver and throb, you hardly have time to make your sketches, one idea chases the heels of the last ...

Sometimes in the midst of this magical process some shock from without awakens you from your somnambulistic state. Someone will call, your servant will come in, the clock will strike to remind you that you must go about your business. Interruptions like these are horrible, inexpressibly horrible. Sometimes inspiration takes off for some time. You have to go after it, sometimes to no avail. Very often a completely cold and calculating technical procedure must come to the rescue. Perhaps it is because of this that even in the works of the greatest masters you can find moments where the organic connection falters, where seams and patches are visible, artificially joined. But there is no escaping it. If that state of the artist's soul which is called *inspiration,* and which I have just tried to describe for you, were to continue without interruption, one wouldn't be able to get through a single day. The strings would all break, and the instrument would be shattered into smithereens! Only one thing is necessary: that the main idea and the general contours of all the individual parts must appear *without being sought,* but rather spontaneously, as a result of that supernatural, incomprehensible, and inexplicable force we call *inspiration.*

But I have strayed from answering your question. In our symphony *there is* a program (that is, the possibility of explaining in words what it seeks to express), and to you and you alone I can and wish to indicate the meaning both of the work as a whole, and of its individual parts. Of course, I can do this here only in general terms.

The Introduction is the *kernel* of the whole symphony, without question its main idea:

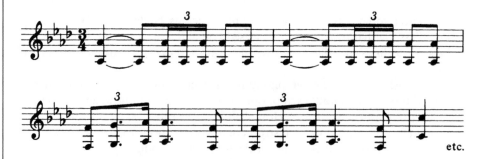

This is Fate, the force of destiny, which ever prevents our pursuit of happiness from reaching its goal, which jealously stands watch lest our peace and well-being be full and cloudless, which hangs like the sword of Damocles over our heads and constantly, ceaselessly poisons our souls. It is invincible, inescapable. One can only resign oneself and lament fruitlessly:

This disconsolate and despairing feeling grows ever stronger and more intense. Would it not be better to turn away from reality and immerse oneself in dreams?

O joy! A sweet, tender dream has appeared. A bright, beneficent human form flits by and beckons us on:

How wonderful! How distant now is the sound of the implacable first theme! Dreams little by little have taken over the soul. All that is dark and bleak is forgotten. There it is, there it is—happiness!

But no! These were only dreams, and *Fate* awakens us from them:

And thus, all life is the ceaseless alternation of bitter reality with evanescent visions and dreams of happiness ... There is no refuge. We are buffeted about by this sea until it seizes us and pulls us down to the bottom. There you have roughly the program of the first movement.

The second movement of the symphony expresses a different aspect of sorrow, that melancholy feeling that arises in the evening as you sit alone, worn out from your labors. You've picked up a book, but it has fallen from your hands. A whole procession of memories goes by. And we are sad that so much already is *over and gone,* and at the same time we remember our youth with pleasure. We regret the past, and yet we have no wish to start life anew. We are weary of life. How pleasant to relax and look back. Much comes to mind! There were blissful moments, when our young blood seethed and life was good. And there were bitter moments of irretrievable loss. But it is all so far off now. It is at once sad and somehow sweet to lose ourselves in the past ...

The third movement does not express definite feelings. These are, rather, capricious arabesques, fugitive images which pass through one's mind when one has had a little wine to drink and is feeling the first effects of intoxication. At heart one is neither merry nor sad. One's mind is a blank: the imagination has free rein and it has come up with these strange and inexplicable designs ... Among them all at once you recognize a tipsy peasant and a street song ... Then somewhere in the distance a military parade goes by. These are the completely unrelated images that pass through one's head as one is about to fall asleep. They have nothing in common with reality; they are strange, wild and incoherent ...

The fourth movement. If you can find no impulse for joy within yourself, look at others. Go out among the people. See how well they know how to rejoice and give themselves up utterly to glad feelings. It is a picture of a popular holiday festivity. [Here, in fact, Chaikovsky introduced a Russian folk song, "The Birch Tree."] But hardly have you succeeded in forgetting yourself and enjoying the spectacle of others' joys, when tireless *Fate* reappears and insinuates itself. But the others pay no heed. They do not even look around to see you standing there, lonely and depressed. Oh, how merry they are! And how fortunate, that all their feelings are direct and simple. Never say that all the world is sad. You have only yourself to blame. There are joys, strong though simple. Why not rejoice through the joys of others? One can live that way, after all.

And that, dear friend, is all I can tell you about the symphony. Of course it's neither a clear nor a complete explanation. But the nature of instrumental music is precisely this, that it resists detailed analysis. *Where words fail, music speaks,* as Heine put it.

Pyotr Ilyich Chaikovsky, *Polnoye sobraniye sochineniy: Literaturniye proizvedeniya i perepiska*, VII (Moscow: Gosudarstvennoye muzïkal'noye izdatel'stvo [Muzgiz], 1962) 124–27. Trans. R. T.

119

Brahms on Composing

The normally tight-lipped Brahms did, on one occasion, reveal to his young friend, the singer and conductor Georg Henschel, how he went about composing. Fortunately, Henschel kept a diary at the time, and he translated and published extracts from it, together with some letters.

Wiesbaden, February 27, 1876

Yesterday Brahms and I left Coblence [after appearing together at a concert there]. We were quite alone in our compartment, and I had the happiness of finding him, in regard to his own self and his way of working, more communicative than ever before. Commencing by speaking of the events of the past days, we soon drifted into talking about art in general and music in particular.

"There is no real *creating*," he said, "without hard work. That which you would call invention, that is to say, a thought, an idea, is simply an inspiration from above, for which I am not responsible, which is no merit of mine. Yea, it is a present, a gift, which I ought even to despise until I have made it my own by right of hard work. And there need be no hurry about that, either. It is as with the seed-corn; it germinates unconsciously and in spite of ourselves. When I, for instance, have found the first phrase of a song, say,

When the sil - ver - y moon. . . .*

*The beginning of the beautiful song "Die Mainacht," op. 43 [Henschel's note].

I might shut the book there and then, go for a walk, do some other work, and perhaps not think of it again for months. Nothing, however, is lost. If afterward I approach the subject again, it is sure to have taken shape; I can now begin to really work at it. But there are composers who sit at the piano with a poem before them, putting music to it from A to Z until it is done. They write themselves into a state of enthusiasm which makes them see something finished, something important, in every bar."

George Henschel, *Personal Recollections of Johannes Brahms* (Boston: Richard G. Badger, 1907), 22–23.

120

The "Brahmin" Point of View

For many, Brahms's chief significance was as upholder of a great tradition—that of German classical instrumental music—at a time when it, along with all classical traditions, was under attack by proponents of "Music of the Future" (see pp. 324–29). Eduard Hanslick's review of Brahms's First Symphony, first performed in Vienna on 17 December 1876, when the composer was forty-three years old, captures well the atmosphere of partisanship that surrounded the event. Hanslick (1825–1904), Vienna's very influential dean of critics for many years, was the first professor of music in the modern liberal-arts sense (he was appointed to Vienna University in 1856, becoming full professor in 1870). He had been notorious since 1854, when his aesthetic tract *On the Beautiful in Music* appeared in response to the writings of Wagner and Liszt. This was the first principled challenge to the late Romantic doctrines that music was to be valued for its emotional or symbolic content, and that the arts found their highest realization in merger. (Stung by Hanslick's polemics, Wagner retaliated by making him the thinly disguised prototype of the pedant Beckmesser in *Die Meistersinger,* who in the original draft of the libretto was named Hanslich.) The symphonies of Brahms were for Hanslick proof positive that absolute musical values could still thrive as before, and were his prime exhibit in opposing what he termed (in his review of the Third Symphony in 1878) the "nonsensical theory" that the symphony had "become superfluous since Wagner transplanted it into the opera." But Hanslick is no narrow formalist: he speaks of "Faustian conflicts" and Romantic nature imagery in his description of Brahms's First, and (along with countless others then and since) complains mildly of the supposed overelaboration of texture and learned contrapuntal artifice in Brahms's style. But his chief points—the continued validity and vitality of the great tradition, and the "ethical" value of pure instrumental music as established above all in the late works of Beethoven—are an excellent summation of Brahms's stature and significance in the eyes of his contemporaries. And in the composer's own eyes, we may confidently add, in view not only of his attitude toward the Neo-German school (see p. 328), but also in view of his famous near-quotation of the choral theme from Beethoven's Ninth Symphony in the finale of his First. Rather pointedly, that theme is brought back within the realm of instrumental music, as if to correct a wrong turn Beethoven had taken, with dire results in what it had suggested to his Romantic followers! (See Wagner, p. 322.)

Seldom, if ever, has the entire musical world awaited a composer's first symphony with such tense anticipation—testimony that the unusual was expected of Brahms in this supreme and ultimately difficult form. But the greater the public expectation and the more importunate the demand for a new symphony, the more deliberate and scrupulous was Brahms. Inexorable conscientiousness and stern self-criticism are among his most outstanding characteristics. He always demands the best of himself and dedicates his whole strength to its achievement. He cannot and will not take it easy.

He hesitated a long time over the composition of string quartets, and more than one symphony was consigned, as a study, to the oblivion of a desk drawer. To the urging of his friends he used to reply that he had too much respect for his forerunners, and that one cannot "fool around" these days with a symphony. This severity with himself, this care for detail, is evident in the admirable workmanship of the new symphony. The listener may, indeed, find it rather too evident. He may miss, in all the astonishing contrapuntal art, the immediate communicative effect. And he will not be wholly wrong. The new symphony is so earnest and complex, so utterly unconcerned with common effects, that it hardly lends itself to quick understanding. This circumstance, although not necessarily a fault, is a misfortune, at least for the first impression. Subsequent repetitions will make it good. The statement of [Franz] Grillparzer [1791–1872; Austrian poet and friend of Beethoven], "I strove for effect, not on the public but on myself," could stand as motto for Brahms's symphony.

Even the layman will immediately recognize it as one of the most individual and magnificent works of the symphonic literature. In the first movement, the listener is held by fervent emotional expression, by Faustian conflicts, and by a contrapuntal art as rich as it is severe. The Andante softens this mood with a long-drawn-out, noble song, which experiences surprising interruptions in the course of the movement. The Scherzo strikes me as inferior to the other movements. The theme is wanting in melodic and rhythmic charm, the whole in animation. The abrupt close is utterly inappropriate. The fourth movement begins most significantly with an Adagio in C minor; from darkening clouds the song of the woodland horn rises clear and sweet above the tremolo of the violins. All hearts tremble with the fiddles in anticipation. The entrance of the Allegro with its simple, beautiful theme, reminiscent of the "Ode to Joy" in the Ninth Symphony, is overpowering as it rises onward and upward, right to the end.

If I say that no composer has come so close to the style of the late Beethoven as Brahms in this finale, I don't mean it as a paradoxical pronouncement but rather as a simple statement of indisputable fact. It is high praise, but it does not necessarily attribute to a composer every virtue, least of all every virtue in the highest degree. One-sided greatness is bought at the expense of other virtues. Mozart would not have been Mozart, and Weber would not have been Weber, had they possessed, in addition to their own peculiar charm, the exaltation and the profundity of Beethoven. The latter, on the other hand, lacked the tender fragrance, the melodic enchantment, the delicate intimacy by which Schumann and Mendelssohn are so directly and simply charming— and they are almost conspicuously lacking in his greatest last works. In Schumann's little Symphony in D minor, and in Mendelssohn's "Italian" Symphony, there is a sweet enchantment, an intoxicating floral fragrance rarely—and then almost surreptitiously— in evidence in Brahms's symphony. But neither Mendelssohn nor Schumann approaches the late Beethoven. Beethoven's third period is not a prerequisite for their symphonies. Mendelssohn and Schumann incline rather to the point of view of Haydn's and Mozart's musical philosophy—and carry it further. Brahms's quartets and the symphony, on the other hand, could not have been were it not for Beethoven's last period.

This outlook is congenial to Brahms by nature, and he has made himself at home in it. He doesn't imitate, but what he creates from his innermost being is similarly felt. Thus, Brahms recalls Beethoven's symphonic style not only in his individually spiritual and suprasensual expression, the beautiful breadth of his melodies, the daring and originality of his modulations, and his sense of polyphonic structure, but also—and above all—in the manly and noble seriousness of the whole. It has been said of Beethoven's music that one of its chief characteristics is an ethical element that would rather convince than charm. This distinguishes it conspicuously from all "entertainment" music—which is not to say that the latter is artistically worthless. This strong ethical character of Beethoven's music, which is serious even in merriment, and betrays a soul dedicated to the eternal, is also decisively evident in Brahms. In the latter's newest works there is even a good deal of the late Beethoven's darker side. Beethoven's style, towards the end, was often unclear, confused, arbitrary, and his subjectivity frequently descended to mere querulous bad humor. The beautiful clarity, the melodic charm, the estimable popularity of his first and second periods vanished. One could reverse the Goethe motto and say: "What Beethoven wanted in his old age (or what one might have wished him) he had in abundance in his youth."

Brahms seems to favor too one-sidedly the great and the serious, the difficult and the complex, and at the expense of sensuous beauty. We would often give the finest contrapuntal device (and they lie bedded away in the symphony by the dozen) for a moment of warm, heart-quickening sunshine. There are three elements—they all play a great role in the most modern German music—for which Brahms has a conspicuous predilection: syncopation, *ritardando,* and simultaneous employment of counter-rhythms. In these three points, and particularly with regard to syncopation, he can hardly go further than he has recently gone.

And so, having relieved myself of these minor reservations, I can continue in the jubilant manner in which I began. The new symphony of Brahms is a possession of which the nation may be proud, an inexhaustible fountain of sincere pleasure and fruitful study.

121

Verdi at the Time of *Otello*

An interesting portrait of Verdi and a remarkably just estimate of his importance were presented in a long article in the London *Musical Times* of 1 February 1887 as the musical world was awaiting news of the first performance of *Otello* in Milan. The following issue (of March 1) gave a detailed account of the work and reported on the public reaction. Excerpts from both articles follow.

VERDI AND HIS NEW OPERA

By the time these words are read Verdi's "Otello" will, in all probability, have been produced at the Milan La Scala. The sooner the better for public curiosity, which is powerfully excited throughout the musical world, and especially for the great mass of musical journalists who, from day to day, or from week to week, feel themselves bound to assume a knowledge though they have it not. The unfortunate persons in question cannot be congratulated upon the accuracy of their vaticinations with regard to "Otello." The secret of the work has been well kept under the stern eye of its composer, whose horror of anything like a *réclame* [publicity] is notorious; and hence the journalists have had little or nothing to exercise their imaginations upon. Of course they have gone wrong. All this comes, we suppose, from competition for news. Journalists nowadays cannot afford to wait for information flowing through its legitimate channel. They must needs go listening at key-holes, overhearing scraps of conversation, taking surreptitious peeps behind the scenes, and, as a last resource, when the story will not hang together, calling upon their fancy for facts. We decline to follow the example, and, therefore, frankly state that we know nothing about the new opera save that it deals with the story of "Otello," that the book has been prepared by Boito, the poet–composer of "Mefistofele," and that the music has been written as a means of relaxation from the duties of a country gentleman, by Giuseppe Verdi, Senator of the Kingdom of Italy, landed proprietor and successful breeder of horses.

We lay stress upon Verdi's position as just stated, because his career is divisible into two powerfully contrasted parts. The first part embraces all the years of his musical activity from 1839 to 1867. During that period the master was a regular worker, and brought forth his yearly crop of music with comparatively few interruptions. There were ten barren years—1841, 1852, 1854, 1856, 1858, 1860, 1861, 1863, 1864, 1866—and eighteen productive ones, some of these being very fertile indeed. In 1844, the crop consisted of two operas; in 1845, of two; in 1847, of three; in 1849, of two; the same in 1853 and 1857. So far, we observe the labours of a professional composer, animated by the ambitions, and struggling with the heavy duties of his calling. But Verdi's life, from 1867, when "Don Carlos" was produced, till the present time, takes a very different complexion. He has left the open mart, with profit; retired from business; devoted himself to rural pursuits, and only resorts for relaxation to that which was once an employment. "Aida" (1871) and now "Otello" are the product of leisure hours spent at the desk when garden, field, and farm made no pressing claims. [Strictly speaking, this was only true of *Otello* and the later *Falstaff*: *Aida*, like nearly all the preceding operas, was written on commission.] The Squire amuses himself at composition. Of course there is no wonder in this. Old men frequently do for pleasure that which they once did for gain, but set about the task in the deliberate fashion born of feeble circulation and failing power. The true marvel is that we are about to receive an opera from a man seventy-three years of age. There are few parallels to this in musical history, and scarcely anything that can fairly be called a parallel in connection with the lyric stage.

To our mind there is something sympathetic in the circumstances under which "Otello" has been written. To begin with, the master has worked at it almost on the spot where, with everything against him, he began the battle of life. An engraving of the house in which he was born is now before us, and shows one of the dwellings with wide low-pitched roofs which are so common in that part of Italy.

In this dwelling Verdi's father carried on the business of a publican and grocer, but could hardly have been more prosperous than the peasants, his customers. The hamlet

Verdi's *Otello*: The Final Scene. A two-page spread from *L'Illustrazione Italiana* of 22 May 1887. The popular Italian weekly had already filled its columns with expectant reports before and glowing reviews (under the heading "The Apotheosis of Giuseppe Verdi") after the first performance, on 5 February of that year. Obviously the opera continued to be news.

of Le Roncole is very small, and inhabited by poor people even now. What must it have been in the devastating years which opened the present century?—in 1814, for example, when Muscovite soldiers descended upon it with fire and sword, outrage and murder, and the infant Giuseppe was only saved as by a miracle. The son of the Cascina [farm house] at Le Roncole was clearly handicapped in the race of life. What could be less promising than his youthful fortunes? As a boy the Fates were hard upon him. Twice he nearly perished; once he suffered from the brutality of a priest at whose altar he served; he began his musical career by playing the organ in the village church for four pounds per year, and when he sought admission to the Milan Conservatoire, submitting to the necessary examination, he was sent back rejected and humiliated.

The little village inn where life opened thus inauspiciously still stands, we believe, and not far from it is a handsome country house, surrounded by beautiful gardens, well-cultivated fields, and every sign of prosperity. The son of the inn-keeper lives there, as one who has conquered in the struggle for existence and for fame, and thence, as the slow fruit of dignified leisure, comes the new opera.

But the contrast just referred to is not the only feature which now excites sympathy. Though, at the moment of writing, his "Otello" is a closed book, the master's whole history invites us to believe that it contains further evidence of a progressive mind. Every student of his works knows that the Verdi of middle life is not the Verdi of an earlier period, and that the composer's advanced years have brought another change, exemplified in his "Aida." With regard to this subject a good deal has been written. On the one hand, enthusiastic Wagnerians have claimed Verdi as a convert to the teachings of their master; on the other, it is denied that any change at all of a radical nature has taken place. For example, Signor Mazzucato, writing in Grove's "Dictionary of Music and Musicians," says:—

No doubt there is a great difference between "Attila," "Ernani," "Rigoletto," and "Aida," but we submit that the difference is to be attributed to the age and development of the composer's mind, and not to a radical change in his way of rendering the subject musically, or to a different conception of the musical drama. The more refined expression of "Aida" compared to "Il Trovatore," and of "Il Trovatore" compared to "Nabucco" or "I Lombardi," answers to the refinement of musical feeling which audiences gradually underwent during the forty years of artistic career of the great composer; he spoke a higher language, because that higher language had become intelligible to the public; but what he said the first day is what he always said, and what he will say again, if he should ever break his long silence. Verdi felt, much more than learnt, that rhythm, the human voice, and brevity were the three elements apt to stir, to please, and not to engender fatigue in his audiences, and on them he built his masterpieces.

This almost amounts to a charge of prostituted genius—a charge with which we have no sympathy. Our belief is that Verdi has always written honestly, and that his wonderful success arose from the fact that he is, or, rather, was some years ago, peculiarly a man of his time. More masculine and capable of stronger feeling than Bellini or Donizetti; of imperfect (in the sense of restricted) musical education and experience; a powerful nature which sought other than the ordinary means of expression, Verdi composed as was natural to him, and had the good luck to reflect the prevailing mood. But the early, rugged, passionate style has undergone a long course of modification, not because the public called for it—they distinctly did nothing of the kind—but because it was the natural outcome of extended experience, clearer perception, and a more cultivated artistic nature. He is not likely in "Otello" to go back from the standpoint of "Aida," and it is interesting to find an old man still progressive, still enlarging his ideas, and amending their expression.

Amateurs everywhere indulge a hope that "Otello" may turn out a masterpiece. Even those who are not among Verdi's admirers must wish for his last effort all the success that he himself desires. The worst of the outlook is that Verdi seems to be the last of the giants. No one, as far as we see, is likely to continue the line.

VERDI'S "OTELLO"
(From Our Special Correspondent)

The long-expected new opera of Giuseppe Verdi was produced at La Scala, Milan, on the 5th ult. [February 5], after one or two postponements, caused, ostensibly, by the illness of the tenor, Tamagno, who had been cast for the title character. [There follows a lengthy, detailed summary of the plot, then a scene-by-scene description of the music, of which the following will serve as a sample.]

The last act will, perhaps, commend itself everywhere as musically the most beautiful. So it ought to do. Every situation on the stage, and every line in the poetry, call for music in an imperative voice, and appeal irresistibly to a composer's instinct. As the curtain rises upon *Desdemona's* chamber, the *cor Anglais* [English horn] takes up a plaintive strain, presently used in the Willow Song. This is developed at some length, with infinite pathos, and so the mind is prepared for the touching scene to follow. After a short dialogue for *Desdemona* and *Emilia,* founded upon the matter of the Introduction, the Willow Song is reached, and at once attention fixes itself upon music as affecting as any ever heard in a theatre. Verdi here adopts the verse form, but with considerable variation in accompaniment; each repetition of the melody thus presenting itself with fresh interest. At the close of the song, *Emilia* takes her leave, and *Desdemona,* left alone, sings the "Ave Maria," beginning with recitative on a single note, accompanied by sustained chords, and passing on to a plain and most moving *cantilena.* Verdi here shows that he rightly estimates the power of simple music. Nothing could be less pretentious than this beautiful strain, and nothing could be more affecting. When first heard at Milan it brought tears to many eyes. *Desdemona* presently sleeps, and *Otello* enters at the back of the stage; standing there, a sinister figure, while the double-basses execute the solo of which every amateur has by this time heard. As he bends over and kisses the woman he is about to kill, the orchestral melody first used at the close of the duet in Act I. re-appears; then *Desdemona* wakes, and the murder scene begins. Verdi does not prolong this unduly. Founding his music for the most part upon a fragment of the double-bass solo, he makes it so forcible that he can afford to pass rapidly on to the catastrophe, and thence to the end. As dramatic music, this *Finale* takes the highest rank. It strikes us as the very feelings of the characters expressed in ordered sound, and it intensifies the situation to a most painful degree. The last bars are the most touching of all, for in them, as *Otello* embraces the body of his wife, re-appears the expressive kiss theme heard first at the moment of their highest happiness. Upon this suggestive reminiscence the curtain finally descends. Our opinion of the work, as a whole, may easily be gathered from the foregoing remarks. To us it exemplifies judicious consideration for dramatic propriety without sacrifice of musical effect, and we must place it among Verdi's finest efforts—in some important respects, at the head of all.

The occasion of the performance was a remarkable one. Repeated delays had intensified interest rather than abated it, and "all the city was moved" because of the opera. The hotels filled with strangers who had secured seats, and others who had come on the chance of obtaining admission; everywhere "Otello" was talked about; the press, annoyed at being shut out from rehearsals, kept up an agitation, and the man who could let out any of the well-guarded secrets of La Scala became for the time a hero. Meanwhile Verdi, superintending the many rehearsals, pursued the even tenor of his way, calm and undisturbed. Visiting nobody, and allowing nobody to visit him, the master reserved all his energy for duty. Rising early each morning, he took a little exercise in the quiet streets; spent most of the day at the theatre, and about ten o'clock went to bed. On the memorable Saturday evening, a crowd gathered before the Hotel de Milan to see him pass to his carriage. This was the beginning of an extraordinary series of demonstrations. A far larger crowd around the theatre cheered Verdi in confident anticipation of an artistic triumph; while within the house and during the performance of the opera, the old composer was summoned at every possible opportunity. So long as the curtain remained up the brilliant gathering let him alone, but whenever it was down they kept him exercised at coming forward, bowing, and retiring. Several times after each act two of the principal artists would lead him on, and then, perhaps by way of suggestion that he had had enough of it, Verdi would step forward alone, hat in hand, with his frock coat tightly buttoned around him. For this the audience reserved their loudest and longest cheer. They became frantic with enthusiasm. At the close there was a special scene of wreaths and flowers and whatnot appropriate to such occasions, but the master preserved his calm demeanour. Agitated he must surely have been, though not a muscle of his face moved, and he appeared as the most unconcerned person in all that delirious assembly. Another ovation awaited Verdi outside, where the constant crowd had become larger and denser. No horses should draw him home that night, but rather the willing arms of his enthusiastic countrymen. The design was fulfilled to the letter, and being able to regulate the pace of the carriage, the people gave their hero an embarrassing example of slow travelling. However, even such a journey must have an end. Verdi reached his hotel, the corridors of which were crowded, and, gaining his apartments, went speedily to bed, where, if he slept, it was not because his lingering admirers in the street failed to make a noise. So ended one of the greatest personal triumphs ever awarded to a composer.

The Musical Times, XXVIII (1887), 73–75, 148–50.

122

Grieg on the Norwegian Element in His Music

On 17 July 1900, Edvard Grieg complied with a request from the American music critic and author Henry T. Finck and sent him a lengthy letter concerning his own music. Understandably, he dealt with the matter of nationalism in music in some detail, since his name was linked with Norwegian folk music in everyone's mind—too much so, he felt—and he wished the relationship to be understood more clearly.

The traditional way of life of the Norwegian people, together with Norway's legends, Norway's history, and Norway's natural scenery, stamped itself on my creative impulse from my earliest years. It was, however, only later in life that I found the way open to immerse myself in the folk songs of my country. When I wrote my early piano compositions, opus 3 and more especially op. 6, pieces in which a national note is variously apparent, I knew next to nothing of our folk songs. Despite certain German pronouncements to the effect that I merely churn out mechanical imitations of Norwegian folk music, this is the truth of the matter and needs to be emphasized. I do not believe myself that these traditional sources have had any crucial influence on my song writing. When local color simply *has* to dominate, the influence is not to be denied—take Solveig's song from "Peer Gynt," for instance. But this is possibly the only one of my songs in which I can clearly be shown to have imitated a folk melody. To one distinctive feature of our folk music I did indeed feel myself drawn: the manner in which the leading note was handled, and most particularly the downward shift of this to the fifth, but a like progression is to be found in the work of other composers. That the spirit of my native land, which has long found a voice in the traditional songs of its people, is a living presence in all I give forth, that is another matter altogether. I find no conscious intention in myself to imitate. Even if I as much as speak my own language (nothing very folk-songy about that!), these conservative German critics have a rude word for that, too. It is "Norsemanship." If my work has reached out across the world in a way I myself can scarcely comprehend, it surely does not owe this to the exclusively national element in it, but rather to the fusion of national and cosmopolitan ingredients. Cultural history shows us that every art form with the throb of life in it has taken on a national character. Like every modern artist who has a purpose, consciously or not I stand fast upon my native ground, and my sensibility. Broadly speaking, I have not sought after the giving of local color. It has come unbidden. I just don't believe a deliberate attempt to import a national element will work. When the national traits are not in the very blood, they have no place in a "creative," but only in a "photographic" art.

Bjarne Kortsen (ed.), *Grieg the Writer,* I (Bergen: B. Kortsen 1972), 36–37.

123

The Post-Wagnerians: Mahler

Here, in a letter to a sympathetic critic (Max Marschalk), are some characteristically earnest thoughts on the state of music at the turn of the century and on his own attitude towards composing by the thirty-six-year-old Mahler. These are followed by a program (and note with what extreme caution it is offered!) for the first three movements of his recently finished Symphony no. 2, the "Resurrection" Symphony. (The remaining two movements, being vocal settings of poetry, required no explanations.) The letter is dated 26 March 1896.

I know, where I am concerned, that so long as I can sum up my experience in words, I would never write any music about it. My need to express myself musicallysymphonically begins only where the *obscure* perceptions hold sway, at the gate that leads into the "other world"; the world in which things are no longer separable through the agency of time and place.

Just as I think it a platitude to invent music to a program, so do I consider it to be unsatisfying and sterile to wish to attach a program to a musical work. This is in no way altered by the fact that the *occasion* for a musical creation is doubtless to be found in an experience of the author's, and an actual one, which for that matter might be concrete enough to be clothed in words.—We stand now—of this I am certain—at the great parting of the ways, where the diverging paths of symphonic and dramatic music separate for ever, and this will soon be plainly visible to those who have a clear understanding of the essence of music.—Wagner, to be sure, made the *expressive means* of symphonic music his own, just as the symphonist, in turn, will now help himself, quite legitimately and quite consciously, to the expressive riches music has gained through Wagner's work. In this sense, all the arts, and even art and nature, are linked together. But this has not yet been given enough thought, since no *perspective* has been gained on the subject so far.—Not that I have erected this "system," as it were, and patterned my work upon it; on the contrary, I finally gained this—personal—view of things after I had written some symphonies (suffering real labor pains in the process)—and after meeting with the same misunderstandings and questions over and over again.—

And so it remains a good idea to let the listener have a few guideboards and milestones for his trip at first, while my manner still seems strange.—But such an explanation cannot offer *more*.

Having expressed myself in the above terms, you can understand that I find it a little awkward to say something to you now concerning the C minor Symphony.—I have named the first movement "Funeral Rite," and, if you are curious, it is the hero of my D major Symphony [No. 1] that I am burying here and whose life I am gathering up in a clear mirror, from a higher vantage point. At the same time it is the great question: *Why have you lived?* Why have you suffered? Is all this merely a great, horrible jest?— We *must* resolve these questions somehow or other, if we are to go on living—indeed, even if we are only to go on dying! Once this call has resounded in anyone's life, he must give an answer; and that answer I give in the last movement.

The 2nd and 3rd movements are conceived as interludes: the 2nd movement, a *memory!* A sunny moment, clear and untroubled, in the life of that hero.

You have surely had the experience of burying a person dear to you; and then, perhaps, as you came away, suddenly the image arose of a happy hour long since vanished, which now settles in your soul like a sunbeam—nothing darkens it—you are almost able to forget what has just occurred! That is the 2nd movement!—Then, if you awaken from this sorrowful dream and have to return to chaotic life, it may well happen that this unendingly mobile, restless, unintelligible bustle of life should strike you as being *ghastly,* like the swaying of dancing figures in a brightly-lit ballroom into which you are peering from the deep night outside—from so *far away* that you *cannot* hear the *music!*—That is the *3rd movement!* What follows after that is perfectly clear to you in any case!— — —

And so, actually, my 2nd symphony is directly connected to my 1st!

Please maintain your friendly interest in me nor think it vanity that I should require this of you. Many, many thanks!

Piero Weiss (ed.), *Letters of Composers Through Six Centuries* (Philadelphia: Chilton Books, 1967), 392–94.

124

The Post-Wagnerians: Richard Strauss

The anguished idealism of Mahler (see the previous reading) contrasts utterly with the cool, practical, sardonic attitude of Strauss towards music and the world. Here are some characteristic musings about *Salomé*, Strauss's scandalously successful opera of 1905, jotted down by the aging composer in 1942.

I went to Max Reinhardt's Little Theatre in Berlin to see Gertrud Eysoldt in [Oscar] Wilde's "Salomé." After the performance I ran into [the cellist] Heinrich Grünfeld, who said, "Strauss, now there's an opera subject for you!" I was able to answer, "I've already begun setting it to music." The Viennese lyric poet Anton Lindner had already sent me that exquisite play, offering to turn it into an "opera text." When I agreed, he sent me a couple of cleverly versified opening scenes; yet I could not make up my mind to begin working on it, till one day the idea dawned on me: Why not simply start right off with "How beautiful is the Princess Salomé tonight" [i.e., with the original prose text]? From that point on, it was not at all difficult to cleanse the play of its most "literary" ornaments, so that it grew into a jolly good "libretto." Now that the Dance [of the Seven Veils] and especially, the last scene are steeped in music, it's all very well to say that the play "simply cries out for music." Yes: but it takes an eye to notice it!

I had long found it a fault in Oriental and Hebrew operas that they lacked the authentic Eastern color and vibrant sunshine. Necessity inspired me with a truly exotic harmony, which shimmered, especially in the strange cadences, like iridescent silk. My desire for the sharpest delineation of character led me into bitonality, since a purely rhythmic characterization, of the kind Mozart uses with the utmost mastery, did not seem strong enough for such opposites as Herod and the Nazarene. It may be thought of as a unique experiment with special material but ought not to be held up as an example for imitation.

Once the excellent [conductor] Schuch had been brave enough to accept "Salomé" for performance, the troubles began: all the soloists came to the first reading rehearsal at the piano, but only to *return* their parts to the conductor—all except the Czech Burian, who, consulted last, replied, "I've got my part memorized." Bravo!—And now the others did feel embarrassed, and the rehearsals began in earnest. At the staging rehearsals, the highly dramatic Frau Wittich, who (because it was a strenuous role and the orchestration was thick) had been entrusted with the part of the 16-year-old princess with the Isolde-voice—You can't write music like that, Mr. Strauss: make up your mind!—went on strike periodically with the indignant objection of a Saxon Burgomaster's wife: "That I refuse to do; I'm a decent woman!" and drove Stage Director Wirk, with his "perverse and wicked" tendencies, to distraction. And yet Frau Wittich, who of course didn't look the part physically, was right, if in a different sense; for the music-hall exoticisms of some of the later productions, with their snake-like writhings and Jochanaan's head twirling aloft, have often exceeded all the bounds of decency and good taste. Anyone who ever visited the Orient and observed the propriety of the ladies there will readily understand that Salomé, as a chaste virgin, as an Oriental princess, can only be played with the simplest, most refined gesticulation, unless she is to awaken only horror and disgust instead of pity, as she disintegrates in the face of the miracle of a sublimer world. Indeed, the acting of all the players should confine itself to the *utmost simplicity,* in contrast with the overly-excited music. Frenzy both on stage and in the pit—that would be too much! The orchestra can manage it quite well alone!—My good father, when I strummed parts of it for him at the piano a couple of months before he died, groaned miserably, "Dear Lord, all this nervous music! It's like having your trousers full of crawling June bugs." He wasn't altogether wrong.

The performance enjoyed the success of all Dresden premières, but the head-shaking soothsayers later that evening in the Bellevue Hotel were unanimous in the opinion that, while the work might perhaps be produced at a couple of the really large theaters, it would soon disappear. Within three weeks it was accepted by, I think, ten theaters and was a sensation in Breslau with only a 70-piece orchestra! Now began the nonsense in the press, the opposition of the clergy (first performance at the Vienna State Opera in October 1918, after a ticklish correspondence with Archbishop Piffl), of the puritans in New York, where the work had to be withdrawn after the first performance at the instigation of a Mr. Morgan. The German Kaiser consented to its performance only after it had occurred to His Excellency [General Manager] Hülsen to let the Star of Bethlehem appear at the end, as a token of the arrival of the Three Kings! On one occasion, Wilhelm II said to his General Manager, "I'm sorry Strauss composed this 'Salomé'; I'm quite fond of him otherwise, but he is going to *do himself a lot of harm* with this." Thanks to this harm, I was able to afford my villa at Garmisch!

Richard Strauss, *Betrachtungen und Erinnerungen,* ed. Willi Schuh (Zürich: Atlantis Verlag, 1949), 180–84. Trans. P. W. Used by permission.

The Twentieth Century

125

Debussy and Musical Impressionism

The first truly representative twentieth-century composer, by common consent, was Claude-Achille Debussy (1862–1918). His innovations in harmony and in formal organization suggested new paths to musicians everywhere, at a time when the prevailing musical mood was one of exhaustion: the "Wagnerian revolution," which had promised to open a door to the future, had in the end only closed the door on the past. Debussy, at first by purely intuitive explorations, sought and found a way out, which he discussed—or rather debated—early in his career with Ernest Guiraud (1837–92), his old teacher (best remembered today for his recitatives to Bizet's *Carmen*). At the time of these conversations all of Debussy's important compositions lay ahead, but his crucial innovations are fully implicit in what he says. He is deeply mistrustful of tradition and "theory," and wishes to replace "learning" with instinct as a guide to the creation of music. These rather typical *fin-de-siècle* attitudes are reminiscent of those of Musorgsky (see p. 336), whose music Debussy knew intimately and loved. We owe our knowledge of these conversations to a set of transcripts made by a student composer named Maurice Emmanuel, who was privileged to overhear them.

DEBUSSY: [I have] no faith in the supremacy of the C major scale. The tonal scale must be enriched by other scales. Nor am I misled by equal temperament. Rhythms are stifling. Rhythms cannot be contained within bars. It is nonsense to speak of "simple" and "compound" time. There should be an interminable flow of both. Relative keys are nonsense, too. Music is neither major nor minor. Minor thirds and major thirds should be combined, modulation thus becoming more flexible. The mode is that which one happens to choose at the moment. It is inconstant. There must be a balance between musical demands and thematic evocation. Themes suggest their orchestral coloring.

GUIRAUD: [Debussy having played a series of chords on the piano] What's that?

DEBUSSY: Incomplete chords, floating. One can travel where one wishes and leave by any door. Greater nuances.

GUIRAUD: But when I play this [a "French sixth" chord on A$^{\flat}$, evidently one of the chords Debussy had played] it has to resolve.

DEBUSSY: I don't see that it should. Why?

GUIRAUD: Well, do you find this lovely? [He plays a series of parallel triads.]

DEBUSSY: Yes, yes, yes!

GUIRAUD: I am not saying that what you do isn't beautiful, but it's theoretically absurd.

DEBUSSY: There is no theory. You merely have to listen. Pleasure is the law.

GUIRAUD: I would agree with you in regard to an exceptional person who has discovered a discipline for himself and who has an instinct which he is able to impose. But how would you teach music to others?

DEBUSSY: Music cannot be learned.

GUIRAUD: Come now, you are forgetting that you yourself were ten years at the Conservatoire.

DEBUSSY: [He agrees and admits that there can after all be a doctrine.] Yes, this is silly. Except that I can't reconcile all this. True enough, I feel free because I have been through the mill, and I don't write in the fugal style because I know it.

Edward Lockspeiser, *Debussy: His Life and Mind*, I (London: Cassell, 1962), 207–208.

Debussy's opera *Pelléas et Mélisande*, along with his orchestral *Prelude to the Afternoon of a Faun* after Mallarmé, was one of the most influential embodiments of his ideals. As he stresses again and again in his writings, his aim was one of naturalness and spontaneity. His aspirations to "formlessness" are reflected in the very nature of his opera, a virtually unaltered setting of Maurice Maeterlinck's drama of the same name, without any allowances for musical "numbers." Debussy's horror of the contrived and the rhetorical is reflected in his sarcastic comparison (from a note written in April 1902) of the natural song-speech at which he aimed with what he saw as the naturalistic bombast of the so-called *verismo* school.

For a long time I had been striving to write music for the theater, but the form in which I wanted it to be was so unusual that after several attempts I had almost given up the idea. Explorations previously made in the realm of pure music had led me towards a hatred of classical development, whose beauty is solely technical and can interest only the mandarins of our profession. I wanted music to have a freedom that was perhaps more inherent than in any other art, for it is not limited to a more or less exact representation of nature, but rather to the mysterious affinity between nature and the Imagination.

After some years of passionate pilgrimages to Bayreuth, I began to have doubts about the Wagnerian formula, or, rather, it seemed to me that it was of use only in the particular case of Wagner's own genius. He was a great collector of formulas, and these he assembled within a framework that appears uniquely his own only because one is not well enough acquainted with music. And without denying his genius, one could say that he put the final period after the music of his time, rather as Victor Hugo summed up all the poetry that had gone before. One should therefore try to be a "post-Wagnerian" rather than a "Wagner follower."

The drama of *Pelléas*—which despite its atmosphere of dreams contains much more humanity than those so-called documents of real life—seemed to suit my purpose admirably. It has an evocative language whose sensibility can easily find an extension in the music and in the orchestral setting. I also tried to obey a law of beauty that seems notably ignored when it comes to dramatic music: the characters of this opera try to sing like real people, and not in an arbitrary language made up of worn-out clichés. That is why the reproach has been made concerning my so-called taste for monotonous declamation, where nothing seems melodic. First of all, it isn't so. And furthermore, a character cannot always express himself melodically: the *dramatic* melody has to be quite different from what is generally called melody. The people who go to listen to music in the theater are really like those crowds you see gathered around street musicians! There you can have your emotions-in-melody for a couple of sous! You can also be sure of a greater degree of attention than is usually found among the patrons of our state theaters, and you will even find a greater wish to understand—something totally lacking in the above-mentioned public.

François Lesure (ed.), *Debussy on Music*, trans. R. L. Smith (New York: Alfred A. Knopf, 1977), 74–75. Translation copyright © 1977 by Martin Secker and Warburg Ltd. and Alfred A. Knopf, Inc. Reprinted by permission of the publisher.

> "Monsieur Croche" (Mr. Eighth-note) was an imaginary character Debussy invented for his critical articles in the *Revue blanche* as a mouthpiece, much as Schumann had used the characters Florestan and Eusebius (see p. 304). In the passage given below, M. Croche gives Debussy a pep talk, and in particular counsels him to ignore critics who would try to dismiss his music by facile comparisons with trends in the other arts. The "term of abuse" has stuck, however, and Debussy is now known to all, for better or worse, as a musical Impressionist. There is some merit in the term—like Debussy, the Impressionist painters had rebelled against academic routine, and had sought in their art a spontaneous and "natural" wedding of content and form.

"Music contains so many impulses you could write a song about them, [said Monsieur Croche]. My favorite music is those few notes an Egyptian shepherd plays on his flute: he is a part of the landscape around him, and he knows harmonies that aren't in our books. The 'musicians' hear only music written by practiced hands, never the music of Nature herself. To see the sun rise does one far more good than hearing the *Pastoral* Symphony. What's the use of such incomprehensible art? Shouldn't all those complications be forbidden? We learn them only because they are as ingenious as a strong-box lock. But you don't agree. Because you know nothing but music and are subject to her obscure and barbarous laws! A lot of clever words are written about you, but you're merely a cross between a monkey and the *domestique*."

I dared point out to him that in poetry and painting alike (and I managed to think of a couple of musicians as well) men had tried to shake off the dust of tradition, but that it had only earned them the labels "symbolist" or "impressionist"—useful terms of abuse.

"It's only journalists doing their job who call them that," continued Monsieur Croche unflinchingly. "That's of no importance. Imbeciles can find something to ridicule in a fundamentally beautiful idea, and you can be certain there is more likely to be beauty in the work of those who have been ridiculed than in those who calmly trail along like sheep to the slaughterhouse for which they have been predestined.

"Remain unique! ... unblemished! Being too influenced by one's milieu spoils an artist: in the end he becomes nothing but the expression of his milieu.

"Search for a discipline within freedom! Don't let yourself be governed by formulae drawn from decadent philosophies: they are for the feeble-minded. Listen to no one's advice except that of the wind in the trees. That can recount the whole history of mankind … "

Ibid., 47–48.

126

Questioning Basic Assumptions

In the early twentieth century, perhaps to a greater extent than ever before in the history of music, composers began rethinking their art not merely from the standpoint of style and technique, but increasingly at the level of the most basic materials and resources. This preoccupation remained a dominant—perhaps it would not be too much to say *the* dominant—characteristic of twentieth-century musical thought. From this point of view one of the truest signs of the times in the first decade of the new century was Ferruccio Busoni's *Sketch of a New Aesthetic of Music,* a strange little pamphlet that appeared in 1906. Its author (1866–1924), a great pianist and respected composer of mixed Italian and German nationality, shows the roots of the early twentieth-century malaise to lie in Romantic strivings after the Infinite. The solution Busoni proposes, though ultimately unfruitful, was typical of the time. Various redivisions of the octave were tried early in the century in hopes of renewing what were widely perceived as the exhausted potentialities of European music. Other parts of Busoni's quirkily prophetic tract seem to presage electronic music, a medium that came into its own only after World War II.

The creator should take over no traditional law in blind belief, for this would make him view his own creative endeavor, from the outset, as an exception contrasting with that law. For his individual case he should seek out and formulate individual laws, which, after the first complete realization, he should annul, that he himself may not be drawn into repetitions when his next work shall be in the making.

So narrow has our tonal range become, so stereotyped its form of expression, that nowadays there is not one familiar motive that cannot be fitted with some other familiar motive so that the two may be played simultaneously.

That which, within our present-day music, most nearly approaches the essential nature of the art, is the Rest and the Hold (Pause). Consummate players, improvisers, know how to employ these instruments of expression in loftier and ampler measure. The tense silence between two movements—*in itself music,* in this environment—leaves wider scope for divination than the more determinate, but therefore less elastic, sound.

What we now call our Tonal System is nothing more than a set of "signs"; an ingenious device to grasp something of the eternal harmony; a meagre pocket-edition of that encyclopedic work; artificial light instead of the sun. We have divided the octave into twelve equidistant degrees, because we had to manage somehow, and have constructed our instruments in such a way that we can never get in above or below or between them. Keyboard instruments, in particular, have so thoroughly schooled our ears that we are no longer capable of hearing anything else—incapable of hearing except through this impure medium. Yet Nature created an *infinite gradation—infinite!* Who still knows it nowadays? And within this duodecimal octave we have marked out a series of fixed intervals, seven in number, and founded thereon our entire art of music. What do I say—*one* series? Two such series, one for each leg: the Major and Minor Scales.

Strange, that one should feel major and minor as opposites. They both present the same face, now more joyous, now more serious; and a mere touch of the brush suffices to turn the one into the other. But when we recognize that major and minor form one Whole with a double meaning, and that the "four-and-twenty keys" are simply an elevenfold transposition of the original twain, we arrive unconstrainedly at a perception of the UNITY *of our system of keys* (tonality). The conceptions of "related" and "foreign" keys vanish, and with them the entire intricate theory of degrees and relations. *We possess one single key.* But it is of the most meagre sort.

However deeply rooted the attachment to the habitual, and inertia, may be in the ways and nature of humankind, in equal measure are energy, and opposition to the existing order, characteristic of all that has life. Nature has her wiles, and persuades man, obstinately opposed though he be to progress and change; Nature progresses continually and changes unremittingly, but with so even and unnoticeable a movement that men perceive only quiescence. Only on looking backward from a distance do they note with astonishment that they have been deceived.

The Reformer of any given period excites irritation for the reason that his changes find men unprepared, and, above all, because these changes are appreciable. The Reformer, in comparison with Nature, is undiplomatic; and, as a wholly logical consequence, his changes do not win general acceptance until Time, with subtle, imperceptible advance, has bridged over the leap of the self-assured leader. Yet we find cases in which the reformer marched abreast of the times, while the rest fell behind. And then they have to be forced and lashed to take the leap across the passage they have missed. I believe that the major-and-minor key with its transpositional relations, our "twelve-semitone system," exhibits such a case of falling behind.

That some few have already felt how the intervals of the Series of Seven might be differently arranged (graduated) is manifested in isolated passages by Liszt, and recently by Debussy and his following, and even by Richard Strauss. Strong impulse, longing, gifted instinct, all speak from these strains. Yet it does not appear to me that a conscious and orderly conception of this intensified means of expression has been formed by these composers.

All signs presage a revolution, and a next step toward that "eternal harmony." Let us once again call to mind, that in this latter the gradation of the octave is *infinite,* and let us strive to draw a little nearer to infinitude. The tripartite tone (third of a tone) has for some time been demanding admittance, and we have left the call unheeded. Whoever has experimented, like myself (in a modest way) with this interval, and introduced (either with voice or with violin) two equidistant intermediate tones between the extremes of a whole tone, schooling his ear and his precision of attack, will not have failed to discern that tripartite tones are wholly independent intervals with a pronounced character, and not to be confounded with ill-tuned semitones. They form a refinement in chromatics based, as at present appears, on the whole-tone scale. Only a long and careful series of experiments, and a continued training of the ear, can render this unfamiliar material approachable and plastic for the coming generation, and for Art.

And what a vista of fair hopes and dreamlike fancies is thus opened for them both! Who has not dreamt that he could float on air? and firmly believed his dream to be reality?—Let us take thought, how music may be restored to its primitive, natural essence; let us free it from architectonic, acoustic and aesthetic dogmas; let it be pure invention and sentiment, in harmonies, in forms, in tone-colors (for invention and sentiment are not the prerogative of melody alone); let it follow the line of the rainbow and vie with the clouds in breaking sunbeams; *let Music be naught else than Nature mirrored by and reflected from the human breast;* for it is sounding air and floats above and beyond the air; within Man himself as universally and absolutely as in Creation entire; for it can gather together and disperse without losing in intensity.

Ferruccio Busoni, "Sketch of a New Aesthetic of Music," trans. Theodore Baker, in *Three Classics in the Aesthetic of Music* (New York: Dover Publications, Inc., 1962), 88–95.

127

From the Writings of Charles Ives

While European musicians philosophized on the need for renewal, an American insurance executive and part-time composer was actually putting some of their most outlandish speculations into practice. Charles Ives was anything but a musical philosopher, although he was often inspired in his compositions by the transcendentalist philosophy of Emerson and Thoreau. Rather, he approached musical innovation in the spirit of the "Yankee tinker," much as he describes his father George Ives, a Civil War bandmaster and New England town musician. Responding above all to a natural curiosity, and unencumbered by the weight of a centuries-old tradition, Ives experimented freely with quarter-tones, polytonality, and polyrhythms at a time when such things were only being dimly imagined elsewhere. In the passage below, taken from an essay of 1925 called "Some Quarter-Tone Impressions," Ives seconds the "back-to-nature" cry of Debussy and Busoni (see the preceding selections)—that is, man should try to break the arbitrary limits he himself has imposed through his musical habits on the infinite variety of sound.

It will be centuries, at least generations, before man will discover all or even most of the value in a quarter-tone extension. And when he does, nature has plenty of other things up her sleeve. And it may be longer than we think before the ear will freely translate what it hears and instinctively arouse and amplify the spiritual consciousness.

But that needn't keep anyone from trying to find out how to use a few more of the myriads of sound waves nature has put around in the air (immune from the radio) for man to catch if he can and "perchance make himself a part with nature," as Thoreau used to say. Even in the limited and awkward way of working with quarter-tones at present, transcendent things may be felt ahead—glimpses into further fields of thought and beauty.

The assimilation of quarter-tones with what we have now into some reasonable and satisfactory basic plan will be, it seems to me, along harmonic lines, with the melodic coming as a kind of collateral, simultaneously perhaps, and just as important, but very closely bound up with the former—in a sense, opposite to the way our present system has developed. It seems to me that a pure quarter-tone melody needs a pure quarter-tone harmony not only to back it up but to help generate it.

This idea may be due to a kind of family prejudice, for my father had a weakness for quarter-tones—in fact he didn't stop even with them. He rigged up a contrivance to stretch 24 or more violin strings and tuned them up to suit the dictates of his own curiosity. He would pick out quarter-tone tunes and try to get the family to sing them, but I remember he gave that up except as a means of punishment—though we got to like some of the tunes which kept to the usual scale and had quarter-tone notes thrown in. But after working for some time he became sure that some quarter-tone chords must be learned before quarter-tone melodies would make much sense and become natural to the ear, and so for the voice. He started to apply a system of bows to be released by weights, which would sustain the chords, but in this process he was suppressed by the family and a few of the neighbors. A little later on he did some experimenting with glasses and bells, and got some sounds as beautiful, sometimes, as they were funny— a complex that only children are old enough to appreciate.

But I remember distinctly one impression (and this about 35 years ago). After getting used to hearing a piano piece when the upper melody, runs, etc., were filled out with quarter-tone notes (as a kind of ornamentation) when the piece was played on the piano alone there was a very keen sense of dissatisfaction—of something wanted but missing—a kind of sensation one has upon hearing a piano after a harpsichord.

Howard Boatwright (ed.), *Essays Before a Sonata, The Majority, and other Writings by Charles Ives* (New York: W. W. Norton & Company, Inc., 1970), 109–11.

One of the salient features of Ives's music—and one of the most controversial—has always been his habit of quoting snatches of all sorts of "vernacular" music in all sorts of unexpected and occasionally outlandish contexts. Ives was not trying to found a style of art music on the characteristics of folk music, like certain European composers (e.g., Bartók—see p. 378). Rather, he was attempting to add a certain communicative dimension to his music through the essentially literary device of allusion. Below, in a passage typical of his blustery style, Ives tries to express his transcendental vision of the essence of music and the role of his quotations in realizing it.

Exception has been taken by some (in other words there have been criticisms, often severe) to my using, as bases for themes, suggestions of old hymns, occasional tunes of past generations, etc. As one routine-minded professor told me, "In music they should have no place. Imagine, in a symphony, hearing suggestions of street tunes like *Marching Through Georgia* or a Moody and Sankey hymn!"—etc. Well, I'll say two things here: 1) That nice professor of music is a musical lily-pad. He never took a chance at himself, or took one coming or going. 2) His opinion is based on something he'd probably never heard, seen, or experienced. He knows little of how these things sounded when they came "blam" off a real man's chest. It was the *way* this music was sung that made them big or little—and I had the chance of hearing them big. And it wasn't the music that did it, and it wasn't the words that did it, and it wasn't the sounds (whatever they were—transcendent, peculiar, bad, some beautifully unmusical)—but they were sung "like the rocks were grown." The singers weren't singers, but they knew what they were doing—it all came from something felt, way down and way up—a man's experience of men!

Once a nice young man (his musical sense having been limited by three years' intensive study at the Boston Conservatory) said to Father, "How can you stand it to hear old John Bell (the best stone-mason in town) sing?" (as he used to at Camp Meetings). Father said, "He is a supreme musician." The young man (nice and educated) was horrified—"Why, he sings off the key, the wrong notes and everything—and that horrible, raucous voice—and he bellows out and hits notes no one else does—it's awful!" Father said, "Watch him closely and reverently, look into his face and hear the music of the ages. Don't pay too much attention to the sounds—for if you do, you may miss the music. You won't get a wild, heroic ride to heaven on pretty little sounds."

I remember, when I was a boy—at the outdoor Camp Meeting services in Redding, all the farmers, their families and field hands, for miles around, would come afoot or in their farm wagons. I remember how the great waves of sound used to come through the trees—when things like *Beulah Land, Woodworth, Nearer My God To Thee, The Shining Shore, Nettleton, In the Sweet Bye and Bye* and the like were sung by thousands of "let out" souls. The music notes and words on paper were about as much like what they "were" (at those moments) as the monogram on a man's necktie may be like his face. Father, who led the singing, sometimes with his cornet or his voice, sometimes with both voice and arms, and sometimes in the quieter hymns with a French horn or violin, would always encourage the people to sing their own way. Most of them knew the words and music (theirs) by heart, and sang it that way. If they threw the poet or the composer around a bit, so much the better for the poetry and the music. There was power and exaltation in these great conclaves of sound from humanity. I've heard the same hymns played by nice celebrated organists and sung by highly known singers in beautifully upholstered churches, and in the process everything in the music was emasculated—precise (usually too fast) even time—"ta ta" down-left-right-up—pretty voices, etc. They take a mountain and make a sponge cake of it, and sometimes, as a result, one of these commercial travellers gets a nice job at the Metropolitan. Today apparently even the Camp Meetings are getting easy-bodied and commercialized. There are not many more of them here in the east, and what is told of some of those that still survive, such as Amy McPherson & Co., seems but a form of easy entertainment and silk cushions—far different from the days of the "stone-fielders."

128

Musical Expressionism

Where Impressionism had at its core an attitude of objectivity (for instance, Debussy's many nature-pictures in tone, especially his orchestral triptych *La Mer*), some of the turn-of-the-century avant-garde was concerned with quite the opposite: a newly intensified subjectivism in which the content of art was mood and emotion pushed to irrationally wild and violent extremes. This last gasp of Romanticism, known as Expressionism, had its musical seat in Vienna, which was by no means coincidentally also the seat of the burgeoning psychoanalytic movement. One might go so far as to characterize Expressionism as the exploration of the human unconscious through art. Its central musical exponent was Arnold Schoenberg (1874–1951), who was moved by the Expressionistic ideal to write music of such an unprecedented and "irrational" complexity that he confessed himself as little able as anyone else to "analyze" his works—a remarkable avowal of the "unconscious" wellsprings of inspiration. In the two passages given below—the first from a letter to Richard Strauss, the second a program note dictated to a follower, Walter Krug—Schoenberg describes his *Five Pieces for Orchestra*, op. 16 (1909; first performed in 1912), one of the most representative Expressionist compositions, and one of the earliest in which Schoenberg wrote music that may be fairly described as "atonal."

The greatest difficulty in performing these pieces is that this time it is really impossible to read the score. It would be almost imperative to perform them through blind faith. I can promise you something really colossal, especially in sound and mood. For that is what they are all about—completely unsymphonic, devoid of architecture or construction, just an uninterrupted change of colors, rhythms and moods.

This music seeks to express all that swells in us subconsciously like a dream; which is a great fluctuant power, and is built upon none of the lines that are familiar to us; which has a rhythm, as blood has its pulsating rhythm, as all life in us has its rhythm; which has a tonality, but only as the sea or the storm has its tonality; which has harmonies, though we cannot grasp or analyze them nor can we trace its themes. All its technical craft is submerged, made one and indivisible with the content of the work.

Nicolas Slonimsky (ed.), *Music Since 1900,* 4th ed. (New York: Charles Scribner's Sons, 1971), 207. Trans. Nicolas Slonimsky. Copyright © 1971 Nicolas Slonimsky. Reprinted with the permission of Charles Scribner's Sons.

The unfriendliness with which such music was received by its early audiences is suggested by some of the reviews that greeted the *Five Pieces* in the London press after the first performance there on 3 September 1912, and, more dismayingly, by the account given by Egon Wellesz (1885–1975)—one of Schoenberg's pupils and later a distinguished composer and musical scholar—of a concert in Vienna the next year at which music by the "New Viennese School" was premiered under Schoenberg's baton.

London Times, 4 September 1912

It was like a poem in Tibetan; not one single soul could possibly have understood it at a first hearing. We can, after all, only progress from the known to the unknown; and as the program writer, who had every reason to know, said, there was not a single consonance from beginning to end. Under such circumstances the listener was like a dweller in Flatland straining his mind to understand the ways of that mysterious occupant of three dimensions, man.

London Daily Mail, 7 September 1912

Arnold Schoenberg evidently revels in the bizarre. According to Dr. Anton von Webern [see p. 368], his music "contains the experience of his emotional life," and that experience must have been of a strange, not to say unpleasant character. Is it really honest music or merely a pose? We are inclined to think the latter. If music at all, it is music of the future, and we hope, of a distant one.

Arnold Schoenberg, "Red Gaze" (1910). Like a few other composers (Mendelssohn, Gershwin), Schoenberg painted on the side. Moreover, his paintings were fully representative of his avant-garde aesthetic leanings. The haunting "Red Gaze" (so called because of its original monochromatic color scheme) is as full-fledged a representative of German Expressionism as are his *Five Pieces for Orchestra*, composed a few years later. *Stadische Galerie im Lebenhaus, Munich (inv. No. F H 139). Used by permission of Belmont Music Publishers, Los Angeles, CA 90049.*

London Daily News, **4 September 1912**

Imagine the scene of the bleating sheep in *Don Quixote,* the sacrificial procession in *Elektra,* and the scene of the opponents in *Heldenleben* [all famously dissonant passages in works by Richard Strauss], all played together, and you will have a faint idea of Schoenberg's idea of orchestral color and harmony. As to theme or subject, it must be supposed that he would consider it an insult to be told that he has any traffic with such things. The pieces have no program or poetic basis. We must be content with the composer's own assertion that he has depicted his own experiences, for which he has our heartfelt sympathy.

Nation, **September 1912 (by Ernest Newman)**

It is not often that an English audience hisses the music it does not like; but a good third of the people the other day permitted themselves that luxury after the performance of the five orchestral pieces of Schoenberg. Another third of the audience was not hissing because it was laughing, and the remaining third seemed too puzzled either to laugh or to hiss. Nevertheless, I take leave to suggest that Schoenberg is not the mere fool or madman that he is generally supposed to be. May it not be that the new composer sees a logic in certain tonal relations that to the rest of us seem chaos at present, but the coherence of which may be clear enough to us all some day?

Ibid., 207–208.

In order to do something for his pupils Anton von Webern and Alban Berg, Schoenberg decided to conduct an orchestral concert that was to be given under the auspices of the Academic Society for Literature and Music. It took place on 31 March 1913 in the large hall of the Musikverein, and included orchestral pieces by Webern, Schoenberg's *Chamber Symphony,* orchestral songs by [Alexander von] Zemlinsky [1872–1942] and Alban Berg, and the *Kindertotenlieder* by Mahler. Apparently one section of the public had come with the intention of creating a scene, for one saw many people, including operetta composers, who had held themselves aloof from performances of modern music. Even during Webern's orchestra pieces and Schoenberg's *Chamber Symphony* there arose an altercation between students, who were enthusiastically applauding, and certain people who sought to disturb the performance by shouts and hisses. When it came to the songs by Berg, however, the noise was so great that one could scarcely hear anything at all. In these circumstances, Schoenberg wanted to discontinue his conducting, but he nevertheless yielded to persuasion; so he made a request, through the superintendent of the Academic Society, that at least the songs of Mahler might be received with the "fitting quiet and respect due to the composer."

As a result of this appeal, several people, who up to that point had disturbed the concert in the most inconsiderate manner conceivable, apparently felt offended and scenes followed which I will not attempt to describe. The performance ended in a wild struggle in which blows were exchanged. It found its echo in the law courts, where a well-known operetta composer, called as a witness, said, "Well, I laughed myself, and why shouldn't one laugh at what is obviously funny?" And another, a practicing doctor, declared that the effect of the music was "for a certain section of the public, so nerve-wracking, and therefore so harmful for the nervous system, that many who were present already showed obvious signs of severe attacks of neurosis."

I do not mention this matter merely to give to a purely local affair an importance it does not deserve—later there were similar scenes in the performances of Schoenberg's works, for instance, at the performance of the *Five Pieces for Orchestra* in Paris in the spring of 1922—but in order to make it clear that, in these circumstances, Schoenberg could not wish to expose himself to such scenes. He became more reserved and more aloof from the world than ever, and it was only with the utmost difficulty that one could persuade him to allow his works to be performed.

Egon Wellesz, *Arnold Schönberg*, trans. W. H. Kerridge (London: J. M. Dent, 1921), 34–35.

129

The Retreat to the Ivory Tower

As a result of the humiliating reception accorded his music and that of his pupils and colleagues, Schoenberg effected a retreat from public concert life. For perhaps the first time a musician of the front rank not only acknowledged, but sought actively to abet, the split that was emerging between "advanced" music and the public to which artists had turned for support since the middle of the eighteenth century. This has been one of the central problems of twentieth-century art: the development of music that—taking its cue from science and scholarship—deliberately addresses itself to a narrow circle of professionals and initiates. The alienation of the creative artist from society, raising thorny questions of aesthetic and social value, is a theme to which our twentieth-century readings will frequently return. Below we give one of the prime documents of this alienation: the Statement of Aims written by Alban Berg (over Schoenberg's signature) for the idealistic Society for Private Musical Performances in Vienna, in which the avant-garde's retreat was forthrightly announced.

The Society was founded in November, 1918, for the purpose of enabling Arnold Schoenberg to carry out his plan to give artists and music-lovers a real and exact knowledge of modern music.

The attitude of the public towards modern music is affected to an immense degree by the circumstance that the impression it receives from that music is inevitably one of obscurity. Aim, tendency, intention, scope and manner of expression, value, essence, and goal, all are obscure; most performances of it lack clarity; and specially lacking in lucidity is the public's consciousness of its own needs and wishes. All works are there-fore valued, considered, judged and lauded, or else misjudged, attacked, and rejected, exclusively upon the basis of one effect which all convey equally—that of obscurity.

This situation can in the long run satisfy no one whose opinion is worthy of consideration, neither the serious composer nor the thoughtful member of an audi-ence. To bring light into this darkness and thus fulfill a justifiable need and desire was one of the motives that led Arnold Schoenberg to found this society.

To attain this goal three things are necessary:

1. Clear, well-rehearsed performances.
2. Frequent repetitions.

3. The performances must be removed from the corrupting influence of publicity; that is, they must not be directed toward the winning of competitions and must be unaccompanied by applause, or demonstrations of disapproval.

Herein lies the essential difference revealed by a comparison of the Society's aims with those of the everyday concert world, from which it is quite distinct in principle. Although it may be possible, in preparing a work for performance, to get along with the strictly limited and always insufficient number of rehearsals hitherto available, for better or worse (usually the latter), yet for the Society the number of rehearsals allotted to works to be performed will be limited only by the attainment of the greatest possible clarity and by the fulfillment of all the composer's intentions as revealed in his work. And if the attainment of these minimum requirements for good performance should necessitate a number of rehearsals that cannot be afforded (as was the case, for example, with a symphony of Mahler, which received its first performance after twelve four-hour rehearsals and was repeated after two more), then the work concerned should not, and will not, be performed by the Society.

In the rehearsal of new works, the performers will be chosen preferably from among the younger and less well-known artists, who place themselves at the Society's disposal out of interest in the cause; artists of high-priced reputation will be used only so far as the music demands and permits; and moreover that kind of virtuosity will be shunned which makes of the work to be performed not the end in itself but merely a means to an end which is not the Society's, namely, the display of irrelevant virtuosity and individuality, and the attainment of a purely personal success. Such things will be rendered automatically impossible by the exclusion (already mentioned) of all demonstrations of applause, disapproval, and thanks. The only success that an artist can have here is that (which should be most important to him) of having made the work, and therewith its composer, intelligible.

While such thoroughly rehearsed performances are a guarantee that each work will be enabled to make itself rightly understood, an even more effective means to this end is given to the Society through the innovation of weekly meetings and by frequent repetitions of every work. Moreover, to ensure equal attendance at each meeting, the program will not be made known beforehand.

Only through the fulfillment of these two requirements—thorough preparation and frequent repetition—can clarity take the place of the obscurity which used to be the only impression remaining after a solitary performance; only thus can an audience establish an attitude towards a modern work that bears any relation to its composer's intention, completely absorb its style and idiom, and achieve that intimacy that is to be gained only through direct study—an intimacy with which the concert-going public can be credited only with respect to the most frequently performed classics.

The third condition for the attainment of the aims of the Society is that the performances shall be in all respects private; that guests (foreign visitors excepted) shall not be admitted, and that members shall be obligated to abstain from giving any public report of the performances and other activities of the Society, and especially not to write or inspire any criticisms, notices, or discussions of them in periodicals.

This rule, that the sessions shall not be publicized, is made necessary by the semi-pedagogic activities of the Society and is in harmony with its tendency to benefit musical works solely through good performance and thus simply through the good effect made by the music itself. Propaganda for works and their composers is not the aim of the Society.

(Signed) President: Arnold Schoenberg, 16 February 1919

Nicolas Slonimsky (ed.), *Music Since 1900*, 4th ed. (New York: Charles Scribner's Sons, 1971), 1307–1308. Trans. Stephen Somervelle. Copyright © 1971 Nicolas Slonimsky. Reprinted with the permission of Charles Scribner's Sons.

130

The Death of Tonality?

Schoenberg's early atonal works created a new crisis in music. By cutting his music loose from its moorings in major-minor tonality, Schoenberg set his art adrift in a sea of limitless possibilities. The infinity of choice was paralyzing. Schoenberg's pupil Anton Webern (1883–1945), in an extract from a series of lectures he gave in the early 1930s, conveys breathtakingly both the exhilaration of the new musical freedom and the desperate search for a new theoretical framework to justify it. What was needed was a new musical "law" that could serve as a guide to compositional practice as the tonal system had served in the past, and that would once again make the construction of coherent large-scale works possible. The result of this quest was the twelve-tone system, which was formulated by Schoenberg shortly after World War I, and which was brought to its greatest peak of creative fruition, in the opinion of many, by Webern. Needless to say, the confidence with which Webern describes the "death" of tonality was not widely shared at the time, and of all the twentieth-century musical innovations, the twelve-tone system was and has perhaps remained the most controversial.

Now I should like to cast a quick glance at the extension of the tonal field. Why do I talk so much about it? Because for the last quarter of a century major and minor have no longer existed! Only, most people still do not know. It was so attractive to fly ever further into the remotest tonal regions, and then to slip back again into the warm nest, the original key! And suddenly one did not come back—such a loose chord is so ambiguous! It was a fine feeling to draw in one's wings; but in the end one found it was no longer so necessary to return to the keynote. Until Beethoven and Brahms, one didn't really get any further—but then a composer appeared who blew the whole thing apart: Wagner. And then Bruckner and Hugo Wolf; and Richard Strauss also came and had his turn—very ingenious!—and many others; and that was the end of major and minor.

Summing up, I would say: just as the church modes disappeared and gave way to only two modes, so these two have also disappeared and made way for a single series: the chromatic scale. Relation to a keynote—tonality—has been lost. The relationship to a keynote had given older structures an essential foundation. It helped to build their form, in a certain sense it produced unity. This relation to a keynote was the essence of tonality. As a result of all the events mentioned, this relationship first became less necessary and then disappeared altogether. Harmonic complexes arose, of a kind that made the relationship to a keynote superfluous. All this happened between Wagner and Schoenberg, whose first works were still tonal. Relationship to a keynote became ever looser. This produced a state in which one could finally dispense with the keynote. The possibility of rapid modulation has nothing to do with this development; in fact just because all this happened in order to safeguard the keynote—to extend tonality—precisely because we took steps to preserve tonality—we broke its neck!

I go out into the hall to knock in a nail. On my way there, I decide I would rather go out. I obey the impulse, get into a train, come to a railway station, go on travelling and finally end up—in America! That is modulation!

In this musical material new laws have come into force, which have made it impossible for a piece to be described as being in one key or another. It was so ambiguous. Things have asserted themselves, which made this "key" simply impossible. We have sensed that the frequent repetition of a note, either directly or in the course of the piece, in some way "got its own back," that this note "came through." It had to be given its due—that was still possible at this stage; but it proved disturbing, for example, if one note occurred a number of times during some run of all twelve. The movement of the individual parts in a polyphonic texture happened chromatically, and no longer in the sense of major or minor. Schoenberg said, "The most important thing in composing is an eraser!" It was a matter of constant testing: "Are these chord progressions the right ones? Am I putting down what I mean? Is the right form emerging?"

What has happened? I can only relate something from my own experience: About 1911 I wrote the *Bagatelles for String Quartet* (op. 9), all very short pieces; perhaps the shortest music so far. I had the feeling here that when all twelve notes had gone by, the piece was over. Much later I discovered that all this was part of a necessary development. In my sketch-book I wrote out the chromatic scale and crossed off individual notes. Why? Because I had convinced myself: this note has been there already. It sounds grotesque, incomprehensible, and it was unbelievably difficult. The inner ear decided quite rightly that the man who wrote out the chromatic scale and crossed off individual notes *was no fool.* In short: a law emerged; until all twelve notes have occurred, none may be repeated. The most important thing is that the single rotation of the twelve notes marked a division within the piece, idea or theme.

All the works created between the disappearance of tonality and the formulation of the new twelve-tone law were short, strikingly short. The longer works written at that time were linked to a text which carried them (Schoenberg's *Erwartung* and *Die Glückliche Hand,* Berg's *Wozzeck*), i.e., really with something extramusical. With the abandonment of tonality the most important means of building up longer pieces was lost. For tonality was supremely important in producing self-contained forms. It seemed as if the light had been put out! (At least, this is how it strikes us today.) At that time everything was in a state of flux—uncertain, dark; very stimulating and exciting, so that there was no time to notice the loss. Only when Schoenberg gave expression to the law were larger forms again possible.

Adherence to the row is strict, often burdensome—but it is *salvation!* The dissolution of tonality wasn't our fault—and we did not create the new law ourselves; it forced itself overwhelmingly upon us. The commitment is so powerful that one must consider very carefully before finally entering into it … almost as if one took the decision to marry; a difficult moment! Trust your inspiration! There is no alternative.

131

Arnold Schoenberg on Composition with Twelve Tones

From the pen of its inventor we have this description of the twelve-tone technique together with a brief account of its gradual formulation. What emerges most forcefully from this little essay—written around 1948 in English, a language Schoenberg never completely mastered—is his burning conviction of the historical legitimacy and necessity of his discovery, as well as its original motivation as a means of achieving long-range coherence in the absence of tonality's all-governing harmonic relationships. Omitted from the essay as given here are a few passages of rather petulant polemic against Josef Matthias Hauer (1883–1959), a Viennese composer who claimed to have beaten Schoenberg to the formulation of the twelve-tone technique (he called his method "Tropen"). Whatever the merits of Hauer's case for priority, and however much it may have nettled Schoenberg, there can be no doubt that it was Schoenberg, not Hauer, who (together with his pupils) made twelve-tone music a viable and genuinely significant creative development.

The method of composing with twelve tones purports reinstatement of the effects formerly furnished by the structural functions of harmony. It cannot replace all that harmony has performed in music from Bach—and his predecessors—unto our time: limitation, subdivision, connection, junction, association, unification, opposition, contrast, variation, culmination, declination, ebbing, liquidation, etc. It also cannot exert influences of similar ways on the inner organization of the smaller segments, of which the greater divisions and the whole work consists.

But in works of Strauss, Mahler and, even more, Debussy, one can already observe reasons for the advance of new formal techniques. Here it is already doubtful, as I have shown in my *Harmonielehre* [*Harmony Textbook,* 1911], whether there is a tonic in power which has control over all these centrifugal tendencies of the harmonies. Certainly, there are still methods employed to establish a tonality, there are even cadences concluding sections which move into the most remote relations of a tonality. But the problem is not whether this number of tonalities can still admit unification, but whether they are controlled by a center of gravitation which has the power to permit their going astray because it also has the power of recalling them. It is quite obvious to the analyst that here compositorial methods have been in function which substitute for the missing power of harmony.

This proves that harmony also in times preceding these masters never had the task of accomplishing all these structural techniques alone, by its own power. There were always several powers at work to produce themes, melodies, and all the larger sections of which a composition consists: the manifold forms of crystallization of intervals and rhythms in their relation to accented or unaccented beats of the measure.

This also proves that many composers working with twelve tones are mistaken when they expect too much from the mere application of a set of twelve tones. This alone could not create music. Doubtless these other formative forces which produce the configurations and variations are even more important. And the history of music shows that harmony was the last contribution to music at a time when there was already great development in existence of melody and rhythm.

The construction of a basic set of twelve tones derives from the intention to postpone the repetition of every tone as long as possible. I have stated in my *Harmonielehre* that the emphasis given to a tone by a premature repetition is capable of heightening it to the rank of a tonic. But the regular application of a set of twelve tones emphasizes all the other tones in the same manner, thus depriving one single tone of the privilege of supremacy. It seemed in the first stages immensely important to avoid a similarity with tonality. The feeling was correct that those free combinations of simultaneously sounding tones—those "chords"—would fit into a tonality. Today's ear has become as tolerant to these dissonances as musicians were to Mozart's dissonances. It is in fact correct to contend that the emancipation of the dissonance is at present accomplished and that twelve-tone music in the near future will no longer be rejected because of "discords."

The other function is the unifying effect of the set. Through the necessity of using besides the basic set, its retrograde, its inversion, and its retrograde inversion, the repetition of tones will occur oftener than expected. But every tone appears always in the neighborhood of two other tones in an unchanging combination which produces an intimate relationship most similar to the relationship of a third and a fifth to its root. It is, of course, a mere relation, but its recurrence can produce psychological effects of a great resemblance to those closer relations.

Such features will appear in every motif, in every theme, in every melody and, though rhythm and phrasing might make it distinctly another melody, it will still have some relationship with all the rest. The unification is here also the result of the relation to a common factor.

The third advantage of composition with a set of twelve tones is that the appearance of dissonances is regulated. Dissonances are not used here as in many other contemporary compositions as an addition to make consonances more "spicy." For the appearance of such dissonant tones there is no conceivable rule, no logic, and no other justification than the dictatorship of taste. If dissonances other than the catalogued ones are admitted at all in music, it seems that the way of referring them all to the order of the basic set is the most logical and controllable procedure toward this end.

This seems to be the appropriate opportunity to tell about the way I arrived at my method.

Ever since 1906–8, when I had started writing compositions which led to the abandonment of tonality, I had been busy finding methods to replace the structural functions of harmony. Nevertheless, my first distinct step toward this goal occurred only in 1915. I had made plans for a great symphony of which *Die Jakobsleiter* should be the last movement. I had sketched many themes, among them one for a scherzo which consisted of all twelve tones. My next step in this direction—in the meantime I had been in the Austrian army—occurred in 1917, when I started to compose *Die Jakobsleiter*. I had contrived the plan to provide for unity—which was always my main motive: to build all the main themes of the whole oratorio from a row of six tones—C-sharp, D,

E, F, G, A-flat. These were probably the six notes with which the composition began, in the following order: C-sharp, D, F, E, A-flat, G. When I built the main themes from these six tones I did not bind myself to the order of their first appearance. I was still at this time far away from the methodical application of a set. Still I believe that also this idea offered the promise of unity to a certain degree. Of course, in order to build up a work of the length of [the opera] *Moses und Aron* from one single set, a technique had to be developed, or rather the fear that this would not succeed had to be conquered. That took several years.

Before I wrote my first strict composition with twelve tones—in 1921—I had still to pass through several stages. This can be noticed in two works which I had partly written preceding the *Piano Suite*, op. 25—partly even in 1919, the *Five Piano Pieces*, op. 23, and the *Serenade*, op. 24. In both these works there are parts composed in 1922 and 1923 which are strict twelve-tone compositions. But the rest represent the aforementioned stages.

In my workshop language, when I talked to myself, I called this procedure "working with tones of the motif." This was obviously an exercise indispensable for the acquisition of a technique to conquer the obstacles which a set of twelve tones opposes to a free production of fluent writing. Similarly, as in the case of *Die Jakobsleiter*, here also all main themes had to be transformations of the first phrase. Already here the basic motif was not only productive in furnishing new motif-forms through developing variations, but also in producing more remote formulations based on the unifying effect of one common factor: the repetition of tonal and intervallic relationships.

It is quite easy to repeat a basic set in one or more voices over and over again. There is no merit in writing canons of two or more voices; even the writing of whole fugues is a little too easy under these circumstances. Composing of these forms in which the highest achievement has already been reached by composers whose form of expression was that of contrapuntal combinations should only be undertaken, for instance, if a composer feels he must calm down a sort of nostalgic longing for old-time beauty, or because in the course of a huge work one of the parts must be in old style.

Arnold Schoenberg, *Style and Idea*, ed. Leonard Stein (New York: St. Martin's Press, 1975), 245–49. Reprinted by permission of Faber and Faber Ltd., London.

132

The Rite of Spring

Quite the most spectacular "event" in the history of the early twentieth-century musical avant-garde was the première of the ballet *The Rite of Spring* (*Le Sacre du Printemps*) by the young Igor Stravinsky (1882–1971), who was then a staff composer for Sergei Diaghilev's Ballets Russes. A musical evocation of the fertility rites of ancient, pagan Russia, this was a work calculated to set the musical world on its ear. Its freedom of dissonance, the crashing force of its "barbaric" orchestration, and above all its hugely resourceful innovations in asymmetrical rhythm, made the work at once bewildering and irresistibly exciting to its early audiences. The result was a historic near-riot at the first performance, which took place in Paris on 29 May 1913.

The Rite of Spring. In this brilliant caricature made by Jean Cocteau in the year of the première, Stravinsky bangs out his ballet at the keyboard and conjures up the ancient elders, youths, and virgins that people it, including the sacrificial dancer at the top. All are rendered with a "cubist" angularity that conveys something of the brusque primitivism of the music. © 2007 *Estate of Jean Cocteau / Artists Rights Society (ARS), NY.*

Below, we give a quartet of readings on this extraordinary work, beginning with an article that appeared over Stravinsky's name in a Paris art magazine on the day of the première. Stravinsky attempted on numerous subsequent occasions to disavow the piece, but letters exist that confirm his authorship beyond doubt. It conveys vividly Stravinsky's own attitude towards his greatest work at the time of its composition.

What I Wished to Express in "The Rite of Spring"

Some years ago the Parisian public was kind enough to receive favorably my *Firebird* and *Petrushka*. My friends have noted the evolution of the underlying idea, which passes from the fantastic fable of one of these works to the purely human generalization of the other. I fear that "The Rite of Spring," in which I appeal neither to the spirit of fairy tales nor to human joy and grief, but in which I strive towards a somewhat greater abstraction, may confuse those who have until now manifested a precious sympathy towards me.

In "The Rite of Spring" I wished to express the sublime uprising of Nature renewing herself—the whole pantheistic uprising of the universal harvest.

In the Prelude, before the curtain rises, I have confided to my orchestra the great fear which weighs on every sensitive soul confronted with potentialities, the "thing in one's self," which may increase and develop infinitely. A feeble flute tone may contain potentiality, spreading throughout the orchestra. It is the obscure and immense sensation of which all things are conscious when Nature renews its forms; it is the vague and profound uneasiness of a universal puberty. Even in my orchestration and my melodic development I have sought to define it.

The whole Prelude is based upon a continuous "mezzo forte." The melody develops in a horizontal line that only masses of instruments (the intense dynamic power of the orchestra and not the melodic line itself) increase or diminish. In consequence, I have not given this melody to the strings, which are too symbolic and representative of the human voice; with the crescendi and diminuendi, I have brought forward the wind instruments which have a drier tone, which are more precise, less endowed with facile expression, and on this account more suitable for my purpose.

In short, I have tried to express in this Prelude the fear of nature before the arising of beauty, a sacred terror at the midday sun, a sort of pagan cry. The musical material itself swells, enlarges, expands. Each instrument is like a bud which grows on the bark of an aged tree; it becomes part of an imposing whole. And the whole orchestra, all this massing of instruments, should have the significance of the Birth of Spring.

In the first scene, some adolescent boys appear with a very old woman, whose age and even whose century is unknown, who knows the secrets of nature, and teaches her sons Divination. She runs, bent over the earth, half-woman, half-beast. The adolescents at her side are Augurs of Spring, who mark in their steps the rhythm of spring, the pulse-beat of spring.

During this time the adolescent girls come from the river. They form a circle which mingles with the boys' circle. They are not entirely formed beings; their sex is single and double like that of the tree. The groups mingle, but in their rhythms one feels the cataclysm of groups about to form. In fact they divide right and left. It is the realization of form, the synthesis of rhythms, and the thing formed produces a new rhythm.

The groups separate and compete, messengers come from one to the other and they quarrel. It is the defining of forces through struggle, that is to say through games. But a Procession arrives. It is the Saint, the Sage, the Pontifex, the oldest of the clan. All are seized with terror. The Sage gives a benediction to the Earth, stretched flat, his arms and legs stretched out, becoming one with the soil. His benediction is as a signal for an eruption of rhythm. Each, covering his head, runs in spirals, pouring forth in numbers, like the new energies of nature. It is the Dance of the Earth.

The second scene begins with an obscure game of the adolescent girls. At the beginning, a musical picture is based upon a song which accompanies the young girls' dances. The latter mark in their dance the place where the Elect will be confined, and whence she cannot move. The Elect is she whom the Spring is to consecrate, and who will give back to Spring the force that youth has taken from it.

The young girls dance about the Elect, a sort of glorification. Then comes the purification of the soil and the Evocation of the Ancestors. The Ancestors gather around the Elect, who begins the "Dance of Consecration." When she is on the point of falling exhausted, the Ancestors recognize it and glide toward her like rapacious monsters in order that she may not touch the ground; they pick her up and raise her toward heaven. The annual cycle of forces which are born again, and which fall again into the bosom of nature, is accomplished in its essential rhythms.

I am happy to have found in [Vaslav] Nijinsky the ideal choreographic collaborator, and in [Nicholas] Roerich the creator of the decorative atmosphere for this work of faith.

Boston Evening Transcript, 12 February 1916. Trans. Edward Burlingame Hill.

As for the première, an eyewitness account by the American writer Carl Van Vechten can hardly be bettered for its immediacy and atmosphere.

My personal impressions of Stravinsky's music and its effect on me are very strong. I attended the first performance in Paris of his anarchistic (against the canons of academic art) ballet, *The Sacrifice to the Spring,* in which primitive emotions are both depicted and aroused by a dependence on barbarous rhythm, in which melody and harmony, as even so late a composer as Richard Strauss understands them, do not enter. A certain part of the audience, thrilled by what it considered a blasphemous attempt to destroy music as an art, and swept away with wrath, began very soon after the rise of the curtain to whistle, to make cat-calls, and to offer audible suggestions as to how the performance should proceed. Others of us, who liked the music and felt that the principles of free speech were at stake, bellowed defiance. It was war over art for the rest of the evening and the orchestra played on unheard, except occasionally when a slight lull occurred. The figures on stage danced in time to music they had to imagine they heard and beautifully out of rhythm with the uproar in the auditorium. I was sitting in a box in which I had rented one seat. Three ladies sat in front of me and a young man occupied the place behind me. He stood up during the course of the ballet to enable himself to see more clearly. The intense excitement under which he was laboring, thanks to the potent force of the music, betrayed itself presently when he began to beat rhythmically on the top of my head with his fists. My emotion was so great that I did not feel the blows for some time. They were perfectly synchronized with the beat of the music. When I did, I turned around. His apology was sincere. We had both been carried beyond ourselves.

Carl Van Vechten, *Music After the Great War* (New York: G. Schirmer, 1915), 87–88.

Although it is easy now to place *The Rite of Spring* in the context of its Russian "nationalist" heritage, particularly the colorful scores of Stravinsky's teacher Rimsky-Korsakov, at first the reaction of the older generation of Russian composers was no different from that of conservative musicians everywhere. Especially interesting is the response of César Cui (1835–1918), the last survivor of the New Russian School (see p. 333). The view of Stravinsky as a kind of musical anarchist or saboteur was widespread.

Recently Sergei Koussevitzky has performed Stravinsky's *Rite of Spring,* which has broken all records for cacophony and hideousness. It is a treasure chest in which Stravinsky has lovingly collected all sorts of musical filth and refuse. This "Rite" has been booed everywhere abroad, but among us it found some applauders—proof that we are ahead of Europe on the path of musical progress.

Letter to M. S. Kerzina, 16 February (1 March, New Style) 1914, in César Cui, *Izbrannye pis'ma* (Leningrad: Muzgiz, 1955), 446. Trans. R. T.

But Stravinsky did not see himself as a monger of filth. And later developments in his career enable us to credit completely the sincerity of his protest at his masterpiece's reception, as reported in the French press shortly after *The Rite*'s première.

Igor Stravinsky is displeased. The audience of the Ballets Russes reacted to his new work *Le Sacre du Printemps* with discordant outcries and laughter, interrupted by the applause of a few initiates. But in all fairness I must say that the composer was not very much upset and did not fulminate too violently against his detractors when we interviewed him yesterday.

Stravinsky is small in stature, but looks tall because he holds his forehead high, so that he dominates his interlocutor; he speaks from an elevation, and his eyes rove over objects and people with a mobility that engulfs them like a sudden shower.

"That my music could not be immediately accepted, I quite understand," he declared backstage at the Théâtre des Champs-Elysées. "What is unjustifiable, however, is the lack of good will on the part of the audience. It seems to me that they should have waited for the end of the performance to express their disapproval. This would have been courteous and honest. I gave them something new, and I fully expected that those who had applauded *Petrushka* and *The Firebird* [presented in previous seasons] would be somewhat dismayed, but I also expected an understanding attitude. I have acted in good faith; my previous works which have been well received were a guarantee of my sincerity, and should have proved that I had no intention whatsoever of making fun of the public. During the première, when the commotion made it impossible for the dancers to hear the music, we all were quite unhappy, not only because of our own pride, but because we feared that we would not be able to go on with the show. And this was the reward for 130 rehearsals and a year of work!"

Henri Postel du Mas in *Gil Blas* (Paris, 4 June 1913), quoted in Nicolas Slonimsky (ed.), *Music Since 1900*, 4th ed. (New York: Charles Scribner's Sons, 1971), 224. Trans. Nicolas Slonimsky. Copyright © 1971 Nicolas Slonimsky. Reprinted with the permission of Charles Scribner's Sons.

133

A Futurist Manifesto

If Stravinsky (see the previous selection) was no musical anarchist, the times certainly did not lack for them. Many of these wild-eyed radicals came from Italy, where they were known as Futurists. Although it is difficult today to suppress a smile when reading manifestos like Luigi Russolo's of 1913, the Futurists did prefigure a serious musical movement of the immediate post-World War II period—that of *musique concrète*, in which the sounds of the everyday world were pressed into musical service through the agency of the tape recorder. This device being unavailable to the earlier Futurists, their "music of noises" remained for the most part an imaginative fantasy. It is worth noting, perhaps, that the author of this fiery condemnation of all musical traditions was no musician himself, but a painter.

Life in ancient times was silent. In the nineteenth century, with the invention of machines, Noise was born. Today Noise is triumphant, and reigns supreme over the senses of men. The art of music at first sought and achieved purity and sweetness of sound; later, it blended diverse sounds, but always with intent to caress the ear with suave harmonies. Today, growing ever more complicated, it seeks those combinations of sounds that fall most dissonantly, strangely, and harshly upon the ear. We thus approach nearer and nearer to the MUSIC OF NOISE. We must break out of this narrow circle of pure musical sounds, and conquer the infinite variety of noise-sounds.

Everyone will recognize that every musical sound carries with it an incrustation of familiar and stale sense associations, which predispose the hearer to boredom, despite all the efforts of innovating musicians. We futurists have all deeply loved the music of the great composers. Beethoven and Wagner for many years wrung our hearts. But now we are sated with them and derive much greater pleasure from ideally combining the noises of streetcars, internal-combustion engines, automobiles, and busy crowds than from re-hearing, for example, the "Eroica" or the "Pastorale."

We cannot see the immense apparatus of the modern orchestra without being profoundly disappointed by its feeble acoustic achievements. Is there anything more absurd than to see twenty men breaking their necks to multiply the meowling of a violin? All this will naturally infuriate the musicomaniacs and perhaps disturb the somnolent atmosphere of our concert halls. Let us enter, as futurists, into one of these institutions for musical anemia. The first measure assails your ear with the boredom of the already-heard and causes you to anticipate the boredom of the measure to come. Thus we sip, from measure to measure, two or three different sorts of boredom, while we await an unusual emotion that never arrives. Meanwhile we are revolted by the monotony of the sensations experienced, combined with the idiotic religious excitement of the listeners, Buddhistically intoxicated by the thousandth repetition of their hypocritical and artificial ecstasy. Away! Let us be gone, since we shall not much longer succeed in restraining a desire to create a new musical realism by a generous distribution of sonorous blows and slaps, leaping nimbly over violins, pianofortes, contrabasses, and groaning organs. Away!

Let us wander through a great modern city with our ears more attentive than our eyes, and distinguish the sounds of water, air, or gas in metal pipes, the purring of motors (which breathe and pulsate with an indubitable animalism), the throbbing of valves, the pounding of pistons, the screeching of gears, the clatter of streetcars on their rails, the cracking of whips, the flapping of awnings and flags. We shall amuse ourselves by orchestrating in our minds the noise of the metal shutters of store windows, the slamming of doors, the bustle and shuffle of crowds, the multitudinous uproar of railroad stations, forges, mills, printing presses, power stations, and underground railways. Nor should the new noises of modern warfare be forgotten.

We must fix the pitch and regulate the harmonies and rhythms of these extraordinarily varied sounds. To fix the pitch of noises does not mean to take away from them all the irregularity of tempo and intensity that characterizes their vibrations, but rather to give definite gradation or pitch to the stronger and more predominant of these vibrations. Indeed, noise is differentiated from musical sound merely in that the vibrations that produce it are confused and irregular, both in tempo and in intensity.

Every manifestation of life is accompanied by noise. Noise is therefore familiar to our ears and has the power to remind us immediately of life itself. Musical sound, a thing extraneous to life and independent of it, an occasional and unnecessary adjunct, has become for our ears what a too familiar face is to our eyes. Noise, on the other hand, which comes to us confused and irregular as life itself, never reveals itself wholly but reserves for us innumerable surprises. We are convinced, therefore, that by selecting, co-ordinating, and controlling noises we shall enrich mankind with a new and unsuspected source of pleasure. Despite the fact that it is characteristic of sound to remind us brutally of life, the ART OF NOISES must not limit itself to reproductive imitation. It will reach its greatest emotional power through the purely acoustic enjoyment which the inspiration of the artist will contrive to evoke from combinations of noises.

These are the futurist orchestra's six families of noises, which we shall soon produce mechanically:

1	2	3	4	5	6
Booms Thunderclaps Explosions Crashes Splashes Roars	Whistles Hisses Snorts	Whispers Murmurs Mutterings Bustling noises Gurgles	Screams Screeches Rustlings Buzzes Cracklings Sounds obtained by friction	Noises obtained by percussion on metals, wood, stone, terracotta	Voices of animals and men: Shouts Shrieks Groans Howls Laughs Wheezes Sobs

I am not a professional musician; I have therefore no acoustic prejudices and no works to defend. I am a futurist painter projecting into an art he loves and has studied his desire to renovate all things. Being therefore more audacious than a professional musician could be, caring nought for my seeming incompetence, and convinced that audacity makes all things lawful and all things possible, I have imagined a great renovation of music through the Art of Noises.

Nicolas Slonimsky (ed.), *Music Since 1900*, 4th ed. (New York: Charles Scribner's Sons, 1971), 1298–1302. Trans. Stephen Somervelle. Copyright © 1971 Nicolas Slonimsky. Reprinted with the permission of Charles Scribner's Sons.

134

The New Folklorism

Among twentieth-century composers who cultivated a "national" style, the Hungarian Béla Bartók (1881–1945) looms largest. A trained folklorist (or, in today's terminology, an ethnomusicologist), Bartók—sometimes in collaboration with a like-minded compatriot, Zoltán Kodály (1882–1967)—collected, transcribed, and analyzed thousands of Hungarian, Romanian, Serbian, Turkish, and North African folk melodies. He attempted systematically to incorporate stylistic features of this music into his own creative work, seeing in this practice a way out of the post-Romantic impasse.

At the beginning of the 20th century there was a turning point in the history of modern music.

The excesses of the Romantics began to be unbearable for many. There were composers who felt: "this road does not lead us anywhere; there is no other solution but a complete break with the 19th century."

Invaluable help was given to this change (or let us rather call it rejuvenation) by a kind of peasant music unknown till then.

The right type of peasant music is most varied and perfect in its forms. Its expressive power is amazing, and at the same time it is devoid of all sentimentality and superfluous ornaments. It is simple, sometimes primitive, but never silly. It is the ideal starting point for a musical renaissance, and a composer in search of new ways cannot be led by a better master. What is the best way for a composer to reap the full benefits of his studies in peasant music? It is to assimilate the idiom of peasant music so completely that he is able to forget all about it and use it as his musical mother tongue.

In order to achieve this, Hungarian composers went into the country and made their collections there. It may be that the Russian Stravinsky and the Spaniard [Manuel de] Falla [1876–1946] did not go on journeys of collection, and mainly drew their material from the collections of others, but they too, I feel sure, must have studied not only books and museums but the living music of their countries.

In my opinion, the effects of peasant music cannot be deep and permanent unless this music is studied in the country as part of a life shared with the peasants. It is not enough to study it as it is stored up in museums. It is the character of peasant music, indescribable in words, that must find its way into our music. It must be pervaded by the very atmosphere of peasant culture. Peasant motives (or imitations of such motives) will only lend our music some new ornaments; nothing more.

Some twenty to twenty-five years ago well-disposed people often marvelled at our enthusiasm. How was it possible, they asked, that trained musicians, fit to give concerts, took upon themselves the "subaltern" task of going into the country and studying the music of the people on the spot. What a pity, they said, that this task was not carried out by people unsuitable for a higher type of musical work. Many thought our perseverance in our work was due to some crazy idea that had got hold of us.

Little did they know how much this work meant to us. We went into the country and obtained first-hand knowledge of a music that opened up new ways to us.

The question is, what are the ways in which peasant music is taken over and becomes transmuted into modern music?

We may, for instance, take over a peasant melody unchanged or only slightly varied, write an accompaniment to it and possibly some opening and concluding phrases. This kind of work would show a certain analogy with Bach's treatment of chorales.

Two main types can be distinguished among works of this character.

In one case accompaniment, introductory and concluding phrases are of secondary importance, and they only serve as an ornamental setting for the precious stone: the peasant melody.

It is the other way round in the second case: the melody only serves as a "motto" while that which is built around it is of real importance.

All shades of transition are possible between these two extremes and sometimes it is not even possible to decide which of the elements is predominant in any given case. But in every case it is of the greatest importance that the musical qualities of the setting should be derived from the musical qualities of the melody, from such characteristics as are contained in it openly or covertly, so that melody and all additions create the impression of complete unity.

It may sound odd, but I do not hesitate to say: the simpler the melody, the more complex and strange may be the harmonization and accompaniment that will go well with it. Let us for instance take a melody that moves on two successive notes only (there are many such melodies in Arab peasant music). It is obvious that we are much freer in the invention of an accompaniment than in the case of a melody of a more complex character. These primitive melodies, moreover, show no trace of the stereotyped joining of triads. That again means greater freedom for us in the treatment of the melody. It allows us to bring out the melody most clearly by building around it harmonies of the widest range varying along different keynotes. I might almost say that the traces of polytonality in modern Hungarian music and in Stravinsky's music are to be explained by this possibility.

Similarly, the strange turnings of melodies in our Eastern European peasant music showed us new ways of harmonization. For instance, the new chord of the seventh which we use as a concord may be traced back to the fact that in our folk melodies of a pentatonic character the seventh appears as an interval of equal importance with the third and fifth. We so often heard these intervals as of equal value in the succession, that nothing was more natural than that we should try to make them sound of equal importance when used simultaneously. We sounded the four notes together in a setting which made us feel it not necessary to break them up. In other words; the four notes were made to form a concord.

The frequent use of fourth-intervals in our old melodies suggested to us the use of fourth chords. Here again what we heard in succession we tried to build up in a simultaneous chord.

Another method by which peasant music becomes transmuted into modern music is the following: the composer does not make use of a real peasant melody but invents his own imitation of such melodies. There is no true difference between this method and the one described above.

Stravinsky never mentions the sources of his themes. Neither in his titles nor in footnotes does he ever allude to whether a theme of his is his own invention or whether it is taken over from folk music. In the same way the old composers never gave any data: let me simply mention the beginning of [Beethoven's] "Pastoral" Symphony [based, so Bartók asserted, on a Croatian folksong]. Stravinsky apparently takes this course deliberately. He wants to demonstrate that it does not matter a jot whether a composer invents his own themes or uses themes from elsewhere. He has a right to use musical material taken from all sources. What he has judged suitable for his purpose has become through this very use his mental property. In maintaining that the question of the origin of a theme is completely unimportant from the artist's point of view, Stravinsky is right. The question of origins can only be interesting from the point of view of musical documentation.

Lacking any data I am unable to tell which themes of Stravinsky's in his so-called "Russian" period are his own inventions and which are borrowed from folk music. This much is certain, that if among the thematic material of Stravinsky's there are some of his own invention (and who can doubt that there are) these are the most faithful and clever imitations of folk songs. It is also notable that during his "Russian" period, from *Le Sacre du Printemps* onward, he seldom uses melodies of a closed form consisting of three or four lines, but short motives of two or three measures, and repeats them *"à la ostinato."* These short recurring primitive motives are very characteristic of Russian music of a certain category. This type of construction occurs in some of our old music for wind instruments and also in Arab peasant dances.

There is yet a third way in which the influence of peasant music can be traced in a composer's work. Neither peasant melodies nor imitations of peasant melodies can be found in his music, but it is pervaded by the atmosphere of peasant music. In this case we may say, he has completely absorbed the idiom of peasant music which has become his musical mother tongue. He masters it as completely as a poet masters his mother tongue.

In Hungarian music the best example of this kind can be found in Kodály's work. It is enough to mention *Psalmus Hungaricus,* which would not have been written without Hungarian peasant music. (Neither, of course, would it have been written without Kodály.)

Benjamin Suchoff (ed.), *The Essays of Béla Bartók* (New York: St. Martin's Press, 1976), 340–44. Reprinted by permission of Faber and Faber Ltd., London.

Bartók's remarks on Stravinsky are penetrating and valid, yet what was a lifelong devotion in Bartók's case was only a passing phase with his Russian contemporary. With his increasing involvement with "neoclassic" music, Stravinsky became less and less sympathetic to musical folklorism and even tried to deny certain aspects of his former enthusiasm for it. Looking back on Bartók in 1959, Stravinsky, while recognizing his late colleague's greatness, wrote that he "couldn't help regretting" the Hungarian's "lifelong gusto for his native folklore." And as early as 1930, in an interview published in a Belgian newspaper, Stravinsky delivered himself of the following acerbic comments:

Some composers have found their most potent inspiration in folk music, but in my opinion popular music has nothing to gain by being taken out of its frame. It is not suitable as a pretext for demonstrations of orchestral effects and complications, and it loses its charm by being *déracinée* [uprooted]. One risks adulterating it and rendering it monotonous.

Vera Stravinsky and Robert Craft, *Stravinsky in Pictures and Documents* (New York: Simon and Schuster, 1978), 202.

England, long sneeringly referred to by Germans as "das Land ohne Musik" (the land without music), suddenly sprang to creative life around the turn of the century, a musical renaissance that coincided not at all by accident with a strong revival of interest in traditional British folk music. Below, Ralph Vaughan Williams (1872–1958), one of the leaders of the English musical rebirth, defends the use of native folk music against the conservative—and largely German-dominated—musical establishment.

I must have made my first contact with English folk songs when I was a boy in the 'eighties, through Stainer and Bramley's *Christmas Carols New and Old.* I remember clearly my reaction to the tune of the "Cherry Tree Carol" which was more than simple admiration for a fine tune, though I did not then naturally realize the implications involved in that sense of intimacy. This sense came upon me more strongly in 1893 when I first discovered "Dives and Lazarus" in *English County Songs.* Here, as before with Wagner, I had that sense of recognition—"here's something which I have known all my life—only I didn't know it!"

There has been a lot of cheap wit expended on "folk song" composers. The matter seems to boil down to two accusations: First that it is "cheating" to make use of folk-song material. This is really nothing more than the old complaint of the vested interests who are annoyed when anyone drinks a glass of pure water which he can get free, rather than a glass of beer which will bring profit to the company. This appears to involve a moral rather than an artistic question; from the point of view of musical experience it seems to me that so long as good music is made it matters very little how it is made or who makes it. If a composer can, by tapping the sources hidden in folk song, make beautiful music, he will be disloyal to his art if he does not make full use of such an avenue of beauty.

The second accusation is made by people who affect to scorn what is "folksy" because it does not come within the ken of their airless smuggeries, because it does not require any highly-paid teachers to inculcate it, or the purchase of text-books with a corresponding royalty to the author. It is really a case of the vested interests once again.

Why should music be "original"? The object of art is to stretch out to the ultimate realities through the medium of beauty. The duty of the composer is to find the *mot juste*. It does not matter if this word has been said a thousand times before as long as it is the right thing to say at that moment. If it is *not* the right thing to say, however unheard of it may be, it is of no artistic value. Music which is unoriginal is so, not simply because it has been said before, but because the composer has not taken the trouble to make sure that this was the right thing to say at the right moment.

My intercourse with Cecil Sharp [1859–1924, folk-song collector and propagandist] crystallized and confirmed what I already vaguely felt about folk song and its relationship to the composer's art. With Sharp it was a case of "Under which King, Bezonian? Speak, or die." You had to be either pro folk song or anti folk song and I came down heavily on the folk song side.

In 1904 I undertook to edit the music of a hymn-book. This meant two years with no "original" work except a few hymn-tunes. I wondered then if I were "wasting my time." The years were passing and I was adding nothing to the sum of musical invention. But I know now that two years of close association with some of the best (as well as some of the worst) tunes in the world was a better musical education than any amount of sonatas and fugues.

Ralph Vaughan Williams, *National Music, and Other Essays* (London: Oxford University Press, 1963), 189–90.

135

The Cataclysm

The complete disruption of European cultural life brought about in the aftermath of the First World War is well described in an essay by Béla Bartók. A sadly persistent twentieth-century theme is introduced: the buffeting art has suffered amid the unstable and oft-times totalitarian political conditions that plagued Europe in recent times. This led certain composers all the more resolutely to renounce public, "establishmentarian" musical outlets, and was a prime factor in turning many of the century's foremost musical minds away from the large forms like symphony and opera, and toward more exclusive and private "chamber" media. Bartók is a case in point: once past his student years he never wrote a symphony, and all his stage works were composed by the time he wrote this article. Thereafter his reputation was to rest on his piano music, his string quartets, and his works for chamber orchestra. This development, of course, has widened the rift between serious music and the mass audience.

Before the war Budapest had a comparatively flourishing musical life. Apart from the performances of the three principal institutions—the High School of Music, the National Opera and the Philharmonic Society (consisting of the Opera orchestra)—a large number of concerts by foreign and home talent stilled the public's craving for good music. Once even Debussy himself came to act as pianist at a Debussy evening. The Vienna orchestral societies were wont to visit us, Richard Strauss's unforgettable conducting being among the chief attractions of these tours. In 1912 even the Russian Ballet was seen here, producing among other things Stravinsky's *Firebird*.

The outbreak of the war naturally brought certain interruptions in its train. At first only the artists hailing from Entente countries held aloof, but since 1919 nearly all foreigners have shunned us. The Opera House remained closed during the season 1914–15. Although it was opened in 1915–16, it had to forgo the assistance of its best conductor, Egisto Tango, of Italian nationality, owing to political intrigues. All these drawbacks were followed in 1916–17 by a very decided improvement. Signor Tango at last was graciously pardoned for happening to be an Italian and enabled to continue his work, which had been so beneficial in every way, and Ernst von Dohnányi [1877–1960], the most eminent Hungarian pianist, left Berlin to take up permanent residence in Budapest. [Tango] was planning the performance of Stravinsky's *Sacre du Printemps* when the revolution broke out in 1918; all connections with other countries were interrupted for a very long time, and it thus became impossible to procure the necessary music.

The Socialists, who then came into power, were very progressively inclined toward all matters pertaining to art, and this soon found its expression in the musical life of the city. The oldest instructors at the High School, no longer able to do justice to their posts, were pensioned and Hungary's two eminent musicians, Dohnányi and Kodály, were entrusted with the management of the institution and the carrying into effect of all those reforms of Dohnányi's which hitherto had been blocked.

Then came the month of March, 1919, and with it the Communist dictatorship. In principle this regime favored the progressive home talent even more than its predecessor. A musical directorate was founded (Dohnányi, Kodály and Bartók) and to its care was committed the guidance of the entire musical life. The artists mentioned, although not avowed Communists, accepted this mission for several reasons: on the one hand they hoped for an improvement of general conditions, and on the other, were desirous of preventing any acts of force that might endanger musical life, and of cutting the ground from under the feet of ungifted musical parvenus.

Unfortunately, the Socialist rule as such was a grave disappointment, and that of the Communists even more so. From November, 1918, onward an absolute delirium to call into being "monumental" institutions seized certain sectors, spreading continuously until it almost took on maniacal proportions, and without any deference to the sparse material resources available. The Soviet revealed its utter ignorance of any planned action in establishing the general and fundamental points according to which the reform of musical instruction, concert life and the publication of musical works were to find their solution. The Trades Union of Musicians (artists) and Musical Craftsmen (both classes were coupled together in one union!) stubbornly—albeit unsuccessfully—attempted, with the backing of the proletariat, to launch its most untalented but noisiest claimants to fame into leading positions. Protectionism and bureaucracy flourished as never before. The Soviet was just as narrow-minded as the former bourgeois administrations had been. Serious and fruitful work was an utter impossibility under such conditions, and a feeling of relief was general when the dictatorship collapsed on July 29, 1919.

But—out of the frying pan into the fire! In the period of conservative reaction that followed, Dohnányi and Kodály were dismissed from their positions as heads of the High School; all their reforms were annulled, the best instructors swept aside, and all this under the false and thin pretense of routing out Bolshevism. Egisto Tango's contract with the Opera was rescinded, and he was allowed to enter the service of Romania as director of the new Romanian National Opera at Cluj. His last performance here (and at the same time the only outstanding musical event during the Communist era) was the new staging of Verdi's *Otello* in a wonderful presentation in May, 1919.

Thus at the present moment—the end of February, 1920—the High School stands deprived of its best instructors, the Opera House of its only good conductor. Complete demoralization reigns at the latter institution since the autumn; it has even happened that the conductor had to interrupt a public performance and start in all over again! The repertory is a hackneyed one, everlastingly *Tannhäuser, Carmen, Butterfly,* and so forth. New works were unknown, barring two unimportant, local one-act productions. But far from being censured for the loss of Tango or for the present inartistic regime, Emil Abrányi, the general director of opera, has merely been accused of possessing too little-marked a sense of "Christian Nationalism"! He was, in all seriousness, accused of having engaged several new Jewish members and of having performed two local works by Jewish composers. For with us at present it is no longer a question of whether a singer, an artist, a savant is of good repute in his especial class of work, but whether he is a Jew or a man of liberal tendencies. For these two sections of humanity are to be excluded as far as possible from all public activity.

Béla Bartók, "Hungary in the Throes of Reaction," *The Musical Courier,* LXXX, no. 18 (April 1920), 42–43.

136

Between the Wars

This remarkable survey by the American composer Roger Sessions (1896–1985) was published in 1933. Sessions saw music in his time as passing through a "crisis" brought about by the breakdown of the common musical language of the eighteenth and nineteenth centuries. He distinguishes three basic trends: "objective" neoclassical ideals; "subjective" twelve-tone composition; and "popular" or "functional" styles that represented an attempt—sometimes spontaneous, sometimes coerced by political authorities—to reestablish ties with the public at large. Sessions leaves no doubt as to where his own sympathies lie, and this is one of the most valuable aspects of his article. For it reminds us that twelve-tone music, which was to stage an extraordinary comeback after World War II (and even seemed for a while to be the basis of a new common-practice period), was widely regarded in the 1930s as a sectarian and moribund movement. It is a matter of some irony that after 1953 Sessions wrote twelve-tone music himself. And he probably lived to regret his sally at the expense of Alban Berg's *Wozzeck*, which, though not a twelve-tone work, was chosen by Sessions as his prime example of musical "Alexandrianism," or esoteric decadence. But that aside, the essay is one of exceptional clarity and intelligence, and its precise characterizations, though close to the tendencies they describe, have scarcely been bettered since.

Perhaps the most obvious symptom of the present crisis is its "confusion of tongues"— the result of nearly a century of musical development before the Great War. What took place during this period was a gradual dissociation of the musical consciousness of Europe (rather, of the Occident) into a multitude of various components. This dissociative process, the last phase of which constituted the "modern music" of twenty years ago, represented for the non-German peoples first of all a breaking-away from the German domination of musical culture, and was the inevitable result of the then latest developments of German music, which, as Nietzsche once so penetratingly wrote, had ceased to be "the voice of Europe's soul" and was instead degenerating into mere *Vaterländerei* ["fatherlandishness"]. The "voice of Europe's soul," however, has never yet been truly recovered; the *Vaterländerei* of which Nietzsche saw the fatal beginnings in Germany began to reproduce itself elsewhere where in a franker and even more accentuated form, in a quantity of national "schools" of picturesquely local significance; the common cultural heritage began to be abandoned in favor of localisms, until by the end of the century a very definite cleavage was perceptible.

It is idle to inquire when and by whom the somewhat sweeping and inexact term "neoclassicism" was first applied to certain contemporary tendencies. It has been applied rather disconcertingly to such essentially different composers as Stravinsky, Hindemith, and [Alfredo] Casella [1883–1947]—composers in each of whom a certain more or less conscious traditionalism (not a new thing in art) is apparent, but who differ widely both in the traditions which they represent, and in the roles which tradition plays in the composition of their styles. There is also sometimes a still more primitive failure to discriminate between the traditionalism which springs from an essential impulse and is animated by a real inner tension, and another traditionalism, also to be found in recent music, which represents the exact contrary of this—a manner, a mode, nourished on *cliché* and fashionable propaganda—a traditionalism of followers and not of independent spirits. It is obviously not the latter that comes into consideration here.

Let us abandon, then, the term "neoclassicism" and consider rather certain features which this term is commonly taken to represent. Many of these features are not traditionalistic in any necessary sense, nor were they so in their origins. The composers in Russia and France who, during the latter half of the last century, made the original break with the specific latter-day German tradition, brought into the varied general current of music a mass of new and at first sometimes not wholly assimilated materials which were in contact with that tradition, or rather with those of its phases against which the break was directed. A more transparent texture, a pronounced emphasis on rhythm and movement, a less emphatic harmonic style, and an instrumentation consisting of sharply defined rather than mixed timbres, were characteristic features of this newer music. What it lacked was first of all depth; it was very often music of association, of mood, of color, with relatively little essential and organic inner life of its own. Taken by and large it represented a collection of various *manners* rather than a style; an exploitation of certain nuances of color and sonority rather than a complete vision, a world in which all possible musical ingredients could find their place.

The new traditionalism, however, can in no real sense be called a "return to the past." Rather should it be considered in the light of a *reprise de contact;* and, in spite of its prophets, essentially nothing more than a point of departure. It was significant chiefly in that it marked the beginning of an instinctive effort to rediscover certain essential qualities of the older music with a view to applying them to the purposes of the new, an experiencing anew of certain laws which are inherent in the nature of music itself, but which had been lost from view in an increasing subjectivism and tendency to lean, even in "pure" music, more and more on association, sensation, and mood.

This traditionalism, then, was essentially a part of a new attitude towards music—new at least for its time. Music began above all to be conceived in a more direct, more impersonal, and more positive fashion; there was a new emphasis on the dynamic, constructive, monumental elements of music, and, so to speak, a revaluation of musical materials. This revaluation has shown itself by no means only in actual compositions, but is perceptible among interpreters also. The function of the interpreter, in fact, has been to some extent reconsidered, and a far greater emphasis is today laid on fidelity to the composer's musical thought than was the case twenty years ago.

It would be inaccurate to define this current, as has been so often done, as an emphasis on "form" at the expense of "content"; it marks rather a change of attitude towards form and content both, which we might describe as a transference of the sphere of consciousness in the creative process. Whereas the earlier tendency was to be more and more conscious in regard to a "meaning behind the notes" and to construct the music according to principles derived from this indirect and not strictly musical source, the composers of the newer music proceeded directly from their musical impulses, seeking to embody these impulses in musical ideas which should have an independent existence of their own, and to develop these ideas according to the impetus inherent in them as musical entities. In other words, with the latter the *musical idea* is the point of departure, whereas with the former extra-musical considerations consciously determine the choice of the idea. The new attitude brought inevitably in its train a new and often laconic form of utterance which was sometimes interpreted as an abandonment of "expression." It was in reality, of course, a new manner of expression, a new sobriety and at its best, as in the finest pages of Stravinsky, a new inwardness. The grandiloquent and neurotic self-importance which characterized so much of the music of the years preceding the war has, in fact, practically disappeared and is only to be found in a few provincial survivals. The contemporary composer, when he wishes to achieve grandeur of utterance, does so by more subtle, monumental means.

While by far the greater part of the more significant contemporary music composed outside of Central Europe, and very much of that composed in Germany as well, may be said to belong in a rough sense to the tendency above described, a large group of composers in the countries once included in the Austrian Empire, together with a perceptible number of Germans, have been following quite other lines. This so-called "Central European" tendency is chiefly embodied in the works of Arnold Schoenberg and his followers, though not strictly confined to them. Nor must the qualification

"Central European" be taken to imply an essentially local or geographical emphasis in the creed itself. Though in our belief it could, for historical reasons, have arisen nowhere else but in Vienna, and represents in fact an inevitable end-stage in Viennese musical culture, it claims for itself a universal validity, a more or less general monopoly, in fact, of what is significant in contemporary music. Far more than any other contemporary tendency it is dominated by a single personality, and its development is closely coincident with that of its leader.

It is hardly necessary to point out that the art of Schoenberg has vital connections with the past. Close acquaintance shows how deeply it is rooted in the chromaticism of [Wagner's] *Tristan* and *Parsifal*. This music may in fact be regarded as pre-eminently a logical development of that chromaticism, and the "twelve-tone system" as, in great part, a bold effort to formulate directive laws for its further development. "Atonality," if its real and not its superficial meaning be understood, is merely another name for that chromaticism and not, as the term would seem to imply, a negation of the necessity for fundamental acoustic unity, based on laws which are the inevitable consequence both of natural phenomena of sound, and of the millennial culture of the Occidental ear.

All that is ambiguous and profoundly problematical in the music of Schoenberg is to be traced to its definitely esoteric character. A contemporary German musician, whose pronouncements in such matters are as authoritative as they are brilliant and profound, has compared certain musical tendencies in present day Germany to the decadent Greek art of Alexandria, remarking that, "There is an Alexandrianism of profundity and an Alexandrianism of superficiality." "Alexandrianism of profundity," indeed, well defines the music of the Central European group in certain respects—its tortured and feverish moods, its overwhelming emphasis on detail, its lack of genuine movement, all signs of a decaying musical culture, without fresh human impulses to keep it alive. The technic of this music, too, is of a curiously ambiguous nature, and often represents an extraordinary lack of coherence between the music *heard* and, so to speak, its theoretical structure—another sign of an art that is rapidly approaching exhaustion. An orchestral movement, for instance, which is constructed according to the most rigid contrapuntal mathematics will turn out to be, in its acoustic realization, a succession of interesting sonorities without audible contrapuntal implication—an impression not to be dispelled by the most conscientious and sympathetic study of the score, the most complete familiarity with both its intellectual and its sonorous content. An opera whose remarkable feature when heard is its fidelity to the text, its responsiveness to every changing psychological nuance, proves on examination to be constructed in its various scenes on the external models of classic forms, without, however, the steady and consistent movement that gives these forms their purpose and their character. Such esoteric and discarded devices as the *cancrizans* [i.e., retrograde] variation of a theme, a technical curiosity which is admittedly inaccessible to the most attentive ear and which was used with the utmost rarity by the classic composers, becomes a regular and essential technical procedure. All of this goes to indicate the presence of a merely speculative element, tending to be completely dissociated from the impression actually received by the ear and the other faculties which contribute to the direct reception of a musical impression, and to produce what is either a fundamentally inessential *jeu d'esprit* of sometimes amazing proportions, or a kind of scaffolding erected as an external substitute for a living and breathing musical line.

Less strictly musical in significance than either of the general currents discussed above, but highly characteristic of our time and therefore worthy of some discussion, is the deliberate movement on the part of musicians, especially in Germany but also to a certain extent elsewhere, to seek a new relationship with the public and to form a great variety of new and direct contacts with it. The past ten years have witnessed the production of a vast quantity of music definitely written for purposes of practical "consumption," and though many of those purposes do not offer a precisely new field for musical production, new, on the other hand, is the scale and extent of the interest which musicians are taking in them.

The movement is only in a partial sense an artistic one. It originated no doubt during the economic chaos in Germany just after the war, in the period of "inflation," when the economic breakdown of the German bourgeoisie led to a profound modification of the musical life of Germany, partly by reducing considerably the public able to attend concerts and operatic performances, and partly by taking the attention of the new generation away from cultural interests—a situation later made more acute by the political, intellectual, and moral unrest which followed. It was under the pressure of such realities that many musicians were forced to take stock of the whole place of music in present-day society and to seek new channels for their activity. They found these new channels in the constructive movements of the time, to which they sought to contribute the energies which music could give. Emphasis was laid above all on the practical purposes of the music thus produced; music was above all to cease to be an article of the luxury or a primarily individual self-expression; to serve rather the ends of education, and especially of political and social propaganda. The same idea, far more drastically applied, will be readily recognized as that underlying the attitude of Soviet Russia towards art.

On perhaps a higher plane, the movement was undoubtedly in part the beginning of a renewed search for a fresh and more actively participating public. Composers busied themselves with the formation of a genuinely popular style, with rendering their music more accessible through a simplification of technic, with applying themselves seriously to the new problems offered by the radio, the cinema and mechanical means of reproduction. New ideals began to appear in the opera; younger composers began to produce works designed definitely for momentary consumption, works which were above all striking and "actual," designed to fulfill a momentary purpose and to be scrapped as soon as that purpose was fulfilled. They recognized, as did Wagner in a wholly different sense before them, the importance and the possibilities of opera in the creation of a public capable of the kind of participation which truly binds the composer to his world and his time.

137

The New Objectivity

With this peremptory manifesto on his actually rather innocuously diverting Octet (French: *Octuor*) for wind instruments in three neo-Baroque movements ("Sinfonia," "Tema con variazioni," "Finale"), Stravinsky threw down a kind of musical gauntlet:

music was not to traffic in "emotions"; it was not to be "interpreted"; "content" was only to be described in terms of "form." Although the position is overstated to a point that is apt to strike one nowadays as belabored if not faintly absurd, in its time (1924) Stravinsky's squib was an important document of a movement in which Stravinsky was by no means the only protagonist—the rediscovery of "purely musical" values after the excesses of Romanticism. Somewhat later, Stravinsky was to insist on the objective "reality" and concreteness of his music in terms even more colorfully extreme: "One's nose is not made: one's nose *is*. So it is with my art." (To which the French poet Paul Valéry responded, *"Vive votre nez!"*) In all of this we see the twentieth-century creator characteristically preoccupied with his materials, and jealous of his rights in the face of a performance tradition that through the nineteenth century had become more and more subjective and indulgent.

My *Octuor* is a musical object.

This object has a form and that form is influenced by the musical matter with which it is composed.

The differences of matter determine the differences of form. One does not do the same with marble that one does with stone.

My *Octuor* is made for an ensemble of wind instruments. Wind instruments seem to me to be more apt to render a certain rigidity of the form I had in mind than other instruments—the string instruments, for example, which are less cold and more vague.

The suppleness of the string instruments can lend itself to more subtle nuances and can serve better the individual sensibility of the executant in works built on an "emotive" basis.

My *Octuor* is not an "emotive" work but a musical composition based on objective elements which are sufficient in themselves.

The reasons why I composed this kind of music for an octet of flute, clarinet, bassoons, trumpets and trombones are the following: First, because this ensemble forms a complete sonorous scale and consequently furnishes me with a sufficiently rich register; second, because the difference of the volume of these instruments renders more evident the musical architecture. And this is the most important question in all my recent musical compositions.

I have excluded from this work all sorts of nuances, which I have replaced by the play of these volumes.

I have excluded all nuances between the *forte* and the *piano;* I have left only the *forte* and the *piano.*

Therefore the *forte* and the *piano* are in my work only the dynamic limit which determines the function of the volumes in play.

The play of these volumes is one of the two active elements on which I have based the action of my musical text, the other element being the movements in their reciprocal connection.

These two elements, which are the object for the musical execution, can only have a meaning if the executant follows strictly the musical text.

This play of movements and volumes that puts into action the musical text constitutes the impelling force of the composition and determines its form.

A musical composition constructed on that basis could not, indeed, admit the introduction of the element of "interpretation" in its execution without risking the complete loss of its meaning.

To interpret a piece is to realize its portrait, and what I demand is the realization of the piece itself and not of its portrait.

It is a fact that all music suffers, in time, a deformation through its execution; this fact would not be regretted if that deformation were done in a manner that would not be in contradiction to the spirit of the work.

A work created with a spirit in which the emotive basis is the nuance is soon deformed in all directions; it soon becomes amorphous, its future is anarchic and its executants become its interpreters. The nuance is a very uncertain basis for a musical composition because its limitations cannot be, even in particular cases, established in a fixed manner.

On the other hand, a musical composition in which the emotive basis resides not in the nuance but in the very form of the composition will risk little in the hand of its executants.

I admit the commercial exploitation of a musical composition, but I do not admit its emotive exploitation. To the author belongs the emotive exploitation of his ideas, the result of which is the composition; to the executant belongs the presentation of that composition in the way designated to him by its own form.

It is not at all with the view of preserving my musical work from deformation that I turn to form as the only emotive basis of a musical composition. I turn to form because I do not conceive nor feel the true emotive force except under coordinated musical sensations.

These sensations only find their objective and living expression in the form which, so to speak, determines their nature.

To understand, or rather feel, the nature of these sensations according to that form (which is, as I said, their expression) is the task of the executant.

Form, in my music, derives from counterpoint. I consider counterpoint as the only means through which the attention of the composer is concentrated on purely musical questions. Its elements also lend themselves perfectly to an architectural construction.

This sort of music has no other aim than to be sufficient in itself. In general, I consider that music is only able to solve musical problems; and nothing else, neither the literary nor the picturesque, can be in music of any real interest. The play of the musical elements is the thing.

I must say that I follow in my art an instinctive logic and that I do not formulate its theory in any other way than *ex post facto*.

Igor Stravinsky, "Some Ideas About My Octuor," reprinted in Eric Walter White, *Stravinsky: The Composer and His Works* (Berkeley: University of California Press, 1966), 528–31.

138

Anti-Romantic Polemics from Stravinsky's Autobiography

Reaction to Romanticism seems to lie at the root of many of the controversial pronouncements so liberally strewn throughout Stravinsky's autobiographical *Chronicles of My Life,* first published in Paris in 1936. First and foremost among them is the classic, characteristically overstated, and still hotly debated denial of music's expressive powers (which, it should be noted, Stravinsky partly retracted in later years). Consciously and deliberately placing himself in the tradition of "formalist" musical aesthetics, Stravinsky delivered himself of a credo that (particularly as expressed in the last paragraph below) might almost have come from the pen of Hanslick himself (see p. 343). What is often overlooked, though, is the fact that Stravinsky by no means excludes emotion from a place of honor in the musical experience. He maintains, however, that emotion is not embodied in music but produced by it, and that this emotion is unique to the musical experience. Stravinsky's insistence on order and structure as the essence of music's "meaning" is connected, obviously, with his neoclassicism, but also seems motivated in part in response to the frequent charges he had to endure of being a musical anarchist and revolutionary—an unwanted reputation that had its origins in the scandalous première of *The Rite of Spring* (see p. 372).

I consider that music is, by its very nature, essentially powerless to *express* anything at all, whether a feeling, an attitude of mind, a psychological mood, a phenomenon of nature, etc. *Expression* has never been an inherent property of music. That is by no means the purpose of its existence. If, as is nearly always the case, music appears to express something, this is only an illusion and not a reality. It is simply an additional attribute which, by tacit and inveterate agreement, we have lent it, thrust upon it, as a label, a convention—in short, an aspect we have come to confuse, unconsciously or by force of habit, with its essential being.

Music is the sole domain in which man realizes the present. By the imperfections of his nature, man is doomed to submit to the passage of time—to its categories of past and future—without ever being able to give substance, and therefore stability, to the category of the present.

The phenomenon of music is given to us with the sole purpose of establishing an order in things, including, and particularly, the coordination between *man* and *time*. To be put into practice, its indispensable and single requirement is construction. Construction once completed, this order has been attained, and there is nothing more to be said. It would be futile to look for, or expect anything else from it. It is precisely this construction, this achieved order, which produces in us a unique emotion having nothing in common with our ordinary sensations and our responses to the impressions of daily life. One could not better define the sensation produced by music than by saying that it is identical with that evoked by contemplation of the interplay of architectural forms. Goethe thoroughly understood that when he called architecture petrified music.

People will always insist upon looking in music for something that is not there. The main thing for them is to know what the piece expresses, and what the author had in mind when he composed it. They never seem to understand that music has an entity of its own apart from anything that it may suggest to them. In other words, music interests them in so far as it touches on elements outside it while evoking sensations with which they are familiar.

Most people like music because it gives them certain emotions, such as joy, grief, sadness, an image of nature, a subject for daydreams, or—still better—oblivion from "everyday life." They want a drug—"dope." It matters little whether this way of thinking of music is expressed directly or is wrapped up in a veil of artificial circumlocutions. Music would not be worth much if it were reduced to such an end. When people have learned to love music for itself, when they listen with other ears, their enjoyment will be of a far higher and more potent order, and they will be able to judge it on a higher plane and realize its intrinsic value. Obviously such an attitude presupposes a certain degree of musical development and intellectual culture, but that is not very difficult of attainment. Unfortunately, the teaching of music, with a few exceptions, is bad from the beginning. One has only to think of all the sentimental twaddle so often talked about Chopin, Beethoven, and even about Bach—and that in schools for the training of professional musicians! Those tedious commentaries on the side issues of music not only do not facilitate its understanding, but, on the contrary, are a serious obstacle which prevents the understanding of its essence and substance.

> Stravinsky's attachment to objectivity and his distrust of "interpreters" in the Romantic tradition made him extremely receptive to new developments in the mechanical reproduction of music, first by mechanical instruments like player pianos, later by electronic recording processes. The result of this interest is an unparalleled body of recorded performances encompassing practically his entire output in authoritative readings whose documentary value can scarcely be overestimated. Stravinsky's concern for the establishment of an inviolate "text" to guide performers, and his indifference to such traditional executant qualities as spontaneity and "personality," are symptomatic of twentieth-century ideas on performance. "Authenticity" in performance style, not only for contemporary music but for music of the past as well, has been uniquely a goal of performers in our own time, and would scarcely have been understood by musicians of the past.

About this time [1928–29] I signed a contract for several years with the great Columbia Gramophone Company, for which I was exclusively to record my work both as pianist and conductor, year by year. This work greatly interested me, for here, far better than with piano rolls, I was able to express all my intentions with real exactitude.

Consequently these records, very successful from a technical point of view, have the importance of documents which can serve as guides to all executants of my music. Unfortunately, very few conductors avail themselves of them. Some do not even inquire whether such records exist. Doubtless their dignity prevents others from consulting them, especially since if once they know the record they could not with a clear conscience conduct as they liked. Is it not amazing that in our times, when a sure means which is accessible to all has been found of learning exactly how the author demands his work to be executed, there should still be those who will not take any notice of such means, but persist in inserting concoctions of their own vintage?

Unfortunately, therefore, the rendering recorded by the author fails to achieve its most important object—that of safeguarding his work by establishing the manner in which it ought to be played. This is all the more regrettable since it is not a question of a haphazard gramophone record of just any performance. Far from that, the very purpose of the work on these records is the elimination of all chance elements by selecting from among the different records those which are most successful. It is obvious that in even the very best records one may come across certain defects such as a crackling, a rough surface, excessive or insufficient resonance. But these defects, which, for that matter, can be more or less corrected by the gramophone and the choice of the needle, do not in the least affect the essential thing, without which it would be impossible to form any idea of the composition—I refer to the pace of the movements and their relationship to one another.

When one thinks of the complexity of making such records, of all the difficulties it presents, of all the accidents to which it is exposed, the constant nervous strain caused by the knowledge that one is continuously at the mercy of some possible stroke of bad luck, some extraneous noise by reason of which it may all have to be done over again, how can one help being embittered by the thought that the fruit of so much labor will be so little used, even as a document, by the very persons who should be most interested?

But, no matter how disappointing the work is when regarded from this point of view, I do not for a moment regret the time and effort spent on it. It gives me the satisfaction of knowing that everyone who listens to my records hears my music free from any distortion of my thought, at least in its essential elements. Moreover, the work did a good deal to develop my technique as a conductor. The frequent repetition of a fragment or even of an entire piece, the sustained effort to allow not the slightest detail to escape attention, as may happen for lack of time at any ordinary rehearsal, the necessity of observing absolute precision of movement as strictly determined by the timing—all this is a hard school in which a musician obtains very valuable training and learns much that is extremely useful.

One of Stravinsky's most explicitly anti-Romantic pronouncements is contained in his recounting of a visit to the Wagnerian "Festspielhaus" in Bayreuth. It begins in a spirit of amiable spoofing, but soon turns into a serious refutation of the Romantic cult of the artist. The closing jeremiad, written almost on the eve of World War II, is chilling.

The very atmosphere of the theatre, its design and its setting, seemed lugubrious. It was like a crematorium, and a very old-fashioned one at that, and one expected to see the gentleman in black who had been entrusted with the task of singing the praises of the departed. The order to devote oneself to contemplation was given by a blast of trumpets. I sat humble and motionless, but at the end of a quarter of an hour I could bear no more. My limbs were numb and I had to change my position. Crack! Now I had done it! My chair had made a noise which drew down on me the furious scowls of a hundred pairs of eyes. Once more I withdrew into myself, but I could think of only one thing, and that was the end of the act which would put an end to my martyrdom. At last the intermission arrived, and I was rewarded by two sausages and a glass of beer. But hardly had I had time to light a cigarette when the trumpet blast sounded again, demanding another period of contemplation. Another act to be got through, when all my thoughts were concentrated on my cigarette, of which I had had barely a whiff. I managed to bear the second act. Then there were more sausages, more beer, another trumpet blast, another period of contemplation, another act—finis!

I do not want to discuss the music of *Parsifal* or the music of Wagner in general. At this date it is too remote from me. What I find revolting in the whole affair is the underlying conception which dictated it—the principle of putting a work of art on the same level as the sacred and symbolic ritual which constitutes a religious service. And, indeed, is not all this comedy of Bayreuth, with its ridiculous formalities, simply an unconscious aping of a religious rite?

Perhaps someone may cite the mysteries of the Middle Ages in contravention of this view. But those performances had religion as their basis and faith as their source. The spirit of the mystery plays did not venture beyond the bosom of the Church which patronized them. They were religious ceremonies bordering on the canonical rites, and such aesthetic qualities as they might contain were merely accessory and unintentional, and in no way affected their substance. Such ceremonies were due to the imperious desire of the faithful to see the objects of their faith incarnate and in palpable form—the same desire as that which created statues and icons in the churches.

It is high time to put an end, once and for all, to this unseemly and sacrilegious conception of art as religion and the theatre as a temple. The following argument will readily show the absurdity of such pitiful aesthetics: one cannot imagine a believer adopting a critical attitude towards a religious service. That would be a contradiction in terms; the believer would cease to be a believer. The attitude of an audience is exactly the opposite. It is not dependent upon faith or blind submission. At a performance one admires or one rejects. One accepts only after having passed judgment, however little one may be aware of it. The critical faculty plays an essential part. To confound these two distinct lines of thought is to give proof of a complete lack of discernment, and certainly of bad taste. But is it at all surprising that such confusion should arise at a time like the present, when the openly irreligious masses in their degradation of spiritual values and debasement of human thought necessarily lead us to utter brutalization? People are, however, apparently fully aware of the sort of monster to which the world is about to give birth, and perceive with annoyance that man cannot live without some kind of cult. An effort is therefore made to refurbish old cults dragged from some revolutionary arsenal, wherewith to enter into competition with the Church.

Igor Stravinsky, *An Autobiography* (New York: M. & J. Steuer, 1958), 38–40, 53–54, 150–52, 162–63. Reprinted by permission.

139

Schoenberg on Stravinsky, Stravinsky on Schoenberg

Often forgotten today is the mutual contempt in which the leading musical "camps" held one another during the period between the wars. Schoenberg, who saw himself as the inheritor of the great tradition of (German-dominated) European music, and whose aesthetic attitudes were largely a continuation of those of the preceding century, saw in Stravinsky and neoclassicism little more than a trivialization of art's purpose and a retreat from the historical exigencies that had brought about, among other things, the twelve-tone system. Among the papers Schoenberg left behind at his death are a couple of rather malicious digs at Stravinsky, in which it is hard not to see a touch of envy at the Russian composer's fashionable position and his huge public prestige. We give one of these below, followed by a little poem Schoenberg set to music in the form of a choral canon. Both date from 1926.

Igor Stravinsky: The Restaurateur

Stravinsky pokes fun at musicians who are anxious (unlike himself—he wants simply to write the *music of today*) to write the *music of the future*. I could not say such a thing without at least giving an inkling of the reasons why any music that is fully and truly of the present must also belong to the future. I am not sure that is what Stravinsky means. He seems rather to find it old-fashioned to regard any work of art as significant for any period beyond the present. And he apparently believes this even though elsewhere he actually admits such significance, constantly finding new points to "take up": Bach, Scarlatti, Clementi, etc. It seems to me, furthermore, that this attitude is no more deeply based than a good many other phenomena of mass psychology.

In all fields of thought there is an undeniable need to produce things to last longer than grease-proof paper and neckties. It may be appropriate to build exhibition buildings to be pulled down after three months; to invent machines for weaving fashionable material; even pyramids need not be planned for all eternity. But, on the other hand, the aim in seeking a cancer cure can only be a permanently effective one; we want to know something unchangingly valid about the course of the stars and the fate of the soul after death.

Maybe for Stravinsky art falls not into this last category but among the fashionable materials and neckties. In that case, he is right in trying merely to satisfy the customers.

I, however, never reckoned to fall among window-dressers. Nor, I think, did any of those who are my models. And I believe not even Muzio Clementi may be so assessed, since he is still good enough to serve as a model for Stravinsky.

Arnold Schoenberg, *Style and Idea,* ed. Leonard Stein (New York: St. Martin's Press, 1975), 481–82, Reprinted by permission of Faber and Faber Ltd., London.

From "Drei Satiren," op. 28:

Ja, wer trommelt denn da?	But who's this beating the drum?
Das ist ja der kleine Modernsky!	Why, it's little Modernsky!
Hat sich ein Bubikopf schneiden lassen;	He's had his hair cut in an old-fashioned queue,
sieht ganz gut aus!	And it looks quite nice!
Wie echt falsches Haar!	Like real false hair!
Wie eine Perücke!	Like a wig!
Ganz (wie sich ihn der kleine Modernsky vorstellt),	Just like (or so little Modernsky likes to think)
ganz der Papa Bach!	Just like Papa Bach!

Translation adapted from Eric Walter White, *Stravinsky: The Composer and His Work* (Berkeley: University of California Press, 1966), 282.

Stravinsky, for his part, had this to say about Schoenberg in an interview he gave the Barcelona newspaper *La Noche* on 12 March 1936:

Schoenberg, in my judgment, is more of a chemist of music than an artistic creator. His investigations are important, since they tend to expand the possibilities of auditory enjoyment, but—as with [Alois] Haba [1893–1973], the discoverer of quarter-tones—they are more concerned with the quantitative than with the qualitative aspects of music. The value of this is evident, but limited, since others will come later and look for and find "eighth-tones," but will *they* be able to make genuine works of art with this? I admire Schoenberg and his followers but I recognize that the chromatic gamut on which they are based only exists scientifically and that, consequently, the dialectic which is derived from this is artificial.

Vera Stravinsky and Robert Craft, *Stravinsky in Pictures and Documents* (New York: Simon and Schuster, 1978), 328.

140

The Cult of Blague:
Satie and "The Six"

Erik Satie (1866–1925) was, by the example of his person as much as by that of his music, one of the most influential figures in French cultural life during the first quarter of the twentieth century. The studied unseriousness for which he was famous is well illustrated in the autobiographical note, characteristically entitled "Memoirs of an Amnesiac," which he wrote as early as 1912. In their merciless debunking of the Romantic mystique, the extracts below engagingly prefigure the more forbidding objectivism of Stravinsky (who acknowledged the influence of Satie's aesthetic attitudes on his own).

Who I Am

Everyone will tell you that I am not a musician. That is correct.

From the very beginning of my career I have classed myself among the phonometrographers. My work has been pure phonometrics. One need only take the *Fils des Étoiles,* or the *Morceaux en forme de poire, En habit de cheval,* or the *Sarabandes,* in order to see that no musical ideas attended the creation of these works. It is scientific thought that rules them.

For the rest, I take greater pleasure in measuring a sound than in hearing it. Phonometer in hand, I work happily and confidently.

What have I not weighed or measured? All of Beethoven, all of Verdi, etc. It's very strange.

The first time I used a phonoscope, I examined a B flat of medium size. I assure you I have never seen anything more revolting. I called in my servant so that he might see it too.

On the phonoscales an ordinary F sharp, very common, reached 214½ pounds. It came from a very fat tenor whom I also weighed.

Do you know how to clean sounds? It's a rather dirty business. Sorting them is neater; to be able to classify them is very exacting and takes very good eyesight. Here we are in the realm of phonotechnics.

As for explosions of sound, often so unpleasant, cotton placed in the ears will attenuate them quite handily. Here we are in the realm of pyrophonics.

In order to write my *Pièces froides,* I used a kaleidophonic recorder. It took seven minutes. I called in my servant so that he might hear it.

I feel I can say that phonology is better than music. It is more varied. The pecuniary rewards are greater. I owe my fortune to it.

In any case, a phonometrist working only moderately hard can easily note down more sounds on the motodynamophone than the most skillful musicians can do in the same time and with the same effort. It is thanks to this that I have written so much.

The future therefore belongs to philophony.

A Musician's Day

An artist must regulate his life. Here then is the precise schedule of my daily activities.

Erik Satie. (Caricature by A. Frueh.) *Paris, Bibliothèque Nationale, C 104041. *

    I get up at 7:18 A.M. I am inspired from 10:23 to 11:47. I have lunch at 12:11 and leave the table at 12:14.

    A ride on my horse for my health's sake, at the rear of my estate, from 1:19 P.M. until 2:53. Another bout of inspiration from 3:12 to 4:07.

Different occupations (fencing, reflection, immobility, visiting, contemplation, dexterity, swimming, etc.) from 4:21 until 6:47.

Dinner is served at 7:16 and over at 7:20. Then come symphonic readings (aloud) from 8:09 until 9:59.

My bedtime is regularly at 10:37. Every week I awaken with a start at 3:19 A.M. (Tuesdays).

I only eat white foods: eggs, sugar, ground bone, the fat of dead animals, veal, salt, coconuts, chicken boiled in white water; fruit mold, rice, turnips, bleached pudding, dough, cheese (white), cotton salad, and certain kinds of fish (without skin).

I have my wine boiled, and drink it cold with fuchsia juice. I have a good appetite, but I never speak while eating for fear of choking.

I breathe carefully (a little at a time). I dance very rarely. When walking I hold my sides and look straight behind me.

Very serious in demeanor, if I laugh it is without meaning to. I apologize all the time and quite affably.

I only close one eye when sleeping; my sleep is very sound. My bed is round, with a hole provided for putting the head through. Every hour my servant takes my temperature and gives me another.

I am a longtime subscriber to a fashion magazine. I wear a white hat, white stockings, and a white vest.

My doctor has always told me to smoke. To this advice he adds, "Smoke, my friend. If you don't, someone else will smoke in your place."

Erik Satie, *Mémoires d'un amnésiaque* (Liège, 1953), 7–10. Trans. R. T.

French music between the wars was dominated by the spirit of Satie: irreverent and insouciant, passionately anti-Germanic, anti-"Impressionist" in its deliberate diatonic simplicity, and full of echoes of jazz bands and music halls. While some of these traits can be found in a few late works by Maurice Ravel (1875–1937) and even in Stravinsky, they received their "classic" embodiment in the music of the next generation. The very young musicians christened the "Group of Six" (on a rather superficial analogy with the Russian "Five") by the critic Henri Collet, were perhaps the most typical (certainly the most publicized) representatives of the Parisian musical mood. Below is a trio of readings dealing with this group and their aesthetic. First, an extract from Collet's original article of 1920:

"I want a French music for France," writes Jean Cocteau [1891–1962, author and artistic trend-setter] in his remarkable little volume *Le Coq et l'Arlequin.* We are happy that he did write that, for it is precisely what we preach ourselves in our tribune, [the magazine] *Comoedia.* "Music that is not national does not exist," writes Rimsky-Korsakov in *My Musical Life,* and continues, "Indeed, all music that is regarded as universal is in fact national." Jean Cocteau and Rimsky-Korsakov tell us what no conservatory can teach: it is necessary to belong to a nation and unite with compatriots. Russian music, cultivated by the illustrious Five—Balakirev, Cui, Borodin, Musorgsky, Rimsky-Korsakov—was united in its aims and became the object of universal admiration because these composers appreciated the initiative of Glinka. The Six Frenchmen, Darius Milhaud [1892–1974], Louis Durey [1888–1979], Georges Auric [1899–1983], Arthur Honegger [1892–1955], Francis Poulenc [1899–1963], and Germaine Tailleferre [1892–1983], henceforth inseparable, as it was demonstrated by an interesting collection of their compositions, as Le Groupe de Six, have by their splendid decision to return to simplicity, brought about a renaissance of French music, because they appreciated the phenomenon of Erik Satie and because they followed the precepts, so lucid, of Jean Cocteau.

Nicolas Slonimsky (ed.), *Music Since 1900,* 4th ed. (New York: Charles Scribner's Sons, 1971), 322. Trans. Nicolas Slonimsky. Copyright © 1971 Nicolas Slonimsky. Reprinted with the permission of Charles Scribner's Sons.

A memoir by Darius Milhaud vividly conveys the atmosphere that reigned over the group's association:

After a concert at the Salle Huyghens, at which Bertin sang Louis Durey's *Images à Crusoë* on words by Saint-Léger Léger, and the Capelle Quartet played my Fourth Quartet, the critic Henri Collet published in *Comoedia* a chronicle entitled "Five Russians and Six Frenchmen." Quite arbitrarily he had chosen six names, merely because we knew one another, were good friends, and had figured on the same programs, quite irrespective of our different temperaments and wholly dissimilar characters. Auric and Poulenc were partisans of Cocteau's ideas, Honegger derived from the German romantics, and I from Mediterranean lyricism. I fundamentally disapproved of joint declarations of aesthetic doctrines and felt them to be a drag, an unreasonable limitation on the imagination of the artist, who must for each new work find different, often contradictory means of expression; but it was useless to protest. Collet's article excited such world-wide interest that the "Group of Six" was launched, and willy-nilly I formed part of it.

The formation of the Group of Six helped to draw the bonds of friendship closer among us. For two years we met regularly at my place every Saturday evening. Paul Morand [1888–1976, novelist] would make the cocktails, and then we would go to a little restaurant at the top of the rue Blanche. The dining room of the Petit Bessonneau was so diminutive that the Saturday customers filled it completely. They gave free rein to their high spirits: After dinner, lured by the steam-driven merry-go-rounds, the mysterious booths, the shooting galleries, the games of chance, the menageries, the din of the mechanical organs with their perforated rolls seeming to grind out simultaneously and implacably all the blaring tunes from the music halls and revues, we would visit the Fair of Montmartre, or occasionally the Cirque Médrano to see the Fratellinis in their sketches, so steeped in poetry and imagination that they were worthy of the *commedia dell'arte*. We finished the evening at my house. The poets would read their poems, and we would play our latest compositions. Some of them, such as Auric's *Adieu New York,* Poulenc's *Cocardes,* and my *Bœuf sur le toit* were continually being played. We even used to insist on Poulenc's playing *Cocardes* every Saturday evening, as he did most readily. Out of these meetings, in which a spirit of carefree gaiety reigned, many a fruitful collaboration was to be born; they also determined the character of several works strongly marked by the influence of the music hall.

And finally, a description by Milhaud of a typically anti-Romantic experiment carried on by Satie with an assist from some of his young admirers:

Just as one's field of vision embraces objects and forms, such as the pattern on the wallpaper, the cornice of the ceiling, or the frame of the mirror, which the eye sees but to which it pays no attention, though they are undoubtedly there, Satie thought that it would be amusing to have music that would not be listened to, *"musique d'ameuble-ment,"* or background music that would vary like the furniture of the rooms in which it was played. Auric and Poulenc disapproved of this suggestion, but it tickled my fancy so much that I experimented with it, in cooperation with Satie, at a concert given in the Galerie Barbazange. During the program, Marcelle Meyer played music by Les Six, and Bertin presented a play by Max Jacob called *Un Figurant au théâtre de Nantes,* which required the services of a trombone. He also sang Stravinsky's *Berceuses du Chat* to the accompaniment of three clarinets, so Satie and I scored our music for the instruments used in the course of these various items of the program. In order that the music might seem to come from all sides at once, we posted the clarinets in three different corners of the theater, the pianist in the fourth, and the trombone in a box on the balcony floor. A program note warned the audience that it was not to pay any more attention to the ritornellos that would be played during the intermissions than to the candelabra, the seats, or the balcony. Contrary to our expectations, however, as soon as the music started up, the audience began to stream back to their seats. It was no use for Satie to shout, "Go on talking! Walk about! Don't listen!" They listened without speaking. The whole effect was spoiled. Satie had not counted on the charm of his own music. Nevertheless Satie wrote another *"ritournelle d'ameublement"* for Mrs. Eugene Meyer of Washington, when she asked him, through me, to give her an autograph. But for this *Musique pour un cabinet préfectoral* to have its full meaning, she should have had it recorded and played over and over again, thus forming part of the furniture of her beautiful library in Crescent Place, adorning it for the ear in the same way as the still life by Manet adorned it for the eye. In any case, the future was to prove that Satie was right: nowadays children and housewives fill their homes with unheeded music, reading and working to the sound of the radio. And in all public places, large stores, and restaurants the customers are drenched in an unending flood of music. In America cafeterias are equipped with a sufficient number of machines for each client to be able, for the modest sum of five cents, to furnish his own solitude with music or supply a background for his conversation with his guest. Is this not *"musique d'ameublement,"* heard, but not listened to?

Darius Milhaud, *Notes Without Music,* trans. Donald Evans (New York: Alfred A. Knopf, 1953), 97–99, 122–23. Copyright 1952, 1953 by Alfred A. Knopf, Inc. Reprinted by permission of the publisher.

141

Polytonality

Widely heralded in its day by musicians in the Parisian orbit was the device of combining chords and keys known as "polytonality." It was seen by its proponents as a way of gaining harmonic enrichment without giving up the "natural" basis of diatonicism in favor of the "artificiality" of atonality. Below, we present a condensation of an extremely systematic exposition of polytonality by Milhaud, its most ardent spokesman. German musicians, whether or not they were adherents of Schoenberg's principles, tended to be extremely skeptical of the methods Milhaud proposes (see Hindemith, p. 412).

Between polytonality and atonality there are the same essential differences as between diatonicism and chromaticism.

Diatonicism implies belief in the perfect triad (root, third, and fifth) as having a concrete reality deriving from major and minor scales which the musician uses in composing his themes. Diatonic melodies, therefore, use only the notes of the scale of the key in which they are written, and the modulations that follow are nothing more than a motion toward other, parallel tonal spheres, whose roots are different, which rest on other scales and other perfect triads, but whose internal workings are the same as those of the original key.

Belief in twelve definite tonalities, having their basis in the twelve degrees of the chromatic scale, would seem to lead—once we admit the possibility, thanks to modulation, of passing from one key to another—to the investigation of the possibilities of superimposing different keys so that they sound simultaneously. Counterpoint leads us in the same direction. The day canons other than at the octave were admitted, the principle of polytonality was established. Often, if one reads the two lines of a canon separately and horizontally, it strikes one that they might well be harmonized in two different keys; the "unitonal" feeling one gets in hearing the canon is the result of each momentary vertical alignment being ruled by the laws of two-part counterpoint and of harmony.

Appoggiaturas and passing tones would seem likewise to suggest the possibility of introducing in a given chord one or more tones foreign to that chord or even to its key. Conventions of voice-leading, the resolution of appoggiaturas and passing tones, may postpone the problem and keep it for now within limits, but as soon as one allows foreign tones to exist stably in a chord, without passing to other tones or resolving, one must find other ways of accounting for them.

Once we admit such an approach it becomes necessary to study methodically the various harmonic combinations that arise from the superimposition of two keys, the inversions of chords thus obtained, and the connections that might be made between them (not to mention the different ways one can combine two simultaneous tonalities: two major keys, two minor keys, one major and one minor). [Here examples are cited from works by Stravinsky, Albert Roussel (1869–1937), Debussy, Ravel, Bartók, Satie, Poulenc, and Milhaud himself.]

The same theoretical work can be done for chords comprising three keys. Each of the 55 chords thus obtained can be expressed in eight different ways according to the principles we have indicated above. The richness of these chords is, as one can see, immense.

If we now were to superimpose all twelve keys we should obtain a chord consisting of all twelve notes of the chromatic scale, which one can space in an infinity of ways (the simplest being by fourths or fifths because of the equidistance of each note in the chord). Here all the keys are reunited and it is as if there were no such thing as key at all: polytonality encroaches here upon the domain of atonality, for a melody constructed on the notes of this chord (the twelve notes of the scale) will be able to employ any note without discrimination, and by virtue of this escape all tonal feeling.

One can see by the different stages which extend from bitonality to the handling of all twelve tones at once, how vast the resources of polytonality are, and how much they enrich the expressive resources of music. The expressive range is considerably expanded, even in the simplest realm of dynamics: the use of polytonality adds subtlety and sweetness to *pianissimi,* while to *fortissimi* it lends greater pungency and force.

There is also a purely contrapuntal polytonality. Instead of superimposing chords or chord progressions, we superimpose melodies written in several keys in a play of counterpoint. This makes for an extremely stark mode of expression, in which the tonal implications of each part are reduced to a minimum, practically to monophony.

This type of writing is particularly well suited to the string quartet or to a small orchestra of solo instruments. I ask to be excused for taking an example from my own work: in my third Symphony for Small Orchestra, published by Universal Edition, there is a passage in which the melodic line played by the flute is in $B^\flat$, that of the clarinet is in F, the bassoon in E, the violin in C, the viola in $B^\flat$, and the cello in D.

One should note that most of the time, if one examines the harmonic whole created by these polytonal counterpoints of diatonic melodies, one obtains vertical aggregations that are unanalyzable and whose harmonic effect is thus atonal.

There are as many different polytonalities as there are composers.

Darius Milhaud, "Polytonalité et atonalité," *Revue musicale,* IV (1923), 29–44. Trans. R. T.

142

The Only Twentieth-Century Aesthetic?

This unashamedly partisan appreciation of Parisian music between the wars by Virgil Thomson (1896–1989), an American composer who was present on the scene, is a document of rare eloquence and perception. Thomson was one of many young American musicians who studied during the period with Nadia Boulanger (1887–1979), a gifted pedagogue who was to a large extent responsible for making America for a time seem a kind of French musical colony (much as, before World War I, it had been a colony of Germany). Thomson's essay, first published in 1941 in the New York *Herald Tribune* (where the author was music critic for fourteen years), is a valuable memento of that moment in American musical history, as well as perhaps the most articulate summary ever made of what Thomson calls "the only twentieth-century musical aesthetic in the Western world."

French and other Parisian music of the 1930's has been but little performed in America. Such of it as has been performed here is usually considered to be mildly pleasant but on the whole not very impressive. This estimate is justified only on the part of persons initiated to its aesthetic. And its aesthetic is derived directly from the words and from the works of Satie, whose firmest conviction was that the only healthy thing music can do in our century is to stop trying to be impressive.

The Satie musical aesthetic is the only twentieth-century musical aesthetic in the Western world. Schoenberg and his school are Romantics; and their twelve-tone syntax, however intriguing one may find it intellectually, is the purest Romantic chromaticism. Hindemith, however gifted, is a neoclassicist, like Brahms, with ears glued firmly to the past. The same is true of the later Stravinsky and of his satellites. Even *Petrushka* and *The Rite of Spring* are the Wagnerian theater symphony and the nineteenth-century cult of nationalistic folklore applied to ballet.

Of all the influential composers of our time, and influence even his detractors cannot deny him, Satie is the only one whose works can be enjoyed and appreciated without any knowledge of the history of music. These lack the prestige of traditional modernism, as they lack the prestige of the Romantic tradition itself, a tradition of constant Revolution. They are as simple, as devastating as the remarks of a child.

In our century French music has eschewed the impressive, the heroic, the oratorical, everything that is aimed at moving mass audiences. Like modern French poetry and painting, it has directed its communication to the individual. It has valued, in consequence, quietude, precision, acuteness of auditory observation, gentleness, sincerity and directness of statement. Persons who admire these qualities in private life are not infrequently embarrassed when they encounter them in public places. It is this embarrassment that gives to all French music, and to the work of Satie and his neophytes in particular, an air of superficiality, as if it were salon music written for the drawing room of some snobbish set.

To suppose this true is to be ignorant of the poverty and the high devotion to art that marked the life of Erik Satie to its very end in a public hospital. And to ignore all art that is not heroic or at least intensely emotional is to commit the greatest of snobberies. For, by a reversal of values that constitutes one of the most surprising phenomena of a century that has so far been occupied almost exclusively with reversing values, the only thing really hermetic and difficult to understand about the music of Erik Satie is the fact that there is nothing hermetic about it at all.

It wears no priestly robes; it mumbles no incantations; it is not painted up by Max Factor to terrify elderly ladies or to give little girls a thrill. Neither is it designed to impress orchestral conductors or to get anybody a job teaching school. It has literally no devious motivation. It is as simple as a friendly conversation and in its better moments exactly as poetic and profound.

These thoughts occurred to me the other evening at a concert of recent works by Milhaud. Not a piece on the program had a climax or a loud ending. Nothing was pretentious or apocalyptical or messianic or overdramatized. And when I remembered the brilliant and theatrically effective works of Milhaud's youth, I realized that after Satie's death he had been led, how unconsciously I cannot say, to assume the mantle of Satie's leadership and to eschew all musical vanity. That, at any rate, is my explanation of how one of the most facile and turbulent talents of our time has become one of the most completely calm of modern masters; and how, by adding thus depth and penetration and simple humanity to his gamut, he has become the first composer of his country and a leader in that musical tradition which of all living musical traditions is the least moribund.

143

The Making of *Wozzeck*

By far the most popular work to emerge from the so-called "New Viennese School" between the wars was Alban Berg's opera *Wozzeck*. Perhaps the ultimate embodiment of musical expressionism in its lurid treatment of an undeniably morbid subject, the opera excited controversy among musicians for its extensive employment of strict and abstract formal procedures. Berg seems to imply in the short apologia he offered in 1928, for a symposium on "problems of opera," that without such external controls, an operatic style that dispenses with "numbers" can easily fail to maintain interest. In any case, Roger Sessions's critique (see p. 387) shows to what extent even progressive musicians found the idea expressed in the final paragraph paradoxical if not perverse.

I never entertained the idea of reforming the artistic structure of the opera with *Wozzeck*. Neither when I started nor when I completed this work did I consider it a model for further operatic efforts, whoever the composer might be. I never assumed or expected that *Wozzeck* should in this sense become the basis of a school.

I wanted to compose good music, to develop musically the contents of Büchner's immortal drama, to translate his poetic language into music; but other than that, when I decided to write an opera, my only intentions, including the technique of composition, were to render unto the theater what belonged to the theater. In other words, the music was to be so formed as consciously to fulfill its duty of serving the action at every moment. Even more, the music should be prepared to furnish whatever the action needed to be transformed into reality on the stage. It was the function of the composer to solve the problems of an ideal stage director. And at the same time, this aim must not prejudice the development of the music as an absolute, purely musical entity. There was to be no interference by externals with its individual existence.

That these purposes should be accomplished by use of musical forms more or less ancient (considered by critics as one of the most important of my ostensible reforms of the opera) was a natural consequence. For the libretto it was necessary to make a selection from twenty-six loosely constructed, sometimes fragmentary scenes by Büchner. Repetitions that did not lend themselves to musical variations had to be avoided. Finally, the scenes had to be brought together, arranged, and grouped in acts. The problem therefore became, utterly apart from my will, more musical than literary, one to be solved by the laws of musical structure rather than by the rules of dramaturgy.

It was impossible to take the fifteen scenes I selected and shape them in different manners so that each would retain its musical coherence and individuality, and at the same time follow the customary method along the lines of their literary content. An absolute music, no matter how rich structurally, no matter how aptly it might fit the dramatic events, would, after a number of scenes so composed, inevitably create musical monotony. The effect would become positively boring with a series of a dozen or so formally composed entr'actes, which offered nothing but this type of illustrative music. Boredom, of course, is the last thing one should experience in the theater.

I obeyed the necessity of giving each scene and each accompanying piece of entr'acte music, whether prelude, postlude, connecting link or interlude, an unmistakable aspect, a rounded and finished character. It was therefore imperative to use every warranted means to create individualizing characteristics on the one hand, and coherence on the other; thus the much discussed utilization of old and new musical forms, including those used only in absolute music.

In one sense, the use of these forms in opera, especially to such an extent, was unusual, even new. But certainly, as conscious intention, it is not at all to my credit, as I have already demonstrated, and consequently I can and must reject the claim that I am a reformer of opera through such innovation. However, I do not wish to depreciate my work through these explanations. Others who do not know it so well can do it much better. I therefore would like to suggest something which I consider my particular accomplishment.

No matter how cognizant any particular individual may be of the musical forms contained in the framework of this opera, of the precision and logic with which everything is worked out and the skill manifested in every detail, from the moment the curtain parts until it closes for the last time, there must be no one in the audience who pays any attention to the various fugues, inventions, suites, sonata movements, variations, and passacaglias—no one who heeds anything but the idea of this opera, which by far transcends the personal destiny of Wozzeck. This I believe to be my achievement.

Alban Berg, "A Word About *Wozzeck*," in Sam Morgenstern (ed.), *Composers on Music* (New York: Pantheon Books, 1956), 461–62. Copyright © 1956 by Pantheon Books, a Division of Random House, Inc. Reprinted by permission of the publisher.

144

Approaching the Limits of Compression

With the mature works of Anton Webern, music seemed to reach a level of concentration and terseness without precedent. Their extreme brevity and thinness of texture have been at once a puzzle and a source of their fascination. The composer himself recognized the problematical aspects of his style, as did his teacher, Schoenberg. Below we give an appreciation of Webern's music by each of them. First, Schoenberg's foreword to the published score of Webern's *Six Bagatelles for String Quartet*, op. 9 (composed in 1911–13, published in 1924):

Though the brevity of these pieces is a persuasive advocate for them, on the other hand that very brevity itself requires an advocate.

Consider what moderation is required to express oneself so briefly. You can stretch every glance out into a poem, every sigh into a novel. But to express a novel in a single gesture, a joy in a breath—such concentration can only be present in proportion to the absence of self-pity.

These pieces will only be understood by those who share the faith that music can say things which can only be expressed by music.

These pieces can face criticism as little as this—or any—belief.

If faith can move mountains, disbelief can deny their existence. And faith is impotent against such impotence.

Does the musician know how to play these pieces, does the listener know how to receive them? Can faithful musicians and listeners fail to surrender themselves to one another?

But what shall we do with the heathen? Fire and sword can keep them down; only believers need to be restrained.

May this silence sound for them.

Die Reihe, II: *Anton Webern* (Bryn Mawr, Pa.: Theodore Presser Company, 1958), 8. Trans. Eric Smith.

Webern's own comments, in a letter to his friend Willi Reich (3 May 1941), concern one of his last works, the *Variations for Orchestra,* op. 30:

On first looking at this score won't the reaction be: why, there really is "nothing in it"!!! Because you will miss the many, many notes you are used to seeing in R. Strauss, etc. Right! But this in fact touches on the most important point: it would be vital to say that here (in my score) a different *style* is present. Yes, but what kind? It does not look like a score from the pre-Wagner period either—Beethoven, for instance—nor does it look like Bach. Are we then to go back still further? Yes—but then *orchestral* scores did not yet exist! But perhaps one could still find a certain similarity to the mode of presentation associated with the Netherlanders. So, something "archaistic"? An orchestrated Josquin perhaps? The answer would have to be an energetic "no!" What, then? Nothing like any of that!

What kind of *style,* then? I believe, to be sure, a new one—following natural law in its material aspects as exactly as earlier forms followed tonality; that is to say, *forming* a tonality, but one that uses the possibilities offered by the nature of sound in a different way, namely on the basis of a system in which the twelve different tones that have been used in Western music up to now "relate only to each other" (as Arnold has put it), but without ignoring the inner laws that govern the nature of sound—namely the relationship of the overtones to a fundamental. At any rate, it is impossible to ignore them if there is still going to be *meaningful* expression in sound! And nobody, really, will maintain that we don't want that!

Now everything that occurs in the piece is based on the two ideas given in the first and second bars (double bass and oboe!). But it is reduced still more, since the second figure is actually a retrograde in itself (the second two tones are the retrograde of the first two, rhythmically augmented). It is followed again immediately on the trombone by the first figure, only in diminution! And in retrograde as to motives and intervals. For that is how my tone row is constructed—it is made up of these thrice four tones. And so it continues throughout the piece, the whole content of which is already present in germinal form in the first twelve tones, that is to say the row! It is pre-formed!!!

Hans Moldenhauer and Rosaleen Moldenhauer, *Anton von Webern: A Chronicle of His Life and Work* (New York: Alfred A. Knopf, 1979), 570–72.

145

The Assimilation of Jazz

George Gershwin (1898–1937) had his start in the world of popular and commercial music ("Tin Pan Alley") and by the 1920s was the foremost composer of the Broadway theater. Beginning with *Rhapsody in Blue* for piano and orchestra (1924), he turned his attention increasingly to the prospect of fusing this type of music (very loosely termed "jazz") with the traditional genres of "concert music." In such a way, he felt (and for a time the opinion was widely shared), a wholly indigenous American art music might be fostered, much as had happened in Russia and in England not long before. The remarks below were "set down" by Henry Cowell and published in a "symposium" on the prospects for American music as of 1933.

The great music of the past in other countries has always been built on folk-music. This is the strongest source of musical fecundity. America is no exception among the countries. The best music being written today is music which comes from folk sources. It is not always recognized that America has folk-music; yet it really has not only one but many different folk-musics. It is a vast land, and different sorts of folk-music have sprung up in different parts, all having validity, and all being a possible foundation for development into art-music. For this reason, I believe that it is possible for a number of distinctive styles to develop in America, all legitimately born of folk-song from different localities. Jazz, ragtime, Negro spirituals and blues, Southern mountain songs, country fiddling, and cowboy songs can all be employed in the creation of American art-music, and are actually used by many composers now. These composers are certain to produce something worthwhile if they have the innate feeling and talent to develop the rich material offered to them. There are also other composers who can be classed as legitimately American who do not make use of folk-music as a base, but who have personally, working in America, developed highly individualized styles and methods. Their new-found materials should be called American, just as an invention is called American if it is made by an American!

Jazz I regard as an American folk-music; not the only one, but a very powerful one which is probably in the blood and feeling of the American people more than any other style of folk-music. I believe that it can be made the basis of serious symphonic works of lasting value, in the hands of a composer with talent for both jazz and symphonic music.

Henry Cowell (ed.), *American Composers on American Music: A Symposium* (Stanford: Stanford University Press, 1933), 186–87.

> Some candid remarks made by Maurice Ravel to an American audience in 1928 remind us of an interesting moment when characteristics of various forms of American music—jazz, ragtime, blues—were enthusiastically adopted by many European composers as yet another way out of the post-Wagnerian dead end. Usually thought of as potential elements of a unique and indigenous American art music (Ravel, an acquaintance and admirer of Gershwin, turns right around and echoes these ideas below), these American traits of harmony and rhythm were absorbed into the cosmopolitan mainstream of between-the-wars "Parisian" music.

Let us now turn to an aspect of my own work which may be of immediate interest to you. To my mind, the "blues" is one of your greatest musical assets, truly American despite earlier contributory influences from Africa and Spain. Musicians have asked me how I came to write "blues" as the second movement of my recently completed sonata for violin and piano. While I adopted this popular form of your music, I venture to say that nevertheless it is French music, Ravel's music, that I have written. Indeed, these popular forms are but the materials of construction, and the work of art appears only on mature conception where no detail has been left to chance. Moreover, minute stylization in the manipulation of these materials is altogether essential. To understand more fully what I mean by the process to which I refer, it would be sufficient to have these same "blues" treated by some of your own musicians and by musicians of European countries other than France, when you would certainly find the resulting compositions to be widely divergent, most of them bearing the national characteristics of their respective composers, despite the unique nationality of their initial material, the American "blues." Think of the striking and essential differences to be noted in the "jazz" and "rags" of Milhaud, Stravinsky, Casella, Hindemith, and so on. The individualities of these composers are stronger than the materials appropriated. They mold popular forms to meet the requirements of their own individual art. Again—nothing left to chance; again—minute stylization of the materials employed, while the styles become as numerous as the composers themselves.

I wish to say again how very happy I am in visiting your country, and all the more so because my journey is enabling me to become still more conversant with those elements which are contributing to the gradual formation of a veritable school of American music. That this school will become notable in its final evolution I have not the slightest doubt, and I am also convinced that it will realize a national expression quite as different from the music of Europeans as you yourselves are different from them. Here again, for the nurture of the most sensitive and imaginative of your young composers we should consider national heritage in all its entirety. There are always self-appointed promoters of nationalism in plenty, who profess their creed with a vengeance, but rarely do they agree as to the means to be employed. Among these nationalists we can always distinguish two distinct clans constantly waging their warfare of criticism. One group believes that folklore is the only requisite to national music; the other predicts the birth of national music in the individual of today. Meanwhile, within the first clan itself dissension goes on: "Folklore? But what in particular is our folklore? Indian tunes? But are they American? Negro spirituals? Blues? But are these American?" and so on, until nothing is left of national background. And the field is at last wide open for those musicians whose greatest fear is to find themselves confronted by mysterious urges to break academic rules rather than belie individual consciousness. Thereupon these musicians, good bourgeois as they are, compose their music according to the classical rules of the European epoch, while the folklorists, apostles of popular airs, shout in their purism: "Can this be American music if inspired by Europe?" We are thus caught up in a vicious and unproductive circle.

In conclusion I would say that even if Negro music is not of purely American origin, nevertheless I believe it will prove to be an effective factor in the founding of an American school of music. At all events, may this national American music of yours embody a great deal of the rich and diverting rhythm of your jazz, a great deal of the emotional expression in your blues, and a great deal of the sentiment and spirit of your popular melodies and songs, worthily deriving from, and in turn contributing to, a noble national heritage in music.

Maurice Ravel, "Contemporary Music," *The Rice Institute Pamphlets,* XV (1928), reprinted in *Revue de musicologie,* L (1964), 216–21. Used by permission of the publisher, Rice University Studies, Houston, Texas.

146

"New Musical Resources"

Henry Cowell (1897–1965) was an enthusiastic musical experimenter whose tireless activity on behalf of what he called "ultramodern" music encompassed—in addition to composing, performing, and teaching—prodigious work as propagandist and publisher. His book *New Musical Resources* (1930) partly described his own music ("tone clusters," for instance, which are produced on the piano with fists and forearms and which gained Cowell most of his early notoriety) and partly described musical effects he imagined but which (particularly the rhythmic ones) he did not consider to be necessarily of immediate practical applicability. There seems to be something peculiarly American about Cowell's devotion to experiment for its own sake, and to a rather abstractly conceived musical "progress," and there is a winning mixture of the visionary and the pragmatic (reminiscent of Ives, who was Cowell's close friend) in his description of the musical novelties he proposed.

Dissonant Counterpoint

Let us meet the question of what would result if we were frankly to shift the center of musical gravity from consonance, on the edge of which it has long been poised, to seeming dissonance, on the edge of which it now rests. The difference might not be, any more than in Bach's practice, a matter of numerical proportion between consonant and dissonant effects, but rather an essential dissonant basis, the consonance being felt to rely on dissonance for resolution. An examination in fact would reveal that all the rules of Bach would seem to have been reversed, not with the result of substituting chaos, but with that of substituting a new order. The first and last chords would be now not consonant, but dissonant; and although consonant chords were admitted, it would be found that conditions were in turn applied to them, on the basis of the essential legitimacy of dissonances as independent intervals. In this system major sevenths and minor sevenths might be used as alternatives; all thirds, fourths, fifths, and sixths would only be permitted as passing or auxiliary notes. Octaves would be so far removed from the fundamental intervals in such a system that they would probably sound inconsistent and might not be used except in the rarest circumstances.

Some of the music of Schoenberg, Ruggles, Hindemith, and Webern seems to denote that they are working out some such procedure as that mentioned above. There is nothing, however, except occasional very good application in their music of the rules that would result from such a counterpoint, to indicate that they use the system consciously, as they have not made public any exposition of their counterpoint.

Rhythm

Assume that we have two melodies moving parallel to each other, the first written in whole notes, and the second in half-notes. If the time for each note were to be indicated by the tapping of a stick, the taps for the second melody would recur with double the rapidity of those for the first. If now the taps were to be increased greatly in rapidity without changing the relative speed, it will be seen that when the taps for the first melody reach sixteen to the second, those for the second melody will be thirty-two to the second. The vibrations from the taps of one melody will give the musical tone C, while those of the other will give the tone C one octave higher. Time has been translated, as it were, into musical tone. Or, as has been shown above, a parallel can be drawn between the ratio of rhythmical beats and the ratio of musical tones by virtue of the common mathematical basis of both musical time and musical tone. The two times, in this view, might be said to be "in harmony," the simplest possible. There is, of course, nothing radical in what is thus far suggested. It is only the interpretation that is new; but

The World's Loudest Pianist. This caricature of Henry Cowell in a Soviet music magazine was inspired by a promotional brochure that advertised him as indicated in our title and described how he put some of the novelties in *New Musical Resources* into practice: "The American composer Henry Cowell startles his audiences with his works, in which new devices predominate: striking the keyboard with fists and elbows, playing with the fingers on the strings, and knocking rhythmically on the top of the piano." The reason why Cowell was singled out for ridicule as a symptom of the decadence of "bourgeois modernism" in the West was because he was well-remembered by Soviet music lovers from his successful concert tour in the 1920s, when Soviet Russia had been hospitable to "revolutionary" artists of all kinds. Cowell's noisiest piano piece, "The Tiger," had actually been brought out in print for the first time by the State Music Publishers of the U.S.S.R. in Moscow. (From *Sovetskaya muzïka*, 1948, no. 5, p. 89.)

when we extend this principle more widely we begin to open up new fields of rhythmical expression in music.

The familiar interval of a fifth represents a vibration ratio of 2:3. Translating this into time, we might have a measure of three equal notes set over another in two. A slight complication is now added. Corresponding to the tone interval of a major third would be a time-ratio of five against four notes; the minor third would be represented by a ratio of six against five notes, and so on. If we were to combine melodies in two (or four) beats, three beats, and five beats to the measure, we should then have three parallel time-systems corresponding to the vibration speeds of a simple consonant harmony. The conductor of such a trio, by giving one beat to a measure, could lead all the voices together; for the measure, no matter what time divisions it included, would begin and end at the same time instant.

Our system of notation is incapable of representing any except the most primary divisions of the whole note. It becomes evident that if we are to have rhythmical progress, or even cope with some rhythms already in use, and particularly if we are to continue with our scheme of related rhythms and harmonies, new ways of writing must be devised to indicate instantly the actual time-value of each note. We are dealing, of course, not with three-fourths meter, five-fourths meter, etc. but with a whole note divided into three or five equal parts.

There is readily suggested, however, a modification of the notation system based upon familiar musical practice. In our present notation the shape of notes is the same; their time-value, whether whole notes, half-notes, quarter-notes, etc., is designated by printing the note as open or solid and by adding stems and hooks. All that need be done, then, is to provide new shapes for notes of a different time value—triangular, diamond-shaped, etc. The use of open and solid notes, of stems, and of hooks is equally applicable to these notes of varied shape. A few adjustments in regard to designating rests would make the system complete.

Tone Clusters

Tone clusters are chords built from major and minor seconds, which in turn may be derived from the upper reaches of the overtone series and have, therefore, a sound foundation. In building up clusters from seconds, it will be seen that since both major and minor seconds are used, just as major and minor thirds are used in the familiar systems in thirds, there is an exact resemblance between the two systems, and the same amount of potential variety in each.

In familiar theory there are certain well-known ways of building with musical material, such as by use of chord-connexions, contrapuntal melodic relationship, canonic imitation, retrograde, thematic structure, etc. All of these methods may be applied to clusters, which also bring with them, however, some new processes of their own.

A characteristic quality of harmony is the possibility of movement within outside tones; that is, in changes of harmony the inner voices usually move to tones which were contained within the outer limits of the tones of the previous chord. But so long as our scale is limited to half-tone intervals, it is obviously impossible to shift tones within the outer limits of a chromatic cluster, except through interchanging the parts. The cluster must be treated like a single unit, as a single tone is treated. All movement must be up or down the scale, as in melody.

[Conclusion]

It is hoped, in putting forth the present outline, that different musicians may take interest in working on the innumerable details of the various subjects. The detailed manner in which each material may be handled is hardly a matter to be decided beforehand and forced upon composers; each one has the right and desire to manage his own materials in such a fashion that they become the best vehicle for his own musical expression.

To disregard the subject of materials, however, does not make for a personal style, or for perfection or freedom of expression. Musical emotions are never so spontaneous as when the forms through which they manifest themselves are so well known to the composer as to be subconscious and can be delicately adjusted to the particular situation. The emotions of a listener with fine perception can never be entirely pleasurable or satisfactory if the composition he is hearing contains crudities of which he cannot but be emotionally as well as intellectually aware.

For the sake of the exquisiteness of emotion which music may express, as well as for the sake of perfection of the music itself, therefore, there is a place for the formalization and co-ordination of different contemporary musical resources by means of their common relationship with the overtone series, which, although it forms a mathematical, acoustical and historical gauge, is not merely a matter of arithmetic, theory and pedantry, but is itself a living essence from which musicality springs.

Henry Cowell, *New Musical Resources* (New York: Alfred A. Knopf, 1930), 38–41, 50–52, 56, 117, 120–21, 138–39. Copyright © 1930 by Alfred A. Knopf, Inc., and renewed 1958 by Henry Cowell. Reprinted by permission of the publisher.

147

Retrenchment

Paul Hindemith (1895–1963) was not only Germany's leading composer in the period between the wars; he was also that rarity among twentieth-century creative musicians, a performing virtuoso (his main instrument was the viola) and an important teacher, both in Europe and in America. As his famous composition textbook of 1937 reveals, it was his devotion to practical musicianship and especially pedagogy that gradually made a traditionalist out of the once-radical musician. In the passage given below, Hindemith reaffirms his faith in "nature," as manifested in the laws of acoustics, as the necessary basis of any valid musical practice, and sets forth his reasons for regarding some of the prestigious styles of the time with suspicion.

Atonality and Polytonality

We have seen that tonal relations are founded in Nature, in the characteristics of sounding materials and of the ear, as well as in the pure relations of abstract numerical groups. We cannot escape the relationship of tones. Whenever two tones sound, either simultaneously or successively, they create a certain interval-value; whenever chords or intervals are connected, they enter into a more or less close relationship. And whenever the relationships of tones are played off one against another, tonal coherence appears. It is thus quite impossible to devise groups of tones without tonal coherence. Tonality is a natural force, like gravity. Indeed, when we consider that the root of a chord, because of its most favorable vibration-ratio to the other tones, and the lowest tone of a chord, because of the actually greater dimension and weight of its wave, have greater importance that the other tones, we recognize at once that it is gravitation itself that draws the tones towards their roots and towards the bass line, and that relates a multiplicity of chords to the strongest among them. If we omit from consideration the widely held notion that everything in which the ear and the understanding are not at once completely at home is atonal (a poor excuse for a lack of musical training and for following the path of least resistance), we may assert that there are but two kinds of music: good music, in which the tonal relations are handled intelligently and skillfully, and bad music, which disregards them and consequently mixes them in aimless fashion. There are many varieties between these two extremes, and of course it does not follow that all music in which the tonal relations are beautifully worked out is good music. But in all good music account is taken of them, and no music which disregards them can be satisfying, any more than could a building in which the most elementary laws of the vertical and horizontal dispositions of masses were disregarded. For the creation of tonality it is all the same, being a matter of style and period, or of the manner in which a composer works, what kind of chord material is employed. A piece that consists primarily of very harsh and grating chords need not be atonal; and, on the other hand, limitation to the purest triads is no guarantee of clean tonal relationships.

The only music which can really be called atonal, therefore, is the work of a composer who is motivated perhaps by a consciousness of the inadequacy of old styles to the musical needs of our day, perhaps by a search for an idiom that will express his own feelings, perhaps by sheer perversity, to invent tonal combinations which do not obey the laws of the medium and cannot be tested by the simplest means of reckoning. Such a man is not impelled by the instinct of the musician, who even in what seems his blindest groping never loses the true path entirely from view.

There are today a considerable number of composers who issue works that they call atonal. Doubtless these composers see in their freedom from tonality a liberty that will lift their art to the infinity of time and space. Apart from the fact that I consider it impossible to abolish the inherent characteristics of the medium, I do not believe that liberty is achieved by substituting mere variety for the principle of natural order. Nowhere does Nature give us any indication that it would be desirable to play off a certain number of tones against one another in a given duration and pitch-range. Arbitrarily conceived rules of that sort can be devised in quantities and if styles of composition were to be based upon them, I can conceive of far more comprehensive and more interesting ones. To limit oneself to home-made tonal systems of this sort seems to me a more doctrinaire proceeding than to follow the strictest diatonic rules of the most dried-up old academic. Is it not strange that the same composers who worship harmonic freedom—or what they mistake for freedom, which is only a dead end which they have not yet recognized as such—have been taken in as regards musical structure by a formalism that makes the artificialities of the early Netherland contrapuntists seem like child's play?

The existence of this style seems to me only to lend final confirmation to the fact, everywhere to be observed, of the disappearance of understanding judgment and critical sense in the field of music. But already a decline is noticeable in the interest manifested in this music based on rules dictated by fashion and contrary to nature.

Anyone to whom a tone is more than a note on paper or a key pressed down, anyone who has ever experienced the intervals in singing, especially with others, as manifestations of bodily tension, of the conquest of space, and of the consumption of energy, anyone who has ever tasted the delights of pure intonation by the continual displacement of the comma in string-quartet playing; must come to the conclusion that there can be no such thing as atonal music, in which the existence of tone-relationships is denied. The decline in the value placed upon tonality is based on the system of equal temperament, a compromise which is presented to us by the keyboard as an aid in mastering the tonal world, and then pretends to be that world itself. One needs only to have seen how the most fanatical lover of the piano will close his ears in horror at the falseness of the tempered chords of his instrument, once he has compared them a few times with those produced by a harmonium in pure intonation, to realize that with the blessing of equal temperament there entered into the world of music—lest the bliss of musical mortals be complete—a curse as well: the curse of too easy achievement of tone-connections. The tremendous growth of piano music in the last century is attributable to it, and in the "atonal" style I see its final fulfillment—the uncritical idolatry of tempered tuning.

There is another catchword that dates from the post-war period: polytonality. The game of letting two or more tonalities run along side by side and so achieving new harmonic effects is, to be sure, very entertaining for the composer, but the listener cannot follow the separate tonalities, for he relates every simultaneous combination of sounds to a root—and thus we see the futility of the game. Every simultaneous combination of sounds must have one root, and only one; one cannot conceive of additional roots somewhere above, belonging to other tonal spheres. Even the craziest harmonic combinations can result in only one root-perception. The ear judges the total sound, and does not ask with what intentions it was produced. Skillful planning of the harmonic fluctuation will eliminate all accidental effects such as always come about when tonal successions belonging to different tonal domains are capriciously combined. But since organic work, growing out of natural roots, will always stand on a firmer basis than the arbitrary combination of different elements, polytonality is not a practical principle of composition.

Paul Hindemith, *The Craft of Musical Composition,* trans. Arthur Mendel (New York: Associated Music Publishers, 1942), 152–56. Copyright © 1942 by Schott Music, copyright renewed. All rights reserved. Used by permission of European American Music Distributors LLC, sole U.S. and Canadian agent for Schott Music.

148

Music and the Social Conscience

Anti-Romantic reaction came from many quarters. In the Germany of the Weimar Republic, post-war idealism combined with adverse economic conditions to produce the widespread conviction that artists must give up the ivory tower and contribute actively to the reconstruction of European society. Composers of the front rank wrote quantities of music for home and school, much of it set to texts of overtly "proletarian" content. Perhaps the most conspicuous art works embodying these principles were the collaborations of playwright Bertolt Brecht (1898–1956) and composer Kurt Weill (1900–50), which ranged from one-act school plays with music to full-length operas. Below, Weill gives expression to his artistic credo in the form of an answer to a questionnaire from the *Berliner Tageblatt,* in which various well-known artists were asked how they would explain their work to an audience of schoolchildren.

I have just played you some music by Wagner and his followers. You have seen that this music consists of so many notes that I was unable to play them all. You would have liked now and then to join in singing the tune, but this proved impossible. You also noticed that the music made you feel sleepy, and drunk, as alcohol or an intoxicating drug might have done. You do not wish to go to sleep. You wish to hear music that can be understood without explanation. You probably wonder why your parents attend concerts. It is, with them, a mere matter of habit. Nowadays, there are matters of greater interest to all; and if music cannot serve the interests of all, its existence is no longer justified.

"Der Musiker Weill," *Berliner Tageblatt,* 25 December 1928, as translated in *The Musical Times,* LXX (1 March 1929), 224.

Though not an adherent of leftist politics, Paul Hindemith shared the sense of social responsibility that motivated such "proletarian" composers as Weill and Hanns Eisler (1898–1962). In a famous statement made in 1927, he expressed himself to the effect that "It is to be regretted that in general so little relationship exists today between the producers and consumers of music. A composer should write today only if he knows for what purpose he is writing. The days of composing for the sake of composing are perhaps gone forever. On the other hand, the demand for music is so great that the composer and consumer ought most emphatically to come to an understanding." Out of this concern Hindemith appropriated a term (actually coined by the musicologist Paul Nettl) that promptly entered the international jargon of twentieth-century music as the very emblem of the aims of "good citizen composers." Later, he came bitterly to resent the word's popularity, and the way it was used by hostile critics to belittle him and his art. Below, in a passage from the preface to the published version of a series of lectures delivered at Harvard University in 1949, Hindemith tries to recant the term and the artistic position it represented. But the passage reveals above all the difference between the artistic climate between the wars and the one that reigned after World War II.

A quarter of a century ago, in a discussion with German choral conductors, I pointed out the danger of an esoteric isolationism in music by using the term *Gebrauchsmusik.* Apart from the ugliness of the word—in German it is as hideous as its English equivalents, workaday music, music for use, utility music, and similar verbal beauties—nobody found anything remarkable in it, since quite obviously music for which no use can be found, that is to say, useless music, is not entitled to public consideration anyway and consequently the *Gebrauch* is taken for granted. Whatever else I had written or said at that time remained deservedly unknown, and of my music very few pieces had reached this country; but that ugly term showed a power of penetration and a vigor that would be desirable for worthier formulations. Some busybody had written a report on that totally unimportant discussion, and when, years later, I first came to this country, I felt like the sorcerer's apprentice who had become the victim of his own conjurations: the slogan *Gebrauchsmusik* hit me wherever I went, it had grown to be as abundant, useless, and disturbing as thousands of dandelions in a lawn. Apparently it met perfectly the common desire for a verbal label which classifies objects, persons and problems, thus exempting anyone from opinions based on knowledge. Up to this day it has been impossible to kill the silly term and the unscrupulous classification that goes with it.

Paul Hindemith, *A Composer's World* (Cambridge, Mass.: Harvard University Press, 1952), x–xi.

> Another notable reaction to the exclusivity of "modern music" and its lack of social utility took place in America during the decade of the Great Depression, and continued to gather force until the end of the Second World War. At its root lay a deep desire to contribute meaningfully to the life of the nation and to see "serious" music fill a real need in American society. Composers like Roy Harris (1898–1979), Virgil Thomson, and, most prominently, Aaron Copland (1900–90) began to write in a style that was basically "neoclassic" and therefore French in orientation (they were all pupils of Nadia Boulanger), but which at the same time attempted to stylize elements of American folk music, especially that of the semimythical American West. They cultivated a deliberate simplicity of form and texture in an effort to win a wider audience for their work. The tendency reached its peak with Copland's ballets *Billy the Kid* (1938), *Rodeo* (1942), and *Appalachian Spring* (1944). By the time Copland wrote the essay we have abridged below (originally delivered as a lecture at Harvard University in 1951), the movement had largely run its course and the composer had been put somewhat on the defensive. The essay remains, however, an eloquent document of a uniquely optimistic and energetic episode in the development of American art music.

The Composer in Industrial America

My own experience I think of as typical because I grew up in an urban community (in my case, New York City) and lived in an environment that had little or no connection with serious music. My discovery of music was rather like coming upon an unsuspected city—like discovering Paris or Rome if you had never before heard of their existence. The excitement of discovery was enhanced because I came upon only a few streets at a time, but before long I began to suspect the full extent of this city. The instinctual drive toward the world of sound must have been very strong in my case, since it triumphed over a commercially minded environment that, so far as I could tell, had never given a thought to art or to art expression as a way of life.

The curious thing, in retrospect, is the extent to which I was undisturbed by the ordinariness of the workaday world about me. It didn't occur to me to revolt against its crassness, for in the last analysis it was the only world I knew, and I simply accepted it for what it was. Music for me was not a refuge or a consolation; it merely gave meaning to my existence, where the world outside had little or none. I couldn't help feeling a little sorry for those to whom music and art in general meant nothing, but that was their own concern. As for myself, I could not imagine my own life without it.

It seems to me now, some thirty-five years later, that music and the life about me did not touch. Music was like the inside of a great building that shut out the street noises. They were the noises natural to a street; but it was good to have the quiet of the great building available, not as a haven or a hiding place, but as a different and more meaningful place.

My years in Europe from the age of twenty to twenty-three made me acutely conscious of the origins of the music I loved. Most of the time I spent in France, where the characteristics of French culture are evident at every turn. The relation of French music to the life around me became increasingly manifest. Gradually, the idea that my personal expression in music ought somehow to be related to my own back-home environment took hold of me. The conviction grew inside me that the two things that seemed always to have been so separate in America—music and the life about me— must be made to touch. This desire to make the music I wanted to write come out of the life I had lived in America became a preoccupation of mine in the twenties. It was not so very different from the experience of other young American artists, in other fields, who had gone abroad to study in that period; in greater or lesser degree, all of us discovered America in Europe.

Sometimes it seems to me that it was the composers who were the very last to take cognizance of a marked change that came over the musical scene after the stimulating decade of the twenties. The change was brought about, of course, by the introduction for the first time of the mass media of distribution in the field of music. First came the phonograph, then the radio, then the sound film, then the tape recorder, and now television. Composers were slow to realize that they were being faced with revolutionary changes: they were no longer merely writing their music within an industrial framework; industrialization itself had entered the framework of what had previously been our comparatively restricted musical life. One of the crucial questions of our times was injected: how are we to make contact with this enormously enlarged potential audience, without sacrificing in any way the highest musical standards?

Jacques Barzun recently called this question the problem of numbers. "A huge increase in the number of people, in the number of activities, and possibilities, of desires and satisfactions, is the great new fact." Composers are free to ignore this "great new fact" if they choose; no one is forcing them to take the large new public into account. But it would be foolish to side-step what is essentially a new situation in music: foolish because musical history teaches us that when the audience changes, music changes. Our present condition is very analogous to that in the field of books. Readers are generally quick to distinguish between the book that is a best seller by type and the book that is meant for the restricted audience of intellectuals. In between there is a considerable body of literature that appeals to the intelligent reader with broad interests. Isn't a similar situation likely to develop in music? Aren't you able even now to name a few best-seller compositions of recent vintage? Certainly the complex piece—the piece that is "born difficult"—is an entirely familiar musical manifestation. But it is the intelligent listener with broad interests who has tastes at the present time which are difficult to define. Composers may have to relinquish old thinking habits and become more consciously aware of the new audience for whom they are writing.

In the past, when I have proffered similar gratuitous advice on this subject, I have often been misinterpreted. Composers of abstruse music thought they were under attack, and claimed that complexities were natural to them— "born that way," a contention that I never meant to dispute. I was simply pointing out that certain modes of expression may not need the full gamut of post-tonal implications, and that certain expressive purposes can be appropriately carried out only by a simple texture in a basically tonal scheme. As I see it, music that is born complex is not inherently better or worse than music that is born simple.

Others took my meaning to be a justification for the watering down of their ideas for the purposes of making their works acceptable for mass consumption. Still others have used my own compositions to prove that I make a sharp distinction between those written in a "severe" and those in a "simple" style. The inference is sometimes drawn that I have consciously abandoned my earlier dissonant manner in order to popularize my style—and this notion is applauded enthusiastically; while those of a different persuasion are convinced that only my so-called "severe" style is really serious.

In my own mind there never was so sharp a dichotomy between the various works I have written. Different purposes produce different kinds of work, that is all. The new mechanization of music's media has emphasized functional requirements, very often in terms of a large audience. That need would naturally induce works in a simpler, more direct style than was customary for concert works of absolute music. But it did not by any means lessen my interest in composing works in an idiom that might be accessible only to cultivated listeners. As I look back, it seems to me that what I was trying for in the simpler works was only partly the writing of compositions that might speak to a broader audience. More than that they gave me an opportunity to try for a more homespun musical idiom, not so different in intention from what attracted me in more hectic fashion in my jazz-influenced works of the twenties. In other words, it was not only musical functionalism that was in question, but also musical language.

This desire of mine to find a musical vernacular, which, as language would cause no difficulties to my listeners, was perhaps nothing more than a recrudescence of my old interest in making a connection between music and the life about me. Our serious composers have not been signally successful at making that kind of connection. Oblivious to their surroundings, they live in constant communion with great works, which in turn seems to make it *de rigueur* for them to attempt to emulate the great works by writing one of their own on an equivalent plane. Do not misunderstand me. I entirely approve of the big gesture for those who can carry it off. What seems to me a waste of time is the self-deceiving "major" effort on the part of many composers who might better serve the community by the writing of a good piece for high school band.

One of the primary problems for the composer in an industrial society like that of America is to achieve integration, to find justification for the life of art in the life about him. I must believe in the ultimate good of the world and of life as I live it in order to create a work of art. Negative emotions cannot produce art; positive emotions bespeak an emotion about something. I cannot imagine an art work without implied convictions; and that is true also for music, the most abstract of the arts.

It is this need for a positive philosophy which is a little frightening in the world as we know it. You cannot make art out of fear and suspicion; you can make it only out of affirmative beliefs. This sense of affirmation can be had only in part from one's inner being; for the rest it must be continually reactivated by a creative and yea-saying atmosphere in the life about one. The artist should feel himself affirmed and buoyed up by his community. In other words, art and the life of art must mean something, in the deepest sense, to the everyday citizen. When that happens, America will have achieved a maturity to which every sincere artist will have contributed.

Aaron Copland, *Music and the Imagination* (Cambridge, Mass.: Harvard University Press, 1952), 96–111. Reprinted by permission of the publishers. Copyright © 1952 by the President and Fellows of Harvard College, © 1980 by Aaron Copland.

149

Music and Ideology

The following manifesto, by the Russian Association of Proletarian Musicians (RAPM), the organization that represented the extreme "left wing" in early Soviet musical politics, presents an interesting (if hopelessly doctrinaire and deterministic) analysis of the post-Wagnerian crisis, and the various early twentieth-century modernisms, in terms of Marxian dialectics. It should be emphasized that this document does not represent an official government or party viewpoint as of 1929. The machinery for imposing party controls on art was implemented three years later, with the establishment of the Writers', Artists', and Composers' "Unions." Official Soviet musical ideology of the Stalin period tended to emphasize nothing like the break with all traditional "classical" heritages advocated by the RAPM, but rather the enforced continuation of the Russian nineteenth-century "national" school. The phrase "a means of communication with people," quoted in connection with the inadequacy of "bourgeois" musical culture, comes from Musorgsky's artistic credo, already cited in this book (see p. 338), while the quotation at the end is from a famous pronouncement (deriving not from Marx but from Tolstoy) by Lenin (real name Vladimir Ilyich Ulyanov, 1870–1924), the founder of the Soviet state.

Music and the Classes

Reflecting the general evolution of class society, the music of the past evolved along two main paths: on the one hand the music of the toilers, the exploited, and the oppressed classes (the so-called folk music), on the other hand the feudal bourgeois music, which comprises virtually the entire bulk of written "cultured" music.

The position of this or that class at a given historical moment determines the development of these two musical cultures.

The brilliant spread of the musical culture of the ruling classes was determined by its possession of the tools of material, technical culture in the domain of everyday life as in that of the special musical field (complicated musical instruments, special technique of their manufacture, special educational institutes, music printing, etc.).

On the contrary, the music of the oppressed and exploited classes, despite its deep musical significance, remains at a primitive stage as far as cultural, technical, and material means are concerned.

The above conditions give the ruling classes the possibility of utilizing the creative forces of the exploited masses. At certain moments of history musicians of the ruling classes address themselves to the art of the oppressed classes and, taking their most valuable possession, nourish their own music entirely with the vitalizing juice of folk music.

Musical Culture of the Past

Bourgeois music in its latest period (that of the entrance of capitalism into its highest stage, financial capitalism) has reflected the process of general decay and disintegration of bourgeois culture. During this period music begins to cultivate decadent moods, and engages in the following pursuits:

a. Cultivation of sensual and pathologically erotic moods emerging as a result of narrowing interests of a bourgeoisie degenerating morally and physically; cultivation of musical materials reflecting primitive psychology of the nations, "colonial" exotic music, etc.

b. Mysticism, feeling of oppressiveness as a premonition on the part of the bourgeoisie of the impending social catastrophe and the end of bourgeois rule.

c. Reproduction in a musical work of the movement of the contemporary capitalist city with its milling humanity and industry. This naturalistic streak in contemporary music is a symptom of its decay and of the inner devastation of the bourgeoisie, the inadequacy of its ideological-emotional world to serve as "a means of communication with people" and inspiration for composers. Hence, the so-called "emotionalist" trends in music and, specifically, urbanist music that reduces itself to a more or less successful reproduction of noises.

d. Cultivation of primitive, coarse subjects as a means, on the part of the bourgeoisie, to slow up the process of degeneration and to fight the proletariat that threatens "anarchy" for the bourgeoisie after the Revolution.

The decadent subject-matter of bourgeois music determines its form. Under the influence of decadent moods the inner meaning of music becomes diluted; technical elements gain ascendancy and music splits into factions according to its formal elements. In contemporary decadent bourgeois music the most characteristic elements are:

a. Hypertrophy of harmonic, vertical concepts, resulting in utter monotony and poverty of metrical, rhythmical design, which leads towards distortion of the musical phrase and loss of dynamic power, and disappearance of melos that caused the vocal crisis of bourgeois opera.

b. Hypertrophy of the polyphonic principle, accompanied by complete negation of the modal groundwork of music (so-called linear music).

c. The pursuit of illogical spasmodic rhythms.

d. The striving towards so-called absolute, self-sufficient "constructivistic" music, mechanistically built, and claiming to produce an emotional response of a predetermined nature. The school of composition inculcating this attitude (the so-called theory of "manufacture" of musical compositions) contributes to the complete disappearance of creative urge, replaced by dead mechanical schematicism.

During this last period the bourgeoisie, disguising its class interests under convenient slogans, makes claim to "objective," formal, technical "attainments," rejects the legacy of the classical past, and promotes "novelty," "contemporaneity," and "progress" in a narrow, formal, technical sense. These trends in contemporary bourgeois music, symptomatic of the psychological distress of the bourgeoisie, are a direct result of its decay and degeneration.

RAPM

The fundamental task of the Proletarian Artistic Associations is to establish the hegemony of the proletariat in various fields of the arts.

In the domain of music, such an organization is embodied in the Russian Association of Proletarian Musicians (RAPM), which unites musicians active in the proletarian advance-guards on the various sectors of the front of class war, among them on the musico-ideological sector.

The ultimate aim of the RAPM is extension of the hegemony of the proletariat to the music field. At present it sets the following concrete tasks:

a. Extension of the proletarian Communist influence to the musical masses, re-education and reorganization of these masses in order to direct their work and creative talents towards Socialist upbuilding.
b. Creation of Marxist musicology and Marxist musical criticism, critical absorption of the musical culture of the past and of contemporary musical literature from the viewpoint of the proletariat.
c. Demonstration of proletarian musical creative productions and creation of necessary conditions for complete development and growth of proletarian music.

In their creative work, composers, members of the Association of Proletarian Musicians, strive above all to reflect the rich, full-blooded psychology of the proletariat, as historically the most advanced, and dialectically the most sensitive and understanding class.

Following the dialectical and not the mechanistic laws of evolution, composers, members of the RAPM, strive to create gradually new musical forms and a new style born of its artistic subject matter.

The interrelation of content and form is regarded by the RAPM as a dialectical unity.

Thus, while not accepting any form of contemporary bourgeois music that in its content is opposed to the proletariat, the RAPM proclaims the slogan of learning the craft first of all from those among composers of the past who reflected in their creative output the subject matter close to the revolutionary ideas of the proletariat.

New musical forms are created and will be created by the proletariat. Proletarian music must "penetrate into the innermost masses of workmen and peasants, unite the thought and the will of these masses and raise them" for further struggle and construction, organizing their class consciousness in the direction of the ultimate victory of the proletariat as builder of Communist society.

"The Ideological Platform of the Russian Association of Proletarian Musicians" (1929), in Nicolas Slonimsky (ed.), *Music Since 1900*, 4th ed. (New York: Charles Scribner's Sons, 1971), 1353–57. Trans. Nicolas Slonimsky (slightly modified on the basis of the original text). Copyright © 1971 Nicolas Slonimsky. Reprinted with the permission of Charles Scribner's Sons.

150

Composers on Trial

The word "totalitarian" was coined in 1925 by the Italian philosopher Giovanni Gentile to describe the sociopolitical system introduced in his country three years earlier by the government of Benito Mussolini, leader of the National Fascist Party. It means a government that assumes *total* responsibility, and seeks *total* control, over all aspects of its citizens' social, cultural, political, and economic activity, both public and private. No government has ever fully achieved such control, but several have tried, and their priorities may be compared. Of all the twentieth-century authoritarian regimes, the Soviet Union best exemplified totalitarianism with respect to the arts. Through its doctrine of Socialist Realism, it promulgated in theory—and, through its many supervisory agencies, enforced in practice—the requirement that art provide an active delivery system for state and party propaganda. The most chilling single instance of that enforcement was among the first: an editorial in *Pravda,* the official organ of the Soviet Communist Party, on 28 January 1936, denouncing an opera, *The Lady Macbeth of the Mtsensk District,* by Dmitry Dmitrievich Shostakovich (1906–75). At the age of twenty-nine, Shostakovich was already a world-famous composer and the outstanding Soviet creative artist of his generation. His opera portrays—and justifies!—the murderous revenge of an oppressed wife against her husband and father-in-law, and, later, against a rival for the love of her paramour. Its exceedingly violent music and its frank portrayal of carnal lust had made it a sensation the world over in the two years since its first performance, and its sudden suppression made headlines everywhere. In the official Soviet press, the editorial, titled "Muddle Instead of Music," was always referred to afterwards as "the historic document," and historic it certainly was: the earliest instance of a mortal threat ("this … could end very badly") directed against an individual creative artist by an omnipotent state. No one has ever been able to define exactly what it was about the opera that so offended the regime, other than the fact that Iosif Stalin (1879–1953), the Soviet dictator, had found the music disagreeable. (He had attended a performance; the composer had been alerted to expect a summons to Stalin's box for congratulations, but Stalin left before the last intermission.) Most likely, an example was being made of the most eminent musician so as to demonstrate that no one's reputation would offer protection against the exercise of totalitarian power. But from now on, Soviet music would be defined by a safe and tame stylistic conservatism ("classicism") that stood in peculiar contrast to the revolutionary image of the regime. The authorship of the editorial remains a mystery. It was probably written by a cultural official at Stalin's behest; the widespread assumption that the dictator wrote it himself is typical of the "conspiracy-theorizing" that official secrecy begets.

With the general growth of culture in our country there has also been a growth in the demand for good music. Nowhere else and never before have composers faced such grateful audiences. The masses await good songs, but also good instrumental works and good operas.

Several theaters have offered Shostakovich's opera *The Lady Macbeth of the Mtsensk District* to this new and culturally advanced Soviet public as both a novelty and a mark of achievement. Obliging music critics have praised the opera to the skies and created a resounding reputation for it. The young composer has heard only enthusiastic compliments, not the sort of practical and serious criticism that might have helped him in his future work.

From its very first minute listeners are deafened by the opera's purposely graceless and jumbled stream of sounds. Little shreds of melody, little stabs at a musical phrase, sink, resurface and disappear once more in the rumbling, grating, screeching din. It is hard enough to follow this "music"; to remember it is impossible.

Thus it continues practically throughout the opera. On the stage singing is replaced by shouting. If the composer should happen by chance upon a simple and comprehensible melody, he immediately, as if alarmed at such a calamity, plunges right back into his musical uproar, which at times turns into a complete cacophony. The expressivity that a music lover demands is replaced by a wild rhythm. This musical racket is supposed to express passion.

СУМБУР ВМЕСТО МУЗЫКИ

Об опере «Леди Макбет Мценского уезда»

Pravda, 28 January 1936: the famous unsigned editorial, "Muddle Instead of Music," which nipped the operatic career of Dmitry Shostakovich in the bud by virtual decree of the Soviet Communist Party.

None of this is the result of any lack of talent in the composer, or of his inability to express simple and powerful feelings in music. This is music deliberately made topsy-turvy so as never to recall classical operatic music, so as never to have anything in common with symphonic sonorities or with the plain language of music that can be understood by all. This is music constructed according to the same principle of rejecting opera as that by which "leftist" art rejects all simplicity, realism and intelligible symbols in the theater, all natural sound of words. This is a leftist muddle instead of natural human music. The ability of good music to seize the imagination of the masses is sacrificed to petty-bourgeois formalistic effects, the pretensions to originality by means of cheap eccentricity. This trifling with serious matters could end very badly.

The danger of such a tendency in Soviet music is clear. Left deformation in opera grows out of the same source as left deviation in painting, poetry, education or science.

Petty bourgeois "innovation" leads to a disengagement from real art, real science, or real literature.

The author of *The Lady Macbeth of the Mtsensk District* has had to borrow from jazz its nervous, convulsive, hysterical idiom in order to lend "passion" to his characters.

At a time when our critics—musical ones included—are declaring their allegiance to Socialist Realism, our stage is offering us, in this creation by Shostakovich, the crudest naturalism. Everyone, merchants and the people alike, is presented in the same monotonously beastly guise. A rapacious merchant wife, who has by means of murder clawed her way to power and riches, is presented as some kind of "victim" of bourgeois society.

It is all so crude, primitive, vulgar. The music croaks and hoots and snorts and pants in order to represent love scenes as naturally as possible. And "love" in its most vulgar form is smeared all over the opera. A merchant double bed occupies center stage. On it all "problems" are solved. Death by poisoning and a flogging are portrayed in the same crudely naturalistic style.

The composer, it seems, has not set himself the task to inquire what our Soviet audience wants and seeks in music. It is as if he has deliberately coded his music, distorted it in such a way that it can appeal only to aesthetes and formalists who have lost all healthy taste. He has ignored the demands of Soviet culture to drive out crudity and disarray from all corners of Soviet life. Some critics have called this paean to merchant-class lasciviousness a satire. But there can be no talk of satire here. With all the means of musical and dramatic expression at his command the author tries to attract the public's sympathy to Katerina Izmailova's crude and vulgar desires and deeds.

The Lady Macbeth is popular with bourgeois audiences abroad. Is it not because the opera is muddled and absolutely apolitical that the bourgeois public praises it? Is it not because it titillates the depraved tastes of the bourgeois audience with its witching, clamorous, neurasthenic music?

Our theaters have spared no pains to give Shostakovich's opera a worthy production. The actors have displayed considerable talent in overcoming the noise, screech and ruckus of the orchestra. They have endeavored to make up for the melodic poverty of the opera with dramatic intensity. Unfortunately, this has only made the crudely naturalistic features of the opera stand out with even greater clarity. Talented acting deserves recognition, but wasted efforts deserve commiseration.

"Sumbur vmesto muzïki," *Pravda*, 28 January 1936, trans. R. T., partially on the basis of the translation in Kurt London, *The Seven Soviet Arts* (New Haven: Yale University Press, 1938), 72–74.

Shostakovich rehabilitated himself the next year—the darkest year of Soviet state terror, full of mass arrests and purges—with his Fifth Symphony (1937), advertised in the Soviet press as "a Soviet artist's creative response to just criticism." Until Stalin's death enabled a measured liberalization of Soviet artistic policy (called "the Thaw"), Shostakovich was a kind of ambassador for Soviet music, sent on official visits abroad (most notably to the Communist-dominated Cultural and Scientific Conference for World Peace, held at New York's Waldorf-Astoria Hotel in 1949). The high point of his world prestige came with his colossal, programmatic Seventh Symphony, composed in 1941–42 during the siege of Leningrad, his native city, and dedicated to its population. It quickly went around the world, just as *The Lady Macbeth* had done a decade earlier, but this time it was the object of feverish morale-building publicity as part of the Allied war effort against the Fascist axis of Germany, Italy, and Japan. Its autograph score was microfilmed and flown, via Teheran and Cairo, to London, thence to New York, where it was given its American première by the NBC Symphony Orchestra under Arturo Toscanini (1867–1957), himself a principled exile from Mussolini's Italy, on 19 July 1942, in a performance that was broadcast live nationwide, and in "transcription," virtually worldwide. It was the very success of the work as a political expression that antagonized many music critics, who were zealous to defend the status of art, and modern art particularly, as "autonomous." That zeal is vividly illustrated by Virgil Thomson's exceedingly hostile review, which could easily compete in harshness with the *Pravda* review of *The Lady Macbeth,* albeit from a diametrically opposite perspective. The main issue in both reviews—on the surface, at least—is, ironically enough, the same: namely, "accessibility." But the surface, in both cases, was obviously just a façade.

Whether one is able to listen without mind-wandering to the Seventh Symphony of Dmitri Shostakovich probably depends on the rapidity of one's musical perceptions. It seems to have been written for the slow-witted, the not very musical and the distracted. In this respect it differs from nearly all those other symphonies in which abnormal length is part and parcel of the composer's concept. Beethoven's Ninth, Mahler's Ninth and Eighth, Bruckner's Seventh, and the great Berlioz "machines" are long because they could not have been made any shorter without eliminating something the author wanted in. Their matter is complex and cannot be expounded briefly.

The Shostakovich piece, on the other hand, is merely a stretching out of material that is in no way deep or difficult to understand. The stretching itself is not even a matter of real, though possibly unnecessary, development. It is for the most part straight repetition. The piece seems to be the length it is not because the substance of it would brook no briefer expression but because, for some reason not inherent in the material, the composer wished it that way. Of what that reason could possibly be I have only the vaguest notion. That the reason was clear to its author I have not the slightest doubt, however, because the piece all through bears the marks of complete assurance. It is no pent-up pouring out of personal feelings and still less an encyclopedic display of musical skill. It is as interminably straightforward and withal as limited in spiritual scope as a film like *The Great Ziegfeld* or *Gone with the Wind.* It could have said what it says in fifteen minutes, or it could have gone on for two hours more. The proportions of the work seem to this auditor, in short, wholly arbitrary.

They do not seem, nevertheless, accidental. Nothing seems accidental in the piece. The themes are clearly thought out and their doings are simplified with a master's hand. The harmonies, the contrapuntal web, the orchestration show no evidence of floundering or of experiment. If the music has no mystery and consequently no real freedom of thought, neither does it contain any obscurity or any evidence of personal frustration. It is as objective as an editorial, as self-assured as the news report of a public ceremony.

The Seventh Symphony has the same formal structure as the rest of its author's work. It is a series of production numbers, interspersed with neutral matter written chiefly in two-part counterpoint. There is a mechanized military march and the usual patriotic ending, neither of them quite as interesting or imaginative as it might be. And the rest of the episodes are even tamer. The pastorale and the Protestant chorale are competent routine stuff, no more; and the continuity counterpoint, though less static than usual, just sort of runs on as if some cinematic narrative were in progress that needed neutral accompaniment. The opening passage, which is said to represent the good Soviet citizen, is bold and buoyant. But nowhere is there any real comedy, which is what Shostakovich does best. It is easy to listen to the piece, equally easy to skip any part of it without missing the sense of the whole. It is excellent journalism, and some of it can even be remembered. But it will probably not make much of a difference to anybody's inner musical life whether he hears it or doesn't.

Shostakovich is an abundant musician, a "natural" composer. Heretofore he has manifested a boyish taste for low comedy (redeemed by patriotic sentiments) that gave gusto to his writing and made listening to it sometimes fun. The present work shows a wish to put boyish things behind him and an ability to do so without losing confidence in himself. That it is less amusing than his previous works is not to its discredit. That it is, in spite of its serious air and pretentious proportions, thin of substance, unoriginal, and shallow indicates that the mature production of this gifted master is likely to be on the stuffy side. That he has so deliberately diluted his matter, adapted it, by both excessive simplification and excessive repetition, to the comprehension of a child of eight, indicates that he is willing to write down to a real or fictitious psychology of mass consumption in a way that may eventually disqualify him for consideration as a serious composer.

Virgil Thomson, "Shostakovich's Seventh," *New York Herald Tribune,* 18 October 1942. Reprinted in Virgil Thomson, *The Musical Scene* (New York: Alfred A. Knopf, 1945), 101–104.

The more complicated career of Sergei Prokofiev (1891–1953), Shostakovich's older contemporary and countryman, was no less emblematic of the fate of composers living in the great twentieth-century totalitarian states. Early an international celebrity both as pianist and composer, Prokofiev spent the decade and a half following the Russian revolution in Western Europe, where he was closely associated for a time, like Stravinsky, with Sergei Diaghilev and the Ballets Russes. He returned to his homeland in 1936, the very year in which Shostakovich was denounced, upon assurances that he would be exempt from the kind of political interference that dogged the younger man. But from the first he experienced difficulties with the authorities, for the period of his Soviet residence happened to coincide precisely with the period of greatest rigidity in Soviet arts policy. (And *precisely* is indeed the word: in a coincidence no novelist would dare contrive, Prokofiev died on the same day as Stalin, 5 March 1953.) Difficulties reached a peak in 1948, when Prokofiev was publicly censured, alongside Shostakovich and all the other most prominent Soviet composers, for *formalism,* defined by a Soviet musical dictionary of the time as "the artificial separation of form from content and the conferring on form or its individual elements of a self-sufficient and primary importance to the detriment of content." This was a code for modernism, of course, and most of Prokofiev's music was placed under a virtual ban. Below, we give the letter with which Prokofiev "greeted" the now-infamous "Resolution on Music" in which he had been indicted by the Central Committee of the Soviet Communist Party, and in which he attempted both to mollify his accusers and maintain the integrity of his musical aesthetic. Prokofiev did not live to see his restoration to official favor and, indeed, his elevation to the status of an unassailable "classic." The opera-in-progress to which he refers, and through which he hoped to exculpate himself, was rejected and prohibited by the Composer's Union and not staged until 1960.

The state of my health prevents me from attending the General Assembly of Soviet Composers. I therefore wish to express my ideas in regard to the Resolution of the Central Committee of the All-Union Communist Party (Bolsheviks) of 10 February 1948, in the present letter. I request that it be read at the Assembly if you find it expedient.

The Resolution of the Central Committee has separated decayed tissue in our composers' creative production from the healthy part. No matter how painful it may be for many composers, myself included, I welcome the Resolution, which establishes the necessary conditions for the return to health of the whole organism of Soviet music. The Resolution is particularly important because it demonstrates that the formalist movement is alien to the Soviet people, that it leads to the impoverishment and decline of music. It points out with ultimate clarity the aims that Soviet composers must attain to be of the greatest service to the Soviet people.

As far as I am concerned, elements of formalism were peculiar to my music as long as fifteen or twenty years ago. Apparently the infection caught from contact with some Western ideas. When formalistic errors in Shostakovich's opera *The Lady Macbeth of the Mtsensk District* were exposed by *Pravda* [in 1936], I gave a great deal of thought to creative devices in my own music, and came to the conclusion that such a method of composition was faulty.

As a result, I began a search for a clearer and more meaningful language. In several of my subsequent works—*Alexander Nevsky, A Toast to Stalin, Romeo and Juliet, Fifth Symphony*—I strove to free myself from elements of formalism and, it seems to me, succeeded to a certain degree. The existence of formalism in some of my works is probably explained by a certain complacency, an insufficient realization of the fact that it is completely unwanted by our people. The Resolution has shaken to the core the social consciousness of our composers, and it has become clear what type of music is needed by our people, and the ways of the eradication of the formalist disease have also become clear.

I have never questioned the importance of melody. I love melody, and I regard it as the most important element in music. I have worked on the improvement of its quality in my compositions for many years. To find a melody instantly understandable even to the uninitiated listener, and at the same time an original one, is the most difficult task for a composer. Here he is beset by a great multitude of dangers: he may fall into the trivial or the banal, or into the rehashing of something already written by him. In this respect, composition of complex melodies is much easier. It may also happen that a composer, fussing over his melody for a long time, and revising it, unwittingly makes it over-refined and complicated, and departs from simplicity. Undoubtedly, I fell into this trap, too, in the process of my work. One must be particularly vigilant to make sure that the melody retains its simplicity without becoming cheap, saccharine, or imitative. It is easy to say, but not so easy to accomplish. All my efforts will be henceforth concentrated to make these words not only a recipe, but to carry them out in my subsequent works.

I must admit that I, too, have indulged in atonality, but I also must say that I have felt an attraction toward tonal music for a considerable time, after I clearly realized that the construction of musical work tonally is like erecting a building on a solid foundation, while a construction without tonality is like building on sand. Besides, tonal and diatonic music lends many more possibilities than atonal and chromatic music, which is evident from the impasse reached by Schoenberg and his disciples. In some of my works in recent years there are sporadic atonal moments. Without much sympathy,

РАБЫ РОБОТА

MODERN

"Slaves to a Robot." This cartoon, which appeared in the leading Soviet music journal in connection with the public hearings at which Prokofiev and Shostakovich, among others, were humiliated, shows some leading music theorists, musicologists, and critics bowing down before a mechanical idol whose Latin-lettered name needs no translation. Is it a coincidence that the robot's face resembles that of Stravinsky, who in this period was particularly reviled in his homeland as an apostate and servile "toady of imperialism"? (From *Sovetskaya muzïka,* 1948, no. 2, p. 152.)

I nevertheless made use of this device, mainly for the sake of contrast, in order to bring tonal passages to the fore. In the future I hope to get rid of this mannerism.

I am highly gratified that the Resolution has pointed out the desirability of polyphony, particularly in choral and ensemble singing. This is indeed an interesting task for a composer, promising a great pleasure to the listener. In my new opera on a contemporary Soviet subject, *The Story of a Real Man* by [Boris] Polevoi, I intend to introduce trios, duets, and contrapuntally developed choruses, for which I will make use of some interesting northern Russian folk songs. Lucid melody, and as far as possible, a simple harmonic language, are elements which I intend to use in my opera.

In conclusion, I should like to express my gratitude to our Party for the precise directives of the Resolution, which will help me in my search of a musical language accessible and natural to our people, worthy of our people and of our great country.

151

Music under and after the Nazis

The National Socialist ("Nazi") government under Adolf Hitler, which ruled an ever-expanding Germany from 1933 to 1945, had a simpler criterion of musical worthiness than the Soviets. It was racial, pure and simple. Music (like Schoenberg's "atonality" but not Stravinsky's "neoclassicism") that was tainted by association with Jews, or music (like "jazz," variously defined) associated with non-white performers, was banned in principle. In practice, both twelve-tone music and American-style dance music were tolerated—the former because it was not always recognized, the latter because it was ineradicably popular—so long as its practitioners were of "Aryan" pedigree. The Nazi index of prohibited music, like the Nazi canon (which of course emphasized the music of Germans, especially Beethoven, Bruckner, and the overtly nationalistic Wagner), was an arbitrary and somewhat negotiable thing, and critics could and often did disagree in public print to a far greater extent than was possible under Soviet power. The first reading below is an abridgment of the booklet that was distributed to visitors to the "Degenerate Music" (*Entartete Musik*) exhibition held at Düsseldorf in 1938, echoing a much more significant exhibition of "Degenerate Art" held the year before in Munich. The author, Hans Severus Ziegler (1893–1978), was a Nazi party hack who had been a follower of Hitler since the mid-1920s and had been rewarded for his faithful service with the directorship of the National Theater in Weimar, Goethe's hometown, and the title of State Commissioner of Theaters for the region of Thuringia in eastern Germany. The exhibition had been his idea. The essay emphasizes race purity, anti-intellectualism, anti-individualism, simple collective virtues, hostility toward modernity and urbanity, and, above all, blind allegiance to Germany, as embodied in the doctrine of "One people, one nation, one leader" (*Ein Volk, ein Staat, ein Führer*). A sideshow to a festival (*Die Reichsmusiktage*) honoring approved new music, Ziegler's "degenerate" exhibit attracted a much more enthusiastic crowd, who delighted in the chance to hear recorded excerpts of works (especially the Weill-Brecht theater pieces) that were otherwise proscribed.

National Socialism has asserted a total claim on all domains of German life and will never relinquish it. We have experienced a revolutionary transformation in our worldview, which in its vast dimensions will take a long time working itself out completely. The point of no return has assuredly been reached, but the full consequences in all parts of German life have not yet been realized. The Führer, as statesman and regenerator of German national life, has called for the revolutionizing of the whole human being and of human nature. After a long period of degeneration it was clear that years and decades of re-education would be needed to bring about the proper spiritual, moral and ethical renewal of Germany.

It is not my intention in organizing this Exhibition to mount attacks on individuals, still less to hinder German musicians in their breadwinning efforts. I only want to give testimony of my wish, in the interests of the present and of the rising generation, to contribute toward elucidating the question of degeneracy in art. It is my ardent wish to cleanse the atmosphere and let in some fresh, liberating air that the future creative and performing musicians of Germany may breathe more freely in their lives and work.

He has no understanding of the task or range of National Socialism who thinks that the hyper-individualism of the liberal past, which has been eliminated from all other walks of the nation's life, might be allowed to persist in the realm of art. He knows nothing of National Socialism who advocates the view that politics has nothing to do with art and that amid the moral and ethical regeneration of the people questions involving the various artistic domains might be exempt from consideration. Cultural politics calls upon us to care for the soul of the people, to foster its creative powers and all the values of character and conviction that we gather under the general term, "the folk." The politician and the cultural politician have the same goal: the creation of a strong nation and the securing of its material and spiritual well-being, the safety of its external existence and the nurturing of its inner existence. Just as the political man must free himself absolutely and entirely from every horrible democratic or Bolshevik way of thinking and reject any and all destructive influences without compromise; just as the politically aware and active German who supports Adolf Hitler must radically repudiate a life that has become inwardly exhausted and decayed; so every responsible agent in the higher reaches of the national life, in the world of artistic activity, must for the sake of cultural reconstruction free himself uncompromisingly from all destructive spirits that would collectively infect the national life with their constant nay-saying.

Anyone who thinks at all clearly must know by now that for over a century, ever since the time of Heinrich Heine [1797–1856, German-Jewish poet of great fame], Jewry has acted as an agent of decomposition and as the disparager of all German values and virtues, and that the subtlest work toward the destruction of our political life is carried out by the Jews through the media of literature, pseudo-science, the arts and the press. These connections, which the Führer has asserted and proved a thousand times over, will be fully uncovered only if all Germans appreciate the consequences and become vigilant.

Ever more emancipated from the beginning of the nineteenth century, and after 1848 altogether unrestrained, Jewry began, at the prompting of its racial will, tirelessly to infiltrate all German thought and feeling, and to palm off on the Germans all kinds of novel ideas stemming from the Jewish race. We must reckon as the most harmful activity of the Jews of the nineteenth century their steadfast efforts to divest the people

The cover of Hans Severus Ziegler's brochure Entartete Musik (Degenerate Music), and the posters for the exhibition of the same name, sported this lovely image, which sythesized all of the objects of Nazi race hatred (Jews, gypsies, and blacks) and attached them to the saxophone, an instrument that evoked not only jazz but many modern concert and opera scores as well, including Alban Berg's *Lulu*, Weill and Brecht's *Three Penny Opera*, and Ernst Krenek's especially popular *Jonny spielt auf* (*Johnny Goes to Town*, 1927), whose title character—a Negro violinist—probably furnished the immediate inspiration for the caricature. *Deutsches Historisches Museum, Berlin* (*R92/715*).

of its creative powers, its talent and genius, and deprive it of its most distinctive racial and national traits.

If Richard Wagner, in his treatise "Jewry in Music" [*Das Judenthum in der Musik*, 1850], could already expose the Jewish charlatans and insipid imitators in the music of his time, with what solidarity did the Jews not rally against German music and its creators, so that we descendents of Wagner still have to unmask the many flabby charlatans of the most recent past who have for decades been ruling our concert and opera life. Our basic error is and has always been to learn nothing either from political history or from cultural history but instead to swim senselessly along in a tide whose currents and influxes all come from sources that should have been easy to detect.

What we have brought together in the Degenerate Music exhibition represents a veritable witches' sabbath of the most frivolous intellectual and artistic culture-Bolshevism, depicting the triumph of subhumanity, of arrogant Jewish impudence and utter spiritual cretinism, the after-effects of which can still be found lingering in today's musical life, albeit steadily diminishing in significance. Degenerate music is thus basically de-Germanized music, for which the healthy element among the people no longer has receptive organs, and can summon up neither sympathy nor susceptibility. It is, finally, the object of snobbish adulation or purely intellectual consideration on the part of more or less decadent scribblers and hacks who write for some of our more fashionable music journals.

No other law exists for the art of a people but that its development be realized *organically*. It might sound all too simple, but the secret of all wisdom consists finally in simplicity: if the greatest masters of music were sensitive to, and created through, the laws of tonality and the manifestly German medium of the triad, then we have the right to brand as a charlatan or dilettante anyone who presumes to overcome these basic properties of sound and by dint of any old sonic combinations improve or extend—but in reality debase—the art.

Together with a whole series of leading musical experts and cultural policymakers I hold the view that atonality, as the result of the destruction of tonality, is evidence of degeneration and culture Bolshevism. And since atonality has its basis in the *Harmonielehre* [Harmony Textbook, 1911] of the Jew Arnold Schoenberg, I declare it to be the product of the Jewish mind. Whoever eats of it will die of it. No one who belongs to the school of Beethoven could possibly cross the threshold into Schoenberg's studio, and anyone who remains for any length of time in this studio of Schoenberg's will of necessity lose his feeling for the purity of Beethoven's German genius. Anyone who compromises in this connection does so at his peril and must one day perish spiritually and creatively. Persons who swear allegiance to "Progress at any price" or to so-called modernity, because they prefer to be counted among the literati as up-to-date instead of joining with the musical ear of the people, will finally learn that true progress proceeds not from the "Zeitgeist" (that Jewish invention!), but only from strong creative personalities. They alone set the pace for the peoples. What Jewish democracy and Marxism have been passing off as "progress" and "Zeitgeist" has really been the doctrine of primitivism and regression to a naked animal tribal life and the renunciation of all culture, or else some sort of witty sloganeering with an ephemeral effect on the taste of the moment.

Even more obviously degenerate is the incursion of brutal jazz rhythms and jazz timbres into the Germanic music world. I do not remotely suppose that the struggle against atonality means rejecting dissonances, even a whole heap of dissonances. It goes without saying that every aesthetic viewpoint is familiar with the law of contrasts. Just as little do we oppose the enrichment of rhythm, but we have every right to assume that the masters of the nineteenth century exhausted all rhythmic possibilities short of admitting, whether instinctively or consciously, rhythms that are racially alien. Whoever meddles with the boundaries of sound combinations risks dissolving our Aryan tonal order. We cannot look upon the great thousand-year development of music as if it were in error, but must see the masterworks of this vast period as the crowning of the Western spirit. Whoever seeks to efface these boundaries will no longer make music the triadic Western way, but will aim to overthrow the dominion of melody. Non-western peoples also make melodic music, but not polyphonic. Polyphonic music-making can only mean for the Westerner the tempering of melodic freedom with the higher and (to us) natural order of the triad. Seldom are we made so clearly and forcibly conscious of belonging to our race than in the naturalness of our music.

So might every man and boy who feels a creative urge within him take counsel from his racial conscience and under its tutelage join ranks with the messengers of the gods, the geniuses of our holy German art. We are doing battle against the deleterious, negating, ice-cold pseudo-spirit, which in recent decades has announced that Beethoven and Wagner have no more to say to us, and we dedicate ourselves to the noble German-Teutonic music whose secret also reverberated in the soul-depths of that greatest of German geniuses and poets Wolfgang Goethe, who once proclaimed, "Song rises heavenward like a spirit and spurs the better self within us to escort it."

Hans Severus Ziegler, *Entartete Musik: Eine Abrechnung* (Düsseldorf: Völkischer Verlag, 1938). Trans. R. T.

The single musical artifact of the Nazi period that remains a part of the standard concert repertory worldwide is *Carmina Burana*, a "scenic cantata" for soloists, chorus and percussion-heavy orchestra (originally meant to accompany dance) by the Munich composer Carl Orff (1895–1982). It is based on medieval Latin (and some old-German) secular poetry celebrating wine, women, and song, the work of vagabond ("goliard") students and clerics, all preserved in a thirteenth-century manuscript once at the Bavarian monastery of Benedictbeuron (from which its name, "Songs of Beuron," was derived), and now at the Bavarian State Library in Munich. Exceedingly popular from the beginning, the cantata gradually won favor and status as an "exemplary" national-socialist artwork—a fact that has to some extent complicated its post-Nazi reception. Below we give two reviews of its first performance. The first is the work of Herbert Gerigk (1905–96), a protégé of Alfred Rosenberg (1893–1946), one of the main Nazi ideologists, later a war criminal condemned by the international tribunal at Nuremberg. Gerigk worked as the regular music reviewer for the *Völkischer Beobachter* (The People's Observer), the official Nazi party organ (as *Pravda* was the official Soviet Communist organ). His review, published not in his usual column but in the main German music monthly, is guarded. The work fell short, in Gerigk's view, of the mass accessibility that a truly *völkisch* art should espouse; the reviewer was troubled by the regressively primitive quality of the music in which he (rather bizarrely) detected echoes of jazz; and at the end he shows signs of the same prudishness that motivated *Pravda*'s denunciation of Shostakovich's *Lady Macbeth of Mtsensk*—a prudishness shared by all totalitarian regimes, which necessarily place the highest premium on the maintenance of public order.

The song texts are juxtaposed without connection, and Orff has generally given them simple strophic settings. He did not use any melodic models (as many a listener assumed) but only relied on a few stylistic formulas from early music, in order to achieve congruence in time between music and subject. The work poses a number of problems.

The first is the texts, sung in monastic Latin and 13th-century German, which no one can understand. Hearing a sung text, one tries to understand it. Otherwise, one might as well sing Chinese or any syllables one pleases. Orff has, from the start, precluded any mass impact of his work by virtue of the incomprehensibility of its language.

Orff's musical style is lapidary. In fact, he merely strings one melody after another. Repetition and rhythmic linkages are the extent of his formal development. The melodic style is often reminiscent of children's songs. But then, despite the deliberate primitiveness, there are passages that unmistakably derive from elite culture. At times one thinks one is hearing the rough vitality of plain musical speech; at other times, the mood is jazz-like.

Yet one must not forget the composer's intention. Orff has written "secular songs for soloists and chorus with the accompaniment of instruments and scenery," conceived as still images in the manner of a magic lantern [i.e., an early light projector]. In Frankfurt it became an opera-oratorio, in which the chorus, in 13th-century costume, sat on benches to the left and right, while in the background the wheel of Goddess Fortune turned between the scenes that the soloists and dancers acted out.

It was an interesting concept, which one might accept as a novelty. But apparently this is to be only the prelude to a whole musical trend. If so, then it would no longer pose a question of art for us but rather one of cultural politics and world-outlook. We shall still have to see how this work affects a naïve mass audience. The texts concern the joy of living, of springtime, drinking and the loose morals of the religious (as early as the 13th century!), and they treat love in a quite unequivocal manner.

Herbert Gerigk, "Das Ende des Allgemeinen deutschen Musikvereins: Rückblick auf das Tonkünstlerfest in Darmstadt und Frankfurt a. Main," *Die Musik*, XXIX, no. 10 (July 1937), 701–702. Translation adapted from that of Steven Moore Whiting.

Far more enthusiastic is the review of Horst Büttner, far less distinguished than Gerigk as a critic but rather an official of the *Reichsmusikkammer* (National Music Office), an arm of the Ministry of Propaganda, and a protégé of Joseph Goebbels (1897–1945), the Propaganda Minister himself and one of Hitler's closest associates. Whether or not because it reflected the view of the more powerful politician, the opinion expressed in Büttner's review, full of sloganeering praise for Orff's "radiant strength-filled life-joy," a typical Nazi locution, is the one that eventually won out. Where Gerigk heard jazz, Büttner hears the healthy exuberance of Aryan folklore. Music so full of the "life-instinct," the review implies, can serve as an antidote to decadence and degeneracy.

We may credit the predominance at this meeting of folkloric methods to the merits of a single composition, which demonstrated the possibilities of using folk-like melodies to shape a large work of a special kind: Carl Orff's scenic cantata *Carmina Burana*. Anyone familiar with this collection of medieval vagabond poetry will have wondered that no one has yet set these songs to music; for they demand music and were certainly sung at the time of their creation. That much of the verse was composed in Latin need not present any barrier, for we have long counted these songs among the most precious possessions of our national literature, and rightly so: this poetry is as typically German as the songs of the Minnesinger Walther von der Vogelweide, and the occasional stanzas of German folk song show clearly enough what expressive domain this wonderful song cycle inhabits: the radiant, strength-filled life-joy of the folk, which here takes multifarious forms, even the elaborate rhyme-games of vagabond students. Orff's text selection places the Ode to the Goddess Fortune at the beginning and end of a three-part scenic cantata, the first part of which interprets in music the joys of nature and love, the second the pleasures of carousing, and the third a cultivated but no less expressive comedy of love. Even though the occasional reference to Gregorian chant or (in the song of the roasting swan) a grotesquely extended melodic line may bring elite musical culture to the fore, the impact of the work nevertheless springs from the self-assurance with which Orff draws on the emotional world of folk song and folk dance. Even the short, indefatigably swirling tonal symbol for the turning wheel of fortune is a masterstroke of folklike inspiration. Later on, the melodic and rhythmic style of the Bavarian-Alpine "two-step" becomes prominent. In the third part, melodic formulas of Romanesque folk song make an appearance. Orff skillfully uses parallel fifths as a folk-music ingredient. The harmony avoids all dissoluteness in favor of block-like force. The instrumentation, despite Orff's refined coloristic sense, aims at clearly defined timbral values. Finally, one may note the stark contrasts between the individual songs. The rhythmic impetus of some is so sweeping precisely because the lyrical contrasts arouse entirely different mental states, like delicate vernal yearning or restrained eroticism. In terms of expression, this cantata is a Song of Songs in praise of the strength of the unbroken life-instinct. Musically, it testifies to the indestructible, irrepressible power of folk song. If German musical creativity in our day can produce such a work, we need not worry that the general yearning for folk-related art will go unfulfilled.

Horst Büttner, "Hochkultur und Volkskunst: 68. Tonkünstlerversammlung des Allgemeinen deutschen Musikvereins vom 8. bis 13. Juni in Darmstadt und Frankfurt a. M.," *Zeitschrift für Music*, CIV, no. 8 (August 1937), 872–73. Translation adapted from that of Steven Moore Whiting.

Our final exhibit is a confidential report filed by a United States Army psychiatrist as part of Carl Orff's "denazification" after World War II. While clearly complicit in the evils of the regime insofar as he was its beneficiary, the composer was found to be ideologically acceptable and allowed to carry on with his career. In part, this finding was the result of a ruse, referred to in item 8, where Orff claimed "innocence by association" by virtue of his friendship with an actual political dissident who was executed, along with some of his pupils (who formed the so-called White Rose organization of resisters), for condemning German military atrocities in wartime. Orff actually had nothing to do with this group, although he did hide out for a while after Kurt Huber's arrest. In the light of Büttner's review of *Carmina Burana*, the statement referred to in item 4 was also less than forthcoming.

1. Orff belonged only to the professional organization, the *Reichsmusikkammer*.

2. He has always been an independent composer without a fixed position except at the Günther School in Munich, of which he was a founder in 1925 and later head of the music department. The owner, Miss Dorothea Günther, a convinced Nazi, became a member of the NSDAP [the *Nationalsozialistiche deutsche Arbeiterpartei*, or Nazi Party] in 1933. He left the school in 1938 because he felt music was becoming less and less important in the school program.

3. He had a fixed income from the municipal theater in Frankfurt and the State Opera in Vienna, for which he had to write operas. He wrote four or five, not all of which are finished.

4. He said that his music was not appreciated by the Nazis and that he never got a favorable review by a Nazi music critic. His great success came after the performance of *Carmina burana* in La Scala [the Milan opera house] in 1942; this performance was not under the auspices of the Propaganda Ministry. During the war his music was played in occupied countries and in [neutral] Switzerland.

5. He composed a festival for children for the opening of the [1936] Olympic games, and a new version of Mendelssohn's "Midsummer Night's Dream." He said that he received no order from Nazi authorities to do so, and that he did it from his own private musical point of view. It was performed twice; then, he withdrew it and wrote a new version which has never been performed. He swears that it was not written to try to replace Mendelssohn's music, and he admits that he chose an unfortunate moment in history to write it.

6. The fact that he was deferred [from military service] during the war is contradictory to his claim that he was not well thought of at the Propaganda Ministry. There were only 12 composers on the deferred list, all more or less known as Nazis. He does not give a very good explanation. He states that he did not know that he was deferred for the first two years, and that since most of the composers had a position in the theater, they did not need to be on this list. He states that he made no request to be placed on the deferred list and had nothing to do with such a list. At this time it is not known whether he was on the list of the so-called "Party-Composers." He said that he does not know who is in the list and believes that he would never have been considered for it.

7. He said that he had never composed for an official Nazi festival or attended one, and never received a prize or title. He also states that he had never had any connection with prominent Nazis. He was introduced to Baldur von Schirach [the head of the Hitler Youth] in Vienna when his opera was performed, and never met Goebbels.

8. Orff's attitudes are not Nazi. One of his best friends, Prof. Carl [*sic*, actually Kurt] Huber, with whom he published *Musik der Landschaft*, a collection of folk songs, was killed by the Nazis in Munich in 1943. Nevertheless he was a "Nutzniesser" [beneficiary] of the Nazis and can at present be classified only as "Grey C," acceptable. In view of his anti-Nazi point of view, his deliberate avoidance of positions and honors which he could have had by cooperating with the Nazis, he may at a future date be reclassified higher.

Confidential political profile, submitted together with a biographical summary and a psychological evaluation, by Major Bertram Schaffner, an interrogator at the Screening Center of the US Army Information Control Division to the Chief of the Intelligence Section of the Office of the Director of Information Control of the Military Government for Germany (US zone), 1 April 1946.

152

The Outlook after World War II

Two perceptive essays by Virgil Thomson give a keen impression of the spectrum of compositional activity just after World War II. In "On Being American" (New York *Herald Tribune,* 25 January 1948), Thomson sharply takes issue with the older idea that American music was to be founded on the cultivation of a self-consciously "national" idiom. The war effectively killed provincial attitudes about the nature of American music at the same time that it made America a musical center on a par with Europe. The presence of so many of the erstwhile leaders of all the various European trends as a direct result of Nazi persecution and then the war—Stravinsky and Schoenberg within a few miles of one another in Los Angeles!—made the United States in a far truer sense than before a musical melting pot.

What is an American composer? The Music Critics' Circle of New York says it is any musical author of American citizenship. This group, however, and also the Pulitzer Prize Committee, finds itself troubled about people like Stravinsky, Schoenberg, and Hindemith. Can these composers be called American, whose styles were formed in Europe and whose most recent work, if it shows any influence of American ways, shows this certainly in no direction that could possibly be called nationalistic? Any award committee would think a second time before handing these men a certificate, as Americans, for musical excellence. The American section of the International Society for Contemporary Music has more than once been reproached in Europe for allowing the United States to be represented at International festivals of the society by composers of wholly European style and formation, such as Ernest Bloch [1880–1959, born in Geneva] and Ernst Krenek [1900–91, born in Vienna]. And yet a transfer of citizenship cannot with justice be held to exclude any artist from the intellectual privileges of the country that has, both parties consenting, adopted him, no matter what kind of music he writes.

Neither can obvious localisms of style be demanded of any composer, native-born or naturalized. If Schoenberg, who writes in an ultrachromatic and even atonal syntax and who practically never uses folk material, even that of his native Austria, is to be excluded by that fact from the ranks of American composers, then we must exclude along with him that stalwart Vermonter, Carl Ruggles [1876–1971], who speaks a not dissimilar musical language. And among the native-born young, Harold Shapero [1920–] and Arthur Berger [1912–2003] are no more American for writing in the international neoclassic manner (fountainhead Stravinsky) than Lou Harrison [1917–2003], who employs the international chromatic techniques (fountainhead Schoenberg). All these gifted young writers of music are American composers, though none employs a nationalistic trademark.

The fact is, of course, that citizens of the United States write music in every known style. From the post-Romantic eclecticism of Howard Hanson [1896–1981] and the post-Romantic expressionism of Bernard Rogers [1893–1968] through the neo-classicized impressionism of Edward Burlingame Hill [1872–1960] and John Alden Carpenter [1876–1951], the strictly Parisian neoclassicism of Walter Piston [1894–1976], the romanticized neoclassicism of Roy Harris and William Schuman [1910–1992], the elegant neo-Romanticism of David Diamond [1915–2005], the folksy neo-Romanticism of Douglas Moore [1893–1969], Randall Thompson [1899–1984], and Henry Cowell, the Germano-eclectic modernism of Roger Sessions, the neo-primitive polytonalism of Charles Ives, and the ecstatic chromaticism of Carl Ruggles, to the percussive and rhythmic research fellows Edgar Varèse and John Cage, we have everything. We have also the world famous European atonalists Schoenberg and Krenek, the neoclassic masters Stravinsky and Hindemith. We have, moreover, a national glory in the form of Aaron Copland, who so skillfully combines, in the Bartók manner, folk feeling with neoclassic techniques that foreigners often fail to recognize his music as American at all.

All this music is American nevertheless, because it is made by Americans. If it has characteristic traits that can be identified as belonging to this continent only, our composers are largely unconscious of them. These are shared, moreover, by composers of all the schools and probably by our South American neighbors. Two devices typical of American practice are the nonaccelerating crescendo and a steady ground-rhythm of equalized eighth notes (expressed or not). Neither of these devices is known to Europeans, though practically all Americans take them for granted. Further study of American music may reveal other characteristics. But there can never be any justice in demanding their presence as a proof of musical Americanism. Any American has the right to write music in any way he wishes or is able to do. If the American school is beginning to be visible to Europeans as something not entirely provincial with regard to Vienna and Paris, something new, fresh, real, and a little strange, none of this novel quality is a monopoly, or even a specialty, of any group among us. It is not limited to the native-born or to the German-trained or to the French-influenced or to the self-taught or to the New York-resident or to the California-bred. It is in the air and belongs to us all. It is a set of basic assumptions so common that everybody takes them for granted. This is why, though there is no dominant style in American music, there is, viewed from afar (say from Europe), an American school.

National feelings and local patriotisms are as sound sources of inspiration as any other. They are not, however, any nobler than any other. At best they are merely the stated or obvious subject of a piece. Music that has life in it always goes deeper than its stated subject or than what its author thought about while writing it. Nobody becomes an American composer by thinking about America while composing. If that were true Georges Auric's charming fox trot *Adieu New York* would be American music and not French music, and *The Road to Mandalay* would be Burmese. The way to write American music is simple. All you have to do is to be an American and then write any kind of music you wish. There is precedent and model here for all the kinds. And any Americanism worth bothering about is everybody's property anyway. Leave it to the unconscious; let nature speak.

Nevertheless, the award-giving committees do have a problem on their hands. I suggest they just hedge and compromise for a while. That, after all, is a way of being American, too.

Virgil Thomson, "On Being American," in *A Virgil Thomson Reader* (New York: Houghton Mifflin, 1981), 304–306. Copyright © 1981 by Virgil Thomson. Reprinted by permission of Houghton Mifflin Company.

In a stimulating, if somewhat oversimplified, account that appeared in the New York *Herald Tribune* on 2 February 1947, Thomson reported and attempted to explain to American readers what was to many a startling and disquieting phenomenon—the adoption, by increasing numbers of young composers on both sides of the Atlantic, of the twelve-tone technique, confidently thought to be moribund a couple of decades before (see Roger Sessions, p. 387). Sympathetic to this manifestation despite his own stylistic conservatism, Thomson was an important early encourager of Pierre Boulez (1925–), one of the first conspicuous "post-Webernians" to emerge.

Musical modernism, as this has been understood for 50 years, is nowadays a pretty dead issue. Its masters are all famous and their works are known to the public. Its libertarian attitude toward dissonance, rhythmic and metrical irregularities, and unconventional sonorities is no longer revolutionary. Children are brought up on these liberties; and even symphony subscribers, a notoriously conservative group, accept them as normal. The only form of modernism that remains to be imposed (or finally refused) is atonality.

In such a situation, with little left to fight for, what future is there for the composing young beyond a prospect of inevitable conformity? How can they avoid being placed in the public's present scheme of things as mere competitors of their elders? How can they be fresh and original and interesting in their own right? Having observed them pretty carefully during the last ten years both here and abroad, I have come to the conclusion that they are doing exactly what anybody could have figured out by pure logic that they would do. They have taken up the only battle left, namely, that of atonality and its allied techniques.

Not all the young, I grant you, are atonalists. There are neoclassicists and neo-Romantics and even a few retarded impressionists among them. But a generation takes its tone from those who branch out, not from those who follow in footsteps. And today's adventurous young, believe me, are mostly atonal. This position has more to offer them in artistic discovery and less in immediate royalties than any other available, excepting only the tradition of pure percussion. The latter is for the present so limited in scope and so completely occupied by John Cage that there is not much room left in it for anybody else.

The atonal techniques, however, are more ample. One can move around in them. And the young of England, France, Italy, and the Americas have recognized that fact. Germany and Russia, on account of their lack of expressive freedom in the last ten and more years, are slower in taking up the new manner. There are still too many older ones that have not been accepted there yet. But in the countries where intellectual freedom is the norm, young composers are busy with nontonal counterpoint.

Nontonal music, any music of which the key and mode are consistently obscure, has so far always turned out to be contrapuntal. It cannot be harmonic in the conventional sense, because chords pull everything back into a tonal syntax. And if harmonic in an unconventional way, through dependence on percussive and other pitchless noises, it becomes contrapuntal through the necessity of writing for these in varied simultaneous rhythmic patterns, these being its only source of formal coherence.

Counterpoint within the conventional scales can be of three kinds. That practiced in Europe from the 12th through the 15th century is known as quintal, which means that, read vertically at the metrical accents, the music will be found to contain chiefly intervals of the fourth and fifth. Tertial counterpoint, which was the official style from the 16th through the 19th century, exhibits principally thirds and sixths when read this way. Secundal counterpoint, which is characteristic of our time, stacks up on the down beats as mostly seconds and sevenths.

Any of these styles can be used with either a diatonic or a chromatic melodic texture. The twelve-tone syntax, the strictest form of chromatic writing, can even be made to come out harmonically as tertial counterpoint. The music of the chief living neoclassicists—Stravinsky, Milhaud, and Hindemith—is diatonic secundal counterpoint. That of Schoenberg is mostly chromatic secundal counterpoint. On account of this music's lack of a full acceptance by the general public such as that of the neoclassicists enjoys, it remains, with regard to the latter, though it was conceived, in point of time, earlier, in an "advanced" position. The more vigorous movements among today's young are, in consequence, all more closely related to Schoenberg than to the others.

The newer music offers a divergence, however, from Schoenberg's practice in its consistent preoccupation with nondifferentiated counterpoint, a style of writing in which all the voices have equal obligations of expressivity and identical rights in rhetoric. The dramatizing of counterpoint into melody, bass, countermelody, and accompaniment is abolished in this style for an equalized texture that recalls the music of the pre-Renaissance period. There are advantages here to intimacy of expression, since the composer can speak in this technique as personally through a vocal or string ensemble as through a solo instrument. The disadvantage of it is that it is not easily applicable to diversified ensembles, where variety of timbre and technique imposes a certain differentiation of melodic style from one voice to another.

The new music, therefore, is mostly homophonic [homogeneous] in sound, or instrumentation. It is personal in expression, too, and contrapuntal in texture. Its counterpoint is secundal and generally chromatic. If it were not the latter, it would resemble more closely than it does official, or neoclassic, modernism. It can appear tonal or nontonal when examined closely; and it can follow or not Schoenberg's twelve-tone syntax, which this composer himself does not always follow. But its chromaticism invariably approaches atonality. This last, let us remember, is not a precise or easily attainable end. It is rather an ultimate state toward which chromaticism has always tended. Its attractiveness to our century comes, I think, from its equalization of harmonic tensions. We like equalized tensions. They are the basis of streamlining and of all those other surface unifications that in art, as in engineering, make a work recognizable as belonging to our time and to no other.

Virgil Thomson, "Modernism Today," in *Music Reviewed 1940–1954* (New York: Random House, 1967), 195–98. Reprinted by permission of the author.

153

New Developments in Serialism

Pierre Boulez achieved his first notoriety in 1952 as a result of a shockingly provocative attack on what he perceived as the incongruity between the just-deceased Schoenberg's great discovery of the "series" and the traditional structural, textural, and rhythmic language he continued to employ to the end of his life. Webern is cited as the fountainhead of a truly integrated serial music, in which structure and texture proceed from the implications of the new ordering principle. Boulez's uncompromising stance and his pugnacious tone ("since the Viennese discovery, every composer outside the serial experiments has been *useless*") immediately made him a spokesman for his generation and a focal point of controversy. Later, Boulez mellowed to the point where he became for six years the conductor of the New York Philharmonic (1969–75).

To take a stand regarding Schoenberg?

To do so is urgently necessary, certainly; it is nonetheless an elusive problem, defying wisdom, perhaps a search without satisfactory result.

It would be vain to deny it: the Schoenberg "case" is irritating, above all because of its freight of flagrant incompatibilities.

For with Schoenberg we attend one of the most important revolutions that has ever affected the musical language. The material, properly speaking, does not change at all: the twelve semitones. But the structural organization is altered: from tonal organization we pass to serial organization. How did the idea of the series materialize? At what exact moment in Schoenberg's oeuvre did it occur?

Suspension of the tonal system is achieved effectively in the Three Pieces for Piano, op. 11. Thereafter, the experiments become more and more penetratingly acute and lead to the renowned *Pierrot lunaire* [op. 21 (1912)]. I note three remarkable phenomena in the writing of these scores: the principle of constant variation, or nonrepetition; the preponderance of "anarchic" intervals—presenting the greatest tension relative to the tonal world—and progressive elimination of the octave, the tonal world par excellence; [finally,] a manifest attempt to construct contrapuntally.

His exploration of the dodecaphonic realm may be bitterly held against Schoenberg, for it went off in the wrong direction so persistently that it would be hard to find an equally mistaken perspective in the entire history of music.

In Schoenberg's serial works, the confusion between "theme" and "series" is explicit enough to show his impotence to foresee the sound-world that the series demands. Dodecaphonism consists only of a rigorous law for controlling chromatic writing; playing [in his works] only the role of regulating instrument, the serial phenomenon itself was not, so to speak, perceived by Schoenberg.

And there, it seems, you have what led to the decrepitude of the larger part of his serial oeuvre. The preclassic or classic forms ruling most of the architectures have no historical link to the dodecaphonic discovery; thus an inadmissible dichotomy arises between infrastructures related to the tonal phenomenon and a language in which one again perceives the laws of organization summarized above. These architectures annihilate the possibilities of organization inherent in the new language. The two worlds are incompatible, and Schoenberg attempted to justify one by the other.

One cannot call such a procedure valid, and it produced results that could have been anticipated: the worst sort of misunderstanding. A warped "romantico-classicism" in which the good intentions are not the least unattractive element. One certainly gave no great credit to the serial organization by not allowing it its own modes of development, but substituting other, apparently surer ones.

The persistence of accompanied melody, for example; of counterpoint based upon a principal part and secondary parts. Nor is it only in the limited conceptions, but equally in the writing itself, that I see reminiscences of a dead world. Under Schoenberg's pen there abounded the clichés of the most ostentatious and obsolete romanticism. I refer to those constant anticipations, with expressive leaning on the key note; I mean those false appoggiaturas; or, again, those formulas of arpeggios, of devices, of repetitions, which sound so terribly hollow. Finally, I refer to the disagreeable use of a contemptibly poor—call it ugly—treatment of rhythm.

At the very beginning, perhaps one should dissociate the serial phenomenon from Schoenberg's oeuvre. It is easy to forget that a certain Webern also labored. Perhaps, like that certain Webern, one could pursue the sound-EVIDENCE by trying to derive the structure from the material. Perhaps one could enlarge the serial domain with intervals other than the semitone. Perhaps one could generalize the serial principle to the four sound-constituents: pitch, duration, intensity and attack, timbre. Perhaps ... perhaps ...

one could demand from a composer some imagination, a certain degree of asceticism, even a little intelligence, and, finally, a sensibility that will not be toppled by the least breeze.

We must keep ourselves from considering Schoenberg as a sort of Moses who died in view of the Promised Land after having brought down the Tables of the Law from a Sinai that some people obstinately want to confuse with Valhalla. [These are mocking references to Schoenberg's opera *Moses und Aron*.] We certainly owe him *Pierrot lunaire* ... and some other very enviable works.

Nonetheless, it has become necessary that we demolish a misunderstanding that is so full of ambiguity and contradictions: it is time to neutralize the setback. Therefore I do not hesitate to write, not out of any desire to provoke a stupid scandal, but equally without bashful hypocrisy and pointless melancholy:

SCHOENBERG IS DEAD.

Pierre Boulez, *Notes of an Apprenticeship*, trans. Herbert Weinstock (New York: Alfred A. Knopf, 1968), 268–76, slightly modified. Copyright © 1968 by Alfred A. Knopf, Inc. Reprinted by permission of Alfred A. Knopf, Inc., and John Calder (Publishers) Ltd., London.

One of the earliest rejoinders to Boulez's intransigent stance came from Theodor Wiesengrund Adorno (1903–69), a German philosopher and sociologist who had studied composition with Alban Berg and who saw the main significance of modernist music in social rather than purely technical terms. That significance, Adorno asserted, lay in the resistance modernist music offered to the homogenizing and dehumanizing effects of the overly rationalized and instrumentalized conditions of modern life. (By *instrumentalized*, Adorno and the other members of the so-called Frankfurt School of sociologists meant the subjection of all human thought and activity to material and pragmatic concerns at the expense of individual growth.) Totalitarianism had been one manifestation or consequence of hyper-rationalization and instrumentalism, whereby human individuals had been turned into the mere means through which the state, a non-human entity, achieved its ends. Advanced capitalist society, working through its cultural institutions (or, in Frankfurt-speak, the "culture industry," whose primary product was popular music), was another agent of dehumanizing instrumentalism. Adorno deemed the great virtue of Schoenberg's atonal (pre-dodecaphonic) music to lie in its most controversial aspect, namely its notorious arbitrariness, in which Adorno saw the triumph of human subjectivity over the many forces that conspired to constrain it, including the demand that it make ordinary or "natural" sense. The rigorous systematization of Schoenberg's achievements that Boulez now proposed in the name of progress, and for which Webern rather than Schoenberg provided the pertinent model, was in Adorno's eyes a regression into the very rationalization and instrumentalism that Schoenberg's expressionist music had implicitly, and heroically, opposed. (The surprising news that emerged in the 1980s, that Webern had been a supporter of the Nazi regime, has been seen by some as corroboration of Adorno's position.) Needless to say, Adorno's claim that social meanings are immanent—inherent and objectively discernable—in musical texts and techniques has been hotly debated from the moment of its first assertion, with no end in sight. The text below is an abridgment of "The Aging of the New Music," a talk Adorno gave in 1954 at a new-music festival in Stuttgart, several years after returning to Germany from wartime exile in Great Britain and America. It was published the next year in *Der Monat*, the German-language organ of the Congress for Cultural Freedom (see p. 457). Adorno's literary style requires comment. Seemingly a parody of German philosophical prose in its near-impenetrability (somewhat mitigated in our version, admittedly against his intentions), it was a deliberate tactic invoked—as he believed it was in the music he advocated—to ward off the possibility of appropriation by popularizers who threatened its freedom of uncompromising dissent. To limit one's thinking and mode of expression for the sake of easy communication was to sacrifice one's personal autonomy to the dictates of social convention. His highly moralistic tone (despite his explicit—inadvertently comical—disclaimer) is another aspect of his work that jars against normal "artistic" discourse and has reminded some readers of the totalitarian writers—e.g., Ziegler (pp. 429–33)—he so passionately opposed.

To speak of the aging of the New Music seems paradoxical. Yet music that has its essence in the refusal to go along with things as they are, and has its justification in giving shape to what the superficial conventions of daily life hid and what is otherwise condemned to silence by the culture industry—which threatens to acquire New Music as a wholly owned subsidiary—precisely this music has begun to show symptoms of false satisfaction. The malicious objection of reactionaries that scholasticism has crept into modernism and is spreading can only be met by the critical reflection sedimented in the works themselves. The concept of New Music is incompatible with an affirmative sound, the confirmation of what is. When music for the first time came to completely doubt all that, it became New Music. The shock it dealt to its audience in its heroic period—at the time of the first performance of the *Altenberg* Songs of Alban Berg or the first performance of the *Sacre du printemps* of Stravinsky in Paris—cannot simply be attributed to unfamiliarity and strangeness, as the good-natured apology would have it; rather it is the result of something actually distressing and confused. Whoever denies this and claims that the new art is as beautiful as the traditional one does it a real disservice; he praises in it what this music rejects so long as it unflinchingly follows its own impulse.

The aging of the New Music means nothing else than that this critical impulse is ebbing away. It is falling into contradiction with its own idea, the price of which is its own aesthetic substance and coherence. The "stabilization of music," the danger of the dangerless, became even stronger after the world catastrophe. Indeed, on no account, as another cliché would have it, has the fermenting mash clarified into ripe, sweet wine. No valid accomplishment, no rounded masterpiece, took the place of the excesses of Storm and Stress. This striving for masterpieces is part of that conformism renounced by New Music. One could hardly claim that the creations of the mid-twentieth century are superior to Schoenberg's *Pierrot lunaire* or *Erwartung*, Berg's *Wozzeck*, the lyrics of Webern or the early outbursts of Stravinsky and Bartók. Even if in the meantime the raw material of composition was purified of slag and unhomogeneous vestiges of the past, and if somehow the possibility developed of a rigorous new musical phase, it is still questionable whether such a purification of all disturbing intrusions would be of service to the cause of music, and not simply to a technocratic attitude, in whose eager concern for consistency something entirely too binding, violent, and unartistic announces itself. In any case, advances in the material have hardly benefited the quality of the works that use them. A blind belief in progress is required not to notice how little progress has been made since the early twenties, how much has been lost, how tame and in many respects how impoverished most music has become. This must be pointed out without hesitation by whoever keeps faith with New Music and hopes to help it better than by accommodation to the *Zeitgeist,* to the servile acknowledgement of the status quo.

The symptoms have worked their way into the compositions of the most gifted and, according to their own principles, most uncompromising composers. Cases like those of Stravinsky and Hindemith, who more or less explicitly abjured what filled their youth, what in them was once so fascinating, are not at issue here. But even Béla Bartók, from whom such inclinations were very distant, began at a certain point to separate himself from his own past. In a speech given in New York, he explained that a composer like him, whose roots were in folk music, could ultimately not do without tonality—an astounding statement for the Bartók who unhesitatingly resisted all populist temptations and chose exile and poverty when the shadow of Fascism passed over Europe.

All the more urgent is it therefore to understand the present situation of what now attracts the disgruntled and rebellious: twelve-tone technique. Schoenberg's own misgivings are enlightening for anyone who is no more pleased by the popularity of twelve-tone technique—as historically necessary as ever—than say, by the popularity of Franz Kafka's works. Twelve-tone technique has its justification only in the presentation of complex musical contents, which cannot otherwise be organized. Separated from this function, it degenerates into a deluded system. Schoenberg himself consistently refused to teach what the music marketplace had falsified into a system. Twelve-tone technique is the inexorable clamp that holds together what no less powerfully strives to break apart. If it is employed without being tested against such contrary forces, if it is employed where there is nothing counteracting it to be organized, then it is simply a waste of energy. Judgment is passed over innumerable contemporary twelve-tone compositions by the fact that in them relatively simple musical occurrences stand in a relatively simple musical interrelation, the establishment of which by no means demanded serial technique in the first place.

Yet among the intransigent, who would as far as possible like to pursue consequentiality beyond Schoenberg, one meets a remarkable mixture of sectarianism and academicism. Among the major exponents of the New Music, including Schoenberg himself, it is not difficult to uncover traditional elements, particularly in its musical language, that is, in its expressive character and the inner construction of the music, in contrast to the entirely transformed musical material itself. The available materials, right up to the present, have all grown out of the soil of tonality. When they are transferred to non-tonal material, certain inconsistencies result, a kind of break between musical subject-matter and the forming of the music. The very concept of a transition, for example, presupposes various harmonic levels of modulation; stripped of its harmonic task it withers up all too easily into a formal reminiscence. Even the central category—the theme—is difficult to maintain when, as in twelve-tone technique, every tone is equally determined, equally thematic; in twelve-tone compositions themes persist largely as rudiments of an older period. On the other hand, it is only by means of these and related traditional categories that the coherence of the music, its sense, the authentic composition, in so far as it is more than mere arrangement, has been preserved in the midst of twelve-tone technique. Schoenberg's conservatism in this respect is not attributable to a lack of consistency, but to his fear that composition would otherwise be sacrificed to the prefabrication of the material. His most recent followers blithely short-circuit the antinomy that he rightly tried to deal with. They are intentionally indifferent to whether the music makes sense and is articulated—a consideration that caused Schoenberg's hesitations—and believe that the preparation of tones is already composition as soon as one has dismissed from composition everything by which it actually becomes a composition. They never get further than abstract negation, and take off on an empty, high-spirited trip, through thinkably complex scores, in which nothing actually happens; this seems to authorize them to write one score after another, without any constraints at all.

This development already set in with Schoenberg's pupil, Anton von Webern. His later works attempt to organize the musical-linguistic means so entirely in accordance with the new subject-matter, the twelve-tone rows, that he occasionally comes very close to renouncing the musical material altogether and reducing music to naked processes in the material, to the fate of the rows as such, though admittedly without ever completely sacrificing musical meaning entirely. Recently a group of composers have pursued this direction further. At their head stands Pierre Boulez, pupil of Olivier Messiaen and René Leibowitz, a highly cultured and exceptionally gifted musician, with the highest sense of form and with a power that is communicated even where he disavows subjectivity altogether. He and his disciples aspire to dispose of every "compositional freedom" as pure caprice, along with every vestige of traditional musical idiom: in fact, every subjective impulse is in music at the same time an impulse of musical language. These composers have above all attempted to bring rhythm under the strict domination of twelve-tone procedure, and ultimately to replace composition altogether with an objective-calculatory ordering of intervals, pitches, long and short durations, degrees of loudness; an integral rationalization such as has never before been envisaged in music. The capriciousness of this legalism, however, the mere semblance of objectivity in a system that has simply been decreed, becomes apparent in the inappropriateness of its rules to the structural interrelations of the music as it develops, relations that rules cannot do away with. The merely thought up is always also too little thought out.

Something in the total rationalization of music seems to appeal strongly to young people. They find their own reflection in the new widespread allergy toward every kind of expression, an allergy that the iconoclastic exponents of "pointillist" music share with their conservative opponents, as with the historicist interpreters of Bach or the collectivist camp followers of the youth movement. Yet it is not expression as such that must be exorcised from music, like an evil demon—otherwise nothing would be left except the designs of [what Eduard Hanslick (see p. 326) called] "sounding forms in motion"—rather the element of transfiguration, the ideological element of expression, has grown threadbare. This ideological element is to be recognized in what fails to become substantial in musical form, what remains ornament and empty gesture. This touches on one of the decisive anthropological grounds for the aging of New Music: young people no longer trust in their youth. Anxiety and pain have grown to an extreme degree, and can no longer be controlled by the individual psyche. Repression becomes a necessity, and this repression, not the positiveness of some higher state of modesty and self-discipline, stands behind the idiosyncratic rejection of expression, which is itself one with suffering. Every impulse not already comprehended under collective schemata necessarily brings to mind what cannot be admitted to consciousness, and is therefore itself forbidden. The belief that through the rationalization of its materials music enters a new scientific stage is naïve, as if with progressive rationalization art would change into science and take part in its triumph; it is one of those hypotheses by which artists undertake to justify, in an amateurishly intellectual way, what they have already begun to do.

These inner aesthetic tendencies accord precisely with those of society as a whole, although the mediation between the two realms is not at every point transparent.

Society not only influences artists externally, not only supervises them—although there is enough of that—it also forms the artist's own essence. Objectivism, which is so vain about its lack of vanity, and so facilely considers itself morally superior, self-righteously puts a premium on the deficiencies of its exponents. But the overcoming of a non-existent self is an all-too-comfortable course. The symptoms of the aging of the New Music are in social terms those of the contraction of freedom, the collapse of individuality that helpless and disintegrated individuals confirm, approve, and re-enact. In this there is a fatal resemblance between the radicals—who turn themselves over to what they mistakenly consider to be the inner law of the material and enthusiastically subtract themselves from the picture—and those who have crawled away into the ruins of a bygone tradition. Nobody really takes a chance any more; all are looking for shelter. The brutal measures taken by the totalitarian states, measures that over-control music and attack all deviation as decadent and subversive, give tangible evidence of what happens less visibly in non-totalitarian countries, of what transpires, indeed, in the interior of art as well as within most human beings. In the face of such profound damage, nothing would be more foolish than to moralize. The simple fact of the matter cannot be kept silent, that today, the alienation between music and the public has so rebounded against music that the material existence of serious musicians is seriously threatened.

The current paralysis of musical forces represents the paralysis of all free initiative in this over-managed world, which will not tolerate anything that would remain outside of it or at least not be integrated as an element of opposition. All this must be brought unsparingly to consciousness, for the sake of the possibility of something better. Whether it will do any good is highly questionable; for the foundation of music, as of every art, the very possibility of taking the aesthetic seriously has been deeply shaken. Since the European catastrophe, culture hangs on like houses in the cities accidentally spared by bombs or indifferently patched together. Nobody really believes in "culture" any more, the backbone of spirit has been broken, and anyone who pays no attention to this and acts as though nothing had happened, must crawl like an insect, not walk upright. The only authentic artworks produced today are those that in their inner organization measure themselves by the fullest experience of horror, and there is scarcely anyone, except Schoenberg or Picasso, who can depend on himself to have the power to do this. Though today all art has and must have a bad conscience to the extent that it does not make itself stupid, nevertheless its abolishment would be false in a world in which what dominates needs art as its corrective: the contradiction between what is and the true, between the management of life and humanity. The possibility of winning back the power of artistic resistance depends on not shrinking from the fact that what is objectively, socially required is now preserved exclusively in hopeless isolation. Only one who was prepared to work in isolation, to support himself by no delusive laws and necessities, would perhaps be granted something more than mirroring the helplessly solitary.

Theodor W. Adorno, "Das Altern der neuen Musik" (1955), trans. Robert Hullot-Kentor and Frederic Will, in T. W. Adorno, *Essays on Music*, ed. Richard Leppert (Berkeley and Los Angeles: University of California Press, 2002), 181–88, 191–92, 199–200.

Adorno's pessimism, redolent of what the Germans called their "zero hour" (*Stunde null*) in the aftermath of the near-total destruction of their culture, found vivid—indeed lurid—echo in some frank remarks by Ernst Krenek (1900–91) about one of his recent compositions. Krenek, a veteran composer who had first made his mark with a "jazz opera" called *Jonny spielt auf* (*Johnny Goes to Town*) in 1926, was one of the oldest musicians to embrace the most recent developments in serial music. In the text below, presented to an audience of composers and musicologists at Princeton University in 1960, Krenek sought to address one of the most commonly made objections to serial music, especially the postwar "total" serialism of the so-called Darmstadt School, in which other measurable features ("parameters") of sound besides pitch, like duration and loudness, were organized in arbitrary sequences like tone rows: namely, the objection that for all its demonstrable organization, the music sounded as though it had been composed by chance. Surprisingly, Krenek agreed, even coming close to saying that it did not matter any more what music sounded like as long as it was highly organized. His justification relied on an analysis of one of Boulez's most rigorously ordered compositions [*Structures 1a* for two pianos] by a Hungarian composer named György Ligeti, whose career will be the subject of a later reading (p. 461).

PREMEDITATED, BUT UNPREDICTABLE

It may be stated that whatever occurs in a serial piece at any given point is premeditated and therefore technically predictable. However, while the preparation and the layout of the material as well as the operations performed therein are the consequence of serial premeditation, the audible results of these procedures [are] not visualized as the purpose of the procedures. Seen from this angle, the results are incidental. They are also practically unpredictable because the simultaneous progress of highly complex rhythmic patterns at various relative speeds together with the corresponding transpositions of equally complex pitch patterns creates situations that defy precise visualization.

THE TIME MECHANISM OF MY "Sestina"

I have addressed the implications of this apparent contradiction in my *Sestina,* op. 161, for soprano and eight instruments (1957). A sestina is one of the poetic forms developed by the Provençal poets of the twelfth century, its original specimen being inscribed by Arnaut Daniel. It may well be called a serial form of poetry, and its essential formative principle is rotation.

The poem consists of six stanzas of six blank verses each. It hinges upon six keywords which appear at the endings of the individual lines. If in the first stanza the order of these words is 1 2 3 4 5 6, the words will appear in the second stanza in the order 6 1 5 2 4 3. The principle of rotation which is applied here consists in switching the position of every two keywords equidistant from the center of the series, proceeding from the end toward the middle. According to the same principle, the positions of the keywords in the subsequent stanzas are 3 6 4 1 2 5; 5 3 2 6 1 4; 4 5 1 3 6 2; 2 4 6 5 3 1. The process ends here, since the next rotation would produce the original series. The six stanzas are followed by a *Tornada* of three lines in which the keywords, one of each pair in the middle and the other at the end of the line, appear in the order 2 5, 4 3, 6 1.

The content of the *Sestina* which I wrote (in German) as text for the present composition is a contemplation of the idea governing the musical construction of the work. The first two stanzas may suffice to indicate the character and form of the poem:

1. Vergangen Klang und Klage, sanfter *Strom.*
   Die Schwingung der Sekunde wird zum *Mass.*
   Was in Geschichte lebt, war's nur ein *Zufall?*
   Verfall, Verhall, zerronnene *Gestalt?*

Die Stunde zeigt Wandel, wendet *Zeit*.
Das Vorgeschrittne ordnet sich der *Zahl*.

2. In Schritten vorgeordnet durch die *Zahl*
gestaltet sich Gedanke, doch zum *Strom*
wird strenge Teilung, uhr-genaue *Zeit*.
Ist es vermessen, solches Mass von *Mass*
dem Leben aufzuzwingen, der *Gestalt*?
Der Zwang zerrinnt, erzeugt den neuen *Zufall*.

In a nearly literal translation which reproduces the positions of the keywords:

Bygone are sound and mourning, tender *stream*.
Vibration of the second becomes the *measure*.
What lives in history, was it only *chance*?
Decline, fading sound, vanished *shape*?
The hour causes change, turns the *time*.
What looks ahead subordinates itself to *number*.

In stages preordained by *number*
thought takes shape, but a *stream*
is (the result of) strict division, of clocklike, precise *time*.
Is it presuming to force such an extent of *measure*
on life, on *shape*?
Force vanishes, brings forth new *chance*.

THE ELEMENT OF CHANCE

The music of my *Sestina* is based on a twelve-tone row divided into two groups of six tones each, which are rotated according to the principle of the sestina. The duration of the tones of the whole composition are derived from the intervals of the row, further subjected to various other permutations to achieve higher rhythmic diversity. "Density," or the number of simultaneously occurring row forms, is another parameter that is determined serially. Another such parameter is the location of the tones within the gamut of six octaves designated as the ambitus of the work. Only the parameter of timbre lies beyond the limits of the serial arrangement. (If this parameter too were organized serially, it would take the instruments out of their practical ranges.)

Now, if the succession of tones is determined by serial regulation (as is the case in the "classical" twelve-tone technique) and, in addition to this, the timing of the entrance into the musical process of these tones is also predetermined by serial calculation (as, for example, in the case of the *Sestina*), it is no longer possible to decide freely (that is, by "inspiration") which tones should sound simultaneously at any given point. In other words, the so-called harmonic aspect of the piece will be entirely the result of operations performed on premises that have nothing to do with concepts of "harmony," be it on the assumption of tonality or atonality or anything else. Whatever happens at any given point is a product of the preconceived serial organization, but by the same token it is a chance occurrence because it is as such not anticipated by the mind that invented the mechanism and set it in motion.

Generally and traditionally "inspiration" is held in great respect as the most distinguished source of the creative process in art. It should be remembered that inspiration by definition is closely related to chance, for it is the very thing that cannot be controlled, manufactured, or premeditated in any way. It is what falls into the mind (according to the German term *Einfall*), unsolicited, unprepared, unrehearsed, coming from nowhere. This obviously answers the definition of chance given, for example, by the *American College Dictionary*: "the absence of any known reason why an event should turn out one way rather than another." Actually the composer has come to distrust his inspiration because it is not really as innocent as it was supposed to be, but rather conditioned by a tremendous body of recollection, tradition, training, and experience. In order to avoid the dictations of such ghosts, he prefers to set up an impersonal mechanism which will furnish, according to premeditated patterns, unpredictable situations. György Ligeti, in his analysis of Boulez's *Structures* for two pianos, characterizes this state of affairs very well: "We stand in front of a row of vending machines ("*Automaten*" in German) and we can choose freely into which one we want to drop our coin, but at the same time we are forced to choose one of them. One constructs his own prison according to his wishes and is afterwards equally freely active within those walls—that is: not entirely free, but not totally constrained either. Thus automation does not function as the opposite of free decision: rather free selection and mechanization are united in the process of selecting the mechanism." In other words, the creative act takes place in an area in which it has so far been entirely unsuspected, namely in setting up the serial statements (selecting the slot machines). What happens afterwards is predetermined by the selection of the mechanism, but not premeditated except as an unconscious result of the predetermined operations. The unexpected happens by necessity. The surprise is built in.

WHAT DOES SERIAL MUSIC "MEAN," IF ANYTHING?

One of the parameters that obviously cannot be controlled by premeditation when those so far discussed are subjected to serial ordering is the expressive, or communicative, aspect of music. If a serial composer were concerned with this problem, he would have to set up a series of "moods," or "ideas," or something of this sort, to begin with, and then let the other parameters fall in line. It so happens that serial composers are not thinking in such terms.

In a more pessimistic attitude than he now seems to entertain, the German composer and philosopher, T. W. Adorno, in an essay called "The Aging of the New Music" (1955), has criticized the recent developments of serial music because in these the (according to him) deep-rooted and essential analogy and affinity of music and speech is abandoned. While it may be true that music from the time of plainchant has been oriented towards speech-like articulation, diction, and over-all structure, and while especially the exploits of Expressionism and atonality point to a very close association with the free articulation of prose, we have to face the fact that under the influence of the constructive rigor that was the very consequence of Expressionistic roaming serial music has turned away from its rhetorical past. Since whatever music seems to communicate is not so much the supposed content of the audible matter as it is the product of the listener's reaction touched off by his auditory experience, there is no reason to assume that the nature of serial music excludes the possibility of interpreting it as a medium of some sort of communication. The interest it may evoke is similar to that elicited by the process of life, to which serial music is related in the paradox of the chaotic appearance of totally and systematically traceable causality. It may mean as much or as little as life itself.

Ernst Krenek, "Extents and Limits of Serial Techniques," in Paul Henry Lang (ed.), *Problems of Modern Music: The Princeton Seminar in Advanced Musical Studies* (New York: W. W. Norton & Company, Inc., 1962), 83–94. Originally published in *The Musical Quarterly*, XLVI (1960), 233–45.

By extreme contrast, the theoretical writings of Milton Babbitt (1916–), the outstanding American theorist of postwar twelve-tone music, exude confidence, optimism—and a notable conservatism, reflecting the very different postwar mood in the United States, which emerged from the war a greater power than ever before, and one with a renewed faith in science and technology. Rather than reject the music of the past (including the prewar serial past) as outmoded, Babbitt—unlike Boulez or Krenek a career academic—devoted a great deal of study to the problems of establishing structural and textural coherence based on specifically and exclusively twelve-tone principles, taking as his point of departure procedures implicit in certain works of Schoenberg and Webern. The two most important of these he has called *combinatoriality* and *derivation*. The first involves the fashioning of twelve-tone sets the pitch content of whose halves (hexachords) can be reproduced or reciprocated by applying the "classical" operations of the system (as described by Schoenberg, p. 370), thus establishing a complementary relationship between various row forms that makes possible a true twelve-tone polyphony and even harmony. The other important device, derivation, consists of ordering the pitches of a tone row in such a way that, for example, its four constituent three-note groups (trichords) will sum up among themselves the classical relationships: inversion, retrograde, retrograde inversion. This kind of row can yield extremely refined and subtle symmetries that can lend to twelve-tone music the kind of structural unity one finds in tonal music. Babbitt also has pioneered methods of applying serial procedures to nonpitch components such as duration and intensity. In the extract given below, from a very influential article of 1955, Babbitt introduces his discussion of "total serialism" by sharply upbraiding his European colleagues for the superficiality of their approach to the problems at hand and their shortsighted attitude toward the classical heritage of serial music. It is not hard to guess that his chief target was Pierre Boulez and his notorious condemnation of Schoenberg.

The first explicit steps in the direction of a "totally organized" twelve-tone music were taken here [in the United States] some fifteen years ago, motivated by the desire for a completely autonomous conception of the twelve-tone system, and for works in which all components, in all dimensions, would be determined by the relations and operations of the system. The specific bases for achieving a total twelve-tone work were arrived at by the end of the war, and when, a short time later, there were reports of a group of young French, Italian and German composers who apparently shared like aims, their work was eagerly awaited. However, their music and technical writings eventually revealed so very different an attitude toward the means, and even so very different means, that the apparent agreement with regard to ends lost its entire significance. The most striking points of divergence can be summarized in terms of the following apparent attributes of the music and the theory associated with it. Mathematics—or, more correctly, arithmetic—is used, not as a means of characterizing or discovering general systematic, pre-compositional relationships, but as a stylistic device, resulting in the most literal sort of "programme music," whose course is determined by a numerical, rather than by a narrative or descriptive, "programme." The alleged "total organization" is achieved by applying dissimilar, essentially unrelated criteria of organization to each of the components, criteria often derived from outside the system, so that—for example—the rhythm is independent of and thus separable from the pitch structure; this is described and justified as a "polyphony" of components, though polyphony is customarily understood to involve, among many other things, a principle of organized simultaneity, while here the mere fact of simultaneity is termed "polyphony." The most crucial problems of twelve-tone music are resolved by being defined out of existence; harmonic structure in all dimensions is proclaimed to be irrelevant, unnecessary, and perhaps, undesirable in any event; so, a principle, or non-principle, of harmony by fortuity reigns. Finally, the music of the past—and virtually all of that of the present, as well—is repudiated for what it is not, rather than examined—if not celebrated—for what it is; admittedly, this is a convenient method for evading confrontation by a multitude of challenging possibles, including—perhaps—a few necessaries. This latter represents a particularly significant point of divergence from the development to be considered here, which has its specific origins in the investigation of the implications of the techniques of the "classics" of twelve-tone music. Indeed, it is a principle that underlies the bulk of Schoenberg's work (namely, combinatoriality), and another, superficially unrelated, principle occupying a similar position in the music of Webern (derivation), that have each been generalized and extended far beyond their immediate functions, finally to the point where, in their most generalized form, they are found to be profoundly interrelated, and in these interrelationships new properties and potentialities of the individual principles are revealed.

Quite naturally, it was the early "American" works of Schoenberg that were the most influential. The familiar Schoenbergian principle of constructing a set in which linear continuity can be effected between sets related by the operation of retrograde inversion, supplies a basis of progression beyond mere set succession. The structural significance of such sets suggests a generalization to the construction of sets in which aggregate structures [that is, those encompassing the total chromatic spectrum] obtain between any two forms of the set. [There follows a detailed discussion of selected passages from Schoenberg's String Quartet no. 4 (1936).]

In addition to the value of such sets in effecting an interrelation of the "vertical" and "horizontal" far beyond mere identity, in generating fixed units of harmonic progression within which the components can in turn generate associative and variable relationships, and in determining transpositional levels, there is a far more fundamental aspect, in that a hierarchy of relationships exists among these sets as determinants of [quasi-tonal] regions, an hierarchical domain closely analogous to the "circle of fifths," and defined similarly by considering the minimum number and the nature of the pitch alterations necessary to reproduce source sets at various transpositional levels.

[As to derivation,] consider the set, so characteristic of Webern, that is used in his *Concerto For Nine Instruments* [op. 24 (1935)]. It is presented in four three-note units: B-B♭-D, E♭-G-F♯, G♯-E-F, C-C♯-A; the first "prime" three-note unit is followed by its retrograde inversion, its retrograde, and its inversion. In this manner, the functional and structural implications of a compositional set can be determined by the derivational interrelationships of such units, in relation to the original set, and to each other, as defined hierarchically by the total domain of source sets. The extraordinary interrelationships that exist within and among the domains so defined emphasize the essential significance of the inherent structure of the set, and the unique compositional stage represented by the fact of the set, as the element with regard to which the generalized operations of the system achieve meaning, and from which the progressive levels of the composition, from detail to totality, can derive.

The twelve-tone structuralization of non-pitch components can be understood only in terms of a rigorously correct definition of the nature of the operations associated with the system. In characterizing the prime set, it is necessary to associate with each note the ordered number couple—order number [within the set], pitch number, measured from the first note as origin—required to define it completely with regard to the set. Then inversion—in the twelve-tone sense—is revealed to be complementation *modulo* 12 of the pitch number. (In other words, pitch number 4 becomes pitch number 8, etc.; naturally, interval numbers are also complemented.) Likewise, retrogression is complementation of the order number, and retrograde inversion is complementation of both order and pitch numbers. Any set of durations—whether the durations be defined in terms of attack, pitch, timbre, dynamics, or register—can be, like the pitch set, uniquely permuted by the operation of complementation, with the *modulus* most logically determined by a factor or multiple of the metric unit. Thus, the rhythmic component, for example, can be structured in precisely the same way, by the identical operations, as the pitch component; rhythmic inversion, retrogression, and retrograde inversion are uniquely defined, and combinatoriality, derivation and related properties are analogously applicable to the durational set. The result can be a structuring of all the durational and other non-pitch components, determined by the operations of the system and uniquely analogous to the specific structuring of the pitch components of the individual work, and thus, utterly nonseparable.

Even this extremely incomplete presentation should indicate the possibility of twelve-tone music, organized linearly, harmonically in the small and in the large, rhythmically—indeed, in all dimensions—in terms of essential assumptions of the system. Certainly, the resources indicated here do not constitute a guarantee of musical coherence, but they should guarantee the possibility of coherence. Above all, it is hoped that they serve to give at least some indication of the extraordinary breadth and depth of the twelve-tone system.

Milton Babbitt, "Some Aspects of Twelve-Tone Composition," *The Score*, no. 12 (June 1955), 53–61. By kind permission of the author.

154

Stravinsky the Serialist

One of the strongest boosts twelve-tone music received in the period following World War II was Igor Stravinsky's famous "conversion" to the technique pioneered by his late arch-rival Schoenberg. In the first of the three extracts given below, Stravinsky expresses to a French reporter a new sympathy for the works of the Viennese atonalists, though he continues to maintain a front of resistance. What he did not tell his interviewer was that even as he spoke, he was at work on his Septet, one of the first works in which he employed a tone row.

The twelve-tone system? Personally, I have enough to do with seven tones. But the twelve-tone composers are the only ones who have a discipline I respect. Whatever else it may be, twelve-tone music is certainly pure music. It is only that twelve-tone composers are prisoners of the number twelve. I feel freer with the number seven.

"Rencontre avec Stravinsky," *Preuves*, II, no. 16 (1952), 37. Trans. R. T.

> The other two passages are from the series of "conversation" books Stravinsky coauthored with the American conductor Robert Craft (1923–), his close associate, who was, perhaps more than anyone else, responsible for arousing his interest in the twelve-tone technique, and the works of Webern in particular. The discussion with Craft of the early serial works emphasizes the continuity of Stravinsky's serial period with his earlier work, while Stravinsky's description of his *Movements for Piano and Orchestra* shows him well embarked on the serial path and betrays a disarming hint of pride in his mastery, so late in life, of some of the more advanced ramifications of his new method.

R[OBERT] C[RAFT]: Do you think of the intervals in your series as tonal intervals; that is, do your intervals always exert tonal pull?

I[GOR] S[TRAVINSKY]: The intervals of my series are attracted by tonality; I compose vertically and that is, in one sense at least, to compose tonally.

R.C.: How has composing with a series affected your own harmonic thinking? Do you work in the same way—that is, hear relationships and then compose them?

I.S.: I hear certain possibilities and I choose. I can create my choice in serial composition just as I can in any tonal contrapuntal form. I hear harmonically, of course, and I compose in the same way I always have.

R.C.: Nevertheless, the Gigue from your *Septet* and the choral canons in the *Canticum Sacrum* are much more difficult to hear harmonically than any earlier music of yours. Hasn't composing with a series therefore affected your harmonic scope?

I.S.: It is certainly more difficult to hear harmonically the music you speak of than my earlier music; but any serial music intended to be heard vertically is more difficult to hear. The rules and restrictions of serial writing differ little from the rigidity of the great contrapuntal schools of old. At the same time they widen and enrich harmonic scope; one starts to hear more things and differently from before. The serial technique I use impels me to greater discipline than ever before.

Igor Stravinsky and Robert Craft, *Conversations with Igor Stravinsky* (New York: Doubleday, 1959), 22.

I have discovered new (to me) serial combinations in the *Movements for Piano and Orchestra* (and I have discovered in the process, too, that I am becoming not less but more of a serial composer; those younger colleagues who already regard "serial" as an indecent word, in their claim to have exhausted all that is meant by it and to have gone far beyond, are, I think, greatly in error), and the *Movements* are the most advanced music from the point of view of construction of anything I have composed. No theorist could determine the spelling of the note order in, for example, the flute solo near the beginning, or the derivation of the three Fs announcing the last movement simply by knowing the original order, no matter how unique the combinatorial properties of this particular series.

Now that I have mentioned my new work, I should add that its rhythmic language is also the most advanced I have so far employed; perhaps some listeners might even detect a hint of serialism in this too. Each section of the piece is confined to a certain range of instrumental timbre (another suggestion of serialism?), but the five movements are related more by tempo than by contrasts of such things as timbre, "mood," "character"; in a span of only twelve minutes, the contrast of an *andante* with an *allegro* would make little sense; construction must replace contrast. Perhaps the most significant development in the *Movements,* however, is the tendency toward anti-tonality—in spite of the long pedal point passages such as the clarinet trill at the end of the third movement, and the sustained string harmonics in the fourth movement. I am amazed at this myself, in view of the fact that in *Threni* [*Threni: Id est Lamentationes Jeremiae Prophetae,* a cantata for soloists, chorus and orchestra (1957–58), the work that immediately preceded *Movements*] simple triadic references occur in every bar.

Igor Stravinsky and Robert Craft, *Memories and Commentaries* (New York: Doubleday, 1960), 100–101.

155

Postwar Compositional "Issues"

Another penetrating survey by Roger Sessions—this one written at a time when he was beginning to enjoy the status of a "grand old man" of American music—states what Sessions saw as the "Problems and Issues Facing the Composer Today." Taking the legitimacy of twelve-tone music for granted as the basis of a new international "common practice"—something no one would have predicted before the war—he focuses on two central concerns: (1) the interest on the part of many composers in extending "serial" modes of organization to areas of music other than pitch, and (2) the prospects for electronic music.

The serial organization of tones must be, and for the most part is, today regarded as a settled fact—the composer is free to take it or leave it, or to adopt it with varying degrees of rigor, as he may choose. The results it can yield are open to all to see and judge as they see fit. More problematical are some attempts that have been made to extend serial organization to other aspects of music—notably to that of rhythmic values and that of dynamics. Any discussion of these matters must emphasize once more that it is only results that matter; that the human imagination works along channels that are frequently unexpected, and that a critical scrutiny of technical premises does not release one in the slightest degree from the responsibility of holding one's mind, ear, and heart open to whatever may reveal genuinely new vistas of musical expression and experience.

With this caution in mind one can easily observe that tones are, for the musical ear, fixed and readily identifiable points in musical space, and that the progress from one

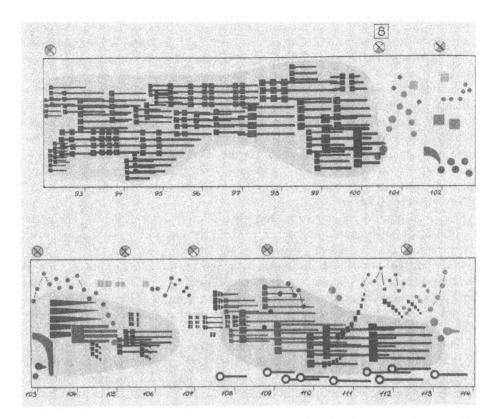

An Electronic "Score." This is a page from the "Hörpartitur," or "aural score," prepared by Rainer Wehinger for *Artikulationen,* an electronic composition by the Hungarian-born GyörgyLigeti (1923–2006), "realized" in 1958 at the Electronic Music Studio of the West German Radio in Cologne. The score shows how the various sounds in the piece relate to one another over time (given in seconds at the bottom of each system). The symbol directly above the score system (circle divided into four quadrants) shows which of the four tracks on the tape carries the sounds notated below. The score is printed in many colors. The various colors and shapes denote the "sound source" (sine wave, noise, filters, etc.), the relative frequency, and the relative intensity. Electronic "scores" like this one do not serve the traditional purpose of musical notation. They are not necessary for performance, but are useful solely for study and for the securing of copyright. Though they possess considerable interest, their relationship to the actual music can be questioned from a standpoint similar to that from which Sessions (see p. 456) questions the relationship of electronic music to human activity. © *B. Schott's Söhne, Mainz, 1970. All rights reserved. Used by permission of European American Music Distributors Corporation, sole U.S. agents for B. Schott's Söhne.*

tone to another has a clear point of departure and arrival. This is partly the result of the fact that within the octave there are only twelve tones, with which the musical ear has familiarized itself over the course of many centuries; and the additional fact that our musical culture has taught us to regard as equivalent tones that occupy the same position within the various octaves. A, for instance, is recognizable as A whether it be played on the open A string of the double-bass, of the cello, or of the violin—or, for that matter, in the high register of the flute or the piccolo. Time values, on the other hand, are by no means fixed; their range is to all intents and purposes infinite. This does not at all exclude the possibility of adopting an arbitrary series of time values for the purposes of any single composition, but it does raise very valid questions regarding the serialization of time values as a general principle. The serialization of dynamics, however, raises questions of a much more fundamental nature. Dynamic values are by their very essence relative, both in an objective and a subjective sense. They have quite different meanings for different media and under different conditions. How can we regard as equivalent, except on the most practical level of balance, a given nuance on, say, the oboe and the violin, or for that matter, the same nuance in different registers of the same instrument; or on the same note on the same instrument, sounded in a small room, a large concert hall, and the open air? What does the indication "*p*" actually mean, and how can we as listeners distinguish in clear terms a transition from "*mf*" to "*f*," or even from "*mp*" to "*ff*"?

The basic question of all is of course—as is often the case—"Why?" The principle of so-called "total organization" raises many questions and answers none, even in theory. First of all, what is being organized, and according to what criterion? Is it not rather a matter of organizing, not music itself, but various facets of music, each independently and on its own terms or at best according to a set of arbitrarily conceived and ultimately quite irrelevant rules of association? Was the music of Beethoven, or who you will, not tonally organized in a sense that is much more real, since it is an organization of musical ideas and not of artificially abstracted elements?

The subject of "total organization" leads naturally to the consideration of electronic media, since the latter make possible the exact control of all musical elements, and make possible in a sense also a partial answer to some of the questions I have raised. Since the potentialities of electronic media in the realm of sound are, at least to all intents and purposes, infinite, it is possible to measure all musical elements in terms of exact quantity, and in fact necessary to do so, since such measurement is the very nature of the instruments and the method by which they are used. A dynamic nuance thus not only can, but must, become a fixed quantity, as can and must, also, any tone in the whole range of pitch or color gradations. Every moment of music not only can but must be the result of the minutest calculation, and the composer for the first time has the whole world of sound at his disposal.

That electronic media will play a vital and possibly even decisive role in the future of music is not to be doubted. I must confess however to skepticism as to what the precise role will be. Two questions seem to me to be crucial. First of all, it is not sufficient to have the whole world at one's disposal—the very infinitude of possibilities cancels out possibilities, as it were, until limitations are discovered. No doubt the limitations are there, and if not there they are certainly in human beings. But the musical media we know thus far derive their whole character and their usefulness as musical media precisely from their limitations—stringed instruments derive their character and utility from not only the fact that they are stringed instruments, that the tone is produced by stroking strings, but from the fact that they are not wind or percussion instruments; and we have learned to use them with great subtlety of effect and power of expression because of that. The dilemma of electronic musical media is a little like that of the psychologist who is reputed once to have said to one of his friends, "Well, I have got my boy to the point where I can condition him for anything I want. What shall I condition him for?"

The other question has to do with the essential nature of music itself. Is music simply a matter of tones and rhythmic patterns, or in the final analysis the organization of time in terms of human gesture and movement? The final question regarding all music that is mechanically reproduced seems to be bound up with the fact that our active sense of time is dependent in large degree on our sense of movement, and that mechanical repetition mitigates and finally destroys this sense of movement in any given instance; it destroys also our sense of expression through movement, which plays so large and obvious a part in our musical experience. This is what lies behind the discussions of the element of "chance," which has so bothered the proponents of "total organization." But the element that "total organization" leaves out of account is not chance at all. It is the organic nature of movement as such, of the fresh and autonomous energy with which the performer invests each musical phrase, every time he sings or plays it, and which gradually disappears for our awareness if we listen so often to a mechanical reproduction of it that we become completely familiar with it, to the point of knowing always exactly what is coming next. It is more than the element of mere "surprise"; it is rather that if the expression of movement is to become effective, we require not only the evidence of movement from one point to the next, but a sense of the motivating energy behind it.

To raise these questions is not in any sense to reject the principle of electronic music as such. In the first place, composers are beginning to feel the need for new instruments. The existing ones, for all their technical perfection, are beginning at times to seem vaguely obsolete as far as some of the composers' musical ideas are concerned. The possibilities electronic music suggest are altogether likely to make this situation more acute.

In my own opinion, electronic media more than justify their existence if only by the new insight one can gain from them into the nature of sound, musical and otherwise, and above all by a vast quantity of fresh experience they can provide, on the purely acoustical level. They are still in a clearly very primitive stage and it is impossible to say what they may contribute in the future. But they raise the above questions and many others, and the questions will certainly become more acute as the media develop.

Roger Sessions, "Problems and Issues Facing the Composer Today," in Paul Henry Lang (ed.), *Problems of Modern Music* (New York: W. W. Norton & Company, Inc., 1962), 30–33. Originally published in *The Musical Quarterly*, XLVI (1960), 159–71. Reprinted by permission of the original publisher.

156

Music and the Cold War

The Congress for Cultural Freedom (*Kongress für kulturelle Freiheit, Congrès pour la Liberté de la Culture*) was the brainchild of Ernst Reuter (1889–1953), the mayor of West Berlin from 1948 to his death. The divided city, in which the Soviet blockade of its western sectors signaled the beginning of the forty-year geopolitical era known as the Cold War, symbolized the new ideological polarization. Antagonism between the Communist east and the liberal democracies that called themselves the "free world" to the west quickly replaced the struggle against fascism as a source of mutual suspicion and anxiety—potentially even scarier than the old, thanks to the possession by both sides of nuclear weapons that (in the jargon of the time) threatened Mutual Assured Destruction. The organization that Reuter envisioned was implemented, for the most part, by American diplomats as part of the propaganda battle between the USA and the USSR for the hearts and minds of Western Europeans. The first conspicuous event sponsored by the Congress was an arts festival in Paris, organized by Nicolas Nabokov (1903–78), a Russian-born composer (and cousin of the better-known novelist Vladimir Nabokov), in which American high culture was put on display alongside European. A close friend and associate of Stravinsky, Nabokov (whose family was of noble rank) had fled postrevolutionary Russia in 1919, lived in Berlin and Paris in the 'twenties, and had worked briefly for Diaghilev's Ballets Russes. He moved to America in 1934 and became an American citizen in 1939. During the war, he worked in military intelligence and, immediately after, as a cultural adviser to the American Military Government in Germany. His cosmopolitan background and his bitter antagonism toward the Bolsheviks made this colorful figure the perfect musical Cold Warrior. Although his two big festivals (1952 in Paris and 1954 in Rome) were ultimately judged wastefully expensive by the Congress and discontinued, they were benchmarks—along with the Darmstadt courses in contemporary music composition, sponsored by the American Military Government at German request—in establishing an American cultural presence in Europe. The first excerpt below is from a letter in which the newly appointed secretary-general of the Congress outlined his festival plans to Irving Brown, an American trade unionist on the Congress's executive committee who was in charge of funding. In 1967, it was revealed (to Nabokov's professed surprise and embarrassment) that the covert source of that funding was America's Central Intelligence Agency.

[The Festival will represent] the first close collaboration of top-ranking American artistic organizations in Europe with European ones and also of American artistic production on a *footing of complete equality* with European artistic production. Hence it is bound to have an extremely beneficial all-round effect upon the cultural life of the free world by showing the cultural solidarity and interdependence of European and American civilization. If successful, it will help to destroy the pernicious European myth (successfully cultivated by the Stalinists) of American cultural inferiority. It will be a challenge of the culture of the free world to the un-culture of the totalitarian world and a source of courage and *"redressement moral"* [restoration of morale], in particular for the French intellectuals, for it will again give a kind of sense and purposefulness to the dislocated and disintegrated cultural life of France and most of Europe.

The political cultural and moral meaning of the Festival and of its program should not be overt. It should be left to the public to make its inevitable logical conclusions. Practically all the works performed belong to the category branded as "formalist, decadent and corrupt" by the Stalinists and the Soviet aestheticians, including the works of Russian composers (Prokofiev, Shostakovich, Scriabin and Stravinsky).

Nicolas Nabokov to Irving Brown (1951), in Frances Stonor Saunders, *The Cultural Cold War* (New York: The New Press, 1999), 113.

Nabokov's introduction to the festival's program booklet begins with the standard modernist account of the history of twentieth-century music, explained however (and for the first time) not as the fruit of audacious enterprise (à la Diaghilev) or benevolent patronage, but as the fruit of political freedom. The Paris festival drove the point home—and despite his claim that the message would be implicit, Nabokov harped on it in the festival publicity—by scouring Western Europe for the score of a suite from

Shostakovich's banned opera, *The Lady Macbeth of the Mtsensk District,* which was performed alongside similarly banned works by the former Parisian Prokofiev, then a Soviet citizen. One of the other main events was the unheard-of pairing of Schoenberg's expressionist "monodrama" (or soliloquy-opera) *Erwartung,* sung by the American soprano Patricia Neway, and Stravinsky's neoclassical opera-oratorio *Œdipus Rex,* narrated by its librettist, Jean Cocteau. The easily read message was that the musical rivalries and antagonisms of the past were now to be put aside in the face of the common totalitarian enemy. The artists in attendance, whether Stravinsky himself (who found *Erwartung* detestable) or the "rowdies" (as Nabokov called them) of Boulez's generation (who hooted and whistled at *Œdipus Rex,* which they regarded as "official" art) seemed as yet a bit less ready than the politicians to grant the point.

L'Œuvre du vingtième siècle (The Works of the Twentieth Century) *is the title of the International Exposition of Art and Thought which is being held in Paris throughout the month of May, 1952 under the aegis of the Congress for Cultural Freedom.*

This association was created in June 1950 by intellectuals, artists and scientists of various countries, united in their desire to defend the freedom of culture against all attempts to subjugate it.

The honorary presidents of the Congress are a group of philosophers from six countries: Benedetto Croce (Italy), John Dewey (USA), Karl Jaspers (Germany), Salvador de Madariaga (Spain), Jacques Maritain (France), and Bertrand Russell (Great Britain); the Swiss philosopher Denis de Rougemont has assumed the presidency of the executive committee and Nicolas Nabokov is secretary-general.

As the Congress conceives it, "L'OEuvre du vingtième siècle" will be a presentation of the most significant masterpieces produced by our civilization over the past half-century in the realms of music, musical theater, painting and literature.

In offering this panorama of unprecedented scope, we hope to demonstrate that Western culture has lost nothing of its creative strength, its diversity and its vitality.

At first glance the evolution of music during the first half of this century shows composers falling prey to the spirit of experimentation and innovation. Since 1900 there has been, everywhere, a search for new ways of arriving at a style and communicating with an audience, whether by dint of new modes of expression and unfamiliar techniques, or by adapting old techniques, like those of medieval polyphony, to the requirements of a modern idiom. But even more striking in retrospect is the violent, appalling and contentious side of these endeavors. The founders of this century's music—that is, the composers of its first two decades—went at it with boundless energy. A veritable plethora of masterpieces arose from this effort, great works of music whose variety of form and meaning never ceases to amaze us. Nevertheless, a pair of common traits lurks beneath all this diversity: all the musicians of this period were reacting against the superficial excitement and extreme conventionality of the last century's declining Romanticism, and—the technical side of the same reaction— against the academic routines taught in nineteenth-century conservatories in matters of harmony and musical form.

There had already been several times in the history of Western music when stylistic conflicts arose—*diatonicism* on the one hand, *chromaticism* on the other—and composers took sides. But this time these old debates led to two opposing tendencies—

toward expression on the one hand and *construction* on the other—the former invoking the most radical chromatic technique, the twelve-tone method of Schoenberg and his school, and the other invoking that reaffirmation of diatonicism known, for want of a more exact term, as neoclassicism. In the twentieth century these techniques appear irreconcilable, and the polemics surrounding these principles have sometimes been heated and theatrical. And yet a goodly number of twentieth-century composers have adapted, each for his own purposes and according to his own personal style, both the discoveries of the atonalists and those of the partisans of diatonicism. Rather than impeding their creative efforts, the mixture of techniques and esthetics has stimulated them. And while the musical trends that have resulted from this effervescence are certainly various and variegated, their sum total is much less incoherent than might appear at first sight. The greatest creative personalities in twentieth-century music, say Schoenberg and Stravinsky, are no more violently opposed than were Palestrina and Gesualdo in the sixteenth.

For the rest, there has been a headlong thrust into the exploration of rhythm—and this, perhaps, is what gives the first quarter of the century its special countenance. At times unconsciously, at times with a naïve ostentation, composers have undertaken to fill their music with the restless, impulsive, dynamic and devouring rhythm of modern life and society. And even more, perhaps, than the emancipation of dissonance or the search for new forms, this nervous rhythm has given this century's music its authenticity.

But once again, as we have already said, what marks the art of this century is the spirit of adventure and experiment, of pursuit and discovery. Novelties of instrumental and orchestral sonority, novelties of syntax and composition—these are what practically every composition from 1900 to 1925 was aiming at. Each new score posed a problem and, if possible, a solution.

And finally—and in this it has been altogether faithful to the tradition that preceded it—the century has been marked by a hypersensitivity to the judgment of History. Never have musicians been more concerned to place themselves within the continuity of Western music. Whether opposed to traditional forms or tempted to evoke some bygone style their eyes are always directed toward the vast horizon of music history that is now available to us in our concerts and our record stores. It has been an undeniable pitfall for contemporary composers. But it has also been one of the sources of versatility, of maturity and of the heroically demanding taste that is ever inclined to compare the offerings of a contemporary master with all the masterpieces of the past.

But there have also been other factors. The world having, thanks to communications media, shrunk considerably, the reach of artists, and of the art market, has been proportionately enlarged. For the first time the mass public has contact, in enormous halls, with symphonic music whose undoubted "popularity" in the nineteenth century was nevertheless the business only of limited and socially privileged audiences: before the end of the last century there were no halls that seated more than 2500 persons. Not even Jules Verne, the science-fiction pioneer, ever imagined symphonies carried by the ether and heard every evening, every hour, over the whole world, by millions of families in their homes. For the first time, vast regions previously isolated have begun to participate in the life of the West, and in the music of the West. Thus, around 1910, Russian music came to be recognized in Europe as a major piece on the musical chessboard. Later, around 1920 or 1925, a remarkable school emerged from the two Americas, bearing an original synthesis of European traditions with American and exotic influences. Exchanges and mutual influences everywhere. The parochial spirit that more than once had infected musicians in the nineteenth century with national or even nationalist tendencies has given way, for better or worse, to universalism.

Naturally, the musical taste of enlarged popular audiences hardly coincides with that of composers. The public is conservative, and slow to open its mind to music more recent than that of the Romantics. Musicians are adventurous and impatient. To win twentieth-century audiences over to twentieth-century music is a task, perhaps the most urgent task of all, that now faces musicians, concert organizers and educators. Many have become conscious of this task. Thus Hindemith has tried, and not without success, to furnish amateur musicians with works at their level, thus taking account in his composing practice of the new conditions of musical life.

* * *

If the music of this century is what it is—extraordinarily lively in sum, and singularly rich in success and promise—it is due, alongside the talent or genius of musicians, to the spirit of freedom that has in various ways presided over their destinies. Freedom to experiment, freedom to express oneself, freedom to choose one's own mentors and make one's own decisions, to choose irony or naïveté, to be esoteric or familiar. During this coming Festival dedicated to the Works of the Twentieth Century and organized for the occasion by the Congress for Cultural Freedom, one will not hear any scores that do not owe their qualities, even their soul, to the fact that they are the music and the art of men who know the value of that freedom.

And those who live today know even better that value because they have seen, in their time, in various parts of the world, how powerful states have denied their citizens, among other material and spiritual freedoms, the freedom to be artists and musicians according to their own taste, their own conviction, their own sense of duty and their own imagination. One had seen music-loving kings and ministers in other times, whose influence could be for good or ill. But only the twentieth century has seen politicians setting themselves up as professors of harmony, composition and esthetics, casting great works into disrepute, covering great artists with insults whose wickedness is exceeded only by their absurdity, and imposing on music a "party line" of servile texts, the most hackneyed style, and "racial" guidelines or "progressive" esthetics patently designed to discourage the human race and the progress of art.

If a festival of modern music has any meaning or any virtue, it is to struggle against discouragement and despair. Neither totalitarian ideologues nor, at the other extreme, anyone's parochial interests, can in any way diminish masterpieces that speak for themselves—and for the civilization in which they were born.

Nicolas Nabokov, "Introduction à l'Œuvre du XXᵉ Siècle," *La Revue musicale*, no. 212 (April 1952), 5–8. Trans. R. T.

Perhaps a more significant and persuasive argument for the "Western" side of the Cold War debate is provided by the example of artists who have defected from the "Eastern" side. The most famous figure of this kind was the Hungarian composer György Ligeti (1923–2006), a refugee after his country's briefly successful anti-Communist revolt of 1956 was violently put down by Soviet tanks in the streets of Budapest. Having surfaced in West Germany and become a habitué of the American-sponsored Darmstadt summer courses, Ligeti immediately became a favorite of the avant-garde, and retained his position at the forefront of contemporary composition to the end of his

life. In the following selection, he recounts his own early career at the request of a
West German record company that had undertaken to issue a comprehensive selection of his works. The composition mentioned at the end, *Atmospheres* for large
orchestra without percussion, has become one of the most celebrated works of the
postwar period, thanks to its adoption (or exploitation as Ligeti, who received no
payment for it, probably thought) seven years after its completion by the director
Stanley Kubrick in the soundtrack of his now-classic movie, *2001: A Space Odyssey*.

It was in around 1950 that I realized that continuing to compose in a post-Bartókian
style, as I had been doing until then, was no longer the right path for me to follow. I was
twenty-seven years old and lived in Budapest, completely isolated from all the new
musical ideas, trends and techniques that had begun to appear in the West after the war.
It was at that time that I first began to imagine a static kind of music that rests within
itself, with no development and no clichéd rhythmic figures. These ideas were vague at
first, and at that time I had neither the courage nor the techniques of composition
necessary to transform them into works. Although the traditional concepts of form
seemed questionable to me, I still adhered to metrical rhythm. In 1951, I began to
experiment with very simple tonal and rhythmical structures and to construct a new
kind of music starting from zero, as it were. I did this using a Cartesian method, so to
speak: by deeming all the music that I knew and loved as not essential to my purposes,
even as no longer valid. I set myself assignments, such as: What can I do with a single
note? Or with its transpositions into different octaves? What can I do with an interval?
Or with two? Or with specific rhythmical relationships which can serve as the basic
elements of a rhythmic-intervallic structure? It was thus that several small pieces came
about, especially works for piano. In these questions and the solutions to them there
were certain traits which had something in common with the ideas of serialism. This
seems remarkable to me, because I proceeded from totally different routes, since I then
had not the slightest notion of the tendencies leading to serial music that were being
developed in Western Europe just at that time. I did not even know about Schoenberg's twelve-tone technique of composition, let alone Webern's procedures.

The decisive turning point in my development as a composer occurred in 1956.
From one day to the next it became possible to make contact with other countries;
sheet-music, records, information about new musical ideas and developments flooded
into Hungary. It is difficult to describe the tremendous speed with which this happened:
it was as though air were streaming into a vacuum that had suddenly been opened up.
After the Uprising I left Budapest shortly before the end of 1956; I arrived in Vienna and
at the beginning of 1957 I was brought to Cologne by Herbert Eimert where I lived as
the guest of Karlheinz Stockhausen for a while. Gottfried Michael Koenig introduced
me to the techniques of electronic music in the Studio of the West German Radio.

Becoming acquainted with serial music and with the other techniques that had
been developed by the avant-garde in the West during the 1950s did not mean that I
automatically adopted these techniques or even the style of serial music; it provided me,
rather, with the possibility of realizing those musical ideas that I had not yet been able
to transpose into music. The essential novelty for me was in fact the awareness that "it
can be done differently."

I soon came to realize that serial music frequently entails indifference to harmonies
and a leveling of intervallic characteristics, so instead of returning to composing with
specific intervals, I sought to take the more radical course: intervals and rhythms should
be completely dissolved, not for the sake of destruction per se, but in order to clear the

way for the composition of finely woven net-formations in which the structural function would be taken over by the texture of these formations. That is not to say that intervals and rhythmical structures do not exist in this kind of music, only that one cannot hear them. They do not determine the form, which is done by something rather more complex, namely by that which results from the intertwining of numerous intervallic and rhythmic parts. What happens musically does thus not manifest itself on the level of harmony and rhythm, but on the level of sonorous net-structures. In doing this, I advanced into a region of subtle sonorities forming an area between sound and noise; the sounds are veiled and blurred by the complex interweaving of the parts. The first orchestral composition in this new style was *Apparitions* (begun in 1956 and completed in 1958–59). In this work there are still traces of rhythmical figures, but fundamental to the character of the music are the changes in the finely meshed web of voices which hold those figures captive, as it were. The progress of the music is borne by the tone-color transformations. In the next orchestral work, *Atmospheres* (Donaueschingen, 1961), this way of composing was extended to the rhythms, so that a totally static music resulted from processes of changes in sonorities and textures.

György Ligeti, *Bericht zur eigenen Arbeit* (1967), trans. Sarah E. Soulsby, slightly adapted to American usage. Booklet accompanying Wergo WER 60.095 (Mainz: Wergo Schallplatten GmbH, 1984).

157

Music and the "New Left"

One of the editors of this book was handed the leaflet reproduced below outside New York's Judson Hall, a small auditorium then facing Carnegie Hall, the city's main classical music venue, on the evening of Tuesday, 8 September 1965, as he was making his way in to a concert of music by the German composer Karlheinz Stockhausen (1928–), a leading figure of the postwar avant-garde, to be performed by Stockhausen's regular ensemble of handpicked musicians under the composer's direction. Distributed by Fluxus, a loose association of New York artists in all media, and seemingly the work of its driving force and spokesman, the architect George Maciunas (1931–78), the leaflet gives aggressive artistic voice to a later Cold War development often referred to, then and since, as the New Left. A youth movement that was initially stimulated by the Cuban revolution in 1959 and by the civil rights struggle within the United States, it flourished, chiefly in Germany and the United States, under the impact of the Vietnam War. The New Left rejected the stark either/or choice of the earlier Cold War. Regarding both the United States and the Soviet Union as self-aggrandizing imperialist powers, New Leftists identified themselves with revolutionary movements in "third world" countries. All high art, emphatically including the avant-garde variety, was seen as complicit (in its elitism) with imperialism and social oppression. Student organizations associated with the New Left caused considerable, occasionally lethal, havoc in the late 1960s and early 1970s. Fluxus (which most regarded as an avant-garde movement in its own right, and which specialized in chaotic spontaneous enactments called happenings) was generally regarded less as a threatening political movement than as an amusing aesthetic sideshow (but then, neither was high art a particularly threatening arm of political reaction). Nevertheless, its tenets, as exemplified in the leaflet, did prefigure the multicultural attitudes of the very late twentieth century.

PICKET STOCKHAUSEN CONCERT!

"Jazz (Black music) is primitive ... barbaric ... beat and a few simple chords ... garbage ... (or words to that effect)" Stockhausen, Lecture, Harvard University, fall 1958

RADICAL INTELLECTUALS:

Of all the world's cultures, aristocratic European Art has developed the most elaborate doctrine of its supremacy to all plebeian and non-European, non-white cultures. It has developed the most elaborate body of "Laws of Music" ever known: Common-Practice Harmony, 12-Tone, and all the rest, not to mention Concert etiquette. And its contempt for musics which break those Laws is limitless. Alfred Einstein, the most famous European Musicologist, said of "jazz" that it is "the most abominable treason," "decadent," and so forth. Aristocratic European Art has had a monstrous success in forcing veneration of itself on all the world, especially in the imperialist period. Everywhere that Bach, Beethoven, Bruckner and Stockhausen are huckstered as "Music of the Masters," "Fine Music," "Music Which Will Ennoble You to Listen to It," white aristocratic European supremacy has triumphed. Its greatest success is in North America, whose rulers take the Art of West Europe's rulers as their own. There is a Brussels European Music Commission to which musicians come from all over the world; why is there no Competition, to which European Musicians come, of Arab Music? (Or Indian, or Classical Chinese, or Yoruba, or Bembey, or Tibetian [*sic*] percussion, or Inca, or hillbilly music?)

STOCKHAUSEN AND HIS KIND

Stockhausen is a characteristic European-North American ruling-class Artist. His magazine The Series [*Die Reihe*], has hardly condescended to mention plebeian or non-European music at all; but when it has, as on the first page of the fourth number, it leaves no category for it except "'light music' that can be summed up by adding a question-mark after 'music.'" Stockhausen's doings are supported by the West German Government, as well as the rich Americans J. Brimberg, J. Blinken and A. Everett. If there were a genuine equality of national cultures in the world today, if there were no discrimination against non-European cultures, Stockhausen couldn't possibly enjoy the status he does now. But Stockhausen's real importance, which separates him from the rich U. S. cretins Leonard Bernstein and Benny Goodman, is that he is a fountainhead of "ideas" to shore up the doctrine of white plutocratic European Art's supremacy, enunciated in his theoretical organ The Series and elsewhere.

BUT THERE IS ANOTHER KIND OF INTELLECTUAL

There are other intellectuals who are restless with the domination of white plutocratic European Art. Maybe they happen to like Bo Diddley or the Everly Brothers. At any rate, they are restless with the Art maintained by the imperialist governments. To them WE SAY: THE DOMINATION OF WHITE PLUTOCRATIC EUROPEAN ART HOLDS YOU TOO IN BONDAGE! You cannot be intellectually honest if you believe the doctrines of plutocratic European Art's supremacy, those "Laws of Art." They are arbitrary myths, maintained ultimately by the repressive violence that keeps oppressed peoples from power. Then, the domination of patrician Art—which is aristocrat-plutocrat in origin, as Opera House etiquette alone shows—condemns you to be surrounded by the stifling cultural mentality of social-climbing snobs. It binds you to the most parochial variety of the small merchant mentality, as promoted by <u>Reader's Digest</u>—"Music That Ennobles You to Listen to It." Even worse, though, the domination of imperialist white European plutocrat Art condemns you to live among white masses who have a sick, helpless fear of being contaminated by the "primitivism" of the colored peoples' cultures. Yes, and this sick cultural racism, not "primitive" musics, is the real barbarism. What these whites fear is actually a kind of vitality the cultures of these oppressed peoples have, which is undreamed of by their white masters. <u>You lose this vitality</u>. Thus, nobody who acquiesces to the domination of patrician European Art can be revolutionary culturally—no matter what else he may be.

> Quite the most spectacular defection from the avant-garde to the New Left was that of the English composer Cornelius Cardew (1936–81), who worked closely with Stockhausen as his assistant at Cologne and Darmstadt from 1958 to 1960, but who in the late 1960s became a disciple of Mao Zedong, the Chinese Communist leader, and repudiated his earlier career and—particularly—his early mentor in a series of strident lectures and essays collected in 1974 in a book called *Stockhausen Serves Imperialism*. The following is an excerpt from the title essay. The work to which it refers, *Refrain*, is a composition for keyboard and mallet instruments. Cardew had participated in its Berlin premiere on 2 October 1959. The term "repressive tolerance," through which Cardew seeks to posit a moral equivalence between the Nazi regime and the liberal-capitalist West German government had been coined by Herbert Marcuse (1898–1979), one of T. W. Adorno's most radical colleagues in the Frankfurt School of sociologists, and (despite his age) an icon of the New Left.

There has always been a mass of talent in the avantgarde and some of this talent is keen to leave the restricted world of the avantgarde and its preoccupations behind and take up a more definite role in the service of imperialism, a role with a larger following and bigger rewards. In 1959, the year he wrote *Refrain*, Stockhausen was ripe for this role. At that time he was a leading figure in the Darmstadt School which had been set up after the Second World War to propagate the music and ideas that the Nazis had banished. The Nazis branded the avantgarde "degenerate" and publicly disgraced it and suppressed it. In postwar Germany a subtler technique was used; instead of suppression, repressive tolerance. The European avantgarde found a nucleus in Darmstadt where its abstruse, pseudo-scientific tendencies were encouraged in ivory tower conditions. By 1959 it was ready to crack from its own internal contradictions and the leading figures were experiencing keenly the need for a broader audience. For this the music had to change. *Refrain* was probably the first manifestation of this change in Stockhausen's work. Since then his work has become quite clearly mystical in character. In a recent interview he says that a musician when he walks on stage "should give that fabulous impression of a man who is doing a sacred service" (note the showmanship underlying that remark). He sees his social function as bringing an "atmosphere of peaceful spiritual work to a society that is under so much strain from technical and commercial forces."

In *Refrain* we can see the beginnings of the tendencies that his present music exhibits alongside the remains of his Darmstadt work.

The score itself is a gimmick typical of Darmstadt thinking. The music is obliged quite mechanically to accommodate itself to a crude piece of mobile two-dimensional design. It is written on a large card with music staves that bow into partial circles centered on the middle of the card. Anchored to this middle point is a strip of transparent plastic with some notations on it. These notations are the recurring refrain that gives the piece its title.

The instrumentation is piano, vibraphone, celeste, each of the three players also using auxiliary instruments as well as vocal exclamations and tongue clicks. Visualizing the kind of musicians required for this, we see the beginnings of the specially trained band of players that are necessary for the presentation of his recent work.

The performance itself creates a situation of intense concentration and listening for the musicians. This listening activity of the musicians communicates itself to the audience and it is this intense concentration and contemplation of sounds for their own sake that reveals the beginnings of the mystical atmosphere that Stockhausen has cultivated more and more theatrically since then.

Some may criticize Stockhausen on the grounds that he presents mystical ideas in a debased and vulgar form. This is true, but it is not enough. To attack debasement and vulgarity in themselves is meaningless. We have to penetrate the nature of the ideas that are being debased and vulgarized and if they are reactionary, attack *them*. What is this mysticism that is being peddled in a thousand guises, lofty and debased, throughout the imperialist world? Throughout its history in India and the Far East, mysticism has been used as a tool for the suppression of the masses. Salesmen like Stockhausen would have you believe that slipping off into cosmic consciousness removes you from the reach of the painful contradictions that surround you in the real world. At bottom, the mystical idea is that the world is illusion, just an idea inside our heads. Then are the millions of oppressed and exploited people throughout the world just another aspect of that illusion in our minds? No, they aren't. The world is real, and so are the people, and they are struggling towards a momentous revolutionary change. Mysticism says "everything that lives is holy," so don't walk on the grass and above all don't harm a hair on the head of an imperialist. It omits to mention that the cells on our bodies are dying daily, that life cannot flourish without death, that holiness disintegrates and vanishes with no trace when it is profaned, and that imperialism has to die so that the people can live.

Cornelius Cardew, *Stockhausen Serves Imperialism, and Other Articles* (London: Latimer, 1974), 48–49.

The most prominent composer to be associated with the New Left was Hans Werner Henze (1926–), a well-established and prolific figure of Stockhausen's own generation, best known for his operas, who began his career alongside Boulez and Stockhausen at Darmstadt. The most notorious single musical event associated with the movement was the 1968 premiere of Henze's oratorio *Das Floss der "Medusa"* (*The Raft of the Frigate Medusa*), which was stopped by the police when the audience began to riot. Henze's memoir of the event, written a year afterward, disavows responsibility for the provocation that caused the disturbance, although most accounts still maintain that it was he who insisted on festooning the podium with the red flags that touched off the newsmaking disruptions. The gesture, as Henze notes regretfully, was futile as well as destructive; nevertheless, the essay ends with a prescient prediction of convergence between "high" and "low" musical genres that may have seemed equally utopian in 1969, but which by the end of the century had become quite normal.

I came to the Left just like anybody else, I imagine. People of my generation, after all, are bound to have a very clear recollection of fascism. To have seen that Hitlerism lived on after the fall of Hitler, that fascism had put on a different mask, has left many people, including myself, with a fascism-trauma. To have seen that fascism lived on in people's mentalities was an enormous shock, especially as one could do virtually nothing against it after 1945. If one did react, one was usually not understood; anti-fascism was *passé*. So all that was left to the majority of German artists and writers of my generation was to emigrate. Our impotence has lasted for a long time. During this period, from 1953 to the present, I have been in Italy, where I have worked with and learned from Italian intellectuals, every one of whom is left-wing.

Turning-points were the National Liberation Front war of liberation in Vietnam, and the liberation struggle of the blacks in the USA, which I have experienced personally and intensely, and still do so today. You ask me about the scandal over the premiere of *Das Floss der Medusa* [*The Raft of the Frigate Medusa,* a requiem for Ernesto Che Guevara] in Hamburg (9 December 1968). This has always been mis-interpreted by the press. Perhaps there is some point in setting the record straight, once and for all. At the start of the concert in the Hamburg Radio there was a demonstration with slogans against consumer culture; the audience was bombarded with thousands of leaflets. All this was organized by three different groups: the "Culture and Revolution" team of the Berlin SDS [*Sozialistischer Deutscher Studentenbund,* modeled after the American *Students for a Democratic Society,* with which it shared its initials], members of the Hamburg College of Music, and of the Hamburg SDS. Then there was the poster of Che Guevara which had been attached to the podium, and which the program director of the radio tore up out of hand. Thus the real protagonist was this enraged radio station boss who, although he knew that the work had been written in honor of Che, was unable to tolerate his picture hanging there.

Students had put the poster up. I had done nothing at all, and hadn't planned anything of the sort; all I wanted to do was to conduct. But that's how it turned out. Then other comrades put up a red flag instead of the Che poster. I was called upon by the Radio's legal adviser to have the flag removed, or else be responsible for the consequences. Thereupon I said I couldn't care less about the consequences, because I was not prepared to submit to such blackmail. The rest was as reported in the press— part of the choir refused to sing in the presence of the red flag (!) and walked off. While negotiations were still going on, heavily armed riot police came in and began to beat up and arrest students as well as Ernst Schnabel, the librettist of *Medusa* (once head of the Hamburg Radio), making the concert physically and morally impossible.

The ending of the work is structured in a way that leads directly from music into reality. Musicians and audiences can carry on from there and continue the evening singing, discussing, taking action. Of course this was a utopian and much too optimistic idea, and as such it will remain as a little monument of that terrible evening. The contradictions emerged more dramatically than ever before.

If a committed artist wishes to articulate his commitment—for instance if he is a composer who writes orchestral music—he has to rely on the modern symphony orchestra if he wants to use the resources of a large ensemble. He has to rely on record companies or radio stations, and to depend for everything on what the system has to offer. He undoubtedly finds himself in a dilemma.

One shouldn't try to fool oneself; the artist is dependent, no matter what, even if only on the dole. If one bears in mind that the revolutionary struggle in Europe is going to last a very long time—unless there are unforeseen and surprising events—I think that simply to hand everything over to the system and opt out borders on counter-revolu-tionary behavior, if it does not actually constitute it. Nothing is achieved by that; on the contrary, one should take advantage of every available opportunity for communication. This also connects with the "long march through the institutions" spoken of by Rudi

Dutschke [a West German radical student leader], and it has something to do with social responsibility. Here are positions that one simply must not give up. This seems to me to be a better strategy than the opposite alternative. Opting out has absolutely no effect on the system.

Practical work includes studying the possibilities for music to move towards street theater, so as to enrich it. But that also means composing quite simple songs. Paul Dessau [a German Communist composer of the older generation and an early mentor of Henze's] is a good example: three times a week he teaches music in a school; he writes pieces for the children and gets them to compose for themselves, which I consider particularly important.

In the course of the development of music I can even see, or rather sense, possibilities that complex orchestral or symphonic music will move in a direction where it will all of a sudden come upon pop music. It could come about one day that the difference will disappear between *musique savante* and the music that young people enjoy so much.

Music would then be something that belongs to all, that is not alien but a part of people's lives. People will no longer be alienated, but will be able to develop; they will be able to open themselves to all the beauties of life. That is one of the things that so moved me in Cuba, this lack of hang-ups about art, this unlimited curiosity about art, and the natural way in which art is approached.

One idea prevalent in the West is altogether wrong. There are those people who say that all previous music has been bourgeois music, and must therefore be done away with. It is not just that it seems odd that, under capitalism, some people want to do away with something that is humanistically essential—while others are trying to do away with capitalism by means of a humanistically essential revolution—but that wanting to do away with art is completely inhuman, unmarxist and monstrous.

Hans Werner Henze, "Musik ist nolens volens politisch" ("Music Cannot Help Being Political," 1969), in *Music and Politics: Collected Writings 1953–81,* trans. Peter Labanyi (Ithaca, N.Y.: Cornell University Press, 1982), 167–71.

158

The Master of "Organized Sound"

Edgar Varèse (1883–1965) was one of the great mavericks of twentieth-century music. Resolutely empirical and intuitive at a time when most composers sought the security of "systems," Varèse remained true to the spirit of untrammeled exploration voiced at the beginning of the century by Busoni, his teacher. He was equally contemptuous of neoclassicism and of twelve-tone techniques, seeking rather to build a new kind of athematic music based on bold juxtapositions of sonorous blocks. Attracted by innovations in technology, Varèse liked to give his pieces "scientific" titles (*Ionization, Hyperprism, Integrals*) and was one of the first to employ such early electronic instruments as the Theremin and the Ondes Martenot. Varèse was the only composer of his generation to master the techniques of postwar electronic music and in the last fifteen years of his life enjoyed his greatest prestige. The passages below all date from this late period; they have been excerpted from a compilation of his writings published shortly after his death.

Because for so many years I crusaded for new instruments with what may have seemed fanatical zeal, I have been accused of desiring nothing less than the destruction of all musical instruments and even of all performers. This is, to say the least, an exaggeration. Our new liberating medium—the electronic—is not meant to replace the old musical instruments which composers, including myself, will continue to use. Electronics is an additive, not a destructive factor in the art and science of music. It is because new instruments have been constantly added to the old ones that Western music has such a rich and varied patrimony.

Grateful as we must be for the new medium, we should not expect miracles from machines. The machine can give out only what we put into it. The musical principles remain the same whether a composer writes for orchestra or tape. Rhythm and Form are still his most important problems and the two elements in music most generally misunderstood.

Rhythm is too often confused with metrics. Cadence or the regular succession of beats and accents has little to do with the rhythm of a composition. Rhythm is the element in music that gives life to the work and holds it together. It is the element of stability, the generator of form. In my own works, for instance, rhythm derives from the simultaneous interplay of unrelated elements that intervene at calculated, but not regular time lapses. This corresponds more nearly to the definition of rhythm in physics and philosophy as "a succession of alternate and opposite or correlative states."

As for form, Busoni once wrote: "Is it not singular to demand of a composer originality in all things and to forbid it as regards form? No wonder that if he is original he is accused of formlessness."

The misunderstanding has come from thinking of form as a point of departure, a pattern to be followed, a mold to be filled. Form is a result—the result of a process. Each of my works discovers its own form. I could never have fitted them into any of the historical containers. If you want to fill a rigid box of a definite shape, you must have something to put into it that is the same shape and size or that is elastic or soft enough to be made to fit in. But if you try to force into it something of a different shape and harder substance, even if its volume and size are the same, it will break the box. My music cannot be made to fit into any of the traditional music boxes.

Conceiving musical form as a resultant—the result of a process, I was struck by what seemed to me an analogy between the formation of my compositions and the phenomenon of crystallization. Let me quote the crystallographic description given me by Nathaniel Arbiter, a professor of mineralogy at Columbia University:

> The crystal is characterized by both a definite external form and a definite internal structure. The internal structure is based on the unit of crystal which is the smallest grouping of the atoms that has the order and composition of the substance. The extension of the unit into space forms the whole crystal. But in spite of the relatively limited variety of internal structures, the external forms of crystals are limitless.

Then Mr. Arbiter added in his own words: "Crystal form itself is a *resultant* (the very word I have always used in reference to musical form) rather than a primary attribute. Crystal form is the consequence of the interaction of attractive and repulsive forces and the ordered packing of the atom."

This, I believe, suggests, better than any explanation I could give, the way my works are formed. There is an idea, the basis of an internal structure, expanded and split into different shapes or groups of sound constantly changing in shape, direction, and speed, attracted and repulsed by various forces. The form of the work is the consequence of this interaction. Possible musical forms are as limitless as the exterior forms of crystals.

I should like you to consider what I believe is the best definition of music, because it is all-inclusive: "the corporealization of the intelligence that is in sound," as proposed by Hoëne Wronsky [1778–1853]. If you think about it you will realize that, unlike most dictionary definitions which make use of such subjective terms as beauty, feelings, etc., it covers all music, Eastern or Western, past or present, including the music of our new electronic medium. Although this new music is being gradually accepted, there are still people who, while admitting that it is "interesting," say, "but is it music?" It is a question I am only too familiar with. Until quite recently I used to hear it so often in regard to my own works, that, as far back as the twenties, I decided to call my music "organized sound" and myself, not a musician, but "a worker in rhythms, frequencies, and intensities." Indeed, to stubbornly conditioned ears, anything new in music has always been called noise. But after all what is music but organized noises? And a composer, like all artists, is an organizer of disparate elements. Subjectively, *noise* is any sound one doesn't like.

Our new medium has brought to composers almost endless possibilities of expression, and opened up for them the whole mysterious world of sound. For instance, I have always felt the need of a kind of continuous flowing curve that instruments could not give me. That is why I used sirens in several of my works. Today such effects are easily obtainable by electronic means. In this connection it is curious to note that it is this lack of flow that seems to disturb Eastern musicians in our Western music. To their ears it does not glide, sounds jerky, composed of edges of intervals and holes and, as an Indian pupil of mine expressed it, "jumping like a bird from branch to branch." To them apparently our Western music seems to sound much as it sounds to us when a record is played backward. But playing a Hindu record of a melodic vocalization backward, I found that it had the same smooth flow as when played normally, scarcely altered at all.

The electronic medium is also adding an unbelievable variety of new timbres to our musical store, but most important of all, it has freed music from the tempered system, which has prevented music from keeping pace with the other arts and with science. Composers are now able, as never before, to satisfy the dictates of that inner ear of the imagination. They are also lucky so far in not being hampered by aesthetic codifications—at least not yet! But I am afraid it will not be long before some musical mortician begins embalming electronic music in rules.

We should also remember that no machine is a wizard, as we are beginning to think, and we must not expect our electronic devices to compose for us. Good music and bad music will be composed by electronic means, just as good and bad music have been composed for instruments. The computing machine is a marvelous invention and seems almost superhuman. But, in reality, it is as limited as the mind of the individual who feeds it material. Like the computer, the machines we use for making music can only give back what we put into them. But, considering the fact that our electronic devices were never meant for making music, but for the sole purpose of measuring and analyzing sound, it is remarkable that what has already been achieved is musically valid. They are still somewhat unwieldy and time-consuming and not entirely satisfactory as an art-medium. But this new art is still in its infancy, and I hope and firmly believe, now that composers and physicists are at last working together, and music is again linked with science, as it was in the Middle Ages, that new and more musically efficient devices will be invented.

I am not impressed by most of today's electronic music. It does not seem to make full use of the unique possibilities of the medium, especially in regard to those questions of space and projection that have always concerned me. I am fascinated by the fact that through electronic means one can generate a sound instantaneously. On an instrument played by a human being you have to impose a musical thought through notation, then, usually much later, the player has to prepare himself in various ways to produce what will—one hopes—emerge as that sound. This is all so indirect compared with electronics, where you generate something "live" that can appear or disappear instantly and unpredictably. Consequently, you aren't programming something musical, something to be done, but using it directly, which gives an entirely different dimension to musical space and projection. For instance, in the use of an oscillator, it is not a question of working against it or taming it, but using it directly, without, of course, letting it use you. The same pertains to mixing and filtering. To me, working with electronic music is composing with living sounds, paradoxical though that may appear.

The essential touchstone for me was Busoni's prophetic book, *Sketch for a New Aesthetic of Music* [see p. 358]. This predicts precisely what is happening today in music—that is, if you pass over the whole dodecaphonic development, which in my view represents a sort of hardening of the arteries. I find the whole twelve-tone approach so limiting, especially in its use of the tempered scale and its rigid pitch organization. I respect the twelve-tone discipline, and those who feel they need such discipline. But it seems much more fruitful to use the total sonic resources available to us. Although there are certain works of Schoenberg that I find magnificent—the *Five Orchestra Pieces* [see p. 363] especially—his orchestration often seems quite thick and fat. Compare this to the transparency and lyricism of Webern!

I respect and admire Milton Babbitt [see p. 450], but he certainly represents a completely different view of electronic music from mine. It seems to me that he wants to exercise maximum control over certain materials, as if he were above them. But I want to be *in* the material, part of the acoustical vibration, so to speak. Babbitt composes his material first and then gives it to the synthesizer, while I want to generate something directly by electronic means. In other words, I think of musical space as open rather than bounded, which is why I speak about projection in the sense that I want simply to project a sound, a musical thought, to initiate it, and then to let it take its own course. I do not want an *a priori* control of all its aspects.

Excerpted from Edgar Varèse, "The Liberation of Sound," and Gunther Schuller, "Conversation with Varèse," in Edward T. Cone and Benjamin Boretz (eds.), *Perspectives on American Composers* (New York: W. W. Norton & Company, Inc., 1971), 29–33, 38–39. Reprinted by permission of the editors of *Perspectives of New Music*.

159

The Music of Chance

Seemingly at the opposite pole from the "total organization" practiced by postwar twelve-tone composers stands the work of John Cage (1912–92). Deeply influenced by Asian religious philosophy, and intrigued by notions of "indeterminacy," which were assuming increasing prominence in contemporary science, Cage—along with a handful of other composers whom he names below—attempted to create a music totally independent of the creator's will. To do this he resorted to chance operations (sometimes whimsical, as in his famous *Imaginary Landscape* for twelve radios), which seemed to challenge the most basic and time-honored assumptions of Western musicians. It was the interest shown Cage in the 1950s by the younger generation of "total serialist" composers like Boulez and Stockhausen, who invited him to lecture at their summer school in Darmstadt, that led to Cage's work being taken seriously by a significant number of his contemporaries. In the extract given below, Cage muses engagingly and candidly about his work and offers an apologia for what has become known as "aleatoric" music (from *alea*, Latin for dice); that is, the music of "unmediated chance." He traces the lineage of his tendency to the Dadaist movement in European art of the post-World-War-I period, but characterizes it nonetheless as a uniquely American manifestation (Henry Cowell is acknowledged as a spiritual forefather) and confidently predicts its decisive impact on European music.

In an article called "New and Electronic Music," Christian Wolff [b. 1934, a pupil and colleague of Cage's] says:

> What is, or seems to be, new in this music? … One finds a concern for a kind of objectivity, almost anonymity—sound come into its own. The "music" is a resultant existing simply in the sounds we hear, given no impulse by expressions of self or personality. It is indifferent in motive, originating in no psychology nor in dramatic intentions, nor in literary or pictorial purposes. For at least some of these composers, then, the final intention is to be free of artistry and taste. But this need not make their work "abstract," for nothing, in the end, is denied. It is simply that personal expression, drama, psychology, and the like are not part of the composer's initial calculation: they are at best gratuitous.
>
> The procedure of composing tends to be radical, going directly to the sounds and their characteristics, to the way in which they are produced and how they are notated.

"Sound come into its own." What does that mean? For one thing: it means that noises are as useful to new music as so-called musical tones, for the simple reason that they are sounds. This decision alters the view of history, so that one is no longer concerned with tonality or atonality, Schoenberg or Stravinsky (the twelve tones or the twelve expressed as seven plus five), nor with consonance and dissonance, but rather with Edgar Varèse who fathered forth noise into twentieth-century music. But it is clear that ways must be discovered that allow noises and tones to be just noises and tones, not exponents subservient to Varèse's imagination.

What is the nature of an experimental action? It is simply an action the outcome of which is not foreseen. It is therefore very useful if one has decided that sounds are to come into their own, rather than being exploited to express sentiments or ideas of order. Among those actions the outcomes of which are not foreseen, actions resulting from chance operations are useful. However, more essential than composing by means of chance operations, it seems to me now, is composing in such a way that what one does is indeterminate of its performance. In such a case one can just work directly, for nothing one does gives rise to anything that is preconceived. This necessitates, of course, a rather great change in habits of notation. I take a sheet of paper and place points on it. Next I make parallel lines on a transparency, say five parallel lines. I establish five categories of sound for the five lines, but I do not say which line is which category. The transparency may be placed on the sheet with points in any position and readings of the points may be taken with regard to all the characteristics one wishes to distinguish. Another transparency may be used for further measurements, even altering the succession of sounds in time. In this situation no chance operations are necessary (for instance, no tossing of coins) for nothing is foreseen, though everything may be later minutely measured or simply taken as a vague suggestion.

Implicit here, it seems to me, are principles familiar from modern painting and architecture: collage and space. What makes this action like Dada are the underlying philosophical views and the collagelike actions. But what makes this action unlike Dada is the space in it. For it is the space and emptiness that is finally urgently necessary at this point in history (not the sounds that happen in it—or their relationships). When I said recently in Darmstadt that one could write music by observing the imperfections in the paper upon which one was writing, a student who did not understand because he was full of musical ideas asked, "Would one piece of paper be better than another: one for instance that had more imperfections?" He was attached to sounds and because of his attachment could not let sounds be just sounds. He needed to attach himself to the emptiness, to the silence. Then things—sounds, that is—would come into being of themselves. Why is this so necessary that sounds should be just sounds? There are many ways of saying why. One is this: In order that each sound may become the Buddha. If that is too Oriental an expression, take the Christian Gnostic statement: "Split the stick and there is Jesus."

We know that sounds and noises are not just frequencies (pitches): that is why so much of European musical studies and even so much of modern music is no longer urgently necessary. It is pleasant if you happen to hear Beethoven or Chopin or whatever, but it isn't urgent to do so any more. Nor is harmony or counterpoint or counting in meters of two, three, or four or any other number.

And in connection with musical continuity, [Henry] Cowell remarked at the New School before a concert of works by Christian Wolff, Earle Brown [1926–2002], Morton Feldman [1926–87] and myself, that here were four composers who were getting rid of glue. That is: Where people had felt the necessity to stick sounds together to make a continuity, we four felt the opposite necessity to get rid of the glue so that sounds would be themselves.

Christian Wolff was the first to do this. He wrote some pieces vertically on the page but recommended their being played horizontally left to right, as is conventional. Later he discovered other geometrical means for freeing his music of intentional continuity. Morton Feldman divided pitches into three areas, high, middle, and low, and established a time unit. Writing on graph paper, he simply inscribed numbers of tones to be played at any time within specified periods of time.

There are people who say, "If music's that easy to write, I could do it." Of course they could, but they don't. I find Feldman's own statement more affirmative. We were driving back from some place in New England where a concert had been given. He is a large man and falls asleep easily. Out of a sound sleep, he awoke to say, "Now that things are so simple, there's so much to do." And then he went back to sleep.

Giving up control so that sounds can be sounds (they are not men: they are sounds) means for instance: the conductor of an orchestra is no longer a policeman. Simply an indicator of time—not in beats—like a chronometer. He has his own part. Actually he is not necessary if all the players have some other way of knowing what time it is and how that time is changing.

Actually America has an intellectual climate suitable for radical experimentation. We are, as Gertrude Stein said, the oldest country of the twentieth century. And I like to add: in our air way of knowing nowness. Buckminster Fuller, the dymaxion architect, in his three-hour lecture on the history of civilization, explains that men leaving Asia to go to Europe went against the wind and developed machines, ideas, and occidental philosophies in accord with a struggle against nature; that, on the other hand, men leaving Asia to go to America went with the wind, put up a sail, and developed ideas and Oriental philosophies in accord with the acceptance of nature. These two tendencies met in America, producing a movement into the air, not bound to the past, traditions, or whatever. Once in Amsterdam, a Dutch musician said to me, "It must be very difficult for you in America to write music, for you are so far away from the centers of tradition." I had to say, "It must be very difficult for you in Europe to write music, for you are so close to the centers of tradition."

The vitality that characterizes the current European musical scene follows from the activities of Boulez, Stockhausen, [Luigi] Nono [1924–90], [Bruno] Maderna [1920–73], [Henri] Pousseur [1929–], [Luciano] Berio [1925–2003], etc. There is in all of this activity an element of tradition, continuity with the past, which is expressed in each work as an interest in continuity whether in terms of discourse or organization. By critics this activity is termed post-Webernian. However, this term apparently means only music written *after* that of Webern, not music written *because of* that of Webern: there is no sign of *klangfarbenmelodie* ["timbre melody"], no concern for discontinuity—rather a surprising acceptance of even the most banal of continuity devices: ascending or descending linear passages, crescendi and diminuendi, passages from tape to orchestra that are made imperceptible. The skills that are required to bring such events about are taught in the academies. However, this scene will change. The silences of American experimental music and even its technical involvements with chance operations are being introduced into new European music. It will not be easy, however, for Europe to give up being Europe. It will, nevertheless, and must: for the world is one world now.

160

New Approaches to the Organization of Time

The innovations in musical rhythm and continuity achieved by Elliott Carter (1908–) have made him one of the more interesting and significant composers to have come into prominence since the end of the Second World War. Adherent of none of the recent tendencies that have dominated the musical world, Carter claims to have addressed more fundamental issues than they have faced. Below, he describes his work in light of its antecedents and in terms of its objectives.

Any technical or aesthetic consideration of music really must *start* with the matter of time. The basic problem has always been that analysts of music tend to treat its elements as static rather than as what they are—that is, *transitive* steps from one formation in time to another. All the materials of music have to be considered in relation to their projection in time, and by time, of course, I mean not visually measured "clock-time," but the medium through which (or way in which) we perceive, understand, and experience events. Music deals with this experiential kind of time, and its vocabulary must be organized by a musical syntax that takes direct account of, and thus can play on, the listener's "time-sense" (which in my opinion is a more illuminating way of referring to the "psychology of musical hearing").

This began to seem important to me around 1944, when I suddenly realized that, at least in my own education, people had always been consciously concerned only with this or that peculiar local rhythmic combination or sound-texture or novel harmony and had forgotten that the really interesting thing about music is the time of it—the way it all goes along. Moreover, it struck me that, despite the newness and variety of the post-tonal musical vocabulary, most modern pieces generally "went along" in an all-too-uniform way on their higher architectonic levels. That is, it seemed to me that, while we had heard every imaginable kind of harmonic and timbral combination, and while there had been a degree of rhythmic innovation on the *local* level in the music of Stravinsky, Bartók, Varèse, and Ives particularly, nonetheless the way all this went together at the next higher and succeeding higher rhythmic levels remained in the orbit of what had begun to seem to me the rather limited rhythmic routine of previous Western music. This fact began to bother me enough so that I tried to think in larger-scale time-continuities of a kind that would be still convincing and yet at the same time *new* in a way commensurate with, and appropriate to, the richness of the modern musical vocabulary. This aim led me to question all the familiar methods of musical presentation and continuation—the whole so-called musical logic based on the statement of themes and their development. In considering constant change-process-evolution as music's prime factor, I found myself in direct opposition to the static repetitiveness of much early twentieth-century music, the squared-off articulation of the neo-classics, and indeed much of what is written today in which "first you do this for a while, then you do that." I wanted to mix up the "this" and the "that" and make them interact in other ways than by linear succession. Too, I questioned the inner shape of the "this" and the "that"—of local musical ideas—as well as their degree of linking and non-linking. Musical discourse, it became obvious to me, required as thorough a rethinking as harmony had been subjected to at the beginning of the century.

Now concretely, in the course of thinking about all of this, I once again—after many years' hiatus—took up interest in Indian *talas,* the Arabic *dureb,* the "tempi" of Balinese *gamelans* (especially the accelerating *gangsar* and *rangkep*), and studied newer recordings of African music, that of the Watusi people in particular. At the same time the music of the *quattrocento,* of Scriabin, and Ives, and the "hypothetical" techniques described in Cowell's *New Musical Resources* [see p. 408] also furnished me with many ideas. The result in my own music was, first of all, the way of evolving rhythms and continuities now called "metric modulation," which I worked out during the composition of my Cello Sonata of 1948.* Now while, as I say, my thinking about musical time was stimulated by a consideration of, among other things, different kinds of rhythmic devices found in non-Western music such as I have mentioned, I feel it is important to point out that these devices interested me as suggestions of many syntactical possibilities that would participate in a very rich and varied large-scale rhythmic continuity such as is *never* found in non-Western music, but *is* suggested by some aspects of Western classical music, starting with Haydn especially. This aim of mine is something very different from that of many European composers who have been influenced by non-Western music and who have tended to be interested in exotic rhythmic devices as "things in themselves"—as local ideas more or less immediately transposable into a (usually) extremely conventional and uninteresting overall rhythmic framework derived from the simplest aspects of older Western music and only slightly more varied than that of the exotic music from which the local ideas have been borrowed. As far as I am concerned, on the contrary, what contemporary music needs is not just raw materials of every kind but a way of relating these—of having them evolve during the course of a work in a sharply meaningful way; that is, what is needed is never just a string of "interesting passages," but works whose central interest is constituted by the way everything that happens in them happens *as* and *when* it does in relation to everything else.

I feel very strongly about this, just because ever since 1944 I have realized that ultimately the matter of musical time is vastly more important than the particulars or the novelty of the musical vocabulary, and that the morphological elements of any music owe their musical effect almost entirely to their specific "placing" in the musical time-continuity. And as I see it, much of the confusion that has arisen in recent discussion of this matter of musical time and, still more, in connection with the many and various mistaken compositional attempts to deal effectively with time in an actual work, has resulted from a refusal on the part of many composers to distinguish between, on the one hand, the given and inescapable structures of experiential time in accordance with which alone, the listener hears and grasps a piece of music (if he hears and grasps it at all); and, on the other hand, certain widespread secondary theorizings about time, of a kind that deny the irreversibility and even the very existence of time. It is certainly a question whether music, as the time-structure it is, can be made to present concretely such theorizings about time and still remain music, any more than a verbal language, say by the introduction of "blanks" or resorting to retrograde word-order, can convey a concrete idea of "non-temporal existence" or an experience (!) of "time going back-wards." All verbal expressions and accounts of anything whatever, including time, require one letter and then one word after another for their presentation, and depend for their meaning on the specific ordering of the words, no matter how unconventional

---

*There is nothing new about metric modulation but the name. To limit brief mention of its derivations to notated Western music: it is implicit in the rhythmic procedures of late fourteenth-century French music, as it is in music of the fifteenth and sixteenth centuries that uses hemiola and other ways of alternating meters, especially duple and triple. From then on, since early sets of variations like those of Byrd and Bull started a tradition of establishing tempo relationships between movements, metric modulation began to relate move-ments of one piece together, as can be seen in many works of Beethoven, not only in the variations of op. 111, but in many places where *doppio movimento* and other terms are used to indicate tempo relationships. In fact, at that very time, the metronome was invented, which establishes relationships between all tempi. In our time, Stravinsky, following Satie, perhaps, wrote a few works around 1920 whose movements were closely linked by a very narrow range of tempo relationships, and much later Webern did the same [author's note].

this ordering may be, just as music requires one sound after another in a determinate order for its presentation and for its particular effect on the listener, if any.

It seems to me that many of the works of the Darmstadt school of composers have suffered greatly from the attempt to apply certain mistaken "philosophic conceptions" of time to music itself, though it is clear that the attractiveness of these conceptions about, say, the "interchangeability of musical moments" has its roots in the kind of visually- and spatially-derived mechanistic thinking that originally produced total serialism and was unconcerned from the outset with the problem of time-continuity and of producing feelings of tension and release and therefore of musical motion in the listener, but dealt rather with unusualness of aural effect, thus reducing music to mere physical sound.

Allen Edwards, *Flawed Words and Stubborn Sounds: A Conversation with Elliott Carter* (New York: W. W. Norton & Company, Inc., 1971), 90–94. Reprinted by permission of W. W. Norton & Company, Inc. Copyright © 1971 by W. W. Norton & Company, Inc.

161

Composer and Society

It is obvious that the music of Varèse, Cage, and Carter—the subjects of the last three readings—derives its justification (like much twentieth-century music) not from the number of listeners it pleases, but from its contribution to the greatly accelerated technical and stylistic development that has characterized modern art in all media. The fact that the development of art resources has outpaced the growth of art audiences is sometimes hailed as evidence of creative vitality (indeed, even as the very definition of art as distinct from entertainment or "kitsch"), and sometimes deplored as evidence of misplaced values. That has always been the debate surrounding modernism. But the rise of totalitarianism (which demanded social relevance) in the first half of the century, and the Cold War (which starkly pitted individual liberty against collective interests) in the second half, has exacerbated and politically polarized the debate. One of the strongest voices on behalf of social responsibility—the more credible for its being uncoerced by political authority—was that of Benjamin Britten (1913–76), a very successful British composer, especially of opera, who consciously decided not to seek refuge in an academic career but rather to put his art at the service of his society. Britten composed a great deal of music for public ceremonies, as well as the kind Paul Hindemith (see p. 412) first upheld and then (responding to Cold War pressures) rejected as *Gebrauchsmusik,* music for more private social use. Britten's social commitment entailed another decision—the voluntary resolve to place limits, abhorrent to modernists, on his own stylistic peregrinations. The reading that follows is an abridgment of Britten's acceptance speech on receiving a prestigious and munificent award from the Aspen Institute for Humanistic Studies, a liberal public policy organization whose purpose, in the words of its founder, Walter P. Paepcke, was to give business executives "the opportunity to understand their role in society and to develop goals and convictions for their lives"—in other words, to give capitalists a social conscience. Although the citation accompanying the award was worded in general and fairly platitudinous terms—"To Benjamin Britten, who, as a brilliant composer, performer, and interpreter through music of human feelings, moods, and thoughts, has truly inspired man to understand, clarify and appreciate more fully his own nature, purpose and destiny"—the timing of the prize makes it apparent that it was granted in appreciation for Britten's *War Requiem* (1964), a setting of the Latin Requiem Mass interspersed with antiwar verses by the English poet Wilfred Owen, who died on the battlefield during World War I. The work was composed for the rededication of Coventry Cathedral, which had been bombed by the Germans during World War II. By specifying that Russian and German vocal soloists participate in the premiere performance, along with the British tenor Peter Pears, the composer's long-standing life companion, Britten (a pacifist and conscientious objector) added to the commemorative intent that of reconciling of former—and potential—enemies. (The designated Russian soloist, the soprano Galina Vishnevskaya, was denied permission by the Soviet government to attend the première; she first performed her part in a recording.)

I certainly write music for human beings—directly and deliberately. I consider their voices, the range, the power, the subtlety, and the color potentialities of them. I consider the instruments they play—their most expressive and suitable individual sonorities. I also take note of the human circumstances of music, of its environment and conventions; for instance, I try to write dramatically effective music for the theatre—I certainly don't think opera is better for not being effective on the stage (some people think that effectiveness *must* be superficial). And then the best music to listen to in a great Gothic church is the polyphony which was written for it, and was calculated for its resonance: this was my approach in the *War Requiem*—I calculated it for a big, reverberant acoustic and that is where it sounds best. I believe, you see, in *occasional* music.

You may ask perhaps: how far can a composer go in thus considering the demands of people, of humanity? At many times in history the artist has made a conscious effort to speak with the voice of the people. Beethoven certainly tried, in works as different as the *Battle of Vittoria* [also known as *Wellington's Victory*] and the Ninth Symphony, to utter the sentiments of a whole community. From the beginning of Christianity there have been musicians who have wanted and tried to be the servants of the church, and to express the devotion and convictions of Christians, as such. Recently, we have had the example of Shostakovich, who set out in his "Leningrad" Symphony to present a monument to his fellow citizens, an explicit expression for them of their own endurance and heroism. At a very different level, one finds composers such as Johann Strauss and George Gershwin aiming at providing people—the people—with the best dance music and songs which they were capable of making. And I can find nothing wrong with the objectives—declared or implicit—of these men; nothing wrong with offering to my fellow-men music which may inspire them or comfort them, which may touch them or entertain them, even educate them—directly and with intention. On the contrary, it is the composer's duty, as a member of society, to speak to or for his fellow human beings.

When I am asked to compose a work for an occasion, great or small, I want to know in some detail the conditions of the place where it will be performed, the size and acoustics, what instruments or singers will be available and suitable, the kind of people who will hear it, and what language they will understand—and even sometimes the age of the listeners and performers. For it is futile to offer children music by which they are bored, or which makes them feel inadequate or frustrated, which may set them against music forever; and it is insulting to address anyone in a language which they do not understand.

During the act of composition one is continually referring back to the conditions of performance—as I have said, the acoustics and the forces available, the techniques of the instruments and the voices—such questions occupy one's attention continuously, and certainly affect the stuff of the music, and in my experience are not only a restriction, but a challenge, an inspiration. Music does not exist in a vacuum, it does not exist until it is performed, and performance imposes conditions. It is the easiest thing in the world to write a piece virtually or totally impossible to perform—but oddly enough that is not what I prefer to do; I prefer to study the conditions of performance and shape my music to them.

There are many dangers which hedge round the unfortunate composer: pressure groups which demand true proletarian music, snobs who demand the latest *avant-garde* tricks, critics who are already trying to document today for tomorrow, to be the first to find the correct pigeon-hole definition. These people are dangerous—not because they are necessarily of any importance in themselves, but because they may make the composer, above all the young composer, self-conscious, and instead of writing his own music, music which springs naturally from his gift and personality, he may be frightened into writing pretentious nonsense or deliberate obscurity. Finding one's place in society as a composer is not a straightforward job. It is not helped by the attitude towards the composer in some societies. But if we in England have to face a considerable indifference, in other countries conditions can have other, equally awkward effects. In totalitarian regimes, we know that great official pressure is used to bring the artist into line and make him conform to the State's ideology. In the richer capitalist countries, money and snobbishness combine to demand the latest, newest manifestations, which I am told go by the name in this country of "Foundation Music."

The *ideal* conditions for an artist or musician will never be found outside the *ideal* society, and when shall we see that? But I think I can tell you some of the things which any artist demands from any society. He demands that his art shall be accepted as an essential part of human activity, and human expression; and that he shall be accepted as a genuine practitioner of that art and consequently of value to the community; reasonably, he demands from society a secure living and a pension when he has worked long enough; this is a basis for society to offer a musician, a modest basis. In actual fact there are very few musicians in my country who will get a pension after forty years' work in an orchestra or in an opera house. This must be changed; we must at least be treated as civil servants. Once we have a material status, we can accept the responsibility of answering society's demands from us. And society should and will demand from us the utmost of our skill and gift in the full range of music-making. (Here we come back to "occasional" music.) There should be special music made and played for all sorts of occasions: football matches, receptions, elections (why not?) and even presentations of awards! I would have been delighted to have been greeted with a special piece composed for today! It might have turned out to be another piece as good as the cantata Bach wrote for the Municipal Election at Mühlhausen, or the Galliard that John Dowland wrote as a compliment to the Earl of Essex! Some of the greatest pieces of music in our possession were written for special occasions, grave or gay.

The wording of your Institute's Constitution implies an effort to present the Arts as a counter-balance to Science in today's life. And though I am sure you do not imagine that there is not a lot of science, knowledge and skill in the art of making music (in the calculation of sound qualities and colors, the knowledge of the technique of instruments and voices, the balance of forms, the creation of moods, and in the development of ideas), I would like to think you are suggesting that what is important in the Arts is *not* the scientific part, the analyzable part of music, but the something which emerges from it but transcends it, which cannot be analyzed because it is not *in* it, but *of* it. It is the quality which cannot be acquired by simply the exercise of a technique or a system: it is something to do with personality, with gift, with spirit. I quite simply call it—magic: a quality which would appear to be by no means unacknowledged by scientists, and which I value more than any other part of music.

This magic comes only with the sounding of the music, with the turning of the written note into sound. The experience will be that much more intense and rewarding if the circumstances correspond to what the composer intended: if the *St. Matthew Passion* is performed on Good Friday in a church, to a congregation of Christians; if the song cycle *Winterreise* [Winter Journey] by Schubert is performed in a room, or in a small hall of truly intimate character to a circle of friends; if Mozart's opera *Don Giovanni* is played to an audience which understands the text and appreciates the musical allusions. The further one departs from these circumstances, the less true and more diluted is the experience likely to be.

One must face the fact that the vast majority of musical performances take place as far away from the original as it is possible to imagine: I do not mean simply Verdi's *Falstaff* being given in Tokyo, or the Mozart Requiem in Madras. I mean of course that such works *can* be audible in any corner of the globe, at any moment of the day or night, through a loudspeaker, without question of suitability or comprehensibility. Anyone, anywhere, at any time, can listen to Bach's B Minor Mass upon one condition only—that they possess a machine. No qualification is required of any sort—faith, virtue, education, experience, age. Music is now free for all. If I say the loudspeaker is the principal enemy of music, I don't mean that I am not grateful to it as a means of education or study, or as an evoker of memories. But it is not part of true musical *experience*. Regarded as such it is simply a substitute, and dangerous because deluding. Music demands more from a listener than simply the possession of a tape-machine or a transistor radio. It demands some preparation, some effort, a journey to a special place, saving up for a ticket, some homework on the program perhaps, some clarification of the ears and sharpening of the instincts. It demands as much effort on the listener's part as the other two corners of the triangle, this holy triangle of composer, performer and listener.

People have already asked me what I am going to do with your money; I have even been told in the post and in the press exactly how I ought to dispose of it. I shall of course pay no attention to these suggestions, however well- or ill-intentioned. But one thing I know I want to do; I should like to give an annual Aspen Prize for a British composition. The conditions would change each year; one year it might be for a work for young voices and a school orchestra, another year for the celebration of a national event or centenary, another time a work for an instrument whose repertory is small; but in any case for specific or general usefulness. And the Jury would be instructed to choose only that work which was a pleasure to perform and inspiriting to listen to. In this way I would try to express my interpretation of the intention behind the Aspen

Institute, and to express my warmest thanks, my most humble thanks, for the unbeliev-able honor which you have awarded me today.

Benjamin Britten, "On Receiving the First Aspen Award" (London: Faber & Faber, 1964).

An equally strong statement from the other side of the ideological divide was Milton Babbitt's "The Composer as Specialist," a talk Babbitt gave one afternoon in the summer of 1957 at the Berkshire Music Center at Tanglewood, near Lenox, Massa-chusetts. (Britten surely knew of it when he gave his Aspen acceptance speech, for it was instantly notorious, thanks especially to the title—"Who Cares If You Listen?"—given to it by its first publisher, a magazine for record collectors.) And ever since, debate over questions of the social value of music and the social responsibility of musicians, aggravated by the unprecedented and voluntary withdrawal of significant numbers of twentieth-century composers into various sorts of "ivory towers," has raged. It is a curious fact that proponents of the retreat, though they are generally looked upon as the advance guard, argue from premises that are directly traceable to nineteenth-century Romanticism. For it is only since the Romantics that there has existed any conception of an artist whose primary obligation is to his art and to its history, not to patrons or consumers of any kind. Babbitt's arguments bring up to date the position of Schoenberg's "Society for Private Performances" (see p. 366) by drawing an analogy between "serious" musical composition and scientific research, and by calling therefore for university support and protection of new music—an idea that has gained enormous acceptance and implementation since the article appeared. Babbitt himself was a member of the faculty at Princeton University. Perhaps signifi-cantly, he taught mathematics there in addition to music.

I am concerned with stating an attitude towards the indisputable facts of the status and condition of the composer of what we will, for the moment, designate as "serious," "advanced," contemporary music. This composer expends an enormous amount of time and energy—and usually, considerable money—on the creation of a commodity which has little, no, or negative commodity value. He is, in essence, a "vanity" composer. The general public is largely unaware of and uninterested in his music. The majority of performers shun it and resent it. Consequently, the music is little performed, and then primarily at poorly attended concerts before an audience consist-ing in the main of fellow professionals.

Towards this condition of musical and societal "isolation," a variety of attitudes has been expressed, usually with the purpose of assigning blame, often to the music itself, occasionally to critics or performers, and very occasionally to the public. But to assign blame is to imply that this isolation is unnecessary and undesirable. It is my contention that, on the contrary, this condition is not only inevitable, but potentially advantageous for the composer and his music. From my point of view, the composer would do well to consider means of realizing, consolidating and extending the advantages.

The unprecedented divergence between contemporary serious music and its lis-teners, on the one hand, and traditional music and its following, on the other, is not accidental and—most probably—not transitory. Rather it is a result of a half-century of revolution in musical thought, a revolution whose nature and consequences can be compared only with, and in many respects are closely analogous to, those of the mid-nineteenth-century revolution in theoretical physics. Apart from the often highly sophisticated and complex constructive methods of any one composition, or group of compositions, the very minimal properties characterizing this body of music are the sources of its "difficulty," "unintelligibility," and—isolation. In indicating the most general of these properties, I shall make reference to no specific works, since I wish to avoid the independent issue of evaluation. The reader is at liberty to supply his own instances.

First. This music employs a tonal vocabulary which is more "efficient" than that of the music of the past, or its derivatives. This is not necessarily a virtue in itself, but it does make possible a greatly increased number of pitch simultaneities, successions, and relationships. This increase in efficiency necessarily reduces the "redundancy" of the language, and as a result the intelligible communication of the work demands increased accuracy from the transmitter (the performer) and activity from the receiver (the listener). Incidentally, it is this circumstance, among many others, that has created the need for purely electronic media of "performance." More importantly for us, it makes ever heavier demands upon the training of the listener's perceptual capacities.

Second. Along with this increase of meaningful pitch materials, the number of functions associated with each component of the musical event also has been multiplied. In the simplest possible terms, each such "atomic" event is located in a five-dimensional musical space determined by pitch-class, register, dynamic, duration, and timbre. These five components not only together define the single event, but, in the course of a work, the successive values of each component create an individually coherent structure, frequently in parallel with the corresponding structures created by each of the other components. Inability to perceive and remember precisely the values of any of these components results in a dislocation of the event in the work's musical space, an alteration of its relation to all other events in the work, and—thus—a falsification of the composition's total structure. For example, an incorrectly performed or perceived dynamic value results in destruction of the work's dynamic pattern, but also in false identification of other components of the event (of which this dynamic value is a part) with corresponding components of other events, so creating incorrect pitch, registral, timbral, and durational associations. It is this high degree of "determinacy" that most strikingly differentiates such music from, for example, a popular song. A popular song is only very partially determined, since it would appear to retain its germane characteristics under considerable alteration of register, rhythmic texture, dynamics, harmonic structure, timbre, and other qualities.

Third. Musical compositions of the kind under discussion possess a high degree of contextuality and autonomy. That is, the structural characteristics of a given work are less representative of a general class of characteristics than they are unique to the individual work itself. Particularly, principles of relatedness, upon which depends immediate coherence of continuity, are more likely to evolve in the course of the work than to be derived from generalized assumptions. Here again greater and new demands are made upon the perceptual and conceptual abilities of the listener.

Fourth, and finally. Although in many fundamental respects this music is "new," it often also represents a vast extension of the methods of other musics, derived from a considered and extensive knowledge of their dynamic principles. For, concomitant with the "revolution in music," perhaps even an integral aspect thereof, has been the development of analytical theory, concerned with the systematic formulation of such principles to the end of greater efficiency, economy and understanding. Compositions so rooted necessarily ask comparable knowledge and experience from the listener. Like all communication, this music presupposes a suitably equipped receptor.

Why should the layman be other than bored and puzzled by what he is unable to understand, music or anything else? It is only the translation of this boredom and puzzlement into resentment and denunciation that seems to me indefensible. The time has passed when the normally well-educated man without special preparation could understand the most advanced work in, for example, mathematics, philosophy, and physics. Advanced music, to the extent that it reflects the knowledge and originality of the informed composer, scarcely can be expected to appear more intelligible than these arts and sciences to the person whose musical education usually has been even less extensive than his background in other fields. But to this, a double standard is invoked, with the words "music is music," implying also that "music is *just* music." Why not, then, equate the activities of the radio repairman with those of the theoretical physicist, on the basis of the dictum that "physics is physics"? It is not difficult to find statements like the following, from the *New York Times* of September 8, 1957: "The scientific level of the conference is so high ... that there are in the world only 120 mathematicians specializing in the field who could contribute." Specialized music on the other hand, far from signifying "height" of musical level, has been charged with "decadence," even as evidence of an insidious "conspiracy."

Imagine, if you can, a layman chancing upon a lecture on "Pointwise Periodic Homeomorphisms." At the conclusion, he announces: "I didn't like it." Social conventions being what they are in such circles, someone might dare inquire: "Why not?" Under duress, our layman discloses precise reasons for his failure to enjoy himself; he found the hall chilly, the lecturer's voice unpleasant, and he was suffering the digestive aftermath of a poor dinner. His interlocutor understandably disqualifies these reasons as irrelevant to the content and value of the lecture, and the development of mathematics is left undisturbed. If the concert-goer is at all versed in the ways of musical lifemanship, he also will offer reasons for his "I didn't like it"—in the form of assertions that the work in question is "inexpressive," "undramatic," "lacking in poetry," etc., etc., tapping that store of vacuous equivalents hallowed by time for: "I don't like it, and I cannot or will not say why."

In search of what to think and how to say it, the layman may turn to newspapers and magazines. Here he finds conclusive evidence for the proposition that "music is music." The science editor of such publications contents himself with straightforward reporting, usually news of the "factual" sciences; books and articles not intended for popular consumption are not reviewed. Whatever the reason, such matters are left to professional journals. The music critic admits no comparable differentiation. He may feel, with some justice, that music which presents itself in the market place of the concert hall automatically offers itself to public approval or disapproval. He may feel, again with some justice, that to omit the expected criticism of the "advanced" work would be to do the composer an injustice in his assumed quest for, if nothing else, public notice and "professional recognition." The critic, at least to this extent, is himself a victim of the leveling of categories.

Here, then, are some of the factors determining the climate of the public world of music. Perhaps we should not have overlooked those pockets of "power" where prizes, awards, and commissions are dispensed, where music is adjudged guilty, not only without the right to be confronted by its accuser, but without the right to be confronted by the accusations. Or those well-meaning souls who exhort the public "just to *listen* to more contemporary music," apparently on the theory that familiarity breeds passive acceptance. Or those, often the same well-meaning souls, who remind the composer of his "obligation to the public," while the public's obligation to the composer is fulfilled, manifestly, by mere physical presence in the concert hall or before a loudspeaker.

I say all this not to present a picture of virtuous music in a sinful world, but to point up the problems of a special music in an alien and inapposite world. And so, I dare suggest that the composer would do himself and his music an immediate and eventual service by total, resolute, and voluntary withdrawal from this public world to one of private performance and electronic media, with its very real possibility of complete elimination of the public and social aspects of musical composition.

But how, it may be asked, will this serve to secure the means of survival for the composer and his music? One answer is that after all such a private life is what the university provides the scholar and the scientist. It is only proper that the university, which—significantly—has provided so many contemporary composers with their professional training and general education, should provide a home for the "complex," "difficult," and "problematical" in music. Indeed, the process has begun.

I do not wish to appear to obscure the obvious differences between musical composition and scholarly research, although it can be contended that these differences are no more fundamental than the differences among the various fields of study. I do question whether these differences, by their nature, justify the denial to music's development of assistance granted these other fields. Immediate "practical" applicability (which may be said to have its musical analogue in "immediate extensibility of a compositional technique") is certainly not a necessary condition for the support of scientific research. And if it be contended that such research is so supported because in the past it has yielded eventual applications, one can counter with, for example, the music of Anton Webern, which during the composer's lifetime was regarded (to the very limited extent that it was regarded at all) as the ultimate in hermetic, specialized, and idiosyncratic composition; today, some dozen years after the composer's death, his complete works have been recorded by a major record company, primarily—I suspect—as a result of the enormous influence this music has had on the postwar, non-popular, musical world. I doubt that scientific research is any more secure against predictions of ultimate significance than is musical composition. Finally, if it be contended that research, even in its least "practical" phases, contributes to the sum of knowledge in the particular realm, what possibly can contribute more to our knowledge of music than a genuinely original composition?

Granting to music the position accorded other arts and sciences promises the sole substantial means of survival for the music I have been describing. Admittedly, if this music is not supported, the whistling repertory of the man in the street will be little affected, the concert-going activity of the conspicuous consumer of musical culture will be little disturbed. But music will cease to evolve, and, in that important sense, will cease to live.

Babbitt's arguments are met head-on by George Rochberg in a speech delivered in 1971. It is significant that this impassioned rejection of "scientific" hermeticism is voiced not by a layman or a critic—whose contentions might easily be dismissed by an inhabitant of the ivory tower—but by a university composer. Rochberg (1918–2005), a professor of music at the University of Pennsylvania, gained considerable notice in the 1970s for breaking with twelve-tone music and reverting to a highly accessible tonal idiom reminiscent of eighteenth- and nineteenth-century classical styles. He attacks the hermetic position on several fronts: its pretension to scientific status; its belief in linear progress in art; its alleged amorality and dehumanization; and above all, its irrelevance to the genuine essence and purposes of art.

It would be presumptuous to attempt or claim to attempt a depth analysis of the aberrations of the contemporary mind, but it seems to me there is a kind of rational madness let loose in the world which delights in manipulation for its own sake, usually, if not always, buttressed by self-justifying, objective principles, a kind of rational madness which understands no theoretical limits to its pursuit of its self-justifying goals and which, worst of all, recognizes none or is blind to all of the possible consequences of its methodology and procedural logic when acted out in real life and among real people. The purest example I know which my description fits in every regard is science; for in science today we see the remarkable phenomenon of an unquestioned, worldwide agreement to pursue knowledge to its absolute limits, regardless of its ultimate consequences for human existence. The horrible paradox in this almost four-century-old play of man's constitutional inability to foresee consequences while in hot pursuit of what he calls "truth" is that as each discovery of this truth has brought man closer and closer to his own extinction either through the prospects of physical destruction or psychological maltransformation or biogenetic tampering, science itself remains supremely and arrogantly confident of its limitless purposes and indeed has the full support and encouragement of governments, industrial entrepreneurs and peoples generally, all of whom continue to believe in its doubtful benefits. As Lewis Mumford has recently pointed out, the "pursuit of scientific truth" is overriding in the twentieth century; and "in this pursuit of truth, the scientist has sanctified his own discipline and —what is more dangerous—placed it above any obligation of morality.... Scientific truth achieved the status of an absolute and the incessant pursuit and expansion of knowledge became the one recognized categorical imperative."

No wonder the world picture of the scientist from Galileo to today still remains as Schrödinger has observed, "without blue, yellow, bitter, sweet, beauty, delight, and sorrow." It was not surprising then, however regrettable it might be, that the dehumanized objectivity of scientific methodology and procedural logic should have gradually entered into and become central to large areas of artistic thought and production.

The emergence of forms of art totally devoid of human content, and therefore meaning, owes everything to a naive, accepting, uncritical belief in the values of machine technology and the scientific premises on which this technology has been firmly based. Humanistic traditions have been abandoned largely in favor of varieties of production which concentrate on consciously devised technical manipulation of the optic nerves, on the application of pure geometric design to the plan of the pictorial or the sculptural space, on the development of factory-produced sculpture for which the artist provides a blueprint, on the emergence of the "happening" as a misapplication of the principles of indeterminacy which permits the artist to indulge himself without restraint or taste, on the establishment of "open theater" and "participatory theater" which, as far as I can see, derive from the principles of behavioral psychology in which stimulus and response play the greatest roles. In short, contemporary art either manipulates the central nervous system, sometimes in bizarre and grotesque, however systematic, ways, or ignores its needs completely by removing itself to realms of abstraction which, though patterned, refuse sense and meaning to the viewer. It is therefore not surprising that we can see the likeness of the dehumanized, morally void spectre of science in contemporary art. The same pretense toward lofty and impersonal objectivity is present in both; the same removal from the consequences of one's actions is present in both; the same preference for reducing the impossible-to-grasp-or-pin-down subject, man, to an eminently manipulable object, automaton, is present in both.

The separation of the immeasurable inside from the measurable outside, i.e., the propensity for converting the world around us into so much machinery to be mastered and controlled, leaving out the dark, subjective nature of the controller, himself an intrinsic part of what he is attempting to control, is the hallmark of the scientific outlook starting with Galileo and Kepler; and while for three centuries painters, sculptors, musicians, poets, writers went their own ways, producing the body of our inherited culture, in the twentieth century, the century in which science itself has finally overtaken and conquered the world, art has succumbed to the ethos which seems to be all pervasive and inescapable. Until the twentieth century it was clear that the worlds of science and art were separate from each other, sharing no basic premise in common. Though Kepler could say:

> As the ear is made to perceive sound and the eye to perceive color, so the mind has been formed to understand not all sorts of things but quantities. It perceives any given thing more clearly in proportion as that thing is close to bare quantities as to its origin, but the further a thing recedes from quantities the more darkness and error inhere in it.

It was precisely in those areas where the mind recedes from quantities and moves freely and intuitively in the realms of qualities that the artist lived and worked his human miracles. It was here that "blue, yellow, bitter, sweet, beauty, delight, and sorrow" held sway and produced their magical images for the eye, the ear, the mind—images which attained a human reality and gave the brutish, hard life of men a possible sense of glory in existence, a sense of the miraculous. But science not only does not believe in miracles; it positively despises them. If one compares the results of the "divine madness" which Plato ascribed to poets with those of the "rational madness" I am ascribing to scientists, it is not difficult to see which is to be preferred in terms of the present and future of man. But the "divine madness" has been almost totally replaced by "rational madness" in the arts of our times; and it is in certain and specific varieties of contemporary music one can see this best.

For music is the most discrete, the most potentially abstract, the most specific of all arts. To Leibnitz it was "unconscious counting," a species of mathematics; to John Ruskin "frozen architecture"; but to musicians it was, until only very recently, "singing." Sound was simply the physical medium, the carrier of the increasingly expanding structures which based themselves primarily on the model of the vocal phrase and its psychology, and projected its human aspirations in clearly shaped, arching melodic lines with or without verbal association. As late as Schoenberg, Webern and Stravinsky, the propensity for "singing" worked its magic even on their purely instrumental works. And where "singing," in the sense of vocal or instrumental lyric expression, was modified to "dancing," in the sense of periodicities with directly felt rhythmic pulsation, music retained its uncanny balance between inner and outer, remained a wholly human creation of human realities, memorable, repeatable, meaningful—if not always beautiful according to individual tastes. By another of the great ironies that pursue premeditating man, as soon as composers began to think of music as sound and sound as quantity, singing and dancing in the traditional musical sense were replaced by conscious counting, going Leibnitz one better, and by literally attaining the condition of "frozen architecture"—sound-events designed in time but not in rhythm. Since present day composers are extremely, if not exclusively, verbal and are given to different varieties of intellection and abstraction, they have fully documented their peregrinations in endless articles and books, few of which ultimately reveal the slightest awareness of the erosion of their own art at their own hands. Because they are fascinated by mathematics, logic, and science and have taken on the rational madness of their scientific confrères, we read much these days about information theory and its relation to the psychology and composition of music; about statistical probabilities, stochastics, and the Markoff Chain and their compositional possibilities, about group and set theory as applied to serial music; about aleatory and indeterminacy and entropy. Every possible scientific metaphor and analogy is invoked. Every possible scientific discipline is ransacked for potential connections with and corroborations of theoretical postulates of how to expand the possibilities of sound itself and its theoretically limitless arrangements, compositionally speaking. Musicians study computer programming, probe the latest linguistic findings, revel in the communication sciences. They read widely in logic; they take courses in advanced mathematics. All this would be admirable if it were for the personal cultural enrichment of those who feel so inclined; but it is in the name of music and exploring its possibilities in every conceivable direction, regardless of where it lands or what outlandish conclusions result, that this incredible display of misguided diligence is carried on. It used to be that a musician who wanted to compose schooled himself in the disciplines of counterpoint and harmony, learned his craft, and went about the uncertain business of producing art. History tells us few succeeded. Today it is enough merely to want to become a composer without benefit of evidence of a musical "ear" to generate a spate of studies which have nothing whatever to do with music as a craft or an art. Observation shows us few are failing. As incredible as it may seem, musicians today have actually come to believe that music is susceptible to analysis and logic, that what it is as acoustical phenomena, as patterns of simultaneous and successive order, as embodiments of structure and design is ultimately knowable by the calculating, measuring, premeditating mind. The presumption of such notions has converted music into a new form of applied science, a kind of acoustical technology.

It is not germane whether the musicians who are deeply involved with scientific ideas and notions understand or apply them correctly to their own production. Here again the scientist can sit on his lofty perch and disclaim any responsibility for what musicians do with his ideas; but the fact remains that his impact on the musician is deep and profound and has had no less deleterious effects on music than on other areas of existence. But like the Chinese box within the box we proceed in depth to ever increasing disregard of consequences. For there are among us composers who renounce any responsibility for what they produce, claiming instead that the very nonrepeatability of their indeterminate works based on chance and/or choice lies in the very nature of physical phenomena, and is therefore of a higher reality than any which pertains to man's limited possibilities, tied down as they are by cultural associations, memory, history. But it is in the area of electronics, magnetic tape, and the computer that music has received today its greatest impress from the technology of science and it is here where composers have entered into pure quantification and measurement of wave lengths, wave combinations, partials and time segments and sequences. That music should thus be subjected to forms of automation is inevitable; and that it should remove itself more and more from singing and dancing and embrace a world of sound devoid of human content is surely the end result of believing that music like everything else today is reducible to formulas, to equations, to statistical probabilities, to predictable and controllable functions and behavior—in short to technology. Any sense of the human limits of music has been lost; and in my view it is not likely it can be regained. At least not until we have passed through the terrors which science and technology have prepared for us and have been driven back by the sheer need to survive to a re-evaluation of priorities in life and a renewed sense of the tragedy of man. The Greeks already understood the nature of this tragedy as the hubris of man, his vaulting pride, his lust for dominion over the very universe which made him. And the Greeks invented the Eumenides, the Fates which, when provoked, cut premeditating man down. Must we wait until we are standing desolate and despairing in a man-made wilderness to understand the words of Dürrenmatt's physicist, Moebius:

> I am poor King Solomon. Once I was immeasurably rich and wise and God-fearing. I was a prince of peace and justice. But my wisdom destroyed my fear of God, and when I no longer feared God, my wisdom destroyed my riches. Now all cities are dead over which I ruled; the empire which was entrusted to me is empty, a desert shimmering in a blue light, and somewhere, around a nameless star, senselessly, eternally, circles the radioactive earth. I am Solomon. I am poor King Solomon.

PART NINE

The Recent Past, and the Present

162

Defection

Ned Rorem (1923–), a composer well known for his gentle art songs and notorious for his garish published diaries, made the biggest splash of his career with the grumpy piece given here in condensed form. Considerable resentment against the academic-modernist establishment (which had looked down on "conservative" musicians like Rorem) seethes behind the welcome it extends to a new pop phenomenon from Britain. (Concerning George Rochberg's defection from the modernist ranks [see p. 484], Rorem grumbled that those who quit smoking get more credit than those who never smoked at all, though the latter are, if anything, the more virtuous.) Now he was taking his revenge. But the appearance of The Beatles, followed by a whole series of other rock bands from across the ocean (widely referred to at the time as the "British invasion") was indeed a watershed event—not so much in the history of popular music as in that of classical music, inspiring as it did a much more serious and potentially disruptive defection than that of a few disgruntled serialists. For the first time it became acceptable, even fashionable, for cultured folk to take the work of commercial musicians seriously, and even critique it seriously. It was a facet of the egalitarian and antiauthoritarian spirit of the sixties—a spirit that had less benign manifestations as well—and a lasting one, marking a permanent change in musical consumption patterns, especially in America, where classical music had always been a somewhat marginal, imported commodity. Where this change mattered most in the creative (or production) history of concert music was its eventual stylistic impact on composers who were children or not yet born at the time of this sea change, who grew up listening to the music of The Beatles and their successors, and who considered it a formative part of their musical upbringing. The newly eclectic spirit surveyed near the end of this book had its origin here.

I never go to classical concerts anymore, and I don't know anyone who does. It's hard still to care whether some virtuoso tonight will perform the "Moonlight Sonata" a bit better or a bit worse than another virtuoso performed it last night.

I do often attend what used to be called avant-garde recitals, though seldom with delight, and inevitably I look around and wonder: What am I doing here? What am I learning? Where are the poets and painters and even composers who used to flock to these things? Well, perhaps what I'm doing here is a duty, keeping an ear on my profession so as to justify the joys of resentment, to steal an idea or two, or just to show charity toward some friend on the program. But I learn less and less. Meanwhile the absent artists are home playing records; they are reacting again, finally, to something they no longer find at concerts.

Reacting to what? To The Beatles, of course—The Beatles, whose arrival has proved one of the healthiest events in music since 1950, a fact which no one sensitive can fail to perceive to some degree. By healthy I mean alive and inspired—two adjectives long out of use. By music I include not only the general areas of jazz, but those expressions subsumed in the categories of chamber, opera, symphonic: in short, all music. And by sensitive I understand not the cultivated listening ability of elite Music Lovers so much as instinctive judgment. (There *are* still people who exclaim: "What's a nice musician like you putting us on about The Beatles for?" They are the same ones who at this late date take theater more seriously than movies and go to symphony concerts because pop insults their intelligence, unaware that the situation is now precisely reversed.)

My approach is that of what once was termed the long-hair composer, somewhat disillusioned, nourished at the conservatory yet exposed all his life (as is any American, of necessity) to jazz. My colleagues and I have been happily torn from a long antiseptic nap by the energy of rock, principally as embodied in The Beatles. Naturally I've grown curious about this energy. What are its origins? What need does it fill? Why should The Beatles—who seem to be the best of a good thing, who in fact are far superior to all the other groups who pretend to copy them, most of which are nevertheless American and perpetuating what once was an essentially American thing—why should The Beatles have erupted from *Liverpool*? Could it be true, as the jazz critic Nat Hentoff suggests, that they "turned millions of American adolescents on to what had been here hurting all the time, but the young here never did want it raw so they absorbed it through the British filter"? Do The Beatles hurt indeed? And are they really so new? Does their attraction, be it pain or pleasure, stem from their words—or even from what's called their *sound*—or quite plainly from their tunes?

The once thriving Art of Song, dormant since the War, is restirring in all corners of the world—which is not the same world that put it to bed. As a result, when Song really becomes wide awake again (the sleep has been nourishing), its composition and interpretation will be of a quite different order and for a quite different public. The artful tradition of great song has been transferred from elite domains to The Beatles and their offshoots who represent—as any non-specialized intellectual will tell you—the finest communicable music of our time. Unlike their "grandparents," all these groups write most of their own material, thus combining the traditions of 12th-century troubadours, 16th-century madrigalists and 18th-century musical artisans who were always composer-performers—in short, combining all sung expression (except opera) as it was before the 20th century. Curiously, it is not through the suave innovations of our sophisticated composers that music is regaining health, but from the old-fashioned lung exercises of gangs of kids.

That the best of these gangs should have come from England is unimportant; they could have come from Arkansas. It seems to me that their attraction has little to do with "what had been here hurting," but on the contrary with enjoyment. No sooner does a culture critic like Susan Sontag [in "One Culture and the New Sensibility," an essay of

1965] explain that "the new sensibility takes a rather dim view of pleasure," than we discover her "new" sensibility growing stale. Her allusion was to a breed of suspiciously articulate composers—suspicious because they spend more time in glib justification than in composition—and who denigrate the *liking* of music, the *bodily* liking of it. Indeed, one doesn't "like" Boulez, does one? To like is not their consideration; to comprehend is. But surely fun is the very core of The Beatles' musically contagious expression: they are antidote to the new (read "old") sensibility, and intellectuals are allowed to admit, without disgrace, that they like this music.

The Beatles are good even though everyone knows they're good, i.e., in spite of those claims of the Under Thirties about their filling a new sociological need like Civil Rights and LSD. Our need for them is neither sociological nor new, but artistic and old, specifically a *renewal,* a renewal of pleasure. All other arts in the past decade have to an extent felt this renewal; but music was not only the last of man's "useless" expressions to develop historically, it is also the last to evolve within any given generation—even when, as today, a generation endures a maximum of five years (that brief span wherein "the new sensibility" was caught).

Why are The Beatles superior? It is easy to say that most of their competition (like most everything everywhere) is junk; more important, their betterness is consistent: each of the songs from their last three albums is memorable. The best of these memorable tunes—and the best is a large percentage ("Here, there and everywhere," "Good day sunshine," "Michelle," "Norwegian Wood" are already classics)—compare with those by composers from great eras of song: Monteverdi, Schumann, Poulenc. Superior melody results from the Distortion of Genius. The Beatles' words often go against the music (the crushing poetry that opens "A Day in the life" intoned to the blandest of tunes), even as Martha Graham's music often contradicts her dance (she gyrates hysterically to utter silence, or stands motionless while all hell breaks loose in the pit). Because The Beatles pervert with naturalness they usually build solid structures, whereas their rivals pervert with affectation, aping the gargoyles but not the cathedral. Genius doesn't lie in not being derivative, but in making right choices instead of wrong ones. It is not in innovation that Paul McCartney's originality lies, but in superiority. It remains to be seen how, if ever, he deals with more spacious forms. But of that miniature scene, Song, he is a modern master. As such he is The Beatles' most significant member.

Just as today my own composition springs more from pristine necessity than driving inspiration (I compose what I want to hear because no one else is doing it), so I listen—sifting and waiting—only to what I need. What I need now seems less embodied in newness than in nostalgia: how many thrilling experiences do we get per year anyway, after a certain age? Such nostalgia appears most clearly engendered by The Beatles. There isn't much more to say, since structurally they're not interesting to analyze: they've added nothing new, simply brought back excitement. The excitement originates (other than, of course, from their talent) in their absolutely insolent—hence innocent—unification of music's disparate components—that is, in using the most conservative devices of harmony, counterpoint, rhythm, melody, orchestration, and making them blend with an infectious freshness.

If (and here's a big if) music at its most healthy is the creative reaction of, and stimulation for, the body, and at its most decadent is the creative reaction of and stimulation for the intellect—if, indeed, health is a desirable feature of art, and if, as

I believe, The Beatles exemplify this feature, then we have reached (strange though it may seem as coincidence with our planet's final years) a new and golden renaissance of song.

Ned Rorem, "The Music of The Beatles," *New York Review of Books,* 18 January 1968. Reprinted in Elizabeth Thomson and David Gutman (eds.), *The Lennon Companion* (New York: Schirmer Books, 1988), 99–109.

163

Minimalism

So taken for granted was the extremism of the postwar avant-garde that advanced composers began to worry about impending dead ends. "How can you make a revolution," Charles Wuorinen asked an interviewer (thinking perhaps of Cage), "when the revolution before last has already said that anything goes?" That was in 1962. By the end of the decade, the answer was clear: "No, it doesn't!" Many of the most self-consciously innovative composers who came into prominence during that decade had begun experimenting with a new kind of radicalism: radically reduced means. Because of that reduction, and because of its reliance on a great deal of (near) repetition of small units, the trend became known (after a comparable tendency in the visual arts) as minimalism. But that term, originally intended (like impressionism or even baroque) as pejorative, has never sat well with the makers of the music, and there are aspects of their products—extravagant length being one—that definitely contradict the convenient label. The way they have talked about it suggests that "pattern and process" might better describe their music. At least the second term in the proposed phrase was explicitly embraced by Steve Reich (1936-), one of the movement's pioneers, in the title of one of his most characteristic statements of principle. The main principle was that the process informing the music's unfolding (unlike the principles informing serial or aleatoric music) should be wholly available to perception. It would be a mistake, however, to regard minimalism, or pattern-and-process music, as a break with the postwar avant-garde rather than a part of it. Its crucial point of likeness with earlier avant-garde attitudes (and even with earlier *isms* like neoprimitivism and neoclassicism, both associated with Stravinsky) was its unequivocally embraced impersonalism, its lack of interest—ringingly declared in Reich's final sentence—in human psychology or subjectivity. Still and all, the trend was distinctive, and highly significant in that it was the first American classical style to exert a strong technical and structural influence on the music of European composers.

Music as a Gradual Process

I do not mean the process of composition but rather pieces of music that are, literally, processes.

The distinctive thing about musical processes is that they determine all the note-to-note (sound-to-sound) details and the overall form simultaneously. (Think of a round or infinite canon.)

I am interested in perceptible processes. I want to be able to hear the process happening throughout the sounding music.

To facilitate closely detailed listening a musical process should happen extremely gradually.

Performing and listening to a gradual musical process resembles:

pulling back a swing, releasing it, and observing it gradually come to rest;

turning over an hour glass and watching the sand slowly run through to the bottom;

placing your feet in the sand by the ocean's edge and watching, feeling, and listening to the waves gradually bury them.

Although I may have the pleasure of discovering musical processes and composing the musical material to run through them, once the process is set up and loaded it runs by itself.

Material may suggest what sort of process it should be run through (content suggests form), and processes may suggest what sort of material should be run through them (form suggests content). If the shoe fits, wear it.

As to whether a musical process is realized through live human performance or through some electromechanical means is not finally the main issue. One of the most beautiful concerts I ever heard consisted of four composers playing their tapes in a dark hall. (A tape is interesting when it's an interesting tape.)

It is quite natural to think about musical processes if one is frequently working with electromechanical sound equipment. All music turns out to be ethnic music.

Musical processes can give one a direct contact with the impersonal and also a kind of complete control, and one doesn't always think of the impersonal and complete control as going together. By "a kind" of complete control, I mean that by running this material through this process I completely control all that results, but also that I accept all that results without changes.

John Cage has used processes and has certainly accepted their results, but the processes he used were compositional ones that could not be heard when the piece was performed. The process of using the *I Ching* or imperfections in a sheet of paper to determine musical parameters can't be heard when listening to music composed that way. The compositional processes and the sounding music have no audible connection. Similarly, in serial music, the series itself is seldom audible. (This is a basic difference between serial—basically European—music, and serial—basically American—art, where the perceived series is usually the focal point of the work.)

James Tenney said in conversation, "Then the composer isn't privy to anything." I don't know any secrets of structure that you can't hear. We all listen to the process together since it's quite audible, and one of the reasons it's quite audible is because it's happening extremely gradually.

The use of hidden structural devices in music never appealed to me. Even when all the cards are on the table and everyone hears what is gradually happening in a musical process, there are still enough mysteries to satisfy all. These mysteries are the impersonal, unintended, psychoacoustic by-products of the intended process. These might include submelodies heard within repeated melodic patterns, stereophonic effects due to listener location, slight irregularities in performance, harmonics, difference tones, and so on.

Listening to an extremely gradual musical process opens my ears to *it*, but *it* always extends farther than I can hear, and that makes it interesting to listen to that musical process again. That area of every gradual (completely controlled) musical process, where one hears the details of the sound moving out away from intentions, occurring for their own acoustic reasons, is *it*.

I begin to perceive these minute details when I can sustain close attention and a gradual process invites my sustained attention. By "gradual" I mean extremely gradual; a process happening so slowly and gradually that listening to it resembles watching a minute hand on a watch—you can perceive it moving after you stay with it a little while.

Several currently popular modal musics like Indian classic and drug-oriented rock and roll may make us aware of minute sound details because in being modal (constant key center, hypnotically droning and repetitious) they naturally focus on these details rather than on key modulation, counterpoint, and other peculiarly Western devices. Nevertheless, these modal musics remain more or less strict frameworks for improvisation. They are not processes.

The distinctive thing about musical processes is that they determine all the note-to-note details and the overall form simultaneously. One can't improvise in a musical process—the concepts are mutually exclusive.

While performing and listening to gradual musical processes, one can participate in a particular liberating and impersonal kind of ritual. Focusing in on the musical process makes possible that shift of attention away from *he* and *she* and *you* and *me* outward toward *it*.

Steve Reich, "Music as a Gradual Process," first published in 1969 in the catalogue to *Anti-Illusion: Procedures/Materials,* Whitney Museum of American Art, New York City. Reprinted in Steve Reich, *Writings on Music 1965–2000,* ed. Paul Hillier (New York: Oxford University Press, 2002), 34–36.

One of the most notable differences between minimalism and other avant-garde styles was the fact that minimalist pieces produced euphoria in audiences and attracted a large following. That fact was used, of course, to impugn it by those who, in keeping with older (Romantic) versions of modernism like that of T. W. Adorno (see p. 442), regarded popularity and avant-garde as mutually exclusive terms. The basis of the style's appeal is well conveyed in a memoir by Ransom Wilson, a flutist and conductor, who attended one of the benchmark events in the history of twentieth-century opera: the now legendary performance of *Einstein on the Beach,* an opera composed by Philip Glass (1937–) and staged by Robert Wilson (1941–), at the Metropolitan Opera House in New York. It was not a presentation by the Metropolitan Opera company; the performers had merely rented the house on a night when it was free. A dozen or so years later, however, the Metropolitan did indeed commission an opera from Glass, called *The Voyage,* to be performed in 1992 to mark the 500th anniversary of Columbus's discovery of the New World. It was only the third Metropolitan Opera première in half a century, and an impressive testimonial to the minimalist movement's success.

My first encounter with "minimalist" music was at the Metropolitan Opera House on November 28, 1976. I was in the audience for one of the sold-out performances of *Einstein on the Beach,* the opera by Philip Glass in collaboration with dramatist Robert Wilson. As I listened to that five-hour performance, I experienced an amazing transformation. At first I was bored—*very* bored. The music seemed to have no direction, almost giving the impression of a gigantic phonograph with a "stuck needle." I was first irritated and then angry that I'd been taken in by this crazy composer who obviously doted on repetition. I thought of leaving. Then, with no conscious awareness, I crossed a threshold and found that the music was touching me, carrying me with it. I began to perceive within it a whole world where change happens so slowly and carefully that each new harmony or rhythmic addition or subtraction seems monumental.

There were no intermissions. The work continued relentlessly in its grip on all of us in that packed house. Suddenly, at a point some four hours into the opera there occurred a completely unexpected harmonic and rhythmic modulation, coupled with a huge jump in the decibel level. People in the audience began to scream with delight and I remember well that my entire body was covered with goose bumps. I left the theater regretting the performance was over, and so excited that I remained awake far into the night.

Ransom Wilson, notes to Angel DS-37340 (1982).

> Like Reich, Glass has formed his own performing ensembles to propagate his work, thus restoring the bond between the creative and recreative roles that romanticism, and then modernism, had rent asunder. Both Reich's ensemble (in which Glass at first participated) and Glass's (in which Reich at first participated) used instruments, like electric organs, that were mainly associated with rock, thus furthering by means of timbre the rapprochement of high and low genres that the sixties had set in motion. Also like Reich, Glass has been a willing explicator of his methods. What follows is his own account of his stylistic development up to the event that Ransom Wilson attended, the effects of which Wilson found so powerful.

The musical forces for *Einstein on the Beach* were built around the ensemble for which so much of my music since 1968 has been written. This consisted of two electric organs, three winds (doubling on saxophones, flute and bass clarinet) and one solo soprano voice. A chamber choir of sixteen mixed voices carries the weight of the vocal music in *Einstein*. A violinist, costumed as Einstein, plays a featured part and completes the lineup.

Einstein was planned as an extended evening performance (four hours, forty minutes) without formal, prescribed intermissions. We knew there would be few people able to sit straight through the entire work, and the audience was expected to take their own breaks (quietly, of course) when needed. Personally, I can say that, after more than fifty performances of *Einstein*, I have never seen the entire work straight through without interruption, though many people constantly assure me they have, as it were, taken it "whole." Still, the work was never intended to be seen as a whole, narrative piece. Its "wholeness" comes from its consistency of subject matter and overall structure and becomes the theatrical equivalent of an "act of faith" for the audience.

The sheer unbroken length of *Einstein* clearly presented musical problems that had to be worked out. With that much music to be performed, the orchestra had to be divided into smaller alternating groups, everyone coming together only occasionally for the big *tutti* numbers. The Knee Plays [i.e., joints, Glass's term for entr'actes], for example, feature the chorus and violin with occasional help from one organ. Since the violinist is sitting halfway between the orchestra pit and the stage, it focuses attention in front of the curtain—a real advantage since there was a scenery change during each of the Knee Plays.

This was actually one of my minor miscalculations in writing *Einstein*. Since the Knee Plays were conceived for smaller groupings of musicians and produced a more intimate effect, they were not very loud. Meanwhile, behind the curtain, huge pieces of scenery were being dragged about, sometimes dropped, and this could often be heard quite clearly over the music. Intermezzo music is always a problem. Just when you would like the music to be quiet, creating a sense of repose between scenes, that's really when it needs to be as loud as you can make it, to cover all the backstage business. (I've continued to write quiet interlude music for other operas, hoping for the best with the backstage crews.)

Music in Twelve Parts, the extended work written between 1971 and 1974, was a catalogue of ideas on rhythmic structure with which I had been working since my Paris pieces of 1965. The two major techniques that had evolved, and that generated the whole of the *Einstein* score, were those I called *additive process* and *cyclic structure.*

Additive process is one of those very simple ideas that can quickly lead to very complicated procedures. It can easily be explained: A musical grouping or measure of, say, five notes is repeated several times, then is followed by a measure of six notes (also repeated), then seven, then eight, and so on. A simple figure can expand and then contract in many different ways, maintaining the same general melodic configuration but, because of the addition (or subtraction) of one note, it takes on a very different rhythmic shape.

I have used rhythmic cycles (repeating fixed rhythmic patterns of specific lengths) to create extended structures in my music by superimposing two different rhythmic patterns of different lengths. Depending on the length of each pattern, they will eventually arrive together back at their starting points, making one complete cycle. This has been described by some writers as sounding like "wheels within wheels," a rather fanciful but not wholly inaccurate way of evoking the resulting effect.

When the cyclic and additive processes are combined, some extremely interesting and complex structures are produced. This was the main overall musical device of *Music in Twelve Parts,* and it is present also in *Einstein.*

In *Another Look at Harmony,* written just before *Einstein* and an important thematic source for the opera, I turned to a new problem. What I was looking for was a way of combining harmonic progressions with the rhythmic structure I had been developing, to produce a new overall structure. This turned out to be a problem of such absorbing interest that it occupied me almost completely for the next ten years, and the results can be heard in all the music I wrote during that time. Each scene in *Einstein,* in fact, presents a different way of "solving" the problem.

One such progression, which recurs throughout the work, appears be a traditional cadential formula, the time-honored closing phrase which, in a variety of forms, became highly developed during the Baroque period and lasted well into the present. However, there is an altered or pivotal chord in the middle that results in a closing chord a half-step below what one would normally expect. It is this lowered resolution of the cadence that motivates its repetition. In the final scene of *Einstein,* this goes on for over eight minutes. What sustains musical interest over that length of time is the additive process which, when applied to the cadence, produces a lengthy and dramatic rhythmic development.

In another progression, a straightforward four-chord sequence is outlined. With each repetition, the length of one chord is increased by a group of short notes as the additive process is applied to the upper part. This can easily be heard as the notes of the bass line become successively longer.

It is worth noting another aspect of the development, in *Einstein on the Beach,* of this new approach of combining rhythmic and harmonic structure into an overall unified process. With the introduction of what is known as "root-movement harmony," (since the "root," or "fundamental," of the chord creates the impression of moving *through* as well as *with* the chord progression), a new element came into play in my music. Harmonic movement is central to our perception of expressiveness. Once this movement had entered my music, it marked a sharp break with the very rhythmically charged, but harmonically static, music I had written before.

In its own way, the pre-*Einstein* music, rigorous and highly reductive, was more "radical" in its departure from the received tradition of Western music than what I have written since. But as I had been preoccupied, at that point, with that more radical-*sounding* music for over ten years, I felt I could add a little more to what I had already done. Again, it is surely no coincidence that it was at the moment that I was embarking upon a major shift in my music to large-scale theater works that I began to develop a new, more expressive language for myself.

Philip Glass, "The Music," in *Music by Philip Glass,* edited and with supplementary material by Robert T. Jones (New York: Harper and Row, 1987), 57–62.

> Finally, here is how Glass accounted to an interviewer for the impact his music made on audiences. His use of the word *biological* is significant, pointing to a feature of the music to which some have objected: namely, its seemingly purely visceral appeal, as if bypassing the rational (or even the conscious) mind. To some, in an age of mass politics (and the use of subliminal "hidden persuaders" in commercial advertising, to use the provocative term coined by the social critic Vance Packard), such an appeal has seemed potentially sinister. Such resistance was not new; it was what had made the music of Wagner so controversial in its time as well.

Q: *In writing about your music, critics have employed several terms: "hypnotic," "minimalist," "trance," "solid state." Do all these terms help clarity what you're doing, or do you think they tend to be misleading?*

A: I think they're almost all misleading, although lately I've come to dislike "minimalist" less than I dislike other descriptions. Insofar as "minimalist music" refers to a specific historical period, let's say from 1965 to 1975, the term is meaningful. But it's rarely meant in a limited way.

When people talk about "hypnotic states" or "trance states" or "druggy states" or "religious states," what they're really saying, in a rather clumsy way, is that the music shares a non-ordinariness with certain other experiences. But you can't say that everyone who doesn't speak English speaks the same language.

For me, what sets the music apart is the fact that it's non-narrative; and because it is non-narrative, we don't hear it within the usual time frame of most musical experiences. As I look at most other music, I see that it takes ordinary time, day-to-day time—what I call colloquial time—as a model for its own musical time. So you have story symphonies and story concertos—even the modernist tradition continues that to a large extent. There's still almost a compulsion with composers to deal with themes and the treatment of themes. The theme becomes the focus of the listener's attention, and then what happens to the theme happens to the listener via a certain psychological trick of identification. This obviously happens in the great concertos of the nineteenth century, with the tortuous journey of the violin and so forth, with happy endings and sad endings.

When music doesn't deal with subjects and treatments, as in my music, which is often a process where the musical material and its evolution becomes part and parcel of the structure of the music, then you don't have the psychological access to the music that I described earlier. That's why we don't hear the music as narrative or as a model of colloquial time. What we're hearing then is music in another time system. Now, we have a lot of experiences in our lives that take place in non-colloquial time systems. Some of them happen to be drug experiences; some are religious experiences; some are nature experiences. So when people say to me that music is druggy or trancey or this or that, I think they're confused; they're confusing a variety of experiences that share in common their difference from ordinary life.

Q: *But non-ordinary time can't be completely dramatic.*

A: No, but even *Einstein* works toward a finale; you can't miss it. I remember when I was talking about the last act, the Spaceship, with Bob [Wilson], I said, "Look, Bob, I think I'm going to write a real finale; a real razzle-dazzle finale." I wanted to see how he felt about it, and he said, "Fine," he liked the idea. With *Einstein*, I decided that I would try to write a piece that left the audience standing, and I've almost never played that music without seeing everyone leave his seat; it's the strangest thing, almost biological. In fact, sometimes I've done concerts where I've played the Spaceship, and then as an encore played the last part of the Spaceship, and the same thing happens again.

Cole Gagne and Tracy Caras, *Soundpieces: Interviews with American Composers* (Metuchen, N.J.: The Scarecrow Press, 1982), 214–16.

164

Fusion

One of the most distinctive features of minimalism was the degree to which its procedures reflected those of non-European music. (In Reich's case, the influences came from Africa and Indonesia; in Glass's, from India.) This influence was no mere matter of allusion or thematic window-dressing (what Reich sneeringly called "Chinoiserie"). The Western component was no longer the unquestioned structural basis. A mutual accommodation of cultures on grounds so much nearer equal than before reflected a general tendency toward multiculturalism in American society, replacing the older ideal of the melting pot, which had emphasized homogeneity over variety. As a political issue it was highly contentious; in the domain of art and entertainment it was less unprecedented. There had been a significant fusionist streak in American music for many decades, especially among composers reared on the West Coast, where the Asian presence was strong. One of the most conspicuous musical multiculturalists was Lou Harrison (1917–2003), a composer who was born in Oregon and raised in California. In the interview excerpted below, when Harrison speaks of "different pitches," he means pitches outside the even-tempered scale, for which he harbored a righteous aversion. In his Concerto for Piano and Gamelan (1987), for example, the piano was tuned to match the gamelan, not the other way round.

The encounter with the other, no matter what it is, is productive. I had a chance at Atlantica, I was in New York for ten years and heard the European repertoire and learned a lot. I did get a great deal of education in New York about Atlantica, but I came back. I am part of Pacifica and as I point out my origins are in the Pacific region. So I have that to draw from and still do. The problem actually, I think, is of graver concern in the East Coast because of the Atlantic connection. The way Schoenberg and Stravinsky solved it was to go to the past of Europe, their own place, whereas here you assume you are American and are fascinated by Japan and Java and China and all around the Pacific basin. When I teach a world music course I teach only the classic music. There were four or five major categories, and they were all Asian nations, even Europe which is only a peninsula of Asia. I didn't do much of the European tradition, but I did do the Chinese tradition, including the Japanese and Korean, and I did do Southeast Asia, predominantly gamelan, and then the Hindu tradition, and the Islamic tradition in several of its aspects. And then, if I had time in class, if I managed to get all that done, then I would do American Indian music, and that brought it around the circle.

When I had the opportunity to study gamelan music, I plunged full speed into it. Why I liked gamelan was that it sounded the way it did traditionally. So I learned the tradition of Javanese gamelan and also a little Sundanese gamelan. I haven't done Bali and I'm not going to—I'm just too old to do anything more. But I'm interested in some of it nonetheless and I can teach Javanese gamelan, the entire orchestra, and produce, you know, a Javanese sounding performance. And Chinese music, when I took that up, I studied several instruments and played them in concerts all over the place.

In my own compositions I never combine a Western instrument with Asian ones unless it can play different pitches, and if it can play pitches that can correspond with gamelan tuning, then fine, otherwise I let it be. I wouldn't dream about combining a gamelan with a Western orchestra because a Western orchestra can't play the same pitches as a gamelan orchestra.

When I taught the world music class, I did approach each of the major sections with at least a good introduction to the ethnic culture of that section. That is to say that they studied Confucius and Buddhism when we were in the Chinese/Japanese/Korean thing. When we were in Indian or Indo they studied a little bit about things like that; Islam, I made an introduction to Islamic thought, and so on. Because it is also reflected in the music, and so that's what I did.

Q: *Right, because it provides a context for what is happening musically. Along these lines, in my own work as a musicologist, I occasionally cross historical boundaries to study various aspects of European and ...*

A: Well, what you're doing is studying the music of Northwest Asia, and the same thing can be done with Javanese music, or Chinese music.

Q: *Right—well, that's pretty much my question: do you find that crossing a historical boundary in dealing with musics of the past is somehow basically the same as crossing geographical boundaries to study the musics of varying regions, or are there fundamental differences?*

A: Oh, I think they're basically the same. Fundamentally we're all humans, what another can do I can try to do. I think it's about the same idea.

Maria Cizmic, "Composing the Pacific: Interviews with Lou Harrison," *Echo* (online journal of the UCLA Musicology Department), I, no. 1 (1999).

One of Harrison's strongest statements on behalf of cultural relativism is this fairly late declaration, published in a collection of essays on the "New Tonality" that, in the name of multiculturalism, was replacing the older academic insistence on a modernist "common practice" based on the twelve-tone technique (which, of course, presupposes an equal-tempered chromatic scale).

Nearly a half-century ago, in one of our many intense musical discussions, Virgil Thomson and I decided that it is part of the tradition of Western music that the composer be able to compose both diatonically and chromatically. We were thinking of this because at the time (at least in New York) the music world seemed quite hostilely divided between "neoclassicists" along with "Americanists" who wrote diatonically, and "twelve-toners" who wrote serial chromaticism. The two groups did not overlap. Looking back from now—the last decade of the twentieth century—we realize that after Hitler's war the chromaticists tended to predominate in intellectual and academic circles. In the last decade, the larger public has grown aware of another movement—"minimalism"— which, from the tonal point of view, reaffirmed centricity and reinstituted periodicity as well. Press notice has recently risen suggesting that nineteenth-century harmonic and/or tonal models from European (actually Northwest Asian) music are currently fashionable. To my mind, all this is indeed simply Fashion among Northwest Asian music lovers, or, lovers of Northwest Asian music. Virgil Thomson also remarked that stylistic periods in Northwest Asian music seem to last about thirty years each.

There are, of course, broader periods and broader problems. All of the above changes, for example, took place within a single tuning period during which the gray veil of industrial twelve-tone equal temperament was drawn across the rich varieties of other tunings. It is, too, principally a keyboard problem, but because so many Western-style composers use the seven-plus-five keyboard, its influence tends to pervade much else. The last time I attended a Percussion Convention, for example, suggested to me that what Cowell, Cage, I and others did had largely gone unheard and unthought, so many were the pieces for twelve-tone marimbas, vibes, xylophones, glockenspiels, muggy-sounding plastic timpani, and so on.

Carl Orff had a beautiful idea in creating his School Music pieces and he even created instruments for them. Surely, educating the young in modes central to their civilization is a fine and good idea. But, he didn't tune them, and again the reality vanishes in the gray mists of industrial temperament. Again, the young are shorted here, because they could learn to hear, and to multiply and subtract ratios when they are learning their fractions.

Although I've always composed both modally and chromatically, I do remember a short period of "squirrel-caging" during the decade I spent in New York City. I would compose a modal ("diatonic") piece entirely as such. Next I'd compose one in which I'd permit myself one accidental. Then in another I'd permit myself two or three accidentals. Shortly, I'd be composing serial twelve-tone music again. I realized then that this was similar to writing in unaltered modes, and I'd do that again. Such revolving came to a halt when Virgil Thomson gave me the first printing of Harry Partch's *Genesis of a Music* [a description of an earlier attempt to reestablish non-equal-tempered tuning for new music] along with the request "See what you can make of this." In a day or so I bought a piano tuning "hammer," began tuning, and haven't looked back. I learned that intervals are real and precise. Again, by this, my interests in world music were reaffirmed and restimulated as well.

I continue to urge fellow musicians to connect their brains with their ears, to know and use precision methods—real ratios, true intervals—and to enter the beautiful humanist garden of musical delights, to enjoy there the sensuous ratios of reason's sunlight, and to share the wings of melody.

It is reasonable to question the superstitions of the misty gray veil. Do so. I rejoice that many, many are.

Lou Harrison, "Entune," *Contemporary Music Review*, VI, no. 2 (1992), 9–10.

165

New Eclecticism

The leveling of distinctions between high and low style (as exemplified in reading No. 162) and between center and periphery (No. 164) point to the general softening of formerly firm boundaries that is often associated with the term *postmodernism*. Perhaps the softest music of all, from this point of view, was that of the late- (and eventually post-) Soviet composer Alfred Schnittke (1934–98). Although born in the USSR, Schnittke was the son of an Austrian-Jewish father and a Volga German mother (i.e., descended from eighteenth-century German settlers in the Russian Empire), and his first language was German. In 1990, after two decades of struggle with the cultural authorities at home (though nothing like the crushing pressure earlier brought to bear on Shostakovich), Schnittke expatriated himself from his native country and lived out his last eight years, amid growing world fame, in Hamburg, Germany. In the article condensed below, Schnittke did as many composers before him had done: namely, recast the history of music in terms that led up to, and justified, his own work. In fact, the degree to which Schnittke's music, beginning in the 1970s, mixed styles and genres that had been thought mutually incompatible was a provocative and (in the most literal sense) transgressive act, whether viewed from the standpoint of Socialist Realism or from that of the Western avant-garde. By the end of the century, however, it looked quite normal. Where Schnittke differed from many other extreme eclectics was the way in which he tended to deploy incompatible styles as binary oppositions, easily (perhaps all-too-easily) read as allegories. In this, he was recognizably in the tradition of his Soviet forebears.

Polystylistic Tendencies in Contemporary Music

It is impossible to treat so broad yet unfamiliar a topic as polystylistics in contemporary music in summary form. Therefore I will limit myself to merely posing a few of the questions raised by the wide diffusion of polystylistic tendencies in music, and refrain from what I regard as premature artistic evaluations.

By polystylistics I mean not only the currently fashionable wave of musical collages [i.e., the use of actual quotations], but also more sophisticated ways of utilizing disparate stylistic elements. Here it is immediately necessary to distinguish two opposing principles: the principle of citation and the principle of allusion.

The principle of citation is manifested in a whole range of devices, beginning with the citation of stereotypical ingredients from a style belonging to another era or another national tradition (characteristic melodic turns, harmonic progressions, cadence formulas) and ending with exact or adapted quotations or pseudo-quotations.

Some examples (deliberately chosen from composers of radically differing aesthetics):

—Shostakovich, Piano Trio: the neoclassical passacaglia theme, with tonic-dominant progressions and a diminished-seventh chord borrowed from the style of eighteenth-century music.

—Berg, Violin Concerto: citation of a Bach chorale (thematically linked with the work's own musical material).

—[Krzysztof] Penderecki, *Stabat Mater* from the *St. Luke Passion*: pseudo-quotation of Gregorian chant as the stylistic basis of the whole work.

—Stockhausen, *Hymnen*: supercollaged mosaic of the contemporary world.

—[Arvo] Pärt, *Pro et contra*: parodistic reliance on Baroque cadence formulas to determine the form of the work.

Here one may refer to the technique of *adaptation*—the paraphrasing of someone else's written score using one's own musical language (analogous to the updating of ancient literary subjects) or else the free development of someone else's material in one's own style:

—Stravinsky, *Pulcinella* or *Canticum sacrum*.

—Webern, *Ricercar:* the music of Bach in multitimbred fragmentation.

—Pärt, *Credo:* notes by Bach, music by Pärt, thanks to rhythmic and textural transformations.

—[Jan] Klusak, *Variations on a Theme by Gustav Mahler:* "What Mahler would have written if he were Klusak."

—[Rodion] Shchedrin, *Carmen Ballet* based on Bizet's music.

And finally, to this category also belongs the citation not of ingredients but of techniques from disparate styles, such as the reproduction of the forms, rhythms, or textures of seventeenth- and eighteenth-century music and even earlier periods in the work of neoclassicists (Stravinsky, Shostakovich, Orff, Penderecki) or the devices of choral polyphony from the fourteenth to the sixteenth century (isorhythm, hocket, antiphony) in serial and postserial music.

—Webern, beginning with Opus 21 (*Symphony*).

—Stockhausen, *Gruppen, Momente*.

—Henze, *Antifone*.

—[Edison] Denisov, *The Sun of the Incas, Italian Songs*.

—[Andrey] Volkonsky, *Suite of Mirrors*.

Often polystylistic hybrids arise in this connection, bearing traits not just of two styles, but of three or four, or even more. An example is Stravinsky's *Apollon musagète*, whose quasi-antique neoclassicism evokes concretely demonstrable associations (as the composer himself acknowledges) with Lully, Gluck, Delibes, Strauss, Chaikovsky and Debussy. Sometimes, as in this work, the interpenetrating elements of one's own style and those of others can be so organic that it crosses the border between citation and allusion.

The principle of allusion can be discerned in subtle hints and unkept promises that hover at the brink of citation but do not cross it. Here classification is impossible, one can only give examples. Allusion is characteristic of the neoclassicism of the 1920s and of the present day; one need only recall Stravinsky or Henze, in whom practically the whole text is elusively colored by references to past styles (vividly individual in the case of the former, unmistakably eclectic in the case of the latter). Leaving Stravinsky (whose paradoxical manner is constructed entirely out of the play of associations and the intentional confusion of musical time and place), one would point to the broad recourse to stylistic hints and allusions in "instrumental theater" (Mauricio Kagel) or the subtle polystylistic humors—scents and shadows of other times—in the music of such contrasting composers as Boulez and Ligeti.

But can one really use the word "polystylistics" in relation to the whimsical play of temporal and spatial associations that any and all music inevitably evokes? In latent form, after all, polystylistic tendencies exist and have always existed in music, for a stylistically sterile music would be a dead music. So is this even worth talking about? Yes, one must talk about it, because lately polystylistics has solidified into a conscious device. Even without citations, the composer often plans polystylistic effects in advance, whether as a shock arising from the collage-collision of different musical eras, or a flexible side-slipping through the stages of music history, or a matter of subtle and seemingly fortuitous allusions.

Today's widespread and conscious use of polystylistic devices in music has roots both technical (the crisis in the 1950s of neo-academicism and purist tendencies, whether serial, aleatoric or sonoristic) and psychological (the strengthening of international contacts and mutual influences, changes in our conception of time and space, the "polyphonization" of human consciousness in connection with the rising tide of information and the polyphonization of art—let us merely recall such terms as stereophony, split-screen, multimedia, etc.).

Polystylistic elements have long existed in European music—not only openly, in parodies, fantasias and variations, but also in the innards, so to speak, of monostylistic genres (as in the contrasts of imagery in musical theater or in programmatic or dramatic symphonic composition). But the degree of consciousness in the use of polystylistics in the past never went beyond the likes of "variations on a theme by so-and-so" or "in the manner of so-and-so." The breakthrough to polystylistics was the product of a tendency, peculiar to the development of European music, toward the broadening of musical space. Its dialectical complement—the tendency toward the growth of organic unity of form—revealed the laws through which this new musical spaciousness could be assimilated. The peculiarity of the present situation is the fact that a new musical dimension has been discovered, but its laws are as yet unknown.

We do not yet know how many layers of stylistic polyphony a listener can process simultaneously; nor do we know the laws of collage, montage, or gradual stylistic modulation—are there indeed any? We do not know where the boundary lies between polystylistics and unoriginality or, for that matter, between polystylistics and plagiarism. The problem of authorship is getting more complicated, not only in the legal sense, but simply as a concept: is there still such a thing as an author's personal and national identity? One would think that an author's individuality will inevitably make itself felt both in the choice or arrangement of cited material and in the overall conception of a given work. In any case the supercollage of Luciano Berio's *Sinfonia* [of 1969, one of whose movements quotes the third movement of Mahler's Second Symphony in its entirety as a background to seemingly incongruous *graffiti*-like superimpositions] is sufficient witness both to his individuality and to his nationality (the richness of his collage polyphony is akin to the mixing of street noises in the soundtracks to Italian neorealist films). Moreover, elements of other styles usually serve as a sort of modified background, a penumbra or periphery around one's own individual style that throws it into relief. There are other difficulties as well: it could be that polystylistics diminishes the absolute, non-associative value of a work, giving rise to the danger of contaminating music with literary effects. The need for well-educated listeners is also increased, since the play of styles has to be recognized as deliberate.

But whatever the difficulties and potential dangers of polystylistics, its virtues are apparent even now. It widens of the range of expressive means, the possibility of integrating "high" and "low" style, the "banal" with the "recherché"—which is to say, it produces a wider musical world and a general democratization of style. It achieves the documentary objectivity of musical reality, represented not only as an individual reflection but in actual citations (in the third movement of Berio's *Sinfonia* one hears apocalyptically threatening reminders about the responsibility of our generation for the fate of the world, expressed through a collage of quotations, musical documents of various eras, in a manner reminiscent of the cinematic advertising techniques of the seventies). It creates new possibilities for the musico-dramatic embodiment of "eternal" problems—war and peace, life and death.

Thus, in Bernd Alois Zimmermann's opera *Die Soldaten* [1965] polystylistics underscores the relevance of the work's underlying humanistic idea to all times—it is a protest not only against the actual German military machine of the eighteenth century that wiped out the heroes of Jakob Michael Reinhold Lenz's original play, but one against all militarism, anywhere at any time. It is precisely the polystylistic nature of the music (in which the author's individual style is interwoven with Gregorian chant and Protestant chorales, the techniques of fourteenth- and fifteenth-century polyphony, jazz, *musique concrète*, and so on) that makes the subject matter relevant not only to the time depicted.

Polystylistics lends an analogous philosophical elevation over the depicted particulars to Sergey Slonimsky's oratorio *A Voice from the Chorus*. Here Alexander Blok's inspired and alarming thoughts about the fate of the world are embodied in a great diversity of means, beginning with a choral passage in the spirit of the sixteenth century and ending with serial and aleatory devices.

One will hardly find a more compelling musical means for conveying the philosophical idea of "links between the ages" than polystylistics.

Alfred Schnittke, "Polistilisticheskiye tendentsii sovremennoy muzïki" (*c.* 1971), in *Besedï s Al'fredom Shnitke*, ed. Alexander Ivashkin (Moscow: Kul'tura, 1994), 143–46. Trans. R. T.

166

New Romanticism

In the 1970s, following George Rochberg's example (see p. 484), a significant number of composers began reappraising the divergence of interests between the makers of twentieth-century concert music and its consumers. The modernist view had cast the rift as the inevitable consequence of historical circumstances. The postmodernist view saw it as a reversible choice. Reversing it meant re-adopting aspects of musical style, including consonant and functional ("tonal") harmony, that had been regarded by many musicians and critics—though never by audiences—as irrevocably outmoded. Both the historical legitimacy of the move and its motivation were in consequence widely suspected. The first reading below is the introductory essay by Jacob Druckman (1928–96), the New York Philharmonic Orchestra's composer-in-residence, to a 1983 festival (repeated in 1984) that put the term *new romanticism* on the musical map, and started the debate. The unfortunate gaffe at the end of the piece (misattributing and misquoting Shelley's "Ode to the West Wind") gave critics some easy ammunition, but the questions it raised proved durable.

Given the enormous profusion of different styles and aesthetics that abound in music today, we might be led to believe that the possibility of viewing its history as a succession of more or less conjunct periods is gone forever. There are even those who argue that the very notion of musical periods was always artificial, an invention of historians superimposed on a simple succession of individual voices. However, we have only to remember that expressions such as *Ars nova, Stile rappresentativo* and *Style galant* were contemporaneous with the music they described and represent their composers' recognition of major shifts in the musical thinking of the time.

The great burgeoning of musical talent in the nineteenth century created a modern tower of Babel and caused the almost total abandonment of the notion of common language. This has continued in our century, compounded by the increasing speed of communication of ideas, and has led to an ever increasing diversity and a constant acceleration of technical and aesthetic change.

Nonetheless, there is a steady underlying rhythm. Just as the surface of the seas can be agitated by storms and smoothed by doldrums while there is a cosmic tide that moves from one pole to another, undisturbed by momentary tempests, so there is a rhythm in the progress of the arts that moves from one pole to another. This great and steady shift seems to happen repeatedly between two distinctly different artistic climates. On the one hand there is the Apollonian, the Classical—logical, rational, chaste and explainable; and on the other hand, the Dionysian, the Romantic—sensual, mysterious, ecstatic, transcending the explainable.

That tide turned twice during the twentieth century. The first time was during the years immediately following the First World War. The most obvious example was Stravinsky, the composer of the savage and primal *Rite of Spring* and *Les Noces* who dismayed his new disciples by suddenly turning around and adapting the harmonies, gestures and forms of the early eighteenth century. The continued swing toward Neo-Classicism was obvious with most of the composers of the post–World War I generation.

During the mid-1960s the tide began to change. Even though new works and new ideas continue to pour out at break-neck speed, we can sense a gradual change of focus, of spirituality and of goals.

No matter how varied the surface of these musics, one can discern a steady re-emergence of those Dionysian qualities: sensuality, mystery, nostalgia, ecstasy, transcendency. Whether this new music will be called "Neo-Romantic" or some other term is yet to be seen, but whatever its name, it is this new music which is the subject of our festival.

There are many parallels to be drawn between the last two decades and the emergence of Romanticism in the 1830s and '40s. The strong but unfocused revolutionary spirit which gripped Europe in the post-Napoleonic years certainly seems to have been reflected in the student uprisings in the late 1960s in the United States, France and Germany. After the disappointments of the culmination of the "Age of Reason" in the nineteenth century and the post-war "cybernetic age" of the twentieth, there seem to have been parallel reachings out to a transcendent state that took many forms. In both centuries there was an intensification of interest in traditional religion as well as new or "exotic" spirituality; in drugs; in the unseen world. (Compare Coleridge and Poe in the nineteenth century with the flower-children of San Francisco in the twentieth; and the dream world of Berlioz's *Symphonie fantastique* with the hypnotic music of Terry Riley, Morton Subotnick or Steve Reich.)

One of the earliest signs of the new aesthetic in the 1960s was the music of the eastern European avant-garde. Krzysztof Penderecki, Witold Lutoslawski and György Ligeti were moving away from an intellectual orientation toward an acoustic sensuality. The poignant nostalgia of Luciano Berio's *Sinfonia* was a masterful example of the general tendency to reach backwards and forwards simultaneously. In Japan, Toru Takemitsu, and in the United States George Crumb and later Joseph Schwantner were leading us into a mysterious and fragrant garden of dreams. Even Stockhausen was talking about the "Age of Aquarius"!

On and on, so many examples—too many and too close to know where it's all heading. There are also many contradictions; but wherever we are going, we know we are in an era of fascinating change. Once again the scent of Byron's "Western Wind" is in the air.

Jacob Druckman, "Music since 1968: A New Romanticism?" *Horizons '83* (New York Philharmonic, June 1–14, 1983), souvenir program, 6–7.

> One of the most conspicuous new Romantics was David Del Tredici (1937–), who began his career as an academic serialist but won enormous public acclaim with a long series of pieces, many for amplified soprano and luscious hyper-Straussian orchestra, based on Lewis Carroll's "Alice" books, culminating (but not ending) in 1975 with a massive vocal-orchestral symphony called *Final Alice*. The first recording of *Final Alice* topped *Variety* magazine's classical sales charts for several weeks—an unprecedented success for a new work. From then on, interviews with Del Tredici inevitably focused on the charge of pandering, as in the excerpts below.

For me tonality was actually a daring discovery. I grew up in a climate in which, for a composer, only dissonance and atonality were acceptable. Right now, tonality is exciting for me. I think I invented it. In a sense, I have. When you're a composer, you've got to feel that, on some level, you're doing something for the first time. Maybe no one will agree, but *you* must feel that way.

About halfway through [*Final Alice*], I thought, "Oh my God, if I just leave it like this, my colleagues will think I'm crazy. But then I thought, "What else can I do? If nothing else occurs to me, I can't go against my instincts." But I was *terrified* my colleagues would think I was an idiot. People think now that I wanted to be tonal and have a big audience. But that was just not true. I *didn't* want to be tonal. My world was my colleagues—my composing friends. The success of *Final Alice* was very defining as to who my real friends were. I think many composers regard success as a threat. It's really better, they think, if *nobody* has any success, to be all in one boat.

I used to play the complete first draft of *Final Alice* just one time each day and then would consider my response: where was it dull, illogical, too much, too little? My *immediate* response was all I valued. I wanted to hear the piece as, eventually, the audience would—once through, without preparation. This aspect of composing is frustrating. So much depends on instinct, the untamable thing, and on proportion, the elusive thing.

Composers now are beginning to realize that if a piece excites an audience, *that doesn't mean it's terrible.* For my generation, it is considered vulgar to have an audience really, *really* like a piece on a first hearing. But why are we writing music except to move people and to be expressive? To have what has moved us move somebody else? Everything is reversed today. If a piece appeals immediately, sensuously, if an audience likes it: all those are "bad things." It is really very *Alice in Wonderland.*

David Del Tredici, interviewed by John Rockwell, in *All American Music: Composition in the Late Twentieth Century* (New York: Alfred A. Knopf, 1983), 77, 82–83; third paragraph from Paul Moravec, "An Interview with David Del Tredici," *Contemporary Music Review,* VI, no. 2 (1992), 21.

> Del Tredici's frank acknowledgment that he adopted the audience's perspective when judging his own work identified the main issue that divided new Romantics from traditional modernists, who could not accept such a community of interests as genuine. In the reading that follows, Matthias Kriesberg, a composer who is actually considerably younger than either Druckman or Del Tredici, impugns their "populist" or "neo-conservative" stance as evidence of false consciousness, seeing the proper source of support for serious music not in the audience as such (unqualified to judge), or in public funding (tainted by totalitarian abuse), but in the time-honored traditions of private patronage. This was another sort of revivalism, perhaps, harking back to the spirit of a famous letter from Schoenberg to one of his patrons, Prince Max Egon von Fürstenberg, extolling the days when: "a prince stood as a protector before an artist, showing the rabble that art, a matter for princes, is beyond the judgment of common people." Meanwhile, despite Kriesberg's optimism, the populist tide has advanced. In 2006, Peter Gelb, the recording executive whose pronouncements come in for some mockery below, took over as general manager of the Metropolitan Opera.

One morning some 25 years ago, the composer Chou Wen-Chung regaled those of us in his music analysis class with reports of musical life in China. So pervasive was the application of Maoist doctrine, we were told, that music was written by committee. When a piece was completed, it was presented to the farmers' collective for criticism. We all had a good laugh. Now consider this sentence from an article by a composer formerly in residence at a top American orchestra, describing a response to a commission: "I walked through my community, knocking on doors, and asked people what sort of piece they would like." (Good thinking: this composer went to the farmers before writing the piece.)

I have often imagined my response if I had received that knock at my door: "You're the composer. You got the commission. Now go home and write the piece you believe in, and don't worry about what I expect." But to suggest today that writing music is about more than pleasing an audience is to commit the most horrific cultural crime of the late, late 20th century: "elitism." There is broad agreement across the political spectrum: wisdom resides in the will of the people. Granted, our embrace of the collective philosophy we used to mock has a new twist; yesterday's masses are today's marketplace. And since the power of the market is the flip side of democracy, you can't challenge one without ostensibly opposing the other. So even contemporary classical composition—not exactly in the mainstream of everyday life—becomes validated in proportion to the number of people served.

Partisans of accessibility flaunt their righteous anger. Some weeks ago, Peter Gelb, the president of Sony Classical, made the perfectly reasonable case that he has a fiduciary obligation to his company to issue recordings that are likely to make a profit, and that he is entitled to advocate the music he believes in. Then he declared, "Serialism will have to start sharing space on concert hall programs with new music of broader appeal." It is telling that this "liberating" musical style is defined by audience response rather than in musical terms. The old new music, we are told, disdained the audience; the new new music does not. (For the record, the opposite is closer to the truth. The bad-old composers naively believed that audiences would eventually hear what the composer heard; the good-new accessibilists assume that audiences are unimaginative and impatient.)

What no one wants to acknowledge publicly is that the current stylistic evolution in contemporary classical music may have more to do with economic forces than with purely musical considerations. Here is part of a letter I received from someone in a position to know the state of mind of one of our prominent New Romantic composers: "His experience as composer-in-residence was an important matter. Once he found that if the conductor, the orchestra, the critics and the audience liked a piece, it was worth 30 or 40 thousand dollars a crack; he and his wife drove better cars. Isn't the long-term problem of every serious composer how to write music that satisfies oneself while making a living doing so?"

Actually, no. The trouble is, we are in love with two contradictory principles. One is that a composer should write music that flows unimpeded from his or her imagination. The other is that "user-friendly" products are superior. It is no accident that the last 20 years have seen an ever stronger demand that composers make their music more directly useful to the needs of the "community." In America today, authority and wealth are won by the endorsement or purchasing power of vast numbers of people. Our decision makers, even in the arts, increasingly come from the ranks of those who find popular success and intrinsic value indistinguishable, who consider successful marketing synonymous with freedom of expression. Uncomfortable with the uneasy fit of serious music into contemporary culture, they proclaim the need to redefine classical music.

Let's recall what drove a century of glorious achievement in painting and sculpture. A relatively small number of collectors followed their own taste and convictions and bought work they believed in. Painting and sculpture are tangible commodities, but the essential point is that artistic success was not achieved because millions of people purchased reproductions. Individuals with the ability to make a difference exercised creative artistic judgment. The same could happen with contemporary composition if even a few people of wealth, appreciating what was at stake, dedicated themselves to the future of serious music. The Los Angeles music patron Betty Freeman should serve as an inspiration to those able to wield the powerful combination of conviction and money. The key is engaging actively in the direct support of creative choices: not leaving to others the selection of composers to support. Only direct involvement will empower composers to resume a position of leadership in their profession.

And that's exactly what is going to happen. The triumph of popular judgment over the power of artistic worth cannot be sustained forever. Sooner or later, individuals of financial means will step forward out of profound dissatisfaction with our parade of new music and its split agenda: to be art and to be nice. The market economy that has obliged new music to conform to popular protocols has also generated nearly unimaginable wealth. It's a safe bet that some of that is in the hands of people who don't want all their music soft.

Matthias Kriesberg, "A Composer's Lament: The Music Goes Soft," *New York Times*, Arts and Leisure, 12 July 1998.

167

Technological Revolution

In July 2000, the American composer and critic Kyle Gann made the provocative claim (in a millennial essay for the *New York Times*) that the year 1983 marked the beginning of a new era in the history of music, a watershed in every way comparable to that marked by the introduction of music printing in 1500 or the invention of staff notation half a millennium before that. The epoch-making innovation was called MIDI, or Musical Instrument Digital Interface, a universal protocol making all electronic sound synthesis devices mutually adaptable, and allowing personal computers to control both electronic and traditional acoustical instruments. It brought to an end the period during which "electronic music" meant something altogether distinct and discrete (and peripheral), it brought pop music into the electronic field in a big way, and it presaged a postliterate future for music, in which notation would no longer be needed for advanced composition. It was an enormous vindication of the faith that a hardy breed of composers and technicians had been placing in computers as a creative tool for music for two lonely decades. While it is obviously far too early to assess the accuracy of epochal claims, the importance and (arguably) the predominance of computer music in early twenty-first-century composition is an established fact. Below are two important documents in its early history. The first is the article, by Max V. Mathews (1926–), an engineer at Bell Telephone Laboratories in Summit, New Jersey, that first brought the musical possibilities of the digital computer to the attention of the scientific community. (The story between the lines: computer music was an offshoot of automation experiments at Bell Telephone, the primary objective of which was the replacement of human operators by machines with sound sensors and synthesized voices.)

With the aid of suitable output equipment, the numbers which a modern digital computer generates can be directly converted to sound waves. The process is completely general, and any perceivable sound can be so produced. This potentiality of the computer has been of considerable use at the Bell Telephone Laboratories in generating stimuli for experiments in the field of hearing, and for generating speech sounds and

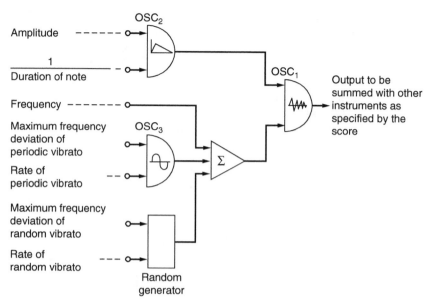

OSC₂

Amplitude

$\dfrac{1}{\text{Duration of note}}$

OSC₁

Output to be summed with other instruments as specified by the score

Frequency

Maximum frequency deviation of periodic vibrato

OSC₃

Rate of periodic vibrato

Σ

Maximum frequency deviation of random vibrato

Rate of random vibrato

Random generator

Schematic diagram of a typical instrument-unit in the computer orchestra. The diagram represents a section of the computer program. In order for the computer to produce a note, numerical values for the note parameters shown at the left of the diagram are stored in the program. The program then generates samples of the sound pressure wave form.

connected speech in investigations of the factors which contribute to the intelligibility and naturalness of speech.

The quality of sound is of great importance in two fields—that of speech and communication and that of music. Our studies at the Bell Laboratories in the first of these fields have led us, over the past few years, to related studies in the production of musical sounds and their organization into musical compositions. I believe that this by-product of our work on speech and hearing may be of considerable value in the world of music, and that further work in this direction will be of substantial value in furthering our understanding of psychoacoustics.

There are no theoretical limitations to the performance of the computer as a source of musical sounds, in contrast to the performance of ordinary instruments. At present, the range of computer music is limited principally by cost and by our knowledge of psychoacoustics. These limits are rapidly receding.

In addition to generating sound, the computer can also function as a machine for composing music. It can either compose pieces based entirely on random numbers generated by itself or it can cooperate with a human composer. It can play its own compositions.

How can the numbers with which a computer deals be converted into sounds the ear can hear? The most general conversion is based upon the use of the numbers as samples of the sound pressure wave. A sequence of numbers from the computer is put into an analog-to-digital converter, which generates a sequence of electric pulses whose amplitudes are proportional to the numbers. These pulses are smoothed with a filter and then converted to a sound wave by means of an ordinary loudspeaker. Intuitively, we feel that if a high enough pulse rate is used and the amplitudes of the pulses are generated with sufficient precision, then any sound wave can be closely approximated by this process. Mathematically, it has been established that this conclusion is correct. Computers deal with a finite number of digits and, hence, have limited accuracy. However, the computer limits are more than sufficient acoustically. For example, amplitudes represented by four-digit decimal numbers, are accurate to within 1 part in 10,000, an accuracy which represents a signal-to-noise ratio of 80 decibels; this is less noise than the ear can hear, and less noise than would be introduced by any audio equipment, such as the best tape recorder. The sampling process just described is theoretically unrestricted, but the generation of sound signals requires very high sampling rates.

The direct conversion of numbers to sound is only one of the ways in which the computer can generate sounds. An alternate procedure is to use the numbers from the computer to control electronic apparatus such as oscillators and filters, which, in turn, generate the sounds. This procedure has the advantage that a much lower rate of output is required from the computer, and hence the computation costs are less. The disadvantage is that the only sounds that can be generated are those produced by the particular electronic apparatus employed, and hence the generality of the sampling process is not attainable.

The central contribution of the Bell Telephone Laboratories to computer music is a program for computing the many samples in a note from the few parameters characterizing it. The program represents a compromise between a general procedure, through which any sound could be produced but which would require an inordinate amount of work on the part of the composer (for to specify individually 10,000 to 30,000 numbers for each second of music is inconceivable), and a very simple procedure, which would too greatly limit the range of musical sounds obtainable. Complexity of the instrument-unit is paid for both in terms of computer time and in terms of the number of parameters the composer must supply for each note. In general, the complicated instrument-units produce the most interesting sounds, and the composer must make his own compromise between interest, cost, and work.

An outstanding advantage is the precision of the computer. Effects are exactly reproducible. The computer is also very flexible. When sufficient effort has been expended in supplying specifications for the instrument-unit, almost any sound effect can be produced, provided the wave form of the sound can be described. It is very easy to use the computer in this way. The electronic equipment (computer and output equipment) has been constructed once and for all. There are no soldering irons, tape-splicings, or even knob-twistings involved, as there are with other electronic equipment for producing music. No manual dexterity is required. Instead, one writes down and gives the computer a sequence of numbers.

The most apparent limitation in the field of computer music results from lack of adequate knowledge of the sound of a given pressure wave. The computer sounds are described in terms of the waveshapes produced by the unit generators in the instrument-units. This method for describing sound is quite different from the method of ordinary music, in which the sound is specified by the instrument which produces it, when certain instructions have been received by the performer. Musicians have had a great deal of experience in listening to the sounds produced by violins, oboes, horns, and other instruments and are well able to predict the contribution of these instruments to the total sound. By comparison, computer musicians have had very little experience in trying to predict the effect of a given harmonic-composition factor or a given attack-and-decay function on the timbre of a note.

Our experience has shown how little we now know about the relation of the quality of sound to various features of waveform. A new body of psychoacoustic data is necessary. These data should relate the properties of the acoustic waves of music to perceived qualities of sound. Part of the task of assembling these data can, of course, be given to the composer, and part of the data can be supplied by interested psychologists. An increase in knowledge in this field is bound to be of value and interest in other fields, including those of speech and hearing.

So far I have described use of the computer solely as a musical instrument. The composer writes one line of parameters for each note he wishes played and hence has complete control of the note. He is omnipotent, except for lack of control over the noise produced by the random-number unit generators. Here a minor liberty is allowed the computer.

However, composing-programs are a reasonable area of computation, and work in this direction has already been done. A number of different approaches can be taken toward composition by computer. At one extreme, the computer can be given a set of rules, plus a random-number generator, and can simply be turned on to generate any amount of music. The work of Lejaren Hiller [1924–94] at the University of Illinois [with programs specifying the rules of first-species modal counterpoint or of twelve-tone composition, among other simple systems] is perhaps closest to this extreme. In the opposite direction, the human composer can maintain close control of the music, using the computer merely to avoid some of the repetitious and tedious work involved in representing his musical ideas. At present, the music-playing program has been modified so as to make transformational development of a theme possible.

A slightly different method has been tried by James C . Tenney [1934–2006] at Bell Labs. His approach is a compromise between a purely random and a completely specified composition. The parameters of the individual notes of the composition are generated as a sequence of independent random numbers by a random-number routine. However, the average value and the variance of these parameters are specified by the composer as functions which change slowly throughout the composition. By this relatively simple algorithm, a long-range structure which can be clearly recognized by the ear is imposed on the composition.

Computer music appears to be very promising technically. However, the method will become significant only if it is used by serious composers. At present, our goal is to interest and educate such musicians in its use. We believe that competent work in the field can benefit not only music but the whole field of psychoacoustics.

Max V. Mathews, "The Digital Computer as a Musical Instrument," *Science*, vol. 142, no. 3592 (1 November 1963), 553–57.

A memoir by Paul Lansky (1944–), a composer who first studied then taught computer music at Princeton University, gives a vividly human idea of what Mathews, above, somewhat dispassionately called the ever-challenging, ever-improving ratio of "interest, cost and work." Enduring the hardships of pioneer life as a member of the latest (and perhaps the last) generation of explorers of genuinely virgin territory for music was something perhaps more enjoyable to look back on from the vantage point of eventual accomplishment than it was to negotiate in real time. Indeed, a bit of forgivable nostalgia for the character-building hard times of old, not uncommon in such recollections, seems to creep in toward the end of our excerpt.

On the face of it, computer music has always seemed like a great idea. On the first day of his computer music course at Princeton in 1966, Godfrey Winham said, with his usual aplomb, "The computer can create any sound you can describe." I was there, partially out of curiosity, partially out of interest, and partially because the graduate adviser twisted my arm, but I wasn't prepared for this degree of futureshock. I quickly learned, however, that there were two large "gotchas" in this statement. The sounds I subsequently "described" were pretty lame—far from what I had in mind—and my relations with the computer consisted of waiting in line to feed a noisy card reader a deck consisting of at least 40 IBM JCL cards, some instrument definitions written in BEFAP, and a bunch of data cards: an "offering" to the big blue IBM 7094 whirling noisily away in the next room. To add insult to injury, I had to come back the next day, fill out a form to remove a digital tape and then drive forty miles to Max Mathews's lab at Bell Labs to hear my feeble efforts. Fortunately there was a great ice cream stop on the way back where I drowned my sorrows in a double-scoop cone. But still, the initial vision never disappeared. We knew somehow that we would get better at "describing sound" even if we had to learn multi-variable calculus (Godfrey did), and that machines would get faster and friendlier. Also, composers such as J. K. Randall and John Chowning were producing some good pieces.

The seventies were a little better. The machines got faster, we now only had to walk across the street with a digital tape; some very interesting things were happening in science and engineering which were giving us new insights into the nature of sound and into the ways in which we might learn to become better at describing it. Milton Babbitt came back from a trip to Stanford in 1973 with rave reviews about a new technique using frequency modulation. And Godfrey and Ken Steiglitz were already beginning to get some interesting results using Linear Predictive Coding for speech synthesis. But still, it was a struggle. Princeton was beginning to put more money into computers. We all were quite pleased when we got an extra megabyte of memory for the IBM 360/91, even though it reportedly cost $1 million! And, though some fancy administrative footwork, the Music Department became the largest non-sponsored user of computer time in the university. We had to learn HP and DEC assembler in order to hear the fruits of our labors. Barry Vercoe showed up and wrote Music 360, which made things a lot easier. And we struggled on, mainly because it seemed like such a good idea, and also because people were getting interesting pieces done. But it was a struggle. We were consoled in our misery when we learned that the guys at Stanford had to get up early in the morning to get to their machines, and we were encouraged when Barry, now at MIT, showed it was possible to do powerful things with minicomputers. The cost seemed to be going down significantly. By 1979 you could probably get a good computer-music studio for $250,000, if you could raise it. Sound hardware was generally custom made, as ours was, and you had to make sure that the guy building it was happy and wasn't about to go off to a commune or to Brazil on vacation. (The engineers we got to work for us were usually more free spirits than nine-to-five types.) But, it still seemed like such a good idea.

In the eighties things started to look even better. Soon we weren't forced to carry tapes, and could actually start to have a degree of reasonableness in our relations with our machines which approached that which we saw our colleagues in the sciences take for granted. Money was always the big problem, but somehow we managed to find it here or there and make things happen. Now we could write in C and LISP under UNIX, and kiss JCL and FORTRAN goodbye. IRCAM [Pierre Boulez's lavishly endowed computer music center in Paris] got underway, and Robert Gross showed us that we could "almost" do computer music without having to use unmounted file systems. UNIX then became a reasonable environment for hearing sound as well as tinkering with it. It was still a struggle, but we kept having glimpses of the possibility that something that was such a good idea would also eventually become a reasonable thing to do. It was also becoming clearer that Godfrey's original supposition was a lot more interesting and complex than we had suspected.

Then along came MIDI! No doubt about it, a great and revolutionary accomplishment. This really created a democratization of computer music in which it was no longer solely the domain of wealthy institutions and professors who could devote years to mastering its intricacies. Yamaha showed us that industry could get its act together a lot more quickly than we could when it came to packaging and functionality. The DX7 is still a marvel of engineering. Those of us who had sweated with software realized quite quickly that to get ninety-six oscillators singing in real time at 50kHz sampling rate, and for less than two thousand dollars, was no trivial accomplishment. And the Macintosh really blew us away. One could only admire this cute little machine that you could lift with one hand and take with you anywhere, that could give you intimate control over those ninety-six oscillators.... I don't think anyone can really appreciate the meaning of this unless they have spent six months getting a PDP11 to go "beep." I still marvel when I am able to open a factory-sealed box and get sound out within twenty minutes.

But there was something wrong. The original vision had gotten cloudy. First of all, things began to happen much too quickly. New machines and software began to emerge so rapidly that the entire field seemed to go into "demonstration mode." The techno-chatter always seemed to consist of terms such as "and now you can ...," or "then it will be possible to ...," or "did you hear about the new...." Very rarely would you hear "let me show you what I've done." Just as one started to learn how to get along without the factory presets, or master some commercial software, a new generation would come along and the learning process would begin all over. In the earlier days I had often told myself and my students that learning to "play" the computer was not unlike learning to play any other instrument. It took a few years in order to start to get returns on your investment of time and tears. Just as you couldn't really expect to make Chopin speak in his native tongue for a few years on the piano, so too on the computer it would take a while before your interactions with the machine began to feel like something other than beating your head against a stone wall. But now it became axiomatic that "real-time" was the ultimate goal, and you made whatever sacrifices were necessary in order to approach this musical zero. The time spent beating your head against the machine was no longer there. Within hours you could be making musical fireworks.

What is troubling is that what is lost by eliminating this frustration is the process in which one develops musically idiosyncratic concepts slowly and over a period of time. Essentially you now take a short-cut and intervene at a much later point. But, the intervention is made by adopting someone else's musical head through machine mediation. This in itself is potentially quite interesting, but it is dangerous to confuse it with original invention. It is a logical consequence of the ability we now have to imbue software with musical intention, whether by design, architecture, or malice aforethought. But what has been happening all too often is that the designers fail to see the extent to which their efforts are musically biased and make claims of universality which are naïve and presumptuous.

I'm not trying to suggest that inefficiency and struggle are necessary for artistic development, but I am saying that the way to higher levels of accomplishment has something to do with being able to take a firm controlling hand over the design of your workshop. What was, and still is, exciting about MIDI is the extent to which a vast number of new people got involved, and often with extraordinary passion and fervor.

Also, a lot of issues relating to performance problems, improvisation, human-machine interaction, artificial intelligence, notation, and so on, could be explored with great ease, and often with no more than a simple synthesizer and a Macintosh. No doubt about it, this is revolutionary, and will have a profound impact on our musical culture and future. But there is a lot about it that clouds the vision and beauty of the computer as the ultimate music machine. To those of us who had a glimpse of the real potential behind this "instrument of the imagination," MIDI seemed to be saying: "Sure, it was a good idea, but you have to accept the fact that it will never be a reasonable one. Accept the limitations and do it my way." The implication was that it was generally foolish to use software generation of sound, because processors, memory, and storage devices were just not capable of satisfying the demands of this activity. To my mind, this kind of bargain-basement thinking is not the way to advance knowledge.

Which brings us to the doorstep of the nineties. The motivation behind this aching prolog is to describe some preliminary impressions of a machine which, I feel, can and will revive the original vision of the computer as the ultimate music machine while at the same time continuing the democratization of computer music begun by MIDI. This machine is, of course ...

Paul Lansky, "It's About Time: Some NeXT Perspectives (Part One)," *Perspectives of New Music*, vol. 27, no. 2 (Summer 1989), 270–74.

168

Postmodernist Paradigms

Vagaries in the politics of style—the relative prestige enjoyed by various practices, the influence exerted by various practitioners—will typically look to practitioners like a response to what Stravinsky called "an irresistible pull within the art," and secondarily, perhaps, to the interaction of strong personalities. Cultural historians also look for paradigms or what the French philosopher Michel Foucault (1926–84) called *epistemes:* the assumptions, usually unspoken (but, when things become unsettled, more likely to be articulated) that govern notions of what is "self-evidently" true. Foucault called the bringing of such things to light the "archeology of knowledge." The ferment surrounding the styles and ideas broached in the last half-dozen readings did bring a couple of modernist epistemes up to fully articulated consciousness. One was the assumption that the arts, like the sciences, progress toward ever-greater perfection (or, at least, ever-greater complexity), and the other was that the intelligibility of musical utterances varies simply and directly with their relative familiarity. According to the first principle, the general state of the arts is defined by their most advanced practitioners, and so the artists using the most novel and esoteric techniques are the most significant and authentic artists at any given time. It is curious that this assumption held as fast as it did in the realm of music history despite the fact that some of the most iconic figures in that history—Bach and Brahms (two of the "three B's"), for example—were anything but technical or stylistic innovators. Their defenders had somehow to finesse this point with arguments that turned them into "progressives" after all (and no less a personage than Arnold Schoenberg performed the task for

Brahms, with a famous essay, published in 1945, called "Brahms the Progressive"). This teleological interpretation of stylistic evolution came under increasingly explicit attack beginning in the 1970s. One of the most effective tactics was to argue not only that it fit the facts of history poorly, but that even on the theoretical plane it had been misconceived because it fundamentally misread the implications of Darwinist evolutionary theory. A characteristic statement of this kind was a fairly lengthy essay (from which we have excerpted two sections) by Scott Johnson (1952–), an American composer interested, like many American composers, in exploring the new relationship between elite genres and popular culture. Johnson's anti-utopian, anti-purist thesis is that a view of style history that sees it as a wholly vertical transmission ignores the true cultural situation of the late twentieth century, in which the vertical is strongly contaminated by horizontal or lateral influences. Style, in other words, is no longer merely an inheritance from one's immediate predecessors (if indeed it ever was that) but rather a response to a vast if not unlimited range of historical and geographical stimuli available via modern communications media; and the validity of styles is something audiences, not historians, decide. The essay's title, "The Counterpoint of Species," gets the idea across by playing cleverly both on "species counterpoint" (known to all music theory students as a method for teaching the rules of sixteenth-century polyphony) and on "The Origin of Species," the title of Darwin's classic exposition of evolutionary theory (1859).

Naming and defining the generations born since World War II has become a popular pastime in recent years, but one feature remains constant. Every group has come of age in a society which acknowledges the Western art music tradition with an increasingly faint and uncertain voice, and which has little use for the composers who are the living offshoots of that tradition. While our indigenous popular musics thrive, the vast majority of educated Americans cannot name a living composer, and most of those who can are likely to know only one or two individuals who emblematically stand for a concept of serious music, in the way that one famous singer can stand for all opera. Composers and their millions of non-listeners alike seem to agree that there is little in common between an elaborately notated piece of music in the European tradition, and a popular piece in which the decisions of band-members, arrangers, or producers flesh out the details left open by the songwriter's art. But during the 1990s, the corrosive side effects of the isolation and near-sacralization of art music became apparent even to those who had not seen the trouble coming. It's no longer unusual to hear academic thinkers or the directors of major classical music institutions soberly acknowledging that the transplanted European tradition of serious music has run into serious problems adapting to the American climate.

At the heart of this *fin de siècle* crisis lies the very set of ideas which provided a solution to the last one. As musical modernism gathered force, the explanatory power of Darwinism and the unprecedented achievements of science and technology combined to create an atmosphere charged with an animating belief in the inevitable march of progress. With both Marxism and Freudianism contributing variations on an underlying theme of the malleability of human nature, the big question was "Why not?" But at the other end of the century, music is not the only field where exaggerated utopian desires have created unforeseen and unwanted side effects. The visionary modernist impulse is now paying the price for its misunderstanding of the nature of cultural evolution.

And yet the perception that there are similarities between cultural change and biological evolution is no mistake. The same basic mechanisms and accidents of evolution which have granted us our survival and the ability to communicate with each other are also at work within seemingly unnecessary "luxuries" like music. It is nearly impossible to listen to or study music for any length of time without noticing both the chains of imitation which link pieces and styles of music together, and the leaps of invention which set them apart. In making these simple observations, we have already identified two of the three classic preconditions for evolution: inheritance and variation. Now off we go to a concert; choose any kind of music, in which we can hear any particular interplay of inheritance and invention. Each decision that you or I make between applauding, not applauding, or leaving the room transforms us briefly into minor ecological forces, making a judgment about relative fitness. At this point all of the Darwinian requirements have been fully met: 1) inheritance, in the style of music; 2) variation, from the personal expression of the musicians or composers; and 3) differential success among the variants, from the assessment that we voted with our palms. "Fitness" is a far more slippery concept in culture than in nature, but in either case it is meaningful only within a particular context or environment. An obscure composer is as "fit" within a hushed roomful of devotees as a popular icon is in the roar of a stadium concert; but that roomful should be cautious about claiming to represent their civilization, rather than merely themselves. And so I'll leave fitness to sort itself out and concentrate on questions of inheritance and variation, which are more interesting and fruitful for the light they throw inward to the workings of musical minds, and outward towards the differences between human beings and the rest of the natural world.

A failure to recognize one of these differences has played a part in leading serious music to its current insignificance in the culture at large. Nature enforces an uncompromising linear purism upon its creatures, because they cannot interbreed with distantly related species. But in the world of ideas, hybridism and cultural cross-pollination play a huge role. Stylistic hybridization has received a very bad press during the second half of the 20th century, and serious music's gradual retreat from its position of importance within 19th-century culture has been marked by bouts of purist fervor from classicists and avant-gardists alike. Both reflect a need to reduce an increasingly complex world to the more manageable proportions of a story, whether one of a golden age lost, or of progress toward some "higher" state; and both stories insist on rejecting the distracting influence of popular vernaculars. The inertia of such monastic attitudes is ample, and even now the sometimes gleefully messy melting pot of the avant-garde community succumbs to occasional fussy fits of house-cleaning.

Our desire for surprise and novelty is balanced against our limited time and energy, and the need to filter the world and focus our attention. Social loyalties which stigmatize influences from less respected sources are one of these filters. Another is that old enemy of avant-gardism, the suspicion that something which is not immediately understood is either a hoax or inept. These conservative and skeptical tendencies are analogous to the body's immune system. They provide social stability, as well as a cast of villains.

But genre definitions are more than artificial constructs, because people do voluntarily sort themselves into predefined categories. The Western classical tradition was so successful at binding together a fairly large group of cultures within a fairly consistent set of practices that it is easy to forget that it began its recorded life as a patchwork of regional styles and segregated genres, with strong feelings about the religious qualities of the human voice, and powerful taboos about when and where and within what style or technique it was appropriate to blend them with instruments. If we think of our own preconceptions about the proper place for saxophones or electric guitars, it is not difficult to imagine what such social conventions might have felt like. The assembly of a common practice was accomplished through gradual and successive transgressions against common sense, which decreed that this technique or sonority does not belong with that one. Much of this could be accomplished by Trojan Horse incursions: "barbarous" Turkish percussion, imported into Viennese classical pieces for sound color and cultural references, gradually lost its exotic connotations and gained a new European one. The ultimate success of these constant borrowings and appropriations depended on a balance between a willingness to accept outside influences and redefine native ones, and the presence of a solid-enough core of common practice to lend structure and to suggest uses for imported material.

Composers like Ravel, Milhaud, or Stravinsky, who participated in the spread of jazz-influenced pieces during the 1920s and '30s didn't get their jazz at all right, but they were not really trying to do that, for it would have required improvisation. They were only making a picture of their surroundings. Since that time the 20th century was filled with messages sent between the European classical tradition and jazz, as populist as Duke Ellington or Leonard Bernstein, or as arcane as Gunther Schuller or Anthony Braxton. But jazz and classical practices have rarely fused in equal parts, and the primary background of each of these composers is usually one or the other. Why has the territory between them, which has been explored so many times from so many angles, been so difficult to settle permanently? The clearest reasons are as much procedural as esthetic: the different skill sets involved in composing and improvising, and the lack of a common practice.

But if we step back and think about the convergence of lineages, we can imagine a sort of sliding scale mediating the practicality of influences, based on the relative complexity of the two genres involved, and the relative ambitions of a given merger. A 50/50 cross-pollination from two complex fields, such as the jazz and classical traditions, is the most ambitious and the most risky of all, as would be a hypothetical convergence of Japanese *gagaku* and Hindustani classical music. But compositions incorporating a more modest influence, we'll say 20/80, are so common in the modern world that failure to recognize their existence flatly contradicts experience. The distaste for eclecticism that continues to bedevil modernism contributes to its cultural isolation.

Rock doesn't put up the same resistance to assimilation into modern post-classical composition that jazz does. Thanks to the very simplicity which excites so much highbrow scorn, rock might offer to the serious music world a relationship which could conceivably become similar to the long-lost relationship that the European tradition once had with its local folk musics. And yet new serious music incorporating rock arrives with a whole new set of electric instruments, technologies, and timbres in tow; and its prolonged success would mean enormous changes in the sound and production of serious music.

Still, over time these differences may not matter very much. To make a simple picture: if a generation of pieces influenced by a previous 20/80 merger engages in another 20/80 merger, their descendents' share of the "pure" heritage is down to 36/64. The next 20/80 change leaves 48.8/51.2, and thus successive approximation has landed us in a 50/50 territory by another route. Obviously these arbitrary numbers are inadequate to describe the unpredictable eddies of nuance where personality touches culturally shared style, but they do draw an outline of the sort of process which alters a living genre. Just as 20th-century percussion pieces can in some way trace their genesis back to the Turkish military incursions into Austria, then so might a future form spring from the borrowings, novelties, or heresies of our day, in a way that is not now foreseeable.

This is not to say that most hybrid mutations won't perish without establishing a lineage. The more distant the leap, the higher the mortality rate is likely to be. But lateral dispersal is inevitable in a complex culture, and inheritance by direct lineage alone is increasingly unlikely. The possibility of lateral dispersion on a truly global plane has radically increased as travel and communication have become easier and more routine.

Scott Johnson, "The Counterpoint of Species," in John Zorn (ed.), *Arcana: Musicians on Music* (New York: Granary Books, 2000), 18–23, 34–40.

The question of what evolutionary model provides the best explanations was also debated within the history of science. In *The Structure of Scientific Revolutions* (1962), Thomas Kuhn argued that not even in the hard sciences is progress steady or linear, but rather proceeds in lurches, when a prevailing paradigm comes up against problems that "normal science" cannot solve. The social costs of stylistic progress produced a crisis of that sort in the arts—and especially music, which does not produce artifacts like paintings that can be individually owned and for that reason command large sums. A comparable crux or crisis was created when old predictions about the assimilability of modernist styles (e.g., Webern: "one day the postman will whistle my tunes") seemed, after a decent interval had passed, to be failing. The ensuing debate resembled one that was going on simultaneously in cognitive psychology and linguistics, between behaviorists like B. F. Skinner, who considered the mind to be a *tabula rasa* on which any kind of information could be inscribed through habituation, and structuralists like Noam Chomsky, who argued that the mind had its own innate structure, and that certain cognitive predispositions, being natural, were not modifiable by habit. Fred Lerdahl (1943–), a composer and music theorist, proposed (at first in collaboration with Ray Jackendoff, a linguist in the Chomskian camp) that the theoretical premises of serial music—its "compositional grammar," as Lerdahl and Jackendoff called it—might be incompatible with the information-processing capabilities of listeners (the "listening grammar") and so might be perceptually opaque, no matter how conceptually elegant. In a much-discussed essay of 1988, the concluding portion of which is given below, Lerdahl broached the most highly fraught of all the questions his theory raised: to wit, its aesthetic implications.

Comprehensibility and Value

There is no obvious relationship between the comprehensibility of a piece and its value. Many masterpieces are esoteric, while most ephemeral music is all too comprehensible. On the other hand, if a piece cannot be understood, how can it be good? Most would agree that comprehensibility is a necessary if not sufficient condition for value.

Care must be taken with this formulation in three respects. First, comprehension presupposes listening competence for the music in question. This competence varies with ability and especially with exposure, but is not less real for that. Second, comprehension pertains to the listening grammar rather than to the compositional grammar. A serial piece may be understood in non-serial ways. Third, we are talking about intuitive rather than analytic comprehension. Along the lines of Jerry Fodor's book, *The Modularity of Mind* (MIT Press, 1983), the mind's music module must be able spontaneously to form mental representations of musical structure from musical surfaces. This is quite different from using the all-purpose reasoning faculty to figure out the structure of a piece.

With these provisos in mind, I think the above formulation stands. Appreciation depends on cognition. I now want to go an aesthetic step further.

Aesthetic Claim 1: The best music utilizes the full potential of our cognitive resources.

This seemingly innocuous statement carries weight because a great deal is becoming known about how musical cognition works. I have outlined aspects of this understanding in the form of seventeen "cognitive constraints on compositional systems," which must be observed if a "compositional grammar"—a set of rules governing the organization of musical information—is to be congruent with "listening grammar," the cognitive realities governing the mental processing of musical information. Following them will not guarantee quality. I maintain only that following them will lead to cognitively transparent musical surfaces, and that this is in itself a positive value; and, conversely, that not following them will lead in varying degrees to cognitively opaque surfaces, and that this is in itself a negative value.

This stance can be refined through the notion of musical "complexity," which is to be contrasted with musical "complicatedness." A musical surface is complicated if it has numerous non-redundant events per unit time. Complexity refers not to musical surfaces but to the richness of the structures inferred from surfaces and to the richness of their (unconscious) derivation by the listener. For example, a grouping structure is complex if it is deeply embedded and reveals structural patterns within and across levels.

The derivation of such a structure is complex if all the grouping preference rules come into play and if they conflict with one another to a certain degree. (Total reinforcement of the rules would produce a stereotypical grouping structure; total conflict would create intolerable ambiguity.) I take complicatedness to be a neutral value and complexity to be a positive one. Many musical surfaces meet the various constraints, but only those that lead to complexity employ "the full potential of our cognitive resources."

All sorts of music satisfy these criteria—for example, Indian raga, Japanese koto, jazz, and most Western art music. Balinese gamelan falls short with respect to its primitive pitch space. Rock music fails on grounds of insufficient complexity. Much contemporary music pursues complicatedness as compensation for a lack of complexity. In short, these criteria allow for infinite variety, but only along certain lines.

I find this conclusion both exciting and—initially, at least—alarming. It is exciting because psychology really does have something substantive to say about how music might be; here is the foundation I was seeking. It is alarming because the constraints are tighter than I had bargained for. Like the old avant-gardists, I dream of the breath of other planets.* Yet my argument has led from pitch hierarchies (Constraints 7–8) to an ap-

---

*An allusion to the opening line of Stefan George's poem, "Entrückung"—*Ich fühle Luft von anderen Planeten,* "I feel the air of another planet"—which Arnold Schoenberg set in 1908 as the final movement of his Second String Quartet, op. 10, in which a soprano soloist joins the instrumental ensemble (thus alluding to a famous earlier step along the "progressivist" path, when Beethoven added voices to a traditionally instrumental genre in the finale of his Ninth Symphony, a move previously celebrated by Wagner; see p. 324).

proximation of pure intervals (Constraint 12), to diatonic scales and the circle of fifths (Constraint 14), and to a pitch space that prominently includes triads (Constraint 17).

However, the constraints do not prescribe outworn styles. Rather they provide a prototype, along lines indicated by Eleanor Rosch in her well-known article, "Cognitive Reference Points" (*Cognitive Psychology* VII [1975], 532–47). Let me give an uncontroversial rhythmic example. A musical surface in which the note values are multiples of 2 is intrinsically more stable and easier to cognize than one in which the note values are multiples of 7 and 11. This does not mean that the latter surface is somehow impermissible. It instead amounts to the observation that, because of the resultant ease in forming a metrical structure, note values that are multiples of smaller prime numbers are easier to process and remember, and therefore that multiples of 2 (or 3) inevitably remain a cognitive reference point for more complicated rhythms. I claim that a similar situation holds for pitch: a structure hierarchically organized around the octave, fifth, triad, and diatonic scale remains a reference point for other kinds of pitch organization, not because of its cultural ubiquity but because it incorporates all of the constraints that govern listening grammars. I take this as a given, with or against which a composer can play creatively. Of course one may opt for a less constrained pitch space. But if a composer chooses the space described above, I am sure there are innumerable and radically new ways to use and extend it. The future is open.

My second aesthetic step has already been implied. I list it here only for the sake of completeness.

Aesthetic Claim 2: The best music arises from an alliance of a compositional grammar with the listening grammar.

This claim does not exclude the artifice hidden in a Bach fugue or a Brahms intermezzo. Such artifice is rooted in the bedrock of a "natural" compositional grammar. At our present musical juncture, however, composers would do well to heed the claim.

This claim carries with it a historical implication. The avant-gardists from Wagner to Boulez thought of music in terms of a "progressivist" philosophy of history: a new work achieved value by its supposed role *en route* to a better (or at least more sophisticated) future. My second aesthetic claim in effect rejects this attitude in favor of the older view that music-making should be based on "nature." For the ancients, nature may have resided in the music of the spheres, but for us it lies in the musical mind. I think the music of the future will emerge less from twentieth-century progressivist aesthetics than from newly acquired knowledge of the structure of musical perception and cognition.

Fred Lerdahl, "Cognitive Constraints on Compositional Systems," in John A. Sloboda (ed.), *Generative Processes in Music* (Oxford University Press, 1988). Reprinted in *Contemporary Music Review*, VI, no. 2 (1992), 97–121. The present extract (appearing on pp. 118–120) has been slightly adapted for the sake of self-sufficiency.

Although Lerdahl stipulated that his aim was descriptive, he was—perhaps inevitably—accused of concealing a prescriptive agenda. The following is an extract from a response to Lerdahl's essay by James Boros (1958–), a composer and computer scientist, that vigorously reasserts the modernist paradigms Lerdahl (and, by implication, Johnson) had questioned, upholds nurture over nature as determinant of cognitive predispositions, and defends the rights of composers (which Lerdahl has denied ever having questioned) to compose as they wish. By invoking the work of Edward Said (1935–2003), a theorist of postcolonialism, Boros implies that politics—contests over power—lurks behind this (and every) ostensibly scientific debate.

We're currently witnessing disturbing efforts on the part of numerous (primarily American) composers and critics to reconstitute tonality as the single, central pillar of Western musical life. On the one hand, such grandiosity is easily dismissed: one need only think back as far as Boulez's laughably narrow-minded and short-sighted statement regarding the "uselessness" of "anyone who has not felt the necessity of the dodecaphonic language" in order to be reminded of the futility of artistic authoritarianism. On the other hand, given the sheer number of viable alternatives to tonality now in existence, one can't help but shudder at the prospect of their being forcibly subsumed within an "official" history in which, together, they are seen simply as an unfortunate "mistake," as a temporary derailment of the merrily rolling choo-choo of "progress."

The most troubling essay [of this kind], Fred Lerdahl's "Cognitive Constraints on Compositional Systems," participates in the fabrication of a lopsided history in which Western tonal music was somehow driven underground during the post–World War II years, only to boldly re-emerge from its "exile" in the present day, thanks to what is described as an irresistible, herd-like gravitation amongst composers everywhere, or what Lerdahl calls "the postmodern resurgence." He ends up making blanket statements—drastic, hideous simplifications which are in no way reflective of the delightful turmoil and uncertainty associated with the current state of cognitive investigation. At one point, he flatly states that "most of human cognition relies on hierarchical structuring." This is a gross misrepresentation: Lerdahl has overlooked or chosen to ignore (1) the fact that no one really knows how human cognition is structured, (2) the fact that when the neat, orderly hierarchies seen in textbooks are transferred to the "real world," they always (in the words of Marvin Minsky, the father of artificial intelligence research) "end up getting tangled and disorderly because there are exceptions and interactions to each classification scheme," and (3) the existence of a large, growing body of literature based on cognitive models in which, depending on the type of processing, hierarchical and nonhierarchical (i.e., network-based) representations may coexist. Things aren't as simple as Lerdahl would have us believe: as Roger Schank puts it, "the world is full of oddities and idiosyncratic events that fail to fit neatly into a pre-established hierarchy."

Even worse, Lerdahl's argument hinges on poorly defined notions of various sorts of "grammars." A "listening grammar" is defined as that which "generates mental representations of the music," and is depicted as a singular, static entity presumably employed by all listeners to a given piece, as if, regardless of differences in gender, ethnicity, cultural and social background, listening environment, and so on, we all listen the same way, each and every time. Lerdahl's major complaint about serial music is that he apparently perceives a lack of connection between this "listening grammar" and what he calls the "compositional grammar"; thus serial music is deemed "cognitively opaque" because listeners "do not hear tone rows," because they supposedly cannot hear "how a piece is serial" due to the "gap between compositional system and cognized result."

Thus, despite the existence of a growing body of theoretical and analytical literature whose goal is to in one way or another empower the listener, Lerdahl seems to be bent on enslaving the listener, who is expected to listen "correctly" by conforming to grammar-dictated conventions. The resulting hodge-podge amounts to a pharmaceutical prescription for composers, the sort of thing that enables the establishment of what Edward Said calls a "narrow circle of what is natural, appropriate, and valid for 'us.'" If it's easy to dismiss Lerdahl's stifling "constraints" as silly and having absolutely nothing to do with either artistic creation or the conditions necessary for its continuance, it's also easy to overlook the way in which he attempts to appropriate the hallmarks of scientific language in order to lend his essay a sheen of respectability. The danger, of course, is that readers may come to equate his opinions with scientific "truths" simply as a result of his carefully chosen method of presentation. As Said succinctly puts it in his *Culture and Imperialism,* "a text purporting to contain knowledge about something actual is not easily dismissed. Expertise is attributed to it. The authority of academics, institutions, and governments can accrue to it, surrounding it with still greater prestige than its practical successes warrant."

The moral smugness and consensus-oriented rhetoric that pervades [such] essays is, I believe, symptomatic of the recent trends about which Said and so many others warn us (and which should be of great interest to anyone concerned with issues of personal freedom), specifically those involving the rise of new types of centrist, conservative dogmas which are particularly seductive because they represent themselves as "the voice of the people," as emanating from the underdog. The prospect of being faced with a pendulum swing which alternately empowers those who shout "Tonality is dead!" and those who should "Atonality is dead!" is indeed an ugly one, not only because it stems from a "black-and-white" mentality which leaves out more than it includes, but also because, as Schoenberg clearly realized, neither method of composition precludes the use, let alone the existence, of the other.

James Boros, "A 'New Totality'?" *Perspectives of New Music,* XXXIII (1995), 538–48.

169

Feminist Perspectives

Broadly speaking, questions about the dominance or (to use the language of cultural studies) the hegemony of social groups in various social contexts have two sorts of answers. The essentialist view locates the causes of dominance in the nature of the groups; the social constructivist view locates them in the social structures and relations that govern the contexts. Male dominance in music composition attracted essentialist explanations (from everyone except women composers) until the 1970s, when the achievements of women composers began to seem normal (that is, unremarkable) as a result of greater equality of opportunity—the most conspicuous and lasting effect, within classical music, of the civil rights revolutions of the 1960s (which included, belatedly and secondarily, a movement toward what was then called "women's liberation"). In the first reading that follows, Pauline Oliveros (1932–), a Texas-born, California-bred composer who has made her mark chiefly in the realms of electro-acoustic music and group improvisation, asserted an early and still vigorous defense of feminine capability in music composition in an article, "And Don't Call Them 'Lady' Composers," solicited by the music editor of the *New York Times* in 1970. This effort at consciousness-raising attacks the hidden essentialism that inhabits the very framing of the familiar question Oliveros considers at the outset. Her argument is closely related to the one given by Betty Friedan in *The Feminine Mystique* (1963), one of the founding documents of modern feminism. Women have not competed successfully in realms of intellectual endeavor, this argument holds, not because of an inferior endowment but because of the way they have been socialized.

Why have there been no "great" women composers? The question is often asked. The answer is no mystery. In the past, talent, education, ability, interests, motivation were irrelevant because being female was a unique qualification for domestic work and for continual obedience to and dependence upon men.

This is no less true today. Women have been taught to despise activity outside of the domestic realm as unfeminine, just as men have been taught to despise domestic duties. For men, independence, mobility and creative action are imperative. Society has perpetuated an unnatural atmosphere which encourages distortions such as "girl" used as a bad word by little boys from the age of nine or ten. From infancy, boys are wrapped in blue blankets and continually directed against what is considered feminine activity. What kind of self-image can little girls have, then, with half their peers despising them because they have been discouraged from so-called masculine activity and wrapped in pink blankets?

The distortion continues when puberty arrives and boys turn to girls as sex objects but do not understand how to relate on other important levels. Consider the divorce rate! No matter what her achievements might be, when the time comes, a woman is expected to knuckle under, pay attention to her feminine duties and obediently follow her husband wherever his endeavor or inclination takes him—no matter how detrimental it might be to her own.

A well-known contemporary composer has a wife who is also a competent composer. They travel together extensively and often return to the same places for performances of his work. She is rarely if ever solicited for her own work and no one seems to see anything wrong with constantly ignoring her output while continually seeking out her husband's work.

Many critics and professors cannot refer to women who are also composers without using cute or condescending language. She is a "lady composer." Rightly, this expression is anathema to many self-respecting women composers. It effectively separates women's efforts from the mainstream. According to the *Dictionary of American Slang*, "lady" used in such a context is almost always insulting or sarcastic. What critic today speaks of a "gentleman composer"?

It is still true that unless she is super-excellent, the woman in music will always be subjugated, while men of the same or lesser talent will find places for themselves. It is not enough that a woman chooses to be a composer, conductor or to play instruments formerly played exclusively by men; she cannot escape being squashed in her efforts—if not directly, then by subtle and insidious exclusion by her male counterparts.

And yet some women do break through. The current Schwann catalog of classical recordings lists over one thousand different composers. Clara Schumann of the Romantic Period and Elisabeth Jacquet de la Guerre of the Baroque are the sole representatives for women composers of the past. But on the positive side, over seventy-five percent of those listed are composers of the present and twenty-four of these are women. These approximate statistics point to two happy trends: 1) that composers of our time are no longer ignored, and 2) that women could be emerging from musical subjugation.

The first of the two trends is developing even though the majority of performers do not include contemporary music in their repertoire and private teachers seldom encourage their students to try new music or even to become acquainted with their local composers. Agencies such as the Rockefeller and Ford Foundation have helped establish centers for new music in universities across the country, and independent organizations such as the Once Group of Ann Arbor and the San Francisco Tape Music Center promoted lively programs of new music throughout the nineteen-sixties. Isolated individual efforts throughout the country have gradually created an active new music network.

The second trend is, of course, dependent on the first because of the cultural deprivation of women in the past. Critics do a great deal of damage by wishing to discover "greatness." It does not matter that not all composers are great composers; it matters that this activity be encouraged among all the population, that we communicate with each other in non-destructive ways. Women composers are very often dismissed as minor or light-weight talents on the basis of one work by critics who have never examined their scores or waited for later developments.

Men do not have to commit sexual suicide in order to encourage their sisters in music. Libraries of women's music should be established. Women need to know what they can achieve. Critics can quit being cute and start studying scores. Near the beginning of this century, Nikola Tesla, electrical engineer and inventor of electrical power from alternating current, predicted that women will some day unleash their enormous creative potential and for a time will excel men in all fields because they have been so long dormant. Certainly the greatest problems of society will never be solved until an egalitarian atmosphere utilizing the total creative energies exists among all men and women.

Pauline Oliveros, "And Don't Call them 'Lady' Composers," *New York Times*, Arts and Leisure, 13 September 1970.

The progression noted in the following exchange between Frank Oteri, a composer, and Tom and Arnold Broido, the heads of Theodore Presser, a major American new-music publisher, carries a strong anti-essentialist implication. It is true that when Ellen Taafe Zwilich (1939–) became the first woman to win the Pulitzer Prize for musical composition in 1983, forty years after the prize was first awarded (to William Schuman [1910–92]) many assumed—that is, grumbled—that she had won *only* because of her gender (although no one had ever argued that a woman had failed to win *only* because of it). The double standard has diminished with repetition.

PRESSER: We're interested in the music. We're not interested in the derivation or the sex or the preferences of the composer. And it would be nice if society weren't interested, either. Woman, I think, is a word that should follow the word composer if it has to be there at all, in a sentence, rather than be in front of it.

OTERI: When Ellen Zwilich won the Pulitzer, it was the first time a woman had ever won the Prize, so that was a big part of the story, and then Shulamit Ran, [in 1991] as the second woman, that was part of the story, but Melinda Wagner [in 1999], I didn't see in any of the articles that I had read, "oh, a woman wins the Pulitzer Prize," because now that she was the third who had done it, I thought that was really great ...

PRESSER: Well, when Ellen did, Bill Schuman asked her, "How does it feel to be the first woman to win the Pulitzer Prize," and she asked him, "How did it feel to be the first man?" [laughs]

OTERI: I love that.

"The State of Music Publishing: Presser's Roster of Composers" (Frank J. Oteri interviewing Tom and Arnold Broido) *NewMusicBox* (American Music Center online magazine), http://lasso.euge.net/index.nmbx (posted 1 February 2000).

Nevertheless, essentialist arguments about feminine aptitude for musical composition have not been abandoned, nor are they invariably advanced invidiously. For example, the *New Grove Dictionary of Music and Musicians* (2nd edition, 2001) states that Pauline Oliveros's compositions "explore concepts such as the self as a non-autonomous entity and value qualities such as intuition commonly thought to be feminine." True, the article in question was written by Timothy D. Taylor, a man, yet Meredith Monk (1942–), one of the most highly respected women composers of the late twentieth century, did not hesitate to point out to an interviewer traits in her own music and her own attitudes that, in her view, distinguished her as a creative figure from her male counterparts.

Q: *How do you feel you relate to the Western musical tradition?*

A: I know there are people very concerned about where they fit into music history. But I would say that's a very male point of view, and it's not one of my big concerns. It's really more an appreciation of something that has gone before me.

Q: *Is that because men wrote that history and gave themselves the "best parts," or because you're not really interested in the concept of history?*

A: I'm very interested in the concept of history, but I think that history as it's presented to us at this point is relative. And it is *his*-story! It doesn't have too much about what women have done over the years, so I don't think it's complete. It is organized in a very linear fashion, so I haven't been able to identify with it that strongly.

Q: *An element of timelessness seems to run through your work. You manage to incorporate the past, present and future all at once. Your work has also been described as being at once "familiar yet foreign, primitive yet contemporary, serene yet alarming"—it's interesting how you manage to evoke all those feelings at the same time.*

A: Well, I always think of time in a circular way, so that the "now" also includes the past and the future. I try to make it so that the experience you have is of being as aware as possible of being here at this moment. But the moment must always include the past and the future for us to appreciate it fully. So I don't cut off roots or eliminate the forward motion of the future. We all have to think very seriously about what we're doing in society. I always think, "Is this useful"—and I think it *is* very useful to remind people of alertness, of aliveness, of seeing things anew, because that is something we lose so quickly. Being awake is difficult, but it is useful to human beings. That's what I've been trying to do. There was a time in the musical theater pieces when I thought the most useful thing was to present the "problem"—you know, what is "wrong." So I did pieces with very apocalyptic aspects. But for the last few years I've found it much more interesting to offer a behavioral alternative, as a kind of prototype, paradigm or template of what human behavior could be. That includes not only the way people are operating but also the energy exchange that can happen in that situation. I think that's really important because the exchange doesn't exist so much any more. The impulse now comes very much from secondary information, sitting at home and listening to a CD or watching movies. There's nothing wrong with that (I make films myself), but it's very important to fight for the "live" situation, for the exchange that happens and the individuality of each person in the audience.

Geoff Smith and Nicola Walker Smith, *New Voices: American Composers Talk about Their Music* (Portland, Ore.: Amadeus Press, 1995), 192–93.

If it is fair to characterize femininity in music in essential terms, then its opposite number should not be merely a default (or universal) position, but should bear traits of actual maleness. Some feminist critics have attempted such an analysis of the standard repertory as created by men. The most prominent such attempt, and perhaps the most ambitious one, is by Susan McClary (1946–), a Harvard-trained musicologist who has analyzed the tonal system of Western common practice from c. 1630 to c. 1900 as being essentially an expression of male sexuality, with a feminine counterweight only possible since (and as a part of) the postmodern, posthierarchical phase of music history.

The tonality that underlies Western concert music is strongly informed by a specific sort of erotic imagery. If music of earlier times presented models of stable order in keeping with the view of the world the Church and courts wished to maintain, music after the Renaissance most frequently appeals to libidinal appetites: during the historical period in which the legitimation of culture moved from the sacred to the secular realm, the "truth" that authorized musical culture became expressly tied to models of sexuality.

When composers of the seventeenth century first turned to the invention of erotic metaphors, they drew upon two distinctly different versions. On the one hand, there were images of pleasure—a quality of timeless, sustained hovering. This quality could be produced through the popular device of ostinato, in which each potential moment of closure is simultaneously the moment that guarantees continuation. The erotic obsessions of Monteverdi's nymph [in *Lamento della ninfa*, from the Eighth Book of Madrigals (1638)], of Purcell's Dido [in the opera *Dido and Aeneas* after Virgil (1689)], or the duet between Poppea and Nero at the conclusion of Monteverdi's *L'Incoronazione di Poppea* of 1643 ["Pur ti miro," now thought to be an interpolation by Francesco Sacrati (1605–50)] are the most celebrated examples of this device. A similar quality could be produced through carefully wrought modal ambiguities that deny the possibility or desirability of closure. Schütz's meditations on texts from the Song of Songs, such as "Anima mea liquefacta est" (*Symphoniae sacrae II* [1647]), create pitch-worlds in which the point is to prolong a kind of pleasure/pain until it melts away in exhaustion.

On the other hand, there were images of desire—desire for the satisfaction of what is experienced as an intolerable lack. The principal innovation of seventeenth-century tonality is its ability to instill in the listener an intense longing for a given event: the cadence. It organizes time by creating an artificial need (in the real world, there is no reason one should crave, for instance, the pitch D; yet by making it the withheld object of musical desire, a good piece of tonal music can—within a mere ten seconds—dictate one's very breathing). After that need is established (after the listener has been conditioned to experience the unbearable absence of some musical configuration), tonal procedures strive to postpone gratification of that need until finally delivering the payoff in what is technically called the "climax," which is quite clearly to be experienced as metaphorical ejaculation.

When these two versions of erotic metaphors first emerged, they were in fact distinguished from each other along lines of gender association. The images of pleasure (and of pleasure/pain) were most often projected onto women: the text of "Anima mea liquefacta est" is uttered by a woman dissolving in her longing for her lover, and most of the famous ostinato pieces were performed by female characters. Male characters could also indulge in this discourse, though when they did so, they indicated that they were giving themselves over to the stupor of erotic transport. Thus Nero's drunken ostinato in praise of Poppea betrays his fundamental absence of patriarchal integrity, his "effeminacy."

Images of desire were more often wielded by male characters, who thereby could demonstrate their rationality, their rhetorical prowess, their ability to set and achieve long-term goals. And it is principally this set of images that wins out historically. The ostinato and the voluptuous pleasure/pain images disappeared after the seventeenth century, as did the early baroque's fascination with female sexuality. The rhetoric of desire and conquest prevails thereafter to such an extent that they come to seem universal—not surprisingly, in the century of the Enlightenment and its categories.

This universalization of what had been marked earlier as only one of several versions of the erotic occurred as well in literature. As a woman I can recognize—and can sometimes even enjoy—such a pattern, both in music and elsewhere in less metaphorical circumstances. But it is only one of many possible erotic experiences I know. Moreover, it is not the only or even necessarily the most intense form of erotic pleasure available to men. Yet it is the form that is most concerned with the exclusive control of sexuality by the male. And that control is, in fact, threatened by the kind of sensual eroticism that involves openness or vulnerability. In other words, the omnipresence of this formal pattern in literature and music is part of a larger cultural tendency to organize sexuality in terms of the phallus, to devalue or even to deny other erotic sensibilities (especially that of the female), to impose and maintain a hierarchy of power based on gender.

A significant factor that contributes to the violence of tonal procedures is that the actual reward—the cadence—can never be commensurate with the anticipation generated or the effort expended in achieving it. The cadence is, in fact, the most banal, most conventionalized cliché available within any given musical style. Moreover, its appearance always spells a kind of death—the cessation of the energy flow that up until that point in the piece had seemed to organize all subjectivity. At the end, the imaginary object of desire remains elusive, and attaining its cadential surrogate necessarily disappoints. But that surrogate is finally all that tonal music (for all its undeniable ability to arouse) has to offer. Beethoven and Mahler quite regularly push mechanisms of frustration to the limit, such that desire in their narratives frequently culminates (as though necessarily) in explosive violence. This may be one of the factors that have caused them to be received as more serious, more virile, more consequential than, say, Haydn or Handel: they don't pull punches, they go all the way to the mat.

For instance, the point of recapitulation in the first movement of Beethoven's Ninth Symphony unleashes one of the most horrifyingly violent episodes in the history of music. The problem Beethoven has constructed for this movement is that it seems to begin before the subject of the symphony has managed to achieve its identity: we witness the emergence of the initial theme and its key out of a womblike void, and we hear it collapse back twice more into that void. It is only by virtue of the subject's constant violent self-assertion that the void can be kept at bay: cadence in the context of this movement spells instant death—or at least loss of subjective identity. Yet the narrative paradigm the movement follows demands the eventual return to the beginning for the recapitulation.

In a more conventional sonata movement, recapitulation would signify simply the reconsolidation of thematic and tonal identity—a kind of formal homecoming that marks the end of a successful adventure. But for the subject of the Ninth, to return to the beginning is to actually regress to a point further back than its own conscious beginnings: it is to be dissolved back into the undifferentiated state from which it originally emerged. And if its hard-won identity means anything, the subject cannot accept such dissolution, even if it is toward that conventional moment of reentry that the whole background structure of the movement has inexorably driven. The desire for cadential arrival that has built up over the course of the development finally erupts, as the subject necessarily (because of narrative tradition) finds itself in the throes of the initial void while refusing to relent: the entire first key area in the recapitulation is pockmarked with explosions. It is the consequent juxtaposition of desire and unspeakable violence in this moment that creates its unparalleled fusion of murderous rage and yet a kind of pleasure in the fulfillment of formal demands.

The point is not to hold up Beethoven as exceptionally monstrous. The Ninth Symphony is probably our most compelling articulation in music of the contradictory impulses that have organized patriarchal culture since the Enlightenment. Moreover, within the parameters of his own musical composition, he may be heard as enacting a critique of narrative obligations. But if Beethoven resists the exigencies of formal necessity at the moment of recapitulation in the opening movement (and again at the beginning of the final movement), he also finally embraces and perpetuates them, and even raises them to a much higher level of violence. And once his successors in the nineteenth century tasted that combination of desire and destruction, they could not get enough of it.

In most post-Renaissance Western music and in virtually all of its critical literature, the climax-principle (like the phallus of the classical Greek column) has been transcendentalized to the status of a value-free universal of form. Despite the prevalence of this pattern, it is rarely even viewed as sexual (let alone masculine) any longer—it is simply the way music is supposed to go. The ostinato-driven clockwork imagery of Janika Vandervelde's piano trio, *Genesis II* (1983), by contrast, provides us with another erotic image: one that combines shared and sustained pleasure, rather than the desire for explosive closure. In the aggressive string parts, the piece also presents the phallic beanstalk image in ways that demonstrate both its exciting appeal and its destructive force. Many of my male students respond immediately and enthusiastically to the violent thrusting of the strings. Some of them only begin to question their enthusiasm after the women have shared their observations (just as many men fail to recognize the phallic dimension of their favorite classics until women, who are situated rather differently with respect to that "universal" experience, point it out).

It might be argued that *Genesis II* has simply reversed the terms of a pernicious binarism: if it is objectionable that in traditional narratives the "feminine" moment must be resolved out as a "large-scale dissonance," then is anything gained by maintaining the same schema but locating the "masculine" as the dissonance? Another potential problem with *Genesis II* is that it may encourage essentialist readings: to map femininity onto nature, cycles, and timeless stability and masculinity onto culture, linear time, and agency is to risk reinscribing these associations that very much need to be interrogated and resisted.

But the significance of Vandervelde's achievement is not *simply* that she has revealed as phallic and sexually violent many of the "value-free" conventions of classical form. Nor is it that she has introduced for the first time some universal, essential woman's voice. For even though our obsession for classifying all music stylistically might make us want to jump impulsively at the chance to codify the distinctive characteristics of a "women's music," there can be no such single thing, just as there is no universal male experience or essence. What Vandervelde has accomplished is an approach to composition that permits her—expressly as a woman—to inhabit a traditional discourse, to call into question its gestures and procedures *from the inside*, and to imagine from that vantage point the possibility of other narrative schemata.

Susan McClary, "Getting Down Off the Beanstalk," in *Feminine Endings: Music, Gender, and Sexuality* (Minneapolis: University of Minnesota Press, 1991), 124–31.

170

New Topicality

Another way in which "high art" traditionally differed from "popular culture" was in its aspirations to "transcendence" or "timelessness" or call it what you will—that is, its claim to inhabit an "autonomous" realm, "beyond good and evil," "disinterestedly" pursuing the beautiful, rather than the good or the true. The derisive quotes surround what were increasingly viewed as a bunch of clichés, mostly inherited from German Romantic philosophy; the derision was timely, given the way in which popular culture had responded to the social pressures of the 1960s in a fashion that seemed to leave high culture not only high but dry. The autonomy of art seemed in danger of shading into irrelevance and its disinterestedness into moral indifference. Such was the view, at any rate, of a group of determined artists who forcibly invested the high-art genres with topical relevance (or, to put it the other way around, interjected high-art projects into contemporary political and social debates) beginning in the 1980s. The one who attracted the most attention was Peter Sellars (1958–), a prolific stage director who followed a series of controversial updatings of traditional operas (notably Mozart's) with a pair of original works in which he teamed up with two artists he had known as students at Harvard in the 1970s: the composer John Adams (1947–), not to be confused with John Luther Adams on p. 540), and the poet Alice Goodman (1958–). The works they produced together, *Nixon in China* (1987) and *The Death of Klinghoffer* (1991), established what was hailed as a veritable new genre. Some wag christened this genre "CNN opera," after the Cable News Network, the first all-news-all-the-time venture on cable TV because of the way it monumentalized stories taken from the daily headlines using high-art methods; these works were consequently open to the sort of lively, at times aggravated, political debate and critique from which traditional art genres (save in totalitarian societies) were usually exempt. The genre certainly justified itself in terms of the notice—or notoriety—that it attracted. Adams, in particular, was launched by *Nixon* on a spectacular career. The downside came out in 2001, when a performance of choruses from *The Death of Klinghoffer*, which dealt head-on with Islamic terrorism, was cancelled by the Boston Symphony Orchestra in the aftermath of the destruction of the World Trade Center, amid charges and countercharges of censorship on the one hand, and moral insensitivity on the other. The interview with Adams below was conducted long in advance of that dénouement by Andrew Porter (1928–), a critic known both for his enthusiasm for Sellars's work, and for his hostility to minimalism, the stylistic milieu from which Adams's work was perceived to derive.

ANDREW PORTER: *Nixon in China is an unusual opera in many ways. One of the most striking is that, so far as I know, it's the only opera ever written about people who are still alive. Whose idea was it to write an historical opera about the historical present?*

JOHN ADAMS: It was Peter Sellars's idea. I think actually two different ideas converged in Peter's mind at about the same time. In the early 1980s he was interested in staging *The Red Detachment of Women*, which is a ballet that has a rather long history in 20th-century China, but which Madame Mao Zedong herself reshaped and rehabilitated in order to express the goals of the Cultural Revolution. The other idea was the actual story of the trip to China, especially as seen through the eyes of someone who was there, in this case Henry Kissinger. Then, when we enlisted Alice Goodman to write the libretto, we all seriously began reading the source material, and as you can imagine, it was just staggering how much literature there was on this event ...

AP: *Yes, it generated everything, didn't it—those newsreels, documentaries ... ?*

JA: Oh yes, and now the opera seems to have generated its own pile of material as well! So, we read a great deal, everything from the Ladies' Home Journal to Mao's poetry to Nixon's own memoirs to hagiography of Chou En-Lai and Mao himself.

AP: *It has turned out to be an important meeting for relations between countries.*

JA: Well, you know it's interesting that every time *Nixon in China* has been produced, some public event has just happened, or is happening: the week of the Houston première was Black Monday on the New York Stock Exchange; when it was playing in Amsterdam, Reagan and Gorbachev were meeting in Moscow; and now here in Edinburgh we're just finishing up the debris of the [1988] Republican National Convention. So there always seems to be something that's tangentially related to this subject going on in the world, which maybe suggests that this is the proper thing for opera to do. It was certainly the case in Verdi and Wagner's time. Opera addressed hotly debated issues that people thought about all the time.

AP: *Yes, but it never did quite in this direct way. I remember writing when the opera first came out that the meeting of Nixon and Chou En-Lai was comparable operatically to the meeting of Wotan and Erda, which is one of the meetings that did change the history of the world as told in Wagner's* Ring, *or perhaps, in Verdi's* Attila, *the meeting between Atilla at the gates of Rome with Pope Leo—the barbarian horde turned back from the gates of Rome, and history again turning on a meeting. Those were allegories, I suppose, of real meetings that were happening, whereas you have chosen real people.*

JA: Yes, they're real people, but yet they're not. One of the things about the story that I found so appealing and why I enjoyed composing it, was the opportunity to move, during the course of three acts, from the plastic cartoon versions of public people that

AP: *Your Richard Nixon and Pat Nixon certainly do have inner lives—characters of their own. To what extent did you invent this for them, or to what extent did you deduce or find it in memoirs?*

JA: There is hardly anything in this opera which is invented. Virtually everything—even in the third act, which most people assume is poetic license—is based on things which Nixon said in his memoirs or that Pat said in interviews.

AP: *Then let me put it another way. Have you used this material critically or not? One of the sharpest criticisms I've heard about* Nixon, *even from people who've enjoyed it very much as a music drama, has been that it produces so favorable an impression of Richard Nixon. I think a lot of people are upset that you seem to present a rather well-meaning man rather than a liar and crook.*

JA: Well, first of all I don't believe that Richard Nixon was a completely mendacious and hopelessly evil person. What we were trying to do with our operatic Nixon was not only to use the historical Richard Nixon but also to try to develop an archetype of an American public leader. One of the principal things that interested me was the typically American sense of assumed superiority. These Americans were coming to China with the tacit assumption that American culture is by far the better one. And that we were bringing progress and democracy and sound marketing principles, and Thomas Jefferson and Abraham Lincoln and Walt Disney to this backward culture. In a sense, what happens in the wonderful scene where Mao and Nixon actually confront each other, is that Nixon—who thinks that by reading a briefing the night before, he can know everything he needs to about China—of course falls completely on his face when he actually encounters the real Mao Zedong who is, to my mind, a far more powerful figure. Beyond that, I think that Nixon's cruelty to Pat was something that we focused on quite a bit, because we feel that this typifies the American idea of what a woman should be. The issue of sexual politics is threaded throughout this opera, both in the relationship between Pat and Dick, and that between Chairman and Madame Mao.

AP: *If you are in* Nixon in China *trying to some extent to criticize what Americans expect, but you present what they do expect, isn't it a type of satire which can backfire?*

JA: But I don't view this as a satirical opera at all. There are elements of satire in it. We hitched up with the word "heroic" at one point, which I somewhat regret—now we're stuck with it—but I think that Alice wanted to use the term "heroic" partly to distinguish the opera from being a satire.

AP: *Yes, it's not satire, but it could fairly be called an epic opera.*

JA: Yes, and of course you know these people did think of themselves as heroes. Nixon saw himself as an astronaut stepping onto the moon, and certainly Mao considered himself as a hero.

AP: *But surely Mao and Chou En-lai were heroes?*

JA: I believe so, yes.

AP: *I'm sure one of the things that people listening to this opera over the air are noticing is that the style develops as it goes along. You don't continue as you begin which—thank heavens!—in this style is something I'm grateful for. Were you conscious of this yourself?*

JA: I'm not exactly sure what you mean? Do you mean that the musical style …

AP: *… becomes more intricate, less repetitive; the blocks become smaller, the interlocking of blocks becomes closer, the working out is tighter …*

JA: I think that the style reflects what's going on poetically. The opening is very repetitive but what I was trying to summon up was the land and the people before all of this event occurred. It seemed to me when I thought of the Long March and of the vastness of the country, and the millions and millions of people, that the repetitive quality of these ascending A minor scales was a perfect way to set that tone. Whereas in Act III we've traveled a great distance and we're no longer talking so much about landscape and simple peasants, we're talking about very complicated human dynamics. We're talking, for example, about the incredibly complicated relationship between Chou En-Lai and Mao, and between Madame Mao and Mao, and hence I thought that the music had to emotionally reflect that, so it's much more complicated music.

AP: *Did you start at the beginning when you composed?*

JA: Yes. I sat down one day and I wrote *Nixon in China* at the top of a blank page of score and I started. I figured that if I didn't I'd never be able to write the opera!

AP: *And then you wrote a scale of A minor?*

JA: Yes.

AP: *And then wrote "x 23" or something?*

JA: Yes … I did!

AP: *Then you came to do the ballet, and I wondered whether you'd listened at all to the music of* The Red Detachment of Women?

JA: I am a little nervous about too much research when it comes to the creative act. I think it's good to have something suggested, but if you get *too* close to your model I think that your original muse gets offended. I had seen not *The Red Detachment of Women,* but a film of another Chinese ballet which was very similar to it called *The White Haired Girl.* But what I recalled from my one and only exposure was that the music was a strange misapprehension, basically of Russian ballet music. It sounded a little bit like a committee had tried to reconstruct by memory a Glinka or perhaps a Tchaikovsky ballet, but there was a tremendous confusion of styles. This was just perfect for me, because stylistic confusion has been one of the fuels that have run my creative engine for years.

AP: *A difference between your music and that of, say, Philip Glass and Steve Reich is that their later instrumental music sounds to me as though it was written for the small ensembles with which they first worked, and has now been transferred into a full orchestra sound, whereas it seems to me that your music has been conceived in orchestral colors right from the start.*

JA: What you must remember about me is that I never had a small ensemble period like Reich or Glass did. I've always been an orchestral composer. The synthesizer is a wonderful instrument for me because it does give a sense of spaciousness and massiveness. I'm a composer who works at the piano like Stravinsky and Copland.

AP: *I wonder if there are any who don't!*

JA: Well there are plenty who claim they don't. I also use an eight track tape recorder. I don't use it in the initial stage. I wrote *Nixon in China* as a piano vocal score—I had to because the singers had to start learning it—and then I went back and orchestrated it. In the orchestration stage I always use an eight-channel tape recorder because I'm able to lay down various tracks of counterpoint, which helps me. I would say that it's created my style—the use of technology—and it's allowed me to develop a very active and very thick and rich texture which I think a lot of minimalist music often lacks.

AP: Nixon in China *is now making its way around the world. Are you meanwhile thinking of what the next opera might be?*

JA: Yes, we're beyond thinking. Actually Alice is hard at work on the libretto of the next opera, and I've been doing a great deal of reading. The subject matter for the new opera is hardly less volatile than *Nixon in China*. It's going to be about the hijacking of the Italian cruise liner the Achille Lauro, and part of that story is the execution of the American Leon Klinghoffer who was confined to a wheelchair. There is a certain similarity to *Nixon*—it's very remote but it's an important one—which is that the opera focuses on Americans abroad, tourists I guess you could say, and the way in which Americans are caught up in world events without really understanding or anticipating what's going to happen to them. I'm an American composer. I'm a very American composer both stylistically and in my attitudes toward my own culture, and I feel that to write an opera about the Palestinian struggle or about Islam versus Judaism is something that is completely outside of my experience, but to write an opera about an *American* confrontation with those forces is something which I can do, and indeed I think this is one of the strongest things that Peter Sellars does as well.

AP: *Whose idea was the subject?*

JA: Oh, it was Peter's again, and I suspect that the subject was suggested to Peter by [the French-Swiss filmmaker] Jean-Luc Godard. Peter and I were talking shortly after he had met with Godard and

	Godard had been talking about terrorism as a form of theater, and that suggested to Peter this idea, and then we all took it up.
AP:	*Do you have to talk to the survivors and participants?*
JA:	This is a very complicated question, and we actually have legal people researching it to find out what our rights are and what their rights are, because of course it's a very volatile issue. It's one thing when you use a public character like Nixon or Mao—you are in the United States protected by the Constitution with public people, in fact there was a very recent Supreme Court decision confirming that—but when you use people who are, theoretically at least, private people then you have much greater possibility of a libel suit.
AP:	*So you're researching not only into the American side but into the terrorists' side as well, I suppose, because they will have to be presented, and you will have to get inside their thoughts in some way or invent them?*
JA:	Yes, this is one reason why writing operas is becoming an obsession for me. I am really hardly interested in anything else at the moment except opera, and one of the reasons is that it commands your attention on every level.

" 'Nixon in China': John Adams in Conversation with Andrew Porter," *Tempo*, no. 167 (December 1988), 25–30. Originally broadcast during the intermissions of an Edinburgh Festival transmission of the opera by the BBC on its British première, 10 September 1988, transcribed by David Allenby.

The First Symphony by John Corigliano (1938–) was another milestone of the new topicality. First performed (by the Chicago Symphony Orchestra) in 1989, when the AIDS epidemic was still largely associated with the gay community and with issues of civil rights for homosexuals, it quickly went around the world in performances by more than 100 orchestras. It uses collage and allusion devices like those associated with Alfred Schnittke (see p. 501), and contains parts for virtuoso piano and cello soloists. It established the composer as a spokesman for an interest group, which was still an unusual role for a classical musician, even though the disproportionate representation of homosexuals in the creative arts was a long- (if not very openly) acknowledged fact. The text that follows was written as an Op-Ed piece for the *New York Times* in the aftermath of 9/11, the terror attack on the World Trade Center that also impinged forcibly, as noted above, on the reception of John Adams's work. Corigliano's piece inspired controversy because of the way in which he linked the perspectives of various minority groups (or "others") with the one to which his name had been attached, and used the perspective of minority rights to inveigh against what he saw as the unjust hegemony of modernism within the world of musical composition. Some hailed the piece as courageous; others denounced it as opportunistic.

"Today we are all Israelis." Is this the closest analogy to the way we live now: shaken by terror, reeling from loss, amazed by hatred, wondering desperately if ours are to be the next deaths? No.

I remember reading, almost 20 years ago on another airliner, the first *New York Times* article about GRID, or gay-related immunological disorder: the only term they had, in those days, for AIDS. That plane, unlike the doomed jets two weeks ago, arrived safely. But the world in which it landed—the 1980's world of New York, of gay men, of the arts—was comparably devastated. With equal surgical precision, the plague slipped through America's proud medical-industrial defenses to slay thousands.

I was startled and moved, then, after the recent disaster, to see on so many senators' lapels the AIDS ribbon—that single loop of red that was for years our lone badge of grief—transformed into a tricolor insignia of everything America lost on Sept. 11. The Israeli analogy is true and apt. But what I thought that Tuesday morning was, "We are all AIDS sufferers now." Of course, a virus is not a jihad: one is a force of nature, the other an act of will. But our responses to each vary less than you might think. As in the early stages of AIDS, we are still searching to define an enemy so that we can understand and defeat it. But even now we can name certain patterns of mind that identify those who hate us, that make their hatred possible.

One such pattern is fundamentalism, which is as distorting to Christianity as it is to Islam. It is also not confined to religion. Fundamentalism is easy to spot when the Rev. Jerry Falwell blames homosexuals and supporters of gay rights for provoking divine retribution in the form of the World Trade Center attack—as well as AIDS. It's horrifically unmissable when Osama bin Laden bids Muslims everywhere to murder Americans for the glory of Allah. Wasn't Nazism, too, fundamentalist: a cult devoted to the purity of German identity? True enough, you may say, but the toxicity of religious extremism is old news. Besides, what has all this to do with New Yorkers, with artists: secular urbanites as likely to turn for spiritual solace at a time like this to their museums, their concert halls, as to their churches and synagogues?

Art, too, suffers its own fundamentalisms, and as we work to respond to this tragedy we must not forget them. Orthodoxies of purity, of hierarchy, of rigidity—theories of music, for example, that politicize its smallest materials, the order of its every pitch—still hold sway over much of our musical life. These orthodoxies are more than nuisances. They support a vision of art as a god devoted to the glory of its priests rather than the other way around. They define music not by what can be added but by what must be subtracted. Dogma drives out free interpretation. Correctness supplants generosity. Religiosity—a fundamentalism of aesthetics—oppresses a true art of the spirit: the only art we need.

Few of my students in the 1990's heeded such dogma. They chose instead to embrace all the sounds around them as well as the new ones they had yet to dream; to name passion, vision, breadth and clarity as music's highest values. Was it the presence of the AIDS tragedy that revealed the academic and political world of this or that musical "ism" as sterile and arbitrary? Or was it simply growing up in American society, the greatness of which cannot be separated from its diversity?

American pluralism remains the most resonant political idea of our epoch. All people of all races, classes and genders have value, can speak truth, deserve respect. The question, and the challenge, is to fuse them all into a society as rich as it is coherent. This political idea has artistic implications. It is too late for a fundamentalism of a master system, just as it is too late for an ideology of a master race. As we respond to the tragedy of Sept. 11, as well as to that of tomorrow, we must struggle to reconcile—imaginatively, flexibly, compassionately, intelligibly—our titanic richness of musical resource with unmistakable structural order. Our nation—the world—demands no less.

John Corigliano, "Music: The Aftermath; We Are All AIDS Sufferers," *New York Times,* 23 September 2001.

171

Millennium's End

The end of the twentieth century did not just mark the end of the arbitrary calendrical entity known as the second millennium. It also marked the end of a rough but actual millennium since the introduction of a writing system—and hence a continuously traceable evolutionary history—in the practice of European music, one that made the notion of classical or art music possible. As that millennium neared completion, many were prompted to reflect on the recent profound changes in the sociology and technology of the art that presaged a historical watershed. Ever since the introduction of electroacoustical methods into musical composition, the prospect of a postliterate period in music history had loomed. The new diversity, both in styles and in the range of its practitioners, also promised foreseeable yet unpredictable change. A new relationship between the literate and nonliterate genres of music, a fact of life since the 1960s, was another pressing yet imponderable issue. Below are a group of millennial ruminations—by two composers, a scholar, and a composer-scholar—on these and other matters of *fin-de-siècle* concern. In the first of them, a composer long associated with the hard-core avant-garde (hence with the most exclusively literate and uncompromisingly hierarchical tendencies in contemporary music) considers a number of implicit challenges to its assumptions. Brian Ferneyhough (1943–) is an English composer who received much of his training on the European continent, taught in Germany and Holland from 1973 to 1987, and has resided in the United States since then, teaching both at the University of California and at Stanford. Until 1994 he remained the coordinator of composition classes at the Summer Courses for New Music at Darmstadt, Germany, the most distinguished European center of avant-garde composition since its founding in 1946. The essay that follows served as the introduction to a biographical encyclopedia containing curricula vitae and work-lists for more than five hundred living composers in the media of Western music from all over the world, including Asia and Africa, as well as the continents more commonly associated with the European tradition and its outposts. The book testified to impressive proliferation, but also to the possibility of overpopulation in a field of elite endeavor and limited public (or even private) economic support. The reference toward the end to "the 'new Unclearness'" is Ferneyhough's wry acknowledgment of his own reputation as a standard bearer for traditional modernism, rechristened (against the minimalist tide) by one of his advocates, the Australian musicologist Richard Toop, as "the new Complexity."

In recent years contemporary music has been undergoing sweeping change more rapidly, both socially and stylistically, than at perhaps any previous period in living memory. At the same time that composition has tended towards a greater internationality (and thus becoming less the province of a smaller group of "traditional" new music-producing nations) the accelerating revolution in electronic media has come to make the world seem both more densely populated and more claustrophobic than hitherto. Most recently, the opening up of Eastern Europe has significantly increased contact and opportunities for interaction and will surely produce many as yet unpredictable changes in our perspective as to where contemporary compositional practice may be heading.

Given the complexity and multifariousness characteristic of the present juncture it would be invidious to attempt to simplify matters with the aid of a few prefabricated categories; nevertheless some important central issues have become clear, not the least pressing of which is the issue of stylistic diversity. Musical style in the twentieth century has never been as conveniently monolithic—even in the 1950s—as many commentators would like to pretend; the current sea change may arguably reflect transformed modes of cultural perception rather than realities of stylistic hegemony. Nevertheless, much ink has been spilled of late over the question of the "total availability" of musical history as a valid object of compositional invention. It seems characteristic of our "Alexandrian" [i.e., creatively exhausted, derivative] epoch that such a dehistoricizing attitude towards material and context should coincide with the attempt to make new music more accessible to larger audiences by couching it in stylistic traits and aesthetic stances characteristic of a much earlier (and perhaps—at least when "creatively misunderstood"—more simple) period. It is a sign of the social power of the newer media that we should have come to appreciate the past as a function of its symbolic transmission, thus robbing it of its perspectival potential. I suppose that many if not most composers today on the threshold of their careers have come to contemporary music via popular, commercial music of one kind or another; this is certainly true on the North American continent. It is extremely interesting to see how such artists manage to grapple with the thicket of issues surrounding such "crossover" phenomena, where "History" is in any case an extremely relative concept.

The remarkable acceleration in the field of music technology has impinged directly on the current state of composing, not least the increasing isolation of composers from organs of public reproduction, the rapid internationalization of research activity and a new focus beginning to emerge in the important area of musical perception and cognition. The instrumental palette, meanwhile, has been rejuvenated through the use of commercially developed electronic equipment (although much remains to be done to persuade the industry to take heed of the specific needs of the non-commercial artist) and major advances have been made in the combination of pre-recorded tape materials and live instruments. Entire new perspectives are being opened with the application of most recent computer technology to real-time manipulation of instrumental and vocal signals, and there are signs that many composers are once more becoming actively involved with the performance of their own works on this basis. While this may indeed represent one major trend, it is also disturbing to the extent that the gap between experimental art forms and those amenable to assimilation by existing vehicles (such as the symphony orchestra) may finally become unbridgeable.

Hand-in-hand with the progressive internationalization of contemporary music comes the notable increase in the number of women composers active in the mainstream. Many women now in their thirties and forties have succeeded in establishing themselves as regular and integral parts of present-day concert life, and a significant number of them come from countries until quite recently not particularly identified as centers of new music activity. Their contribution is certain to grow even more rapidly in the coming decade, in spite of the tendency of music publishers to abdicate their traditional role as disseminators of new works and artists. That this is an enforced abdication is clear, stemming as it does both from the economic marginality of new music and the sheer impossibility of keeping up with the expansion in the number of composers now active on the professional scene. Although a few major publishers do indeed maintain this traditional role as best they may, there is little hope for the vast majority of young composers to be adopted and supported in this fashion. One immediate result of this change has been the tendency of many individuals to set themselves up as the publishers of their own music—something that has become a practical possibility only in the last few years. Even major publishers are beginning to resort to electronic means of servicing large catalogues, thus eliminating the need to maintain costly storage space for products that typically sell very slowly. The primary advantage of this situation from the point of view of composers is that most income from the hire, sales and performance of works remains in their own hands. Problematic, on the other hand, is the sheer effort involved in publicizing oneself, in making individual voices heard to the degree necessary for a career to "take off."

Several pressing issues continue to concern those active, in whatever capacity, in new music circles. One of the most weighty of these is the tendency, already far advanced, for recent works to be eliminated from the programming of the majority of radio stations. To be sure, there are notable exceptions, especially in smaller countries, where the creative artist is often in more direct and active contact with those responsible for planning. Unfortunately they remain exceptions, and the compact for mutual support that carried much new music programming since World War II has been eroded to the point where a thoroughgoing redefinition of goals and possibilities seems unavoidable. Another concern has been the parallel dilution of journals actively propagating contemporary issues, in particular those aimed at a non-specialist readership. Music, ephemeral by definition, is in great need of support by the written word to maintain a constant profile in the public eye.

On the positive side, official support for young composers seems to be growing, to judge by the plethora of competitions and scholarships on offer. At the same time, it is difficult not to see the present juncture as extremely difficult for such individuals in view of the "new Unclearness" of both aesthetic and economic situations. Composers from Eastern Europe in particular will surely come to feel this when suddenly freed from socio-political constraints and exposed to the tender mercies of the market at large.

Few generally recognized "hubs" of contemporary music pretend any longer to the sort of hegemony prevalent a decade or two ago. The major festivals of the 1970s and early 1980s have, by and large, made way for a decentralized network of lower-key events, often supported by local rather than national institutions. Although several names are still current—Donaueschingen, Darmstadt, Holland Festival, Metz, Warsaw, the International Society for Contemporary Music, etc.—their status has come to be seen as increasingly problematic in a time of general belt-tightening and reduced expectations. It might be argued that this is a wholly positive phenomenon, insofar as the future belongs to a different species of internationalization (by implication more modest, realistic and egalitarian). My own feeling, though, is that the elimination of the sort of collision of resources and vision which such major events have often occasioned would ultimately prove a serious impoverishment, leaving the field of large-scale productions to opera and smorgasbords of "personality cult"-influenced television spectacles, themselves often enough the instruments of political or industrial interests.

Brian Ferneyhough, "Preface," in Brian Morton and Pamela Collins (eds.), *Contemporary Composers* (Chicago: St. James Press, 1992), ix–x.

Kyle Gann (1955–), American born and trained, is a representative of more recent, less elitist traditions than those with which Ferneyhough has been associated. As he and other Americans of his generation like to put it, theirs is the "downtown" scene (as distinct from the high-modernist, Eurocentric "uptown"). Perhaps for that reason, his millennial assessment, at the end of a historical survey of American classical music, is correspondingly less elegiac, even exuberant. His radical distinction between old Europe and young America may seem a little cocky and overdrawn, but it is one to which many Americans do subscribe at the beginning of the third millennium, even in the traditionally old-European precincts of classical music. Perhaps characteristically American, too, is Gann's faith in the Internet, a phenomenon both touted and feared as a democratizer of knowledge, as a support network for American classical music.

So many music writers are pessimistic about the future and present state of music. It is true that the audiences for classical music are falling off, that more and more young people don't attend live concerts, that symphony orchestras are folding, that university departments are increasingly forced to cater to rock and commercial music to attract students. But such oft-quoted statistics have primarily to do with the decline of interest in *European* music. How about *American* music? Are the fates of the two continents chained together? Or does the death of the prestige of European music offer American music an opportunity it has been yearning for since the influx of immigrants before World War II?

If it were possible to kill off American music through lack of audience, lack of funding, and lack of institutional support, American music would have died a thousand deaths over the last 150 years. American composers are accustomed to surviving on virtually nothing. One European's book of interviews with American composers was entitled *Desert Plants,* acknowledging that they can get by on infinitesimal amounts of support that European artists would consider starvation rations [Walter Zimmermann, *Desert Plants: Conversations with 23 American Musicians* (Vancouver: ARC Publications, 1976)]. Our educational institutions have barely tried to expose students to American music to find whether they are attracted to it or not. How can the impending death of European music's support system in America possibly hurt any American composers except those tied in to European performance practice? Aside from their constitutional rights as citizens and the occasional small grant, what do most American composers possess that can be taken away?

Were I forced to choose the decades that I thought were the most fertile in American music, in terms of excellence and beauty, I would quickly pick the 1920s and 1990s, less certainly the 1930s and 1980s. John Cage himself named 1952 as the low point in American culture—significantly, the year he composed *4'33"*. Since that year—if *4'33"* can be considered a kind of death of music that renders a rebirth possible —American music has been reforming itself, building up a new, firmer, more solidly indigenous tradition. That frustrating gap between composers and audiences? It's gone, or else kept alive only by virtue of an artificial life support system that our institutions keep it on. There is nothing complicated or off-putting or opaque about the music of Eve Beglarian, Mikel Rouse, Glenn Branca, John Luther Adams, Peter Garland, William Duckworth, Pamela Z, Joshua Fried. Anyone who's curious can comprehend their musics *more* easily than they can understand Mozart.

It is true that, as the classical music establishment sinks, American composers will have to fight in order not to sink with it. But the fight cannot be more difficult than the struggle already has been to be included and well represented within the Euro-classical world in the first place. The battleground is shifting—American composers have established a much stronger foothold on the Internet than they possessed in orchestra programs or classical record stores, and much of their music is more easily available via the Web than it has been through standard retail outlets. In order to survive, composers and their slim support system will have to create a public perception that classical (European) music is one thing, and the world of American composition something else altogether, unhampered by the elitist and class associations that make Mozart and Brahms seem more irrelevant with each passing year.

The problem is that, as the theorist Mihaly Csikszentmihaly has written, a creative culture is a triangle requiring three points: individual artists, a tradition to work within and against, and a public with an adequate amount of disposable attention. The third variable is what is lacking today. As corporate control over the economy necessitates ever more work and income to keep up with technology and ahead of inflation, people have less time than ever to explore the art springing up around them. And, paradoxically, just as disposable attention plummets toward zero, there has never been so much exciting music, there have never been so many imaginative composers. Our music scene is collapsing under the weight of more good work than our current stressed-out and distracted audiences can assimilate.

Art cannot solve the problems of society—at least, most of us reflexively assume that it can't. In recent years, politicians and administrators have attempted to use art to ameliorate social ills, mostly by increasing the programming of art by members of designated minorities so that those minorities will feel included by our cultural institutions. Whether this strategy really does improve collective self-esteem, or whether it is a sop thrown to minorities in lieu of political change that would materially benefit them, remains to be decided. But can't Thelonius Monk's music uplift and inspire a white person, and couldn't Copland's music have the same effect on an African- or Asian-American? Doesn't the enormous impact of gamelan and Indian ragas on late twentieth-century American music prove that art's meaning isn't limited by ethnic categories?

Say for a minute that artists are, as they have so often been described, the antennae of the race, the first people to register and reflect undercurrents of collective psychological change. If so, then the composers of the 1990s, in once again creating music in which intellectual, physical, and emotional appeal are no longer separated, may be pointing toward an upcoming rebirth in American society. Perhaps the road from *4'33"* to Meredith Monk's *Atlas* and Mikel Rouse's *Dennis Cleveland* and John Luther Adams's *Dream of White on White* is a road that society itself is slowly and belatedly traversing, a road that starts with the simple, egoless act of stopping to listen, and that points toward a reintegration of personality, toward restoring playfulness and emotiveness to creativity. If any of this is true, isn't it possible that the music of these 1990s might be indeed supremely useful, if nothing more, as a psychological model, operating on deeper terms than any orchestra-sponsored questionnaire would be able to measure?

I believe so. I further believe that composers and audiences alike have forgotten how crucially important music can be to nonmusicians and that they, composers and audiences both, are resisting remembering because of the tremendous responsibility that importance entails on both sides. However, every few years bring a new crop of composers whose music has wide and lasting appeal, each crop larger than the last. As Cage said so often, "We need not fear for the future of music." And if the music described here falls into disuse in the twenty-first century, it will be because twenty-first-century composers stood on our shoulders to create a music so heavenly that there was no longer any need for the past.

Kyle Gann, "Postlude: The Road from *4'33"*," *American Music in the Twentieth Century* (New York: Schirmer Books, 1997), 384–86.

Meredith Monk is one of the first late twentieth-century composers frankly to view herself within, and celebrate, a postliterate musical culture; but even she, at the end of the passage quoted below, voices a bit of ambivalence at the loss of permanence that postliteracy might imply.

Q: *Do you have complete control over all aspects of your work, or do you allow input from other people you're working with?*

A: I always do a lot of preparation, either sitting at the piano or sometimes laying down tracks myself. I've been doing that for about ten years—laying down tracks of my own voice, trying some of the ensemble work or counterpoint, and then going into rehearsal. Particularly with the older members of my ensemble who I have been working with for a long time, there's a give and take in the rehearsals where we try variations and different configurations of who's singing what. There are some sections where the structural element is very precise, but there are always others where a singer can play with it—that comes from having sung together for a long time. If you heard two performances of *Dolmen Music* [1980], the overall structure would be the same but phrase by phrase there would always be a place for a singer either to compress or expand a little bit.

Q: *In that case, how do you notate?*

A: I never notated a piece until my opera *Atlas* [1992]. I use notation as a memory device after I'm happy with the overall structure of a piece. The point about doing music and live performances is that things grow in a very organic way. People who come to an opening night of mine, expecting to see some kind of European concept of perfection, will get a surprise if they come back two weeks later—they will see how the form has grown through the act of performing it. With me, there's a certain point where I feel that the piece has grown into a form that feels stable, where the overall form feels very satisfying. It's at that point I would notate it.

Q: *What form does that notation take?*

A: Notation is something I'm struggling with right now. I've always been very skeptical of it, and now that I'm getting older, I'm having to cope with the problem of how much I'm leaving to other people. How much can you really get from looking at a piece of paper? It's so sketchy in relation to what we're doing, especially the vocal work. For *Atlas*, the orchestral score is very clear, though instrumentalists did some wonderful things with different performances of it. But basically, what you see on the page is what you get. I don't know how you would notate some of the vocal work, and I don't know if I want to or not. I'm struggling with that right now because I do want to pass my work on. It's not that I don't want to have other people do it, but I think that the way it's made comes from a primal, oral tradition that is much more about music for the ears. In Western culture, paper has sometimes taken over the function of what music always was. I feel that my music is between the barlines: what is really happening is underneath the page, and I don't know how to deal with that.

Geoff Smith and Nicola Walker Smith, *New Voices: American Composers Talk about Their Music* (Portland, Ore.: Amadeus Press, 1995), 188–89 (interview with Meredith Monk).

Postliteracy, a novelty for classical music, could be seen in a larger context as a reversion to a norm rather than an unprecedented departure; for most of the music of the world's cultures has been, and still is, nonliterate in its methods of creation and dissemination. That is one of the reasons why ethnomusicologists, who study non-literate musics as a matter of course, are among the most perceptive analysts and interpreters of the most recent developments in Euro-American art music. The little essay that follows is the preface to a study by Mark Slobin (1943–), an ethnomusicol-ogist who has studied the oral musical traditions of Central Asia and of diaspora Jews in America, of what he calls *micromusics*, idiosyncratic (and syncretic) individual musical styles that naturally multiply under the new technological and social condi-tions. This may reach the point, Slobin implies, where it may become impossible or superfluous to look for dominant trends. The questions that loom behind this study— as they do behind most of the developments we are considering here—are questions of values. Is ever-greater diversity and idiosyncrasy something to celebrate as a sign of vigorous creativity or something to deplore as a sign of lessened community and loss of interpersonal (let alone intercultural) communication? Does ever-greater differen-tiation breed ever-greater mutual tolerance or the opposite? Above all, what does the ever-greater instability of concepts and values augur for the future of our musical culture?

I began my work as an ethnomusicologist in Afghanistan in 1967, and moved slowly westward through Europe to the United States. Everywhere I went I noticed small musics living in big systems. Groups of people in neighborhoods, in clusters across entire countries, or even in diaspora seem to think that certain musical styles, instru-ments, songs, ways of singing or playing, ideas about what music is or might be, were somehow "ours." And what's "ours" was always set apart from what's not: "mine," "theirs," or "everybody's."

This fascinating counterpoint of near and far, large and small, neighborhood and national, home and away, has haunted me as I work on specialized situations in particular places. Nowhere is it safe to draw conclusions about what belongs to whom, because it isn't how the music *sounds*, but how it can be *thought* that counts: outsiders—even if certified by doctorates in music—all have tin ears. To show just how tangled music really is, let me offer three metaphors:

1. *Homespun.* We are all individual music cultures, using patchworks of compiled sounds stitched into a cultural quilt to help keep us warm. But we are restless sleep-ers; from time to time we throw off the covers, change the linen, look for sleeping pills, or even buy an electric blanket, which leads us to:

2. *Electronic.* Our musical antennae are always waving about in the atmosphere, ignoring some sounds and hauling in others for future reference, although we still don't have a clue as to how we do so or why. We have stored away countless live and recorded sounds, tied to kin, friends, moments, and often the music triggers the memories rather than the other way round. Yet we are not freestanding, factory-fresh equipment; *contexts* matter to us as much as inputs, which takes us to:

3. *Environmental.* Amid a set of personal landscapes we can identify formations, musical Stonehenges, that stand free and look communal. Like that ancient pile, such structures are cryptic, mutely posing puzzles of who shaped them and what they represent. Unlike those changeless megaliths, musical monuments are mobile, flexible, more like a mirage. The nearer you get, the more their rigid outlines shift in the shimmering air. Less poetically, what I mean is that we make temporary shelters of our musical materials, not only personally, but collectively. Up close, what's

"Irish," "American," or "Irish-American" looks like the work of tent-dwellers, not stone-raisers after all.

I'm collecting metaphors here to make a point that I'll keep returning to below: we need to think of music as coming from many places and moving among many levels of today's societies, just as we have learned to think of groups and nations as volatile, mutable social substances rather than as fixed units for instant analysis. Yet at any moment, we can see music at work in rather specific ways, creating temporary force-fields of desire, belonging, and, at times, transcendence.

Let me get away from metaphors and down to cases, of which Andy Statman's might make the point. When I first met Andy in the late 1970s, he had just switched over from being a leading mandolinist in bluegrass music to helping found the fledgling *klezmer* movement. This movement was a drive by younger Jewish-American musicians of differing pasts and persuasions to forge a new "ethnic" style based on their neglected "Jewish" roots. Fifteen years later, the *New York Times* (April 12, 1992) finds Statman in "a home resonant with delightful sounds" as "a man of many talents and strong [Orthodox Jewish] faith." Meanwhile, his music has branched out past the older *klezmer* sound to include not only his old favorite, bluegrass, but beyond. As Statman says, "the orchestra plays traditional Jewish European music, but we also flow freely into bits and pieces of what we like.... It's our own form of improvisation, and folk music and the bluegrass influence is right there." "Indeed," says the reporter, "his music is so varied he jokingly calls it 'Moroccan African Mongolian klezmer music.'" In figuring out this stance, remember that the "traditional Jewish European music" itself was a blend of styles including Moldavian, Ukrainian, and shades of Balkan, all transformed in New York in the 1920s and 30s.

Even a brief attempt at understanding Andy Statman shows us: (1) any essentialist analysis of music will not hold; (2) interchange among small musics is rampant these days, and always was; (3) musicians, like the rest of us, negotiate individuality in very complex ways (there the process involves an unpredictable knotting of aesthetics, professionalism, and multiple allegiances); (4) units like Statman's orchestra are the fulcrum on which individual and group identities turn and balance precariously in the cultural and subcultural winds.

The point is emphatically *not* to make sense of the iceberg of which Statman is the tip—such an attempt would rapidly run aground—but rather to try out ways of systematic viewing. Only by pretending that things are stable can we see how they change. Above all, I am interested in *interaction,* within small groups, between social groupings, and with the powers that be (industry and ideology, bureaucrats and bankers) that set the tone, make the rules, and provide the resources. There are no "simple" societies any longer, yet "complex" is too flat a word to describe the nestings and foldings, the cracks and crannies of the lands of Euro-America. In this time of radical reshaping, after the collapse of the East-West structure that defined the political, economic, and human landscape of the region for two generations, we badly need a framework for further thought. The "advanced" North Atlantic area has turned out to be as confused as the "developing" or "backward" zones it once defined by supposed superiority. Meanwhile, the fragmenting and regluing of the eastern zones proceeds fitfully and unpredictably. Overall, the music of Euro-America in the 1990s is at least as complicated as that of anyplace on the planet, especially since Euro-America is the place to which much of the rest of the world has moved or longs to migrate. In transit, in process, and even in their dreams they all sing—or at least wear headphones to mask exterior noise with interior sounds.

Mark Slobin, "Preface," *Subcultural Sounds: Micromusics of the West* (Hanover, N.H.: University Press of New England, 1993), ix–xi.

172

A Glimpse of the Future?

Whether the idea of music without composers is utopian or dystopian is not something we need to decide, perhaps, but it is the ultimate postmodernist fantasy, and it is already within today's technological reach, as a bemused but perceptive report by a New York critic, who attended a kind of musical science fair in the year 2000, attests. It jibes quite neatly, if fortuitously, with a musicopolitical fantasy that attracted attention in the 1980s: *Noise: The Political Economy of Music,* by Jacques Attali, first published in French (as *Bruits*) in 1977. The author was a French economist and political adviser whose career met an inglorious end in 1993 when he was forced to resign as president of the European Bank for Reconstruction and Development over an embezzlement scandal. An amateur musician, he reconceptualized the history of world music in four stages, each prophetically heralding an epoch in the history of economic and political relations: (1) the *sacrificial,* wherein music was the property of the hereditary and clerical elites and was primarily a medium of propitiation and social control; (2) the *representational,* wherein music became the property of the bourgeoisie and a medium of social emancipation; (3) the *repetitive,* wherein music became the property of capitalist exploiters and a medium of commercial exchange; and (4) the age of *composition,* not yet achieved but foreseen, wherein music would became the property of everyone and a medium of individual empowerment. The last stage would witness the "negation of the division of roles and labor as constructed by the old codes." There would no longer be any distinctions among composers, performers, and listeners. Everyone would be all three at once. Attali was a bit vague as to how that would be achieved. And he was no longer around to tell us how the situation described below might correspond to that achievement. But we can end our survey of the musical past with a hint of at least one possible musical future.

The Lincoln Center Festival's five-concert Electronic Evolution series last month surveyed the history of electronic music, starting with the 1920 invention of the theremin, the electronic instrument that looks like a radio transmitter and was once a staple of sci-fi movie soundtracks. These rewarding concerts showed where electronic music has come from. But a free preconcert event in the Low Library at Columbia University showed where electronic music, maybe music as a whole, could be going. It was a multimedia display of six interactive sound and image installations, and it was packed with mostly young adults. For this veteran concert-goer, the glimpse into the interactive musical future was at once fascinating and disconcerting.

The gizmos on display were not inventions of computer geeks who had drifted into music. All of the creators are composers pursuing advanced degrees who have gotten increasingly involved with computer software. Yet these interactive inventions may someday put composers out of business, at least those who cling to the quaint idea that composing means one person in private putting notes and sounds together for later public performance.

Just compare that passive, laughably outmoded way of experiencing new music with the fun and challenge of "Soundscape Navigator," an experimental installation by R. Luke DuBois and Mark McNamara. It allows you to navigate through a virtual-reality space, a kind of room where wildly varied sounds with corresponding images, like amazing sonograms, appear, collide and vanish on wall-size panels. Moving around the "room" with a hand-held lever changes the way the sounds are "spatialized," to quote the composers, though perhaps "designers" would be a more apt billing. In a way "Soundscape Navigator" turns Olivier Messiaen's conviction that harmonies have colors into glaring, fast-paced reality. Instead of just hearing sounds, "it's as if you are driving around in them," said Douglas Irving Repetto, the producer of the exhibit and the creator of "BeatyBeatyBeaty and the Infinite Grid," a software-based instrument that allows the user to improvise highly complex music. Or so I was told. Try as I did to follow the explanations of "gains," "frequency curves" and "multitrack graphical interface," I had no idea what the instrument really does, though it's surely ingenious.

"Tinkering With Speech," an installation by Timothy Polashek, was easy to use and attracted lots of partakers. It enables you to collaborate in the creation of a text-sound work by speaking into a microphone and watching the computer-generated results. The sounds of the words are fragmented in every way imaginable: syllables get shifted around, vowels are substituted for one another, parts of words are combined into new words, some as nonsensical as anything in Gertrude Stein. Jason Freeman's "Locust Tree in Flower," the title taken from a William Carlos Williams poem, is essentially a four-minute "composition," an aural and visual representation of the poem. Listening through earphones, the "audience member," to use Mr. Freeman's term, is asked to speak selected syllables and words from the short poem into a microphone. The software responds by mixing, looping and otherwise altering the speech sounds and corresponding images.

The biggest hit was "Interactions," by David Birchfield. The user—again, just one at a time—begins by typing into a computer an Internet address of his or her choice. This generates a burst of images on two adjoining screens. Concurrently, the installation presents the user with two sets of sounds triggered by the imagery, one in each cup of the earphones. The user indicates a preference by tapping one of two small drums with a mallet. This causes the rejected sound source to alter its content more in line with the chosen one. But when the sneaky rejected source gets too similar, the previously chosen one changes drastically. So in a sense the two sides are constantly fighting for the fickle user's favor. Watching people thwacking the drums with glints in their eyes, you could sense the seductive allure of "Interactions." All concertgoers have had the experience of sitting impatiently through pieces they didn't much like, thinking: "What's the music doing now?" "Why can't it repeat that pretty good thing it did before?" "I wish the pace would pick up." "What a bore!" "Ah, I like that; it's sort of neat." With this installation, the listener finally has the power to change the piece immediately, to cater to his or her own taste, mood and attention span.

Give listeners this degree of choice, and they are likely to use it. Of course, advanced interactive technology, we are told, will not eliminate the need for composers but simply expand available sound resources and create a role for newly engaged audiences. I would say to the composer-computer whizzes who are inventing this stuff, "Be careful what you wish for." I will not soon forget the giddy sense of empowerment that every user of "Interactions" projected while I stood by, sort of nervous. I mean, who will care what critics think when music becomes an interactive endeavor?

For those of us who persist in thinking of a musical composition as a creative statement of a trained and artistic individual, there was one reassuring thing: though the users of these interactive installations worked alone, having witnesses watching and listening on extra earphones seemed a large part of the enjoyment. So composers as we have known them may disappear someday. Yet perhaps the concert, or at least a new kind of collective listening experience, will continue.

Anthony Tommasini, "Music, Minus Those Pesky Composers," *New York Times,* Arts and Leisure (6 August 2000), 28.

Defined here are only those terms that are not defined in the context of the reading in which they occur. For terms that are defined in the readings, consult the Index.

4'33" Composition by John Cage in which a performer enters a performance space, initiates a performance by some recognizable gesture (most often, by opening or closing the keyboard lid on a piano), but makes no intentional sound. The title specifies the duration of the performance.

accidentals Signs ("sharp" and "flat") used to indicate chromaticism (q.v.); they direct that a given pitch be raised or lowered a half step.

Agnus Dei The last of the fixed texts (Ordinary) of the Mass. It accompanies the taking of communion.

aleatoric From alea, Latin for "dice"; denotes music composed according to chance operations.

allegro (Italian: happy) A brisk tempo; a piece or section played at a brisk tempo.

Alleluia The highly melismatic Gregorian chant that precedes the reading of the Gospel at Mass.

antiphon A short verse appended to psalms as a refrain in early Christian use.

antiphonal A mode of performance originating in psalmody, in which two or more choruses sing in alternation; by extension, any performing situation, vocal or instrumental, in which such alternation takes place.

antiphoner, *Antiphonale* (Latin), **antiphonary** Book containing the Gregorian chants for the liturgical hours or Divine Office (q.v.).

antiphony The use of antiphonal (q.v.) performing forces.

archlute A large lute, used to play harmonic accompaniments in the late Renaissance and early Baroque (also known as chitarrone or theorbo).

aria 1. As Caccini uses it in the 17th century, the word means a song consisting of stanzas sung over a repetitious musical accompaniment (ground bass). 2. In common parlance, any extended solo number in an opera, cantata, or oratorio.

Ars nova The title of a fourteenth-century French treatise on musical notation, now used to designate the style of fourteenth-century French music generally.

atonality The absence of a functional tonic or tonal center to govern the harmony in a composition.

aulos The principal wind (reed) instrument of the ancient Greeks. It often had a double bore.

ballade (medieval) A form of courtly song in which the musical sections are in the scheme AAB. This form has proved especially durable and has been given many other names (e.g., "bar form").

ballata An Italian dance-song form similar to the French virelai (q.v.).

bassadanza, basse danse (French) A ballroom dance of the 15th and 16th centuries in which the couples moved in procession; usually the opening number in a formal ball.

bluegrass A style of American country music that originated in the 1940s. The name comes from the nickname of the state of Kentucky, as incorporated into the name of the group that popularized the style, Bill Monroe and the Blue Grass Boys.

branle A ballroom dance of the 15th and 16th centuries in which the couples formed a circle.

caccia A 14th-century genre in which a poem about hunting (Italian: *caccia*) is set to music in which one part "chases" another (Italian: *cacciare*) in imitation; by extension, any medieval texture of two canonic parts over a harmonic bass line.

cadence The end of a phrase, section, or entire composition, usually signalled by a conventional formula; hence, a way of articulating musical structure, comparable to punctuation.

cadential Pertaining to cadence.

cadenza (Italian: cadence) A showy passage of virtuosity near the end of a concerto movement or aria; in the 18th and 19th centuries often improvised by performers; nowadays usually sung or played from memory.

canon 1. Any verbal rubric or performance direction in a medieval or Renaissance musical manuscript. 2. A polyphonic piece that could be realized in performance from a single notated line by applying such a rule. 3. By extension, any piece in which all the parts have the same music but start at different times and/or at different pitch levels (a "round" is a form of canon).

canticle A Gregorian chant performed in the manner of a psalm, with verses recited to a tone (q.v.) and with a framing antiphon (q.v.).

cantus firmus A Gregorian chant on which a piece of medieval or Renaissance polyphony was constructed (usually held out in longer note values than the accompanying parts); by extension, any melody so used, or any texture in which one voice moves noticeably more slowly than the others.

chanson (French: song) In music historiography the term is usually restricted to denote the French courtly part songs (secular polyphonic songs) of the 15th and 16th centuries.

chorale congregational hymn, especially as set by composers for the Protestant church in simple chordal harmony; by extension, a piece or passage resembling such a hymn-setting in texture.

chord A composite sonority produced by the simultaneous sounding of different pitches; the basic unit of harmony.

chromatic scale A scale encompassing all the notes on the keyboard rather than just the seven in diatonic scales (q.v.)

chromaticism The use of pitches that lie outside the normal scale of a given mode or key; a common means of achieving vivid expressivity in much texted or programmatic music since the Renaissance.

circle of fifths A representation of the harmonic relationships within a scale or mode in the form of a chain of cadences.

cithara See kithara.

cittern A small mandolin-like fretted instrument of the Elizabethan period; chords were usually strummed on it as accompaniment for other instruments or voices.

clavichord A very soft-spoken, intimate keyboard instrument, obsolete since the late 18th century, in which the tone was produced by a metal tangent attached to a lever activated by the key, which struck the string directly.

clavier A keyboard; a keyboard instrument.

clef A sign placed on the musical staff to define the specific pitches represented by the lines and spaces.

close In 18th-century English, a cadence, or, more commonly, a cadenza (q.v.).

concerto Since the late eighteenth century, an extended work for a virtuoso soloist with orchestral accompaniment; earlier the term had designated a number of genres, beginning in the late sixteenth century, in which disparate instrumental (or vocal and instrumental) forces cooperated.

conductus A medieval composition to a Latin text but without a Gregorian cantus firmus; its texture was monophonic (q.v.) or homophonic (q.v.) and it was often used to accompany processions (which may account for its name).

contrapuntal Making use of counterpoint—that is, the combination of two or more melodic lines in a single texture.

contratenor A voice part in medieval polyphony set in counterpoint with the tenor.

cornett A wind instrument like a woodwind in its fingering system but like a brass instrument in its mouthpiece and embouchure (q.v.); in use through the 17th century.

courante A 17th-century French court dance in triple meter and stately tempo.

da capo (Italian: from the top) A direction to begin again, used in many pieces (like Baroque operatic arias) in ABA from, to save the trouble of writing out the last section. Hence "da capo aria" means an aria in ABA form.

diatonic scales (e.g., major and minor, medieval modes) whose distribution of intervals (whole and half steps) conforms to that of the white keys of the piano.

dissonance A combination of pitches that produces a harmonic clash according to the rules of composition in force at a given time. Dissonances are by no means avoided or prohibited in any musical style—indeed, their use is often highly expressive—but their handling is subject to restriction and their movement to consonance is normally effected by means of conventional procedures (called "resolutions").

Divine office The daily round of Christian monastic services.

dodecaphonic A fancy (Greek-derived) equivalent of "twelve-tone" (q.v.).

dodecaphonism The technique or practice of twelve-tone composition.

dominant The pitch, triad (q.v.), or key on the fifth degree of the scale; the dominant triad has a strong sense of implied progression to the tonic, and is the initiator, therefore, of cadences in tonal music.

dotted (rhythm) A radical alternation of long and short notes, giving a majestic effect (if slow) or an agitated one (if fast). The term is derived from the notation of such rhythms (the dot lengthens the long note beyond its normal value).

double bar The sign drawn through the staff to denote the end of a piece or of a major constituent section.

dulcian The 16th-centruy prototype of the modern bassoon.

embellishment Decorative additions to or departures from notated music or well-known tunes. Often these are stereotyped "graces" indicated by special conventions of notation.

embouchure The positioning of the lips in playing a wind instrument; in Burney's description of Frederick the Great's flute playing, the word refers figuratively to the quality of tone produced through the application of the embouchure.

enharmonic 1. In Greek music, a genus (tuning system) that included intervals smaller than a half-step. 2. In common practice, the designation of the same actual pitch by different notational signs (e.g., F-sharp vs. G-flat); enharmonic relationships are tools in constructing complex or "remote" modulations (q.v.).

estampie A medieval dance, consisting of a number of repeated strains (i.e., sections), with or without refrain. Its name suggest that it was of a vigorous, "stamping" character.

even (or equal) **temperament** A tuning, especially of keyboards, in which all the intervals are of uniform size.

figural music In the Renaissance, metrically organized music notated in "mensural" notation (as opposed to plainchant, notated in neumes [q.v.]).

finale Concluding scene of an operatic act or final movement of an instrumental composition.

flageolet A simple wind instrument of the recorder family, used generally not for art music but for accompanying dancing.

formalism (formalist, formalistic, etc.) In Soviet music journalism, the use of advanced or esoteric compositional techniques at the expense of direct expression or accessibility.

frottola An Italian partsong (secular polyphonic song in the vernacular) of the late 15th and early 16th century; the equivalent of the French courtly chanson.

gagaku The ancient traditional music of the Japanese imperial court.

galliard A Renaissance dance in a lively triple meter. When Francis Bacon writes "galliard time," he means, simply, triple meter.

gamelan Indonesian percussion orchestra.

genre A type (cf. *genus*) or category of composition.

German flute The transverse, cross-blown flute, as distinguished (in the 18th century) from the vertically held recorder.

Gradual 1. The highly melismatic Gregorian chant that follows the reading of the Epistle at Mass. 2. A book containing the repertoire of chant for the Mass (cf. antiphoner).

ground bass A repeating cadential phrase in the bass, over which continual melodic variations are played, as in the Baroque dance forms *chaconne* and *passacaglia*; by extension, any unvaryingly repeated (*ostinato*) bass pattern.

gruppi In early Italian Baroque songs, melismas or roulades.

harmony 1. The practice and technique of combining simultaneous pitches in chords. 2. As Plato uses it, the word is roughly equivalent to mode (q.v.).

hautboy The 18th-century English term for oboe, more clearly showing its derivation from the French *haut bois* (*"loud wood [wind]"*).

hocket, *hoquetus* A rather virtuosic musical genre of the 13th and 14th centuries in which a musical line was seemingly broken up among two or more performers, who alternated and exchanged notes and rests very rapidly. The effect of such a manner of singing was whimsical, even comical, as is reflected in the term itself, which comes from the Latin for hiccup.

homophony A polyphonic texture in which all the parts move rhythmically together, producing chords; also, a texture in which one part is clearly the leading melodic one, the other parts providing harmonic support.

horizontal Refers to the successive or linear aspect of musical texture (by analogy with the appearance of musical notation, in which succeeding notes are written from left to right). Cf. vertical.

hymn A metrical song in praise of God, usually meant for congregational singing in unison.

imitation A texture in which different voices or instruments make successive entries singing or playing the same theme.

intabulate To arrange a polyphonic vocal piece for performance on lute or keyboard. *See* tablature.

interval A frequency difference between two pitches, generally measured in terms of the steps of the scale. For example, the octave, which actually represents a frequency ratio of 2:1, is so called because the two tones it comprises are located eight scale steps apart (and so it goes for the fifth [3:2], the fourth [4:3], etc.).

Introit The opening variable section of the Mass (Proper), consisting of a psalm verse and an antiphon. It accompanies the entrance of the celebrants (hence the name).

inversion A form of melodic variation in which the contour is reversed (e.g., a progression to a higher pitch is replaced by an equidistant progression to a lower one).

isorhythm The casting of the tenor in a fourteenth-century motet in a repeating rhythmic pattern.

jack The lever mechanism, activated by the keys, that causes the quill to pluck the string in harpsichords or related instruments; in Shakespeare's sonnet the word refers, synecdochically, to the keys of the virginal themselves.

Kapellmeister The German term for choir master or conductor, derived from the Italian *Maestro di cappella* (q.v.).

kithara The harplike instrument of the ancient Greeks, usually associated with Apollo.

klezmer A performing instrumentalist in the Ashkenazi (Eastern European) Jewish tradition; by extension, the music such musicians make, especially in wedding bands.

krummhorn, crumhorn, cromorne A capped reed instrument with a curved (German: *krumm*) bore, used chiefly in the 16th century.

legato Manner of performance in which tones are smoothly connected.

Lied (plural: **Lieder**) (German: song) This word is used in English to denote settings of lyric poetry by German composers.

lira da braccio A bowed string instrument on which chords were performed, in Italian Renaissance and early Baroque music, to accompany singing actors in intermedii and early operas.

lute Gourd-shaped plucked-string instrument, in use in Europe from the time of the Crusades until the 17th century; the prime soloist and accompanying instrument of the Renaissance.

lyre A smaller instrument of the kithara family.

madrigal An Italian vernacular poem set to sophisticated music. The madrigal had two main periods of vogue: the late 14th century and the late 16th (in the early 17th century it was imitated by English composers). The two repertoires, of course, are extremely dissimilar stylistically.

Maestro di cappella (Italian) The leader of a choir; by extension, the director of any musical establishment.

Matins The first service in the daily round of the Divine Office (q.v.), observed in the early morning hours.

melisma A melodic flourish sung to a single syllable.

menuet, minuet A French court dance of the 17th and 18th centuries in triple meter and moderate tempo. It survived long after its ballroom days as a part of the Baroque suite and the Classical symphony.

mezza voce (Italian: half-voice) In an undertone (usually with reference to singing; Liszt uses it in a figurative sense).

modal A modern term denoting the use of diatonic scales (modes) other than major or minor, most of them reminiscent or evocative of premodern, non-Western, or folk musics.

mode 1. A collection of pitches, and characteristic functional relations among them, that provides the raw material for composition. The pure pitch content of a mode is usually summed up or demonstrated by means of a scale (i.e., the arrangement of the constituent pitches in ascending or descending order of frequency). 2. With special reference to Medieval and Renaissance notation of rhythm, mode denotes the interrelationship of the note values.

modulation A change of key; a musical passage that effects such a change. Modulations are "near" or "remote" depending on how many tones the scales of the two keys have in common.

monochord A one-stringed contrivance used by medieval theorists or trainers of singers to demonstrate intervals.

monophonic A texture consisting of a single melodic line without counterpoint or harmonic support.

mordent An embellishment usually consisting of a single (but occasionally multiple) alternation of a written note with the one directly below it in the scale.

musique concrète Electronic music that manipulates pre-recorded natural or musical sounds rather than specially synthesized ones.

mutatio The process of applying the rules of solmization (q.v.) in the Middle Ages.

neoclassicism The use of musical gestures or stylistic references that deliberately evoke obsolete or "historical" genres or repertories in modern music.

neumes The earliest form of Western musical notation (found in Gregorian chant manuscripts from the 9th century on and still in use for the notation of church chant). In their most primitive form neumes indicated the rise and fall of the melodic contour but not fixed pitch. For the latter, the staff was invented. Whether neumes ever encoded rhythmic information is a matter of debate.

Nocturn A cycle of readings, hymns, and responsorial chants originating in Christian vigils; several are performed in the course of the Matins service.

octave Because an octave is the most consonant interval (q.v.), two notes an octave apart are regarded as having so great an affinity that they are called by the same letter name; thus the word octave is often used, by extension, to mean pitch register.

Office *See* Divine Office.

opéra comique A French comic opera with spoken dialogue.

organum Originally, the harmonic enrichment of a chant through doubling at a constant consonant interval; later, a more elaborate melismatic composition over a cantus firmus (11th through 13th centuries).

partials In acoustics, the members of the harmonic series engendered by any natural sound-producing vibration (fundamental). The relative prominence of the various partials in musical sounds is what largely determines timbre (q.v.).

pastorale A piece that evokes a rural scene, or emotions associated with such a scene.

perfect/imperfect consonance In medieval theory, perfect consonances were those that had frequency ratios of a simple arithmetic kind (i.e., the ones putatively discovered by Pythagoras); imperfect consonances were frequency ratios that were more complex (with the result that the two tones stood out from one another more). In practical terms, the perfect consonances were the octave, the fifth, and the fourth; the imperfect, the third and the sixth.

pitch-class The class of all musical pitches or frequencies denoted by a given letter name (e.g. A, B-flat) regardless of register or octave (q.v.).

plainchant, *cantus planus* Christian medieval ("Gregorian") chant, sung in unison and in free rhythm, as opposed to figural (i.e., polyphonic and/or metrical) music.

polyphony A texture consisting of a multiplicity of simultaneous sounds. Polyphonic textures are extremely various and some have their own names (e.g., homophony [q.v.], imitation [q.v.], etc.).

positive (or **portative**) **organ** A small, movable organ (as opposed to the large ones that were built into churches).

pricksong, pricking Pricksong was the Renaissance English term for figural music (q.v.); pricking was the term for copying music into manuscripts (from the scratching of quill on parchment).

programmatic Instrumental music written to convey a narrative or pictorial content that is specified by a title or subtitle, or in words (the program, or programme) accompanying the score.

psalmody The ritual singing of psalms.

raga Roughly, the Hindi equivalent of the English term "mode." In Indian classical music, ragas are differentiated not only by intervallic content but also by mood and by the time of day to which they are appropriate.

rauschpfeife A loud capped-reed instrument used in Germany in the 16th century; except for the capped mouthpiece, identical to the shawm (q.v.).

rebec(k) A small, pear-shaped bowed string instrument of the Middle Ages and Renaissance. By Milton's time it had passed out of "art music" usage altogether and was a rustic instrument used (like the flageolet) to accompany folk dancing.

recorder An end-blown flute with a whistle mouthpiece, in widespread European use from the Middle Ages until the early eighteenth century and revived both as an educational tool and as a performance instrument in the twentieth century.

regal A kind of positive organ (q.v.) that had reed pipes instead of open ones; it produced a very penetrating, rasping sound. Regals were used in the Middle Ages and Renaissance to train choirboys and, later, Monteverdi specified it to accompany the ferryman Charon's aria in his opera *Orfeo*.

relative major/minor The major and minor scales that share a common pitch collection and hence a common key signature. The tonic of the relative major scale is the third note (mediant) of its relative minor.

report A 17th-century English term for a ricercar (q.v.), or any passage using imitation.

Responsory A chant in which a soloist is answered by a group; by extension, a responsorial mode of performance is any situation, vocal or instrumental, in which such an alternation obtains.

retrograde A form of melodic variation in which the notes of a melody are presented in reversed order. Medieval and Renaissance musicians called the technique *cancrizans*, after what they took to be the way a crab walked.

ricercar, *ricercata* A polyphonic, imitative piece, usually based on a single theme, and usually of a complicated, "learned" character.

rondeau (medieval) One of the medieval dance-song forms with refrain, known as *formes fixes*. Its scheme is ABaAabAB, where the capital letters stand for the refrains (i.e., repetitions of text and music together), while the small letters stand for repetition of music to new words. The presence of complete refrains at the beginning and the end accounts for the name of this form: it is symmetrically "rounded."

roulade A virtuosic, decorative melisma (q.v.).

sackbut An older, smaller form of trombone, in use through the 17th century.

Sanctus The section of the Mass Ordinary that precedes the Elevation of the Host (cf. Agnus Dei).

schola A Gregorian chant choir.

sequence 1. An elaborate medieval hymn sung after the Alleluia in the Mass, most widespread from the 12th to the mid-16th centuries; only five remain in liturgical use today. 2. A short phrase which is repeated at different pitch levels, usually ascending or descending by step.

serial music Any music (including but not limited to twelve-tone music) that is organized on the basis of an arbitrary series (or "row") of pitch-classes; as used in the immediate post–World War II period, the term often denoted music in which other elements besides pitch were ordered according to an arbitrary series.

serpent The bass member of the cornett family, so called after its S-curved shape; serpents survived in military bands (and to a limited extent, in the opera pit) until the mid-19th century.

set In twelve-tone music, another word for tone row (q.v.).

shawm A double-reed instrument of the Middle Ages and Renaissance; ancestor of the modern oboe. Cf. *rauschpfeife*.

Singspiel A German comic opera with spoken dialogue (18th–19th centuries).

solmization The technique of singing at sight by the use of paradigm syllables: Ut(do)-re-mi, etc.

sonorist A style, pioneered by eastern European composers in the late 1950s and 1960s, that makes conspicuous use of extended instrumental techniques and novel sonorities, many of them inspired by the sounds of electronic music.

staccato Manner of performance in which the tones are sharply detached.

stile rappresentativo The recitative style of early seventeenth-century Italian opera, which sought to represent emotion truthfully by imitating the sound of human speech.

style galant Literally, "well-mannered" or "courtly style": a light, airy, simple-textured style cultivated in the mid-eighteenth century and reflecting the tastes of polite society.

suspension A form of expressive or cadential dissonance produced by holding a pitch while the surrounding voices change to a new harmony, then resolving the held pitch to one that accords with the new harmony.

syncopation A rhythm that conflicts with the prevailing meter. Typically, a syncopated note is an accented note on a weak beat, which is then held past the next strong beat. Syncopated rhythms have been a source of inventive experimentation, for the sake of expressivity or of simple delight in patterns, since the 13th century.

tablature A method of notation for fretted and keyed instruments that indicated not the note to be played but the fret to be stopped or key to be depressed. It survives in the "guitar chords" of today's popular sheet music.

tempo What is loosely thought of as the "speed" of a piece of music; actually it is the duration of the various notes as measured in actual time.

tenor 1. In medieval and Renaissance music, the part that holds out (Latin: *tenere*) the cantus firmus (q.v.). 2. By extension, the voice that sang such a part. 3. By further extension, in common usage, a high male voice, or a male singer with a high voice.

theme A melody whose transformations and recurrences determine the form of a musical composition; in musical analysis, material that is formally significant in this way is called *thematic*.

tibia An ancient flute, originally made from an animal's leg bone.

timbre "Tone-color"; the characteristic quality of sound by which, for example, two instruments playing identical pitches can be distinguished.

tonality 1. The system of functional harmonic relations that governs musical syntax in most music written since the Renaissance; the organization of music around a tonic (q.v.). 2. A key (e.g., G major).

tone In Gregorian chant, a formula to which a psalm or canticle is recited.

tone row (or **series**) An arrangement of the twelve notes of the chromatic scale into a specified order of intervals which then provided the raw materials for the construction of a twelve-tone composition.

tonic The governing (key-defining) pitch in tonal music; the pitch required for a sense of completion or repose.

transpose As C. P. E. Bach uses the term, it means to play a piece in a different key from the one in which it is notated.

triad The basic unit of tonal harmony since the 16th century; it is a three-note chord consisting of intervals respectively three and five scale steps from the lowest tone (called the root).

trill A rapid alternation between two adjacent notes of the scale.

tripla A tempo relationship common in Renaissance music (namely, three times as fast). As Bacon uses the term, it means, simply, any arithmetical (i.e., proportional) coordination of tempos.

triplum The highest voice (and last to be composed) in a medieval polyphonic composition.

troubadour A noble poet-musician of medieval southern France (then called Aquitaine or Languedoc) who wrote and sang in Provençal; the troubadours created the earliest body of literate secular music in the West.

twelve-tone music Music composed (following a method devised by Arnold Schoenberg in the early 1920s) on the basis of an arbitrary ordering of the twelve pitch-classes (q.v.) of the even-tempered chromatic scale.

vertical Refers to the simultaneous aspect of musical texture (by analogy with the appearance of musical notation, in which simultaneously sounding notes are written one on top of the other). Cf. horizontal.

vibrato Rapid, minute, regular fluctuations in frequency and/or intensity, applied to musical tones to make them more pleasing or expressive.

vielle A medieval bowed string instrument; the ancestor of the violin family.

viol The main bowed string family from the 15th to the 18th centuries. One member (the so-called double bass) survives today.

viola da gamba The Italian term for viol; whatever the size, viols were held between the legs (*gambe*).

virelai One of the medieval dance-song forms with refrain. Its model stanza is *AbbaA,* where *A* is the refrain and *a* is the music of the refrain sung to the third line of the stanza.

virginal A small, often pentagonal English keyboard instrument of the harpsichord family. Sets of virginals, often piled one atop another in order of size, were very popular domestic instruments in Shakespeare's time.

Boldface page numbers denote passages authored by the person or persons indexed; italic page numbers denote illustrations. The source titles, which appear regularly in the main body of the text, are not repeated here.